CW00968394

AVRO
MANCHESTER

The Legend
Behind the Lancaster

AVRO MANCHESTER

The Legend behind the Lancaster

Robert Kirby
BSc PhD C.Geol FGS

Midland Publishing
Limited

Dedicated to
the air and ground crews of
RAF Bomber Command

© Robert Kirby 1995

Design concept and editorial layout
© Midland Publishing Limited
and Stephen Thompson Associates

Typeset in
ITC Cheltenham Book
and Bramley

Edited by Ken Ellis

First published 1995 by
Midland Publishing Limited,
24 The Hollow, Earl Shilton,
Leicester, LE9 7NA
England
Tel: 01455 847 256 Fax 01455 841 805

ISBN 1 85780 028 1

All rights reserved. No part of this
publication may be reproduced, stored in
a retrieval system, transmitted in any form
or by any means, electronic, mechanical
or photo-copied, recorded or otherwise,
without the written permission of the
copyright owners.

Printed and bound by
WBC Book Manufacturers Limited
Bridgend, Mid-Glamorgan

Half-title page illustration:
**Beautifully proportioned lines of
207 Squadron Manchester Mk.IA L7515 'EM-S'.**
via Philip Jarrett

Photograph on previous page:
**Aircrews of 106 Squadron, Coningsby,
looking exuberant, as well they might, on the
morning of 31st May 1942. The previous
night's thousand bomber raid had been a
stunning success and the unit suffered no
casualties. A Mk.I and a Mk.IA are at rest
in the background. Wing Commander Guy
Gibson is centre foreground and Flight
Lieutenant John Wooldridge is second row,
third from the right.**
via Aerospace Publishing

Contents

Jacket illustration –
From a specially commissioned painting by
Keith Woodcock GAvA

Foreword

Wing Commander T C Weir DFC

It was March 1941 when, at last, Avro Manchesters began arriving in 61 Squadron. They came to us with great expectations, and we gazed on them with awe and respect. No longer need we envy those squadrons that had been privileged to receive and operate their Manchesters before us. Needless to say we felt some degree of inferiority.

We had high hopes for the Manchester. Its size, bomb-carrying capacity, operating range, the enormous 2,000 hp Rolls-Royce Vulture engines, the huge airscrews were all very impressive to us who had been flying Handley Page Hampdens for so long. The luxury and sophistication of gun turrets provided a special feeling of protection from enemy attack.

Squadron conversion to the new aircraft was slow over the next three months. Training was periodically interrupted because Manchesters were being grounded for engine modifications. The Vulture engines were not standing up under normal training and intensive flying conditions. Engines were seizing up, dense fumes and white metal particles spewed from exhausts, and on occasion the failure of airscrews to feather, all contributed to a number of crashes and loss of life among Manchester squadrons during this period.

It was always a disappointment when the Manchesters were grounded although we knew it was for safety reasons, and only for a short time. Morale among the crews was maintained to a reasonable level by operating the few Hampdens we still had on strength in the squadron until the Manchesters returned to service. We had faith in each of the modifications and in the ability of our maintenance crews to make the aircraft safe for us. But there were disturbing stories circulating that height could not be maintained on one engine, and that crews had been forced to abandon their aircraft. Nevertheless, our desire to fly our Manchesters did not diminish. We were aware that a problem with the Vulture engine existed but, with supreme confidence, we believed that we could handle any situation. Besides, whatever the problem, it was always something that would happen to one of the other crews.

Some of our training flights involved intensive flying tests in which the engines were subjected to overload conditions, war load climbs and airscrew feathering. On one such

flight I had on board a valuable cargo of 13 aircrew members of the squadron, mostly pilots, to observe the tests. Suddenly, toward the end of the test, it happened. The port engine failed 20 miles from base at about 1,000 feet. Fortunately, the port airscrew feathered perfectly. Then followed a harrowing 20 minutes nursing the aircraft back to base, where we landed safely to the great relief of all on board. Rolls-Royce technicians were especially pleased to get a defective engine intact.

The Manchester responded lazily to the controls in the air. It had poor climbing ability because the Vultures were underpowered and inefficient for such a large aircraft, especially under bomb load conditions. Also, operating height over enemy territory was much lower than desired. However, we accepted these failings knowing we were

One of many Canadian aircrew in 5 Group, Wing Commander T C Weir DFC was a flight commander in No 61 Squadron when the first Manchesters were received. He became Commanding Officer on 5th September 1941 when Wing Commander G E Valentine was killed and he remained in command until June 1942, by which time 61 had relinquished their Manchesters (for Lancasters).
via Wing Commander T C Weir

delivering a much heavier bomb load than we had been accustomed to with our Hampdens.

Late in June 1941 the squadron carried out a few operational sorties in Manchesters but this period was short-lived. The Manchesters again were grounded and the squadron reverted to operating the Hampdens during the next three months. Manchester air time during this period consisted mostly of a limited number of intensive flying tests. This was a particularly difficult time for the squadron. There were two upheavals: first, the squadron moved from Hemswell to North Luffenham, followed shortly afterwards to Woolfox Lodge. I was wounded one night by anti-aircraft fire, and while on sick leave was informed that our Squadron Commander, Wing Commander George Valentine, had gone missing on a Berlin trip in a Manchester, taking with him the station commander and several key station and squadron members. I was recalled immediately to take command of 61 Squadron. At this time we did not seem to be a very effective part of the war effort. Morale was at a low level.

In October 1941, when it seemed that the Vulture engine problems had been solved, flying hours on Manchesters increased, consisting mainly of training flights and conversion of more crews. Our confidence in the Manchester improved, and with the increased activity morale also began to improve.

We began to take part in operations again in December. The Manchester was capable of sustaining considerable flak and machine gun damage and still remaining under control in the air. Miraculously, many machines returned from operations severely damaged by enemy action. We were not always aware of the actual reason that some machines failed to return. Enemy action was usually considered the main reason but, in retrospect, it is possible that engine failure on a long, arduous flight could have contributed to losses.

Most pilots had their own favoured method of making their bombing run over the target. It was like believing in the benefit of a good luck charm. Some tried to follow closely an aircraft ahead, believing the first aircraft would get most of the attention from the flak gunners. Some glided, with reduced throttle, over the target. My plan was to study the pattern of flak concentration as I approached the target from some distance away. I imagined it was rhythmic with heavy and light concentrations, so I would time my run over the target as the flak concentration appeared to die down momentarily. Right or wrong, I convinced myself that these tactics were infallible.

Soon we began receiving additional Manchesters, exceeding our squadron establishment. These were transferred to us from other squadrons which were converting at that time to Lancasters. In addition the squadron swelled with a heavy intake of newly graduated aircrews from Operational Training Units. The burden of converting these crews onto Manchesters rested with the squadron. Allocating flying time to such a large number of crews, and air time per serviceable aircraft required good organising ability by the two flight commanders, Squadron Leaders Paape and West. These two officers had provided long, efficient service in the squadron, and their operational tours were stretching out. I was hoping they would soon complete their lengthy tours and go on well-deserved rest periods. We had several good, experienced officers who could be recommended to take their places. In addition, the demand for flying hours put a great strain on our maintenance personnel to keep serviceability of aircraft at a high level for both operational and training duties.

In March 1942 we started conversion to Lancasters and April saw the last of the Manchesters in 61 Squadron. It had been 13 months alternating between optimism and frustration; a difficult time for any commander to maintain squadron morale, especially among aircrews.

I had a young Canadian air gunner in my crew who often provided a little lift for me. He would poke his head through my office doorway to ask if we were flying on operations that night. If the answer was 'No', I could clearly hear him muttering as he turned away, 'Ah, heck!'

That completes the story of the Manchester during its period of service in 61 Squadron. It is sad to relate that the Manchester did not make its way into greatness, but it did leave its mark. Perhaps its most notable claim to fame is that its weaknesses gave birth to the magnificent Avro Lancaster.

Dr Kirby has studied the Avro Manchester and the Rolls-Royce Vulture engine for many years. He researched manufacturer's records, RAF records, and all Manchester equipped squadrons in 5 Group, Bomber Command, gaining a thorough knowledge and under-

standing of the service history of the Manchester. Dr Kirby has been instrumental in awakening the memories of former members of aircrews, and in doing so has brought some interesting and exciting stories to light. Of special note, he has brought some aircrew members into contact with each other again

after so many years. In particular, in at least one case, one crew member found another whom he believed had not survived the war.

The 'Wingco's crew. Wing Commander Weir and crew walking out to a 61 Squadron Manchester at Woolfox Lodge. *L Boot*

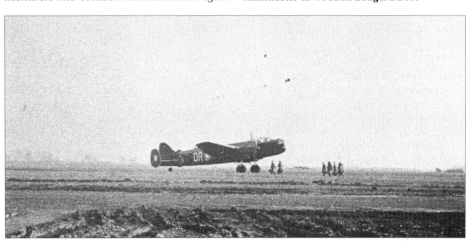

Hidden for 50 years and never previously published, is this gem from a small batch of photographs taken at Waddington on 17th July 1941 by Sir Cecil Beaton. Five unknown aircrew members from 207 Squadron pose with L7378 'EM-A'. This evocative picture serves as a fine tribute to all Manchester aircrew. *Cecil Beaton, courtesy Sotheby's, London*

Preface
and Acknowledgements

I have maintained a lifelong interest in aviation, especially concerning the Second World War. In the last 13 years this has become focused upon the development and service history of the Avro Manchester.

Over that prolonged period of time, the search for material became a single-minded one. The Manchester has proved elusive, doubtless because of its 'unloved' nature. Despite this, I am pleased at the depth of information that has come to light, and this is in no small way courtesy of those individuals and organisations I name below. Much of the information unearthed was previously unknown, despite the fact that the type served only in the United Kingdom.

The tale of the Manchester has never been presented in such detail and only now can the real story be told. Previous narratives have always been by way of a brief preface to a history of the Lancaster, necessarily lessening the story of human endeavour that filled the short career of its predecessor. For the first time, it can be made clear the extensive nature of airframe development accomplished and the small additional step needed to realise the world-beating Lancaster.

The account presented is constrained in a number of ways. First and foremost, many of the RAF aircrew involved were either killed flying Manchesters or on subsequent bomber tours later in the war. In addition, the Manchester was in front line service from November 1940 to June 1942, a period in the early war when Britain's fortunes were at their lowest. Security was very strict, cameras were frowned upon or forbidden, film was difficult to obtain and get developed. As a result, few unofficial photographs of Manchesters were taken. In respect of official records of the development and service history of the aircraft, two files were devoted to the Manchester. These are 627801/37, which related to the period 1936-39, and AVIA 15/2323 for 1939-42. Regrettably, 627801/37 was destroyed in the late 1940s, fortunately not before Professor Lindhoff had made a brief summary for the Ministry of Supply. AVIA 15/2323 remains available in the Public Record Office in Kew. The situation with respect to the aircraft and engine manufacturer is little better. Most Avro drawings and records related to the Manchester were destroyed in a fire at Chadderton in 1959, whilst the drawings and documentation

related to the Rolls-Royce Vulture were disposed of by an over-zealous manager in recent years. Records of A&AEE trials at Boscombe Down remain in place and have been consulted, but regrettably the archives of the Catapult & Arrested Landing Department of RAE Farnborough were transferred when that department moved out to RAE Bedford in the 1950s. When Bedford closed the trail went cold. Operational records in the various unit Form 540 and 541s are complete, although skeletal, at the Public Record Office. Complementary Luftwaffe records were destroyed or are difficult to gain access to.

Acknowledgements

Much of this book is based on personal recollections and experiences of former servicemen. My researches have extended beyond the United Kingdom to Australia, Canada, New Zealand, South Africa and the USA. Without exception they responded to my questions with patience and, where independent checking was possible, with commendable understatement of their experiences. If I have done them justice my main objective will be fulfiled. It is invidious to single out individuals but it is necessary to acknowledge the late Jim M Duncan, and Jim A Taylor (ex 207 Squadron) who motivated and encouraged my early researches. I also thank Canadians 'Mike' W J Lewis (ex 207 Squadron) and Bill H Shorrock and T C Cam Weir (ex 61 Squadron) for their assistance, friendship and hospitality.

The author has received guidance, encouragement and information from a large number of organisations and individuals: Richard Bateman, David Birch, Roy Bonser, Michael J F Bowyer, Chaz Bowyer, W 'Bill' R Chorley, Andrew Clarke, Mrs Margaret Dove, Sid Finn, John Foreman, Peter Green, Peter Hall, Mr & Mrs Alec Harvey-Bailey (Jnr), Charles Hawes, Harry Holmes, George A Jenks, Mr & Mrs Bob Howell, Ray E Leach, Francis K Mason, Geoff Page, Simon Parry, Bryan Philpott, Bruce Robertson and Ray Sturtivant. The following historical co-workers overseas: Denmark: Birger Hansen; Belgium: Jacques de Vos, Peter Loncke; Germany: Herbert Scholl, Eric Nonnenmacher, Horst Diener, Horst Amberg, Gebhard Aders, H Frhr von Friesen, Heinrich Griese; Netherlands: Gerry Zwanenberg, Ab Jensen, Chris Timmer, J G T Hans de Haan, Co Marschalkerweerd.

Squadron Associations: No.49, Tom Gatfield; Nos 50 & 61, Eddie Davidson, Doug McKinnon and Skip Welford; No 83, Ron Low and Frank Harper; No 106, Des Richards; No 207, Raymond Glynne-Owen.

Thanks are due to the following institutions: Aeroplane & Armament Experimental Establishment, Boscombe Down (now the Aircraft & Armament Evaluation Establishment); Aerospace Publishing, publishers of World Air Power Journal and Wings of Fame; Air Historical Branch, Whitehall; British Aerospace; Dept of Health & Social Security, Newcastle; Imperial War Museum, Lambeth; Personnel Management Centre, Innsworth; Postmaster General's Office, Crawley; Prisoners of War Association; Public Record Office, Kew; Rolls-Royce; Royal Aircraft Establishment, Farnborough (later the Royal Aerospace Establishment and now part of the Defence Research Agency); Royal Air Force Escaping Society; Royal Air Force Museum, Hendon.

The original manuscript was typed by Mrs Janet A Edis. Much of the photography was undertaken by Alain Lockyer. Computer discs were translated by Tim M Buckley.

Many individuals, too numerous to thank individually, provided photographic materials. Their contributions are credited in the captions.

I am indebted to all of them.

Robert Kirby
Taunton, Somerset
August, 1995

Chapter One

A Difficult Birth

Avro's Type 679 Manchester was a disappointment and a failure in service. As such it ranks in obscurity alongside such other early war British types as the Blackburn Botha, Boulton Paul Defiant, Fairey Battle, Saunders-Roe Lerwick and Vickers Warwick, aircraft specified and developed during the same 1930s desperate race to re-arm. Yet to place the Avro design in the same category as these five is both harsh and unjustified.

Largely due to the efforts of the Avro chief designer, Roy Chadwick, the Avro Type 679 Manchester was a triple triumph. First, it was a triumph of innovative aeronautical design. Second, it was a triumph of engineering, for Chadwick not only designed and built the aircraft, but also many of the lathes and machines on which it was constructed.

Third, and as importantly, it employed a breakdown construction which represented a major advance in mass production techniques, putting it streets ahead of its rivals. This technique not only produced huge benefits in terms of sub-contracting and dispersing production, but in speeding repair and returning to service damaged or 'weary' examples.

At a very advanced stage in the continuous development programme, Avro wisely changed the Manchester's name to the Lancaster. The Battle, Botha, Defiant, Lerwick and Warwick went no further. The Manchester evolved into a new form. Aircrew morale was restored, and a legend was born.

Chadwick not only designed and built the Manchester, and out of it the Type 683 Lancaster, but went on to design the Type 685 York, the Type 694 Lincoln and the Type 696 Shackleton, all types that were directly descended from the Manchester and the thinking that it embodied. Each was a success story in its own right. Unlike any other bomber design of the Second World War, a dynasty stemmed from the Manchester.

The advanced nature of the design and the extent to which so many of the Manchester's systems and roles represented major steps into the unknown tend to be lost in the type's problematical service history. The type helped to refine the role of the strategic bomber. Paralleling this are the development history and problems arising from design of its new and for the time, extraordinarily powerful, Rolls-Royce Vulture engines. In this connection the Manchester was unique in

being the only aircraft to employ the Vulture on operations. Arising from the under-developed nature of the latter the Manchester might justifiably lay claim to being the only British engine test bed to undertake 1,263 sorties over occupied Europe!

The initial phase of the Manchester story, however, belongs to the bureaucrats and Air Ministry officials, to Rolls-Royce and to Avro staff. Hindsight allows the many blind alleys and mistakes during the development to be highlighted clearly, but all three were striving to bring to reality a heavy strategic bomber, something which simply did not exist prior to that time. Nobody in that era of galloping technological change knew where the limits lay and what such a bomber could or could not accomplish. As initially specified the Manchester had a variety of roles and requirements. Amongst these were the capability of being catapulted from an airfield, a role envisaging torpedo bombing with a multiple load and dive bombing from an angle of 60°.

Model of the Avro Type 679 submitted with the company's tender to specification P13/36 in late February 1937. *G A Jenks collection*

In the end two major problems led to the abandonment of the Manchester. Firstly, it was a victim of its 1936 twin-engine specification and the two under-developed Rolls-Royce Vultures, and secondly it became weighed down by an unsupportable middle-age spread. Other recurring themes are the multitude of difficulties which bedevilled the project and the oscillation in the ascendancy of the Manchester in comparison to the design of the Handley Page Halifax and Short Stirling. Starting as the leading contender, the Manchester fell behind and became poorly regarded to the point where it was on the brink of cancellation in favour of the Halifax. Saved by a few visionaries it was regarded as worthy of continuation only on grounds that it was cheaper and faster to progress than to switch wholly to the Halifax. Only later, when transformed into the Lancaster, did it achieve its true ascendancy over the Halifax and Stirling. A final aspect of this initial phase which runs through the entire history of the type are the Herculean efforts, on an almost continuous basis, by the principal participants and their staffs.

During the mid-1930s the concept of a bomber with a really long range and heavy bomb load was still evolving and in summer 1936 the Air Staff formulated operational

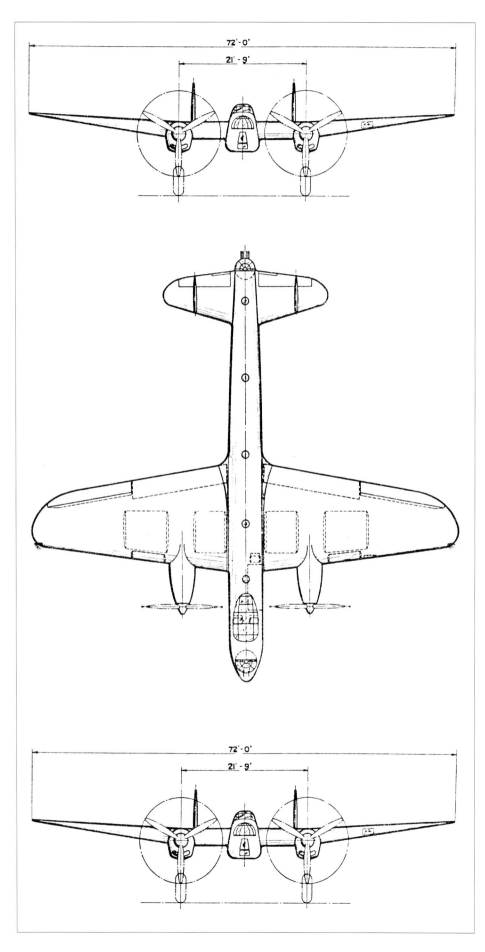

requirements for a new heavy bomber. This was later to be issued as Specification P13/36 to which the Manchester would be designed. At this time the Air Staff were formulating Expansion Programme 'F' and were influenced by three criteria:

1 Most important was a requirement for a substantial striking force of heavy bombers.
2 Every enterprise was hampered by financial constraints.
3 In view of limitations imposed by No. 2, every aircraft was required to have as great an offensive capability as possible.

Whilst Specification P13/36 was still being appraised it was calculated that the aircraft would be the operational equivalent of three Fairey Battles in range, speed and bomb load. This estimate went part of the way towards satisfying criteria No. 1 and No. 2 and in an endeavour to satisfy No. 3, it was hoped to combine in the new bomber the roles of torpedo carrier, general reconnaissance and general purposes aircraft. Fortunately for P13/36 these alternative roles were never allowed to spoil the design.

The requirements were approved by the Chief of the Air Staff in August 1936 and represented a big improvement over the bomber specification issued only one year previously, the B1/35, which was to emerge eventually as the Warwick. This in itself is a mark of the pace of technical development in the 1930s.

B1/35 and P13/36 Compared

Spec.	Cruising Speed	Max. Range	Max. Bomb Load
B1/35	230mph at 15,000ft	2,000 miles with 2,000 lb	4,000 lb with 1,000 mile range
P13/36	275mph at 15,000ft	3,000 miles with 3,000 lb	8,000 lb with 2,000 mile range

The all up weight of the P13/36 was to be approximately the same as the B1/35, but the former was to be a good deal smaller and faster. The heaviest bomb load or longest range was to be realised by catapult take-off, for no engine then being developed was powerful enough to meet the needs of a twin-engined type to this requirement.

Operational requirements were sent in advance of formal specification on 24th August 1936 to six firms, A V Roe, Boulton Paul, Bristol, Handley Page, Short Brothers and Vickers. The final specification was approved by the Director of Technical Development in September and when this was issued by Contracts Branch in November copies were also sent to Fairey and Hawker.

Three view general arrangement of the P13/36, dated January 1937 that appeared in the tender document. Note the format of the tailplane, fins and rudders. *G A Jenks collection*

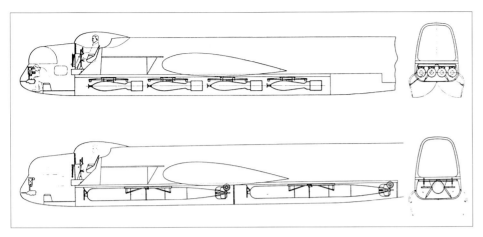

Diagrams taken from the P13/36 tender document showing how the bomb bay could take up to 16 bombs or two 18in torpedoes.
G A Jenks collection

The specification represented a major challenge to Avro, which was then working on the wooden framed, later welded steel tube, and canvas covered Anson. P13/36 called for an all metal, stressed skin twin-engined bomber of 45,000 lb all up weight powered by two of the new 1,700hp Rolls-Royce Vulture liquid cooled, 24 cylinder engines. The successful competitor would need to achieve a speed of not less than 275mph at 15,000ft on two-thirds power. Its service ceiling was to be 28,000ft and in the event of one engine becoming unserviceable the aircraft needed to be able to fly and maintain height at 10,000ft.

Bearing in mind restrictions at existing airfields, the aircraft had to be capable of taking off within 500 yards with a 1,000 lb bomb load and fuel for 1,000 miles or 700 yards with a 3,000 lb load and fuel for 2,000 miles. The size of existing airfields was partly behind the requirement for an accelerated take-off capability, carrying the maximum bomb load of 8,000 lb with a range of 2,000 miles. Also envisaged in this same requirement though, was the need to carry the heaviest bomb load over the longest distance.

A multiple role was envisaged for the aircraft. The bomber must be able to operate in the strategic role, when the longer range and more modest bomb load would be carried, or alternatively as a short range, tactical bomber with a heavy bomb load. In the latter role the aircraft must, for reasons of accuracy of bomb delivery and its own security, be capable of diving at angles up to 60°. Indeed, the loads required had to be even more diverse, envisaging as a further option two 18 in torpedoes to be carried internally. Since these weapons were each 18ft 3in long this implied an extraordinarily long bomb bay, unless the weapons could be slung side by side or one above the other. A final option envisaged the carriage of 16 fully armed

troops, with no bomb load. This was a daunting specification for the period. To fly the aircraft, a crew of four was called for, whilst the latest power-operated turrets, mounting twin guns in the nose and quadruple guns in the tail, were required.

The specification stressed particularly that good all-round visibility was required for the pilot, together with excellent manoeuvring characteristics at high speed. Emphasis was placed upon designing, constructing and testing all the services of the aircraft at the greatest possible speed. Amongst other requirements was a suitability for easy quantity production and certain restrictions on overall sizes and those of major components. The central span and longest fuselage section must not exceed 35ft, with other wing and fuselage sections limited to 22ft. The latter restrictions were imposed by the existing RAF vehicles, buildings and packing cases in which the aircraft or its components might be transported or housed.

Urged on by Roy Dobson, the Managing Director of Avros, Roy Chadwick, the Chief Designer, immediately set to work every designer and draughtsman who could be spared. So many new things had to be evaluated and designed, but by late February 1937 the Design Tender to P13/36 was ready and within a few days submitted to the Air Ministry. The tender submitted was accompanied by a large number of detailed drawings and included a scale model of the aircraft. The Avro Type 679 envisaged a rather diminutive 'Medium' mid-winged monoplane with, as yet, little resemblance to the final Type 679 Manchester which emerged.

The demanding specification could only be met by employment of the most advanced design characteristics. All metal construction, including a light alloy monocoque fuselage built up on a framework of hoops and stringers was to be employed, with flush

riveted skin. The performance was to be achieved by employing the smallest possible size and highest safe wing loading, together with special attention to surface smoothness, in overall design but also in skin finish, and the use of cellulose lacquer paint to minimise drag. In addition to its small size, the use of the new and advanced constant-speed, fully feathering airscrews was envisaged. Furthermore, all three of the undercarriage legs and wheels were to be fully retractable and enclosed by doors. Extensive use of hydraulic power was envisaged to control flaps, bomb doors and the fully feathering propellers but also to drive the heavily armed, power operated gun turrets. The aircraft spanned a mere 72ft. The wing was of twin main spar construction and had an equal taper on leading and trailing edges, but an asymmetrical curve to the tip, which left the maximum span close to the leading edge. The tail had a similar planform and was surmounted by inset fins rising from the upper surface only.

The narrative within the tender informed the Air Ministry that the requirements of the bombing task had dictated the basic design, but the general reconnaissance and general purposes requirements had also been catered for. The problem of exploiting the alternatives between long range and very heavy bomb load, made possible by catapulting, had been accommodated by a simple design in which all the bombs were carried in the fuselage and all fuel and oil in the wings.

The cavernous bomb bay extended for two-thirds of the length of the fuselage and it was this requirement that had necessitated the mid-wing design. In respect of the bomb carrying capacity the tender outlined that the 8,000 lb requirement had been accommodated in a considerable number of alternatives. In the case of the 2,000 lb bombs, six of which could be lifted, making a total of 12,000 lb, the specification had been improved on by a large margin. Even with 12,000 lb of bombs, catapulting permitted a range of 1,000 miles to be attained. Avro stated the view that the bomb provisioning was one of the best attributes of the design.

Sketch of the proposed portable engine hoist from the original Avro tender.
G A Jenks collection

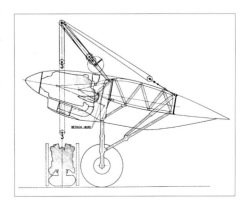

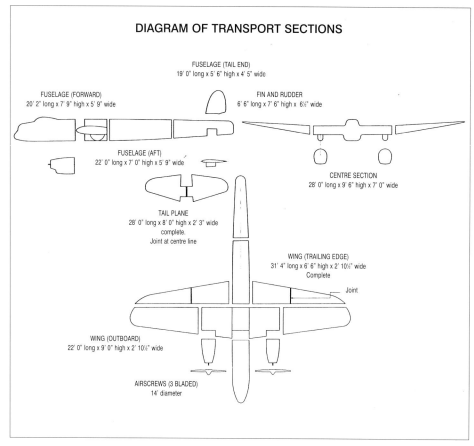

DIAGRAM OF TRANSPORT SECTIONS

FUSELAGE (TAIL END)
19' 0" long x 5' 6" high x 4' 5" wide

FUSELAGE (FORWARD)
20' 2" long x 7' 9" high x 5' 9" wide

FIN AND RUDDER
6' 6" long x 7' 6" high x 6½" wide

FUSELAGE (AFT)
22' 0" long x 7' 0" high x 5' 9" wide

CENTRE SECTION
28' 0" long x 9' 6" high x 7' 0" wide

TAIL PLANE
28' 0" long x 8' 0" high x 2' 3" wide
complete.
Joint at centre line

WING (TRAILING EDGE)
31' 4" long x 6' 6" high x 2' 10½" wide
Complete

Joint

WING (OUTBOARD)
22' 0" long x 9' 0" high x 2' 10½" wide

AIRSCREWS (3 BLADED)
14' diameter

Diagram showing the breakdown of major components for ease of production and transport, appearing in the P13/36 tender. The ability of the Type 679 to be broken down in this way shows not only the attention to practical detail by the design team but was also to render both the Manchester and the Lancaster ideal for mass, dispersed production.

Detail drawing from the P13/36 tender showing interior details. The all-encompassing specification is apparent in the rear fuselage where the originally requested message pick-up hook can be seen in stowed position immediately forward of the tail wheel.
Both G A Jenks collection

The small size and careful attention to clean lines was expected to result in a high cruising speed of 294mph at 15,000ft and a corresponding maximum speed of 341mph. The company announced it had developed a rapid and effective method of flush riveting, which would form the countersink in the plating and head the rivet in one operation. The skin of the aircraft would thus be flush riveted in its entirety.

Detailed consideration had been given to wing spar extrusions and eventually the decision was made to produce these by cutting fabrications of appropriate section diagonally along their length to produce two tapering booms. This required a large costly machine. Chadwick was unimpressed with the speed at which the available machines worked and set-to, in co-operation with the woodworking firm Wadkins, to design a faster method. This eventually came to fruition as a machine which worked the metal five times faster than previous examples. Chadwick's involvement not only concerned these background machine-tool designs but later such standard equipment as bomb carriers and gun installations. His involvement truly reached every facet of the design.

In order to ensure adequate space and freedom of movement for the crew, three mock ups of the front fuselage had been constructed and evaluated at the Newton Heath works. The four man crew included pilot, navigator, and wireless operator accommodated in close proximity and a bomb-aimer-gunner. A sound-proofed rest room equipped with two couches or reclining chairs was planned in the centre section for two additional crew members, who could relieve the duty crew during long flights.

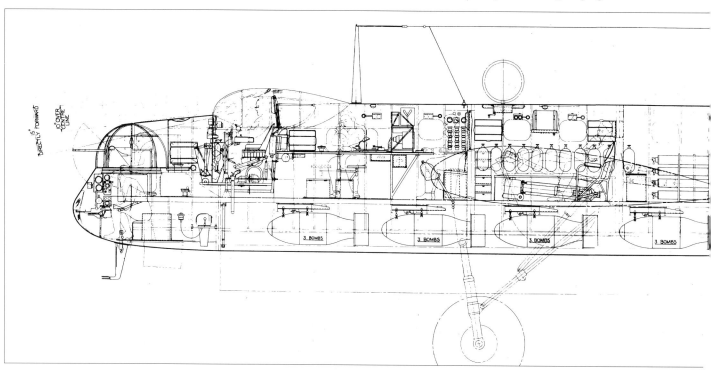

DIRECTLY 15° FORWARD

10° OVER CENTRE LINE

3. BOMBS   3. BOMBS   3. BOMBS   3. BOMBS

Nash and Thompson gun turrets were incorporated in the nose and tail as required by the specification, but in addition, space was provided for a retractable mid-under turret if considered necessary.

The high speed had been attained by employing a high wing loading. This in turn had raised the problem of which trailing edge flaps should be used. These were planned to double as dive brakes and for this reason, to withstand the heavy loads imposed on them and their operating mechanism, split trailing-edge flaps were recommended.

The tender then gave a general description and performance estimate, parts of which are reproduced below. The figures merit attention because in them can be seen unmistakably the seeds of the ultimate failure of the type. Whilst the output of the twin Vulture engines was correctly specified within a few horse-power, the weight would increase disproportionately, leaving the aircraft fatally underpowered.

Avro Type 679 Design Tender

Principal dimensions

Span	72ft 0in
Length	69ft 0in
Height	16ft 6in
Wheel track	21ft 9in
Wing area (gross)	930 sq ft
Tail area	165 sq ft
Fin and rudder area	70 sq ft

Weight estimate

Structure	10,150 lb
Power units	7,120 lb
Empty weight	17,270 lb

Gross weight of aircraft - normal load
Range 1,000 miles, bomb load 1,000 lb.

Weight empty	17,270 lb
Fixed military load	1,353 lb
Removable military load (incl. 4 crew)	2,820 lb
Fuel (562 gallons)	4,330 lb
Oil (30 gallons)	270 lb
Total gross weight	26,043 lb

Gross weight of aircraft - overload
Range 2,000 miles, bomb load 8,000 lb.

Weight empty	17,270 lb
Fixed military load	1,353 lb
Removable military load (incl. 6 crew)	10,464 lb

Fuel (1068 gallons)	8,240 lb
Oil (50 gallons)	450 lb
Total gross weight overload	37,777 lb

(Two intermediate loads were also presented.)

Engines	Two Rolls-Royce Vultures
Engine power, max	1,710 bhp at 3,000 rpm at 15,000 ft
Max. climb	1,680 bhp at 2,850 rpm at 13,500 ft
Take-off	1,480 bhp at 3,000 rpm at sea level

Performance with Normal Load - Level speed

Max. speed	at sea level	266 mph
	at 5000ft	290 mph
	at 10,000ft	315 mph
	at 15,000ft	341 mph
	at 20,000ft	331 mph
	at 25,000ft	306 mph

Cruising speed at two-thirds max power at 2,600rpm

	at sea level	231 mph
	at 5,000ft	252 mph
	at 10,000ft	273 mph
	at 15,000ft	294 mph
	at 20,000ft	282 mph
	at 25,000ft	263 mph

Take-off, still air	without flap	305 yds
	with 30° flap	245 yds
	with 60° flap	225 yds

Distance to clear 50ft obstacle		
	without flap	415 yards
	with 30° flap	365 yards
	with 60° flap	345 yards

Landing run with brakes and flaps	250 yds
Service ceiling	31,400ft
Absolute ceiling	32,400ft
Wing loading (on gross area)	28 lb/sq ft

Performance on one engine – Level speed

Max speed at sea level	185 mph
Climb rate at sea level	512 ft/min
Service ceiling	19,300ft
Absolute ceiling	20,600ft

Performance with maximum overload was specified and only diminished by about 8–11 mph across the range of height and power.

Take-off with maximum overload if catapult not used
Take-off run in still air with

no flaps	775 yards
30° flaps	615 yards
60° flaps	550 yards

Distance from rest to clear 50ft obstacle with

no flaps	1,085 yards
30° flaps	935 yards
60° flaps	880 yards

Performance with maximum overload

Climb rate at sea level	1,050 ft/min
Time to 5,000ft	5.02 minutes
Service ceiling	24,250ft
Absolute ceiling	25,400ft
Wing loading (on gross wing area)	40.60 lb/sq ft
Engine loading (on max power)	11.05 lb/bhp

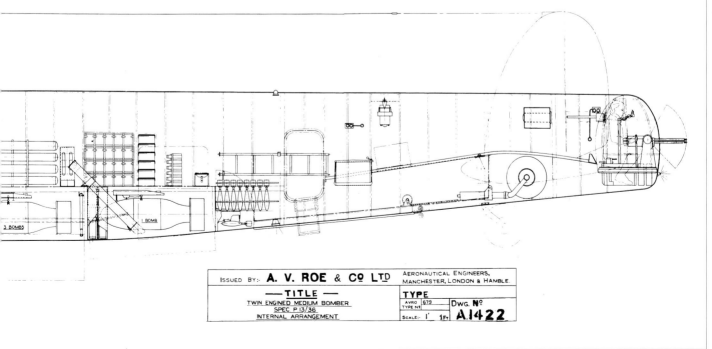

ISSUED BY:- A. V. ROE & Cº LTD	AERONAUTICAL ENGINEERS, MANCHESTER, LONDON & HAMBLE.
— TITLE — TWIN ENGINED MEDIUM BOMBER SPEC P 13/36 INTERNAL ARRANGEMENT	TYPE AVRO TYPE N° 679 DWG. N° SCALE:- 1' 1FT A.1422

With assurances of good stability and responsiveness to the controls in all axes, having been tested on the company's Anson and a projected speed which would leave the Hawker Hurricane, still two years away, standing and prove a good match even for the sleeker Supermarine Spitfire, the tender went on its way. If the proposed aircraft lived up to expectations it looked as if Avro would have a world beater on its hands. At the tender design conference in February 1937 all the designs were analysed and first and second places went to Avro and Handley Page respectively.

A bare eight weeks after the tender was submitted, on 30th April 1937, the Air Ministry informed the winning companies that their tender was successful. Two prototypes of each of the Type 679 and HP.56 aircraft were required. The race was on in earnest. There was intense pressure from the Air Ministry to foreshorten the timescale of development as well as competition between Avros and Handley Page and Shorts, who had a contract to develop the larger 55,000 lb all up weight, four engined heavy bomber to specification B12/36 on the same timescale.

Avros immediately launched into a major expansion to cope with the design and development work required. During the design stage the appearance of the aircraft changed. The inset fins were replaced by end plate fins, whilst the original 72ft span was increased to 80ft 2 in. Wind tunnel models show the outline of the aircraft at this time and the Manchester look is clearly already apparent.

Whilst Avros were overjoyed that they had been successful and had beaten such well established designers of large aircraft as Fairey, Handley Page, Shorts and Vickers, it is as well to pause for sober reflection. Although the Type 679 had won the tender competition and was hence initially the favourite, Chadwick's relative inexperience had led to unwarranted optimism in a number of respects. Whilst the timescale from receipt of an instruction to proceed and the first flight was pegged at 12 months, it actually took 21 months. Whereas emphasis had been placed on speed and a calculated maximum of 341mph at 15,000ft with normal load, 265mph was to be closer to the eventual mark, whilst at various stages the wing was to be stretched twice by a significant 18ft, tailplane span was to increase by five feet and the fin design was to change several times and bedevil the design. Furthermore and fatally, weight was to escalate dramatically. In addition to his great skill, Chadwick was a realist and later, with those he knew he could trust, quite open.

When the problems with the Manchester became apparent and the need to switch to the Merlin evident, Chadwick told Air Vice-Marshal Wilfred Freeman and the Director and Deputy Directors of Technical Develop-

ment, W Farren and N E Rowe, that it was his inexperience in designing large all-metal aircraft of the rigidity demanded by the specification which had led, in part, to the aircraft coming out overweight. All this was in the future because, however advanced the aircraft was, it would only perform as well as its engines permitted. Here too, although in common with a number of other new types, the Manchester would be breaking new ground.

During the early 1930s it had steadily become apparent at Rolls-Royce that the Air Ministry would soon be launching specifications for larger aircraft for which the power available from existing engines would be inadequate. To anticipate this, Rolls commenced the design of a bigger engine in September 1935. One factor which is likely to have influenced the design is that it would have to run on 87 octane petrol. At this stage only the United States had 100 octane fuels and arising from the neutrality act it was anticipated that this might not be available in the event of war.

Considering what sort of engine this might be it was recognised that it was desirable to keep within the bore sizes on which the company had experience. Cylinder size would thus be controlled by the desired bore/stroke ratio. Increased capacity over existing engines had to come from increasing the number of cylinders. A G Elliott, the Chief Designer, may have considered V16 or V24 engines as well as 'H' and 'X' pattern cylinder layouts, but eventually opted for the X24 cylinder concept having four banks of six cylinders. Moreover the bore of 5in and stroke of 5½ in chosen permitted the frontal area to be kept to a minimum.

Rolls' policy in engine design was to build on existing and known technology, keeping innovatory aspects in each design few at a time. This led to a design based on the existing Kestrel and the Peregrine which had evolved from it. The same bore and stroke was chosen with the two V crankcases placed back to back driving a single crankshaft. The angle between the blocks was to be 90°, giving a swept volume of 2,590 cu in. The cylinder and piston design were similar to the Kestrel but here the similarity ended. The light alloy crankcase was new, the two halves being located by shallow tongue and groove dowels at each main bearing panel, of which there would be seven.

The crankshaft had six throws on the seven bearings and whereas Royce, in his earlier Eagle X16 pattern engine, had tackled the connecting rod problem by using two pairs of fork and blade rods on a common crankpin and thus staggered the cylinders, Elliott opted for a 'star-rod' design, with a master and three articulated rods. The implication of this was of four pistons and cylinders per bearing and herein lay an intrinsic defect of the design. The star-rod concept

implied some variation in cylinder stroke, whilst the chosen design of the rods was complex, one articulated rod was located on the master and the other two were in the cap, giving a split line for the big end at an angle to the master rod. (See page 83.) To close the con-rods around the bearing thus required two long and two very short bolts. This design concept too was untried and provided a further Achilles' heel. The loadings of the four con-rods were such that a high brinell nickel-chrome steel, probably S65, was used for the bolts. This was a major departure from Rolls-Royce experience, since all their 'V' engines used a more ductile 3.5% nickel steel for their con-rod bolts, giving a tensile strength approaching 55 tons.

The engine was to have a two-speed supercharger of the Farman pattern, adapted by Rolls-Royce and similar to those previously used by the company. The supercharger downdraft intake was adapted from the Peregrine, except for the outlets to the two trunk pipes. The reduction gear was of a layshaft design and was also new. The cylinders would each have four valves operated by an overhead cam-shaft and two sparking plugs. Each engine consequently had 48 plugs and each Manchester 96!

Design and construction proceeded during 1936-37, with the first engine being test run on the bench on 1st September 1937. In the first year of development testing over 860 hours running was completed with the engine reaching its design power of about 1,750hp. By this time the engine was at the heart of a number of new aircraft designs. However, development did not proceed without problems. Possibly the main development problems involved crankcase distortion and main bearing reliability. In view of the resulting delays and Rolls-Royce's increasing importance to the future war effort, with its Merlin, Griffon, Exe and Peregrine engines, Vulture development did not get the highest priority within the company.

In the original Vulture design the two crankcase halves were secured by diagonal bolts and with the somewhat small dowels it was easy to distort the crankcase assembly as the nuts were tightened. The main bearing materials then in general use were lead bronze with 1% tin and a similar material with 0.5% silver. The 1% tin lead bronze had good mechanical properties, but was prone to seize if there were any breakdown in lubrication. The 0.5% silver lead bronze had good bearing properties, but tended to crack just above the bond with the steel shell causing the surface to break up. The crankcase distortion was tackled by replacing the existing dowels with large 'cheese' dowels on either side of the main bearing bore in the crankcase panels. This enabled production engines to be built without excessive distortion.

Concern was also expressed about the cylinder top-end condition. With the single piece block, deterioration in this top joint would allow a coolant leak into the cylinder or a gas leak into the cooling system. In the Vulture saddle studs were introduced in an effort to maintain the seal at this point. The rest of the engine seems to have worked reasonably well during development, although the originally proposed coil ignition was abandoned in favour of magneto ignition, which also gave rise to problems later.

Meanwhile, although design work was still in an early stage, Avros received a great stimulus with an order, to the modified Air Ministry Specification 19/37, for 200 of the Type 679, now named 'Manchester'. The contract, No. 648770/37/C4(c) arrived on 1st July 1937. A very large scale logistics exercise was required, involving hiring and training designers and engineers. Planning for production also had to be organised and scheduled; parts had to be designed and assembled, materials ordered, tools designed, built and bought, sub-contractors appointed and the factory floor space extended. Planning and preparation took so much time that the first metal was not cut until mid-1938. In addition to the thousands of drawings, the myriad of structural items had to go through rigorous strength tests.

By early 1938, doubts had arisen concerning the development of the Rolls-Royce Vulture and alternative power plants were considered. Not only were there problems with the engine itself, but doubt arose as to the production capacity of the Rolls parent factory. The Air Ministry, accordingly, directed Handley Page to re-configure their HP.56 to take four Merlin engines on a stretched wing. The new design was redesignated as the HP.57 and ultimately became the Halifax. Human perversity being what it is, Sir Frederick Handley Page complained vehemently over the delays induced by forcing him to redesign for the four Merlin configuration. Later, as Vulture delays proliferated, Dobson and Chadwick of Avro were to complain equally strongly when Air Ministry initially refused to consider switching to four Merlins on the Manchester. As a consequence the Manchester was left as the sole successful contender to specification P13/36.

The pace of development was such that numerous meetings were required with Air Ministry and RAF officials and suppliers at London, Derby, High Duty Alloys and George Dowty, etc. Thus during 1937 and early 1938 emphasis was on designing and building machine tools, jigs, making drawings and refinements to the design. A number of milestones en route were as follows:

Rolls-Royce Vulture. *Rolls-Royce*

One of three wooden mock ups built or evaluated at Avro's Newton Heath works to test crew positions and freedom of movement.
G A Jenks collection

Manchester Design Milestones

18 Mar 37	Advisory design conference
26 Apr 37	Preliminary examination of mock up of front fuselage
4 May 37	Final mock up conference
1 Jul 37	First production order off the drawing board
4 Aug 37	Decision that the first prototype will have Bristol Hercules engines and the second Rolls-Royce Vultures
26 Aug 37	Torpedo requirement cancelled
4 Jul 38	Catapult requirement cancelled
11 Aug 38	Dive bombing requirement cancelled

Taking these in chronological order, it would seem that two mock up noses were scrapped before final approval for the crew disposition was given. The principal change was replacement of the prone bomb aiming position by a seated and later, a kneeling one. The proposal to adopt the Bristol Hercules was merely a stop-gap to enable flying experience to be gained with the first prototype. Vulture development was already lagging in mid-1937, but even so with the Hercules at this time outputting only 1,350hp it is unlikely the Manchester would have got airborne with such units. As its role evolved, and also arising from the extreme pressures which were building up for the bomber to reach the production line, it is notable that the ancillary roles were progressively laid to one side. In addition to the extra design work entailed, Coastal Command had assessed the Manchester and decided it would be too large, too unmanoeuvrable and unsuited to control in a dive to accomplish torpedo attacks safely.

A year later the catapulting and dive bombing requirements were cancelled. By this time the design had been frozen and the great additional strength and weight demanded by these two requirements was an intrinsic part of the design. It had originally been agreed that catapult launching facilities in the aircraft were to be designed by Avro in collaboration with the Royal Aircraft Establishment (RAE). By May 1938 Avro had proposals agreed for the structural integrity of the airframe, and the catapult strong points. Some two months later, when the option was cancelled, the first 20 aircraft on the production line were already too advanced to take account of the weight saving offered. Whether this requirement was ever designed out of the aircraft has not been established. Despite the importance of reducing weight Chadwick estimated it would lead to a six to nine month delay and £50,000 extra cost in jigs and tools.

Indeed, the first prototype was employed on accelerated take-off trials, as distinct from catapulting, and the dive-bombing requirement re-emerged for a short period in April 1940. It was finally cancelled only when the 60° angle considered essential for bombing accuracy was judged unattainable. Of all ancillary requirements it was the troop carrying which persisted longest, not being abandoned until 31st January 1940.

These are three major items of design to provide examples, but in fact during 1937 and 1938 the design changes were too numerous to list. Undoubtedly the most far-reaching was the decision to set aside the catapult requirement. Together with the changes in requirement, the cumulative effect of the extra design and constructional effort must have retarded progress on the two prototypes very considerably and in turn adversely affected production. The work load on Chadwick and his staff must have been ferocious and, reading between the lines, the patience of a saint must have been an essential requirement in dealing with some Air Ministry and RAF requests.

A typical, if rather extreme, example is the letter Avro received from the Air Ministry dated 17th January 1938 under the heading 'Duplicate Engine Policy'. It informed Chadwick, 'In future it will be a fundamental policy of Air Ministry that all aircraft will be specifically designed to take alternative types of engine'. The P13/36 design for the Hercules and Vulture now had to be capable of conversion to either the Napier Sabre or Bristol Centaurus within 48 hours. In a classic of bureaucracy the writer concluded 'I do not wish to be informed of the difficulties to be overcome'! Another requirement, stemming this time from concerns over the availability of light alloys, targeted the Manchester specifically. All firms were to consider alternatives to light alloys including steel, reinforced synthetic resins, plywood, pigmented cellulose acetate sheet and laminated paper. The Manchester was highlighted as its design was at the critical stage when substitutions might be made.

Requirements piled on requirements at fever pitch. The Director of Repair insisted on additional design effort in a number of areas, including the requirement that fuel tanks, not only be removable but interchangeable. Avro designed the aircraft to accept standard bomb hoisting carriers, but Air Ministry later changed the requirement again so that Avro had to redesign and stress a large part of the cabin floor once more. Avro's own bomb carriers offered better flexibility and were eventually adopted. A misunderstanding in respect of take-off loads necessitated larger undercarriage members, which in turn entailed redesign of the stowage space in the engine nacelles.

These few individual changes must be anticipated to have multiplied up through the entire design, providing a glimpse of just what a massive undertaking the Manchester was. Of the multitude of changes, perhaps the most visually obvious were the replacement of the inset fins by elliptical fins and rudders at the ends of the tailplane and the extension of the wing span from 72ft 0in to 80ft 2in. The latter modification is particularly significant, in that, bearing in mind the marginal take-off and flying performance, necessitating further wing extension, it seems unlikely with the original wing that the aircraft would have left the ground at all. Later, on reflection, it was considered that the delays in getting the Manchester into production stemmed sequentially from the initial need to design and build machines on which the aircraft itself was in turn built, then from the multitudinous changes in design and finally due to the problems incurred with the Rolls-Royce Vulture engines.

At the end of 1938 Expansion Programme 'L' projected the acquisition of 3,500 medium and heavy bombers for the RAF, 1,500 of which would be Manchesters. To achieve this, the Manchester Production Group was

Differences in cockpit framing indicate another of the wooden mock ups at Newton Heath. Note the 'collar' being worn by the pilot. *G A Jenks collection*

established involving not only Avro but also Armstrong Whitworth, Fairey and Metropolitan-Vickers (known as Metrovick). A second batch of 200 Manchesters was ordered from Avro, 100 from Metrovick in 1939 and plans made to bring Armstrong Whitworth at Coventry and Fairey at Manchester into the production group. Orders for 300 Manchesters were placed with each of these companies in late 1939 or 1940. Part of these orders seem to have been as outlined in the table below. Eventually many of these orders were to emerge as Lancasters.

Manchester Production Group Initial Orders

Serials	Qty	Contractor	Date
R4525 to R4744	150	Fairey Aviation	Sep 39
R5273 to R5477	150	Armstrong Whitworth	Sep 39
R5482 to R5763	200	A V Roe	Sep 39
W1280 to W1498	150	Armstrong Whitworth	Dec 39
W4102 to W4700	450	A V Roe	Jan 40

As 1938 had progressed, the Air Ministry also began to give increasingly urgent thought to the defensive armament to be carried by its three new heavy bombers. Historians and analysts have frequently criticised RAF Bomber Command for sticking to the small calibre 0.303in gun, power operated turrets, whilst heavy calibre cannon were ranged against them by opposing German fighters. In fact the Air Ministry Directorate of Armament Development (DArmD), were to carry out a long and intensive development programme to equip RAF bombers with two 20mm power operated cannon turrets. The development programme came to nothing and it was not until the very late stages of the war that even the twin 0.5in calibre turret was available for rear defence, long after the Manchester had passed into oblivion. The history of these endeavours is beyond the scope of this book, save to point out that what was lacking was not the vision, but rather the technology to implement it.

Between 1938 and 1941 the intensive development programme produced nothing usable and Air Vice-Marshal Robert Saundby of Bomber Command Headquarters and one of the leading proponents of heavy cannon turrets, summarised the main problems in a letter to Air Vice-Marshal J Slessor of 5 Group Headquarters in May 1941. These were:

1 A reduced rate of fire compared to the 0.303in, although the sighting accuracy was equal.
2 The excessive weight of adequate ammunition supply and its bulkier stowage.
3 These considerations necessitated both the turrets and stowage of spare ammunition being close to the centre of gravity (cg) of the aircraft. Tail installation was hence precluded.
4 The absorption of the recoil stresses added greatly to the aircraft structural weight.

5 The increased drag of the exposed barrel, or barrels, required much greater horse power for traversing or elevating.
6 Throughout this era, severe difficulties were experienced with handling and reloading the heavy cylindrical magazines, whilst belt feeding for cannon was not available until 1941.

Initially plans had been made to provide twin 20mm Hispano cannon power operated turrets in mid-upper and mid-under installations in the Manchester. A design conference was held at the Air Ministry on 15th May 1939 to draw up a specification from which the Nash and Thompson company would design and build the installations. Space mock ups based on a 48in diameter ring had already been constructed.

The problems of such powerful turrets were prodigious. In respect of the above list, each 20mm gun weighed 110lb and just two 60 round magazines weighed 132lb. The estimated total weight of a turret, less ammunition, gunner or accessories was at least 500lb. Such weight considerations suggested a reduction to a single 20mm Hispano cannon, but the rate of fire achievable would then be inadequate.

The 15th May 1939 meeting considered ammunition supplies. Thirty or 60-round magazines were available, with the 60-round desirable for daylight work or sustained engagements. The turret would need to carry four 60-round drums with an approximate weight of 224lb. A further ten 60-round drums of reserve ammunition were required and increased the weight by a further 560lb. Much design and development work was carried out, but the problems proved insuperable. The 20mm Hispano Suiza was naturally much larger than the 0.303in Browning. It had a length of 8ft 2½in. At least 5ft 6in would protrude from any turret and in addition to the drag, problems with barrel whip would be encountered. One palliative was to shorten the barrel length, but then problems with excessive muzzle flash blinding the gunner were encountered. It was discovered that Anti-Aircraft (AA) Command had secured exclusive access to scarce supplies of flashless propellant. The power requirements were stated to be 2hp for two 20mm, greater than the Manchester had available. A further limitation was that depressing the guns below the horizontal on the beam was found to present serious design and structural problems.

Wind tunnel model of the Type 679. The design has evolved to embrace the end plate fins and rudders and the bomb aimer's 'blister' in the lower nose. *G A Jenks collection*

Recruiting and Training Programme model of the P13/36, dated March 1938. *via Peter Green*

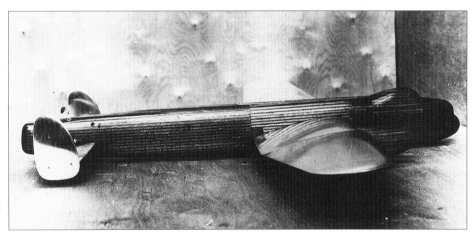

Throughout this period manhandling the heavy ammunition drums in aircraft taking any evasive action proved a severe limitation. As initially formulated, Nash and Thompson informed the meeting that to reload it would be essential to align the turret fore and aft, train the guns vertically and use a mechanically powered drive to disconnect the expended and reconnect the next 30-round or 60-round drum. These requirements were not attainable in a Manchester. Later belt feeding for larger calibre guns was developed, but the higher gun ammunition and power unit weight requirements precluded multiple turret installations aft of the Manchester centre of gravity.

When Lord Beaverbrook shelved all further development work on the B1/39 'Ideal Bomber' and F11/37 turret fighter projects the work on 20mm turrets was also suspended. Nevertheless, as operational experience with the Manchester was gained, serious efforts to substantially increase the defensive armament re-emerged, in May/June and October/November 1941 particularly.

Construction of the Manchester prototypes proceeded during late 1938 and early 1939, but all this time Vulture development had been falling steadily behind. The problems with crankcase distortion during construction and a welter of other problems had limited even bench running. After first rescheduling the HP.56 to take four Merlins, which Avros initially did not object to because it allowed them to leap ahead in the unofficial race, serious consideration was given to switching to either Napier Sabre or Bristol Centaurus engines in the Manchester. Nacelle design apparently reached an advanced stage, but since neither engine was as advanced as the Vulture, neither offered realistic options. It was already clear to Chadwick that at the pace the Manchester was evolving and with the number of changes imposed upon the company undiminished, modifications would have to be incorporated into aircraft on the assembly line as and when they became finalised.

Whilst the two prototype Manchesters began to come together rapidly as 1939 advanced, it became obvious that a delay was going to arise from late delivery of the

L7246 after towing out for its first flight. The tow rope is still attached to the main wheels. A ring bolt and escape hatch, soon to be obstructed by the addition of a centre fin, are located in the upper rear fuselage.
British Aerospace

Opposite page: **First prototype L7246 with main and tail wheels well lashed and weighed down during its initial engine runs at Ringway in mid July 1940. Note that the spinners, propellers and turret fairings remain in aluminium finish.**

L7246 being towed out, immediately prior to its first flight at Ringway. The date is close to 20th July 1939. Note what appear to be two lights, as opposed to a perspex window, beneath the bomb aimer's blister, the painted turret fairings, and the lack of fin flashes.
Both British Aerospace

Rolls-Royce Vulture engines, which would, moreover, end up more than a ton per pair heavier than originally envisaged. The first prototype, L7246, had 80ft 2in span wings, the 28ft span tail and twin end plate fins.

Early in 1939 flight test engines had finally become available for evaluation on the Hawker Henley test beds. The engine in the first Henley, K5115, suffered the problem of insufficient coolant flow, leading to aeration, which was thought to have been cured by fitting a larger capacity header tank in the aircraft. However, the problem subsequently recurred on several occasions in the Manchester. The second Vulture Henley, L3302, suffered another of the typical lubrication problems with the engine, namely a fall in oil pressure with altitude, accompanied by excessive oil aeration. The aircraft later force-landed on the beach at Borth, Wales when a con-rod broke. Soon, too, engines were released for the Vickers B1/35 Warwick and the Manchester. Chadwick is recorded asserting that only 1,630 to 1,650hp was available from the Vultures at this stage in their development.

L7246 had finally come together at Ringway in April 1939, by which time weight had risen alarmingly. Following several days taken up with ground running and engine testing, L7246 was made ready for its first flight on 25th July 1939. Avro staff and the various Air Ministry officials seconded to the company had by now been living with the project for approaching three years. This, combined with the variety of novel and complex systems in the aircraft, led to an unusually heightened tension as preparation for the initial test was completed. Chief test pilot, Captain H A 'Sam' Brown, accompanied by assistant Bill Thorn and two engineers boarded the aircraft, watched not only by Dobson, Chadwick and other senior staff but small

knots of workers all round the airfield. L7246 looked unusually smooth and clean with its faired over front and rear turret positions as it taxied to the end of the runway and began a protracted take-off run. The aircraft roared into the sky and disappeared from view. In the absence of any radio link those on the ground were left in suspense until its return and safe landing a mere 17 minutes later. As it taxied in Sam Brown offered a quick thumbs up to Dobson and Chadwick, but after the engines were shut down there was clearly much to discuss and of a more than superficial nature.

For a start, both engines had run very hot and Brown had to nurse and watch these closely. More directly relevant to Chadwick, however, was that even lightly loaded, the take-off had been unusually protracted and the climb rate disappointingly below that initially specified. Indeed performance in this respect was sufficiently marginal that a substantial increase in wing area was obviously essential. A major redesign effort was necessary. Furthermore, lack of directional stability indicated that tail fin area had also been seriously underestimated. Subsequent flights over the next few days allowed various aspects of performance to be evaluated more fully. A top speed of 265mph was recorded, way below that initially forecast. The original all-metal elevators were also considered unsatisfactory. Investigations revealed that the elevator shape, hinge point and construction were all wanting and work was put in progress to redesign a new metal framed elevator with fabric covering.

Clearly, as opposed to nearing the end of the design phase, Avro had a great deal of rethinking to do. Much of this can have been no surprise to Chadwick, although the extent to which the aircraft had underperformed must have been worrying. Chadwick must also have been conscious of the fundamental dilemma facing the design. Over the three year period the fixed military load had escalated sharply, as had structural weight. In contrast, not only had power availability in the Vulture not kept pace with the weight escalation, it did not as yet meet its initial design power output.

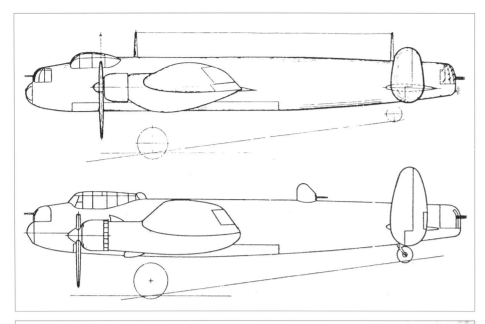

Engine options were almost constantly being considered. Top view shows Drawing No. A1491 dated 29th April 1937 to 27th January 1938 showing the Type 679 with Bristol Hercules radials. Lower view is A1605, dated 25th August 1941 and the Manchester II Bristol Centaurus radial installation.
via Chaz Bowyer

A Manchester main spar showing the undercarriage mounts and a bare Vulture on the engine bearers. *British Aerospace*

Chadwick's dilemma was that to improve flying performance it was now estimated that a further span increase to 90ft 1in and enlarged tail surfaces were required. This in turn meant even greater weight. Moreover, much of the military load, including the turrets, had yet to be installed.

On the plus side the aircraft had, in general, handled quite well and indeed good flying characteristics and well co-ordinated controls were later to become an acknowledged feature of the Manchester and Lancaster. For the moment Chadwick and Dobson had more serious and immediate problems to deal with. These were the related ones of continued lack of progress with Vulture development and power output, coupled with the steady and apparently inexorable weight increase. Indeed these two problems were to continue to bedevil the aircraft throughout its service life.

Consideration of longer term options must have become more sharply focused in Chadwick's mind from this time onwards. It was never possible to judge quite how close Rolls-Royce were to fully overcoming the Vulture problems and the company were naturally optimistic, at least publicly, on prospects. The Sabre and Centaurus options were serious possibilities, if only in view of the limitations of the Vulture. Possibly around this time Chadwick began to seriously explore a more radical enlargement to four engines. Certainly, as the more pessimistic prospects emerging from Avro became known, Bomber Command preference began steadily to swing in favour of the second placed design in the tender competition, the Handley Page Halifax.

From this time onwards, Avros continued to struggle to maintain a flight test and development programme, frustrated by long periods of unserviceability due to engine problems. Rolls-Royce too at this stage were investing a massive manpower effort in Vulture development, which was still at the heart of a number of vital aircraft programmes, not least amongst which were the Hawker Tornado fighter and the Manchester. Although all documents relating to these have not been tracked down, Chadwick was later to explain to Professor Michael E W Postan and Mr R Lubbock in 1944 that flight trials on the Manchester prototypes had been protracted and difficult owing to the terrible powerplant problems which persisted during the second half of 1939 and 1940. One Vulture after another had blown up and been destroyed completely, until half a dozen had been consumed over this period. In Rolls-Royce's case, however, they were never able to input anything like the effort into Vulture development as was contributed to the even more important Merlin programme. These facts point clearly, not only to the roots of the Manchester problem, but to the eventual solution.

Avro's giant step forward into new techniques, as represented in the Manchester, was further complicated by a range of other problems, of which the most serious seem to have been hydraulic failures in the aircraft. On 28th September 1939, after L7246 had been grounded for a month due to hydraulic and engine problems, a 43 minute flight was accomplished. On this occasion a quill shaft failed in the port engine, incapacitating the hydraulic system. At this time flexible hydraulic pipes were installed in a number of places in an effort to overcome the hydraulic failures, which perpetually occurred in flight and not on the ground. Pressure fluctuations were suspected to be the cause, but finally vibrations in the air were found to be the origin. At Boscombe Down, the A&AEE (Aeroplane & Armament Experimental Establishment) were standing by to evaluate the aircraft, but clearly it was far from ready. As the war began in September 1939 the major programme to refine and improve the Manchester was not the only issue to occupy Avro design staff, major though this was.

During 1939 wide ranging discussions had been held in the Air Ministry concerning the needs for defensive armament in the three heavy bombers, the Halifax, Manchester and Stirling, then under development. A radical alternative to the power operated nose and tail turrets with relatively small calibre guns, or the 20mm cannon in conventional turrets had been proposed. This involved very large diameter, low drag cannon-armed turrets located close to the centre of gravity of such aircraft in mid-upper and mid-lower positions. At this time development of the Manchester was more advanced than its two rivals and the type was chosen for the long term development of such turrets. On 6th April 1939 Mr W S Farren had written to the Director General of Research and Development setting out the concept. The requirement was considered at this time of such high priority that four of the Manchesters, Nos. 10, 14, 18 and 22, were to be requisitioned from the production line for the development. The task was a major one, involving not only redesign and streamlined fairing of the nose and tail positions, but also a probable swelling around the centre fuselage station to accept a variety of development turrets up to 10 feet in diameter!

A Rolls-Royce Vulture with all ancillary services installed, but with cowlings removed. Almost certainly this is the prototype, L7246; note the aluminium finish to the propeller and the spinner. *British Aerospace*

At a meeting on 21st September 1939 held at Avro, Chadwick informed the assembled Air Ministry and turret manufacturers' representatives that the revised Manchester fuselage, designated Mk.II, was largely designed, other than for turret specifications from the various manufacturers. The concept involved upper and lower twin cannon turrets. Avro would manufacture a belly bulge capable of taking the largest of the three turrets and would install a standard diameter ring in the special fuselage to take the largest turret. The other two manufacturers would have to supply adapter rings with their turrets to fit this standard ring. The three turret manufacturers involved offered different alternatives.

Nash and Thompson had designed the 90in ring upper and lower turrets with either 37–40mm or 20mm guns. Boulton and Paul proposed 78in ring upper and lower, four Hispano cannon turrets and Bristol a 96¼in ring, four Hispano upper and lower turrets. The latter two turrets were also scheduled for installation in a new bomber to specification B1/39.

Avro were to be responsible for any necessary fairings and a 30hp Scott air-cooled engine was to be installed in the fuselage to drive the turrets. In each case the mid-under gunner would be able to abandon the aircraft without entering the fuselage. Avros were also to provide a rest position and oxygen point for the gun loader adjacent to the upper and lower turrets. Quite how much further design and development work was put into this concept is unclear, but doubt was expressed of the necessity of the Manchester Mk.II concept in May 1940 and it was cancelled on 12th June 1940.

These diversions cannot have assisted Chadwick in the autumn of 1939 as Avros struggled to come to terms with the range of fundamental problems still besetting the design. However, not all was doom and gloom. In early 1939 a visiting team from the Directorate of Aeronautical Inspectors had carried out a preliminary critical report on the suitability of the two prototypes, L7246 and L7247, then under assembly, for quantity production. They declared themselves to be generally satisfied and were especially impressed on account of the limited previous experience at Avros in all-metal aircraft construction.

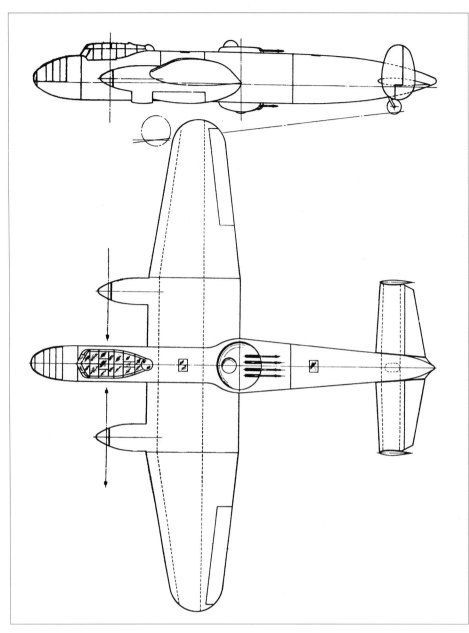

Side and top views of the Manchester armament development aircraft. This is Drawing No. 1528, dated 29th August 1939, showing upper and under Boulton Paul turrets each with four cannons. Note the bulbous effect to the mid-fuselage. *via Chaz Bowyer*

By late 1939 Chadwick finally believed reliability in the Vultures, the hydraulic system and the aircraft in general was improved sufficiently for L7246, still unarmed and with short span wings and the small, twin fin tail to proceed on to its next major hurdle, at A&AEE. Time was to reveal a major contrast between Avro's expectations and unfolding events.

In anticipation of delivery to Boscombe Down, Captain Sam Brown carried out a final test flight in L7246 from Woodford on 25th November 1939. The aircraft was loaded to 32,500 lb. His report praises the good and simple take-off performance, requiring only the advancement of the starboard throttle ahead of the port to counteract the swing to starboard. Aileron and rudder control was assessed as light and effective at all speeds, although the elevator was acknowledged as somewhat heavy, especially at high speeds. The machine was reported both laterally and directionally stable although fore and aft stability was questionable. Brown concluded that the Manchester was easy to handle and had no vices whatever, apart from the easily controlled tendency to swing on take-off.

On 29th November L7246 began its delivery flight to Boscombe Down. En route over Staffordshire the port engine cut out and Bill Thorn, the pilot, was unable to maintain height on the remaining engine. Fortunately he was able to effect a safe wheels down

landing in a large field at Charnes Hall, Wetwood village in Staffordshire, about 8 miles east of Market Drayton. There were red faces at Avros when it was discovered that the fuel cock of the port engine had been inadvertently turned to reserve instead of main tank. Fortunately the precious prototype was undamaged and after a ditch had been filled and six big trees cut down, the aircraft was able to take off at 2.45pm on 1st December and return to Ringway for checking. On 10th December, this time flown by Sam Brown, L7246 took off for Boscombe Down, landing safely after a two hour flight.

At Boscombe, Avro had made arrangements to increase the vertical tail surface area, first with an unusually shaped shark-fin mounted on the centre rear fuselage, but within a few days by a larger, more oval shaped fin, more in keeping with the general contours of the aircraft.

Trials evaluation flying commenced with great urgency at Boscombe Down but within two days, on 12th December, disaster struck the programme when the aircraft experienced engine failure at 300ft soon after take-off. The pilot was unable to maintain height and return to the airfield, but skilfully force landed in a cabbage field with the undercarriage retracted. Again damage to the aircraft was relatively limited. L7246 was recovered from the field and the engine on this occasion rapidly repaired. The urgent trials programme was resumed, but on 23rd December another engine failure occurred. Despite being at 3,000ft, height could not be maintained on the remaining engine and the aircraft crash landed in a field short of the boundary of Boscombe Down. This time, examination of the defective engine disclosed that a complete internal failure had occurred, with two con-rods protruding from the crankcase. Evidently the Manchester problems were far from solved and the aircraft was dismantled and returned to Woodford. It seemed wise to defer further testing and risk to the sole prototype until the serious engine and airframe problems had been attended to. The A&AEE had accomplished enough trials flying to at least provide an initial report and this provided a stark contrast with that of the Avro chief test pilot only two weeks earlier.

Initial trials in L7246 were carried out at weights of 34,000 lb and 40,000 lb. On take-off the elevators were very heavy and excessive force was required to raise the tail and then to unstick the aeroplane. At 40,000 lb the take-off performance was most unsatisfactory. The aircraft took 580 yards to take-off and had only reached 20ft after 1,070 yards, so that the distance required to clear a 50ft screen could not be obtained. Take-off performance was considered one of the most unsatisfactory aspects. Whereas the ailerons were light and effective at all speeds, the rudder only became effective at speeds in excess of 100mph. The elevators were excessively heavy and ineffective below 100mph and over 260mph in the dive. In view of the instability of the aircraft throughout the speed range, it was considered that a larger tailplane was necessary.

The aircraft would maintain height on one engine at 3,000ft at a load of 32,400lb but not at 40,000lb. On approach and landing, lowering the undercarriage produced nose heaviness and the flaps, tail heaviness. The tail heaviness became greater with increase in engine power on approach and it was difficult to hold the aircraft in a glide. Approach with full flap and little engine was straightforward until the aircraft was flared prior to touch down, when the elevator became very heavy indeed. As a result a controlled landing was considered virtually impossible. The general conclusion seems to have been that serious problems had still to be overcome in the Manchester.

As 1940 began, the feverish pace of Manchester development continued, but its focus was now shifted. Whilst pressing Rolls-Royce as hard as was possible to come up with solutions to the serious engine problems, stress was imposed on Avros in two directions, towards reducing weight and improving aerodynamic performance. By 6th May Rolls-Royce appeared to have overcome their problems to a large extent and an Air Ministry minute reports that the maximum rpm available for take-off had increased to 3,200 and the company were now satisfied that these latest engines would behave satisfactorily. Time was to be a harsh judge of this ill-placed confidence.

In February and March 1940 correspondence passed repeatedly between Norman E Rowe, the Deputy Director of Technical Development, and Roy Chadwick in connection with a major revision in design with a view to substantially cutting the all up weight of the aircraft. Only a major weight-saving

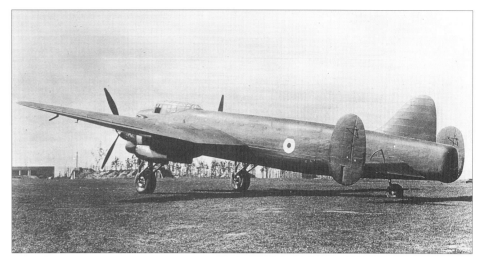

L7246 at Boscombe Down, probably in December 1939, with definitive form of centre fin. Note that the propellers and spinners have been painted, the underwing serials deleted and underwing roundels applied. *A&AEE Boscombe Down HA447-2*

The prototype after one of its two forced landings near Boscombe Down in December 1939, most likely the one on 12th December 1939. *via R C B Ashworth*

was considered capable of rescuing the flagging fortunes of the aircraft. In reviewing the situation in May 1940, Director General of Research and Development reported to the Air Ministry Directorate of Planning that since February 1939 the equipped weight of the Manchester had increased by 4,485lb, whilst a further 550lb was about to be added. As unassisted take-off was not assured at weights in excess of 45,000lb, this steady escalation in equipment had to be pegged back and indeed reduced if any significant bomb carrying capability was to be retained.

Chadwick immediately set to work. Little could be achieved on the initial 20 aircraft, which were already at an advanced stage of construction, but by various radical changes, mainly a reduction in the gauge of metal used in the aircraft skin, a substantial improvement was achieved. On 24th April Rowe wrote to Chadwick congratulating him on the 1,550lb total weight saving proposed and instructing him to set these in hand immediately. These further alterations, and others soon to follow to the design and equipment of the aircraft, would ultimately require Avro to restress the aircraft six times. However, despite his efforts in this direction, Chadwick was now engrossed in a more radical and revolutionary solution.

From March 1940 the Avro team began to press harder for the adoption of the four engined solution to the Manchester dilemma. On 18th April 1940 Chadwick wrote to the Air Ministry setting out his proposed mark numbers for the various Manchester subtypes then under active development, ending with the Manchester III powered by four Merlins and with the rider 'This type will probably be given another name later'.

The reality of the Manchester's position was only too apparent. Having started as the leading contender and achieving most of its development milestones earlier than its two rivals, the Manchester now looked a very poor second compared to the Halifax. It was all too evident that the Manchester, with its two Vultures and all up weight of 45,000 lb, would not compare with the four Merlin Halifax, which was designed to operate at 50,000 lb at this stage. Worse was to follow, for by the summer of 1940 Vulture development and production, and the technical position of the Manchester itself, were such that the whole future of the type was in jeopardy. Yet delivery of the first pre-production aircraft had still to be made! For the rest of the year, and especially during the critical discussion period of autumn 1940, the Halifax would become the yardstick by which the Manchester, and more importantly the four Merlin Manchester III, would be judged. Thus, even before it reached RAF service, much of 1940 was to be a crisis period for the design. Although Manchester production would outpace that of the Halifax, only much later, from early 1942, would the design regain its ascendancy over the Halifax and indeed achieve its true and deserved superiority.

For the moment, in Spring 1940, Chadwick and Avro's design staff were fully occupied with more immediate issues. In the shorter term the dominating weight problems had been tackled with the proposed crash weight reduction programme, whereas in the longer term Chadwick hoped to eradicate these completely by switching to the four Merlin configuration.

Weight was only one of the Manchester's problems. Equally serious were the take-off, climb, single-engined and general flying characteristics. In order to improve the first three, plans were well advanced to stretch the span of the outer wings to 90ft 1in. This was achieved by leaving the centre section to outboard of the engines unchanged, but then machining new main spars to the new length and spacing the ribs at wider centres along the wing. This was the second such extension from the initial design span of 72ft and would become the standard for the entire Manchester force. Using the same basic idea, Chadwick gained permission for a further tip extension to 95ft on 24th April 1940 and used the same idea a fourth time to finally stretch the wing to 102ft, the final production form of the Manchester III.

The urgent need for type testing of L7246 meant that when repairs were completed in May 1940 the 80ft wings and short span tail were retained, as they were initially on the second prototype, L7247. Opportunity was, however, taken to improve the longitudinal stability of L7247 as rapidly as possible. As an interim measure, and by way of obtaining design information, two small ancillary control surfaces were mounted on struts beneath the elevators of L7247. A more permanent and radical solution involved scrapping the 28ft metal tailplanes and elevators entirely and replacing them with a new 33ft metal tailplane and steel-framed, fabric covered elevator. This increased tailplane area by 20% whilst the root and tip chords were unchanged. To improve elevator effectiveness the hinge was set back by 24% at the same time. Whilst all this was going on, plans were confirmed to fit all production Manchesters with the enlarged third fin located on the top rear fuselage. In this configuration the Manchester would be further tested and ultimately go to war.

Around this time plans were finalised to incorporate the large twin gun Fraser Nash F.N.21A 'Low drag' mid-under turret. This naturally went a significant way towards nullifying any weight saving gained by Chadwick in pursuit of improved take-off, climb and single engined performance. The total weight of the F.N.21A was 608 lb so whether this is the 550 lb item complained of by Tedder in May 1940 is uncertain.

Whilst these many changes were being specified, designed, built, incorporated and tested, pressure from Bomber Command was becoming even more insistent in respect of its need for the aircraft. It was to this end that the Director General of Research and Development, Air Vice-Marshal Arthur Tedder, authorised Avro on 27th May 1940 to delete certain essential items of operational equipment from the first production batch of 20 aircraft, then at an advanced stage of construction at Woodford. The Air Ministry had taken this step with a view to hastening the introduction of the first batch, with the intention of using these as bombing and gunnery training aircraft so that crews could become familiar with the new type. As a temporary expedient, it had been decided that only one in three of these first 20 aircraft should be completely equipped and a list of 22 small items to be deleted was handed to Avro on 28th May 1940. The action was thus unrelated to the weight reduction programme then in progress and furthermore recognised that the aircraft would need later retrospective modification. Resignedly, Chadwick concurred with this latest edict.

On 26th May 1940 the second prototype, L7247, now fully equipped with its three gun turrets, but retaining 80ft span wings, made its first flight and joined the test programme. Its initial shark fin was soon replaced with the standard centre fin.

When the impact of each of these new changes filtered through to Avro it was accepted that the first 20 aircraft were already too advanced for the long span tailplane to be incorporated on the production line and it would need to be a retrofitted item. Deliveries and installations of F.N.21A mid-under turrets had barely got underway when, on 1st July 1940, a further Air Ministry instruction was received to have F.N.21As on the Manchester and Halifax deleted and replaced by two hand-held Browning or Vickers gas operated guns in this position.

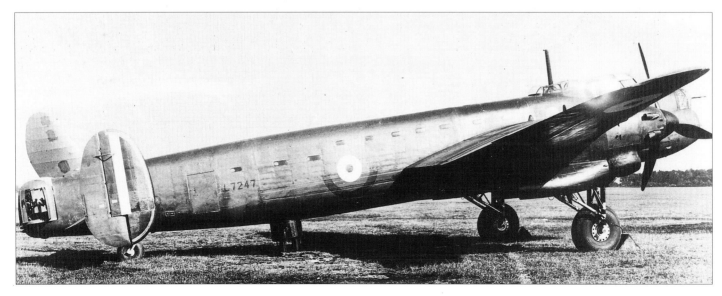

Magnificent shot of the second prototype, L7247, apparently prior to first engine runs. The nose F.N.5 turret is shown to advantage. Wingspan 80ft. Tailspan 28ft. Note the 'bench seat' ancillary elevators.
No.207 Squadron archives

Comparative views of the F.N.21A 'low drag' mid-under turret in extended and retracted positions. Heath Robinson would have been immensely proud, but in mitigation it was one of the very earliest attempts at a powered mid-under installation. Note the vertical stowage of the gun barrels.
British Aerospace

Opposite page: The first armed Manchester, second prototype L7247, with interim 'shark' fin fitted. This was soon replaced by the definitive centre fin. Yellow underside and fuselage roundel are rendered black by the Orthochromatic film. Note the rear F.N.4A turret trained fully to port and the lowered mid-under F.N.21A. *G A Jenks collection*

The Manchester's immense bomb bay, also showing the extended F.N.21A turret. The flat bottomed inner surface of the early bomb doors, which proved unable to close around the 4,000 lb 'Cookie', is evident.
British Aerospace

Experimental F.N.4 with early 'D' shaped cupola rotated to port, showing positions for the four 0.303in Browning guns.
Crown Copyright 10123(B)

Trial installations of the F.N.7A mid-upper turrets in the Stirling, Manchester and Halifax were to proceed. More than 100 of these had become available following the cancellation of the Blackburn Botha. Pending a final decision on the latter, hand-held beam mounted guns were to be provided.

Accordingly and patiently, Chadwick instructed that no more F.N.21As were to be installed, although between nine and eleven from the initial batch of 20 already had these incorporated. Indeed, the saga of Manchester defensive armament was far from over. This recently scheduled, mid-under, hand-held gun installation was objected to by the RAF in that it obstructed the vacant mid-under position which now needed to be retained as an escape hatch. Chadwick obligingly designed Avro's own retractable, mid-under, hand-held installation. All this effort eventually came to nothing for in service the F.N.21As were soon removed and subsequent aircraft delivered until March 1941 had no mid-positioned armament of any kind.

It is hard to believe that in the summer of 1940, with production so advanced and the RAF set to receive the aircraft for service, that virtually no type-testing of any significance had been accomplished at the A&AEE at Boscombe Down. With handling and performance trials of only the most perfunctory nature carried out and a range of urgent modifications in prospect, pressure was extreme to get some testing of the Manchester carried out. Accordingly, in May 1940, still without turrets, with 80ft wings and 28ft tail and the same elevators but now with take-off power conditions altered to 3,200rpm and +6lb/sq in boost, L7246 was returned to Boscombe Down for the vital take-off trials. These immediately confirmed that, even with more powerful engines, take-off, climb and single engine performance were all unacceptable and the 90ft wing was essential. In addition, longitudinal stability was so inferior that a longer span tail was essential for the 21st and subsequent Manchesters. Further tests were made on L7246 in July and August with the 90ft wing and with the new elevator design, although these still spanned the original 28ft. Take-offs were repeated at +6lb/sq in and +9lb/sq in boost. The 90ft span, combined with greater power, had clearly resulted in a considerable improvement in performance and operating safety margins. Control loads on the elevators were also greatly reduced with significant improvement in general handling.

The second Manchester prototype, L7247, was also allocated to A&AEE in late June 1940 for urgent armament trials. It, too, had the original 80ft wing, 28ft tail, but had the interim auxiliary aerofoil balance beneath the elevators to lighten control forces. Ground trials loading all specified combinations of bombs were carried out, with good results, other than for a number of superficial and readily rectified complaints. In the final design the bomb aimer knelt on a specially provided cushion beneath the front turret. The complaint was made that the front turret could not be manned simultaneously with the bomb aiming station. Furthermore, a large collecting box and chute for spent cartridges largely blocked the view for the bomb

Mock up Manchester rear fuselage hung inverted from the roof of the 24ft wind tunnel at the Royal Aircraft Establishment to evaluate aerodynamic behaviour of the F.N.20 Stirling-type cupola. This was never adopted.
Crown Copyright 31848

View of the mock up rear fuselage and circular cupola, tested inverted at RAE, July 1940.
Crown Copyright 32000

aimer and had to be removed and stowed to permit access to the bombsight. It was recommended that this be replaced by permanent, less obstructive canvas chutes with cartridge containers either side and behind the bomb aimer, and that both crew must be able to carry out their duties immediately and simultaneously. Even better were the results of bombing trials. In the air low level bombing trials from 1,000 feet produced a very high accuracy with a mean error of eight bombs of 24 yards. This was attributed to the Manchester being such a steady bombing platform.

Preliminary results of the turret trials at A&AEE were less encouraging, especially in the case of the rear turret installation. Clearly, the Manchester was one aircraft which would not be 'right first time'. As originally specified, the first batch of Manchesters were to have the F.N.4 tail turret with a specially-designed, metal-framed and perspex cupola streamlined into the rear fuselage lines. The second and subsequent batches would have the later, more advanced, F.N.20 turret with servo ammunition feed. In a later departure and attempt at standardisation in aircraft turret armament, it was decided to

adopt a 'mean' cupola with a circular section in plan view. This standard turret would equip not only Manchesters but also Stirlings, Short Sunderlands and Vickers Wellingtons. Unfortunately, the circular cupola was oversize on the Manchester and in full scale mock up wind tunnel tests produced drag increases of 7–11 lb or more. The additional weight and drag of the F.N.20 led Avros, already acutely concerned in respect of the escalating weight, to protest. The timing of the installation of the F.N.20 with circular cupola was steadily put back during 1940 and eventually the cupola was abandoned on the Manchester and later on the Lancaster.

Initial flight trials with the F.N.4 with D-shaped cupola on L7247 and later L7278 had alarming consequences. In the first tests on L7247, turret rotation in level flight at 232mph led to vibration and buffeting in the rear fuselage, which was readily detected in the pilot's controls. The vibration led to hesitation in the speed of turret rotation. Even worse, when a further trial involving a dive to 280mph and rotation of the F.N.4 was repeated, a violent and uncontrollable trim change in the Manchester was induced. Rotation in one direction led to a nose down pitching, which could not be corrected using the controls until the turret rotated back fore and aft. Rotation in the opposite direction induced a violent nose-up attitude followed by a stall. Turret rotation became jerky in both modes. At this speed, as rotation continued, vibration of the turret and buffeting became steadily more violent and transmitted itself to the entire rear fuselage, especially from the tail spar aft. Nash and Thompson representatives became sufficiently scared that, fearing a complete structural failure of the aircraft, they called for the test to be terminated.

In a similar trial a few days later a rigger

stationed in the rear fuselage encountered actual jamming of the turret at two points in its rotation and jerky rotation between. Accompanying the savage vibration he noted the fuselage itself twisting with the imposed stresses. The trial was again abandoned and a landing made at Boscombe Down.

Examination proved that the port elevator aerodynamic balance had collapsed, the complete structure supporting the turret was loose and the entire cupola could be rocked from side to side and made to touch the fuselage sides! The rear of the aircraft had been close to total disintegration. A series of countersunk screws and nuts fastening the curved cover to the fuselage end and the turret mounting had come loose.

RAE Farnborough examined the problem, which they immediately suspected had the same source as similar effects encountered on the Lerwick and Sunderland. The wind tunnel tests took account of the fact that the Manchester elevators were in close proximity to the turret and the violent nose down pitching was due to the rapid development of a region of high pressure above the elevator and in front of the protruding turret shoulder, forcing the elevator downwards. Dr J Seddon, who carried out the wind tunnel tests, was unable to induce the nose up pitching, possibly because of the absence of prop wash in his model tests. These would be present on the full-scale aircraft, however. Possible cures included:

1 Fitting deflectors to the fuselage ahead of the turret to smooth the airflow over the turret on rotation.
2 Cutting a wedge from the inboard edge of the elevator where the high pressure region was concentrated.
3 Moving the tailplane forward or downward from the disturbed region.

Thus informed, considerable restressing and beefing-up of the Manchester was undertaken. The rear fuselage was lengthened and the rear turret located six inches further aft, obviating the need to move the tailplane forward. A wedge-shaped section was cut from each inboard elevator and deflectors fitted to the extreme rear fuselage to flare it out in front of the turret. The countersunk screws and nuts in the curved turret housing were replaced by rivets, the nuts having become slackened by vibration. Hoop and transverse stiffeners were fitted within the curved turret housing. Finally, struts were fitted between the lugs on the turret mounting and the fuselage sides, to eliminate lateral rocking of the turret. With these modifications the F.N.4 was refitted and the trials programme resumed. At all airspeeds and turret rotation speeds vibration and buffeting were eliminated and the turret turned smoothly and evenly.

Finally in the trials programme, the elevator appendages had proved unsatisfactory, but the new steel frame and fabric-covered elevator which replaced it had both nose balance and inset geared balance tabs. These new elevators resulted in a great improvement in control at both low and high speeds, including in the dive. L7247 returned to Boscombe Down in September for the first tests with the new 33ft tail and redesigned elevator, and with the standard triple fin tail. A further significant improvement in longitudinal stability with the new tail was found. Also evaluated at the same time were the strengthened rear turret housing. It is evident that even with the severely limited flying programme attained, Chadwick was coming close to ironing out the aerodynamic problems with the design. Had engine availability

and reliability been at all reasonable, it seems inevitable this satisfactory situation would have been accomplished much earlier. No one could possibly have appreciated at the time that, whilst these airframe problems were close to solution, the mechanical problems with the new aircraft, especially the hydraulic system and the engine problems, had barely been recognised, even at this advanced stage.

The next trials programme at Boscombe Down provided both a major milestone in performance as well as a warning of things to come. On or close to the 23rd August, the first production Manchester, L7276, arrived to carry out the long delayed type testing to its 45,000 lb design weight. The aircraft was fitted with the production 90ft wings and two Vulture II engines modified to the latest standard and with power output increased to 1,850bhp and a two speed supercharger. For these trials the 28ft span tail was retained because the new 33ft tail had only just been tested and would only be introduced in production from the 21st aircraft onwards, but the latest elevator modification, albeit at 28ft, was incorporated.

It is worth pausing to review the findings of the testing of L7276. With the new engines operating at 3,200rpm and +9lb/sq in boost, L7276 took off at the maximum all up weight of 45,000 lb in 660 yards and cleared a 50ft screen in 1,175 yards, a great improvement on L7246 in the initial condition. Landing run was 845 yards. The aircraft attained a maximum speed of 261mph at 17,000 feet and a ceiling of 22,100ft. A range of 1,700 miles with 8,000 lb of bombs and 1,000 miles with the maximum load of 11,000 lb was achieved. Best climbing indicated airspeed at 45,000 lb was 135mph. Nett and gross wing loadings

Three quarter rear view of L7247 in the green/brown/yellow camouflage.
G A Jenks collection

were 43.5 lb/sq ft and 40 lb/sq ft respectively. L7246's maximum all up weight was disposed as follows:

Tare weight	29,360 lb
Typical Service Load	3,070 lb
Fuel and Bombs	12,570 lb
Fully Loaded Weight	45,000 lb

The extensive report evaluated many aspects of the operation of the aircraft. Ground handling was reported as good and straightforward. Take-off, climb and single engine performance were still indifferent but now within acceptable limits. Handling qualities in the air were found to be good and controls light and effective. Night flying characteristics and view from the cockpit were all excellent and a great compliment to Chadwick. In many respects the docile Manchester was to be likened by crews to a big Anson, quite a commendation for a heavy aircraft.

Of the very few problems amongst the many pages, the engine noise at the pilot's seat was found to be very high and accompanied by 'drumming'. Fatigue set in after two to three hours flying as a result. At the nearby navigator's and wireless operator's stations noise levels reduced by about a third. The control column was too high, causing difficulties in seeing the instruments and the aircraft leaked in a number of places, notably the front and rear turrets, radio mast and position and the top escape hatches. Front and rear turret operation was now considered satisfactory with latest changes incorporated, but the mid-under F.N.21A was a quite shocking affair.

A&AEE produced evaluations of Manchester gun turrets on 31st July 1940, 21st August 1940 and finally on 11th January 1941 and it was these which finally buried the F.N.21A. The clear view areas were at best restricted. Rotation through 360° was possible, but downward search angles were limited to 30° to 80°. In practice oil from the leaking bomb door rams perpetually smeared the perspex so that the gunner could see very little. During firing, an additional crew member had to be stationed in the fuselage looking through the fuselage windows and directing the gunner to the danger area! Worse still, the 'Low Drag' notation attached by the manufacturers was a distinct misnomer. During initial tests at 220mph, lowering the turret resulted in a speed loss of 16mph, a speed reduction sufficiently major that the crew would be forgiven for believing the aircraft had stopped in midair. Subsequent modifications to the footwells reduced this speed loss, but other, equally serious, problems were manifest. During firing whilst the turret was trained on the beam, the forward of the two guns frequently ceased firing due to links and empty cases blowing back into the gun body and fouling the breech block. The balancing fin was of insufficient size and interfered with rotation at high speed, whilst the two retractable footwells distorted on rotation.

Finally, it was not found possible to retract the turret at normal cruising speeds. The turret jammed on the port side and it was necessary for three crewmen to lift very strenuously to raise it back into the aircraft! The port turret ram was ineffective. It was clear the turret was far more of a hindrance than an asset and the findings of the tests merely served to reinforce the decision promulgated on 1st July 1940 to delete the F.N.21A from production Manchesters.

A warning, if such were needed by Rolls-Royce and Avro, was contained in the recorded maximum oil inlet temperatures. The port engine had hovered at 85°C and the starboard at 83°C against a permissible maximum of 90°C for half an hour only!

Reality intruded into this generally upbeat assessment as early as 12th September, when an engine failed in L7276 on take-off once more and the aircraft had to force land. The crew were unhurt and the damage to the aircraft relatively limited, but it was clear that Vulture reliability still had a long way to go. Ironically, as the Manchester's subsequent history was to reveal, A&AEE turned disorder

into something of a benefit by describing their first hand experience in salvaging Manchesters from the field. They had already had two to deal with and others would follow.

Soon L7277 and L7281 arrived at Boscombe Down for further trials, but in September and October 1940 the focus began to swing away from A&AEE and to Bomber Command itself, where urgent preparations for introducing the aircraft to service were being made. Despite many of his short term problems with the Manchester being overcome by the recent spate of modifications and trials, Chadwick remained deeply sceptical of the Vulture and the autumn was to provide the ultimate decision in respect of the long term future of the type.

Indeed, much more than scepticism over the Vulture was worrying Dobson and Chadwick at this time. On 28th August, Air Vice-Marshal Charles Portal had advised the Air Staff that henceforth, as a matter of policy, all the Command's heavy bombers were to have four engines. With the future of their twin-engined brainchild already looking bleak, this policy decision turned the Manchester into an anachronism overnight and before it had even reached service. There were many things about the Manchester that the 5 Group aircrews would never know. In retrospect one can only observe that this was just as well. Now it was crystal clear to Avros that the only long term future for the aircraft was the four Merlin Manchester III, or Lancaster.

In an unexpected diversion on 9th September 1940, Bomber Command called a conference to review the inadequacies of the Manchester arising from the many essential items omitted from the first 20 machines. In an unnecessary show of petulance, Portal wrote to Saundby that the aircraft was deemed 'completely useless' for operations.

Sight had apparently been lost that it was the Ministry itself which had authorised the deletions a mere three months earlier! Certainly at this stage Portal was no friend of the Manchester. The situation was made worse because Squadron Leader Hyde, Commanding Officer designate of the first Manchester squadron, had been invited as an observer. Chadwick's deep well of diplomacy must have been severely tested. It was agreed that retrospective fitting would be carried out at the earliest convenient date and that, meanwhile, deliveries should continue.

Much more serious was that on 6th October 1940 Rolls-Royce commenced delivery to Avro of what it once more was hoped would be the final and definitive version of the Vulture II, with all development problems allegedly cured. Within a few days it was clear that this was not the case when L7277 was found to persistently throw large quantities of oil from the crankcase breather of one of its Vultures at high rpm. A hurriedly convened meeting on 19th October 1940 learned from Rolls-Royce that the oil loss was caused by frothing, the cause of which the company had tracked down in the last few days to a defect in the oil pump. The problem was in all probability cured and no delay would ensue on this account.

Whilst production of Manchesters proceeded apace at Woodford, and was now well underway at nearby Metropolitan Vickers, Dobson and Chadwick's sternest test, possibly of their entire careers, was at hand. With squadron service imminent, the long term future of the project hung by a thread. Powerful forces such as Lord Beaverbrook, the Minister for Aircraft Production (MAP), and others, encouraged in no small measure by Sir Frederick Handley Page, were determined to cancel the aircraft and switch the factory space created to Halifax production.

Close up of the F.N.4 four gun rear turret in L7247. In this state, the aircraft is as initially delivered, with the 28ft span tail, no diagonal chamfer on the inner edge of the elevators and lacking flared deflector on the extreme rear fuselage. Chronic vibration problems were experienced with this configuration. *via Chaz Bowyer*

The expectation in MAP and in Bomber Command was that the Halifax would be a superior aircraft and that the Manchester III would never match it in performance. The Halifax was expected to operate at an all up weight of 57,000 lb at this time. Mr Farren, the Director of Technical Development, reported to Patrick Hennesey, Beaverbrook's deputy at MAP, that the Manchester development, the Lancaster, could not operate at this all up weight and would never quite catch up on the Halifax. Hennesey did not readily accept this view, even though Sir Wilfred Freeman had also expressed similar reservations. Mr Rowe, the Deputy Director of Technical Development, went to Manchester on 15th November 1940 and came back satisfied that Chadwick could indeed produce a 55-57,000 lb capability from the development.

Furthermore, on 19th November 1940 Farren reported again to Hennesey that the change in all up weight was a big job, but nothing like as big as the change from Manchester to Halifax production. He judged that the two types would eventually be equally acceptable to the Air Staff. It was safe to plan for production of whichever type was most convenient.

Those two weeks in November were the climax of the debate over the future of the Manchester/Lancaster and ended in victory for Mr Hennesey and those directing Lancaster production at Avro. At no time was it ever suggested that the Lancaster might be better, indeed the aircraft had yet to fly, merely that it would be no worse than the Halifax.

What seems to have swung the argument is the assurance that the aircraft would merely be quicker into production with the many existing jigs and tools already common to the Manchester. That the production techniques developed by Avros were infinitely better than those at Handley Page never seems to have crossed anyone's mind, or if it did it was never recorded.

Although the records appear to reveal Hennesey as an open-minded individual susceptible to rational argument, Chadwick himself, in 1944, was to be adamant in crediting Sir Wilfred Freeman with the vision to push ahead with the Lancaster, whilst Hennessey was of no material assistance. No doubt what is most important in all this is that, whoever deserves the credit and whatever the reasons dictating it at the time, history shows that the right decision was made. Clearly it was a close run thing and it would still be a long time before the Avro development of P13/36 would be reinstated in the minds of Air Ministry and Bomber Command as the better design.

With the Manchester poised to enter service it is appropriate to consider its progress beside that of its contemporaries, the Handley Page Halifax and the Short Stirling. Their developments and chronology are virtually coincident:

Manchester, Halifax and Stirling Compared.

	Avro 679 Manchester	HP.57 Halifax	Short S.29 Stirling
Specification	P13/36	P13/36	B12/36
Issue date	24.8.36	24.8.36	24.8.36
Prototypes	2	2 (as HP.56)	2
Ordered	30.4.37	30.4.37	30.4.37(?)
First flight	25.7.39	25.11.39	14.5.39
First del to RAF	6.11.40	13.11.40	2.7.40
First operation	24/25.2.41	10/11.3.41	10/11.2.41

Despite the many and variable trials and tribulations of achieving the transition from first specification to their operational baptism, the chronological histories of the three aircraft had run remarkably in parallel. At this stage the many intrinsic advantages to the Avro airframe had not become manifest.

Comparison with a near contemporary American bomber, the Martin B-26 Marauder, is also instructive.

While the Manchester specification was issued in 1936 and that to which the Marauder was designed as late as January 1939, the two appeared in service at a similar time. Manchester operations and delivery of the first four Marauders to the USAAC both took place in February 1941. The two aircraft had comparable engine power in the two Rolls-Royce Vulture engines at 1,780hp each and the Pratt & Whitney R-2400 Double Wasp at 1,850hp apiece.

As initially designed operating weights were also similar at 26,043 lb for the Manchester and 27,200 lb for the Marauder. Here the similarities end and these statistics hold the key to the respective failure and success of the two types in service. Whereas the Vulture was underdeveloped and unreliable, the Double Wasp was not only developed and thoroughly reliable, but a robust radial.

The contrast in the aircraft is even more stark. Whereas the Marauder was a comparatively diminutive aircraft with an initial span of 65ft and length of 56ft, the Manchester was much larger, spanning 90ft 1in and having a length of 69ft 4¼in. In keeping with their size the Marauder initially operated at an all up weight of only 27,200 lb, whereas the RAF were soon attempting to operate the Manchester at 45,000 lb. Even when latterly some semblance of reliability was available in the Vulture, the Manchester thus had a weight penalty approaching 18,000 lb in comparison to its lighter near-contemporary.

Amongst the serving aircrews there was an impatience and excitement at the prospect of the introduction of the three new 'secret' types. The RAF had decided to allocate the Stirling to 3 Group, the Halifax to 4 Group and the Manchester to 5 Group. Whilst 3 and 4 Groups elected to make the transition to service by equipping existing operational units, 5 Group chose to create a new unit, 207 Squadron, to achieve the transition.

No. 5 Group aircrews knew little of the new aircraft, but from that which filtered out they were eager at the prospect of a change in their fortunes. They had been operating Handley Page Hampdens, aircraft with a span of 69ft and length of 53ft and a maximum bomb load of 4,000lb at 1,200 mile range, with manual gun positions, no propeller feathering mechanism and extremely cramped crew positions for four.

To ease and speed the transition to service 5 Group was prepared to attach the aircrews allocated to the new 207 Squadron to A&AEE so that they could make the earliest possible start on learning the complexities of these large, new and sophisticated aircraft. So many new systems had to be learned. In comparison to the Hampden, the six man crew of the Manchester had comparatively luxurious accommodation, there were two pilots and aircrew could readily change positions in flight.

The Vulture engines, with their 16ft diameter propellers, were considered so powerful that it was judged unsafe for personnel or vehicles to pass behind aircraft whilst these monsters were being run up on test. After a Commer pickup truck had allegedly been blown over whilst passing behind a Manchester during engine tests, a new regulation was promulgated that a prohibited entry area, staked out with red flags, must be established for 50 yards behind each of the powerful new behemoths! Crews were no doubt taken by this impression of barely suppressed power.

Noel C Hyde, who was operational with 44 Squadron, flying Hampdens from Waddington, was sent for by Air Vice-Marshal 'Bert' Harris at Headquarters, 5 Group at Grantham in late August 1940. Ushered in, the Air Officer Commanding (AOC) informed Hyde that he had been chosen to reform 207 Squadron, at that time absorbed into 12 Operational Conversion Unit (OTU), at Waddington with the new heavy bomber. Hyde promptly went off on attachment to A&AEE at Boscombe Down in order to learn everything he could about the Manchester. Hyde began familiarisation flying on 1st September 1940 in the first production aircraft, L7276.

Test and development flying continued from Boscombe Down at a pace dictated by the many serviceability problems and modifications needed by the aircraft and during the same period Hyde was also busy seeking out experienced captains who would be sufficiently proficient to bring the new aircraft up to an operational status. He was fortunate in that a number of pre-war pilots were completing their first operational tours on Hampdens at this time. The first he acquired was Flying Officer Johnny Siebert, an excellent Australian pilot, who had been in Hyde's flight on 44 Squadron. With the assistance of Avro flight personnel, Rolls-Royce engineers and their own crews, Hyde and Siebert

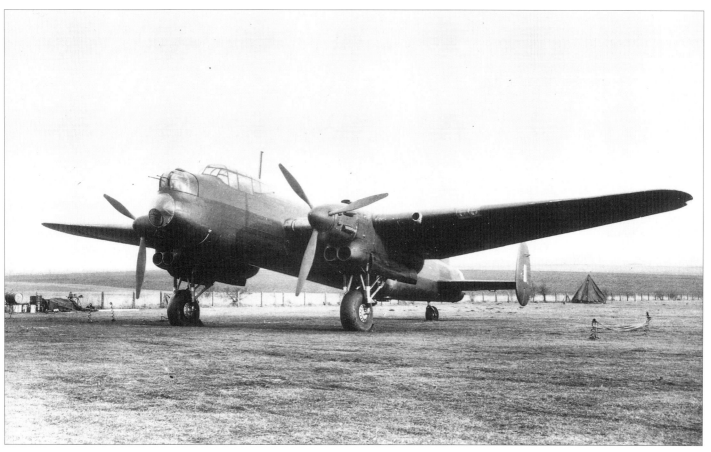

Delivered to Boscombe Down on 25th October 1940, with the very latest modifications to its Vulture II engines, L7277 was soon grounded due to aeration and frothing of its lubricant system. An urgent enquiry laid the blame on the oil pump on this occasion.
RAF Museum P6298

began regular handling flights on the second prototype, L7247, in early September. On 9th September 1940, Hyde took L7247 from Boscombe to Grantham. With him in the aircraft were Johnnie Siebert, Freddie Rowarth the chief engineer at A&AEE and two crew. The purpose of the flight was to allow the AOC of 5 Group, Harris, to inspect the aircraft. RAF aircrews rapidly found themselves drawn into the development programme of the aircraft, testing L7277 with a modified petrol pump on 17th September 1940. Frequent flights to the Avro factory at Woodford to discuss the progress of development and to the all grass airfield at Waddington commenced.

However, all was not frantic activity. Sergeant Eddy Edmonds, an air gunner, remembers the long periods of inactivity when the aircraft were grounded for engine or airframe modification. Then they would

report to the duty officer early in the morning and in the absence of any requirements wander across to the aircraft, where their activities were confined to sitting in their future crew positions trying to familiarise themselves with their new surroundings.

The Rolls-Royce Vulture engines were still far from satisfactory. On 24th September 1940 Hyde took L7247 to Ringway. Whilst they were there it was decided to ground all the Manchesters in the flight test programme until a minor engine modification was carried out. In September 1940 a breakdown in coolant flow to two banks of cylinders in the Vulture-powered Vickers Warwick K8178 led the Rolls-Royce test pilot, Reg Kirlew, to make an emergency landing at the small grass airfield at Burnaston, on the outskirts of Derby, when an engine overheated and caught fire, the cylinder blocks themselves burning like Thermite. Subsequently the Warwick was re-engined, first with Pratt & Whitney Double Wasp and later with Bristol Centaurus engines. K8178 was the only Vulture powered version.

The coolant problems were not easy to track down because they were not replicated in all Vulture engines simultaneously. Whilst Manchester production got into its stride in late 1940 and plans for the introduction of the aircraft to RAF service were hurriedly progressed, a Rolls-Royce minute dated September 1940 seemed finally to come to grips with one of the elusive coolant

problems. Overheating arose, it was decided, when the coolant became contaminated by small amounts of oil, which coated the internal coolant passages and provided an insulation. The coating prevented the coolant from picking up the heat from the cylinder liners.

Finding the source of the oil was difficult to establish but it possibly had an external source, as opposed to one within the engine itself. This line of enquiry seems to have arisen by analogy with experience with the Merlin. Early Merlins used 100% ethylene glycol cooling and no problems had arisen, whereas overheating began to show itself in certain engines when the coolant was changed to a 30% glycol/pressurised water mixture. Skilful detective work showed that the manufacturing process left small quantities of oil in the coolant passages. 100% ethylene glycol dissolved the oil films whereas the 30% mixture did not.

The problems with the Merlin were cured by employing a sodium metasilicate flush of the cooling system prior to test. It is possible that the Vulture problems were alleviated in this way too. Whilst the exclusion of the oil from the coolant system alleviated the coolant problem to some extent the operating temperatures were still unacceptably high, especially in local hot spots. These not only put strain on these areas but also had a deleterious effect on oil temperatures and thus pressures.

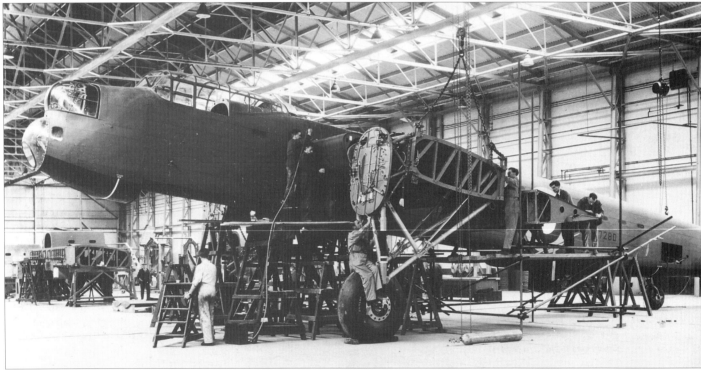

Presumably as a consequence of the grounding Hyde did not fly in another Manchester until 25th October 1940. He had meanwhile been busy hunting more experienced flight crews and in the intervening period acquired Squadron Leader Charles Kydd, destined to be one of the giants of the Manchester period, and his crew. Within a few days another highly experienced captain, Flying Officer Peter Burton-Gyles, and his crew joined the unit working up at Boscombe Down. This was the state of play at the end of October 1940 when the first Manchester deliveries to 207 Squadron and RAF service commenced. After the protracted development, the great range of problems encountered and overcome, and the advanced nature of the new technologies intrinsic to the design, there might have been reason to expect a bright future for the aircraft.

The reality would prove more brutal.

L7247 with forward F.N.5 turret traversed fully to starboard, again photographed with Orthochromatic film. *G A Jenks*

Sixth production Manchester, L7280, coming together rapidly at Woodford, mid 1940. It is fitted with the mid-under F.N.21A turret. Note early colour scheme. *British Aerospace*

Chapter Two

Into Service

On 1st November 1940, 207 Squadron was reformed at Waddington as part of 5 Group Bomber Command to introduce the Avro Manchester I into RAF service. As of that date the squadron had no aircraft allocated to it. A note in the Operational Record Book (ORB) reads as follows: 'Several Officers and NCOs have been attached to A&AEE Boscombe Down to gain experience of these aircraft. Owing to engine unserviceability very little flying has been done, but maintenance personnel have gained useful experience'. No one could have realised at the time what a prophetic judgement on the subsequent flying career of the Manchester these few words were to be.

On 6th November, L7279, the squadron's first aircraft, was collected from 6 Maintenance Unit (MU) Brize Norton and flown to Boscombe Down. On the 8th, Squadron Leader 'Hettie' Hyde, Squadron Leader Kydd and Pilot Officer McCabe, the Engineering Officer, flew L7279 to Waddington for the first time and all squadron personnel were moved by air and rail to join them; approximately 75 airmen of all trades. That very night, coincidentally, Waddington was bombed by a German intruder, without any damage to the Manchester. On the 10th the Squadron's second aircraft, L7278, was collected from 27 MU Shawbury.

In the meantime, more air and ground crews were arriving at a rapid rate and the NCOs trained at the Aeroplane & Armament Experimental Establishment (A&AEE) began passing on their knowledge to the new recruits – Acting Flight Lieutenant D J French, Flying Officer F E 'Frankie' Eustace DFC, Flying Officer W J 'Mike' Lewis DFC.

A note in the 207 Squadron ORB for 12th November specifies that representatives of Rolls-Royce had arrived to carry out urgent modifications to the aircraft cooling system.

Eight days later, on the 20th, the book records that little flying had been accomplished due to the need for engine modifications, whilst next day orders were received that L7278 and L7279 were to fly intensively until 500 hours had been achieved on both aircraft to test the modifications which had been incorporated.

Leading up to this spate of activity, Rolls-Royce had run to earth another problem with the cooling system. The Vulture had two coolant pumps, each serving two banks of cylinders independently from the other. Air-locks within the cylinder blocks caused poor distribution of the coolant. The air-locks arose, it was discovered, by cavitation within the pump which centrifuged the water. Air accumulated progressively in the pump and in exceptional circumstances built up to such an extent that the coolant could no longer pass through it. Rapid seizure of the engine followed. The air-locks were eliminated by the fitting of a balance pipe linking the two pumps. This permitted one pump to feed the other two banks of cylinders if required and at a stroke eliminated the air locks and hot spots.

Rolls-Royce records indicate that the first balance pipe modification was incorporated into 207 Squadron's first Manchester, L7279, and flown on 20th November 1940. It seems likely that both L7279 and L7278 were so fitted and that this refinement was the one to be proved during the intensive flying programme. This modification did turn out to rectify the deficiency and at the same time reduced oil temperatures to some extent. No. 207 were later to lose a Manchester at

Perranporth in May. Rolls-Royce themselves lost their own trials aircraft at Tern Hill in June 1941 due to coolant problems and in that crash the test pilot lost his life. Possibly these later defects had a different origin.

A photograph of L7279 taken soon after delivery shows the general configuration of these first aircraft. They were the triple finned Mk.I variety with 28ft span tailplanes. Compared to the prototype aircraft, the colour scheme had already undergone a change, the demarcation line between the brown and green shadow-shaded upper surface and the night black underside was moved to a position half way up the fuselage sides, the actual separation line being straight. With an establishment of only one flight and eight aircraft the initial two aircraft soon received code letters: L7278 'EM-A', L7279 'EM-B'. The code letters were painted grey and serials soon repainted grey on the squadron. Fuselage roundels were type A1.

Most notable feature of L7278 and L7279, as initially delivered, was that they had the original Frazer-Nash F.N.21A retractable 'dustbin' mid-under turret. In July 1940 a policy decision had been made to delete the F.N.21A after the tenth airframe on the production line, but available records variously state that nine, ten or eleven aircraft were actually fitted.

Both the Rolls-Royce Vulture engines and the Manchester airframes had a range of novel features being introduced to service aircraft for the first time. These items were as new and untried as the aircraft itself and many were to prove sources of unserviceability in the future.

No. 207 Squadron's first Manchester, L7279 'EM-B', photographed at Waddington soon after its delivery. It carries the initial camouflage scheme, grey codes and a red serial behind the code letter 'M'. The F.N.21A mid-under turret is retracted. It was agreed to remove these on 9th December 1940 and work commenced on 25th January 1941. L7279 undertook a single operation before being relegated to training duties.
No. 207 Squadron archives / R Glynne-Owen

A gunner getting acquainted with the F.N.4 rear turret in one of 207 Squadron's first Manchesters.
No. 207 Squadron archives / R Glynne-Owen

services in the Manchester were hydraulically operated, this presented frequent problems.

Another deficiency indicative of the desperate urgency with which the aircraft was introduced was that these early aircraft, possibly the first 20, had no engine driven air compressors. These were necessary to maintain the air pressure in the pneumatic wheel brakes at the required level. In these aircraft the ground crews therefore had the task of topping up the air bottles after every two landings to maintain the pressure.

By the end of November only 25 hours flying had been accomplished. With the allocation of L7283 and L7284 to the squadron, however, the aircraft strength had risen to four Manchesters.

A disservice to the war effort was provided by non-flying personnel at about this time. On 24th November 1940 when Flying Officer Siebert, Flight Lieutenant French and crew were again participating in the intensive flight test programme, they were briefed to carry out an endurance test in L7279. The test required them to fly at ceiling height of approximately 17,000ft between turning points at Waddington, Trowbridge, Shrewsbury, Gainsborough and Northallerton in Yorkshire. The crew was supplemented by two army officers. After almost three hours of monotonous flying, with fuel running low at the end of the northern leg, French decided to terminate the test, break cloud and return to Waddington. Everything was calm on board, the wireless operator and one of the army officers were playing noughts and crosses, when they had the misfortune to emerge directly over Linton-on-Ouse airfield, where a German air raid was in progress. They immediately came under intense anti-aircraft fire from the airfield defences and by a rare chance one of the first shells burst close-by, tearing off part of the wing tip.

Feverish activity ensued whilst evasive action was taken and Siebert fired off a volley of colours of the day, accompanied by unprintable remarks regarding the aircraft recognition capabilities of the anti-aircraft crews. Various suggestions were made including landing and taking issue with the belligerents, but good sense prevailed and the aircraft returned safely to Waddington.

Whilst 207 Squadron pilots began their earliest tentative flight trials with the Manchester, back at Ringway on 27th November a new Manchester, L7292, gave a pilot inexperienced on the type a virtuoso performance of the full range of problems it was to inflict on aircrews over the next three years. A ferry pilot and skeleton crew collected L7292

For example, the initial Manchesters had no cabin heating system, although it was intended to install a system in later aircraft. In the meantime crews were each issued with the Irvin electrically heated trousers, jackets, gloves and boots. These had electrical leads joining with a master lead which plugged into a socket at each crew station. During the service training and development flying, carried out from November onwards, the suits were also evaluated and found seriously wanting. Crews constantly experienced shorts and burn-outs, especially in the boots and gloves and as a result they regularly flew five or six hour test flights at 15,000ft with nothing to warm them whatsoever.

These initial aircraft had an untried method of joining their long runs of hydraulic piping together, called Ermeto couplings which replaced the earlier Aircraft General Spares (AGS) couplings. In the latter the pipe ends were belled out to accept a metal 'olive', the assembly then being clamped together by male and female nuts and locked in place with wire. Ermeto couplings, once made, could not be undone and did not require wire locking, hence speeding up production of airframes. The couplings had been tested under workshop conditions, but the vibrations in the airframes when flying led to frequent fracturing of the hydraulic pipes at the Ermeto joints. Since many of the at the Woodford works on this day. It seems that very soon after take-off an Ermeto hydraulic coupling behind the pilot's seat failed. A dense and fierce mist of fluid then sprayed into the cockpit as the aircraft was beginning to climb away, temporarily blinding the pilot. The entire contents of the system sprayed over the pilot and crew, the inside of the perspex canopy and all the flight instruments.

No sooner had the spray begun to die away than the starboard engine ran away. The revs rose to 3,600rpm and the engine noise reached a deafening howl as the propeller feathering mechanism failed, sending the airscrew into the fully fine position. The drenched, shocked and deafened pilot was unable to obtain any response from the constant speed unit, nor either would the starboard engine respond to movements of the throttle lever. Miraculously, the pilot kept the aircraft level, meanwhile heading with desperate urgency for Ringway and an emergency landing.

Test assembly of the first Metropolitan Vickers Manchester, R5768, on 21st December 1940 at Trafford Park. Two nights later R5768, together with major components of the next twelve in line, were destroyed in an air raid.
G A Jenks collection

En route the pilot deliberated whether he should shut down the overheating and racing starboard engine by switching off its fuel supply, but recognised that such action would leave him in a worse situation, with a dead engine and windmilling propeller. The engine continued to race uncontrollably for nine minutes until it finally seized on finals for Ringway, where a safe wheels-down landing was effected. No damage to the aircraft or occupants was reportedly occasioned, although one Vulture was wrecked. The pilot no doubt departed hence, a nervous wreck in urgent need of de-greasing solvents and a clean pair of underpants!

The accident report stresses that clear thought by the pilot was impeded by his unfamiliarity with this new type of aircraft, the unexpected drenching from the Ermeto failure and the extremely high noise level, which made it very difficult for him to pass any instructions for the operation of the emergency flap and undercarriage system to the other crew members.

Investigation proved that the cause of the high revs was a failure of the Hallite washer joining the constant speed unit to the engine. This denied pressure oil to the pitch mechanism such that the blades remained against the fine pitch stop. De Havilland were requested to undertake a modification to prevent a recurrence, but feathering failures

were to plague the Manchester for much of its life. The Ermeto problem was already appreciated it appears because the report merely re-emphasises the urgency of replacing it with the tried and tested AGS system.

During December 1940 flight testing and development flying continued and additional aircraft, L7280 and L7286, and personnel joined the squadron. The problems being experienced with the new systems in the aircraft, and especially with the engines, were sufficiently serious and intractable that a meeting to consider these was held at Waddington on 9th December 1940. This was attended by the new Air Officer Commanding (AOC) of 5 Group, Air Vice-Marshal N H Bottomley, and Sir Robert Renwick of the Ministry of Aircraft Production (MAP). They discussed the modifications and additional equipment which would be essential before the Manchester could become operationally fit.

Worrying as the underdeveloped state of the Manchester and the serious hydraulic problems were, the over-riding problem was that it was so grossly underpowered. When the squadron received their first aircraft they were flown at a maximum all up weight of 45,000lb. The aircraft was powered by two 1,760hp Vultures. Indeed the Manchester was the largest British twin-engined aircraft of the war and therein lay its Achilles' heel.

1 BOMB-AIMER'S PANEL
2 BOMB SIGHT
3 BOMB-AIMER'S CUSHION
4 BOMB-AIMER
5 CAMERA
6 FORWARD GUN TURRET (2 BROWNING GUNS)
7 RUDDER BAR
8 MAP CASE AND COURSE AND HEIGHT INDICATOR STOWAGE
9 AIRSCREW, THROTTLE AND FUEL CONTROL LEVERS
10 SEAT ADJUSTING LEVER

74 RECONNAISSANCE FLARES (PORT AND STARD.)
75 OXYGEN BOTTLES
76 PARACHUTE STOWAGE (REST ROOM)
77 REST BED (STOWED)
78 DINGHY STOWAGE
79 HYDRAULIC HEADER TANK
80 BOMB WINCH HANDLE
81 AIR HEATER (REST ROOM)
82 OXYGEN BOTTLES (PORT AND STARD.)
83 WIRELESS OPERATOR
84 DE-ICING PANEL
85 TRANSMITTER-RECEIVER
86 OBSERVATION DOME
87 AERIAL MAST (DE-ICING ON LEADING EDGE)
88 D. F. LOOP (RETRACTABLE)

60 FIRST AID OUTFIT
61 FIREMAN'S AXE
62 ACCESS LADDER
63 FUSELAGE ENTRANCE DOOR
64 TWO FLARE CHUTES
65 WATER BOTTLES
66 SEA MARKERS
67 AMMUNITION DUCTS
68 PARACHUTE STOWAGE (MID GUN
69 AMMUNITION (REAR TURRET)
70 BOMB COMPARTMENT
71 FLARE CHUTE EXTENSION (STO
72 FLAP JACK MOUNTING
73 REST CHAIR

11 DUAL-CONTROL COLUMN
12 PILOT
13 FOLDING SEAT
14 EMERGENCY UNDERCARRIAGE LEVER
15 OBSERVER'S INSTRUMENT PANEL
16 SEXTANT STOWAGE
17 NAVIGATOR
18 NAVIGATOR'S TABLE
19 VOLTAGE CONTROL PANEL
20 TRAILING AERIAL WINCH
21 ACCUMULATORS
22 COOLANT TANK
23 CARBURETTOR AIR INTAKE
24 VULTURE ENGINE
25 RADIATOR (COOLANT)
26 SELF SEALING FUEL TANK
27 OIL COOLER AIR OUTLET
28 OIL COOLER AIR INTAKE
29 LANDING WHEEL
30 OIL TANK
31 DE-ICING EQUIPMENT
32 TWIN LANDING LAMPS
33 PORT NAVIGATION LAMP
34 AILERON
35 FORMATION KEEPING LAMP
36 MID GUN TURRET (2 BROWNING GUNS)
37 MID TURRET STEP
38 AIR HEATER (MID GUNNER)
39 MID GUNNER
40 EMERGENCY RATIONS
41 VACUUM FLASKS

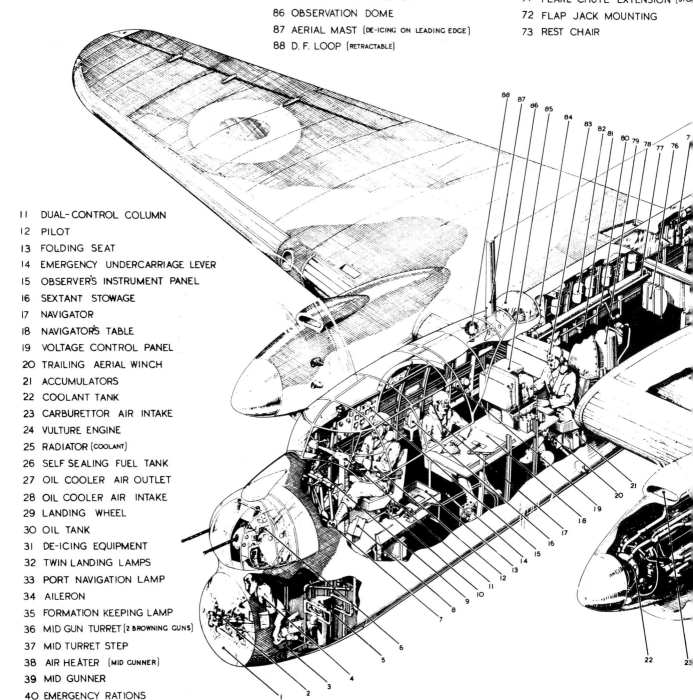

DRAWING PREPARED BY MESSRS A.V. ROE LTD.

Illustration from the frontispiece of Air Publication A.P. 1600A Volume 1– *The Manchester I Aeroplane*. The cutaway shows an aircraft with 80ft wings, 28ft tail and a mid-under turret, appropriate only to the second prototype.

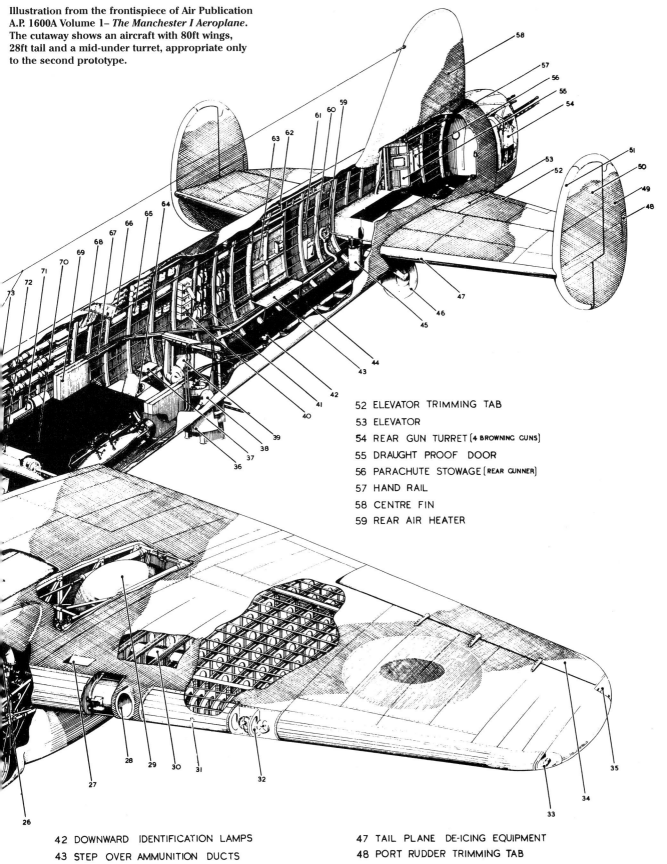

52 ELEVATOR TRIMMING TAB
53 ELEVATOR
54 REAR GUN TURRET (4 BROWNING GUNS)
55 DRAUGHT PROOF DOOR
56 PARACHUTE STOWAGE (REAR GUNNER)
57 HAND RAIL
58 CENTRE FIN
59 REAR AIR HEATER

42 DOWNWARD IDENTIFICATION LAMPS
43 STEP OVER AMMUNITION DUCTS
44 WALK WAY
45 ELSAN CLOSET
46 FIXED TAIL WHEEL

47 TAIL PLANE DE-ICING EQUIPMENT
48 PORT RUDDER TRIMMING TAB
49 PORT RUDDER
50 PORT FIN
51 PORT FIN DE-ICING EQUIPMENT

Subsequent to the meeting of 9th December, agreement was reached on the essential modifications required by all Manchesters and on further intensive flight trials. As has been described, desperate measures had been required to get the Manchester into service and requirements were changing on an almost daily basis. Many deletions had been permitted in order to get the first batch of 20 into service and at that moment on the production line aircraft were still being fitted with the original 28ft span tailplane. These aircraft were not considered operationally fit by Bomber Command and a long and indeed ever-lengthening list of modifications was demanded. As of this date a Bomber Command letter lists:

Manchester In-service Modifications

Items which are recent or new requirements considered essential by the Command
Resin Lights
Improvement in fuel content determination
Deletion of under turret and provision of escape hatch in same position
Strengthen W/Op table
Reposition W/Op key
Reposition 3 x 24 volt accumulators
Neutralising unit repositioning
Separation of aerials for TR9f and R1082
New carriers for 2,000lb AP bombs, 1,800lb GP and mines
Modification to accommodate 1,000lb bomb in 500lb carriers

Items considered desirable by Command
Glycol spray for bomb aimer's panel
Wiper for bomb aimer's panel
Anti-dazzle plate for landing lamp

Items discussed at meeting with Command at Manchester on 22nd October 1940
Cabin heating OR Electrically heated clothing (Gloves and boots provided for first 38 aircraft. 39th and subsequent aircraft will have cabin heating system)
Armour plate & draught proof bulkhead (Retrofit)
Barrage Balloon Cutters (Retrofit)
Exhaust flame dampers
Curtain at navigator's table
Perspex blister at navigator's station
Distant reading compass (51st and subsequent aircraft)
Hot and cold air intake
Bomb aiming, increased downward vision
Provision of extra fire extinguishers
First aid box
Fuel jettison system (Installation ready for 21st aircraft)
Increased vision for rear turret (Nash & Thompson) modification ready for test

Other Items
Oxygen and intercom for nose turret
Wireless mast deicer, also wings and tail
Fitting IFF R3003
Introduction of H type 1000 generator
Automatic controls Mk.IV (Impractical on first 20 aircraft)
F24 camera stowage (Impractical on first 20 aircraft)
Marconi T1154 - R1155 (Impractical on first 20 aircraft)
Lorenz Blind Approach equipment (Investigate to see if can be fitted)

'The 26th aircraft is expected in mid-January 1941 and will have all operational requirements, including cabin heating [note discrepancy with list – Author]. It is intended to withdraw the early aircraft and modify them at Avros or Maintenance Units.' Comments about the status of the Stirling and Halifax were also included. Eight Manchesters had so far reached 207 Squadron whereas only two Halifaxes had reached 35 Squadron. The letter recorded that these two had completed very little flying due to tail wheel problems, but that Bomber Command considered that it may turn out to be the best of the three aircraft operationally. It was agreed that 207 Squadron would receive the 21st and subsequent machines, and L7296, the 21st production airframe, became the first with the 33ft span triple fin tail and all current operational equipment. Avro had tested this example satisfactorily on 18th December.

An itemised list of Avro Works Modifications from this period details:

Avro Works Modifications

Mod No.	Item
119	Wing tips 90ft span – all aircraft
108	Large tailplane – 21st and subsequent (and retrofit to earlier batch)
11	Self-sealing petrol and oil tanks – all aircraft
45	Barrage Balloon Protection – 21st and subsequent aircraft
13	Armour protection for crew
93	Armour plate bulkhead at Former No. 8 – 21st and subsequent aircraft
121	Bulletproof glass
?	Twin beam guns pending
?	Under gun mount pending
?	Cabin heating (being designed)
86	Oxygen regulator
80	Regulator restrainer
70	Wiring for bomb aiming panel
35	Heated panel for bomb aimer
75	Heated boots and gloves
?	Autopilot – 21st and subsequent aircraft
?	Bombsight CSBS Mk.9A
106	R3003 IFF
85	T1154 & R1155 W/T
110	1000 Watt Generator
24	Lorenz beam approach equipment – all aircraft
83	Mixing box – 21st and subsequent aircraft
116	Aerial feeder
30	Airscrew deicer
32	Tail deicer
33	W/T mast deicer

Headquarters Bomber Command also required 207 Squadron to intensively fly six aircraft until 500 hours on each had been completed. The following aircraft were selected, L7278, L7279, L7280, L7283, L7284 and L7286. Take-off, climb, all up weight, and single engine performance were all to be

evaluated. However, it was already clear that the desired increase in power was unlikely to be forthcoming.

The intensive test flying programme commenced, but fairly soon one aircraft was in trouble. One morning the squadron's first crew, that of Flying Officer Johnny Siebert, were allocated the task of testing the single engine performance of L7286 from Waddington. The four or five crew were supplemented by two or three soldiers from the airfield defence force along for a joy ride. Over Lincoln at about 7,000ft the captain and second pilot, all former Handley Page Hampden aircrew with no previous experience of feathering airscrews, finding single engine flying rather tame and tedious, decided for the hell of it to feather the other airscrew and glide. It was certainly a novel experience for them and seemed fun.

When the aircraft was down to 3–4,000ft the crew initiated the procedure to unfeather the propellers and restart the engines. Regrettably, the feathering mechanism had failed, either because of flat batteries or jammed solenoid valves, and neither propeller could be unfeathered, despite increasingly feverish efforts. At the gliding angle of a Manchester the ground was approaching rapidly and Siebert called for everyone to assume their crash positions at the rear of the aircraft.

There was no large field ahead but without power they had no options. The pilot made his approach, lowered the flaps and undercarriage and touched down in a ploughed field. Before their forward speed had decreased significantly, and with the tail still up, the River Witham appeared across their path. In desperation Siebert hauled back on the stick, jumped the river and pulled up in another ploughed field beyond, near the Bardney sugar beet factory. With considerable sighs of relief the crew climbed out to take stock of the damage. This turned out to be confined to the loss of the long trailing aerial, which was wound fully out at the time of the incident.

Other arrivals, quickly on the scene, were the village police force and a couple of armed farmers, who had initially mistaken the Manchester for a German aircraft. The Wireless Operator, Sergeant Jim Taylor, called Waddington on the radio and they were collected by a vehicle sent out from the airfield. The impact of the incident on the army passengers was not recorded!

On 22nd December 1940 after the greater proportion of the fuel had been drained, the ground had firmed up with the frost, and with the wind in the right quarter the Commanding Officer, Squadron Leader Hyde, flew the Manchester out solo and returned safely to Waddington some 15 minutes later. The only disciplinary action resulting from this misadventure was that Jim Taylor received a bill from the RAF for the loss of the trailing aerial.

Meanwhile, Flight Lieutenant Dereck French experienced one of the first serious hydraulic problems in 207. On 19th December French, Burton-Gyles and three crew took off in L7280 on a local test flight. Immediately after the wheels left the ground the pipe carrying hydraulic oil to the port engine radiator shutters burst, spraying the fluid onto the hot exhaust pipe. The engine burst into flames. French aborted the test and completed the shortest possible full circuit, landing back at Waddington some 15 minutes later with the port engine still blazing. Fire engines were already standing by as the aircraft rolled to a halt and the flames were quickly extinguished with little further damage to the airframe. It had been a narrow escape.

Whilst production at Woodford began to get into a rhythm, aircraft deliveries seemed on the point of a major boost with the coming on stream of the Metropolitan Vickers assembly line. Construction had commenced earlier in 1940 and the first deliveries were scheduled before the year end. The Metrovick factory at Trafford Park in Manchester had no adjacent airfield and instead it was intended that completed broken down major components would be moved to Woodford for final assembly and flight testing alongside Avro built machines. It was agreed that Metrovick's first Manchester, R5768, should undergo a test assembly at the factory as a one-off operation to ensure that everything fitted, prior to disassembly and final completion at Woodford. R5768 eventually came together on 21st December 1940, to the satisfaction of management and workforce, and was photographed inside the factory next day. On the night of 23rd December, a German air raid by KG1, and led by pathfinding Heinkel He 111s from KG100, attacked Manchester. By coincidence, or otherwise, the Metrovick factory was heavily bombed and the assembled R5768 and components for the next twelve in line (R5769 to R5780) were destroyed or damaged beyond repair, along with essential jigs and tools. It was a cruel setback at such a crucial moment.

Following building repairs Metrovick production soon resumed. The serial numbers R5768 to R5780 were reallocated to the next aircraft on the production line, but it was three months later, on 31st March, before the new R5768 was assembled at Woodford. The Germans had provided a lesson in strategic bombing and R5768 became the only Manchester to appear twice as a complete aircraft.

On 31st December the Air Ministry Overseer, Resident Technical Officer and Chief Designer of A V Roe arrived for a conference on Manchester modifications and equipment. The Group and Station Engineer Officers also attended. The squadron strength at the end of the year had risen to eleven Manchesters. These were probably: L7278, L7279,

Very rare photograph showing wrecked fuse-lage sub-assemblies from the initial production batch, R5769 to R5780, lying outside the Metrovick factory at Trafford Park soon after the German air raid of 23rd December 1940.
via G A Jenks

L7280, L7282, L7283, L7284, L7286, L7288, L7290, L7291 and L7292.

Instead of accomplishing 500 hours of intensive flying on its six aircraft by the last day of the year, 207 Squadron had achieved a mere 78 hours on all aircraft for the whole month of December. The low flying hours did not reflect a lack of effort, however, since Avro, Rolls-Royce and the squadron air and ground crews were working at an intense pace.

The winter of 1940-41 was one of the coldest on record and the Manchester was presenting the ground crews of 207 Squadron with quite desperate problems as a result of the early stage of its development. Pilot Officer McCabe and his colleagues did, however, discover that they had cause to be grateful for two features of the Rolls-Royce Vulture. The engine turned out to be one of the easiest piston engines of all time to start in cold weather, which was one factor to be grateful for when the ground crews of 44 Squadron at Waddington were struggling with the Bristol Pegasus engines of their Hampdens. Also, when the Rolls-Royce Vultures were running they were as smooth as a turbine, unlike the highly tuned, but by comparison rough, Merlin from the same stable.

Former Sergeant Bill Buck recalls one take-off early in the Manchester work-up period, when a young Rolls-Royce development engineer was on board to monitor engine performance. By a not unusual coincidence one engine began streaming smoke as they accelerated on their take-off run. With no apparent power loss, but increasing trepidation amongst the crew, the take-off was completed. Suspecting that the smoking engine might pack up at any moment Buck tackled the engineer and asked, with com-

mendable understatement, whether the presence of such volumes of smoke was altogether safe and normal. The engineer replied with disarming reassurance that there was no need for concern and that the smoke was perfectly normal for an engine at this stage of development. Buck was not taken in by a single word and speculated on whether the engineer would be so relaxed had the smoke materialised with him on board over Berlin instead of the airspace around Waddington.

The Vulture problems became no better during January 1941. Whilst the flight testing and training continued at a hectic pace, slowed only by the fight to keep the Manchesters airworthy, no major failure had occurred so far to a Vulture engine whilst airborne. This changed when, at about this time, Flying Officer Frankie Eustace had an engine fail at the most crucial period – on take-off. In these circumstances the pilot had to be either extremely fortunate or capable, preferably both, to avoid a crash. Control became critical and the golden rule said at all costs maintain the heading and under no circumstances turn into the 'dead' engine. On this occasion Frankie Eustace feathered the dead engine but then committed the cardinal sin of turning back to the airfield. Generally an aircraft at this stage could be expected to spin in and crash, but on this occasion Eustace got away with his mistake and managed a successful downwind landing back at Waddington.

After this providential escape the Manchester was towed in from the airfield and parked directly outside the flight office. A number of pilots, including Frankie Eustace and 'Mike' Lewis, were relaxing in the flight office when the Manchester was towed in. The aircraft had the first of the de Havilland fully feathering propellers. The pilots sat around digesting the good fortune of Eustace's survival. As 'Mike' Lewis recalls, one of the assembled group suddenly noticed that the propeller of the seized engine was unfeathered.

Thinking that the unfeathering had been done by a ground crew member whilst their attention was diverted, they continued their discussion. However, a few moments later someone else noticed that the propeller was feathered again. To a man they leapt up and, forming a posse, sought out the engineering officer immediately. Together they inspected the aircraft and found to their surprise that nobody had been near or had entered the aircraft since it was towed in. A technical inspection revealed that the feathering solenoid had stuck closed and as long as the battery lasted the propeller would have continued to feather and unfeather itself.

So the aircraft not only had engine but also propeller troubles. What if this had occurred some distance from base? Emergency calls to de Havilland resulted in a party of engineers from the company arriving and disconnecting the feathering circuits until such time as they devised a solenoid which would not stick closed. Regrettably this was not to be the last of the propeller feathering problems to be encountered by the squadron.

Whilst the development flying progressed and decisions were being made to implement the modification programme specified on 15th December, preparations for operational flying continued in parallel. On 16th January 1941 the ORB notes that a detachment was being formed at Driffield to speed air firing training.

On 21st January 1941 the AOC, Air Vice-Marshal Bottomley, visited the station to discuss the possibility of the squadron undertaking restricted operational flying and it was agreed that this should be implemented. By the 24th the initial plans were prepared and the AOC 5 Group was informed that the squadron would try to have four aircraft and crews fit for operations on 14th February. The ORB noted that six aircraft and crews were being prepared.

Manchesters had continued to arrive at Waddington during this period from various maintenance units, including 6 MU Brize Norton, 27 MU Shawbury and 46 MU at Lossiemouth. Subsequent to the first few Manchesters received by the squadron with the F.N.21A mid-under turret, the next aircraft had no mid-positioned armament of any kind fitted and these were destined to be the aircraft with which the first tentative operations were flown. This was despite the undertakings of 9th December 1940 which had promised that the later, operationally fit aircraft were to be issued to the squadron for these initial operations.

These early aircraft maintained the colour scheme of the first aircraft to be received by the squadron in having the upper and lower surface colours meeting in a straight line mid-way up the fuselage side. The well known photographs of L7284 'EM-D' and L7288 'EM-H' show such Manchesters to good advantage and were probably taken very early in 1941. The loss of the weight of the mid-positioned turret offered a marginal improvement in performance of these aircraft. The last Manchester to be received by the squadron with no mid-position turrets is unknown but the rest of the batch at least up to and including L7302, some 20-21 aircraft, were delivered without any mid-position armament.

On 25th January 1941 an Avro working party arrived at Waddington to carry out the agreed modifications to the Manchesters. The modifications were to be done at the rate of five aircraft per week and would require the aircraft to be housed in the hangar. A total of 14 aircraft were to be modified at Waddington, a further nine awaiting delivery at Woodford and four still at the MUs.

Mr Burke of the Ministry of Aircraft Production (MAP) visited the station to discuss the situation with respect to modifications

L7282 'EM-J', one of the initial batch of pre-production, non-operationally fit aircraft, at Waddington *circa* January 1941, in the early paint scheme with mid-under F.N.21A turret retracted. The outer profile of the original bomb doors is well displayed.
RAF Museum P022535

and equipment for the aircraft to make them operationally fit. Several very desirable modifications, such as the fitting of autopilots, balloon cable cutters etc. would not be included.

A member of 207 groundcrew in the Maintenance 'M' Flight, 2nd Aircraftman Norman Rushton, recalls that another necessary modification carried out on some aircraft was the fitting of self-sealing fuel tanks in place of the original unprotected tanks. Possibly this related to the first few pre-production aircraft which were originally envisaged as test, development and crew conversion trainers. To facilitate this modification the lower mainplane skin was detached to allow the tanks to be removed. Three groundcrew then raised the new self-sealing tanks into place, bracing these upwards into the space whilst the rest of the team fastened the metal retaining straps and tightened them with turnbuckles. Finally the wing skin was pop-riveted back in place.

The FN.21A turrets were removed by the squadron armourers and airframe fitters working with the Avro party, the circular holes being infilled with a neat removable hatch. Norman Rushton remembers constructing these from wood. They were of the correct depth to span the gap between the floor and the outer skin of the aircraft, being flat on the top and curved to blend with the fuselage contours beneath. The hatches were closed by an interior spring-loaded bolt and had a ring handle and cable to lift them clear in an emergency.

L7288 'EM-H' at Waddington with squadron codes overprinting the serial. Note trestle in place around the starboard Vulture. The F.N.21A mid-under turret was never fitted to this aircraft. *No. 207 Squadron archives / R Glynne-Owen*

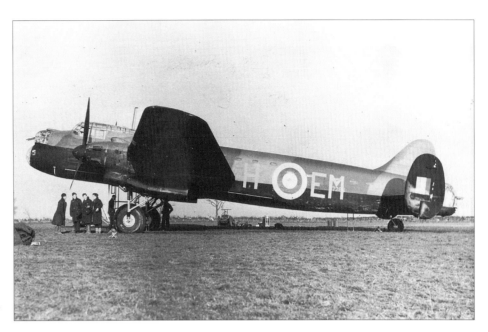

A 'press ganged' scratch crew assembled in front of L7288 'EM-H', circa December 1940 to January 1941. Left to right: Flying Officer Peter Burton-Gyles (captain); Sergeant J A Taylor (wireless operator); unknown; Sergeant Hudson, (observer); Sergeant J Scott (wireless operator/air gunner). The aircraft joined 207 on 7th December 1940, and passed to 97 on 26th February 1941. *No. 207 Squadron archives / R Glynne-Owen*

Installation of the cabin heating system was not such a simple matter. A square hole was cut in each wing leading edge between the fuselage and engine cowling inboard of which a radiator was located. A duct was run directly from the engine to this radiator conducting coolant through the radiator and returning it to the engine cooling radiators located beneath the engine nacelle. Air introduced through the leading edge intake was led through this radiator and thence straight into the aircraft in the wing root one to each side of the fuselage.

On test it was found that both ducts projected a terrific blast of hot air directly at the radio operator at his seat on the port side just in front of the main spar. Thus, after trials and further complaints from the aircrew a thin steel deflector plate was fitted over each inlet to distribute the heat laterally to some extent. However, there was no internal ducting to direct the heat forward to the front turret and bomb aiming position, nor towards the rear for the tail gunner. Consequently, although the centre section became reasonably warm there was no significant benefit at the extremities of the aircraft.

An internal Avro minute records the items involved and the progress of the modification programme.

Manchester Modification State, January/February 1941

Item	Status
Mine Carriers	All
Wireless R3003	All
Cabin Heating	L7311 onward
Armour Plate	L7300 onward
Flame Dampers	All
Resin Lights	All
Lorenz	All
Heated bomb aiming panel	All
Perspex blisters	All
Remove F.N.21A	First nine aircraft
Completed by 23rd January	L7288, L7284, L7292, L7294, L7286, L7300, L7282, L7299.
Completed by 21st February	L7279, L7298
Completed by 28th February	L7278, L7280, L7283, L7290, L7291.

On 30th January 1941 the Senior Air Staff Officer (SASO) of Headquarters 5 Group, Group Captain A P Richie, visited Waddington to discuss the status of the training, the modification programme and the establishment of the squadron. Meanwhile the Avro working parties continued the intensive modification programme. The 14 Manchesters at Waddington were: L7278, L7279, L7280, L7282, L7283, L7284, L7286, L7288, L7290, L7291, L7292, L7294, L7298, L7299.

During early February the number of pilots and aircraft continued to increase rapidly. On 11th February 1941 seven modified Manchesters were allotted to the squadron. The precise date of delivery is uncertain but the aircraft possibly included L7300 and certainly included L7302, L7303 and L7304.

By this time a decision had been taken to form a new Manchester squadron, 97, from 'B' Flight of 207. The new squadron was to utilise aircraft from the original batch of 20 which, despite the modification programme, would still not be considered suitable for operations. No. 207 was to operate the newer, better-equipped aircraft from subsequent batches. For the moment aircraft and personnel continued to arrive at Waddington, where the Avro working party and squadron ground crews continued their intensive modification programme. Optimism for the Manchester was still running at a high level. Sir Robert Renwick had estimated that the Manchesters in 5 Group would be fully modified to current operational status by 1st March 1941.

Left: **View of L7288 'EM-H' at Waddington. Photograph must have been taken pre-February 1941 because the aircraft lacks the lower bomb aimer's window, balloon cable cutters, cabin heater intakes and cockpit side blister. Engine covers are off the starboard Vulture.** *No. 207 Squadron archives / R Glynne-Owen*

Bottom: **L7282 reached 207 on 21 December 1940 and is seen here without armament. It passed to 97 on 20th February 1941 as a crew trainer and went for upgrading by Avro on 17th August 1941. It was never re-issued from storage.** *RAF Museum*

Opposite page: **Wireless operator Sergeant J A Taylor and wireless operator/air gunner Sergeant J Scott pose at the radio position in L7288. No. 207** *No. 207 Squadron archives / R Glynne-Owen*

By then Avro would have similarly modified a further 25 aircraft prior to delivery and produced a further 12 to current status. If this had been realised, both 207 and 97 would have their 18 initial establishment plus one in reserve and there would be a further 34 fully operational Manchesters available.

Avro production was to have reached three per week by this time and plans were laid to form a new squadron or re-equip an existing Hampden unit. No. 61 was eventually chosen, but events were to overtake these optimistic plans. On 14th February 1941, despite the allocation of the new aircraft to the squadron, the ORB records that the four operationally fit aircraft promised to the AOC 14 days previously were still not available.

On 15th February the squadron at last had six operationally fit crews and aircraft. No operations were required and so the crews undertook night cross-country training in the Manchesters. On the same day more experienced pilots, Pilot Officers W G Gardiner DFC, W S Herring DFM and Flying Officer G R Taylor DFC arrived on posting from a spell as instructors at 16 Operational Training Unit (OTU), Upper Heyford.

No. 207 was poised for operations against the Third Reich. The RAF's intention of providing a core of experienced and high calibre aircrews to introduce the Manchester into service, as intimated by newly-promoted Wing Commander 'Hettie' Hyde, had been implemented. Regrettably it was to prove a much more intractable task to achieve the transition of the Manchester to a successful service aircraft.

Up to this date, although the transition had proved far from routine, there had been no significant accidents. There was still a good deal of enthusiasm for the aircraft. By comparison with the Hampdens most aircrew were accustomed to, the Manchester was a much larger and very advanced aircraft.

At the time of their introduction to operations the aircraft standardised on a crew of six. These were a first and second pilot, an observer (navigator), who also aimed the bombs and manned the front gun turret, two wireless operators/air gunners (W/Op AG) and a rear gunner. The captain was invariably an experienced second tour officer, whilst the second pilots were freshly trained sergeant pilots straight from Hampden OTUs. Having gained Manchester and operational experience under the direction of the captain it was envisaged that these second pilots

would then go on to form their own crews. Part of the second pilot's duty was to monitor the engine instruments.

At this time the trade of navigator did not exist and neither was a front gunner, bomb aimer or flight engineer carried. Similarly, the 1st W/Op was a second tour man and the 2nd W/Op AG was a new boy completing his training on operations before transferring to a crew in his own right. The 2nd W/Op AG occupied the mid-upper F.N.7A, soon to be introduced. In those aircraft which continued to operate without the mid-upper turret, the 2nd W/Op AG occupied the front turret.

The Vulture engines were rated at 1,760hp each. The aircraft had an empty weight of 29,432 lb, a mean weight of 41,315 lb and a maximum loaded weight of up to 45,000 lb. A maximum bomb load of 10,350 lb could be lifted but more usually 8,000 lb or 6,000 lb of bombs were carried. With an 8,000 lb load the range was 1,630 miles. On trials a top speed of 265mph at 17,000ft was recorded. The best cruising speed was 185mph at 15,000ft. Take-off performance was marginal, supposedly requiring a 1,300 yard run to clear a 50ft obstacle in calm conditions. In practice a fully loaded Manchester was unlikely to clear six feet at 1,400 yards in warm weather, whilst the average landing run was 1,050 yards.

By this time 'Mike' Lewis had a large number of flying hours in Manchesters, including the testing and development work done on the squadron, the training of the less experienced second pilots allocated to the unit and the preparation for operations. Lewis recalls the Manchester as an exceedingly stable bombing platform. The triple-finned Mk.I was especially stable laterally. Once the aircraft had settled onto the desired heading it would hold it until the cows came home, almost as if an automatic pilot was engaged. In comparison, Lewis later found its offspring, the Lancaster, was less stable in that even with the most precise flying from the pilot the nose continually described a gentle rotary motion in the sky. This spiralling motion must have been the bane of bomb aimers.

The ailerons of the Manchester were also very light and responsive. Lewis found that the aileron feel became lighter as speed increased in a dive. At an indicated airspeed (IAS) of about 250mph in a dive the aircraft could be rocked up to 30-45° either side of horizontal using only one finger of each hand on the control column. In comparison the Lancaster with the same ailerons and a very similar wing plan was much heavier, the weight increasing progressively as speed built up.

In contrast, the elevators of the Manchester I with short span tail were extremely heavy. Although this had some virtues when the aircraft was trimmed to fly straight and level it was altogether unsatisfactory for carrying out evasive manoeuvres and when engaged on circuits and landings. Receiving dual instruction on the early Mk.I was a physically demanding task for the trainee pilot. Quite excessive force was necessary to raise and lower the nose, to the extent that pilots rapidly exhausted their physical resources. Pilots under instruction found that three take-offs and landings was the limit they could achieve at one session and this was rarely sufficient to accomplish a complete check out of a new pilot.

Lewis found he could speed the task of converting new pilots onto the type by carrying two trainees on each flight. When one pilot had carried out three circuits and landings he changed seats with the other trainee until he had recovered his strength.

Flying the classic corkscrew evasive manoeuvre in the early Mk.I for any length of time was very demanding on the pilot. Pilots learnt to use a combination of gentle corkscrew with simultaneous use of flying and engine controls if rapid changes of flight direction or height were required in the event of a fighter attack.

Flying Officer Peter Burton-Gyles in the captain's seat of L7288. 'Unknown' in second pilot's seat and gunner Sergeant J 'Scotty' Scott in an unaccustomed place by the navigator's table. *No. 207 Squadron archives / R Glynne-Owen*

Balsdon arrived on attachment at Waddington from Headquarters 3 Group to gain experience on Manchesters. He was to command the reformed 97 Squadron scheduled to be based at Coningsby. No. 207 Squadron was to transfer the necessary aircraft, aircrews ('B' Flight) and maintenance personnel to form the nucleus of the new unit.

To this end, aircrews continued to assemble at Waddington for training. On 20th February 1941 Flying Officers Paape DFC and Ayton, Flying Officers Blakeman and Romans, all experienced, decorated second tour pilots, arrived. The squadron's work-up to operations continued at a feverish pace, embracing many aspects. On 22nd February it was noted that four new aircraft were collected from Woodford, L7310, L7311, L7312, L7313. L7313 was the first squadron Manchester to be fitted with the F.N.7A mid-upper turret, but on a visit on the 24th the Director of Technical Development (DTD) Inspector noted that this remained unserviceable as the firing cut out cams had yet to be fitted.

By now the airfield at Waddington had become so crowded that nine aircraft were dispersed to nearby Coleby. At the same time it was arranged for the squadron air firing detachment to be recalled from Driffield. To ease and speed the training Headquarters 5 Group had agreed to the allocation of two Fairey Battle target tugs to Waddington so that air firing training could continue at the nearby Wainfleet Ranges. Meanwhile, the intensive night flying training, bombing and operational preparation continued. The milestone of the squadron's – and the Manchester's – first operation was at hand.

Whilst the squadron was poised expectantly to carry out its first operation the contrast between this anticipation and their true predicament was stark. A decision to abandon the Manchester had been made in November 1940 and the Lancaster prototype had flown in January 1941. Before they flew their first operation their aircraft was already obsolete. No. 207 and the 5 Group units in its wake were about to endure almost a year and a half of operations with, thankfully unbeknown to them, no significant prospect that the problems would be sorted out. Unwittingly, they were the victims of the grave and desperate position the Allies were in – every aeroplane was needed, even if it was of doubtful serviceability.

For the moment, pilots satisfied themselves in regard to the flying characteristics of the aircraft, which proved generally adequate, whereas their major concern centred around the engines. Being so seriously underpowered was a major limitation on performance, and reliability was at best marginal.

By late February 1941, at about the time they first operated, many Manchesters underwent a further and hasty field modification to their colour scheme. The demarcation between the upper surface colours and the black undersides was raised again, this time to the top of the fuselage. On the tailplane, wings and cowlings the actual junction was a straight line. In contrast, on the fuselage top decking the junction was wavy. The central fin was coloured black to match the twin

endplate fin and rudder assemblies. Colour schemes differed slightly from aircraft to aircraft. Generally the wavy black underside colour swept up to the leading edge of the central fin leaving the whole of the rear fuselage black. On at least two aircraft, L7309 and L7319, although having a black central fin, the wavy demarcation on the fuselage ran all the way through to the rear turret. On these aircraft the unit codes and individual aircraft letters and the serials were grey. This colour scheme remained unchanged until September 1941.

On 18th February 1941 Squadron Leader R D Stubbs arrived from 144 Squadron, Hemswell, with a view to assuming command of 'B' Flight of 207 Squadron. The ORB for this day also noted that Squadron Leader D F

Chapter Three

First Operations

Over a prolonged period, Bomber Command had been contributing a large effort to the bottling up of the German Battle Fleet in Brest.

On 24th February 1941 the Command was briefed for an attack on a 'Hipper' class cruiser known to be tied up in the port. Some 30 aircraft from 3 Group, 25 Handley Page Hampdens and six Manchesters from 5 Group and some Coastal Command aircraft were involved.

For 207 Squadron's memorable first operation of the war there was a state of high excitement. In addition to the squadron personnel, high ranking officers from 5 Group and distinguished guests from Avro and Rolls-Royce were invited to witness the operational debut of their protégé, the Manchester. The aircraft were mainly from the original batch delivered to the squadron. They lacked the mid-upper turrets, still had the 28ft span tailplane and saw only limited operational flying. Bomb loads consisted of 12 x 500 lb semi-armour piercing bombs, with the exception of L7300 which for some reason only carried eleven.

Crews operationally fit at this time were those of Flight Lieutenant Dereck French, Squadron Leader Charles Kydd, Flying Officers Johnnie Siebert, Peter Burton-Gyles, Frankie Eustace and 'Mike' Lewis. Typically of the man, Wing Commander 'Hettie' Hyde was not going to miss this first operation. He did not have a crew of his own and so 'borrowed' French's crew for the occasion leaving the dejected Flight Lieutenant behind. 'Hettie' was to earn the undivided respect of his crews by being the only commanding officer the squadron had during the 18 month period it operated Manchesters to fly the aircraft regularly on operations. A very experienced pilot, he had a tremendous rapport with both his air and groundcrews. French remained on the ground to play host to the distinguished visitors, retaining vivid memories of the unit's first operational sortie. It was a bad night with poor visibility, storms, snow lying on the ground and still falling.

The aircraft took off at closely spaced intervals between 1835 and 1850 hours. Four aircraft recorded a take-off time of 1840 hours. The aircraft made their way individually to the target area, as was the procedure at this stage of the war, there was no 'forming up'.

Operational Debut, Brest – 24th February 1941

Serial	Code	Sqn	Captain
L7300	EM-*	207	W/C N C Hyde
L7288	EM-*	207	S/L C J F Kydd
L7279	EM-*	207	F/O J A Siebert
L7284	EM-*	207	F/O P R Burton-Gyles
L7286	EM-*	207	F/O F E Eustace
L7294	EM-*	207	F/O W J Lewis

* In this and subsequent raid tables, an asterisk indicates that the individual aircraft code has not been confirmed.

In L7284 the second pilot, Sergeant Les Syrett, received his first surprise soon after take-off. Having completed his post take-off checks, established their designated course and reached a height of 1,500ft, Flying Officer 'BG' Burton-Gyles turned to Syrett and, indicating the controls, called 'It's all yours, call me when you reach the target'. With this he slipped out of the pilot's seat and steadied the controls whilst Syrett took his place. Syrett had expected to undertake maybe half a dozen trips before he was allowed to do any other than relieve the pilot for short spells during the safer and more routine legs of the flight. Yet here he was only a few minutes into the flight on his first operation in command of a fully loaded Manchester.

Syrett climbed to the briefed flying height and set a new course with mixed feelings of excitement and apprehension. The feeling was heightened by the fact that 'BG' had already disappeared aft. These early Manchesters had no second pilot's seat and consequently the captain could only stand beside him and observe. This indeed was Syrett's normal crew position. While Syrett felt some trepidation at his responsibilities, 'BG' felt none. For four months he had been training and flying with this crew. During the time he had watched each one closely and progressively gave the newcomers more to do as their ability and confidence developed. On their long endurance and test flights 'BG' had increasingly encouraged Syrett to do the flying. He would not have been sitting there if 'BG' had harboured any doubts. The outward flight was uneventful and as they approached Brest Syrett called 'BG' telling him the target was dead ahead.

The squadron Operational Record Book (ORB) records all aircraft as making individual 'high level' bombing attacks, although the debriefing reports show that in general

the height reached was around 10,000ft. Wing Commander Hyde reached 15,000ft, some 4,000ft higher than the next Manchester. Over the target area and to the north, south and west the aircraft encountered searchlights, light and heavy flak, but night fighters were not in evidence.

As Burton-Gyles took L7284 across Brest, Sergeant Syrett had his second great surprise of the night. 'BG' was flying at his favourite height of 8,000ft and the flak, particularly the lighter guns, which were firing mainly tracer, seemed so dense to the newcomer that he could not imagine them completing the attack without being hit. Syrett had expected the captain to put the nose down a little, traverse the target area as rapidly as possible, dump the bombs and go.

Not Peter Burton-Gyles. He circled the target, trying to establish the best direction of approach for his bomb run. Having satisfied himself on the location of the target and the best approach, he next did a dummy run across the area. All this time the flak was hammering away around them and 'BG' and the experienced crew members with him appeared to be completely unperturbed.

Burton-Gyles then made two further attacks during which, on the instructions of the observer, Sergeant Houghton, in the bomb aiming position, they released a stick of six bombs on each run. The reason for this was to prevent the Germans calculating the bomb load of the new bomber. Owing to a design fault, the bomb aimer could not observe the fall of bombs and thus Syrett was ordered to look down through the starboard blister in the cockpit. Syrett found he could see the weapons falling away for some time because of the sky being brightly illuminated by searchlights and flak.

With the attack completed, Houghton tried to close the bomb doors. At this point a second problem with the design became apparent, because, as a result of a flak hit or a leak, the hydraulics had failed and the bomb doors could not be closed. 'BG' turned for home and once clear of the target area handed control over to Syrett. He ordered 'Take over and call me when you reach base'. Syrett regained the seat and began setting his new course, checking time and the fuel situation. To his surprise and concern he found they had been over the target for exactly 40 minutes.

This was a bit disturbing because the maximum bomb load and short range of the target had meant them not carrying a full fuel load. In addition to the time spent over the target, Syrett had to contend with the additional drag of the open bomb doors.

All six Manchesters bombed what they believed to be the target, two dropped the bombs in two separate runs of six bombs per stick. Further hydraulic problems with the attack force, which were to prove more intractable than the observation of the fall of bombs, manifested themselves during the return flight. L7300, Hyde's aircraft, developed a serious hydraulic leak, which resulted in a film of hydraulic fluid spreading over the windscreen. As a result 'Hettie' had to complete his return flying almost blind. Before the situation deteriorated further he wisely decided to make a precautionary landing, which was successfully accomplished at Boscombe Down at 2255 hours. Frankie Eustace diverted to Middle Wallop for unexplained reasons. The four remaining aircraft flew on towards Waddington where Johnnie Siebert landed at 2345 before the assembled VIPs, 'Mike' Lewis touched down at 2355 followed by Charles Kydd 35 minutes later at 0030 hours.

Meanwhile L7284 was plodding back across England under the control of Les Syrett. Although delayed by the drag of the enormous bomb bay the fuel situation appeared to be marginal, but sufficient. They arrived last of all in the circuit at Waddington where control was returned to Burton-Gyles for the landing. Entering the circuit, 'BG' called the control tower and obtained permission to land. Below, the various dignitaries assembled for the occasion strained to catch sight of the approaching aircraft.

At this point the seriousness of the hydraulic leak became apparent when they were unable to lower the undercarriage. Following the failure over Brest this had not been unexpected and was not a cause for concern because the emergency pneumatic system to lower and lock the legs was available as a back up. When directed at the appropriate time, Syrett operated the emergency system. To their dismay the undercarriage warning lights showed green on the port side and red on the starboard. The starboard undercarriage leg had failed to lock down. Aborting the landing approach, 'BG' overflew the control tower where a visual check confirmed that this was not a check light failure but the starboard leg was indeed stubbornly retracted. 'BG' tried everything possible to get the remaining leg down, but without success. Avro's Chief Designer, Roy Chadwick, was one of the invited guests and he established radio contact with the aircraft, making a further series of suggestions as to how the reluctant undercarriage might be released. These options were exhausted in turn and eventually with the fuel situation

critical and the engines faltering, 'BG' informed the tower of his intention to make a one wheel landing. The crew were sent to crash stations. The rear gunner, 'Eddy' Edmonds, left his turret and sat on the floor with his back to the mainspar, facing aft.

They descended towards the snow-covered grass runway at about 30° to it. As they crossed the perimeter and entered the flare path funnels 'BG' turned into line with the runway and dropped the port wing as low as possible. Flaring out with the left wing low they touched down onto the port main wheel and tail wheel simultaneously. 'BG' fought with rudders and ailerons to keep them straight and gave full left aileron to keep the starboard wing up. At a critical speed he trod on the brakes and the right wing descended gently onto the ground. By this time the speed had dropped away to such an extent that they merely slewed round to starboard, coming to rest facing across the runway. Damage was confined to the bomb doors, starboard wing tip and propeller. Nobody was hurt and the aircraft was repaired within a few days. It had been a magnificent landing. L7284 was the first Manchester to be damaged in the course of operational flying.

As well as the damage to L7284 there was an embarrassing sidelight to the incident. Examination proved that the reason for the failure of the emergency undercarriage system was due to its incorrect assembly by the Avro working party.

A tragic perspective on this first operation is that of the six captains involved, four were eventually killed and the other two became prisoners of war. Of the second pilots, Sergeant Pendrill was killed, Syrett badly injured, Hugh Morgan, John Nunn, and Robson were taken prisoner. The fate of Sergeant Rowlands has not so far been established.

With Roy Chadwick on this occasion was Sandy Jacks, the Avro Chief Inspector. Both had maintained a close liaison with the squadron, in particular Jacks was a frequent visitor to Waddington. Chadwick had flown to Waddington in an Anson and both Avro employees stayed on the station overnight. Next morning bad weather grounded the Anson and Chadwick and Jacks travelled back to Woodford by car. The two discussed the events of the previous night during their journey. They knew they had an urgent problem on their hands. The hydraulic failures they had witnessed were serious but surmountable, the crews' reaction at debriefing was generally enthusiastic. Jacks recalled that some of the Manchesters had suffered superficial flak damage, although this is not reported in the ORB. What was clear was that the aircraft were not able to climb above the light and medium flak. Whether all the crews had deliberately chosen to bomb from such a low height cannot be ascertained, but this seems unlikely. Chadwick voiced his worries to Jacks, 'If they are in the flak now,

they will be no good a year from now, even if the engine power can be increased'. Chadwick's concern was centred on the Vulture engines, even if their reliability could be improved they would still not be capable of providing the Manchester with a satisfactory operational ceiling. The German flak gunners would slaughter them.

As a result of the first operation Avro's rushed ahead with fabrication of the perspex insert to the lower fuselage immediately behind the bomb aiming bubble. Along with other urgent modifications this was incorporated at Waddington by the hard pressed Avro working parties.

On 25th February 1941 the 207 Squadron ORB records the formal establishment of 97 Squadron at Waddington and that it was planned to transfer sufficient aircraft and crews to form a flight of eight aircraft as a nucleus.

The following day, 26th February, five Manchesters were detailed for night bombing operations to Cologne. For this raid the five Manchesters were to join 72 aircraft from 2 and 3 Groups, whilst 5 Group provided nine Hampdens from Hemswell, 10 from Scampton and 10 from Lindholme. The target was the industrial centre of Cologne and the bomb load of each aircraft 12 x 500 lb general purpose (GP) bombs. The aircraft took off in a group between 1910 and 1915 hours.

Cologne – 26th February 1941

Serial	Code	Sqn	Captain
L7300	EM-*	207	F/L D J French
L7292	EM-*	207	F/O J A Siebert
L7288	EM-*	207	F/O P R Burton-Gyles
L7286	EM-*	207	F/O F E Eustace
L7294	EM-*	207	F/O W J Lewis

Three aircraft believed they had located the target area, each making two separate runs and bombing from heights between 8,000ft and 13,000ft for five of the six runs. In L7288 Les Syrett had again taken over from Burton-Gyles soon after take-off. This operation was to be a more severe test for him than the last, involving as it did several hours flying over occupied territory including German airspace itself. On reaching the target 'BG' took over and, looking ahead and below, the crew could see fires burning everywhere and bombs from other aircraft exploding every few seconds. Surprisingly there was no sign of flak, searchlights or fighters. All this indicated they were really over a decoy target, but a careful check appeared to confirm they were indeed over Cologne. The first stick of bombs was duly released with no response whatever from the ground below.

Remaining unconvinced of their precise target, 'BG' turned away and having withdrawn to a suitable position turned back and dived on the target to have a closer look. The observer in the nose, Ken Houghton, and the rear gunner, 'Eddy' Edmonds, were told to stand by and at 2,000ft over the designated aiming point 'BG', satisfied that this appeared to be a built-up area, levelled out and ordered Houghton to release the bomb load. Taking advantage of their proximity to the ground, Edmonds blazed away with his four Brownings for good measure.

By this time the rear gunners had cut a kite-shaped clear-vision panel in the perspex between the guns. As soon as he ceased firing, Edmonds stood up in his turret and stuck his head through the panel to have a look at the effects of the attack on the built-up area below. Unbeknown to him, as he stretched forward his intercom plug came out, isolating him from the rest of the crew. When 'BG' called each crew station in turn there was consequently no response from the rear turret. As Edmonds sat down and plugged in his intercom connection again he was startled when the turret doors suddenly burst open as a crew member arrived to check whether he was still around.

There can be little doubt that Burton-Gyles, along with the other operational captains in 207, fully appreciated by this stage the unreliability of the Vulture engines and the degree to which they were underpowered. Many Manchesters on test proved to be unable to maintain height on one engine. Even when lightly loaded, carefully trimmed and with the throttle of the remaining engine fully advanced, many still sank, some at a more alarming rate than others. To take the risk of diving to a low altitude over enemy territory, as 'BG' did and other Manchester captains were to do subsequently, was to court

certain disaster in the event of an engine failure. The fact that they were prepared to go to such lengths to ensure their bombs were laid on target, in full awareness of the risks, speaks legions for the enthusiasm and 'press on' spirit of the aircrews, operating against almost insuperable odds in their Manchesters. Almost before L7288 had crossed the town and whilst still at 2,000ft, 'BG' called on Syrett standing beside him to change seats. Having done so, Syrett wasted no time in climbing to a respectable height and heading for home.

The remaining two aircraft engaged in the operation both experienced equipment failures, necessitating early returns. Close to the enemy coast, Frankie Eustace, in L7286, experienced a serious drop in oil pressure in the port engine, a common Vulture problem at this time. He diverted to Flushing and dropped his bomb load in two sticks from 10,000ft and 9,000ft, returning safely to Waddington at 2210 hours.

'Mike' Lewis in L7294 was even more unfortunate. A serious hydraulic failure developed within an hour of take-off. The bombs were jettisoned in the North Sea and the aircraft returned to Waddington, effecting a safe landing at 2110 hours.

Bomber Command records indicate 353 high explosive (HE) and 15,060 incendiaries dropped from the 106 aircraft which bombed. The German archivist in Cologne reported only 10 HE and 90 incendiaries actually fell within the city limits.

Meanwhile, on 27th February 1941 the actual transfer of 'B' Flight, 207 Squadron to form the cadre of 97 Squadron took place.

The aircraft involved comprised: L7282, L7283, L7290, L7291, L7292, L7294, L7298 and L7299.

The 12 officers transferred to provide a nucleus of trained crews were: Squadron Leader R D Stubbs DFC; Flight Lieutenants G O L Bird DFC and J S Sherwood, Flying Officers F E Eustace DFC, W J Lewis DFC, M J C Harwood DFC and Pilot Officers R S Ayton DFM, H S Blakeman DFM, W A Brown, F G Reid (observer), A A Morgan (observer) and J Trueman (gunner).

On that day 97 Squadron nominally had three Manchesters available for operations although the unit would not have been able to sustain any intensive pressure in this regard. Established initially on a single flight basis, three Manchesters were in the maintenance hangar having their bomb compartments modified by Avro whilst the remaining two aircraft were dispersed at Coleby awaiting modifications. The aircraft in any case still lacked many essential refinements. Fully trained crews were heavily engaged test flying aircraft and collecting new ones. Fresh crews were arriving and required training. By early March the Squadron still did not have an engineer or armaments officer and the aircraft were plagued with many minor problems, mostly to the hydraulic systems.

Mk.I L7288 'EM-H' of 207 Squadron at Waddington, circa January/February 1941.
No.207 Squadron archives / R Glynne-Owen

On 10th March 1941 the pressure on Waddington eased to some extent when 97 Squadron personnel moved out to Coningsby. Here the grass airfield was flooded and boggy, precluding transfer of the aircraft. Eventually aircraft were flown in between 15th and 18th March but by the 27th all had become bogged down after further heavy rain, preventing any air activity for some days.

Although limited operational flying with these initial batch of aircraft was undertaken by 97, as with 207, they lacked mid-upper turrets and various other refinements and most retained the 28ft span tail. Later batches of more operationally fit Manchesters were collected in dribs and drabs as they became available.

An indication of the feverish pace of activity for the squadrons during this work-up period was that on 1st March 1941 two complete aircrews and 15 maintenance personnel were attached to 207 from 61 Squadron at Hemswell for this unit to gain experience on the Manchester. The crews were those of Flying Officer Geoff Hall and Pilot Officer Peter Casement and their training began in earnest next day. No. 97 was to pass on its pre-production aircraft to this unit in turn during March so that conversion could begin.

This rapid expansion of the Manchester force concealed an impending crisis of catastrophic proportion – engines! At this stage it was merely the case that Rolls-Royce were unable to maintain even the output to satisfy production of this one type. Avro had set up frequent internal Manchester production meetings. In February 1941 they recorded the position as critical, with Avro themselves nine Vultures short and Metrovick four short of the promised output. By 17th March the shortfall had risen to ten for Avro and six for Metrovick. The situation was shortly to worsen and threaten the entire future of the aircraft.

On 2nd March 1941, Johnnie Siebert with his crew in L7303 and maintenance personnel were detached to the Air Fighting Development Unit at Duxford for trials. By this time serious serviceability problems with the remaining Manchesters, especially with the hydraulic systems and the oil cooling system of the engines, had reduced the available Manchesters to a minimum. For 207 Squadron's third operation on 3rd March only two aircraft could be raised for another attack on a 'Hipper' class cruiser at Brest. The main operation for the night was a force of 71 aircraft dispatched to Cologne. The two squadron aircraft joined five others in a diversionary raid to the French port.

Brest – 3rd March 1941

Serial	Code	Sqn	Captain
L7302	EM-R	207	F/L D J French
L7313	EM-C	207	F/O P R Burton-Gyles

Both aircraft carried 11 x 500 lb semi-armour piercing (SAP) bombs, but although they remained serviceable they were unable to locate the target, owing to low cloud over the continent. The crews were aware of the general locality of the target owing to the intense flak coming up through the cloud layer. However, aiming SAP bombs on pinpoint targets such as ships was out of the question in such circumstances.

Peter Burton-Gyles as captain of L7313 'EM-C' had elected to allow Les Syrett to fly the entire operation, changing seats as they waited on the runway for the green light from the Aldis lamp. The outward trip had been uneventful, but target location proved impossible. Turning aside from the immediate target area and over the sea they did a climb from low level, establishing that the cloud base was well below 1,000ft and extended to well above their ceiling. There was no possibility of bombing in such conditions without danger to the French civilian population in the neighbourhood. Accordingly, with the weather extremely bad and no secondary target specified, they aborted the operation and turned towards England.

In L7302 'EM-R' Dereck French, with a total crew of only five had been flying for over an hour on instruments. As he approached the target area the weather deteriorated further with a series of violent thunder storms and much lightning. In what he estimated to be the target area, L7302 was struck by lightning, which hit the fuselage near to the identification, friend or foe (IFF) set. To ensure its security in the event of a forced landing in enemy territory the IFF was fitted with a small Thermite explosive charge which could be detonated by pressing the appropriate button. The lightning strike exploded the charge, destroying the set, blowing a jagged hole in the side of the aircraft. Inspection by torchlight revealed a small heap of molten metal on the fuselage floor beneath the site.

In these extreme conditions it was impossible to locate the target and French decided there was a better chance of regaining base without the bomb load. Having crossed the French coast he jettisoned the load 'safe'. In the bad weather conditions he found the aircraft easier to handle, eventually landing back at base 5hr 45min after take-off.

On reaching base, Syrett assumed Burton-Gyles would wish to land the aircraft as the full bomb load remained on board. However, 'BG' stood beside him in the second pilot's position and supervised Syrett making the landing himself. 'BG' advised on the timing of the lowering of the flaps and undercarriage, the engine revolutions and propeller settings and continued to encourage his protégé all the way into a smooth landing. As soon as this was effected, 'BG' nipped into the pilot's seat and taxied the aircraft to its dispersal.

By this time an experienced pilot with approaching 1,000 hours flying and a tour on

Hampdens behind him, French was well equipped to make the decision to jettison the bombs in the interests of saving the aircraft and its crew. He was accordingly outraged to be 'carpeted' next morning by an insensitive Station Commander who abused him for 'Throwing away bombs to the value of his annual salary'. French could hardly believe his ears. Incredulously he tried to explain that in terrible weather, jettisoning the bombs had possibly made the difference between saving and losing the aircraft. He rapidly recognised that reason and commonsense was not one of that officer's strong points.

On 4th March Sir Robert Renwick, Group Captain Anderson and Mr Rosenberg of the Ministry of Aircraft Production (MAP) visited 207 Squadron to discuss the Manchester's hydraulic system. At the meeting, confirmation was given of the decision to scrap the Ermeto-type hydraulic joint and if possible to retrospectively modify the existing aircraft. In the meantime, the squadron would have to carry on with the existing system.

A further problem stemming from the defective hydraulic system was capable of solution. Oil from the persistent leaks was also found to be affecting the undercarriage micro-switches, whose operation provided the visual cockpit indication that the main wheels were locked in position. Hydraulic oil penetrated the micro-switches causing them to malfunction and preventing the green indicator lights from illuminating when the undercarriage was lowered. The pilot therefore was not aware whether the hydraulic fluid in the retraction system of the undercart had leaked away, or whether the wheels were locked but the micro-switches were simply not operating.

Only a few days before, on 28th February 1941, perhaps as a direct consequence of these difficulties, Sergeant Harwood had the misfortune to have the undercarriage on L7312 collapse on a normal landing at Waddington. There were no casualties. An answer was required urgently. Lockheed engineers were called in to advise on the hydraulic systems, whilst a staff member from Pye Ltd went to Manchester to advise Avro on the micro-switches. The short term solution devised was to integrate the press button of the switches within an oilskin diaphragm sealed into the sides of the switch.

At the same time, a system of testing the integrity of the switches was devised. This involved a bicycle pump mounted on a board connected through tubes to a suction pad, while a connection went to a large glass 'U' tube. If pumping air through a hole drilled in the case raised the level of red ink in the tube and then held steady, then the switch was airtight. The hole was finally plugged with whalebone and sealed with resin. These modified micro-switches made it possible to distinguish true hydraulic failures from micro-switch failures once more.

Early March 1941 was a period of continued, almost non-stop pressure on the ground-crews. Serviceability of the Manchesters continued to be poor despite their most urgent endeavours. Modification to the existing aircraft continued. In the meantime small numbers of serviceable Manchesters were detailed for operations which were invariably called off.

On 6th March 1941 a 207 Squadron Manchester was prepared for an attack on Brest, which was later cancelled. On the 8th, three aircraft were prepared for an attack on the oil refinery at Gelsenkirchen, but the operation was cancelled at 1700 hours owing to bad weather. Finally on the 11th four aircraft were detailed for a raid on Kiel. The weather caused this operation to be abandoned also.

By now the original crews knew each other very well. Wing Commander Hyde had already earned the respect of air and ground crews alike. Introducing a new aircraft to operations was a demanding task at the best of times. The almost insurmountable number of technical problems, both large and small must have made the situation doubly difficult. To these problems was added the continual need to train new aircrews, as well as lose existing experienced crews to the squadrons designated for conversion. At this period 207 was an experimental and test unit, a conversion unit and an operational squadron all rolled into one. On the few occasions when these pressures allowed Hyde to get away he could be seen in the mess. He was renowned for his liking for pink gins, which he invariably ordered in threes. A typical posture was to be deep in conversation, a glass in each hand and the third at the ready in the crook of his elbow.

Squadron commanders in Bomber Command were not established with a personal crew as they were not supposed to fly regularly on operations. By this stage, Hyde had almost as many hours on Manchesters as anyone and when he felt the need to gain experience of flying the aircraft on operations he took the simple expedient of 'borrowing' a crew.

During their detachment to Duxford for fighter affiliation duties Johnnie Siebert and his crew had another little adventure. Arriving at their dispersal point one morning from their briefing they could find no sign of their maintenance personnel. Siebert and the other three crew members, Fomison (observer), Taylor (wireless operator) and Gurnell (rear gunner) were impatient to be on their way and decided they could pre-flight L7303 themselves. They removed the covers, ran the checks and, priming the engines with the low-geared manual handles provided, started them with self-starter and internal batteries. All the instrument readings rose to normal levels and with no more ado they removed the chocks and taxied out. L7303 was carrying a full dummy bomb load.

They lined up on the live runway and received a 'green' from the control tower. Siebert advanced the throttles and soon they were belting down the runway. The pilot concentrated on keeping the aircraft straight, the tail came up and the boundary fence was approaching fast. Siebert glanced at the airspeed indicator to judge precisely the moment of lift-off – no airspeed! Consternation ensued. They lifted off and Johnnie kept the aircraft down to build up flying speed. A quick glance confirmed their worst fears – the cover was still on the pitot head.

A landing back at Duxford was considered unwise and they agreed to make for Newmarket with its longer runway. En route, construction work in progress at another airfield, Waterbeach, drew their attention. What was also apparent was that, save for the construction workers, the airfield was unoccupied. Following their failure to carry out the pre-flight checks correctly Waterbeach apparently offered an opportunity to save face. They could land unobserved, remove the pitot head cover and take-off again so nobody would be aware of their error.

Manchester I L7284 'EM-D' during a photocall in February 1941. Tailspan 28ft but it is uncertain whether the F.N.21A mid-under turret was ever fitted to this aircraft. L7284 was, in many respects, not operationally fit when it participated in the first operation on 24th February 1941. It never operated again, passing to **No. 61 Squadron in mid-April.** *No.207 Squadron archives / R Glynne-Owen*

The decision to land was endorsed by those on board and Siebert made a wide circuit before lining them up with the long deserted runway. The approach was difficult without an airspeed indicator and as a precaution against the fatal stall Siebert kept the speed well up. Everything went smoothly until at the moment of their high speed touch down they suddenly realised that the runway was coated with loose gravel. They careered down the strip in their overloaded condition with the brakes having little effect in checking their progress. The aircraft overshot the runway and charged on through an unoccupied perimeter gunpost. In passing, the spinning propellers picked up many strands of barbed wire and the coils flew everywhere before they tangled themselves tightly around the propeller bosses. A truck was sent to retrieve the shamefaced crew and L7303 was later recovered with only minor damage.

No. 207 Squadron undertook an uneventful operation to Hamburg with four aircraft on 12th/13th March 1941. With continued favourable weather Bomber Command maintained its offensive on Hamburg the very next night, the 13th/14th. This operation was to prove far more eventful. No. 207 was called on to provide two Manchesters, but managed to produce five, including L7313 'EM-C', possibly still the only aircraft on the squadron with a mid-upper turret and L7278 'EM-A', the latter one of the earlier batch not passed on to 97 Squadron. Squadron Leader Kydd, Flight Lieutenant French and Sergeant Harwood and their crews were to operate for the second consecutive night and were joined by Wing Commander Hyde and Flying Officer Matthews.

Hamburg – 12th/13th March 1941

Serial	Code	Sqn	Captain
L7313	EM-C	207	F/O H V Matthews
L7310	EM-H	207	S/L C J F Kydd
L7303	EM-P	207	W/C N C Hyde
L7302	EM-R	207	F/L D J French
L7278	EM-A	207	F/Sgt F B Harwood

The aircraft again carried 10 x 500 lb GP bomb loads and although no take-off times are noted in the ORB it is believed that they assembled for take-off around 2000 hours. Four aircraft took off safely, but the fifth, L7313 'EM-C' piloted by Matthews, burst its tail wheel tyre due to undercarriage leg shimmy whilst taxying. Take-off times were not rigidly controlled during this period and it was decided to replace the tail wheel out on the aerodrome, a task which took about 30 minutes.

Matthews restarted the engines, taxied to the take-off point and, having received a 'green' from the control truck Aldis, set off in pursuit of his colleagues. Activity on the flarepath had been detected by a lurking intruder. A Junkers Ju 88A-2 or 'A-4, possibly coded 'R4+NL' of I/NJG2 at Gilze-Rijen in Holland and crewed by Feldwebel Hans Hahn (pilot), Unteroffizier Ernst Meissler (wireless operator) and Uffz. Helmut Scheidt (engineer) was patrolling the Lincolnshire airfields. Undetected, Fw Hahn timed his attack to coincide with the moment the Manchester became airborne and was at its most vulnerable. The crew never had a chance and L7313 was riddled with cannon and machine gun fire soon after crossing the airfield boundary.

The noise of the firing and low flying combat brought many people rushing to their windows on the airfield and in the town of Lincoln. The wife of Sergeant Jim Bryce, himself a wireless operator under training and serving with 207, saw the blazing Manchester pass low over the roof tops, closely followed by the Ju 88. The scene was also witnessed by Flight Sergeant John Wells from the window of the aircrew quarters on the airfield at Waddington. He saw the navigation lights of L7313 as it took off, the sudden sharp brilliant lines of tracer from the fighter and the glare from the crash as the aircraft hit the ground behind trees.

L7313 crashed at Whisby some five miles west of Waddington and continued to burn on the ground, part of the bomb load exploding. Flying Officer Matthews, Sergeants Redgrave, Welch and Hemingway were killed outright. Flight Sergeants W A W Cox, the wireless operator and Marsden were thrown clear, but received multiple injuries. They were taken to Lincoln hospital where Marsden later died. Bill Cox survived although with the loss of a leg.

The remaining aircraft attacked the Blohm und Voss shipyards at Hamburg in fine weather and returned safely. The entire raid caused 119 fires, including one in a timber yard. The casualty list, 51 killed and 139 injured, was the heaviest in the city to date. No. 207 Squadron had suffered its first loss and the whole unit was stunned to have seen the savagery and finality with which death could strike right on their own doorstep.

Incensed by the loss of their comrades, Wing Commander Hyde and Squadron Leader Kydd conspired with the Squadron Intelligence Officer, who believed he knew where the intruders were based. It was agreed to arm two aircraft and each put in a spare trip to retaliate. The prospect of using a Manchester as a night intruder may seem incongruous now and the existence of the aircraft was still being kept secret from the Germans at this time. Fortunately good sense prevailed and the beat-up never took place. Flying Officer Matthews and Sergeants Redgrave and Welch were buried at Waddington Parish Church on 18th March 1941.

For some reason all previous Manchester histories have wrongly identified this first operational Manchester loss as L7319. Why this should have occurred is unknown since the ORB, Air Historical Branch aircraft record cards and the records of the War Graves Commission are quite clear that L7313 'EM-C' was the aircraft concerned. Indeed L7319 'EM-X' went on to have a long and active career before being struck off charge on 1st January 1943.

On the 18th March Flying Officer Geoff Hall went to 46 Maintenance Unit (MU) at Lossiemouth to collect 61 Squadron's first Manchester, L7307, and deliver it to Hemswell. The entire squadron crowded round to inspect the aircraft, from which great things were expected. In order to safeguard the few valuable aircraft becoming available, only crews having more than 100 operational hours on Hampdens were allowed to fly Manchesters at night. Within days and to further conserve the operationally fit aircraft, L7276, L7292 and L7294 from the pre-production batch were allocated as crew trainers. L7315, L7387 and L7388 came later in anticipation of operational flying.

Two days later, on 20th March 1941, 207 suffered its second Manchester loss, again on operations. The squadron produced three aircraft which joined 21 Armstrong Whitworth Whitleys for a minor operation to the Lorient submarine base in France. Take-off was arranged for 1850 but delayed by group until 0200 hours.

Lorient – 20th March 1941

Serial	Code	Sqn	Captain
L7310	EM-H	207	S/L C J F Kydd
L7302	EM-R	207	F/L D J French
L7278	EM-A	207	F/Sgt F B Harwood

A closely guarded secret was that the squadron took two observers from the still neutral USA on the operation. The two US Navy servicemen attended the briefing and Commander McDonnell accompanied Kydd, whilst Lieutenant Commander Wannamaker flew in L7302 with French. The reason for US Navy, rather than Army Air Force personnel being involved may have been to do with the target. Both American servicemen flew in full US Naval uniform and several mused at the consequences if either had been killed over occupied Europe or captured.

The bomb loads were 10 x 500 lb SAP bombs intended for the concrete U-boat pens. As usual, the take-off of the heavily loaded Manchesters was a very marginal affair. Harwood took the aircraft to the extreme end of the airfield and took off over the hangars and administrative buildings.

L7278 had by this time been shorn of its mid-under F.N.21A turret and so the second wireless operator/air gunner, Sergeant Aitken, was flying in the front turret. No mid-upper turret was fitted. Owing to the continued engine problems the observer, Flight Sergeant Roy Holland, had been given the extra duty of watching the oil pressure gauges mounted on the starboard side of the fuselage, adjacent to the navigators position, but directly behind his seat.

The night was dark and moonless such that as the crew settled down to their routines they had only the altimeter to reveal how painfully slowly the Manchester was gaining height. The route ahead involved flying south to the English Channel and on into occupied France. After only 30 minutes flying Holland, on one of his periodic checks, was startled to see a major drop in oil pressure on the port engine accompanied by rough running, which he reported immediately to the captain. Whilst the two pilots debated whether to return, the rough running of the engine disappeared. Half a minute later the rough running recommenced, temperature rose off the dial and the engine caught fire. The aircraft had struggled to a mere 1,200ft by this time and as soon as the engine failed began to lose height rapidly. Quick action was required to avert a certain catastrophe and Harwood ordered the crew to bale out whilst he held the machine steady.

The rear gunner, Hallam, left his turret and baled out from the rear entry door on the starboard side. Aitken, from the front turret was the first to leave the escape hatch in the bomb aimer's position, followed in succession by Holland. The second pilot, Sergeant Birch, was helping Harwood maintain the aircraft on an even keel as Holland passed him. By the time Holland had collected his parachute stowed near the hatch, clipped it on and jumped Birch was right behind and escaped directly after him.

Holland, aware of the extremely close proximity of the ground, pulled his ripcord the instant he vacated the hatch. He felt a tremendous jerk as the 'chute opened and immediately afterwards hit the ground in the middle of a ploughed field.

In the aircraft the wireless operator, Sergeant Hogg, had remained to try and assist Harwood with the forced landing. There was no prospect that the captain could have escaped from such a low level and there had been no time to drop the bomb load safe. The fire had by this time spread and the whole port wing was alight. In the total pitch darkness Harwood had no choice but to land blind with no knowledge of the terrain ahead. Regrettably the landscape was heavily wooded and the port wing hit two large trees causing the aircraft to slew round and crash in the adjacent field. L7278 continued to burn and several bombs exploded. The two crew members remaining in the aircraft were killed. Birch and Aitken were later found dead and it appeared they had been unable to open their parachutes before impact with the ground. Only Holland and Hallam survived.

Holland found to his surprise that he was completely unhurt and stood up to release his parachute. About half a mile away he saw the flames from the crashed Manchester and heard the first of the bombs detonate. In the distance, a farmhouse was just visible in the intense darkness and he made his way there. Transport was obtained and he was taken to nearby Cottesmore, where he spent the night in the sick bay alongside Hallam. They returned to Waddington next day. L7278 had crashed just west of the A1, 1½ miles east of Wymondham in Leicestershire, five miles north west of Cottesmore. (This crash has previously been incorrectly reported as occurring on return from the operation and at Wymondham in Norfolk.)

The port engine had been flung clear in the crash and initial examination revealed it to have two holes in the crankcase where broken con-rods had hit it. Subsequent investigation showed the cause of the failure of the port engine to be a break up of the 0.5% silver main engine bearing. No. 207 had lost its second Manchester.

The remaining two aircraft claimed to have located the target area and both dropped their bomb loads at the estimated time of arrival through cloud from only 10,000ft in two separate sticks. On the second run over the presumed target area the navigator in French's aircraft, Sergeant Wells, inadvertently knocked off the fusing switches at the last moment before the second stick was released with the result that the remaining three 500lb SAPs fell away safe.

Since all the aircrew positions were occupied, Wannamaker, the US Navy observer in French's aircraft, had to stand for the whole flight other than on take-off and landing. Near the target he had tapped Wells on the shoulder and asked what the fireworks were. 'Flak', came the reply. Following their safe return the American had remarked 'Good Show', whether in relief at getting his feet safely back on the ground or in praise of the operation is uncertain. What the observers learned can't have been a great deal, but at least they had survived the experience.

Personnel of 207 Squadron were shocked at another loss so soon after that of Flying Officer Matthews and bitter that it was the result of engine failure, not enemy action. Another blow fell soon after. On 27th March the squadron was called upon to provide four of the 39 aircraft raised by Bomber Command for operations to Dusseldorf. The Manchesters were still plagued with a host of problems of which lack of power and persistent bearing and crankshaft failures in the engines were merely the worst.

Dusseldorf – 27th March 1941

Serial	Code	Sqn	Captain
L7311	EM-F	207	S/L C J F Kydd
L7302	EM-R	207	F/O D A A Romans
L7303	EM-P	207	F/L J A Siebert
L7318	EM-K	207	F/O A M Paape

'Mike' Lewis remembers what a heart stopping experience a take-off in a fully loaded Manchester could be with an occasion reminiscent of the 27th March and of many others, when he watched other pilots fighting to become airborne. Dave Romans and the other pilots were using the long runway to the north east. Having reached the extremity of the available runway, Romans began his take-off run. The run seemed interminable with even the tail reluctant to rise. Eventually, and with little runway remaining, the Manchester unstuck, but it continued to sit there in a more or less three-point attitude showing no inclination whatever to climb, even to the height of the airfield boundary hedge. With great presence of mind and skill, when he came within 100 to 200ft of the hedge, Romans rammed the stick hard forward, causing the aircraft to drop its wheels onto the ground and bounce. At full power Romans hauled back on the stick once more to hold the aircraft at the top of the bounce, cleared the hedge by a whisker and was then able to raise the undercarriage and climb laboriously away!

'Mike' Lewis himself observed that even on the longest take-off run (north east – south west) he considered things going normally for a Manchester take-off if he passed the Lorenz hut with his port wing tip just above the hut obstruction light. Off the south western end of this runway some 3½ miles distant lies the small country church of Coleby. The normal climbing performance when fully loaded was such that they expected to pass over this church at little over 100ft with the wheels and flaps up. Little wonder that the ground staff also awaited each departure with bated breath, never quite being certain when they might expect a Manchester to lose power and join them in the building.

On the night of 27th March 1941 the four Manchester crews briefed for the Dusseldorf raid were seen off at around 1930 hours by Group Captain Boothman, the new station CO. His parting words as the crews climbed into the lorry which took them to their dispersed aircraft were to the observer in Johnnie Siebert's aircraft, Sergeant George Fomison. Fomison was wryly advised to be sure to pick out a nice, fat maternity hospital in Dusseldorf as his aiming point. This was a sarcastic jibe at 'Lord Haw Haw', who was claiming in propaganda broadcasts at that time that the RAF only bombed hospitals and non-military targets. In other ways this was ironic since Bomber Command at this time would most dearly have loved the ability to exercise any degree of selectivity over the targets it bombed!

Soon after take-off Flying Officer Paape DFC in L7318 'EM-K' experienced a major drop in oil pressure in one of the Vultures, which necessitated an early return. The aircraft landed back at Waddington with its bomb load intact before the engine failed and caught fire. The remaining three aircraft located Dusseldorf without undue difficulty, Kydd and Romans dropped four 1,000 lb GP and 420 x 4 lb incendiaries from 10,000 ft and 7,500 ft respectively, each in two approaches to the target area.

Siebert bombed the target at around 2230 hours also making two approaches and dropping a stick of bombs on each run. Very intense flak was encountered in the target area, as was to be expected in 'Happy Valley'. One flak shell burst sufficiently close to the aircraft to jolt the starboard wing up in the air. After the shock, level flight was resumed and course set for the return. The crew speculated as to whether they had merely experienced a near miss or whether any damage had occurred on the starboard side – all instruments were giving expected readings.

As they approached the searchlight belt over the Dutch border the flak died down and fighter attacks were expected, a careful lookout was maintained. Suddenly, the starboard engine began to smoke and lost power. The propeller was promptly feathered and the engine shut down. L7303 'EM-P' immediately began to lose height and within a few seconds the port engine, which had been advanced to full power in an attempt to maintain height, started to lose thrust too. The, by now, notorious Vulture engines were proving inadequate to the task.

Johnnie Siebert was heard to call that he could not hold the aircraft up any longer and the Manchester fell into a sideslip to port, nose down but still under some semblance of control. Jim Taylor in the wireless operator's position slammed the key of his wireless set over to transmit and without waiting for the 15 seconds necessary for the set to warm up began transmitting their position to base. As he did this he suddenly noticed air-to-air tracer passing the aircraft on the port side.

The crippled Manchester had been intercepted by a Messerschmitt Me 110 night fighter of III/NJG1 from Eindhoven in Holland, piloted by Oberfeldwebel Herzog. (Note: While the prefix 'Bf' is historically correct, this work will use the contemporarily accepted 'Me' prefix for the Messerschmitt 109 and 110.) The time was 11.30pm, Herzog had already shot down a Whitley of 78 Squadron at 11.05pm, although in his combat reports he was to identify both of the aircraft he attacked as Wellingtons.

Taylor was temporarily cut off from the intercom as he transmitted and missed the captain's first order to abandon. The starboard engine had by this time caught fire and a hydraulic failure was experienced. Neither of these were unusual experiences in Manchesters at this time and there is no absolute certainty that Herzog's fire actually hit the aircraft to cause further damage.

Jim Taylor was then firmly slapped on the shoulder as the second wireless operator/air gunner, Sergeant McDougal, hastened forward from his position in the mid-upper turret to the escape hatch in the nose, struggling into his parachute as he went. Taylor slipped the clip over his Morse key to clamp it on 'transmit', ripped out his intercom lead and oxygen connection and followed McDougal.

By this time the triple-finned aircraft was side-slipping viciously, diving steeply and one engine was racing. The hydraulic failure had severed the power to the rear turret and the main undercarriage had flopped down. As Taylor dived through the hatch he was closely followed by Pete Gurnell, the rear gunner, who, without power to his turret had also been unable to rotate it by hand. McDougal had elected to hasten forward to the lower escape hatch despite his proximity to the rear entry door. On leaving the rear turret, Pete Gurnell looked for the quickest way out. Having reached the crew entry door he wrenched the handle intending to bale out from there. To his dismay the handle came away in his hand and he later decided that in his haste to escape he had probably twisted it the wrong way.

The starboard main wheel narrowly missed Taylor and Gurnell as the aircraft side-slipped over them. They were the last crew members out alive. It is likely that the gallant captain escaped the same way but was hit by the main wheel. His body was located next day in a depression which testified to the force of the impact. His parachute was unopened.

As the surviving five aircrew floated down on their parachutes the abandoned aircraft dived away beneath them, an engine still racing, and crashed on a farmhouse at Bakel north east of Helmond and near Eindhoven. Oberfeldwebel Herzog had attacked the Manchester from below and as he broke away he observed the parachutes of the survivors in the glow of the searchlights. He then dropped or fired a flare, which burst beneath the descending airmen. In its light they could see that they were falling into an area of open water. Taylor and Gurnell were feverishly blowing up their 'Mae Wests' when they splashed down into four inches of water overlying a further two feet of mud. Taylor sprained an ankle in the landing and after disposing of his 'chute waded alone for about an hour before reaching firm ground and eventually a village. Here he was taken in by the residents of the local cafe, given first aid and fed before being sent on his way with the name of a contact in the Dutch underground movement in Eindhoven.

Early next morning he was spotted and arrested by a German patrol and taken to the nearby airfield at Eindhoven. Here he was reunited with the survivors of his own crew and that of a Wellington shot down nearby.

By a strange coincidence in the early hours of the morning one of the two pigeons carried by L7303 arrived back in its loft in the very street in Lincoln where Taylor's girl-friend of the time, later his wife, then lived. How the pigeon escaped will never be known.

At Eindhoven the crew met Herzog who described to them his combat with their 'Wellington'. Many knowing glances were exchanged amongst the crew as they knew that no Manchester had previously fallen in occupied territory. Following this meeting Taylor and Robson had the tragic task of identifying the body of their pilot brought in by the Germans. They were later kept in solitary confinement, deprived of cigarettes and interrogated for almost three days.

The Germans must by then have inspected the wreckage of their aircraft and in the absence of any of the distinctive geodetic structure perhaps began to suspect that they had shot down a new type of aircraft and not a Wellington. The airmen were threatened with a firing squad if they did not talk and quizzed closely about the names of the Dutch citizens who aided them. Throughout the ordeal they managed to stick to their story of wading through the swamp all night and not meeting any of the local population.

No. 207 Squadron had lost its third Manchester and L7303 became the first to fall in enemy territory. It is likely that the aircraft was sufficiently fragmented in the crash that the Germans learned little from it. L7303 was lost to a combination of flak damage, engine failure and fighter attack although the aircraft was clearly already doomed when Herzog came upon it.

Following night flying tests on the afternoon of 30th March 1941, 207 Squadron produced four aircraft for a further attack on the *Scharnhorst* and *Gneisenau* at Brest. All aircraft located the target, where two sticks each of 6 x 500 lb SAP bombs were dropped from heights ranging from 15,000 to 9,500 ft. Three aircraft claimed that their bombs hit the dock whilst the crew of 'EM-J' were unable to observe the result of their attack.

Brest – 30th March 1941

Serial	Code	Sqn	Captain
L7302	EM-R	207	F/L D J French
L7319	EM-X	207	F/O D A A Romans
L7309	EM-J	207	F/O A M Paape
L7311	EM-F	207	P/O W G Gardiner

Paape and crew had a frightening experience when they arrived back in the vicinity of Waddington. The controllers refused to light the flarepath on account of a reported prowling intruder. The tower advised Paape to divert to Digby, where a landing was successfully accomplished. Afterwards, whilst unwinding in the mess, they received a severe shock when one of the station Bristol Beaufighter pilots came over. Having established that they were a recently arrived Manchester crew he told them he had just landed

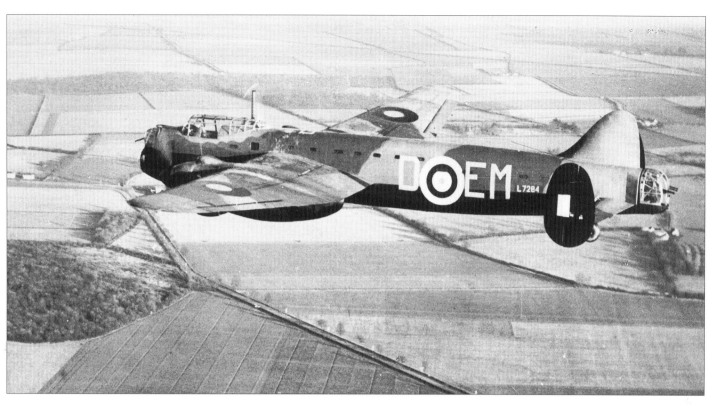

from an operational patrol immediately behind them and had come within a whisker of shooting them down. Keyed up from the chase for intruders he had completed his circuit to land and lined up on finals directly behind this strange and indistinct shape ahead. As the Manchester had throttled back the Vultures produced showers of sparks, which streamed out behind in a trail and rushed back towards the Beaufighter. For several seconds the pilot had mis-identified the sparks as tracer from an intruder. Only in the last fraction of a second before he attacked the aircraft ahead did the pilot correct his identification. It was a stark demonstration to the crew of L7309 that they were never safe until they had landed and vacated their aircraft.

March had been a difficult month for 207. Three Manchesters had been lost on operations with many crew members killed or taken prisoner, serviceability continued to be poor with a wide range of serious problems, of which the problems with the Rolls-Royce Vultures were the worst. Things were soon to take a significantly greater turn for the worse. In March one flight of 61 Squadron had begun to work up on the Manchester to join 207 and 97. Events were to prevent 61 Squadron flying its first operation in the Manchester until late June.

The 19th Manchester production meeting on 31st March itemised delays in Vulture delivery as the major stumbling block, whilst the loss of L7278 on operations was to herald a desperate crisis for Rolls-Royce and the Vulture. Evidently the engine was far from being safe to fly let alone operate over Ger-

many. Paradoxically it is reported that the Vulture II was type-tested at 2,010hp and +9lb boost on 100 octane fuel for the first time during March. Moreover, R5768, the first Metrovick Manchester, was finally complete. In the event, again dictated by the impending engine crisis, R5768 did not reach the RAF until 18th April a year later in 1942.

April 1941 began with 207 Squadron continuing its operations at a feverish pace in the hope of bottling up the German Navy in the European ports. On the 4th five Manchesters were prepared for an attack on the battle cruisers at Brest.

Brest – 4th April 1941

Serial	Code	Sqn	Captain
L7314	EM-T	207	F/O D E Pinchbeck
L7317	EM-C	207	F/L P R Burton-Gyles
L7311	EM-F	207	F/O A M Paape
L7319	EM-X	207	F/O D A A Romans
L7302	EM-R	207	P/O W G Gardiner

Serious technical problems continued. L7314 failed to take-off owing to engine trouble, whilst Paape in L7311 had to turn back after eleven minutes with hydraulic trouble, landing back at Waddington with the bomb load intact.

Each Manchester carried three 2,000lb SAP bombs with the intention of making a precision attack on the ships themselves. Brest was located and attacked in good visibility. The three remaining aircraft which reached the target bombed from between 8,000 and 11,000ft. Burton-Gyles and Gardiner believed their bombs fell in the dock

Another view of L7284, showing the effectiveness of the camouflage on the starboard wing against the wintry Lincolnshire countryside. *No.207 Squadron archives / R Glynne-Owen*

area but the crew of Romans' aircraft were unable to observe the results of their attack.

Returning crews claimed a direct hit on one of the German cruisers. German records which have become available show that one bomb fell in the dry dock in which *Gneisenau* was lying but failed to explode. Bombs also fell on the Continental Hotel in Brest just as the evening meal was being served. Several German naval officers from both *Scharnhorst* and *Gneisenau* were killed.

Next day the captain of *Gneisenau*, perhaps uncertain whether the bomb was a dud or a delayed action device, and influenced by the continual harassment campaign, decided it would be safer if his ship were moved to a buoy mooring in the harbour. This later proved to be an unwise move because it allowed the torpedo bombers of Coastal Command to take a crack at the ship. On the 6th, Flying Officer Kenneth Campbell of 22 Squadron carried out an ultra-low level torpedo attack in a Bristol Beaufort operating out of St Eval. This resulted in a direct hit and damage of a sufficiently serious nature that six months was necessary to repair the ship. Met with a vast array of anti-aircraft fire from all quarters, the Beaufort was destroyed in the raid. Campbell was awarded a posthumous Victoria Cross.

On 6th April, 207 Squadron returned to Brest for a follow up precision attack on the enemy cruisers. In reality the chances of finding and hitting such small targets with the equipment available and at night were minuscule in the extreme and on this occasion the target was found to be blanketed in 10/10ths cloud. There would have been more chance of finding a needle in a haystack. Bomber Command had still to learn its hardest lessons. It was nonetheless an eventful operation. Following night flying tests, four Manchesters were serviceable. Once more, each of the aircraft carried three 2,000 lb APs.

Brest – 6th April 1941

Serial	Code	Sqn	Captain
L7322	EM-B	207	F/L P R Burton-Gyles
L7311	EM-E	207	F/O W J Lewis
L7310	EM-H	207	F/O A M Paape
L7314	EM-T	207	F/O D E Pinchbeck

'Mike' Lewis' description of his experiences provides the best insight into the difficulties experienced trying to employ such an under-developed aircraft on operations.

'During the early days of April, I formed up a new crew, composed of Flying Officer Nunn as my co-pilot, Pilot Officer Sheen as navigator, Sergeants Riddell as wireless operator, Roberts as the second wireless operator/air gunner and McPhail as my rear gunner and with that crew, however, I carried out only one operation that being a bombing raid on April 6th to Brest.'

'Three quite separate technical problems manifest themselves during this operation to Brest. The first of these was the on-going

Flying Officer Peter Burton-Gyles (hatted) and crew being debriefed at Waddington following an operation. *No. 207 Squadron archives / R Glynne-Owen*

problem we were having at this time with the hydraulic system. We regularly had hydraulic leaks and hydraulic line failures, which we found out could be mainly attributed to the fact that all the joints, especially the 90° joints in the hydraulic lines, were built without any 'olives'. These joints did not always hold under the 400 and 600 lbs per square inch pressure on the hydraulic system and we had hydraulic failures. When we had these failures we realised we had a second problem and that was that we could not get the bomb doors open. To correct this Avro drilled holes in the lower portion of the bomb door jacks and inserted pins in these holes, which were connected by a wire to a loop or bracket on the front of the bomb bay. The theory was that if we experienced a hydraulic failure, by pulling on the wire we would remove the pins, thereby causing the oil in the lower portion of the bomb door jacks to leak out. The weight of the oil on the upper part of the jacks would then crack the bomb doors open and once they were cracked open the slipstream would pull them open all the way.'

'The operation to Brest introduced us to a third problem, which had not previously occurred. This was the seal on the control for the radiator flaps. The control was a two position rotary switch by which the pilot could either select the flaps to fully open or to the automatic position, where the position of the flap was controlled by the temperature in the radiator. We found very early in operations that in the trail or automatic position the undercarriage would not retract completely as the undercarriage doors caught on the radiator flap. Hence, all take-offs and landings had to be carried out with the radiator flap in the fully open position.'

'Back to the matter of the radiator control. As I was taking off that night, I pulled up the undercarriage after lift-off, the undercarriage retracted and it was a characteristic of the hydraulics system that it operated normally at 400 lbs per square inch. The correct mode of operation was that after the undercarriage completed its retraction the pumps continued to build up pressure until they reached 600 lbs, at which time a relief valve cut in and the system went back to idle at 400 lbs. This night, when the pressure had reached the point of probably about 500 lbs, the seal on the engineer's panel which controlled the radiator flaps burst and the pumps sprayed the whole contents of the hydraulic system into the cockpit, squirting it all over the entire crew and the area forward of the main spar and there was not a thing we could do about it. I might say that that was one take-off that was certainly blind, even my instrument panel was completely covered by a film of oil to the extent that I could not clearly read the instruments.'

'Despite having lost the use of the complete hydraulic system and with those crew members in the cockpit area soaked in

hydraulic oil we continued with the operation on the understanding that on reaching Brest, instead of opening the bomb doors hydraulically we could initiate the famous Avro manual 'pull-the-wire' system, and open the bomb doors. So on reaching the target we pulled the pins and the wires and we pulled and we pulled and we shook the airplane and in no way could we get the bomb doors open. We had on board three 2,000 lb AP bombs and there was no way we could get rid of them. So, after about half an hour in the target area, during which we failed to get the bomb doors open, we turned around and headed back for Waddington.'

'About half way across the English Channel the bomb doors came open. By this stage we did not have enough gasoline left to turn around and return to Brest and drop the bombs and then get back home again, so I decided the best thing to do was just take the aircraft home as it was. This we did with the three 2,000 lb bombs dangling in the open bomb bay. We avoided all cities and towns en route and we were able to return to base and carry out a safe landing at Waddington.'

'So, the emergency bomb door opening system did not work, but furthermore, we found out a more fundamental weakness in the hydraulic system of the aircraft. The seal that let go on the control panel on the starboard side of the aircraft, that is the control that operated the radiator flaps, was made of pressed paper. It only stood to reason that after a short period of operation that pressed paper seal was going to fail, as it did in my case, and empty the whole contents of the hydraulic system into the aircraft. So, once again, emergency modifications were made and all the paper seals were removed and proper seals replaced them.'

'It is impossible to recall the proper sequence, dates, etc of all the modifications etc that were made to the airplane, but eventually all of the joints in the hydraulic system were replaced with proper joints containing 'olives', good seals were placed in all the hydraulic system, but they never did modify that radiator flap to the point that it could be left in the automatic position at take-off and still permit the undercarriage doors to open and close.'

As with 'Mike' Lewis, when the other three 207 Squadron aircraft reached what they estimated to be the target area they found it completely obscured by cloud. Indeed Brest itself was only vaguely detectable from the flak coming up through the solid overcast. They stooged around until, despairing of finding a hole in the cloud, both 'Pappy' Paape and Derek Pinchbeck dropped an armour piercing bomb in the general area of the flak concentration. Later, for good measure, Paape dropped the remaining two, this time having the satisfaction of seeing the glow of a fire through the cloud as some consolation for his efforts.

Meanwhile, in L7322, Les Syrett had flown to the target area where Peter Burton-Gyles changed places with him. They had been briefed to be as accurate as possible because near misses would do no harm to the two battle cruisers. There was 10/10ths cloud and the target was only detectable from the flak bursts and occasional bomb flashes beneath the cloud layer. Using these as a guide the crew released the first stick of AP bombs, but this was too much 'faith and blind hope' to suit the likes of 'BG'. Roy Holland, the observer that night, explained the obvious, that he could not bomb what he could not see. As with their first operation to Brest, 'BG' withdrew to a safer distance to formulate an alternative plan.

Off to seaward from the flak barrage they descended to discover the cloud base, finding it at 2,000ft. Below this height the searchlight concentration was intense and dazzling and 'BG' quickly popped back into the enveloping murk.

As they climbed back up to 8,000ft, 'BG' decided on a diving attack. He advised the crew that he would be giving them one chance and one only. The observer, second pilot and captain would have to operate as a well trained team. Holland was instructed to set 2,000ft and 200mph on his bomb sight and Syrett was to stand beside the captain calling out the height and speed as they descended. Having reached 8,000ft 'BG' pointed the aircraft at the colourful commotion and entered a shallow dive. In the bomb aimer's position Holland was poised, 'BG' concentrated on maintaining their heading, hoping he would not have to hunt for the ships once they emerged. As they descended their speed built up and soon exceeded 200mph showing no sign of easing the rate of increase. Syrett called 'Skip, we're diving too fast, you'll never slow down to 200 at this rate'. 'BG' replied that it could not be helped so Syrett kept calling out their height and speed as they descended. As they broke cloud at 2,000ft they flew straight into the glare of what seemed like 50 searchlights just waiting for them.

'BG' headed for the ships whilst Syrett called to the observer 'Any moment now we will be at 1,500ft and doing 300 plus – can you cope?' Holland responded instantly, 'Do what I can, hold it level Skip, right, more right, too much, left a bit, hold it, steady – bombs gone'. By this time they were below 1,000ft and had to climb hard to regain the sanctuary of the cloud. Syrett marked the fall of bombs and thought they had achieved at least one direct hit, although other crew members believed they had probably overshot.

Sergeant Syrett then flew back to Waddington, where Peter Burton-Gyles made a safe landing. On disembarking the crew observed to their amazement that their dive onto the ships at Brest had resulted in the fabric covering being stripped completely from

the central fin to leave the fragile skeleton exposed. For his skill and determination 'BG' was awarded a bar to his DFC.

It was a futile gesture. In the unlikely event that the ships had been hit, armour piercing bombs needed to fall at least 7,000ft to reach a speed at which they would penetrate armour. To many of the aircrews it must have seemed that even when they were, by input of the most determined efforts, able to overcome the almost insuperable problems of operating their Manchesters, that Bomber Command was squandering their efforts to very little effect. Nevertheless the endeavours of the aircrew were undiminished. Many young men were beginning to feel that they were not just fighting the Germans, but Avro, Rolls-Royce and the whole dumb air force. Such was their spirit at this time that they actually expected to win!

Next day and naturally unbeknown to the crews, Avro's had their regular production meeting. Three new Vulture engines were out of commission at Woodford due to carburettor trouble. Avro listed their requirement as two Vultures per day until the 24th of the month whilst Metrovick were desperate for six engines immediately. The bottleneck was becoming more accentuated.

The intensive pace of flying continued for the moment and a day later, on 8th April 1941, 207 Squadron made available the largest number of Manchesters yet achieved, joining a force of 229 aircraft for an operation to the shipyards at Kiel. Each Manchester carried a load of four 1,000 lb GP and 240 x 4 lb incendiaries.

As 207 were undertaking their largest operation to date, 97 Squadron embarked on its first Manchester operation from Coningsby, also to Kiel. Although aircraft from batches beyond the first 20 airframes were beginning to arrive at Coningsby the earlier

Wing Commander Noel 'Hettie' Hyde (second left) photographed in a prisoner of war camp. He failed to return from the Kiel raid of 8th April 1941. *No. 207 Squadron archives / R Glynne-Owen*

aircraft, chiefly with the experienced crews posted in from 207 were mainly preferred. Each aircraft is recorded as carrying a load of 12 x 1,000 lb GP and 840 x 4 lb incendiaries but it is more likely that the GPs were 500 pounders.

Kiel – 97's Debut, 8th April 1941

Serial	Code	Sqn	Captain
L7290	OF-*	97	F/L G O L Bird
L7291	OF-*	97	F/O J S Sherwood
L7308	OF-*	97	F/Sgt G E A Pendrill
L7294	OF-*	97	P/O H S Blakeman
L7302	EM-R	207	W/C N C Hyde
L7300	EM-S	207	F/L G R Taylor
L7309	EM-J	207	F/O W J Lewis
L7314	EM-Y	207	F/O D E Pinchbeck
L7319	EM-X	207	F/O D A A Romans
L7317	EM-C	207	P/O W G Gardiner
L7322	EM-B	207	P/O W S Herring
L7310	EM-H	207	S/L C J F Kydd

In pursuit of his insistence on keeping abreast with operating problems Wing Commander 'Hettie' Hyde had again borrowed Dereck French's crew, although they had remained 'headless' for a few days after French was posted to 97 Squadron. Hyde had with him Flying Officer H T Morgan (second pilot), and Sergeants J Wells (observer) Buck (wireless operator), D Budden (second wireless operator/air gunner), and L 'Lofty' Hedges (rear gunner). L7302 had no mid-positioned turret with the result that Budden occupied the front turret.

The eight 207 and four 97 Squadron aircraft took off between 2100 and 2200 hours in good weather. Hugh Morgan remembers the outward crossing of the North Sea in full moonlight all the way. Crossing the enemy coast just north of Kiel Bay the East Frisian Islands provided a beautiful sight, black on a silver sea. Their route then took them along Kiel Bay to approach the dockyards themselves. The aircraft was possibly flying as high as 17,000ft. They had no trouble on the outward flight and there seemed to be nothing going on ahead over Kiel as they approached. Probably they were one of the first aircraft to arrive on target. This happy situation changed dramatically as soon as they began their final run in to the outskirts of Kiel, for they were suddenly illuminated by what seemed like 50 searchlights and coned. Flak promptly began bursting and Hyde took desperate evasive action, throwing the cumbersome Manchester around as if it were a light aircraft. They were, however, unable to escape the merciless beams.

Fortunately, most of the heavy flak seemed to be bursting behind the aircraft, possibly on account of the speed built up on approach and during the evasive action. A few bursts looking as big as houses came close enough to buffet the aircraft and they were also troubled by tracer from smaller calibre flak guns, fragments from which penetrated the fuselage. Blinded by the searchlights, unable to identify the target or escape the groping fingers there was no alternative and Hyde called the navigator in the bomb aimer's position to get rid of the bomb load, holding L7302 straight and level for a few seconds until they tumbled away into the night. Hyde then pushed the nose down, speed built up rapidly and they were soon out of range of the lights and enveloped once more in the protective darkness.

Hyde turned the aircraft onto the course planned for their return flight. Turning away north from the bay they headed up towards Flensburg with the intention of turning west again and overflying the narrowest part of Schleswig Holstein.

Things had calmed down and none of the cockpit instruments showed any sign of damage to the systems of the aircraft. They were halfway across the narrow neck of Schleswig south of Flensburg when Morgan next turned to check the engine instruments mounted on the starboard side behind the observer's chair. The starboard glycol temperature gauge was way above normal, but his attention was drawn from this immediately by the sight of the starboard engine. The exhaust ports and all other thin pieces of the starboard engine nacelle were glowing with a dull red heat. Turning swiftly he tapped Hyde on the shoulder but within seconds flames had burst out of the engine.

Hyde immediately feathered the starboard propeller, turned off the fuel supply and pressed the extinguisher button. If the extinguisher worked at all it had no effect and soon flames were streaming out 50 yards behind the wing trailing edge and showing signs of spreading. It was difficult to gauge how long the flames might take to reach the starboard wing tank, but on account of the fire remaining undiminished Hyde soon had no alternative but to order the crew to bale out.

Later they were to be thankful that they did not have to come down in Kiel in the midst of a raid and that the engine should choose to catch fire 50 miles away directly over the narrow part of Schleswig Holstein. There was no sign of enemy activity and they believed the fire to be a delayed result of flak damage resulting in an oil or glycol leak. For the moment there was feverish activity as the crew hurried to vacate the aircraft. John Wells recalls that for no apparent reason when his turn came to bale out of the front hatch he chose to throw his helmet through ahead of him.

Morgan put on his breast type parachute and was third or fourth in line to reach the hatch. He straddled the opening and was helped out by a shove in the behind from the next in line – no time to think of the 14,000ft of nothing between himself and the ground. Outside it was still bright moonlight with unlimited visibility and, having checked the altimeter before leaving, Morgan decided there was height enough in hand to free fall clear of the aircraft. Having made the decision partly out of curiosity, he found the sensation rather pleasant. He consequently held on for quite a while, perhaps until 10,000ft before he felt it must be time to check whether the parachute would actually work. It did. Pulling the ripcord produced an explosion of white silk in front of his face followed by a tremendous jerk and there he was apparently stationary in space. A few searchlights were playing some distance off and occasional flak bursts were in evidence over Flensburg.

Back in the aircraft 'Hettie' Hyde was more at ease once the crew were safely out of the aircraft. He waited at the controls, hanging on with baited breath on the off chance that by some miracle the fire would die out of its own accord. He had more experience of flying the Manchester solo than perhaps any other pilot and might just get back on the remaining engine. However, the fire showed no sign of abating and so within a short while he too followed the crew down into Schleswig Holstein.

With Hyde out of the aircraft it was now out of control, Morgan could hear the sound of the engines and it was coming closer. He looked around and saw it above him in a spiral dive trailing a banner of flames like a comet. With the engines making a loud rising and falling 'wow-oo-wow-oo-wow-oo' the aircraft swooped close beside him. Another

interesting experience! Morgan continued to watch as the Manchester picked up speed and soon hit the ground below him with a tremendous bang. The flaming wreckage spread out in pieces over an acre or two of ground. Clearly the Germans would not make much out of that.

Above, Morgan could see the cluster of parachutes from the rest of the crew, from whom he was separated on account of his free fall. Hyde too was separated from the rest as a consequence of his later escape from the aircraft. Buck, Budden, Wells and Hedges landed within a few seconds of each other in a village, Morgan touched down gently in a ploughed field some distance away, whilst Hyde landed with a bump in a frosty field even further separated from the main group. Hyde made off and remained at liberty for two days and nights during which he walked into Flensburg under cover of darkness. He had hatched a plan to stow away on a Swedish ship he hoped to find moored in the port and so make good his escape. No such luck, he was spotted in the town by the police whilst trying to locate the port area and arrested, going first to the local Luftwaffe station.

Morgan too started to walk north hoping to reach Denmark and establish contact with the resistance network. He navigated by the pole star. Within a few hours of starting the journey he was confronted by a canal, some way off was a bridge. He was dressed only in his thin black flying overalls complete with Cambridge University Air Squadron badge. The bridge beckoned. He approached with what he thought was extreme caution, and waited, it seemed unmanned. He was almost across when with a sudden shock he became aware of an armed German sentry motionless in the shadows watching his every move. Bluff seemed to be the only remaining option open, he approached what proved to be a middle aged Private armed with a rifle. 'Guten Abend' called out Morgan with a cheery wave. 'Komm', replied the sentry.

Taken first to some guardroom or police station he was surprised to be handed over to the Luftwaffe and was driven by them to the officers' mess of the night fighter squadron based at Flensburg. He was ushered into the ante-room where a number of young officers crowded around him and plied him with Sekt (German champagne), meanwhile trying to persuade him that one of their night fighters had shot them down, not the flak. They were charming and it was all very 'Beau Geste' and unreal. He slept comfortably in one of their guest rooms, his real life as a PoW only beginning the next day when he was reunited with the main group of his fellow crew members.

They had had an entirely different experience. John Wells watched the buildings of the village as he drifted down towards them

and was unable to avoid landing heavily on the sloping roof of a farm building. The parachute collapsed and before he could obtain a safe handhold he slid down and off the roof, landing softly but with mixed fortune in a pile of manure.

Having had a hardly silent and unannounced arrival he decided to knock at a nearby farmhouse door. The door opened. Raising his eyebrows he asked in his best English 'Is this Denmark?' The man in the doorway fixed him with a hostile stare, there was no sign of being welcomed across the threshold in the first glance. 'Nein, Deutschland' came the reply. Still the penny didn't drop. Wells was a young and not much travelled airman with no European experience and had no idea where Deutschland was, but there was certainly no sign that he was welcome, he turned away and wandered off in confusion.

A hue and cry had obviously been raised and he was soon rounded up by an armed soldier. The soldier gestured to him and made it clear that he was to pick up his parachute and march ahead down the lane away from the village. Within a short while Wells decided not to carry the parachute and threw it into the ditch alongside. The escort became a little excited and indicated he should retrieve it. Wells stood his ground. The soldier pointed to him 'Officer?' Wells drew himself up to his full height and replied in a loud voice 'Non-Commissioned Officer'.

This seemed to settle the dispute and the guard thereupon sent for a young boy, who appeared with a bicycle with a pannier on the front. The boy retrieved the 'chute and, putting it on the pannier, marched along behind them to the local school hall. Here he was reunited with Buck, Budden and Hedges, one of whom handed Wells back his flying helmet, which he had picked up in a nearby lane. Eventually the crew were reunited in the Dulag Luft interrogation camp before Hyde departed for the officers' camp.

Following the early bird Hyde, the rest of the squadron aircraft located Kiel in turn. They bombed from heights ranging from 12,000 to 14,000ft with the exception of Dave Romans who came down to an almost suicidal 3,500ft before releasing his bombs. All crews found the visibility nearly unlimited but later crews, including Romans, had difficulty identifying the target and observing the results of their attack as the dock area became obscured by smoke.

L7309 was one of the early Manchesters lacking any mid-positioned armament. Lewis was flying his first operation with the crew and in the absence of a mid-upper turret Bill Wetherill was flying in the front turret that night. Amongst the crews and the intelligence community in the RAF there was a belief at this time that most of the German flak batteries were directed by sound locators and 'Mike' Lewis had been busy thinking up a new idea to try to fox these predictors. His tactic was to climb as high as possible upwind of the target, whereupon he would pull back the throttles to full idle and set the propellers to fully coarse pitch and then glide more or less silently down across the target to avoid detection by the sound locators, releasing the bomb load at 9-10,000ft. Lewis had tried out the idea locally in the skies around Waddington and decided to test the new technique that night – it did not work.

It was a beautiful clear night and having reached a location just south east of the target they did a wind finding triangle at 15,000ft. The observer, Belfitt, confirmed a south east wind, which he had previously calculated from observations made en route to the target.

Thus prepared, at about 7-8 miles south east of Kiel, Lewis went into the planned attack. Everything went according to plan until they got down to about 11,000ft and were almost directly over the target when they realised that the wind at low altitude was from the north west and their ground

'EM-X' L7319 of 207 Squadron on 25th March 1941, possibly at the Air Fighting Development Unit. The early straight line camouflage demarcation has already been raised. The wavy separation runs through to the rear turret. L7319 was one of the longest serving and most successful Manchesters. It flew 31 operations with three Manchester squadrons and continued in use at 1654 Conversion Unit until February 1943. *via R J Edmonds*

speed was becoming very low. They carried on and had just released the bombs at about 9,000ft when the searchlights suddenly homed onto them and locked on. Attempting to climb out of the danger proved fruitless and the flak began to rise and burst close around them. The defences of Kiel were well prepared and had other, more efficient, location devices by this time.

The only way out before the flak pin-pointed them fatally was to dive down the searchlight beams and with this in mind Lewis called the front gunner, Wetherill, and told him to stand by to shoot out the lights. Thus prepared, Lewis stuffed the nose down and went for the deck. As he did so, Wetherill blazed away at the blinding sources of the beams, being successful in dowsing more than one of their tormentors, before the guns jammed. Flak continued to rise and Wetherill, now unoccupied, was feeling very exposed in the front turret. He obtained permission to vacate the turret and in an instant appeared in the cockpit to sit in the parachute rack behind the pilot's armoured seat, facing aft. As the descent continued the unattended front turret swung slowly on to the beam, setting up an increasing buffeting as it did so. Wetherill had to return to the turret and traverse it to the fore and aft position and then lock it. Never having flown in this position, Wetherill had not appreciated the necessity for such action.

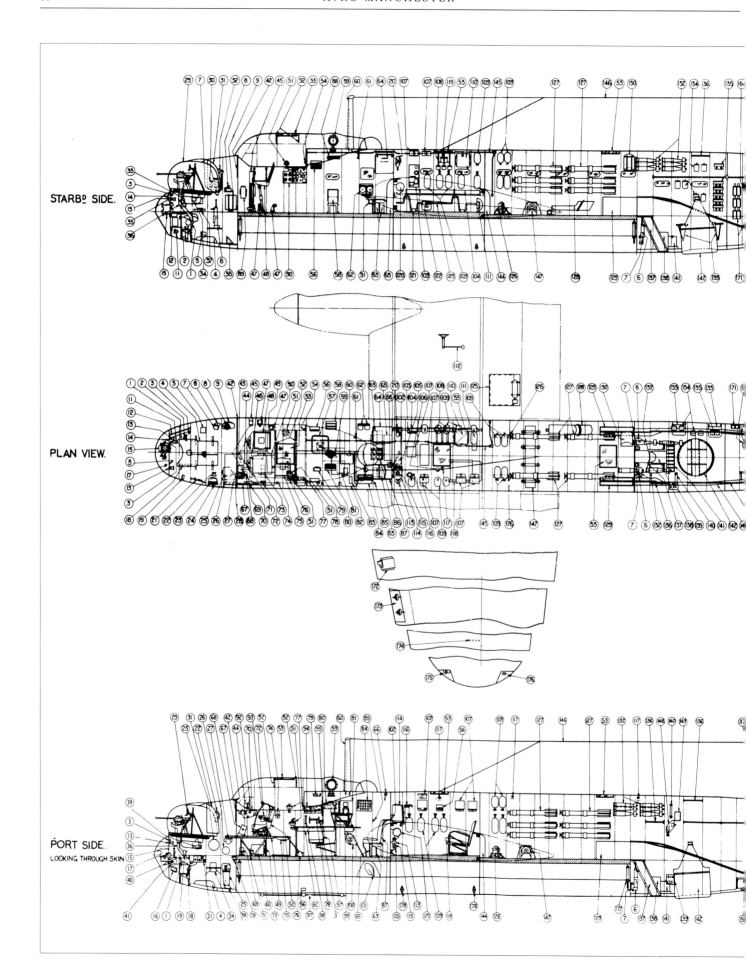

STARBᴰ SIDE.

PLAN VIEW.

PORT SIDE.
LOOKING THROUGH SKIN

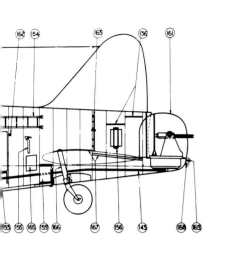

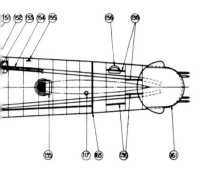

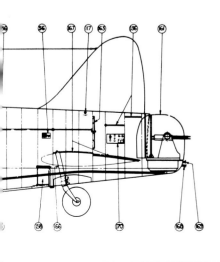

Another illustration from Avro Manchester, Air Publication A.P.1600A (*Fig.1*). It provides a good insight into the location of the complex array of fittings inside a Manchester Mk.I. The second prototype or a pre-production aircraft with mid-under turret is illustrated.

Key:

1   Bomb aimer's support.
2   Tail drift sight.
3   Dimmer switch.
4   Door and cushions.
5   Immersion switch.
6   Recuperator.
7   Oil filter.
8   Aldis signal lamp and stowage.
9   Front gunner's parachute stowage.
10 Not annotated.
11 Stowage for bomb firing switch and bomb sight lead.
12 Automatic distributor and bomb selector switch panel.
13 Cockpit lamp.
14 Headlamp.
15 Automatic bomb sight.
16 Bomb sight control panel.
17 Steering control (auto controls).
18 Target map case.
19 Turn regulator (auto controls).
20 Fire extinguisher.
21 Bomb aimer's port instrument panel.
22 Rudder servo (auto controls).
23 Elevator and rudder gyro (auto controls).
24 Gyro azimuth.
25 Camera F24.
26. Aileron gyro (auto controls).
27 Elevator servo (auto controls)
28 Camera motor.
29 Front gun turret.
30 Inspection lamp and lead stowage.
31 Draught screen.
32 Stowage for dual control rudder pedals.
33 Inertia switch (fire extinguisher).
34 Gravity switch (fire extinguisher).
35 Bomb aimer's writing pad and pencil stowage.

36 Empty cartridge chute.
37 Tail drift sight stowage.
38 Bomb aimer's foot ramp.
39 Suppressor.
40 Course setting bomb sight.
41 Azimuth bracket.
42 Pilot's instrument panel.
43 Junction box (blind approach).
44 Control column and dual control handwheel.
45 Flying control locking gear stowage.
46 Main receiver (blind approach).
47 Stowage for O.2 compass brackets.
48 2nd pilot's folding seat.
49 Pilot's floor.
50 Pilot's seat.
51 O.2 compass positions.
52 Sun blinds.
53 Emergency exit.
54 2nd pilot's oxygen socket.
55 Not annotated.
56 Oxygen regulator panel.
57 Navigator's swivelling seat.
58 Sextant stowage.
59 DF loop aerial.
60 Aerial mast.
61 Navigator's oxygen socket.
62 Voltage regulators.
63 Accumulator stowage.
64 Electrical services panel.
65 Step and cover at front spar.
66 Upward firing Very pistol mounting.
67 Automatic control panel.
68 Map case and course and height indicator stowage.
69 Rotary transformer (blind approach).
70 Pilot's oxygen socket.
71 Aileron servo (auto controls).
72 Control unit (blind approach).
73 Signal receiver (blind approach).
74 Undercarriage warning buzzer.
75 Observer's tip up seat.
76 Emergency hand pump.
77 Observer's oxygen socket.
78 Navigator's pencil tray.
79 Height and speed computer stowage.
80 Douglas protractor and course and speed calculator stowage.
81 Wireless apparatus and equipment.
82 Navigator and wireless operator's table.
83 Wireless operator's instrument panel.
84 Wireless receiver coil stowage.
85 Wireless operator's oxygen socket.
86 Wireless transmitter coil stowage.
87 Wireless operator's seat.
88 Very pistol cartridge stowage.
89 Junction box.
90 Observer's instrument panel.
91 Rheostat.
92 Pilot's bomb firing switch.
93 Sutton harness (pilot's).
94 Navigator's instrument panel.
95 Navigator's table, lamp.
96 Terminal block (blind approach).
97 Dipole aerial (blind approach).
98 Navigator's torch.
99 Wireless operator's drawer.
100 Winch aerial.
101 Fairing for winch aerial fairlead.
102 Very pistol stowage.
103 De-icing services panel.
104 Rest bed.
105 Hydraulic accumulator.

106 Aerial lead-in insulator.
107 Flying rations.
108 Marine distress signals.
109 Oxygen bottles.
110 Drinking water tank.
111 Rest room parachute stowage.
112 Fuel gauge transmitter.
113 High pressure filter.
114 Oil reservoir.
115 Automatic cut-out (hydraulic system).
116 Low pressure filter.
117 Cabin lamp.
118 Rest chair.
119 Hand shields for marine distress signals.
120 Emergency air bottles.
121 Bomb winch handle (short).
122 Bomb carrier crutch handle stowage.
123 Bomb winch handle (long).
124 Not annotated.
125 Dinghy stowage.
126 Bomb winch stowage position.
127 Reconnaissance flares.
128 Flare chute extension.
129 Ammunition boxes for rear turret.
130 Parachute stowage.
131 Not annotated.
132 Sea markers.
133 Step at mid-turret.
134 Water bottles.
135 Emergency rations.
136 Hand rail.
137 Flare chutes
138 Step on flare chutes.
139 Mid-gunner's instrument panel.
140 Oil reservoir.
141 Ammunition boxes for mid-turret.
142 Mid-gun turret.
143 Ammunition duct.
144 Cover at rear spar.
145 Dinghy manual release.
146 Aerial.
147 Flap jack mounting and cover.
148 Pump for mid-turret.
149 Instruction label for mid-turret.
150 D. R. compass.
151 Downward identification lights.
152 Door.
153 Step over ammunition ducts.
154 Access ladder.
155 Fireman's axe.
156 Parachute for rear gunner.
157 Step at D. R. compass.
158 Upward identification lamp.
159 Lavatory.
160 Not annotated.
161 Rear gun turret.
162 Switch.
163 Draughtproof door.
164 D. R. compass correction card.
165 First aid outfit.
166 Tail wheel.
167 Walkway.
168 Tail formation-keeping lamp.
169 Tail navigation lamp.
170 Rear gunner's instrument panel.
171 Vacuum flasks.
172 Oil cooler.
173 Landing lamps (port only).
174 A.S.I. pressure head (port only).
175 Navigation lamp.
176 Wing formation-keeping lamp.
177 Bomb door jacks.
178 Bomb door latch jacks.

As they finally escaped the beams and pulled out of the dive, Wetherill returned to his station behind the pilot's seat. As he did so he glanced out of the cockpit window just in time to see an 88mm flak shell pass straight through the starboard wing tip, tearing upwards large sections of the wing skin before carrying on up to explode perhaps 10-12,000ft above them.

It was a lucky escape, but the torn and twisted upper wing skin was now standing straight up and forming a 'dive brake', resulting in a serious disturbance of the airflow over the right aileron. The aileron was induced to flap uncontrollably by the turbulent air flow. Lewis and the second pilot, Brailsford, were hard pressed to hold the wildly flailing control column, whilst the aircraft was vibrating so badly that Lewis feared for a structural failure of the airframe.

Looking down, Wetherill saw they were now so low that in the bright moonlight he could make out, not only farmhouses and treetops, but signposts. Eventually Lewis and Brailsford managed to lift the shuddering Manchester to 300ft, at which point they inadvertently overflew a fully alerted German airfield. Light flak from the airfield defence force was soon bursting around them. Lewis could do no more than return rapidly to treetop level and no further damage occurred.

The vibration in the airframe had continued unabated and both pilots were rapidly losing the remaining strength in their arms. Shortly afterwards, however, the force of the airflow on the upstanding section of wing skin bent it back over itself until it came to lie flat over the surface behind. The vibration suddenly died away almost completely and the pilots were then able to recover their strength and take turns flying the aircraft back across the North Sea.

They returned at low level and landed back at Waddington. Needless to say the tactic of a silent diving approach was abandoned. On reflection the crew were able to tease Wetherill over the speed with which he had moved from the turret to get the substantial armour plate of the pilot's seat between himself and the flak. He countered by remarking that he hadn't joined to see flak shells coming through the wings or for a guided tour of the byways of Northern Germany. It was obvious they had had a lucky escape.

In comparison 97 Squadron crews had a more gentle introduction to Manchester operations. The good visibility made target identification easy and Sherwood identified Kiel from the fires whilst still 60 miles distant. Blakeman had the misfortune to have his incendiaries hang up.

So the remaining Manchesters came home to Waddington and Coningsby. Next morning the news of Wing Commander Hyde's loss swept through 207 Squadron. All were devas-tated at the loss of their popular commanding officer, who had done more than anyone to bring the Manchester into operational service. As a temporary measure, Squadron Leader Charles Kydd was given command of the squadron until Bomber Command decided upon a replacement.

Although even the Intelligence Units were not aware of it, this was one of the most successful raids of the early night bombing campaign. The attack had lasted for nearly five hours and towards the end the town's electricity supply broke down completely. Many fires were started and the local brigade had to call in reinforcements from all the surrounding areas. Bomb damage was focused on the Eastern Dock Area with the Deutsche Werkes and Germania Werkes prevented from building U-boats for several days. Naval, industrial and civilian damage was widespread and 88 Germans were killed and 184 injured in the attack.

During the afternoon, amidst the continued training and test flying still in progress, the squadron prepared one aircraft for operations. This involved L7319 'EM-X' captained by Flight Lieutenant Burton-Gyles. The target was the Vagesack shipyard downstream from Bremen on the River Weser. The operation was unusual in the respect that only one aircraft was made available and joined eight other aircraft from other units in a diversionary raid. The operation was also unusual in that the aircraft carried a chest of packaged tea with instructions that the route should involve overflying Leeuwarden and Groningen in Holland where the tea was to be dropped in small packages. The bomb load is reported in the ORB to have made up of four 1,000lb GPs and 420 x 4lb incendiaries.

'Eddy' Edmonds, the rear gunner that night, suggests the aircraft to have been carrying a 4,000lb high capacity (HC) bomb and to have been allocated the Vagesack target to attack as a lone aircraft under cover of a larger attack being carried out upriver. The purpose of the solo effort was suggested to be to permit subsequent damage assessments to be made in the absence of the complication of bomb damage caused by other aircraft. However, the ORB notes a normal bomb load and it is unlikely that L7319 was modified to carry a 4000lb 'Cookie' at this time. The 80-strong main force aircraft attacked Berlin.

En route to the target Les Syrett was given the job of dispatching the tea down the flare chute. On paper it should have been a simple and easily accomplished task. In the rear fuselage by the flare chute were stowed two plywood tea chests bound by the usual metal strips. Taking the aircraft's crash axe Syrett prized off the metal bands and opened the chests. In the dark and cramped conditions this took quite a time. Inside he found a large number of tightly packed paper packages each containing about four ounces of tea.

After circling for Syrett to gain access to the provisions, 'BG' then made his first run over Leeuwarden. On receiving the call to start discharging Syrett removed the cover from the chute and thrust in the first handful of packets. These promptly flew back in the blast of outside air into the face of the dispatcher before bursting on the fuselage roof and spraying loose tea everywhere. They never trained aircrews for this humanitarian operation.

By experiment, Syrett found that if he rammed in a handful of bags and clapped the cover straight back onto the chute he could prevent the blowback. After waiting for a few seconds to ensure that the bags had been discharged he could re-open the cover and push in more bags. The operation was laborious in the extreme and despite circling for a prolonged period Syrett had only discharged half a chest full by the time 'BG' calculated they must continue their main mission to Vagesack.

During the period when the tea was being dispatched the aircraft must have been a sitting target for any prowling night fighter. Only the weakness of the German night fighter defences, possibly coupled with the fact that other RAF bombers were concentrating their attention elsewhere, led to the aircraft being able to undertake the humanitarian element of the sortie. Later in the war such a task would never have been contemplated. Whether any of the tea packets cleared the aircraft without being ripped to tatters and whether any were recovered by the oppressed Dutch population for whom they were intended will never be known.

Syrett opened the second chest to save time later. They encountered no serious opposition over the target, which was bombed from 10,000ft. The bombs were estimated to have fallen a quarter mile short of the target. The remainder of the tea was dropped on the return leg and the aircraft landed safely back at Waddington 5hr 35min after take-off. Les Syrett had alternated between flying the big bomber and throwing the tea bags about. It was sometimes a strange war.

During daylight on 10th April 1941, 61 Squadron experienced at first hand one of the more terminal problems the Manchesters were liable to. Flying Officer Geoff Hall took off from Hemswell in L7307 with the commanding officer, Wing Commander Valentine, and ten crew for air firing practice. Immediately after lift-off and whilst still at maximum power the starboard engine blew up in a spectacular way and caught fire. Hall immediately went for the feathering button and fire extinguisher, but neither had any effect. The failure was sufficiently complete that flying con-rods and pistons had destroyed the feathering and extinguisher lines. Hall managed to achieve a complete circuit and landed back at base, hotly pursued by the fire engine, which managed to contain the fire.

On the night of 10/11th April 1941, 97 Squadron dispatched its second operation with its Manchesters when five were allocated to the usual target at Brest. Again, all five aircraft remained serviceable and reached the primary target.

Brest – 10/11th April 1941

Serial	Code	Sqn	Captain
L7323	OF-*	97	S/L R D Stubbs
L7294	OF-*	97	F/L J S Sherwood
L7308	OF-*	97	F/O C P D Price
L7292	OF-*	97	F/L D J French
L7298	OF-*	97	F/O F E Eustace

The only incident which upset an otherwise uneventful operation occurred soon after 0200 hours when Sherwood's aircraft was attacked without warning by an intruder as it approached to land at Coningsby. The first attack was wide of the mark. Sherwood immediately took evasive action and raised the flaps and undercarriage. The control tower diverted them to a nearby beacon which they orbited for some time before returning to land undamaged. Next day many machine gun and cannon shell cases which had fallen from the intruder's ejectors were picked up on the airfield.

By the time 207 Squadron was called upon to operate again on 12th April 1941, it could produce six aircraft for a further attack on the *Scharnhorst* and *Gneisenau* in Brest. The attack force numbered 66 RAF bombers. The aircraft concerned were:

Brest – 12th April 1941

Serial	Code	Sqn	Captain
L7317	EM-C	207	F/L P R Burton-Gyles
L7309	EM-J	207	F/O J L Nunn
L7322	EM-B	207	P/O W S Herring
L7311	EM-F	207	F/L G R Taylor
L7314	EM-T	207	F/O D E Pinchbeck
L7319	EM-X	207	P/O W G Gardiner

Each aircraft carried a load of 10 x 500 lb SAP bombs. Only a direct hit from some considerable height could possibly produce some worthwhile damage with such a bomb load.

The operation got off to a bad start for the Manchesters as Flying Officer Pinchbeck returned to Waddington after only 30 minutes due to another hydraulic leak, this time in L7314. Over the continent dense cloud cover was encountered and all aircraft experienced difficulty in finding the target. Locating what was believed to be the general target area, Dicky Taylor was making his bomb run when a hydraulic failure occurred in his aircraft, L7311. This resulted in the bombs being jettisoned on the approach,

although Taylor later estimated them to have fallen in the target area. Whether the hydraulic failure caused the bombs to be released automatically, or whether the failure was of a type similar to that experienced by 'Mike' Lewis on take-off a few days previously, making jettisoning of the load prudent, is not known.

Gardiner gave up any hope of locating the target after a prolonged search and returned to Waddington with bomb load intact. Herring and Nunn dropped their bombs through cloud from 10,000 and 12,000ft respectively being unable to observe any result, whilst 'BG' came down to 7,000ft and claimed to have made two visual attacks on the target. The first of these was estimated to have straddled the *Gneisenau* and the second to have fallen in the target area. All in all, it was not a successful raid and only 37 aircraft claimed to have attacked the target area.

In view of the failure to resolve the extreme difficulties being experienced with the Rolls-Royce Vulture engines, the Air Ministry announced next day, 13th April 1941, that forthwith all Manchesters were to be grounded pending investigation of the bearing trouble in the engines.

Following earlier failures Rolls-Royce engineers had descended on Waddington and found that many of the Vulture engines had faulty main bearings. By the 13th, a sufficiently large number of faulty bearings had been isolated that 207, 97 and 61 Squadrons were grounded to permit rectification of this major defect.

The bearings in the engine had been suspect for some considerable period and it seems likely that Rolls-Royce were following several separate lines of enquiry at the time, all of which led back ultimately to damage to the bearings themselves. Investigations prior to this period had focused in two particular areas, namely the suitability of the metal alloy from which the bearings were turned and the oil system in the aircraft.

Taking these two problems in turn it had been recognised that the original 1% tin lead-bronze bearings tended to break up, a problem exacerbated by the unrelated problems of low oil-pressure. At some stage the standard bearings were replaced by 0.5% silver lead-bronze bearings, which did not prove to be much better. These had led to several failures, for example the crash of L7278 on 20/21st March 1941 was specifically attributed to a failure of this material by the Defect Investigation Department of Rolls-Royce.

Arising from this and earlier failures the metallurgists at Rolls had embarked upon a research programme to discover a suitable alternative. Eventually an LA4-type material containing 4% silver alloyed with the lead-bronze was developed and seemed to offer promising prospects. A batch of bearings sufficient to equip a large number of engines was produced, the first of which, Nos. 30 and

78, were made ready and installed in L7295, the Rolls-Royce development aircraft.

In addition to the use of the new LA4 material, the opportunity was taken to turn the bearings slightly undersize, the gap between bearing and crankshaft being reduced from 0.0047in to the range 0.0030-0.0035in. The purpose of the reduced gap was to promote an increase in oil pressure in the region, lack of which was believed to have seriously increased the bearing problems.

Such was the level of urgency that Rolls-Royce immediately commenced installation of the new bearings purely on the result of bench testing. L7295 was about to start its initial flight testing exactly at the time of the April grounding. The aircraft was set to accumulate 120 hours flying over as short a period as possible.

After 112hr 30min the test flying was curtailed when the port engine developed a leak, lost its coolant in the air and overheated. Reg Kirlew, the test pilot, landed the aircraft successfully and both engines were removed and returned to Derby for inspection. L7275 later had the engines reinstalled but had only completed a further seven hours before the overheating and engine fire which this time killed Kirlew. (See page 74.)

Sir Robert Renwick, Group Captain Roberts and Mr Fielding visited 5 Group on 19th April to arrange the replacement of defective engines in all group Manchesters. Avros and Rolls-Royce delivery schedules, already seriously behind, were put further adrift. A Rolls-Royce minute of 28th April specified:

Manchester captain Flying Officer W. J. 'Mike' Lewis, framed in the flak hole made in the starboard wingtip of L7309 'EM-J' of 207 Squadron during operations to Kiel on 8/9th April 1941. The wingtip was replaced next day at Waddington. *W Wetherill*

'Two LA4 engines, numbers 360 and 206, have been delivered to Avro's and these are being fitted to L7393, which is being prepared for dispatch to 207 Squadron. Fourteen LA4 engines have been delivered to 207 Squadron, Nos. 44, 240, 250, 356, 358, 362, 364, 366, 368, 370, 372, 374, 382 and 390. Two LA4 engines have been delivered to A&AEE for L7373, Nos. 352 and 386. The engines probably arrived at Waddington on or before 14th April and engine replacement and flight testing began'.

Arising from the bench running of the LA4-type bearings and the results of the inspection of Vultures Nos. 30 and 78, confidence was building at Derby that a successful material had been found. Eventually the Vulture was to be the only engine to utilise the LA4-type bearing materials.

In April 1941, Rolls-Royce's major attention, at least as far as it was perceived and communicated to the RAF, was focused not so much on the bearing material itself but elsewhere in the engine, namely upon its oil system. The oil system was subject to a number of inadequacies, which were difficult to isolate one from another, but it is likely that a major step towards rectifying these was accomplished during the April groundings.

The oil system inadequacies had become familiar to all Manchester crews and included a pronounced tendency for oil pressure to decline with altitude, accompanied by critically high and fluctuating oil temperatures and in extreme cases, failures of oil supply to the big end bearings. In exceptional circumstances the oil pressure would suddenly fall to zero at altitude leading to overheating, engine failure and fire. Such sudden pressure drops were traced to air-locking of the scavenge pumps by an accumulation of bubbles.

Overcoming these problems involved a prolonged effort and was not made easier by the fact that both Rolls-Royce and Avro systems were involved. Not only did a natural tendency arise for both companies to blame the other for problems, but suspicion at times fell on the RAF groundcrews and their maintenance procedures.

Establishing the precise sequence and timing of the recognition of the problems and the development of solutions has not been possible.

The reason for the declining and low oil pressure with altitude was traced to air entering the oil system. The source of the air proved difficult to track down and turned out to arise in several unrelated ways. The first source was eventually traced to shrinkage of a fibre washer in the oil pump suction union. Shrinkage allowed the connection to become loose and air to be drawn in. Aerated oil is a very poor lubricant and a contemporary report concluded that this was most probably the cause of the fall in oil pressure

in Vulture engines in Manchesters on operations. Avro implemented an immediate and simple solution, which was the replacement of the fibre washer with a soft aluminium one.

At about the same time it came to light that Avro's had deleted the extension suction pipe in the oil tanks of the first 56 aircraft because of a lack of the necessary castings. As a consequence, frothy oil from the top of the oil tanks, instead of de-aired oil from lower levels of the tanks, tended to be drawn off. Rolls-Royce recommended that all such affected oil tanks should be modified immediately and on 24th April the Manchesters were grounded completely to permit the oil tanks to be removed for this to be accomplished.

The aeration problem was only one of the major problems with the oil system of the engine. In the Vulture system, oil was fed to the main bearing journals on the crankshaft and from there it passed through drilled passages to the big-end bearings. Failures of the main bearings had arisen, it was suspected, due to oil starvation. Centrifugal forces generated by the crankshaft led to air collecting in the main bearing journals, displacing the oil. The risk of big-end failure was consequently greatly increased.

At the same time as the LA4 bearing material was being developed, consideration was given to increasing the oil flow and pressure to the big-end bearings. It was thought that this might be achieved by grooving of some kind. Various forms of grooved bearings were experimented with, including partial grooving, shallow continuous grooves, and deep narrow grooves. Experiments showed that the deep narrow continuous grooves supplied the greatest quantity of oil and hence provided the best lubrication. These trials may have been concluded in early 1941. It seems likely that the new LA4 bearings incorporated the deep narrow continuous grooves and were built with their clearance reduced to the range 0.0030-0.0035in.

Aeration, failure of oil supply to the main bearings, inadequate oil pressure, excessive oil temperature, all these aspects of the oil system had taken many months to recognise and, it was hoped, put right. The 22nd Manchester production meeting on 26th April noted that Rolls-Royce and Avro were supervising the engine changing programme. Notwithstanding these unscheduled diversions, Avro had delivered five Manchesters, L7390 to L7394, in the last seven days and in addition three Metrovick aircraft were at various stages of assembly at Woodford.

Amongst all this engineering mayhem the squadrons were standing-by, waiting to resume operations to Germany. Nothing provides so stark a reminder of the desperation of Britain's plight in early 1941 than this placing of an aircraft at so early a stage in its development in the very front line of Bomber

Command. Such knowledge as can be assembled today makes the endeavours of the aircrews that much more worthy of respect.

With this wide range of modifications confidence was high that the major problems were finally resolved. Sadly, even at this late stage, it proved not to be the case. The oil system itself, despite its extensive reworking, still continued to be subject to a range of problems. In July Avro were to attempt a radical solution to this, which had disastrous side effects on the already marginal climbing and flying characteristics of the aircraft. Coolant problems and con-rod bolt problems were still to be recognised and overcome, whilst serious propeller malfunctions remained to be isolated and remedied. All this mercifully was unknown to 5 Group and the aircrews as they began testing their modified Manchesters in April 1941.

Whilst the Manchesters had been grounded for engine changes and modifications to be incorporated, advantage of the time had been taken to carry forward other improvements. The suspect paper seals in the hydraulic system were replaced. The Ermeto coupling had also proved unsatisfactory. It has been suggested that the Ermeto couplings were replaced at this time by the older, proven, AGS system. It was now agreed that in the interests of quick production wire locking of all the AGS joints was to be dispensed with.

Retrospective action was not taken on the earlier aircraft, which were either not used on operations or perhaps returned to Avro or the Maintenance Units for replacement of the hydraulic piping.

The precise timescale over which these modifications to the hydraulic system were carried out is not clear, but by the late summer the greasy-floored Manchester was becoming a thing of the past. One memory of such aircraft relates to Peter Burton-Gyles and his pet terrier, which invariably accompanied him on training flights. Jim Duncan, his wireless operator, recalled that one day the dog took up its usual station on its haunches alongside 'BG's seat in a particularly oily Manchester. As they started up and taxied out the dog stayed put but as the aircraft accelerated for take-off the friction between dog fur and oily floor was suddenly overcome with the result that the startled dog, still in upright position, slid aft, latterly accompanied by much scrabbling of feet, until it came to an abrupt halt with its rump against the main spar.

Whilst these more fundamental problems of the engines and hydraulic system were keeping the aircraft away from operational commitments, other developments and testing continued apace.

As early as 10th April 1941 the Air Officer Commanding 5 Group and Wing Commander Butler had visited Waddington to inspect the 4,000 lb bomb installation in one of the first 207 Squadron aircraft to be equipped to carry this new bomb, the thin cased high capacity 'Cookie'. The aircraft concerned was L7379, destined to have a very short lifespan. On 13th April 1941 the ORB notes that aircraft (number and identity undefined) with special bomb racks for 4,000 lb bombs were collected from Woodford. It is almost certain that L7377, L7378 and L7380 were the aircraft concerned, followed two days later by L7381.

When these aircraft reached the squadron a bomb stowage problem was immediately manifest. With the bomb installed the doors would not quite close. The reason for this was that the doors were absolutely flat along the bottom of the aircraft on their inner surfaces and the circumference of the bomb was just enough to bear on this flat bottomed section, preventing them closing snuggly into the belly of the aircraft. To overcome this a section of each door was cut out. This cut out section was further modified by having a wedge shaped piece on the centre line on the inside all along the door cut away and a flat piece of Alclad skin was then inserted into each door. Finally this cut-out section was hinged back in place in the aperture in the bomb door. An air deflector or streamlined combing was added at the front and rear of the bomb doors, which were now held shut by lengths of heavy duty elastic cord.

To load the 'Cookie' the doors had to be forced open against the tension of the elastic and clamped. Then the bomb was winched into position on the bomb hook, following which the doors were allowed to close around it, being finally held with a pin.

When the bomb was to be dropped the doors were no longer opened from within the aircraft. Instead the bomb was simply released in the normal way by the bomb aimer, whereupon it fell onto the hinged door inserts, which sprung open with the weight of the bomb and allowed it to fall free from the aircraft. Immediately the tension in the rubber cords would pull the inserted bomb door panels closed. On test and later in operational use it was found that the slipstream would sometimes prevent these inserts in the main doors from closing simultaneously.

This whole procedure produced a weird series of noises and sensations in the aircraft. Firstly, there was the jolt and bang of the 'Cookie' falling on the bomb door inserts, followed by a shudder in the airframe as the inserts were forced open and finally by two bumps as each door was pulled closed individually by the heavy rubber cords. No. 207 operated with this 'Heath Robinson' modification for some time before Avro came up with the curved bomb doors which eventually became standard on the Manchester and later the Lancaster.

Whilst work on these problems was in progress Group Captain Boothman AFC, the station commanding officer at Waddington, carried out a test on 15th April 1941 on a mid-upper turret of a Manchester. Crews had complained that rotation of the mid-upper turrets installed on their latest batch of Manchesters caused a severe tail flutter to be set up in the canvas covered central fin. The vibration was sufficiently severe that for a time 97 Squadron at Coningsby operated its Manchesters with the mid-upper turret unarmed. The early installations of the F.N.7A allowed the unit to project high out of the fuselage and it may have been these aircraft too which lacked the fairing around the turret. It is possible that some mid-upper turret installations were actually undertaken retrospectively on squadron aircraft at Waddington and perhaps it was these early installations which gave the greatest trouble.

The tests, undertaken by John Boothman, as second pilot, involved L7321 with Flight Lieutenant, as he had become, Burton-Gyles as pilot and 'Eddy' Edmonds in the mid-upper turret. The object of the test was to investigate the effects of the turret on the fin at various speeds. 'BG' climbed to altitude and put the aircraft into a dive, maintaining a steady speed. Edmonds then had to rotate the mid-upper onto the beam and check what was happening to the centre fin. The procedure was repeated at progressive increments of speed until, at around 320 knots and with the turret abeam the fin started to deform.

The unit thus obtained some information about the safe operating envelope of the mid-upper turret. Later aircraft had the F.N.7A set lower in the fuselage and surrounded by a streamlined fairing, which decreased, but never eliminated, the vibration set up in the central fin by rotation. Nevertheless, Manchesters continued to shed the canvas coverings to their central fins and return, gingerly at first, to Waddington and Coningsby with just the flimsy metal framework left in place. On more than one occa-

sion the disturbance to the airflow actually caused an aircraft to shed the entire centre fin in flight. Despite initial great alarm it was found that the aircraft remained controllable. Flight Lieutenant French of 97 Squadron had found that the mid-upper turrets also decreased the sensitivity of the rudder control such that it became impossible to make a turn with the certain knowledge that the aircraft would end up on the desired bearing.

During operations the pilot of a Manchester would always know in advance when his mid-upper gunner was ready to test his weapons since the turret would first be traversed until the guns were directed on the beam. As the F.N.7A turret rotated, it disturbed the airflow across the central fin to such a marked degree that a perceptible tremor ran through the airframe and was even detectable in a small rocking pressure of the control column in the pilot's hands.

The unsatisfactory situation with the mid-upper turrets continued to alarm 5 Group. Trials were hurriedly set up with the test aircraft, L7320, at Boscombe Down. Tests showed that when the F.N.7A 'Botha' turret was rotated, buffeting was so serious that the centre fin of the aircraft was very largely destroyed. A number of problems had been chasing each other around, so to speak. When inadequate lateral stability dictated the fitting of the third fin it did so at the expense of the only other emergency exit in the rear fuselage upper decking.

Mk.I L7380 'EM-W' at Waddington with a revised, but still interim, colour scheme. The demarcation between upper and lower camouflage is raised to the upper fuselage decking, but, anticipating a later version, is straight. By September 1941 the join had been oversprayed wavy. Unit codes are now ahead of the roundel on the port side and very pale grey. Serial is red. Delivered on 13th April 1941 it undertook five sorties before it failed to return with Flight Lieutenant W J 'Mike' Lewis on 7/8th September 1941.
No. 207 Squadron archives / R Glynne-Owen

Only the removal of the F.N.21A mid-under turret had made an aperture available for an escape hatch. Absence of mid-positioned armament then led to installation of the F.N.7A mid-upper turret, whose rotation in turn compromised the centre fin itself. Furthermore the centre fin limited the field of fire of the F.N.7A. Given more time Avros might have progressed more rapidly to the twin fin 'Lancaster' tail fin configuration. Time was one thing Avros did not have.

Bomber Command had completely lost patience and on 30th April 1941 issued an edict stating that they either wanted mid-uppers which worked or no turret at all. Whilst Avro cast around for a solution, an instruction, Mod 243 of Avros, called for the removal of all mid-upper F.N.7A turrets from Manchesters. The weary Avro work parties and squadron groundcrew buckled down to yet another desperately urgent task. Avros were considering two options, either a strengthening of the fin or a change of turret, but in the intervening period out they had to come. A number of pilots viewed this with some satisfaction, anything to decrease the weight and ease the strain on the underpowered aircraft was a bonus.

On 15th April 1941 207 Squadron also passed on three of its older aircraft to 61 Squadron, which was in line to be the third Manchester unit. L7279, L7281 and L7304 were collected and flown to Hemswell.

No. 207 Squadron armourers, Spooner (left) and Smith pose in front of a 207 Manchester. Behind are a 44 Squadron Handley Page Hampden and a Fairey Swordfish. The latter was used by the Navy to bring the naval armourer to fuse sea mines. Only the Hampdens carried mines at this time. Photograph probably taken between February and 15th April 1941. *E B Spooner*

During Spring of 1941 pressure for improvements in Manchester armament at squadron and group level intensified. It is clear that Air Vice-Marshal Jack Slessor at 5 Group Headquarters in Grantham was one of the major driving forces and he had the active support of Air Vice-Marshal Saundby at Bomber Command Headquarters in High Wycombe. No. 5 Group had been let down by the Directorate of Armament Development (DArmD) in the defensive armament for the Hampden. In desperation they had turned to two local British firms in their area, British Manufacturing and Research Company (MARC) of Grantham and Messrs Rose Brothers of Gainsborough. Mr Kendall, the managing director of British MARC, and Mr Rose had got together and quickly built the electrically operated, but hand held, RB3 installation for two Vickers Gas Operated 0.303in machine guns. These had greatly improved rear defence in the Hampden. Now faced with the limitations of the defunct F.N.21A and the obsolete F.N.7A, 5 Group turned once more to these unofficial saviours.

Mr Rose and a British MARC representative were guided around a 207 Squadron Manchester at Waddington by Wing Commander Butler of 5 Group on 26th and 29th April 1941. They recommended a radical solution in which the F.N.7A would be scrapped and replaced by twin hand held, but electrically traversed, 0.5in Hispano cannon with shortened barrels and a belt feed system. No. 5 Group sent these recommendations to a receptive Saundby at High Wycombe with a request to proceed. DArmD, who had been informed as a courtesy, replied sourly and obstructively that a shortened 0.5in cannon did not exist, nor could it be belt fed and in any case, their own extensive experimentation proved that only hydraulic power was adequate to such a task. Slessor responded by pointing out that the short barrelled 0.5in Hispano cannon was already operational in Coastal Command Anson and Bristol Beaufort aircraft for anti-submarine and E-boat operations! A belt-feed system for cannon had recently been tested successfully on the Hurricane II wing at Air Fighting Development Unit Martlesham Heath and the RB3 mounting was giving excellent service! In a phrase that demonstrates 5 Group's ambitions for the strategic bomber, Slessor stressed 'We must get these big heavies onto day work as soon as possible and we do want the heavier metal for that'.

In the short term, 0.5in guns in power turrets were not likely to be available. As an interim measure a power assisted and lighter twin 0.5in installation on a more robust scarf ring was proposed. The installation was to be enclosed in a perspex and metal cupola which would project no more than 18in into the slipstream and rotate through the rear-

ward arc as the guns themselves traversed. Belt feeding was to be incorporated in order to maintain an adequate continuous defence without the awkward drum feeds with their intrinsic defenceless periods whilst reloading was in progress. When the time came to progress this development, 5 Group requested the damaged fuselage section from Squadron Leader Mackintosh's Perranporth crash on the 18th May. (See page 73.) The undamaged upper section would be ideal for Rose and Kendall to play with.

Slessor acknowledged that this course of action would be very unorthodox, but pointed out that Rose and Kendall had agreed to provide all materials and labour free of charge. He quoted the precedent of the RB3 as an example of previous achievements. Quite what became of these proposals is unclear because the 0.5in Hispano installation never materialised in the Manchester. The squadron engineering officer, Flight Lieutenant Eric McCabe, and fitter gun armourer, Sergeant Hodgkinson, both recall assisting in some trials with 0.5in Hispano cannon but in respect of the rear turret.

In 97 Squadron, concern had been focused on the continuing inability to man and operate the F.N.5A nose turret when the bomb aimer was kneeling at this sight, a factor which was of much greater significance with 5 Group anxious to use Manchesters for daylight operations. By late May, as a temporary field modification, 97 Squadron had lowered the bomb sight mountings of all squadron Manchesters by 2½in and at the same time dispensed with the cumbersome shell case collector chute and boxes. Thus modified, the F.N.5A could operate whilst the Manchester was on the bomb run. The hot empty shell cases fell on the bomb aimer's back and littered the bomb compartment, but 97 considered this a minor inconvenience compared to the benefit gained.

During this period 207 and 97 Squadrons' roles as test and development, or guinea pig, units were well to the fore. Manchesters were declared airworthy again and on 1st May 1941 three of 207 Squadron's aircraft were prepared for operations to Hamburg, which were later cancelled due to the weather. A period of intensive, but still extremely frustrating, activity was about to commence.

Almost as if it were a token to mark this return to operations, Bomber Command notified Avro on 3rd May of the third change in camouflage markings consistent with the field modifications to the camouflage scheme which had been introduced on the squadrons in late February. The divide between the upper and lower colours was to be moved to the top of the fuselage decking and the straight separation changed to a wavy one. Any unmodified service aircraft were to be repainted on the squadrons as opportunity permitted.

Chapter Four

Catastrophe

For the first time, the Manchester was destined to carry the new 4,000 lb high capacity (HC) bombs operationally. On 2nd May 1941 three aircraft from 207 Squadron were serviceable for a raid on Hamburg and their bomb bays were to carry 'Cookies'. These joined the force of 95 aircraft dispatched.

Hamburg with the first 'Cookies' – 2nd May 1941

Serial	Code	Sqn	Captain
L7377	EM-G	207	S/L C J F Kydd
L7317	EM-C	207	F/O D A A Romans
L7379	EM-T	207	F/O D E Pinchbeck

The three aircraft took off at intervals during the course of the evening. The crew of L7379 were a little excited knowing that the mission was on, but that on return they were all going on leave. The observer, Sergeant S E Panton, was flying with the crew for the first time having returned from leave to find that his own crew, that of Pilot Officer Gardiner, were on a course at Cottesmore. At briefing they were issued with the standard warning – all gun turrets were to be manned on take-off, over target and on landing. Also a close watch had to be maintained on engine oil pressure. If the pressure fell into the red area they were to return.

At this time one of Bomber Command's philosophies was still to extend the duration of the attack in an attempt to keep the German workforce from their beds. Accordingly, L7379 was the second aircraft to take-off, departing with its 4,000 lb 'Cookie' at around 2200 hours. Panton gave Pinchbeck a course for the 'gate' on the English coast near Skegness. There was to be the usual strict wireless silence until the aircraft crossed the enemy coast on the way back home, with the exception of all Manchesters. These aircraft were required to broadcast their call sign every hour. This was part of the investigation set up to establish whether Manchesters were being lost due to engine failure or enemy action. The other standing instruction to the wireless operators at this time was that in the event of their aircraft having to go down over enemy territory they were to broadcast their position and one of three coded words for 'flak', 'fighters', or 'engines' to indicate the cause of their demise. One source claims that there is only one example of such a message ever being received and

that said 'engines'. This claim has not been substantiated. It was clear that, along with the crews, the Command was acutely sensitive to the reliability of the Vulture engines.

At the briefing, Sergeant W M McGregor, the wireless operator in L7379, had been given a list of German beacon stations operating for the use of their own aircraft and submarines. To assist Panton, McGregor tuned in to them in turn and kept taking direction finding (D/F) bearings to provide the observer with running fixes and so pinpoint their position all the way across the North Sea. The flow of slips of paper with station name and position continued. Panton also monitored the oil pressure regularly and although it fluctuated during the crossing it did not fall to danger point.

They were behind time but decided to press on. Suddenly McGregor was surprised to see and feel the effects of flak bursting around them at a time when he thought they should be still well out to sea. He stood up and glanced at Panton's chart and saw they were over the island of Heligoland. From this inadvertent pinpoint they set course for the mouth of the Elbe river. This too was a surprise as McGregor had expected them to make a landfall to the north near Flensburg and then turn south to come down on Hamburg through the 'back door'. The banks of the Elbe were heavily industrialised and thus protected by a corridor of flak guns – this was the 'front door'. On their approach to the target along the Elbe they were consequently detected by the defences and received their close attention, taking quite a number of near misses from flak in the process. Fortunately they remained undetected by the searchlights. They found the weather at the target to be fair with ground haze and extreme darkness making it difficult to identify the aiming point.

Panton went forward to the bomb aiming position. The flak was increasing in intensity as they reached the outskirts of Hamburg. Suddenly all the searchlights lit up and L7379 was coned and held in the beams. The flak continued to rise and became increasingly accurate, Panton felt a shudder of at least one hit from the fire. As they steadied on the bombing run close to 0100 hours and at 12,000ft another flak hit was received and the aircraft immediately lifted as it rid itself of the 4,000 lb 'Cookie', toggled away by Panton.

Almost as soon as this happened and before he could leave the bomb aiming position a sliver of flak came through the perspex dome of the bomb aiming position, hit the bombing panel and splintered it.

As Panton began to return to his navigating position he was shocked to see that the port engine was on fire, with flames streaming back from the cowling. Pinchbeck operated the Graviner extinguisher and feathered the propeller, whereupon the fire in the port engine seemed to abate to some extent.

Pinchbeck turned the aircraft away to the north in an attempt to clear the target area and pick up a course for home. Already they were losing height. The remaining Vulture was not proving adequate to the task. The pilot called Panton to say he could not get the aircraft round onto its new westerly course for home, to which Panton replied that in that case they would end up in the Shetlands. At this moment the starboard engine too burst into flames, with fire already creeping along the leading edge of the wing towards the fuselage. Pinchbeck gave the inevitable order to bale out; fortunately no one had been wounded.

Unaware of what was happening up front, when the flak slowly died down McGregor had started to set up his transmitter and receiver and to reel out the trailing aerial. He would then be ready to transmit a message to 5 Group saying L7379 had bombed the primary target and was crossing the enemy coast on the way home. Sergeant A S Duncan, the second wireless operator/air gunner, was standing in the walkway behind the navigator's seat with his head in the perspex bubble on the starboard side looking down on Hamburg. At this moment McGregor was on the wireless, not the intercom, and Duncan, who had been moving around the aircraft, was not plugged into the intercom either. Suddenly Duncan turned round and started kicking McGregor's boot to attract attention. He was shouting. McGregor tried to lip read as he spoke but the only word he could make out was 'fire'.

Thinking Duncan was getting excited about the fires of Hamburg down below them, and being and 'old stager' himself, McGregor thought he would have seen it all before and so didn't even bother looking out. The flak had more or less stopped and he continued reeling out what remained of the trailing aerial in preparation for transmitting his message. Turning next to his radio equipment he finished setting it up. Having completed this task, he looked round the partition in his compartment to get a time from Panton for crossing the enemy coast. He was dumbfounded to see only Pinchbeck, alone in the aircraft, struggling in his seat.

Following the order to bale out, which McGregor had missed, Panton proceeded immediately to the forward escape hatch. Releasing the hatch, he held it for a moment before pitching it out and watching it tumble end over end in the slipstream as it dropped away. He tightened his parachute harness and waited for the rest of the crew. When he saw Lee, the second pilot, leave his seat he sat on the edge of the hatch and dropped free, the first crew member to leave. He was quickly followed by Lee and then Duncan. When McGregor saw Pinchbeck was alone the realisation of their predicament and the fact that he should clearly be long gone was naturally instantaneous. Discarding his helmet he put on his parachute and moved forward to the now vacant second pilot's position. Entering the cockpit area he noticed for the first time the starboard wing well ablaze – his first intimation of the cause of the rest of the crews' hasty exit.

Reaching the second pilot's position, McGregor saw that the skipper had not fastened his parachute harness and his right

Squadron Leader Charles Kydd, 'A' Flight commander and commanding officer of 207 Squadron after Wing Commander Hyde failed to return on 8/9th April 1941. Kydd died following the crash of L7310 on 21st June 1941.
No.207 Squadron archives / R Glynne-Owen

hand lap strap had fallen between the flap and undercarriage levers. Instead of turning the harness and lifting it out of the narrow gap the preoccupied and desperate pilot was tugging frantically at the strap, which was jamming across the gap.

McGregor reached over and took the stick in his hands, holding the descending Manchester on an even keel and allowing the pilot to use both hands to release the buckle of his harness and get it securely fastened. What McGregor did not notice at the time was that Pinchbeck was flying in an observer-type parachute harness, owing to the fact that his own parachute was being repacked. Instead of sitting on his pilot-type 'chute Pinchbeck had placed a cushion in the bucket seat of the aircraft. Obviously Pinchbeck had no realisation of what lay ahead for him, for as soon as his harness was fastened up tight he gave McGregor the thumbs up. With the starboard wing burning furiously and the port engine still alight the risk of an explosion appeared imminent and the wireless operator wanted no further encouragement! Turning round, he dived from the step to the second pilot's position, head first, straight through the open forward escape hatch after his three colleagues.

As he dived through the hatch one visual image burned itself into his brain. Turning his head, he had seen an observer-type parachute in the camera hatch. He pulled his ripcord as soon as he vacated the aircraft and the canopy jerked open, leaving him swinging suspended beneath. As the aircraft passed above him he had noted that the undercarriage was in the down position and that the aircraft was carrying full flap. These factors, added to the loss of the engines, no doubt contributed to the extremely rapid sink rate.

On the way down, McGregor dwelt on which crew member he presumed must have jumped from the forward hatch without a parachute. He could not imagine Lee, Panton or Duncan having done so and to salve his conscience he decided it must probably have been left in the aircraft from a previous flight. This would be unusual, but not impossible, he judged.

Back in the aircraft, Pinchbeck and the rear gunner, Sergeant C N Barron, had still not escaped, although neither knew that the other was still on board. When Barron got the order to bale out he found the hydraulic supply to the rear turret had failed and he was unable to traverse the turret. Reaching inside the aircraft he took his parachute and spent some time clipping it to his chest. Outside he could see the flames streaming back from the blazing wing and expected the aircraft to explode at any moment.

Barron then tried to traverse the turret manually with the emergency system. The rate of turn seemed painfully slow and before he had achieved the 90° traverse on to

the beam to allow him to tumble out backwards he changed his mind. In his desperation it seemed the rear door offered a quicker exit route. Traversing the turret back to the fore and aft position he accordingly scrambled out and rushed forward to the rear entry door on the starboard side. He pulled the handle and threw all his weight onto the rear door but it appeared to be completely jammed.

With time passing and his anxiety rising with every passing second he abandoned this course of action and returned once more to the turret. Once inside he began the painfully slow business of traversing it onto the beam. Despite what seemed to be his most feverish activity, no doubt by this time with every second seeming like a year, he was unable to swing the turret at a speed which appeared to provide him any early prospect of escape. Once more he changed his mind, surely by chopping off the handle of the rear door with the fire axe he could force it open and effect a rapid exit. He could not recollect any sign that the door was distorted or damaged.

Traversing the turret back to the fore and aft position again he hurled himself back along the fuselage a second time. He grabbed the fire axe but as he did so he was immediately thrown to the floor and held there by tremendous 'g' forces. The immediate thought which came to him was that he was too late and that with the pilot finally vacating the aircraft it had commenced its final uncontrollable plunge to destruction. He could do nothing more than wait for the final impact.

Meanwhile, up in the cockpit following McGregor's escape, Pinchbeck's next move was to reach behind himself to the parachute storage position behind his seat, where he had placed his parachute. This was difficult to achieve since he had to release the stick to turn around and reach into the stowage rack. The aircraft was either not fitted with an autopilot or alternatively it was not working. Eventually reaching the rack Pinchbeck discovered, to his abject horror, that it was empty. Subsequently it transpired that Duncan, who had been moving around the aircraft taking his parachute with him, had gone into the nose compartment and put his parachute in the camera hatch whilst he busied himself with another task. On returning to the main deck he left his 'chute behind and on receiving the order to bale out did not appreciate that the pilot was using the unusual observer-type 'chute and harness. Accordingly he had mistaken the 'chute in the stowage rack behind the pilot's seat for his own and in his haste grabbed it, buckled it on and went.

Derek Pinchbeck now realised where Duncan's 'chute was, presumably being able to see it lying there from his position in the cockpit. His only chance seemed to be to release the controls and rush forward and grab the 'chute before the aircraft went out of control. Unbeknown to Pinchbeck, however, L7379 had on full flap and the undercarriage was down. Consequently as soon as he released the controls and moved towards the forward compartment the Manchester put its nose down and went into an almost vertical dive.

More than one unsuccessful attempt was made to leave the controls with, unknown to him, rear gunner Barron bouncing around in the tail section. Finally, Pinchbeck made a last desperate attempt and succeeding in getting hold of the 'chute, however the aircraft had by this time entered a vertical power dive, pinning them both down. It was clear to Pinchbeck that he was not going to be able to clip on the parachute and climb down against the 'g' forces to the forward hatch and bale out.

The aircraft had by this time lost a great deal of height and little time appeared to be left if he was to save himself. Pinchbeck dropped the 'chute and forced himself, with an almost superhuman effort, back to his seat. Desperate measures were called for and so, placing his feet on the instrument panel, he linked his forearms around the stick and heaved. Slowly his straining began to have some effect and he finally managed to recover the aircraft onto an even keel at about 2,000ft. He knew then that alone he would have no other option but to carry out a forced landing in the dark in open country.

Back in the rear fuselage, Barron could hardly believe his deliverance. Acting automatically he jumped up, chopped the lock from the rear door with a few axe blows and jumped out. He had no idea of the altitude and it is likely the Manchester was down to 1,000ft or less by the time he baled out.

Pulling the ripcord immediately, the parachute blossomed above him and he was suffused in a mixture of immense relief and embarrassment. In his panic to escape he had been trying to force the door outwards whilst actually it was designed, as he well knew, to open inwards. All in all it had been a lucky escape for him.

Up front, Pinchbeck prepared himself for the forced landing, the wing was still ablaze, it was completely dark outside and he had no idea of what lay ahead in his path. He had no power and a rapid sink rate and so no opportunity of choosing his land-fall. It would be first and final. Still unaware that the undercarriage was down he anticipated a belly landing. The aircraft sank lower until it was only 15-20ft above the ground. This was it. Suddenly ahead, directly in his path, and his first sight of ground, a farmhouse loomed up in the darkness. He was almost on to it before it became distinguishable. This must be it, death was staring him in the face once more and this time he could do nothing. At this point chance took a hand and the subse-

quent few seconds passed with no one other than fate in control.

Instead of hitting the farmhouse or descending on to its belly, at its high sink rate the main undercarriage wheels chose this moment to meet the ground hard. The aircraft still had plenty of speed and a high bounce ensued which lifted the Manchester clean over the farmhouse without so much as disturbing a slate. On the second touchdown, which was fortunately on open ground behind the house, the undercarriage collapsed and L7379 descended onto its belly, skidding along for some distance before stopping.

Pinchbeck was practically unhurt and immediately climbed out of the upper escape hatch in the cockpit canopy, jumped down and raced away from the still blazing aircraft. He had covered about 150 yards when the petrol tanks exploded, destroying what remained of the wreck.

Instead of being last, Pinchbeck turned out to be the first to find his feet on the ground, followed soon afterwards by Barron. Panton, who was first out, was able to glimpse the aircraft towing a banner of fire as it plunged earthwards. He had escaped from quite a high level, perhaps 10,000ft and eventually landed at Stade at 0315 hours.

L7309 'EM-J' of 207 Squadron back from the wars again, this time with its tail feathers shredded. The crew fought a prolonged engagement with two Messerschmitt Me110s and sustained damage to the tailplane, fins, fuselage, wings, fuel tanks and undercarriage doors entailing some 360 skin perforations en route to Berlin, 10/11th May 1941. Squadron Leader Kydd made a successful early return. *via E McCabe*

McGregor, too, heard the noise of the Manchester's remaining engine as it flew over him in his parachute. There was no flak or noise other than the wind in the rigging lines. He was absolutely freezing as the only outer flying clothes he was wearing at his overheated station were flying boots. He heard the aircraft go into a vertical dive and then a minute or two later a loud explosion as the petrol tanks ignited on the ground. He landed safely in a ploughed field and as it would soon be dawn he found a wood, stuffed his parachute, 'Mae West' and harness into a rabbit hole and hid in some bracken along the edge of the wood nearby. L7379 had crashed at the village of Bremervorde over 30 miles due west of Hamburg.

From inside an F.N.4A rear turret such as this, Sgt Oliver of 207 Squadron claimed two Messerschmitt Me 110s on the night of 10/11th May 1941. *via Aerospace Publishing*

Ahead of L7379, Flying Officer Romans dropped four 1,000 lb general purpose (GP) and seven small bomb carriers (SBC) containing 420 x 4 lb incendiaries from 12,000 ft. The bombs were not seen to burst but the incendiaries straddled the docks. Romans' aircraft, L7317, was also hit by flak, but managed to reach Waddington and land safely.

Meanwhile Squadron Leader Kydd had been briefed to make a dawn sortie to Hamburg. Following the night's heavy raid it was intended to keep the weary defenders on their toes by triggering the early warning

radar, sounding the air raid siren and raising the city-dwellers from their beds they had so recently returned to. Take-off time was 2310 hours. This was to be an operation calling for all Charles Kydd's unrivalled qualities of leadership and coolness.

Following an extremely dark night the rising dawn still presented target identification problems due to a persistent ground haze over the city. The observer, Pilot Officer Sheen, now in the bomb aiming position, searched desperately for the aiming point as they held a steady course at 15,000 ft on their bomb run. The defences were well and truly roused and the flak was intense. It seemed as if every gun in Hamburg was concentrating on this lone Manchester. The wireless operator, 'Scotty' Scott, was sweating profusely at

Kydd's dedication and praying second by second for the cry of 'bombs away'. The incantations over the intercom as Sheen conned Kydd towards the aiming point appeared to come from one totally detached from the hell all round them.

Suddenly Sheen called 'I think we're overshooting'. Kydd calmly replied 'Alright, we'll go round again'. Scott's hopes were dashed. Kydd turned and made a second bombing run through what Scott recalled as the heaviest anti-aircraft fire he had ever experienced. Kydd never flinched or deviated from his determination to fly straight and level. The 4,000 lb 'Cookie' fell away on Aiming Point 'B'. As the short night lifted, Kydd dived away from the seething, thoroughly roused, target and finally escaped the jolting flak. Descending to ground level to take advantage of the last vestiges of twilight, Kydd hedge-hopped across Germany towards the coast.

In addition to the flak defences the Luftwaffe were also thoroughly alerted. As Kydd concentrated on following the terrain a few feet beneath, the gunners and lookouts could clearly see the day fighters overhead quartering the sky in a desperate search for them. They escaped detection and crossed the coast without further incident, reaching Waddington at 0510 hours. They never came cooler or more efficient than Charles Kydd. The Hamburg Authorities in their own report noted 26 fires, 13 of them large. Three people were killed and 16 injured.

Of the aircraft which failed to return, L7379, the whole crew, especially Pinchbeck and Barron, had had a quite shocking experience and were lucky to have all escaped with their lives. The degree to which engine failure contributed to the loss of L7379 is impossible to judge. At least the port engine appears to have been set on fire by flak and the aircraft was clearly losing height even before the starboard engine took light. A third Manchester had now fallen in occupied Europe but as yet the Germans had been left with precious little on the ground

Back at Waddington, three aircraft of 207 Squadron were required for operations the very next day, 3rd May 1941. Two were briefed to attack Cologne with 4,000 lb HC bombs and the third was to go to Brest to keep up the pressure on the *Scharnhorst* and *Gneisenau*, carrying three 2,000 lb armour piercing (AP) bombs. This night, Bomber Command split its forces, allocating 101 aircraft to Cologne and a further 33 to Brest.

Brest – 3rd May 1941

Serial	Code	Sqn	Captain
L7377	EM-G	207	F/O W J Lewis
L7378	EM-A	207	F/O A M Paape
L7316	EM-U	207	P/O W G Gardiner

Lewis and Paape attacked Cologne with their 4,000 lb bombs. Lewis attacked from

12,000 ft and observed his bomb bursting near the aiming point. Subsequent to releasing the bomb, Lewis dived on the target to give the gunners a chance to suppress the town defences. The wireless operator/air gunner, Sergeant Jim Duncan (not to be confused with A S Duncan who was on board L7379 during the horrific sortie of 2nd May), records in his logbook that they overflew the target area at 2,000 ft and the gunners blazed away at searchlights, flak batteries and the empty streets. Such an action was not uncommon, but the more remarkable in that none of the Manchester crews doubted the certain outcome of losing an engine at that height over Germany. Paape dropped his 'Cookie' from 7,000 ft but was unable to see the effect. Similarly, Gardiner dropped his three 2,000 lb AP bombs in his attack on Brest but was unable to ascertain any effect. Heavy cloud had led to problems for the Cologne force and from the aircraft dispatched only 8–10 bombs fell within city limits, causing minor damage and casualties.

No. 207 Squadron had operated on virtually every night in May and on the 9/10th were called upon again. This time four aircraft were made ready, of which one was allocated to Mannheim, whilst the remaining three were detailed to attack 'The Big City', Berlin, for the first time in the Manchester's history. The tactical plan involved aircraft attacking Mannheim with a diversion to Berlin by five bombers. It was by far the deepest penetration so far and no mean return journey for an underpowered aircraft with such unreliable and underdeveloped engines. Three experienced captains were to attack Berlin, whilst the new 'B' Flight commander, Flying Officer T C Murray, took on Mannheim.

Berlin the first 'Big City' raid – 9/10th May 1941

Serial	Code	Sqn	Captain
L7309	EM-J	207	F/L P R Burton-Gyles
L7381	EM-R	207	F/O T C Murray
L7316	EM-U	207	P/O W S Herring
L7393	EM-V	207	F/L G R Taylor

Murray had an uneventful mission to Mannheim where the 4,000 lb bomb was dropped in the target area from 17,000 ft. The flash of the explosion was readily distinguished and large fires reported. Local records document that a large number of buildings of all types were destroyed or damaged, 64 persons were killed and 122 injured.

From the Berlin force, Taylor's aircraft, L7393, returned after an hour with wireless transmitter failure, an unusual fault in the midst of so many engine and hydraulic problems. Herring and crew in L7316 were heading eastwards over the North Sea towards the enemy coast and had reached 10,000 ft when they were intercepted at 2320 hours by a night fighter, identified as a Messerschmitt Me 110. After a brief encounter the '110 was

claimed shot down by the rear gunner, Sergeant 'Tiny' Hallam, and L7316 was able to proceed, apparently undamaged. Flashes of other bombs exploding were observed in the target area and L7316 released six 1,000 lb bombs on the aiming point. The aircraft was hit by heavy flak and, although it is not recorded, it is likely that the damage occurred in the target area. The flak must have missed the vital parts and the delicate engines, for L7316 was able to return safely to Waddington. Burton-Gyles also reached Berlin in L7309 and his six 1,000 lb GP load was dropped in the target area from 18,000 ft.

The following night, 10/11th May, 207 Squadron was again called for a follow up raid to Berlin. In its turn, 97 Squadron raised four Manchesters. In all, 119 aircraft were dispatched to Hamburg and the Berlin force numbered 23. Only two aircraft were available from 207 Squadron, L7316 missing out perhaps due to the flak damage it incurred the previous night. Major R A Holmes of the Anti-Aircraft Liaison with 5 Group accompanied Kydd as an observer. He was to have an eventful night, although not at the hands of the flak batteries.

Berlin – 10/11th May 1941

Serial	Code	Sqn	Captain
L7383	OF-*	97	P/O H S Blakeman
L7374	OF-*	97	F/O F E Eustace
L7323	OF-*	97	P/O R S Ayton
L7324	OF-*	97	F/L G O L Bird
L7309	EM-J	207	S/L C J F Kydd
L7393	EM-V	207	F/O D A A Romans.

It was a clear, moonlight night. Frankie Eustace of 97 Squadron experienced a series of serviceability problems and eventually diverted to Borkum. German night fighters were very active. Soon after crossing the enemy coast and whilst flying at 17,000 ft between Rensburg and Husum in Schleswig Holstein L7309 was intercepted by two Me 110 night fighters, apparently operating as a pair. At the moment of interception Kydd and Flying Officer Nunn were flying the aircraft, Pilot Officer Sheen was at the navigator's table, Sergeant Scott was manning the front turret, whilst the second wireless operator/air gunner, Sergeant Linklater, was on the radio and Sergeant Oliver was vigilant in the rear turret. As soon as the interceptors were spotted Linklater climbed up into the astrodome to observe the proceedings. In the action which followed Kydd was blind to the attacks and depended entirely on instructions from behind, whilst Oliver was fully occupied trying to repulse attacks and keep an eye on two Me 110s at once. Consequently, Linklater fell naturally into the role of attack co-ordinator.

He commenced a running commentary on the ranges and manoeuvres of the attack-

ers. As they closed in, he instructed Kydd when and in which direction to break and the pilot began to throw the overloaded bomber around the sky in a spirited fashion, losing height all the while. Scott could do little but sit and wait, listen and watch in trepidation as the tracer fire periodically flew past him. It was a desperate battle for the ultimate stakes. After two passes one of the fighters made a mistake, allowing Oliver to get in a telling shot. The aircraft dived away, apparently out of control. Oliver claimed this aircraft destroyed. Linklater was getting excited; although his commentary remained unbroken it was frequently interspersed with expletives, pronounced with the greatest emphasis, 'Bugger Me!', he shouted, 'Jesus Christ!'.

The second Me 110 carried out seven separate attacks, throughout which Kydd's evasive manoeuvres persisted with undiminished vigour. Despite this, the enemy pilot knew his stuff and on each approach the Manchester staggered under the impact of cannon and machine gun hits. They were hit in the tailplanes, fins, fuselage, wings and undercarriage doors. Kydd continually monitored the engine instruments. So far the vulnerable engines and vital services remained miraculously intact, but there was a serious fuel leak in the port wing tank.

Finally Oliver was able to draw a bead and the fighter was seen to disengage immediately. Oliver claimed this as a probable. Later they were to learn that the entire episode had been witnessed by other British aircraft in the vicinity who confirmed that this interceptor crashed, apparently into the sea.

As they slipped away into the night the crew of L7309 found that the combat had extended down to low altitude and as they took stock of the situation they found every system apparently serviceable, but there was an all pervading smell of aviation spirit. The petrol gauges indicated a rapid loss of fuel and in the circumstances Kydd had no alternative but to abort the operation and make an early return.

On arrival back at base Kydd made a normal approach but found the aircraft virtually without elevator control. Consequently when he flared for landing the aircraft flew more or less straight on into the ground, making what for him was an unusually heavy landing. The six 1,000 lb GP bomb load was still intact. Inspection on the ground showed that the canvas covering on the central fin, shredded by the fire from the night fighter, had been all but torn off by the slipstream. The fabric was largely torn from the elevators accounting for the heavy landing. In the circumstances they marvelled that Oliver had escaped without a scratch. The self-sealing in the two tanks had worked to some extent, staunching the main leaks sufficiently for the Manchester to race back to base before they became dry completely.

Next day the airframe fitters counted some 360 perforations to the skin of the aircraft. Following their debriefing, Sergeant Oliver was awarded the DFC whilst Sergeant Linklater received the DFM, the citation eulogising the 'brilliant commentary' which had been a major contribution to their success.

Two 97 Squadron crews, L7388 and L7324 were also intercepted, this time by Junkers Ju 88 night fighters en route to the target. Both Blakeman and Bird managed to evade the attacks and went on to bomb Berlin successfully, as did Herring.

The night was to provide the first loss for 97 Squadron and the first of three consecutive encounters with the cold, pitiless North Sea. Earlier in the day the 'A' Flight Commander, Squadron Leader Ronnie Stubbs, had carried out a night flying test in his personal aircraft, L7323 'OF-A'. Its performance, especially the power available from the two Vultures, was below normal and Stubbs had reservations about Pilot Officer Ayton taking it to Berlin, especially since this would be Ayton's first Manchester operation.

The crew of six consisted of Paddy Ayton (captain), Sergeants Jack Chantler (second pilot), 'Jock' Bryce (observer), Bill Sykes (wireless operator), Bob Anderson (rear gunner), and Dennis Harvey (front gunner), the latter on his first ever operation. At briefing the crews were given the German parliament buildings, the Reichstag, as their aiming point. The bomb load consisted of six 1,000 lb GPs with 12 hour delayed action fuses. For the first time the bombs were to have small rockets attached which would erupt on impact, permitting the fall of bombs to be observed. The course to be followed in and out was the same northerly route via the Baltic.

Normally at his station at the navigator's table, 'Jock' Bryce wore only his uniform tunic, as the blast of hot air from either side of the fuselage to his left was terrific. Some quirk this Saturday night made Bryce break his usual routine and don not only a white polo neck sweater but also his outer flying suit and flying boots. When all the preparations, drawing 'Mae West' and parachute, completing pre-flight log and checking his charts, were complete he and the crews climbed aboard the tenders and were driven to the aircraft.

At the dispersal L7323 was waiting, bomb doors still agape. Their ground crew, with several WAAF girls along to see them off, had chalked messages on the bombs. Bryce looked up at the load they were to carry to Berlin for the squadron's first visit. 'Ow's this for size Adolf?' said one, 'Up yer Jacksie, Goebbels', read another. Bryce's scan also took in the novelty of the rockets mounted on the bombs. The girls wished them good luck and a safe return and their presence led to them overlooking their ritual pee on the tail wheel.

In the failing light the Manchesters started up and taxied out into line, snaking to the north end of Coningsby airfield. Last in line, Paddy Ayton's crew watched the Manchesters on their headlong southerly run, each lifting off when some two thirds of the way down the grass runway. Ayton swung 'A-Apple' onto the grass runway and gunned the engines. The run seemed interminable and the aircraft had only just begun to lighten when they passed the two-thirds marker. Slowly the wheels unstuck, but 'A-Apple' immediately sank back and bounced. The bounces became further apart as the boundary hedge approached. Ayton was committed and still L7323 steadfastly refused to rise. The crew would never forget streaking over the boundary hedge just as their undercarriage began to retract.

A sea of shocked civilian faces zipped past just below eye level. At Waddington the local population were accustomed to aircraft departing for operations, but Coningsby was a new station and half the population of Boston and neighbouring villages had turned out to cheer them on. Had they known the identity of the target their encouragement would have been more enthusiastic still. Adrenalin continued to flow as L7323 clipped and carried away a radio aerial from a cottage roof.

Ayton commenced a tentative climbing shallow turn to port onto course and with the setting sun now behind them they made out their three comrades ahead and already way above. Despite rpm and air speed being as recommended and with the flaps still down, L7323 'A-Apple' was a ground bird and steadfastly refused to rise. Slowly and almost imperceptibly, however, the aircraft did begin to lift and at midnight, as they passed Heligoland on the port beam, they had achieved 7,000ft.

A full moon rose, illuminating the night sky, its brightness unsettling for an overloaded bomber whose main defence was its invisibility in the dark sky. As they kept a vigilant lookout the two pilots and front gunner all cried out in unison – 'Vapour trails'. These appeared momentarily and persisted for short intervals before fading again as different air masses were traversed. L7323 had reached 10,000ft and could be coaxed no higher on its existing fuel and bomb load.

Jim Bryce, the observer, was taking a running series of bearings from Radio Hilversum and plotting these against compass bearings as they map read across the coast of occupied Europe. The visibility was virtually unlimited making him doubt his calculations from time to time. Soon after crossing the coast they altered course for Potsdam. Approaching the western suburbs of Berlin they were behind on the estimated time of arrival but relieved to have escaped any interference by searchlights, flak or fighters. Now the lights and flak began to rise, alarming because there was neither mist nor cloud

to disguise it. Their lowly height had the consolation that most of the flak was bursting above them.

The great distance at which landmarks were perceptible was still causing Bryce concern, but suddenly Dennis Harvey, the front gunner, spotted a lake ahead, by which Bryce was able to establish that they were five miles to the west of the proposed track. Ayton swung east and made for the final turning point. Occasional vapour trails were still evident over the target; they had not been singled out by the defences and were only a few minutes late.

Turning onto the final leg, Bryce descended to the bomb aimer's position, set the flying height, wind speed and direction and other inputs. The city beneath was laid out like a map and the front gunner and Bryce, with the eye not glued to the bomb sight, began quartering the suburbs for a sighting of Templehof aerodrome. The searchlight and flak activity had become intense and the crew were keyed up during this crucial run up. Everyone leapt when the rear gunner shouted suddenly over the intercom 'Holy Christ! Are we that big?'. An urgent query from the pilot. 'A bloody big Manchester just cut across our tail', replied the gunner. 'That's alright then, just keep quiet!' said Ayton restoring calm and concentration on board.

In the final few seconds an industrial haze made map reading difficult, a distinctive north west to south east highway gave a pinpoint but the Reichstag had not been located and Bryce gave a 'Left, left, steady' to the pilot before pressing the button.

The automatic sight was moving fast, an indication that the bombs would undershoot the aiming point. The aircraft jolted and bucked as the bombs fell away in a neat stick over about ten seconds. Following the release, Bryce immediately called 'Bombs gone, close bomb doors, course 330 compass'. After the short delay Anderson saw the rockets explode with orange flashes at the point of impact 10,000ft below.

Their briefed course led them on a north westerly heading out towards the Baltic and a return flight mainly over water. After a few minutes on this heading Ayton requested a new and more direct course pretty much due west back to Coningsby. On this return leg they soon picked up the distinctive outline of the Elbe, and as they continued, searchlights and flak defences sprang up to the north west as a second Bomber Command attack on the port of Hamburg developed. To avoid meeting the attacking force head on, Bryce suggested a further south westerly diversion to pick up a familiar pinpoint over a lake west of Hanover.

With the lake in view the return flight was uneventful until the second pilot, Chantler, up in the mid-upper turret, watching for night fighters, called to report oil flowing back from the starboard nacelle across the wing upper surface. Bryce checked the oil and temperature gauges on the starboard Vulture, which were still normal and then looked out to see the heavy flow rippling in the slipstream. Immediately rechecking the engine instruments Bryce was dismayed to see that within those few seconds the oil pressure had dropped and the temperature had risen off the dial. Before he could alert the pilot there was a tremendous explosion in the engine and flames shot out to be carried behind like a fiery comet. Anderson noted these extended aft of his position at least two aircraft lengths. Ayton immediately hit the extinguisher button. Fortunately the fire died rapidly. The feathering mechanism had also remained undamaged, permitting the propeller blades to be turned edge-on to the airflow.

An interesting sidelight was that, arising probably from the vibration problems in the centre fin induced by rotating the mid-upper turrets, L7323 was flying this night with the turret unarmed, the squadron groundcrew had not had time to remove it in accordance with Bomber Command instructions.

Despite the immediate emergency receding, their situation was unpromising, the airspeed dropped to 110mph and from their height of 10,000ft they began a steady and inexorable descent. Bryce gave Ayton a course to the nearest point on the English coast at Cromer. A slight consolation arising from the sudden course change and loss in speed and height was that fresh bursts of flak began to explode above and to the right on their previous course.

There was initially little concern, by common consent they agreed that without the bomb load and with much of the fuel gone, as they descended the denser air would progressively provide more lift and they would make it. Ayton trimmed the aircraft so that it would lose the least height possible, all removable equipment, save for one Browning and 100 rounds in the rear turret was jettisoned, but their descent continued. They crossed the Dutch-German border and continued out over the Zuider Zee. Speed dropped almost to the stall and the aircraft kept yawing towards the dead engine. Ayton was fighting for every foot of altitude. They could have done without the dead weight of

the useless F.N.7A turret. They continued in this manner westward for about 15 minutes, the rev counter on the remaining port Vulture had packed up and the boost reading steady at +3lb.

When the altimeter reading reached 50ft, Ayton threw caution to the winds and rammed the throttle lever through the gate. The boost reading fell to -0.5lb and the glycol immediately began boiling out of the breather like frothing milk. The options exhausted, L7323 was set to descend right into the sea.

Manchester I of 207 Squadron at West Raynham on 6th June 1941 for inspection of examples of RAF aircraft by Prime Minister, Winston Churchill. Aircraft captain, at extreme right and half cut off, was Squadron Leader Charles Kydd. Crew, from the left: Nunn, Oliver, Goldstraw, Scott, Linklater plus three groundcrew. Note the retention of the old style, mid-fuselage, colour separation. Aircrew logbooks list this aircraft as L7310 or L7322. *No.207 Squadron archives / R Glynne-Owen*

They were low enough to determine that the sea was fairly smooth and unbroken by white caps. Ayton was fully occupied and it was Chantler, the second pilot, who called the front and rear gunners to the mid-section. Bryce went to the rest seat and strapped in whilst Chantler joined the gunners. Sykes, the wireless operator, was stationed behind the pilot with instructions to link his arms around him at the moment of impact.

Ayton dropped the flaps and cut the throttle, raising the nose as he did so, 'A-Apple's' tail made contact and rose again so that the next contact was nose down, accompanied by a violent deceleration. Bryce jack-knifed forwards across the lap strap and banged his head violently against the armour plated doors ahead. Coming round in a daze he heard screaming coming from aft. Anderson had left his ditching station to retrieve sandwiches and chocolate from the parachute rack by the rear spar and had been thrown violently forward by the impact, injuring his ribs. Ayton was also pitched forward, breaking an ankle and losing his boot in the process.

The aircraft settled quickly, but each man took up his assigned role. Ayton was soon standing in the escape hatch in the cockpit roof directing the release and inflation of the dinghy; astern the second wireless operator/air gunner was releasing the pigeons. Bryce called to the wireless operator in the cockpit to retrieve his navigation satchel which he had stuffed with maps, Very pistol and cartridges in anticipation of the ditching. However, it was immediately obvious that the satchel was already underwater and the Manchester was settling quickly. Ayton just had time to recover his parachute from the rack to use as a sail. A small wave broke across the mainplane and washed the slowly inflating dinghy into the sea. It was time to leave.

The crew scrambled out and hauled the dinghy alongside by its static line. They embarked, easing the groaning rear gunner in on top last of all. The next shock was the sudden appreciation that nobody knew how to release the static line or had given any thought till now to a knife. Here a minor and highly opportune miracle manifest itself because, when Bill Sykes thrust his hands into the Irvin jacket he had borrowed for the flight, he found a pen-knife placed there by its more thoughtful owner. With this they cast the dinghy adrift and were well clear when L7323 sank seven minutes after ditching close to 52°30'N 4°15'E, 22 miles west of Bergen am Zee at 0410 hours.

Next day Wing Commander Balsdon and Squadron Leader Stubbs carried out air sea rescue searches for Paddy Ayton and his crew, but they were searching well to the north along the briefed return route. Despite Sykes' best efforts, their SOS message was not received and it is likely the radio was

unserviceable. Having ditched early on Sunday morning the 13th May they remained at sea for four and a half days until they were seen and picked up by a group of small Dutch trawlers at about 1830 hours on Thursday 17th May and were landed early on Friday back at Ijmuiden and captivity.

In the long running battle with the Luftwaffe, the night had more or less belonged to the Manchesters. No. 97 Squadron's crews had evaded their assailants and gone on to complete their operations whilst Sergeant Oliver of 207 Squadron had claimed two night fighters shot down.

Again, on 12th May 1941, 5 Group called on 207 to operate its Manchesters, Squadron Leader Kydd was still acting commanding officer and the pace of operations remained feverish. Three aircraft were prepared for an operation to Mannheim. In the event it was an unsuccessful operation even by the Manchester's standards. L7310 failed to take-off due to unspecified unserviceability at the last moment.

Mannheim – 12th May 1941

Serial	Code	Sqn	Captain
L7310	EM-H	207	Unknown
L7322	EM-B	207	F/O W J Lewis
L7316	EM-U	207	F/O T C Murray

In L7316 Flying Officer Murray and crew had serious navigational problems partly due to thick ground haze over the Ruhr. Instead they diverted to Cologne where an aiming point (AP) was attacked from 16,000ft with six 1,000 lb GPs. These were seen to explode slightly north of the AP. Immediately prior to their arrival the crew witnessed and reported an enormous flash three miles east of the town.

'Mike' Lewis in L7322, a Manchester stripped of its F.N.7A, experienced another of the engine problems which plagued the squadron as he relates:

'On May 12th I acquired a new aircraft, L7322, which as far as I was concerned, was the best Manchester I ever flew and it became pretty well my personal aircraft until I completed my tour. However, it had its teething problems. On this night we set out for a raid on Mannheim, but by the time we got well south of Cologne, the starboard engine oil temperature rose to the danger mark, the pressure dropped and I was forced to drop my bomb load from 16,000ft on my alternate target, which was the railway station at Koblenz, and return to base. The arrival back at base was far more hair-raising than the operational trip in and out over enemy territory. We arrived back at base still with low oil pressure and the temperature in the starboard engine nearly off the clock, to find an intruder in the circuit. The flying control officer at Waddington refused to put on any lights whatsoever whereby I could carry

out a landing. The wind was in the east that night, which necessitated coming around to the west and turning over the village of Waddington, the airfield married quarters and landing towards the east.'

'Of course, of all the things that had to happen, the local air defence corps on the airfield operating one of their searchlights decided to illuminate me and having done so sat with the light on me for a considerable time, naturally providing a nice target for the intruder as well as blinding me. I could only get rid of the thing by firing off the colour of the day, which was a most undesirable act as the intruder would obviously see it and could possibly copy it.'

'I did a very tight circuit and used no lights until I arrived over the boundary of the airfield, at which time I turned on the landing lights and put L7322 down. As soon as I landed I turned the lights off again. I had no sooner accomplished this and was still braking on my landing run when the intruder laid down a stick of four bombs, about 400 yards to my starboard side and parallel with my heading. We ended up taxying to our dispersal using flashlights to find our way through the hedges. The searchlight crew were *persona non grata* for some time.'

Of the 105 aircraft dispatched not more than ten aircraft dropped their bombs within the city limits causing light damage and few casualties. However, 92 soldiers were killed in Cologne when a bomb hit their barracks.

On 13th and 14th May 207 Squadron was allowed a brief respite from operations. The only major flying reported by 207 Squadron on the 13th was that Flight Lieutenant Burton-Gyles visited the de Havilland factory at Hatfield to procure new washers for the constant speed units in the propellers of the aircraft. The precise reason for the change being necessary is not made clear but at about this date Flying Officer Nunn had a bad experience whilst engaged on a training flight in L7377 when the constant speed unit in one engine packed up. The engine promptly over-revved itself and on trying to feather the propeller Nunn found it moving instead to the fully fine position, resulting in excessive drag on one side. Fortunately Scampton was spotted just within reach and an emergency forced landing was successfully accomplished between the hangars. This was another serious fault with the aircraft, which further lowered the crews' confidence in the Manchesters.

On the 15th 207 Squadron found four Manchesters available and 97 Squadron a further four for a repeat operation to Berlin. Only 14 aircraft were detailed for this diversion to Berlin, whilst 101 aircraft raided Hanover. It was to prove the last operation for some weeks and was a disaster for the two squadrons. Some hundreds of personnel had spent thousands of hours to get just these eight aircraft serviceable.

Berlin – 15th May 1941

Serial	Code	Sqn	Captain
L7324	OF-*	97	F/L G O L Bird
L7306	OF-*	97	F/O J S Sherwood
L7374	OF-*	97	F/O C P D Price
L7383	OF-*	97	F/O H S Blakeman
L7322	EM-B	207	F/L P R Burton-Gyles
L7321	EM-D	207	F/O J L Nunn
L7393	EM-V	207	F/L G R Taylor
L7316	EM-U	207	F/O W G Gardiner

Following their take-off the first casualty was with 207 Squadron. Flying Officer Nunn, in L7321, which encountered engine trouble necessitating an early return after only one hour 35 minutes flying. When some 150 miles out Flying Officer Price lost power in his starboard engine, necessitating the bomb load being jettisoned. Fortunately he was able to return to Coningsby still nursing the failing starboard Vulture.

Flight Lieutenant Bird, was less fortunate. Several radio messages were received from the aircraft, the last an SOS message from a position about 20 miles off Borkum in the Frisian Isles timed at 2300. The message told its own story 'Starboard engine cut and the other giving trouble. Changing to Heston, please tell them'. The message was passed on and the squadron remained optimistic, but the hopes were misplaced. Bird and his crew were never heard of again and are presumed to have drowned in the North Sea, their final moments never to be established.

Next, as they laboured eastwards dragging L7393 up to the best altitude they could achieve, Flight Lieutenant Taylor and crew became sufficiently concerned about the high fuel consumption that they finally abandoned the attempt to reach the primary target and diverted to Hanover, where they dropped their six 1,000 lb bombs, but did not observe any of them to burst.

Most frustrating of all, in L7322 Burton-Gyles, having lugged his six 1,000 lb bombs all the way to Berlin, found the bomb doors jammed. Despite all his manoeuvres they would not budge. They had to be happy with jettisoning one package of NICKLES (propaganda leaflets) over Berlin before carrying the whole bomb load back to Waddington. In L7316 Gardiner located what he believed to be the Berlin area and dropped six 1,000 lb bombs from 16,000ft in what was reported as north Berlin, although the designated aiming point was not distinguishable. Sherwood and Blakeman completed their operations but without observing any results.

During the return flight the Manchesters ran into a severe electrical storm. For Flight Sergeant Bob Fletcher, the second pilot to Flight Lieutenant Sherwood in L7306, it was his first experience of St Elmo's fire. The leading edges of the mainplanes and other areas glowed as if red hot. Fork lightning danced from the propellers and gun barrels. Suddenly the static which had built up discharged with a terrific flash, temporarily blinding the entire crew. After what seemed an eternity the eyesight started to return and the two pilots slowly began to discern the instruments. The only damage was to the radio set which was put out of commission. Eventually they landed back at Coningsby almost on dry tanks after 7hr 15min in the air.

The whole raid was a dismal failure. In tying up so many trained servicemen it was difficult to see at this time that the Manchester was not more of a help to Germans and a hindrance to the British. Despite being in service for almost 7½ months the aircraft were of extremely limited usefulness and plagued by a multitude of most serious operational short-comings. Of the eight Manchesters dispatched, only three bombed Berlin, the remaining five having serviceability problems of varying degrees of seriousness.

Sergeant Harwood, possibly Flight Lieutenant Siebert, Flying Officer Ayton and now Flight Lieutenant Bird, all experienced second tour pilots, had all been lost in a few weeks due to engine failures. Despite the adoption of LA4 bearings it was clear that other equally serious problems remained to be cured. It had to stop.

On 16th May 1941 three aircraft were detailed by 207 Squadron for a raid on Hamburg, which was mercifully cancelled at 2030 hours. On the 17th, orders were once more received that Manchesters were to be withdrawn from operations for a second time, whilst intensive investigations were carried out to try to overcome the engine problems. Intensive test flights at full load were to begin immediately on a few selected aircraft.

On a sunny and clear late spring day on 18th May 1941, Squadron Leader Mackintosh embarked upon one of the earliest flights of this intensive test programme. L7393 was loaded with a full dummy bomb and fuel load and was to fly a three-legged cross country at maximum height to test the engines under the most arduous conditions. The route involved turning points at Land's End and the Isle of Man, starting and finishing at Waddington. The flight crew of six was supplemented by two or three additional aircrew along for a joy ride. No second pilot was carried. The aircraft climbed to a height of 16,000ft and the leg down to Land's End passed without incident.

Mackintosh turned north and set course across the Celtic Sea en route to the Isle of Man. They had reached perhaps 30 miles along this track, mid-way between Land's End and the Welsh coast, when a sudden rise in glycol temperature was noticed in the starboard Vulture. The engine rapidly overheated and caught fire. Mackintosh immediately turned off the fuel supply to the engine, feathered the propeller and hit the Graviner button. To their intense relief the fire died down and went out. Their plight was still acute because the bomber was heavily laden and its power reduced by half. L7393 began to lose height rapidly and Mackintosh executed a quick turn to port. A crew member went down into the nose to release the bomb load and decrease the all up weight.

The rate of descent was appreciably diminished but Mackintosh immediately set course for the nearest airfield, the small grass strip at Perranporth, only just large enough for its resident Spitfires. A radio call alerted the airfield and the ambulance and fire engine were deployed in anticipation of their arrival. Their inexorable descent continued, Perranporth could clearly be seen ahead. As they approached Mackintosh suddenly became aware that they were unlikely to clear the towering cliffs above which Perranporth was perched. He immediately commenced a flat turn to port whilst the crew rapidly dismantled the guns from the three turrets, ditching them and their ammunition from the various hatches. At the same time the bulk of the remaining fuel load was jettisoned. As they completed the turn Mackintosh headed in to Perranporth. There was no beach visible along the coast to either side. It was Perranporth or bust.

L7393 was now able to maintain its height and in a very flat circuit at low speed Mackintosh dragged the aircraft into its final approach. The flaps were only lowered partially to avoid increasing the descent rate and they crossed the cliff top with only a few feet in hand. As they rapidly gobbled up the available open space it became clear they would not stop within the airfield boundary. Accordingly, Mackintosh raised the undercarriage and dropped the aircraft on its belly in an attempt to stop. Earth, turf and sparks flew around them as they skidded first through the boundary hedge, crossed a road and went through another hedge into an adjacent field. After slithering a further 50–100 yards, their forward motion was diminished when the port wing hit a parked lorry and they slewed to the left before finally grinding to a halt.

The aircraft was still more or less intact but severely battered. By good fortune it did not catch fire and the crew, although badly shaken, were able to scramble out. Sergeant Nisbet was the only crew member with a significant injury, the rest being superficial and they were able to make their way to the ambulance which had come to a halt by the newly created gap in the hedge.

L7393 was a write off and L7280, flown by Flight Lieutenant Taylor, carrying Mr Walker and Mr Nicholson of Rolls-Royce was sent to Perranporth to make an early investigation of the faulty engine. It was decided that the starboard engine should be transported by road to the Rolls-Royce factory at Derby, where a complete strip down and detailed investigation could proceed.

Despite the almost terminal nature of the Vulture problems Manchester production was proceeding apace. In the week up to 5th May 1941 L7395, L7396, L7386 and L7398 were built, whilst R5770, R5771 and R5772 were in an advanced stage of assembly or delivered. By the 19th, deliveries in the previous week had included L7401, L7402, L7415, L7416 and L7417 whilst components for R5773 were arriving at the assembly shop at Ringway.

It was clear however that Rolls-Royce were beginning to come to terms with yet another potentially fatal engine problem, even though only a little over two weeks had elapsed since the Manchester was returned to operations, in that the 25th production meeting were advised that not only were Rolls-Royce 31 engines behind on their agreed Vulture delivery schedule, but also serious delays were being incurred by a further and fresh programme to change every single Vulture engine. The indications are that Rolls-Royce engineers, like the Avro workforce and the aircrews making Herculean efforts, had pinpointed and thought they had devised a solution for yet another Vulture problem. What was desperately needed now was a breathing space to manufacture modified parts and then yet again strip and rebuild every Vulture. Small wonder delivery schedules had slipped. For the immediate future no time was to be allocated. Miraculous though it may seem, other departments involved with the Manchester had made some progress and on 20th May all units received formal authority to increase the take-off weight of the Manchester to 47,000 lb.

On 21st May 1941 Wing Commander K Purdon Lewis finally took command of 207 Squadron from the acting CO, Squadron Leader Kydd, and that very day all aircraft were held on the ground so that the oil filters could be examined and for removal of the viscosity valves from the engines. It was established that every oil filter was unserviceable, being between 0.25in and 0.375in too short. The following day Kydd flew to Avro's Woodford factory and returned with 86 serviceable oil filters for immediate installation. Clearly, this was an Avro rather than a Rolls-Royce component. These filters and the viscosity valves were installed over the next day or so in all 207 and 97 Squadron aircraft and between the 23rd and the 25th all aircraft did war load climbs. This was a different and parallel problem clearly not requiring engine removal.

Despite the fact that Manchesters were officially grounded, in the next couple of days the urgency of the war situation necessitated all serviceable aircraft being kept available for immediate take-off with a load of 10x500lb semi-armour piercing (SAP) bombs. The *Bismarck* and the *Prinz Eugen* were out in the Atlantic and every possible aircraft was required to cover all conceivable contingencies. Fortunately the Manchesters were not required and on the afternoon of the 27th they were stood down completely.

On 29th May 1941, in pursuit of the pressing engine problems, Wing Commander Lewis, Flight Lieutenant McCabe and the 'resident' Rolls representative at Waddington visited the Rolls-Royce factory at Derby to inspect the engine of L7393, which had meanwhile been taken apart by the engineers. No definite reason for the failure seemed to be established at this stage and the party returned still with no satisfactory diagnosis of the problem.

The Manchester allocated to Rolls-Royce for engine investigations had itself crashed on 26th May in similar circumstances to L7393. Reg Kirlew, the Rolls-Royce test pilot, had already survived several emergency landings following Vulture failures in the Manchester. At 1420 hours on the 26th the starboard engine of L7295 caught fire and Kirlew attempted to land the aircraft at Tern Hill instead of simply abandoning the valuable test-bed with the evidence. One mile north of Tern Hill they ran out of altitude, the starboard wing and engine were torn off and thrown clear on impact with a large tree and the remainder of the aircraft burnt out. The pilot died and his three compatriots in the aircraft were injured.

Fortunately the vital damaged starboard engine remained for Rolls-Royce engineers to carry out their meticulous forensic examination. This showed that a similar failure to the one at Perranporth had occurred. By now four Manchesters had crashed in May alone due to engine failure. Those of Paddy Ayton and 'Golly' Bird of 97 Squadron were lost in the North Sea but the Vultures from Mackintosh's and Kirlew's aircraft were available. In a fifth Manchester, that of Derek Pinchbeck, an engine failure was the contributory factor in the loss.

With the Manchesters still grounded, a conference was held on 31st May 1941 to consider the engine failures. The conclusion of Rolls-Royce engineers was that the oil system was the primary cause. They concluded that the engine fires were secondary and resulted from overheating. The overheating was considered to be most likely due to the DTD (Director of Technical Development specification) 1094 oil used as a lubricant tending to gum up the pistons, leading to partial seizures and coolant leaks.

During a more prolonged investigation Rolls-Royce eventually discovered that the real reason was that oil was leaving the scavenge pump contaminated by air bubbles, which with the standard aircraft system did not disengage from the oil once it reached the main oil tanks. The restriction caused by the viscosity element of the viscosity valve was also found to promote aeration by further breaking up the air bubbles into smaller ones. The function of this valve was to bypass oil when it was cold so that it kept circulating through the engine until it warmed, when its flow was diverted through the oil coolers located in the wing leading edge, outboard of the engines.

The aeration leading to oil-pressure reductions, oil temperature rises and ultimately airlocking of the scavenge pumps was tackled in a range of ways. Firstly and importantly the oil pump was recognised as not being large enough. Rolls-Royce discovered that by replacing the existing Roloid gears with new Rolls gears the flow rate was improved by 50%. This required some opening up of the casings, the new gears featuring large tooth spaces and short pitch contacts to benefit capacity, but having only marginally greater diameter than the Roloid units.

Secondly, the aircraft oil scavenge line was re-engineered. A Vokes filter was installed before the oil cooler, whilst the original viscosity valve, with its aeration creating constriction, was replaced by a simple spring-loaded relief valve allowing freer passage of the oil.

The filter eliminated much of the aeration, evidently by causing the smaller bubbles passing through the filter felt to aggregate into larger bubbles, which were more easily disengaged from the oil once it reached the tank. Oil pressure was also substantially increased. After this prolonged investigation some of the more disconcerting attributes of the Vulture were overcome.

In addition to the crisis at 5 Group caused by the Manchester grounding, which had placed in abeyance the entire Manchester re-equipment programme, there was by now a crisis of a different nature at Avro. The combination of shortfall in Vulture deliveries, together with the current serviceability problem led to completed aircraft accumulating at the Woodford and Ringway factories to such an extent that both space considerations and the ever present threat of German attack were causing acute anxiety. Yet without serviceable engines how could the aircraft be dispersed?

Despite its gross inefficiency the course of action eventually taken, following agreement on 31st May, proved the best option. A small batch of special 'slave' engines, modified to the latest but still interim, Rolls-Royce standard were installed into the waiting aircraft in turn, permitting them to be more widely dispersed to such localities as Cranage and Tollerton. There the engines were removed and returned to Avro to permit other Manchesters to be steadily and slowly dispersed into storage. In only four short months 5 Group's and the aircrew's optimism for their new Manchesters had been dashed in a drastic manner.

On the first day of June, another Vulture on a 207 Squadron Manchester failed in the air. Flight Lieutenant Peter Burton-Gyles was gliding down from bombing height after a test flight in L7317 when a coolant leak in one engine led to overheating. He landed at Waddington before the engine finally seized. This was another permutation on the engine problems and investigation on this aspect was intensified, whilst the other problems were still under examination.

Next morning, the 2nd, yet another engine failure occurred, this time of a terminal nature. After starting L7318 at Waddington a con-rod went through the sump on the port engine, which then proceeded to catch fire. A large piece of the con-rod assembly buried itself in the ground between the fortuitously placed feet of Rex Nicholson, the resident Rolls-Royce representative. Fortunately quick action with an extinguisher saved the aircraft. This time a big-end bolt failure was suspected. Yet another fundamental Vulture problem was beginning to be appreciated.

Elsewhere on the aerodrome at Waddington and in the presence of Rolls-Royce engineers eight gallons of coolant was added to the suspect starboard engine of L7317, which had overheated the day before and the coolant system was then pressure tested. Extensive leaks were manifest at the bottom of the guard tubes and water drained from the sump. Unfortunately at the same period the thermostatic overflow valves fitted in the coolant header tanks of the Vultures also began to misbehave, the valve sticking in the open position and coolant being lost. In extreme cases engines would seize up.

Problems seemed to be occurring at a more rapid rate than could be investigated. It was a very depressing situation, with no indication that a realisation of the underlying problems had been isolated, or that effective action was being taken. Propellers, cooling, oil filters, oil and possible big-end failures, the engine problems seemed never ending.

Although the aircraft were still 'grounded' much test flying of modified Manchesters was still required. To give the crews something else to do whilst trundling around the sky for hours on end Bomber Command found two liaison exercises with the ground defences for them to participate in.

It seemed that Anti-Aircraft Command had become concerned that enemy aircraft may have been able to evade detection by feathering their engines and gliding down on their targets. Whether it was in the belief that the bombers could simply evade the outdated sound locators, or alternatively that the new ground-to-air radars then coming into use for directing the anti-aircraft batteries onto their targets would thus become less effective is not altogether established.

No. 207 Squadron was instructed to undertake a series of dummy silent approach attacks on Nottingham. This city had apparently been chosen as it was one of the first areas in central England to be issued with radar-guided guns.

Consequently on 4th June, Flight Lieutenant Burton-Gyles, Flight Sergeants Syrett and Houghton, accompanied by the squadron engineering officer, Flight Lieutenant Eric McCabe, and Mr Hook, undertook the first silent approach attack on the city in Manchester I L7377. The attack procedure involved climbing as high as the Manchester would reach, generally 18–19,000ft upwind of the target. The aircraft was then headed for the city and the engines stopped, both propellers were feathered, the stick pushed forward and the aircraft was to glide down across the 'target'.

This in itself was a hardly appropriate procedure in a Manchester, in that all the instruments were power-driven off the engines and so once these were shut down the blind flying instruments ceased operation. Uppermost in the minds of the Manchester crews was whether, having glided across the target to 20 miles beyond, there would be enough power left in the aircraft batteries to unfeather the propellers after such a lengthy time stopped.

On the 4th 'BG' glided down towards Nottingham, simulated a bomb run at 12,000ft culminating in Ken Houghton dropping a photoflash whose ignition was recorded on the ground, and carried on beyond the target to below 8,000ft. At 6,000ft he initiated the procedure to unfeather the propellers and restart the engines. The starboard engine started, but the propeller of the port Vulture steadfastly refused to unfeather. The aircraft would not maintain height on the one engine and it was clear they would not reach Waddington. They began looking for a very large field and, as they got even lower, any size of field. At this moment they came within sight of the flying training school at Harlaxton. Unannounced and with precious little height in hand they dumped the undercarriage and flaps and lobbed in over the hedge, crosswind. As they touched down Syrett saw several Airspeed Oxfords on their take-off runs crossing their paths from left to right. The Oxfords were on a collision course, but as they accelerated and the Manchester slowed the trainers passed under the nose, missing them by a mere 50ft. The crew breathed a sigh of relief at this close shave.

Inspection showed that a failure of the Gaco washer in the propeller feathering mechanism had caused the problem. This was an oil sealing washer fitted inside the propeller. When this ruptured, oil was prevented from reaching the right side of the operating mechanism which altered the pitch of the propeller. The silent approach trials went on until 12th June. Flying Officer Lewis and others participated in them, each being ever more nervous over the possibility of a propeller feathering failure.

At this time the German blitz was in full swing and desperate measures were being considered to combat the bombing, which was becoming ever more accurate. For the moment there was little that could be done to distract the German bomb aimers once the target finding radio beams were laid on. One of the precautions that Anti-Aircraft Command was considering at this time was large-scale smoke screens over British cities and other military targets, the idea being that once the authorities identified which target the beams were laid over they could ignite a large smoke making operation up-wind of the city and completely blanket the city with smoke.

To test the idea smoke screens were set up over several selected areas and on 10th and 12th June 'Mike' Lewis and other pilots carried out smoke screen recces over these areas. Quite how obscuring the target area would have made the target less visible to the radio beams is unclear, possibly it was hoped to obscure fires from incendiary bombs released by the pathfinders which the less experienced crews could otherwise home in on.

After this intensive series of trials the crews flew down to Hendon on 16th June 1941 for a conference at the Air Ministry regarding the effectiveness of the smoke screens and the silent approach attacks on Nottingham. The smoke screens were destined not to be implemented and presumably the Anti-Aircraft Command proved able to detect the Manchesters. The aircrews were no doubt most relieved that they were never required to employ the silent approach technique in an offensive fashion over occupied Europe. 'Mike' Lewis was no doubt able to give first hand experiences of the results of using similar techniques over Kiel.

On 16th June 1941, the Manchesters, which had only been allowed to carry out very limited flying, were completely grounded for modifications to the coolant, cabin heating systems and the thermostatic overflow valves.

Another suite of engine problems was being overcome but major difficulties still remained. Following the series of engine fires leading to the forced-landings at Perranporth, Tern Hill and elsewhere, and a prolonged enquiry into their causes, which entailed a number of false leads, the source was finally appreciated.

The sequence of failure was believed to stem from a combination of poor distribution of coolant through the cylinder blocks, exacerbated at times by leaks of coolant from a gland on the water pump. Overheating of the areas not adequately supplied with coolant led to piston seizure, followed fractionally later by con-rod failure. Very often prior to the seizure the cylinder liners got so hot that the liner-to-head seal was destroyed. The water/glycol coolant then entered the cylinder and produced the white smoke from the exhaust manifold so characteristic of this type of failure.

In the case of the Perranporth and Tern Hill crashes the con-rod failures were rapidly followed by engine fire, which in the case of the Tern Hill aircraft was sufficiently intense for the aluminium cylinder block to flare and burn.

To further improve coolant distribution locally within the crankcase it was also deemed necessary to fit baffles between the cylinder liners. These distributed the coolant more evenly within the cylinder blocks, especially around the sparking plugs and exhaust port areas. An internal baffle system was developed and tested but never incorporated into production engines.

At this same period in mid-June 1941 the opportunity was taken to modify the thermostatic valves in the coolant system. Leaks, lack of balancing pipes between the upper and lower banks of cylinders, uneven distribution and suspect thermostatic valves had all contributed to the severe cooling problems, the various inadequacies being difficult to isolate and overcome.

Mid-June 1941 represented a low-point in the fortunes of the Manchester, with worse to come until the eventual, but by no means ideal solution to the Vulture problems in early August. Perhaps surprisingly, the situation with respect to Handley Page Halifax and Short Stirling availability at this moment was worse. In Air Marshal Linnell's second weekly report on progress in clearing troubles with service aircraft on 18th June, a review undertaken two days earlier revealed that only 16 Halifaxes and 14 Stirlings were available for operations. In contrast, three squadrons of Manchesters, numbers unspecified, were available. On their return to operations a few days later, 207, 97 and 61 raised 18 serviceable Manchesters.

By 11th July, preserved records of the complete engine changing programme then found necessary, lists the total completed Manchesters at 94, disposed as follows:

Waddington	20	Burtonwood	2
Coningsby	12	Woodford	14
Hemswell	9	Ringway	9
Finningley	7	Bracebridge Heath	4
Boscombe Down	2	Cranage	7
Brize Norton	2	Tollerton	6

Avro had done well to achieve such an output in view of the many setbacks. Had Rolls-Royce had the capacity to overcome the Vulture problems, Bomber Command would have had a Manchester force of four to five squadrons at its disposal by this time.

The host of engine modifications and constant attempts at improvement created a bottleneck in component supply. Availability of Vulture spares was always a major problem, but with the spate of changes it became acute. Obtaining items through normal Rolls-Royce channels and Air Ministry bureaucracy would have introduced an unacceptable

delay and it is here, to his eternal credit, that the Rolls-Royce Service Engineer at Waddington, Rex Nicholson, became a key man in the Manchester serviceability story.

Being the Rolls-Royce 'rep' at the sharp end must have been an unenviable task, requiring a deep well of tact and diplomacy. The company had obviously chosen wisely. Nicholson had identified closely with the aircrew from the beginning. One of Nicholson's offices in Waddington's hangars became a veritable treasure trove of the latest spares, unobtainable through the RAF stores procedure. He maintained the stock by regular visits to the Derby and Ilkeston factories of Rolls-Royce, mostly in the dead of night, where various colleagues supported his clandestine activities in acquiring factory-fresh spares straight out of the back door of the company. As he has acknowledged, in any other circumstances he would have been charged with theft on a large scale.

The myth arose amongst the Engineering Officers of 207, 97 and 61 Squadrons that Nicholson had the power to perform miracles of no less magnitude than that of the loaves and fishes. This unorthodox short-circuiting of the spares supply route significantly eased some of the more critical shortages and gave the units at least a fighting chance of mounting operations on a limited scale.

By 20th June 1941, the modifications completed, the aircraft were air-tested during the day and declared available for operations once more. Nobody was to know, but 207 Squadron was facing one of the bitterest and most tragic days in the 18 month period it was to operate Manchesters, with the Germans no more than waiting in the wings.

Pilot Officer Les Syrett had already undertaken a number of operations with the experienced captains in the squadron, Flight Lieutenant Burton-Gyles, Squadron Leader Kydd and Flying Officer Nunn. The crew under training included Sergeants Jim Duncan, at that time a second wireless operator, 'Scotty' Scott, observer Ken Houghton, and rear gunner 'Eddy' Edmonds. On the 21st June Kydd was due to give Syrett his final dual check out. Syrett had asked the crew if they would be willing to operate with him if he was accepted and checked out as a first pilot. They agreed and during the morning Syrett visited the flight office asking if they would accompany him on the check out. It was a hectic morning, since it was already known that a maximum effort would be required from 207 and 97 Squadrons on their return to operations and that 61 Squadron was to undertake its first Manchester operation. Preparations for night flying tests and the multitude of tasks this entailed was in progress.

Several of the crew were missing, but Syrett buttonholed 'Eddy' Edmonds, who was living in Lincoln at the time and had already arranged to go home to lunch. He agreed that

if Syrett could delay the test, that after lunch he would rustle up the crew and they would accompany him during the afternoon. It would be their first ever flight with Syrett as captain. Thus agreed, they went their separate ways to make their plans.

Unfortunately it was not to be. 'Scotty' Scott had made himself scarce earlier in the day having been forewarned that a gas mask practice was to be held. Such practices entailed wearing the masks for an hour whilst carrying out normal duties. Scott abhorred such practices and accordingly was skulking in his room. He was, however, not essential to the air test.

Kydd was perhaps unable to delay the test until later in the afternoon and at 1300 hours Manchester L7310, Kydd's 'own' aircraft, was made ready for the check. In addition to the two pilots only the wireless operator, Sergeant Arnott, accompanied them.

Night flying tests were already in progress at Waddington and one of Kydd's closest friends, Flying Officer 'Pappy' Paape, a New Zealander, was already in the air carrying out the necessary check of all the systems in L7322. Sergeant Bill Wetherill was acting as wireless operator on that test.

The radio was switched so that the crews could talk to each other, as well as to the watch tower and Paape and his crew could both see L7310 lining up for take-off and hear the patter between Kydd and the flying control officer. Syrett was strapped in the left hand pilot's seat, Kydd was standing in the second pilot's position and Arnott was at the wireless operator's station.

They commenced their take-off run towards the south, parallel to the Sleaford Road, on the east side of Waddington aerodrome. The take-off took the aircraft between the old First World War hangars on the south side of the airfield and the bomb dump. L7310 became airborne about in line with the hangars and the bomb dump and had achieved perhaps 150ft above the boundary when the port engine failed. The problem was the usual, terminal one of complete disintegration, through causes not at that time established, which resulted in a piston coming right out through the side of the crankcase.

It was the single most critical moment of the whole flight. The port airscrew was immediately feathered. Paape saw a wisp of smoke and heard the clipped voice of Kydd 'Returning to base, engine failure'. Everyone looked on with bated breath as L7310 fought a battle for precious speed and height. Syrett had 10° of flap on and had retracted the undercart, but as the aircraft was only 5mph above stalling speed he could neither take-off the flap nor lower the wheels or even change course. The aircraft was descending almost as fast as it was going forward. Within seconds, Paape and all in radio contact heard Kydd's final transmission 'Losing

Looking forward inside the cockpit of a 61 Squadron Manchester. The second pilot's seat is stowed. *L Boot*

Looking forward inside the cockpit of a 61 Squadron Manchester. The second pilot's seat is stowed. *L Boot*

height, have to go down'. Paape, in helpless frustration, called into the radio 'Be careful, Charles'. It was not to be. L7310 had run out of options.

Syrett headed for a field which was guarded by a row of trees directly in his path. Unable to increase speed or climb to clear the trees, Syrett called to the other two to brace themselves.

The aircraft flew into and through the trees, stalling as it did so. It crashed heavily into the field beyond, where its forward motion was further checked by a grassy bank. The deceleration forces and impact were tremendous. They were on the east side of the Sleaford Road at Dunston Pillar.

Syrett did not lose consciousness but immediately after the impact saw that his left arm was broken, as it was bent the wrong way at the elbow. He found he could move his right arm and used it to move his left arm, cradling it in his lap.

Only seconds it seemed after the impact an ambulance came tearing across the field. It had apparently been on the nearby road, the crew saw the crash and simply turned in through the open gate. Miraculously the aircraft had not caught fire, but their situation was dire. Syrett felt very weak and detached and could hear Arnott yelling for morphia. There was no sound from Kydd.

Two soldiers had managed to climb in through a hole in the nose. Syrett instructed them to get the other two out first and give them morphia. Having extracted Kydd and Arnott the rescuers returned for Syrett.

Even after 45 years Syrett could recall his precise directions: 'My left arm's broken, something else too I think, I can't move. Undo these harness straps. No, don't take them right off. Take hold of each end and carry me out. Use it as a stretcher. Careful please I feel very fragile somehow'.

Syrett was grievously injured and in deep shock, his responses were detached and automatic and were not logically worked out in any way. He recalls asking how the others were and was told they were OK, as was he. Paape had landed immediately but was, like the rest, totally unable to help.

The three were loaded in the ambulance. Syrett has no further recollections beyond this until he came round in hospital with an army officer scrutinising his identity disc. The officer asked his home address and Syrett was able to give it. Suddenly, realising why it was required, Syrett shouted at the departing officer that he would break his neck if he sent

any alarming telegrams to his home.

Syrett had the feeling Kydd and Arnott were in the beds beside him, but within hours an ambulance arrived to move him from Bracebridge Heath to the larger Raunceby Hospital 40 miles away. Sadly Kydd and Arnott were beyond help and died shortly afterwards.

The whole squadron was shocked and depressed by the incident. Squadron Leader Kydd was the 'A' Flight commander, one of the most capable and experienced pilots in 207 Squadron and the main force in keeping the unit together when Wing Commander

Hyde was lost. Liked and greatly respected by everyone, there were never enough of his sort around.

The incident showed as well how random and blind was the hand of fate, a chance arrangement, unthinkingly made, had saved 'Eddy' Edmonds and others in the crew. The most inconsequential and commonplace decisions in wartime could spell the difference between life and a horrifying death.

The crew mourned and grieved the loss of their comrades and at the same time felt overwhelming bitterness and frustration at the waste and pointlessness of war.

Top: **Radio position of Manchester I R5786 of 61 Squadron.**

Centre: **Controls and instruments of a 61 Squadron Manchester. Note the second pilot's control yoke was directly connected to the captain's.**

Bottom: **Throttle box and instrument panel facing the pilot's seat, 61 Squadron aircraft.** *All L Boot*

Meanwhile at Waddington, Coningsby and Hemswell, despite the apparent evidence that the previous month of groundings had done little or nothing to cure the serious problems with the Vulture engines, preparations for their return to operations on 21st June continued. As a concession, 5 Group had given them only a shallow penetration attack on shipping and the docks at Boulogne on the occupied coast of France. A total of 18 Manchesters were allocated to Boulogne, by far the largest force assembled to date, and ten Wellingtons were to raid Dunkirk. Meanwhile, the main force bombers were divided, 68 being allocated to Cologne and 56 to Dusseldorf.

It was to be the 24th 207 Squadron operation with Manchesters and employed originally eight aircraft. The eighth, L7310 with Pilot Officer Syrett was the one missing – with good reason – when the Manchesters lined up. No. 61 Squadron had by now had some Manchesters on strength for almost four months and had witnessed their problems with increasing trepidation. Nevertheless a rising sense of expectation was apparent at Hemswell as six were prepared. Wing Commander Valentine, the commanding officer, and Squadron Leader Weir, the flight commander, had made themselves available.

Boulogne, the largest yet – 21st June 1941

Serial	Code	Sqn	Captain
L7387	QR-*	61	W/C G E Valentine
L7388	QR-*	61	S/L T C Weir
L7389	QR-*	61	F/O M Parry
L7307	QR-*	61	F/O G Hall
L7304	QR-*	61	F/O K G Webb
L7315	QR-*	61	F/L J L Riley
L7308	OF-*	97	S/L R D Stubbs
L7325	OF-*	97	F/L R A Fletcher
L7324	OF-*	97	F/L D J French
L7382	OF-*	97	F/O F E Eustace
L7383	OF-*	97	P/O H S Blakeman
L7316	EM-U	207	F/O D A A Romans
L7322	EM-B	207	F/O A M Paape
L7378	EM-A	207	F/O J L Nunn
L7311	EM-F	207	F/O W M R Smith
L7321	EM-D	207	F/O W J Lewis
L7312	EM-L	207	F/L R W Reynolds
L7314	EM-Y	207	F/O J D G Withers

On this occasion each 61 Squadron aircraft was limited to a load of 7,500 lb of 500 lb GP bombs. In keeping with their excitement, Flying Officer Parry had his port rev counter go unserviceable on starting engines, but elected to keep quiet about it and press on regardless.

No. 207 Squadron's Manchesters were loaded with 12 x 500 lb GP bombs and headed individually towards their target. The route was south past the west side of London before turning south eastwards to Boulogne. The operation began to go amiss from an early stage. Flying Officer Withers was outward bound on track at around 6,000ft. German intruders were active over Lincolnshire and one, which was being tracked by the Lincolnshire Air Observer Corps, by chance followed a course overlapping that of L7314.

No. 10 Group, Fighter Command, had scrambled a number of night fighters, including aircraft interception radar equipped Bristol Beaufighters from 25 Squadron at Wittering, to counter the threat posed by the German intruders. The controller at 10 Group was homing one of the Beaufighters along the presumed track of the intruder and when the two tracks closed the Beaufighter was mistakenly homed onto the track of L7314.

It appeared that in addition to this mischance another was to contribute to the events of the next few minutes. The 5 Group operations plan for that night, giving times and routes etc. had gone via Bomber Command to Fighter Command, arriving at 10 Group Headquarters just at the time of the change of controllers. The new controller had received the operations plan, but it had become covered by other papers on his desk and the details within it had not therefore been extracted and placed on the operations board. Consequently he had no information before him to indicate the presence of friendly aircraft at the vital location.

Accordingly, the controller homed the Beaufighter onto the 'hostile' until the pilot was able to obtain a visual on the aircraft ahead in the darkness. Squadron personnel believe that what happened next was that the Beaufighter pilot identified the aircraft as an RAF bomber and relayed this to the controller. The controller was unwilling to accept this identification. Cautiously the Beaufighter moved closer, recognising roundel markings and RAF squadron codes in pale letters on the fuselage. Clearly the bomber crew had also seen the Beaufighter for they fired off the correct colours of the day. This was passed to the ground station, where the controller still insisted the aircraft to be hostile and instructed the pilot to complete the interception and shoot the aircraft down.

Although in two minds, the Beaufighter pilot dropped back before finally closing in again and giving the Manchester, still flying slowly and straight and level, a burst with the fixed forward cannon and machine guns.

The Manchester was fatally hit and plunged to the ground at Wollaston, Northamptonshire, at 0155 hours. If not killed by the fire from the Beaufighter, the crew must have died instantly in the crash. The wreckage burnt fiercely and part of the bomb load exploded. Next day only traces of five separate bodies and the identity disc of Sergeant James, the second pilot, could be found in the burnt out wreckage. It was a tragic mistake which should never have happened and for which safeguards were in operation, yet under the stress of war such human errors were likely. Flying Officer Withers and crew had had only about 20 minutes of operational flying experience before being so brutally and mistakenly cut down.

Further on down the track, 207 Squadron's contribution was dogged by other unforced errors. As Flying Officer Mike Smith in L7311 approached the south coast, his front gunner inadvertently pulled the parachute ripcord. The silk spilled out all over the bomb aimer's station and billowed back into the pilot's cockpit in the many draughts streaming into the aircraft. The lower escape hatch was blocked by silk and rigging and there was the chance of the controls becoming fouled and jammed by the wayward cords and material. Wisely, Smith aborted the operation and returned to Waddington with the bomb load intact.

Over the target there was some interference from flak and searchlights but the remaining 207, 97 and 61 Squadron aircraft carried out the planned attack. On return, Flying Officer Romans diverted to Biggin Hill where, as he was landing, the starboard engine suddenly caught fire. The fire was fortunately extinguished, whether by Graviner or the station fire service is not recorded, before any serious damage was done to the aircraft or crew.

On examination next morning the fire was found to be caused by the 'banjo' fitting for the petrol gauge on the engine coming loose with the result that petrol dripped onto the hot exhaust pipes.

To crown a day of almost unmitigated disaster for the Manchesters, as Flight Lieutenant Sherwood was returning from Boulogne in L7325 the aircraft was intercepted by a Boulton Paul Defiant night fighter, also from Wittering. L7325 had reached a position 50 miles south of Coningsby at 4,000ft and the crew were letting down and making initial preparations for the landing. Suddenly, and without any warning, the aircraft was enveloped in a welter of machine gun ball and incendiary bullets rising up from almost directly underneath. The aircraft received many hits and the incendiaries also seemed to explode both above and beneath the aircraft. Initially the crew suspected anti-aircraft fire from the ground and there was great relief when soon after Bob Fletcher had fired off the colours of the day the firing ceased.

Sherwood quickly established that, miraculously it seemed, there were no injuries on board and none of the vital systems had been destroyed. Sherwood carried on to Coningsby with all haste, where he carried out a landing directly onto the flarepath without the usual circuit of the airfield. It was a wise precaution because the damage they had incurred immediately began to manifest itself. One engine failed as they approached the end of their landing run, and clouds of steam were rising from the pierced coolant system of the other Vulture. Hydraulic fluid was squirting from nicks in the hydraulic lines. In the circumstances they were very fortunate to have reached Coningsby at all on two failing engines and to have lowered the flaps and undercart with the remainder of the hydraulic pressure still in the system. They had no alternative but to stop on the flarepath and shut down the remaining engine, whose temperature had rapidly risen above the danger level. A tractor came to tow them back to dispersal. Next day they counted over 300 holes in the aircraft.

The Defiant crew were court martialled and Sherwood and his crew were called to Wittering to give evidence. It was here that they learnt the night fighter crew's side of the story. It had been a clear night over the United Kingdom and the patrolling aircraft had been warned that German intruders had already dropped bombs in several localities. The crew had detected a large aircraft and managed to infiltrate themselves directly beneath it without being seen. Whilst doing this they had called up their ground controller to enquire if any friendly aircraft were in the vicinity. On receiving a negative, they immediately opened fire, riddling the centre section of L7325. On seeing the colours of the day fired they broke off the attack and rechecked with the controller who belatedly recognised the aircraft as friendly. The crew of the Defiant got off with a severe reprimand as it was considered that the main fault lay with the ground controller.

The remaining aircraft returned to Waddington, Coningsby, and Hemswell landing between 0420 and 0535 hours. When the events of the last 24 hours filtered back, a mood of deep gloom and depression, mixed with intense frustration and anger settled on the squadrons. They had reached perhaps the lowest ebb in the whole difficult period over which they operated the Manchester. No. 61 Squadron crew, at least, had completed their first operation without any of the incidents which had marred the return of the two senior squadrons.

On the night of 23rd/24th June 1941 seven aircraft were detailed from 207 Squadron, taking off between 2328 and 2350 hours, and five from 61, taking off between 2314 and 2325, for operations to Dusseldorf. 'B' Flight of 61 Squadron dispatched five Handley Page Hampdens.

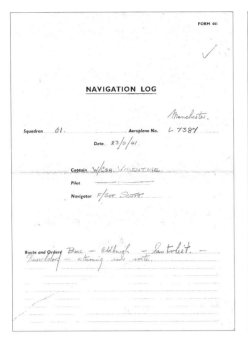

The Navigation Log (Form 441) reproduced above was completed by F/Sgt Scott, during an Operation which routed Hemswell - Aldburgh - Santoliet - Dusseldorf, returning same route, in L7387, on the night of 23/24th June 1941. The aircraft captain was Wing Commander G E Valentine, the 61 Squadron CO. Although there is no mention of engine trouble on this occasion, there was certainly drama. At 0143 hours the log reveals 'Ht 4,000ft, could not pin-point pos[itio]n, caught in searchlights, shooting them out' and at 0200 it indicates 'S/C [set course] 274. Front turret on fire, using extinguishers'.

The ticks and 'good log' comments are the work of Flight Lieutenant A B Harrison, the 61 Squadron navigation leader, confirming that Bomber Command was doing its best with methods then available, to achieve quality control on its operational flying. Ten weeks later both Wing Commander Valentine and Flight Lieutenant Harrison were lost with all on board L7388, when shot down over Berlin on the night of 2nd/3rd September.

The height profile for this entire operation – Hemswell-Dusseldorf and return – noted in column five of the centre page, ranged between 4,000 and 6,000ft. This, juxtaposed to such severe engine problems requires no further explanation.

The four page Form 441 document is itself interesting, on two counts. As expected, and in line with the economies of the time, it is printed on MF, a cheap mechanical woodpulp, yet its size (10⅞ x 8¼ in when folded) is a non-standard sub-division of the Imperial paper sizes then in use. It seems likely to have been printed several to view on double or quad 'Cap (Foolscap), but even this would have been bordering on the wasteful, and surprising for the times.

Minute details at the foot of page 4 (not reproduced here) show it to be part of a '1000M' (1 million) print order placed (by the HMSO?) in December 1939 with C P Ltd (Co-op Printers?). *Author's collection*

Dusseldorf – 23rd/24th June 1941

Serial	Code	Sqn	Captain
L7387	QR-*	61	W/C G E Valentine
L7388	QR-*	61	S/L T C Weir
L7389	QR-*	61	F/O M Parry
L7304	QR-*	61	F/O K G Webb
L7315	QR-*	61	F/L J L Riley
L7311	EM-F	207	F/O W M R Smith
L7378	EM-A	207	F/O J L Nunn
L7381	EM-R	207	F/O W G Gardiner
L7322	EM-B	207	P/O W S Herring
L7380	EM-W	207	P/O A W Hills
L7319	EM-X	207	F/O T C Murray

The usual severe lack of power for take-off was exaggerated even more this night by the high summer temperatures. Fortunately, all became airborne safely. These high temperatures led to overheating, power and performance losses and consequently the Manchesters were barely able to climb.

As a result of the overheating and the recent continued engine failures the pilots were naturally unwilling to 'cane' the engines for fear of further seizures. They avoided using full boost and 3,200 revs in the hope of nursing their aircraft to a height safe enough to permit a return to base from occupied Europe in the event of an engine failure. The deaths of the crews lost in the preceding months were too vivid and real to permit any other course.

Flying Officer Mike Smith was unable, despite his best endeavours, to lift L7311 above 7,000ft even though he had been airborne for 1½ hours. It would be suicidal to attack Dusseldorf from such a height and the chances of getting far if an overheated engine did finally fail were remote. Reluc-

tantly, but wisely, he unloaded his six 1,000lb GPs and 180 x 4lb incendiaries on the airfield at Flushing. Three other 207 Squadron Manchesters encountered the same problem to a serious extent. Flying Officer Murray in L7319 lightened the load by dropping a 1,000lb GP on Haamstede aerodrome in Holland. This permitted a climb to a safer height and he was then able to complete the attack on Dusseldorf. Flying Officer Herring, having used up some fuel, finally reached 10,000ft by the time he was in the target area.

Reports from only one 61 Squadron aircraft are available but as with the initial operation all returned safely. Flight Lieutenant Riley was unable to locate either the primary or any last resort target and brought his bombs back to Hemswell. Those reaching Dusseldorf returned to base between 0350 and 0518 hours. Nos. 207 and 97 Squadrons returned to Dusseldorf again the next night.

On the 26th, 207 and 97 Squadrons, along with 61 Squadron on its third operation, were off again, this time to Kiel, along with 51 aircraft to Cologne, and 44 to Dusseldorf. Again, 18 aircraft were involved. The eighth aircraft assigned to the operation from 207 Squadron burst a tail wheel tyre taxying for take-off and consequently was left behind when the remaining group departed in a bunch between 2310 and 2325 hours.

Over an hour after take-off, Coningsby received a desperate message from the wireless operator of Flying Officer Frankie Eustace's L7374, to the effect that the rear gunner, Sergeant McLaren had been killed by enemy fire. No further transmissions were received and it is known that the aircraft later crashed on the coast at Süderkoog in the German Frisian Isles with the loss of the seven man crew. One body was found washed up at nearby Westerhever.

German night fighters had become very active in the approaches to the German coastline at this time, possibly aided by ground radar tracking and one of these was indeed the assailant. Whether the final crash owed itself to damage incurred in the initial attack or from a subsequent engagement is not known.

Kiel – 26th June, 1941

Serial	Code	Sqn	Captain
L7387	QR-*	61	W/C G E Valentine
L7388	QR-*	61	S/L T C Weir
L7389	QR-*	61	F/O G Hall
L7304	QR-*	61	F/O K G Webb
L7315	QR-*	61	F/L I A Stewart
L7423	OF-*	97	S/L R D Stubbs
L7424	OF-*	97	F/L D J French
L7375	OF-*	97	F/O J A Little
L7374	OF-*	97	F/O F E Eustace
L7383	OF-*	97	P/O H S Blakeman
L7382	OF-*	97	F/Sgt D H Rowlands
L7312	EM-L	207	F/L R W Reynolds
L7378	EM-A	207	F/O J L Nunn
L7381	EM-R	207	F/O W G Gardiner
L7319	EM-X	207	F/O T C Murray
L7317	EM-C	207	F/L G R Taylor
L7322	EM-B	207	P/O W S Herring
L7311	EM-F	207	F/O W M R Smith

An anxious Coningsby awaited the return of the Manchesters and when it became undeniable that Frankie Eustace was the latest victim, many 5 Group aircrews were deeply saddened. Frankie was well known to many in 5 Group, who recalled the night he was over the North Sea returning from an 'op' in a Hampden when the windscreen suddenly shattered and flew back into his face, following a bird strike. Having no goggles, he flew for the remainder of the flight with the wind blasting straight into his face. His eyes looked like two raw hamburgers for a week after the incident. A great character, New Zealander Frankie was engaged to be married. Frankie's beautiful golden Cocker spaniel, Jill, was given to his grieving fiancé and his friends tried desperately to put this latest loss behind them.

Sergeant Rowlands was attacked by a Me 110 night fighter approaching the enemy coast approximately 30 miles west of Tonning. The aircraft was hit in several places and one crew member, Sergeant Harvey, received a slight head wound. By excellent co-ordination and effective fire control the crew were able to damage the attacker. Smoke was seen issuing from the enemy fighter which broke off the attack. L7382 then carried on to bomb Kiel successfully.

Flying Officer Little's aircraft, L7375, was heavily engaged by flak at its attacking height of 14–15,000ft. The aircraft was hit in many places but sustained no serious damage and returned to base.

No. 61 Squadron sustained its first operational casualty when L7304, piloted by Flying Officer Webb, crashed near the North Sea coast at Brunsbuttel in Germany. All the crew were killed and no details of how their aircraft met its fate have emerged. Possibly they were another victim of the rising menace of German night fighters.

Aircraft had no difficulty locating the target and the reports indicate the attacking aircraft reached heights ranging between 13,000ft and 16,000ft. None of the reports indicate any problem with climbing, perhaps because the air temperature had decreased. On the 26th, the attack was wide of the mark as the authorities reported slight damage and no casualties.

Few photographs of Manchesters serving with 97 Squadron have come to light, so this view of 'OF-Z' is a particular delight. There are two candidates for the identity of this machine; L7474 was 'OF-Z', but close scrutiny suggests this may be L7424 (no previously known code) lost with Flying Officer Little on 12/13th August 1941. *Wells via Vincent / Merrick*

Despite the occasional faltering morale arising from losses such as Flying Officer Eustace, spirits were generally high and it was necessary to curb the exuberance of individual crew members, who from time to time smuggled on board large quantities of house bricks or empty beer bottles. The bricks were reputed to be very effective when they fell in built-up areas, whilst the tumbling bottles produced a scream or wail like a siren as they fell.

Despite the personal interest this gave to individual crew members themselves, efforts had to be made to moderate the practice because the Manchesters were already so overloaded on take-off.

Following this operation, on 28th June 1941, 207 and 97 Squadrons received orders to commence daylight formation practice, including both formation bombing and gunnery practice. The objective of the training was to prepare them for participation in a major daylight operation against the *Gneisenau* in Brest and the *Scharnhorst* in La Pallice. In the event the attack took place on 24th July 1941 involving RAF Boeing (Flying) Fortresses, Hampdens, Wellingtons and Halifaxes. Although the *Gneisenau* was not damaged the *Scharnhorst* was hit by five AP bombs, three of which went straight through the ship. It was incapacitated for four months.

Flying Officer W Mike R Smith and Flight Lieutenant W J 'Mike' Lewis, close friends and pilots with 207 Squadron, in front of the mess at Waddington. Mike Smith was killed on his 50th 'op' on 12/13th August 1941 and 'Mike' Lewis failed to return from an operation on 7/8th September 1941, becoming a prisoner of war. *W J Lewis*

Finally, on 29/30th June 1941, 207 Squadron took part in its last operation for this period. Eight aircraft were detailed for a raid on Hamburg, joining a diversionary force which totalled 28 aircraft. The main raid went to Bremen, with 106 aircraft. In the event, only six Manchesters took off since one burst a tail wheel tyre taxying out, the third time such a problem had occurred, whilst another developed electrical trouble which could not be cured in time for the aircraft to participate. It was to be another eventful operation for the squadron, although, as with so many times before, the Germans had no part to play in the difficulties experienced. Two aircraft carried 4,000 lb HC bombs whilst the remainder carried five 1,000 lb GPs. They took off between 2300 and 2326 hours.

Hamburg – 29/30th June 1941

Serial	Code	Sqn	Captain
L7319	EM-X	207	F/L T C Murray
L7316	EM-U	207	P/O A W Hills
L7321	EM-D	207	F/O W J Lewis
L7381	EM-R	207	F/O W G Gardiner
L7322	EM-B	207	F/L R W Reynolds
L7373	EM-T	207	P/O H G Keartland

Of the six which proceeded, one, L7316 'EM-U', flown by Pilot Officer Bill Hills, with Pilot Officer Bowes-Cavanagh (second pilot), Sergeants Glenn (observer), Smith (first wireless operator), van Puyenbroek (front gunner) and Spindler (rear gunner), was gaining height painfully slowly as usual as they crossed the North Sea en route to the target. By the time they had reached a position 40 miles north of Terschelling they had still only reached 5,000ft.

Suddenly, Bowes-Cavanagh gestured with his hand towards the starboard engine and called Hills on the intercom. 'Do you see what I see?' Craning his neck and looking across the second pilot, Hills saw that the starboard engine was on fire. The flames were already shooting back over the engine nacelle and upper surface of the mainplane.

The nervous tension rose to fever pitch, things had to, and did, happen quickly. 'Jettison bombs,' called Hills and the navigator, Glenn, rushed forward to the bomb aiming position in the nose to rid them of the load, which would otherwise rapidly bring them down to ditch in the sea on the one remaining engine. Before further action was initiated though, the most immediate problem was the fire.

'Feather starboard propeller', called Hills, at the same time reaching out to cover the port propeller feathering switch to prevent it being inadvertently feathered in the dimly lit cockpit. His action was both seen and misinterpreted by an agitated Bowes-Cavanagh, who immediately reached across and knocked Hills' hand away, calling 'Not that one'. Bowes-Cavanagh then feathered the starboard propeller, stopped the engine, and pressed the fire extinguisher. The propeller feathered and began to windmill slowly and at about the same time they felt the pronounced lift as the bombs fell away safe from the open bays.

'Parachutes', shouted Bowes-Cavanagh on the intercom, beginning to leave his seat. Obviously he was convinced that the fire was not going to be extinguished and that perhaps only seconds remained before the wing spar burnt through.

'No, you fool', called Hills, 'it's a bloody long swim from here.' Bowes-Cavanagh resumed his seat, Glenn closed the bomb doors and both pilots continued to watch the burning engine. In accordance with standing orders related to action in the event of engine failure, Charles 'Smudger' Smith, the wireless operator, hurried to send the specially abbreviated code which had been worked out so that group could be informed of the reason for an aircraft going down. The aircraft began to lose height but within a short period they were relieved to see the fire first die down and then go out altogether. Hills immediately began a gentle turn to port into the live engine and requested a course for the nearest point on the English coast.

Whilst Glenn worked out the best course Hills trimmed the aircraft to conserve every precious foot of altitude. Despite his best efforts the aircraft continued to lose height. The urgency of the initial emergency was over, but the tension remained high and the crew sat with bated breath as the Manchester descended almost imperceptibly towards the English coast. After many minutes flying, a comparison of height and distance travelled made it clear that, provided the port engine maintained power, there was a chance that the coast would be reached before they ran out of airspace.

The Manchester could only make 120 knots on one engine and was now flying into a headwind. It was a long and tense flight, the only conversation being the regular checking of height loss versus distance remaining. Eventually the British coast appeared ahead, but another difficult decision now faced Hills. The aircraft was continuing to lose height despite everything he did to trim the aircraft and use the best engine settings. They were already below 2,000ft and could not be sure they would reach base. Hills knew that 1,000ft, which they would soon be down to, was a crucial height at which they must either be within certain contact with an airfield, otherwise he would have to bale the crew out. If he waited until they were lower there was a strong chance they would not all escape from the aircraft in time.

Hills informed the crew that he was going to restart the starboard engine in the hope of gaining more altitude. This was risky, normally an engine which had been on fire would never be restarted because the chances of the fire flaring up again were so high. Hills judged that if the crew were all ready to jump there was no significant additional risk, for at their present sink-rate they would all be in their parachutes within a few minutes anyway.

Having prepared the crew, the restart procedure was initiated. To their mingled surprise and relief the engine restarted and did not catch fire. Hills advanced the starboard throttle up to that of the port engine and was able to climb for the first time since the fire. Keeping a careful eye on the starboard Vulture, they ascended to a safe height, at which point he then throttled back. Immediately, and for no apparent reason, the starboard engine stopped and subsequently resisted all attempts to restart it a second time. Nevertheless, the engine had done what was required of it and they now had precious altitude in hand. Hills feathered the dead starboard engine, and having called Waddington to tell them he was coming in on one, carried out a safe landing back at base. In respect of this incident the squadron Operational Record Book notes 'Left [inner?] starboard engine manifold was found to have a large hole through which flames played on the engine cowling'.

A second aircraft, L7322 'EM-B', captained by Flight Lieutenant Reynolds, reached the target area where the crew found, as so often happened in the Manchester, that a hydraulic leak had developed which prevented the bomb doors opening. Despite their best efforts they were unable to open the doors manually and they reluctantly and disconsolately returned to Waddington with all of the bombs still on board.

The remaining four aircraft eventually fought their way up to altitudes ranging between 14,000ft and 16,000ft to drop their bombs on the target area. They returned to Waddington and landed between 0430 and 0530 hours on 30th June 1941. The part played by these four cannot be ascertained but Hamburg reports chronicle much damage on this small raid, with eight killed and 115 injured. A large fire destroyed a big stockpile of rice in a foodstore. Three bombers were shot down by night fighters over the town, the crash of one of these possibly caused the fire in the rice store.

On 30th June the Manchesters were grounded yet again. They had been operational for only eight days since the previous 4½ weeks grounding. This time they were off operations for five weeks but the final serious problem with the filter was cured to the extent that was possible. Problems with the Vulture were so varied and multifaceted that they overlapped in time. Whilst the cooling problems had finally begun to be solved, a new and equally serious defect had started to make its presence felt.

First of all the engine from Squadron Leader Kydd's aircraft was inspected and the failure which led to this crash found to be a 'red herring', in the search for the continued Vulture problems, although a no less fatal one. A loose tappet nut had led to a valve blockage and then in turn induced a complete engine failure. In direct line with the spate of most recent accidents the port engine of L7318 of 207 Squadron which failed during ground running on 2nd June had been received and inspected by the Defect Investigation Department of Rolls-Royce at Derby. Initial inspection suggested that the two short big-end bolts had sheared.

On 29th June 1941 L7315 of 61 Squadron had an uncontrollable engine fire causing the crew to bale out near Grantham. The aircraft crashed and was written off, killing the pilot, Pilot Officer C G Colborne. This fire was also tied to the same con-rod bolts failing. Next, L7389 'QR-J' of 61 Squadron had an engine fire in the air and force-landed in a wheat field near Fowlmere. There were no casualties on this occasion. This engine failure too was traced to a similar con-rod bolt failure.

Following such bolt failures the unrestrained con-rods would then flail around, break loose and smash through the crankcase, sometimes almost severing the engine in two. Even worse, such catastrophic dam-

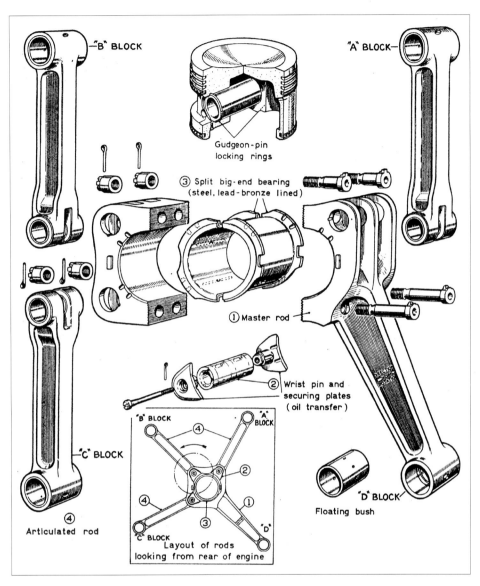

age frequently destroyed the propeller feathering line, with the result that the dead engine's propeller could not be feathered. The drag from the windmilling blades, plus the loss of 50% of the total engine power, was too much and the remaining engine could not keep the aircraft airborne. Following the 30th June grounding it was decided that four aircraft each from 61, 97 and 207 Squadrons were to carry out intensive flying to investigate the problem.

Manchester L7427 of 97 Squadron force-landed on or before 3rd July 1941. No-one was injured but con-rod bolt failure was to blame. By 6th July the number of aircraft had been reduced to one per unit to fly until 240 hours had been achieved on all engines.

During June, the Defect Investigation Department of Rolls-Royce had become aware that the cause of the bolt failures was uneven and, in some cases, excessive tightening of the bolts. Lovesay, the Chief Development Engineer, had the bolt loads at maximum rpm recalculated, which showed them to be higher than was thought. Mean-

Heart of the Vulture's problems, the main big-end bearing and star rod design. The diagonal split line between the master rod and cap and the unequal length con-rod bolts are shown to advantage. *Taken from AP.1801A, Volume I, Rolls-Royce Vulture.*

while, the engines of every Manchester had to be removed once more and returned to Rolls-Royce, who were to issue replacement engines with new con-rod bolts, which were now to be tightened to a lower and carefully monitored value to ensure the precise degree of stretch required to give adequate bolt tension.

A second contributory factor to bolt failures was considered to be a conflict between the saw-tooth location in the master con-rod and cap, and the fitting diameter of the bolts. The powerful control of the saw-teeth tended to dog-leg the connecting rod bolts, affecting their tension. Rolls-Royce rectified this as Modification No. 44 and it was to be the modification following which the engines finally became reliable.

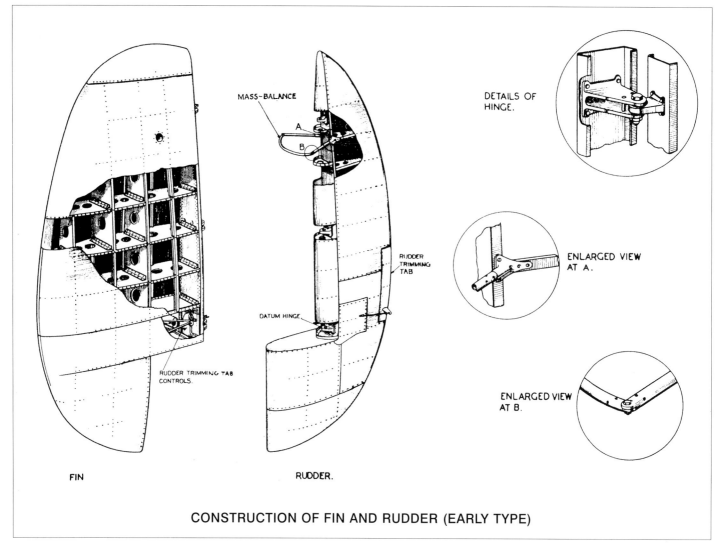

MASS~BALANCE

DETAILS OF
HINGE.

RUDDER
TRIMMING
TAB

ENLARGED VIEW
AT A.

DATUM HINGE

RUDDER TRIMMING TAB
CONTROLS.

ENLARGED VIEW
AT B.

FIN   RUDDER.

CONSTRUCTION OF FIN AND RUDDER (EARLY TYPE)

A contributory factor to the excessive strain on the single bearing imposed by the four con-rods was the high loading at 3,200rpm. Accordingly, as part of Mod No. 44 and to protect the short con-rod bolts, the maximum rpm was reduced to 2,850, giving the suggestion of de-rating. At the same time, however, the boost pressure was increased to 9lb, effectively restoring take-off power, so the derating referred only to rpm and not to power. The combination of modified tightening techniques, relieved fitting diameters and reduced rpm produced a reliable operation at overhaul lives initially of 120 hours, subsequently rising to 180 hours. An added bonus to this change was that the engine actually operated better at this rating and gave a little more power and shorter take-off run.

During June, whilst Rolls-Royce strove so doggedly to track down the range of serious defects still popping up in the Vulture, Avro had opportunity to consolidate their efforts. By the 10th all F.N.7A mid-upper turrets had been shorn from service aircraft, whilst consideration was given to overcoming the rotation/vibration interaction of the turret and centre fin. By 27th June all the options had

been evaluated. Both Bomber Command and Avro had recognised that the centre fin could not be strengthened and the only option was to bring in the final tail modification, the deletion of the three fins and their replacement with two new 'Lancaster' end-plate fins and rudders of larger area. This was Avro Mod No. 390. The only drawback was that this modification would not be available until mid-July at the earliest. It was agreed to bring this modification in at the earliest moment on the production line and also provide additional sets to retrofit existing aircraft as and when possible.

Accordingly, permission was given to refit the F.N.7A, but to restrict its arc of traverse. The principle reason for re-introducing the F.N.7A was that it offered the only beam defence for the aircraft. Groundcrews and armourers set-to once more. Notwithstanding this instruction some Manchesters which had never had this item fitted continued without it (eg. L7300), others which had been temporarily stripped had the item re-instated and yet others, like L7309 which had not previously carried the turret, now had it installed. Aircrew preference and pressure of

Above and right : **The summer of 1941 also saw approval given to build from-new Manchesters with the enlarged 'Lancaster' fin and rudder and the modification in the field, where practical, of others in the operational fleet.**
Taken from A.P.1600A, Avro Manchester.

other modifications and normal routine maintenance seem to have influenced the situation.

At the 27th Manchester production meeting on 9th June 1941, aircraft completed and the serious state of the engine delivery and modification programme were stressed. By the next meeting, on 14th June, Manchesters L7427 to L7430 had been completed whilst R5772 to R5774 were being erected. The firm were 32 engines short for new construction and the state of flux in respect of the engine modification was causing further disruption. On 18th June A M Linnell reported that Rolls-Royce were 96 Vultures behind the initially projected schedule but some good news was that the company had promised 18 modified engines per week for the next three weeks. The running to ground of the con-rod bolt failure further delayed this programme.

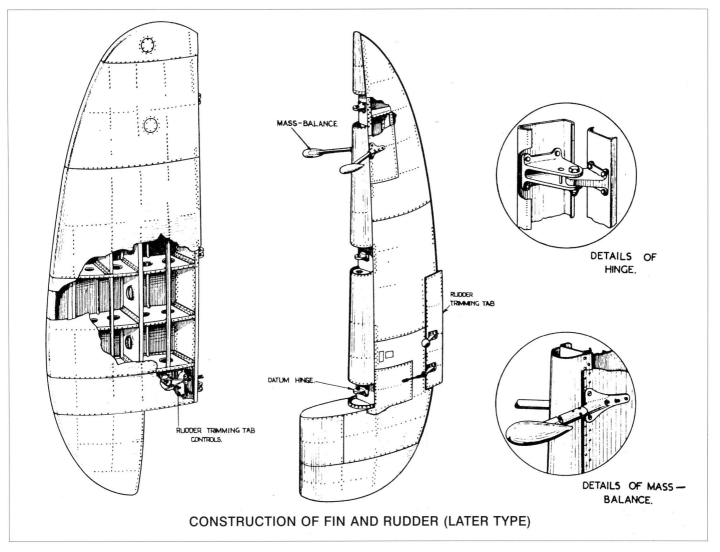

MASS-BALANCE

RUDDER TRIMMING TAB

DATUM HINGE.

RUDDER TRIMMING TAB CONTROLS.

DETAILS OF HINGE.

DETAILS OF MASS — BALANCE.

CONSTRUCTION OF FIN AND RUDDER (LATER TYPE)

In the meantime, during late May and June and possibly arising from the increasing threat of the German night fighter force, Bomber Command was reviewing crew policy on the Manchester. By 27th June a decision had been made to raise the complement by one to make seven man crews. Within days the policy was promulgated, requiring every turret to be permanently manned, whilst a wireless operator had to be continuously on watch. There were to be two pilots, an observer to do the navigating and bomb aiming, a wireless operator/gunner in the radio position and a second in the front gun turret. Two air gunners were to man the dorsal and rear turrets.

This was in line with the planned refitting of the F.N.7A 'Botha' turret, but conceivably more lay behind it. Possibly Bomber Command was still hoping to make use of the Manchester in daylight because Avro had been asked to reconsider the possibility of designing a retractable and hand-held gun mounting for a pair of Brownings in the vacant mid-under position. In an apparent conflict with the new policy it was suggested that these could be manned as necessary by

the first wireless operator/air gunner. In the event crew complement was increased by one, to further reduce the already marginal performance of the beleaguered aircraft. The hand-held mid-under assembly never materialised, which was probably just as well.

On 12/13th July 1941, engines incorporating Mod No. 44 were received, one each day, at Waddington for 207 Squadron's intensive flying Manchester, L7419. No.97 Squadron contributed L7425 and 61 Squadron L7388.

At the same time as the aircraft was grounded, Avro attempted to effect a further modification to improve the persistent problem with oil cooling in the Vulture. The modification was to the oil cooler ducting and involved a technique for improving airflow through the system. This entailed placing a lip in front of the exit duct on the upper surface of the wing, outboard of the engine. The purpose of the lip was to increase the air flow through the system and increase cooling.

In mid-July, from the 17th onwards, three crews in each of the three squadrons were taken off operations for a week to take turns to fly five hours per day in their designated

aircraft, each trip included a climb to 17,000ft at +6 boost and 2,850rpm.

In the meantime, again anticipating success, from 19th July onwards the installation of new engines in all squadron Manchesters commenced.

Rolls-Royce delivered 16 Vultures to Waddington by 19th July, eleven incorporating both LA4 bearings and a Mod 44 con-rod assembly. Sixteen were delivered to Coningsby by 26th July, 18 more for 207 Squadron at Waddington by 2nd August, together with 12 for 25 Operational Training Unit at Finningley. Finally, four were delivered to Hemswell for the Manchester Flight of 61 Squadron by 9th August. To permit this flow rate the squadrons had to return Vultures from their aircraft at a rate of four a day from 16th July.

On 28th July the engines of L7419, having flown 120½ hours in nine days were removed and dispatched to Rolls-Royce for dismantling and investigation. The engines of the 97 Squadron aircraft were similarly sent away. Following feverish stripping and inspection the engines were reassembled and the fleet of Manchester aircraft in 5 Group were declared fit for operations once more.

Night fighter's eye view of the elegant proportions of the Allies' largest twin engined bomber. It is not possible to distinguish the Mk.I and Mk.IA from this aspect.
J Simpson

Nobody could have known it at the time, but Mod 44 was to prove the final key to the Vulture becoming a reasonably reliable engine. Further problems were to occur, especially a spate of propeller feathering failures, but these were not Rolls-Royce problems. In respect of the Avro cooling lip modification, the effect was by no means as satisfactory, as will be apparent later. So, in mid-summer, the Manchesters returned to operations.

Up to this time the engine had experienced four major and a host of minor problems. The major problems involved the bearings, the oil system, the coolant system and the con-rod bolts. Not only the bearings themselves, but also the other three problems had a direct effect upon the bearings too, with the result that failures of quite different origins led to similar types of damage to the engine.

A major associated consequence already alluded to, which greatly exacerbated even these very terminal failures, was that on occasions the liberated con-rods would sever the line to the feathering mechanism leaving the dead engine windmilling at fine pitch and greatly increasing the drag.

During this grounding, between the end of June and 7th August, different contingency plans were made for the aircrews. With the Manchesters stood down, they were to be temporarily seconded to nearby Hampden squadrons to carry on operating. Later the squadrons were temporarily issued with a number of Hampdens and carried on operating using these aircraft for a while. What was in fact a retrograde step must have seemed like a deliverance.

In June New Zealander Flying Officer 'Pappy' Paape had been posted on to 61 to assist them working up their Manchesters to operational status. Paape did not survive the war. Flying Officer Dave Romans, the Canadian, was posted on, having participated in his last operation with 207 Squadron on 21st June 1941. Romans was killed soon afterwards, on 8th September 1941, flying an RAF Fortress I in daylight with 90 Squadron, when he was attacked by two Messerschmitt Me109 fighters and crashed, in Norway.

Despite not being able to do anything about the fundamental underpowering of the Manchester there was some glimmer of hope that engine reliability would at last be improved from the catastrophic low experienced between 13th April and 7th August. In almost four months 207 Squadron's Manchesters had attempted a mere 61 operational Manchester sorties, whilst 97 and 61 had attempted 38 and 16 respectively.

Many crews were feeling that just to get the aircraft in the air deserved a medal. Yet during the seven months 207 Squadron had flown its Manchesters the crews had received precious little recognition in the form of decorations. The Stirlings and Halifaxes were, in contrast, going from strength to strength in both day and night operations and their crews were the 'glamour boys' of Bomber Command. As usual with human endeavour, recognition, praise and awards went hand in hand with achievement and no honour attended determination, application and effort. Many directly involved felt it took considerably more courage and bravery to fly over occupied Europe in their Manchesters than in either of the four engined 'heavies'. The crews were distinguished from the rest of the aircrews of Bomber Command by their continual operation in a totally unreliable aircraft.

Compared to watching the oil temperature and pressure continually fluctuating and rising so close to, and at times past, the danger mark, the dangers presented by the Germans often seemed modest and certainly short lived in proportion. There was little in wartime to compare with the sweet torture of perpetually speculating on which system was going to fail first. Perhaps the nearest comparable situation was the crews in the Atlantic convoys spending days at a time wondering with every beat of the engines whether a German torpedo was coming through the ships plates to join them. The crews of the Manchester squadrons were the forgotten airmen, feeling the RAF was as ashamed of them as it was embarrassed and humiliated by the continual disappointments they had encountered with the aircraft in their charge.

By this time 5 Group had drastically revised its schedule for re-equipping its squadrons with Manchesters. After 97 Squadron received its first Manchesters on 27th February 1941 and 61 its initial complement early in March, no further squadrons had been converted. Indeed 61 never had more than ten Manchesters on strength until October. Nos. 207, 97 and 61 had spent much of their time grounded and non-effective. The remaining 5 Group squadrons soldiered on with their obsolescent Hampdens. A decision had long ago been made to transfer all Manchester orders to Lancasters.

With Manchesters returning to operations, Avro could concentrate on the remaining aircraft on order as well as tooling up for Lancaster production. For Rolls-Royce, effort on the Vulture was soon to terminate almost completely. In the case of the groundings, 207 Squadron engineering personnel in particular had put in a magnificent effort. Wilfred Freeman, Vice Chief of the Air Staff at Air Ministry, had recognised the tremendous dedication of the squadron, writing to Air Vice-Marshal Jack Slessor the Air Officer Commanding 5 Group on 1st August 1941 to commend him on the 249 hours 25 minutes of flying the Manchesters of the three squadrons had achieved in such a short period of time. In turn, Slessor passed on these commendations to Group Captain Boothman, the officer commanding RAF Waddington, conveyed these commendations, with his own praise and thanks to Wing Commander Purdon Lewis, adding the rider that the main bouquet was due to Eric McCabe and his engineers, as their aircraft had achieved 120 hours of the total 249 flown.

The Manchester crews could not have realised that the period June and July 1941 also represented one of the all time low points in the fortunes of the whole of Bomber Command. Before war commenced the Air Staff had calculated that the average expected bomb aiming error in daylight would be 300 yards. By 1940 this was, in some unexplained manner, transformed into an expectation for night bombing too. A pious hope.

During 1940, photo-reconnaissance showed little evidence of damage to targets reportedly heavily attacked. Similarly, reports filtering back from occupied Europe were at odds with the claims of returning bomber crews. There was apparently a gulf between what Bomber Command was achieving and that which a superficial assessment and the propaganda it led to claimed. Quite how large was the gulf was soon to be made clear.

By April 1941 Air Staff studies for night bombing revised the average aiming error for moonlight from 300 yards up to 1,000 yards. An Air Staff directive of 9th July 1941 indicated that this implied that precision targets, such as transportation systems and the oil industry, could thus be attacked on a quarter of the nights of any month, with large working class and industrial areas allocated for the remaining three quarters of any month.

No. 207 Squadron 'A' Flight commander, Acting Squadron Leader G R 'Dicky' Taylor. He was killed on his 47th 'op', to Berlin, on 12/13th August 1941. *via M B Taylor*

Squadron Leader Charles Kydd's crew being debriefed. *No. 207 Squadron archives / R Glynne Owen*

Throughout the winter of 1940-41 and on into spring 1941. Prime Minister Winston Churchill had followed the progress of the bombing offensive. He was aware of its shortcomings, especially in its inability to do effective damage even against the invasion barges in the channel ports. Lord Cherwell (Professor Lindeman), Churchill's scientific advisor, shared his concern. To allow an independent and objective assessment of the problem, Lindeman had arranged for cameras to be made available for installation in RAF night bombers. By use of a photoflash dropped with the bomb load and timed to ignite at the instant the shutter in the camera opened, the intention was to photograph the ground in the area where the bombs had fallen. Subsequent photo interpretation was used to identify the spot and relate this position to the designated aiming point.

An intensive bombing survey campaign using this technique was mounted in June and July 1941, the resulting material generated being passed to Lindeman's secretary, D M B Butt. Having analysed the data, Butt published his results in early August 1941 in what became known as 'The Butt Report'. Its findings were devastating. Butt had analysed the photographs from 6,105 sorties undertaken mainly to the French ports and the Ruhr area of Germany. He found that close to a third of sorties dispatched had failed to attack the designated primary. He therefore concentrated his analyses on the two thirds which reported they had attacked the primary target. Dividing these sorties by target area, he found that only one third of sorties to French coastal targets came within five miles of the aiming point. Against targets in the Ruhr the statistics were even worse, with only a tenth of sorties claiming to have hit the primary actually plotted within five miles of the aiming point. Reduced to easier terms, of every

100 aircraft dispatched only 22 bombed within five miles on French targets and a mere 6.6 over the Ruhr.

The report had an immediate effect upon Churchill and an initially incredulous Air Staff. The implication was that for deeper penetration operations the statistics may be even worse, although the persistent industrial smog blanketing the Ruhr was a significant factor in the difficulty of identifying such targets.

Divided up using different criteria, Butt showed that on moonlight nights two crews in five came within five miles of the aiming point whereas on moonless nights the ratio fell to 1 in 15. At the very moment when perceptive airmen, aware of the intensified German night fighter capability, already foresaw the end of bombing operations in bright moonlight, the Butt Report found their capability for moonless nights to be negligible. Submission of the Butt Report thus signalled the low water mark in the fortunes of Bomber Command.

When Professor Blackett, writing on 18th February 1942, made his assessment of Bomber Command's achievements in terms of German casualties he reported that during the entire previous year the British bomber force had been killing Germans at about the same rate that the German defences were killing highly trained British aircrew. It was a dismal outcome for all the efforts.

For the very first time it was starkly clear that Bomber Command had not yet reached the stage of having a bomb aiming problem, as the over-riding navigation problem prevented the aircraft reaching the target area in the first place. The report was to lead Air Vice-Marshal Saunders, the Senior Air Staff Officer of Bomber Command, to equate the bombing effort with 'exporting bombs in the general direction of Germany'.

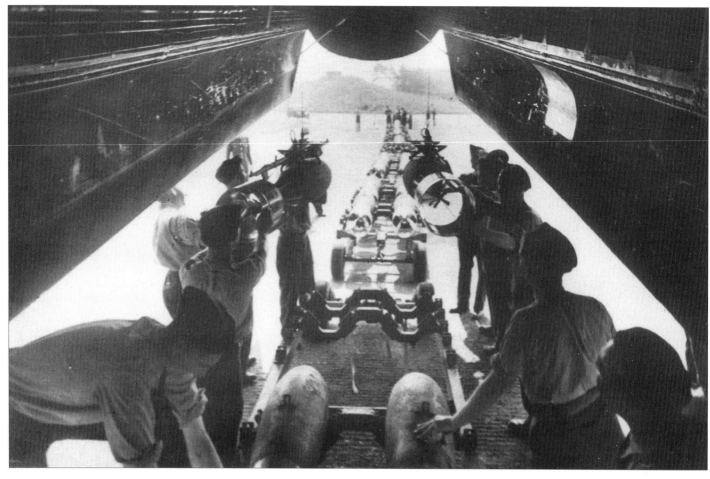

Unusual shot from inside the bomb bay during bombing-up. *P Beauchamp*

As a result of this, although Bomber Command specified particular buildings as the aiming points to crews in the future, from then onwards it was tacitly understood that most were merely carting bombs to the surrounding suburbs. The area bombing policy was taking shape.

Although the Butt Report concentrated minds admirably on the total inadequacy of astro-navigation, dead reckoning and radio beacons, in one respect salvation was at hand, albeit at some distance. By coincidence, the first of Bomber Command's target finding aids, GEE, was under trial in August 1941. Regrettably for Bomber Command, navigational deficiencies were not the only factor impeding its effectiveness.

The British bombs of this period were both defective and inefficient, with the result that when they did go off they did very little harm. The range of GPs, which were the principal weapons of the RAF at this time were badly designed. When dropped they were likely to bury themselves in the ground, with the result that much of the blast went harm-

lessly upwards rather than outwards. It was also found that these bombs had a casing far too thick, with a casing to charge ratio of 27% compared to 50% for the bombs currently in use by the Germans. Much of the explosive force was consequently used in blowing the case apart. Even worse than this, throughout 1941, and on into 1942 and 1943 the proportions of dud British high explosive bombs remained steady at 25%.

Whilst many of these deficiencies were progressively becoming apparent and being overcome, indeed from as early as March 1941 the thin-cased high capacity 4,000 lb blast bomb, the so-called 'Cookie' or 'Dangerous Dustbin' was already coming into service, one further deficiency of staggering proportions was to remain overlooked until as late as September 1943. Only during the planning of British defences against the threat of the German 'V' weapons did it finally come to light that the explosives used by the Germans were 80% more efficient than those used in British bombs. This was the more appalling when it was appreciated that virtually all concerned, other than the Air Ministry, was aware of this fact.

In the inquiry which followed it emerged that the Ministry of Supply, Armament Research Department in Sevenoaks had proposed in April 1940 a programme of testing aluminised explosives. The programme was

turned down due to an aluminium shortage. However, despite this the Navy was well aware of the value of aluminium as an explosive enhancer, using this in the Torpex in torpedoes and the Minol in depth charges. Following these revelations the first aluminised explosive-filled bombs finally reached operational squadrons on 4th December 1943. It was a galling failure of basic communications.

As far as the immediate situation in August 1941 was concerned, Churchill was in despair 'I find it an awful thought that three quarters of our bombs go astray. If only we could make it half and half we would have doubled our bombing power'. Despite these setbacks, Churchill remained undaunted – he had not promised or expected quick solutions.

Mercifully unaware of these doubts and deficiencies, the squadrons were about to emerge from the longest period of grounding of the Manchester since its service introduction. They had more than their fair share of problems within their own microcosm. For the moment there was some optimism that Rolls-Royce had finally grasped the nettle as far as the problems with the Vulture were concerned. With LA4 bearings and correctly tensioned con-rod bolts to Mod 44, the aircrews were all set to give the Manchester another chance.

Chapter Five

A Faltering Return

Bomber Command wasted no time; on 7th August 1941 the Avro Manchester was declared fit for operations once more and on that very day No. 207 Squadron was called upon to join in a planned raid by 106 aircraft to Essen. Three Manchesters and seven Handley Page Hampdens were given the Krupp works itself as their aiming point. Each Manchester carried five 1,000 lb general purpose (GP) bombs and 60 x 4 lb incendiaries. Take-off was 0040 to 0100 hours.

Essen – 7th August 1941

Serial	Code	Sqn	Captain
L7381	EM-K	207	F/O W M R Smith
L7422	EM-V	207	F/L W J Lewis
L7373	EM-T	207	F/L T C Murray

Once in the air, there was some confidence that Vulture engine reliability was improved in the Manchesters. Yet this was the very day on which yet another problem became manifest. The aircraft experienced tail flutter in various degrees of severity. Flight Lieutenant Murray in L7373 experienced severe tail flutter on the outward flight which forced him to abandon the attempt to reach Essen and instead attack the first 'SEMO' he located. A SEMO was one of the Command's euphemisms to cover its inability to find and pinpoint precise targets. The acronym stood for Self-Evident Military Objective – how this could be established in the cloudy, smog-laden darkness over the Ruhr was not made clear. The bombs dropped by Murray were believed to have fallen on Duisburg. Flak batteries engaged the aircraft whilst it was on its bombing run and it finally landed back at 0600 hours.

L7381 and L7422 encountered severe static and icing conditions en route to the target. Over Essen a ground haze prevented precise target location, but both dropped five 1,000 lb GPs and 60 x 4 lb incendiaries, which were estimated to have fallen in the general area of the target. A large fire was seen near Essen.

Flying Officer Smith's aircraft iced up badly on the return flight, but he still managed to land back at 0445 hours. All the Hampdens also returned safely. Following this operation the Hampdens were withdrawn from 207. Unlike the Manchesters, they had not encountered any serviceability problems

and none were lost on operations with the squadron. Consistent with the cloud and industrial haze, Essen reported a light raid with only 39 high explosive and 200 incendiaries falling in the town. There were no casualties. For the moment both 97 and 61 continued with one Manchester and one Hampden flight.

Up until this time the aircraft losses in the squadrons were mainly due to flak. Despite the concern felt in the Command over Manchester losses on operations due to engine failure, only the aircraft of Sergeant Harwood, Pilot Officer Ayton and Flight Lieutenant Bird had been lost solely due to this cause. German flak defences were already very efficient and few of the aircrew had encountered German night fighters in combat. Although RAF Fighter Command had been operating aircraft interception (AI) airborne radar equipped night fighters since July 1940, their German equivalents were lagging behind in this area. The German night fighter force was still relatively small at this stage of the war, having approximately 170 serviceable aircraft.

This was a situation which was soon to change, as the Manchester squadrons were to find to their cost during the month of August. On 12th August 1941 Bomber Command laid on a deep penetration raid to Berlin and 207 Squadron was called to provide six Manchesters with 97 offering three more. The total force was 70 aircraft to Berlin, 78 to Hanover and 36 to Magdeburg.

Berlin – 12th August 1941

Serial	Code	Sqn	Captain
L7306	OF-*	97	Sgt D H Rowlands
L7383	OF-*	97	F/O H S Blakeman
L7424	OF-*	97	F/O J A Little
L7422	EM-V	207	F/L W J Lewis
L7373	EM-T	207	P/O A W Hills
L7316	EM-U	207	P/O H G Keartland
L7380	EM-W	207†	F/O W G Gardiner
L7381	EM-R	207	F/O W M R Smith
L7377	EM-G	207	S/L G R Taylor

† With Wing Commander Purdon-Lewis as second pilot.

On the morning when the crew lists were posted at Waddington Sergeant Bill Wetherill found himself listed to fly as wireless operator in Squadron Leader Dickie Taylor's crew. Initially a member of Flying Officer Paape's

crew until the latter was posted in June, Wetherill had flown several operations with Acting Squadron Leader Taylor in July in Hampdens. This would be their first operation together in Manchesters and an enlarged crew would be required. The nucleus of the crew was Taylor (pilot), Sergeants Beattie (observer), McPhail (rear gunner) and Wetherill (wireless operator). Sergeant Nottidge was to be second pilot and Sergeant G R Birt was listed as the second wireless operator/air gunner.

As the preparations advanced, Wetherill was approached by a wireless operator he did not know. The newcomer introduced himself as Bob Birt and remarked that he was down to fly with Taylor as the second wireless op/gunner. On the grounds that he was senior to Wetherill he proposed that he should be first wireless op/gunner and occupy the radio position, whilst Wetherill should take his place in the mid-upper turret and be on hand to take the coffee round to the various crew positions from time to time. Wetherill countered by pointing out that he was already the 'regular' in the crew. In gentlemanly fashion this little difficulty was resolved when the two agreed that the best way out of the dilemma was a compromise in which Wetherill would be first op/gunner on the way to the target and after they had cleared the target area they would swap so that Birt could be the same for the return flight.

Neither were to know, but this agreement was to be the first of three occasions during the next 12 hours when Wetherill's life was to be saved by pure chance. From one of the other crews, the captain, Flight Lieutenant 'Mike' Lewis was to recall this as one of the saddest days of his life.

Consistent with the deeper penetration, the take-off time was commensurately earlier than for the Ruhr operations. Pilot Officers Hills and Keartland, and Flying Officers Gardiner and Smith took off very close to 2130 hours and it is likely that Flight Lieutenant Lewis was last away at 2135. No. 97 Squadron Manchesters took off from Coningsby between 2102 and 2111 hours. On account of the anticipated fuel consumption, most pilots chose a route to the north of the Ruhr via a more or less direct line from Waddington to Berlin. It was a beautifully clear night with absolutely unlimited visibility.

As the nine Manchesters headed east-wards across the North Sea one aircraft was already in trouble. Gardiner was discovering that despite his most determined efforts, L7380 was quite unable to climb to a reason-able flying height, added to which excessive tail flutter was experienced. L7380 was one of the Manchesters with the poorest perfor-mance. With no alternative, Gardiner divert-ed to nearby Emden and dropped his bombs on the port area and landed back safely at Waddington at 0250 hours.

As they crossed the enemy coast crews could already see, flicking across the sky miles ahead, the fingers of the lights in the searchlight belt over Holland, like gigantic cobwebs reaching out to trap them. In a fore-taste of what was soon to follow for another Manchester, L7306 of 97 Squadron, piloted by Sgt Rowlands, was intercepted by an uniden-tified night fighter over Holland. The alert gunners fortunately spotted the interceptor as it closed and L7306 nipped smartly into nearby cloud. The same aircraft was spotted on the starboard quarter three to four min-utes later but Rowlands slipped away to port and no further attack materialised.

Bringing up the rear of the phalanx after crossing the Dutch coast, 'Mike' Lewis was concentrating on the airspace ahead, whilst the gunners kept a sharp look out for other aircraft in their designated sectors of sky. There was no protective cloud to blanket them by the time 207 reached the area and fighter attacks had to be expected.

Suddenly, directly ahead, Lewis regis-tered a stream of tracer fired between one aircraft and another. This was immediately followed by a large, distinctive, pinkish-cen-tred flash of a 'Cookie' exploding in a bomber and then the awful brilliant yellow flare of the aircraft's fuel tanks exploding. The disinte-grating, shattered wreck tumbled earth-wards, shedding blazing fragments until it fell below Lewis' line of vision under the nose.

He had witnessed the instantaneous destruction of an RAF bomber caught naked by a German night fighter. The awful sight was imprinted in his memory and on return he learned that his best friend, Mike Smith, just 21 years and a few days old, had been killed on his 50th operation over occupied Europe, together with his entire crew. His enquiries on return led him to believe that he had almost certainly witnessed his friend's death, but only recently has the evidence been assembled to prove the truth of this supposition.

L7381 had fallen to one of the most experi-enced German night fighter aces of the time, Oberleutnant Ludwig Becker. Becker was doubly famous, being credited as the first German night fighter pilot to obtain a victory with the AN ground radar guidance system back on 16th October 1940. The action in which he obtained his second 'first' had come only three days before he shot down

Mike Smith. Following his successes in 1940, Becker pulled some strings and arranged to be transferred to Berlin-Werneuchen, the German experimental night fighter centre. Here he did much of the development flying on the 'Liechtenstein' airborne interception system. Many German night fighter pilots were bitterly opposed to this equipment when it was first issued to operational units. Its serviceability was poor, and its weight and the drag of its cumbersome external aerial array significantly impaired the already mar-ginal speed advantage of the makeshift night fighters then in use. These radar-equipped aircraft were thus commonly left on the ground while the crews, not experienced in the use of the radar, preferred their earlier, more manoeuvrable aircraft.

This situation persisted for quite some time in mid-1941 but when Becker was post-ed to a front line unit, IV/NJG1 at Leeuwar-den in Holland in July 1941, the situation changed dramatically. Becker and his radar operator, Feldwebel Staub, were so compe-tent and experienced with the 'Liechten-stein' equipment that very soon the other crews had christened Becker the 'Nacht-jagdprofessor'.

On the night of 8/9th August he took off from Leeuwarden in a Dornier Do 215 equip-ped with 'Liechtenstein'. With him were Feldwebel Staub as wireless and radar oper-ator and Obergefreiter Wilhelm Gaensler as air gunner. Shortly after midnight, with the aid of the Seeburg plotting system and 'Freya' ground radar station, he was guided onto the tail of an incoming RAF bomber. At a range of a few kilometres they detected the raider on their 'Liechtenstein' set and Staub was able to direct Becker close enough to obtain a visual sighting. Becker fired at the gently weaving bomber and Vickers Wellington T2625 'GR-B' of 301 Squadron crashed near Bunde just across the German border, the first ever airborne radar victory by a German night fighter.

No record of Becker's operational flights or victories has yet to come to light but it is pos-sible that L7381 'EM-R' was the second Ger-man airborne radar assisted victory of the war. A copy of the combat report submitted by Becker following this action has survived. In translation it reads:

'On 12th August 1941 I took off at 2320 hours in Do 215 'G9+OM' for night operations in the vicinity of Leeuwarden. (The crew were Becker, Staub and Gaensler). I was guided by means of the Seeburg table (con-troller Lt Maier) and picked up the target on 'Liechtenstein' radar at a height of 4,700 metres and at a distance of 2,500 metres and at 0125 I distinguished high in front of us the enemy aircraft, a type unknown to me. I attacked from down and behind, one single attack, firing several bursts of fire. My burst of fire went exactly through the centre of the fuselage. Target disappeared downwards into

clouds and I could not observe how the air-craft crashed on the ground. The aircraft, an 'Avro Manchester' was found with numerous hits by machine gun and cannon near Slochteren [east of the town of Groningen] by the Aircraft Recovery Commando from Leeuwarden. I landed at 0202 hours at Leeu-warden'.

A confirmation of the destruction was obtained from Oberfeldwebel Reinthal who was flying over Schiermonnikoog with Leut-nant Gehring at that time. He observed the firing and its result and recorded it at 0125 hours. At the end of September the 'Liecht-enstein' radar in Becker's Do 215 became unserviceable and it was apparently well into 1942 before the next airborne radar assisted kill was achieved.

Local reports say that the Manchester exploded with the bomb load and the enor-mous load of petrol. Burning pieces came down behind the Apostolic Church at Froom-bosch near Kolham and a real rain of fire from the petrol fell on the land. All around lay the bodies of the six airmen. Flying Officer W M R Smith from Knebworth, Hertfordshire, was found in a ditch, still sitting in his seat. One other airman had come down in a stub-ble field, making in it the impression of his body. The six airmen were buried on the afternoon of 14th August 1941 in the ceme-tery near the Hoofdweg at Kolham. In 1951 they were reburied at the Central Allied Cemetery at Holten in the Province of Over-ijssel. There can be no doubt that none of the six knew what had hit them.

Oberleutnant Becker went on to claim 44 victories, rising to the rank of Hauptmann and Staffelkapitän of NJG1. His life was squ-andered for no benefit when he died with Oberfeldwebel Staub at his side on 26th Feb-ruary 1943 during his first daylight operation over the North Sea. The 'Nachtjagdprofessor' had no familiarity with the tactics required to attack massed American bomber forma-tions.

Perhaps the most surprising factor of the Do 215 *versus* Manchester combat is that although neither of the crews involved sur-vived the war such a complete record of the incident from eye witnesses and combat reports on both sides can be assembled more than 50 years later.

Following the return of Flying Officer Gar-diner and the loss of Flying Officer Smith, the seven remaining Manchesters continued their mission to Berlin, cloaked in the anon-ymity of darkness. En route over Hanover Sergeant Rowlands was heavily engaged by flak and released his bombs on that city to enable him to escape the barrage. On locat-ing the target area Lewis, Keartland, Hills and Blakeman all received a hot reception from the flak defences. Lewis dropped his five 1,000 lb GPs on the west side of Berlin observing three fires on the ground caused by earlier bombers. Keartland unloaded his

5 x 1,000 lb GPs north east of the aiming point. Hills carried a 4,000 lb high capacity (HC) and 240 x 4 lb incendiaries and also found the searchlights very accurate on his bombing run. For a period he was coned by approximately 30 searchlights and held for five minutes. He eventually evaded the beams and his 4,000 lb bomb, dropped through the 207-designed bomb aperture in the bays, fell on the north side of the city. Flying Officer Blakeman dived to bomb a fire in the position his observer calculated Berlin to be.

Meanwhile, Squadron Leader Taylor was also approaching the target area at about 12,000 ft. Other than a brief encounter with searchlights and flak in the defensive belt at the Dutch coast their outward flight had been uneventful. Each of the experienced captains had their own philosophy for survival on operations, developed from the lessons of their first tours. Taylor had explained his to Sergeant Wetherill during their preparations for previous flights. He believed that when caught by accurate flak barrages the best course of action was to fly absolutely straight and level. Statistically, he claimed, the aircraft was just as likely to jink into a flak burst as away from one.

Perhaps his was an appropriate philosophy for the early days of the war when the threat of night fighter interception was relatively remote and radar predicted flak was in its infancy. The Achilles' heel of this approach to anti-aircraft fire was soon to become manifest.

Bill Wetherill's most vivid memory is of their approach to the target area. The search-lights seemed more numerous, active and dangerous than ever before. They appeared to be working in groups and in close co-ordination with the heavy flak batteries. The flak guns were also working in unison, throwing up box barrages into the apex of those searchlights which had located and held a bomber.

On the bomb run Taylor continued to hold L7377 straight and level whilst 'Tam' Beattie in the bomb aimer's position conned them towards their designated aiming point. Their load was a single 4,000 lb HC 'Cookie', which Beattie duly dropped on what was believed to be the aiming point. The aircraft was equipped with the modified bomb doors which Wetherill recalls as being canvas covered and they all felt the bump as the bomb fell on the doors, prising them open, followed immediately by the reverberation as the aperture sprang closed once more. Beattie left the bomb aiming position and made his way back to his navigator's seat, hooking up his intercom.

Suddenly they were illuminated by a searchlight, joined in rapid succession by others. They were coned and held by the mercilessly bright beams. It almost appeared to Wetherill that the release of the bomb was a signal which activated the lights. Within a few seconds an intense and co-ordinated flak barrage opened up on them. Wetherill felt the concussion of the first burst, not one but a number of shells exploding together in a small area of sky. Beattie called on the intercom that the first burst was well ahead and above the aircraft.

Taylor continued to fly his steady course and at intervals of several seconds further barrages exploded. It became apparent that although the gunners had initially over estimated their speed they were gradually getting closer with each burst. Then a burst jolted them from such a close distance ahead and above that they immediately flew through the smoke, smelling the distinctive acrid cordite which had yet to disperse. They waited with baited breath, still held like a fly at the centre of a spider's web, but the next burst was even closer, immediately above the nose inducing a tremendous shock and shudder in the aircraft. A shower of splintered perspex flew from flak shards penetrating the cockpit canopy.

In the absence of any call Wetherill could not be certain what damage had been caused. Consequently he left his radio position and moved forward into the cockpit. Dicky Taylor had been hit in the wrist by a flak splinter which had severed an artery. 'Tam' Beattie was already standing between the pilots, Wetherill could see he was trying to fasten a temporary tourniquet above the spurting artery to staunch the flow of blood, Sergeant Nottidge had taken over control and was flying the aircraft.

Wetherill offered assistance but received an assurance from Beattie that he could cope. Further bursts of flak continued to buffet the airframe but at this stage Wetherill could discern no further damage. Beattie, an experienced and senior observer, had taken control of the situation, as he continued to work on Taylor's wound. At the same time he was calmly directing the inexperienced Nottidge in a series of evasive manoeuvres in an attempt to escape the clinging lights.

Wetherill returned to his position and was standing watching for any evidence that they might be shaking off the flak, to no avail. The next group of shells burst with a loud explosion and concussion beneath, which shook the aircraft again. With the blast the armour plating doors behind Wetherill's seat, providing access aft, burst open. Turning, Wetherill saw to his horror that the whole of the inside of the fuselage aft of his position was already a raging inferno.

The size and intensity of the conflagration immediately after the shells had burst surprised Wetherill. This was no small fire, but already an enveloping blow-torch of flame. Wetherill could only surmise that perhaps the flak had set off the flares stored immediately beneath Bob Birt, trapping him in his position in the mid-upper turret. The rapidity with which they had been engaged by the flak gunners had prevented Birt and Wetherill effecting their agreed exchange of crew stations.

This one look down the 'blow-lamp' of a rear fuselage convinced Wetherill that the aircraft was doomed and that his only hope of survival was to escape from the aircraft as quickly as possible. He grabbed and fitted his observer's chest-type parachute and made to move to the forward escape hatch beneath the nose. He was dismayed to find his exit completely blocked by the three aircrew struggling in the cockpit. In desperation he flung off his leather flying helmet, pulled open the armoured doors, and tried to force a way to the rear entry door instead. He was met by a veritable ball of fire which set his hair smouldering. By now the fire was spreading to the wings and the flames began to shoot forward through the armoured doors into the cockpit area. There could, it seemed to Wetherill, be but a few seconds remaining to effect an escape.

Returning to the cockpit area he found it deserted. Fortunately the aircraft was still flying straight and level in a gentle dive, perhaps under control of the autopilot. By this time Taylor, Nottidge and Beattie were crouched around the forward escape hatch, but were still not getting out. Beattie was still tending to the tourniquet on Taylor's wrist, effectively blocking Wetherill's escape. The whole airframe was hot and fire was licking at Wetherill who, without his leather flying suit, was already beginning to burn.

The only possible escape from a certain and horrific death in the blazing coffin of L7377 seemed to be the starboard cockpit window. In desperation Wetherill grabbed the catch and slid it backwards. A searing pain shot through his hands as he found the catch so hot his flesh stuck to it. Ripping his hand away and leaving the skin behind he pushed the chest-type 'chute through the narrow opening. By now the fire was shooting into the cockpit area, forcing him into frenzied activity in an attempt to escape it. He stuck his head through the aperture, then worked his shoulders through one at a time. Heaving himself outward, his feet left the cockpit floor and he was out of the aircraft almost to his waist.

Having momentarily escaped the worst of the fire a sudden chilling fear gripped him when he noticed for the first time the starboard propeller still turning at maximum revolutions some 18 in behind his right shoulder. Any further progress in this direction and he would inevitably fall directly into the arc of the airscrew and certain death. He must retreat, despite the advancing fire. In his last desperate lunge through the cockpit window he had lost the purchase of his feet on the cockpit floor. Indeed, he discovered, in blind panic, that he could now no longer move forward or back into the aircraft, but was stuck tight in the window.

The fire had by now reached his legs and he felt them burning, he continued his frenzied efforts to get back into the cockpit, with his mind focused on the forward escape hatch which must, surely, by now be vacant. Shock and exhaustion combined to weaken him and he was now trapped, totally unable to help himself. His face a few inches from the spinning propeller blade tips, his legs burning, he was a helpless victim of fate. He fainted. Fate took a hand in an incredible fashion, for Wetherill's next conscious memory is one of feeling very sick and dizzy whilst tumbling over and over through the air as he fell. His immediate thought was quite obtuse. A few nights earlier he had had his first experience of drinking too much, with the attendant, detached stupor of finding all about him spinning. Determining later never to do it ever again he was now irrationally angry to find himself in the same state.

Cold reality quickly dawned on him, the only possibility can be that the flames had finally reached the fuel tanks, exploded the aircraft and thrown him clear. It was his second escape from death during the operation. Wetherill raised his hands, which were skinned from the wrist down, and took the D-ring in his grasp. Despite excruciating pain he pulled the rip-cord and to his relief the parachute blossomed unburnt above him. The whole action, from illumination to hanging in his parachute, had seemed an eternity, although in truth it is likely to have occupied only two minutes or so.

Following the last gentle dive of L7377 and his own free fall, Wetherill found himself still quite high, perhaps 10,000ft. He became aware of material flapping in his face. Despite his burns he could discern it to be the two legs of his battledress trousers. Whilst trapped in the cockpit these had completely burnt through all the way down the back to leave the fronts as loose strips of cloth, as soon as he was hanging upright in his harness they rose up into his face. One flying boot was missing and on the way down he kicked off the other. Overhead he could hear the raid still in progress and see the searchlights quartering the sky for their next quarry. Soon he could see the ground, and as the features grew nearer and larger, realised he was heading for an area of trees. Unable to use his burnt hands he reached up vainly with an elbow to try and shorten the suspension cords and steer the 'chute to one side. He succeeded merely in inducing a violent swing and fearing the 'chute might collapse, he left it to its own devices. Thus he was unable to prevent himself from crashing through a large tree at Gross-Beeren Teltow, on the southern outskirts of Berlin.

The parachute stuck high in the tree and Wetherill was left swinging in the air still suspended some distance from the ground. Looking down he saw he was in the top of a hedge bordering a lane. He reached up for the quick release buckle of the parachute at his waist. Despite exerting as much force as the pain in his hands would allow, he was unable to turn it. His full weight was on the buckle and he had no strength left in his hands. After several attempts he gave up, slumped exhausted in the harness, and waited to be found. Above he could still hear aircraft engines, bombs exploding and the flak.

After only a few minutes he heard and then saw people out searching for him with torches. His descent had obviously been witnessed from below. They progressed along the lane beside him but could not find him. In shock and pain from his burns, realising the urgency with which he needed medical attention, he abandoned all prospect of escape and called out to the search party in his best schoolboy German. They stopped. 'Wo sind Sie?' (Where are you?) 'In dem baum' (In the tree) replied Wetherill. Shining their torches aloft they soon located him. A group reached up and took hold of him, with an unceremonious tug they pulled him down from the tree, parachute and all. Seeing the seriousness of his burns the party realised he was unable to undo his parachute buckle and removed the 'chute for him.

Subsequent memories are fragmentary and incomplete and it seems that Wetherill lost consciousness from time to time during the next few days. As he drifted between oblivion and reality some vivid memories remain. He came round as the search party tried to get him on this feet, there were a number of them, including one middle-aged man in a Sturm Abteilung (SA, the 'Storm Troopers') brownshirt uniform and a teenage boy of about 16 years of age. As they were escorting him along the lane he overheard and understood that they were discussing where best to take him. Suddenly the 'Brownshirt' stopped the procession and, drawing a gun, spoke to the rest of the party 'Uberlassen sie ihn mir, ich erledige ihn um die ecke'. (Leave him to me, I will take him round the corner). His eyes dropped illustratively to the Luger, Wetherill understood only too well what was being proposed.

To his surprise and immense relief the teenage boy immediately intervened on his behalf, standing between airman and 'Brownshirt' and condemning the adult in strident tones. The rest of the party sided with the teenager and so, humbled and thwarted, the 'Brownshirt' backed down and holstered his gun. Wetherill could breath again, an adolescent and enemy stranger had just saved his life, and in the middle of an air raid at that. Not having exchanged places with the mid-upper gunner, being blown clear of the doomed aircraft and now saved from murder, this was the third life-saving moment since the Manchester had been caught in the searchlights. Turning, the boy spoke in English 'You will be safe when some military come', he smiled reassuringly.

After a short walk they reached what Wetherill took to be an underground first aid post or air raid shelter. There nurses appeared and cut off what remained of his trousers. They bathed his burns, which extended down the whole length of the backs of both legs and bandaged them. His badly burnt hands were also dressed and loosely bandaged. His face was less severely burnt and therefore left uncovered. Wetherill fainted again and has confused memories of being laid down on what he took to be a pile of sawdust. Many people, each it seemed in a different style military uniform, came to look down at him, shaking their heads and clicking their tongues at his condition.

Some time later it became apparent that another wounded airman had been brought in and Wetherill was asked if he could identify the newcomer. The man was badly burned and his features unrecognisable, with a start Wetherill suddenly recognised an unburnt section of Fair Isle pullover on the chest of the person lying before him. It was McPhail, the rear gunner. Doug McPhail was a short, stocky chap with red hair and a distinctive handlebar moustache. The hair and moustache were gone now and the features puffed up and distorted by the fire so that only the sweater gave a clue to his identity.

Wetherill never discovered how McPhail managed to vacate the aircraft, since the crew believed he was sufficiently wide in his flying suit to have difficulty falling out of the turret doors during ground practices. It is presumed that McPhail escaped by parachute despite his burns and the difficulty of vacating the turret. Shortly afterwards a German officer arrived in an Opel and took custody of Wetherill. McPhail stayed behind since his first aid was still not completed.

Wetherill accompanied the officer alone, whilst the initial treatment of McPhail's grievous burns continued. In the back of the Opel the officer addressed Wetherill, the English impeccable. 'I'm sorry, old boy, that it had to be my flak battery that shot you down'. Wetherill speculated on just how sorry the officer really was but managed to reply diplomatically 'Well never mind, thus are the fortunes of war'.

Wetherill was taken first to a German Military Hospital where his burns could be properly treated. He had the great good fortune to be attended by an extremely considerate and sympathetic German doctor, who apologised profusely for the necessity of causing him pain and discomfort. All the bandages on his legs and hands were removed, the wounds cleaned and redressed, strips of hanging skin were picked or cut off. Owing to his lapses of consciousness the timescale is uncertain but Wetherill believed he remained in the hospital all that night.

His next recollection is of travelling in a military ambulance over the cobbled streets of Berlin to a French prisoner of war (PoW) hospital somewhere in or near the city. This was a very uncomfortable journey as the bumpiness of the ride aggravated his wounds and caused great pain, such that before he had arrived he had lost consciousness once more. The main wards were taken up by wounded and sick French PoWs and he was put in a small room as he was the only English person in the hospital.

At some stage McPhail was brought into the ward beside him. McPhail was not only severely burned but also deeply traumatised by his experience. He was in the main conscious, although far from lucid, fighting all attempts to give him the medication he so desperately needed. The attendants tried to attach McPhail to a saline drip but he resisted. Wetherill tried to reason with him, but McPhail continued to toss and turn until the drip came out of his arm.

McPhail clearly recognised Wetherill, calling out 'They're trying to kill us Bill' and 'Don't let them do this to us'. Wetherill tried in turn to reason with McPhail 'No Mac, they're French, they're trying to help us'. It was to no avail, McPhail died later that day.

Wetherill, too, was seriously burned and continued to experience periods of lucidity interspersed with losses of consciousness. Under the devoted care of the French doctors and nurses he slowly began to improve. One nurse told him later he was the one not expected to pull through. The treatment of such severe burns was virtually an unknown area of medicine. When he was sufficiently recovered the doctors began their attempts at skin grafts on his burns. By no means all of the skin grafts attempted on him were successful. His injuries would require very prolonged hospitalisation.

With time he became more mobile and eventually became quite well acquainted with the German officer-in-charge, Statfeldwebel Salmon. When be became well enough to be mobile, Salmon would allow Wetherill into his room to listen to the BBC, although he always returned before the news was due and switched off the set. From time to time Salmon would also give him a tot of Schnapps to drink and showed him many kindnesses without ever forgetting that they must, unfortunately, remain enemies.

One day, during the early part of his convalescence, a Luftwaffe officer arrived at the hospital to interrogate Wetherill. He had a sheaf of papers with details the Germans had gleaned already about their aircraft. Looking over the German's shoulder, Wetherill could read under aircraft type the words 'Manchester' and under captain 'Squadron Leader Taylor'. He asked many questions which Wetherill was unwilling to answer, amongst the most important, and a question he kept returning to was 'How many engines did your aircraft have? Two or four?' The wreckage must have been very scattered, but clearly the Germans were perplexed, believ-

ing such a big aeroplane should really have required four engines. Up to this time the Germans had only had the opportunity to examine the wreckage of Siebert, Hyde, Pinchbeck, Webb, Little, Smith and Taylor's Manchesters and in every case the aircraft were almost totally destroyed.

When the German was unable to obtain the answers he wanted, Wetherill eventually felt able to ask him, in turn, what had become of the rest of his crew. The interrogator told him that Taylor, Nottidge and Beattie had all drowned in the lakes around the city of Berlin. It has not been possible to corroborate from any source what Wetherill was told, but if there is any truth at all in the information it would perhaps imply that the three did successfully parachute from the front hatch before the aircraft disintegrated. Since all three were wearing their 'Mae Wests' and the water temperatures in August must have been relatively high, it would seem, to a degree surprising, if all had drowned as the German claimed.

The Germans had also found the body of Bob Birt, in what circumstances is not known. From the body they took a photograph, which was burnt at the edges, of Birt with a girlfriend sitting in the gateway of a field on his motorcycle. The interrogator told Wetherill that Birt was dead too and gave him the photograph for safekeeping.

Wetherill remained in hospital for more than five months before being sent to Stalag 88 PoW camp near Breslau in January 1942. His wounds were far from healed and he very quickly went back to the camp hospital. In Stalag 88 he met Jim Taylor, the wireless operator from Johnny Siebert's crew.

Taylor had been a good friend of Bob Birt and so Wetherill offered him the scorched and burnt photograph. Taylor took the photograph and cared for it amongst his personal possessions all through his time in PoW camps. With him it survived harsh winters in Stalag Luft 3 in Upper Silesia when the inmates had no heating and ice from the prisoners' breath built up to six inches on the inside walls of the barracks. It survived a forced march right across northern Germany before the advancing Russians in the winter of 1944 and more than 50 years later was still kept in Taylor's wallet.

Wetherill still required further hospital treatment and in 1943 he finally went before a neutral Red Cross medical board. On the panel were a German military doctor, a British (PoW) doctor and a Red Cross doctor, who jointly considered the medical condition of wounded prisoners with a view to repatriating those whose medical condition warranted it. In October 1943 Wetherill was repatriated to Sweden and on to England via an hospital ship. So 207 Squadron had lost their 'A' Flight commander, Acting Squadron Leader Taylor, on his 47th operation.

From the 97 Squadron force Flying Officer

J A Little and crew failed to return. L7424 encountered its problem on the return flight. Signals were received from the aircraft at 0135 and 0222 hours requesting fixes. The signals were sufficiently far apart to imply that the aircraft may have become lost but the reasons for its final demise have not been established. A last signal, received at 0228 at Coningsby, said the crew were preparing to bale out and the entire crew descended successfully in the Nordhorn-Schuthorf area of the Dutch-German border to become prisoners of war. The remaining Manchesters of the Berlin force made their way back to Waddington and Coningsby and landed safely. They had been badly mauled by the flak defences over the 'Big City'

More seriously, although unknown to them, a new and potent force had been deployed effectively against them for the first time. Smith and possibly Little both having been lost to night fighters, the aircrews which came after them would have good reason in future to be more fearful of the radar equipped night fighter than the flak defences, which in the main were to prove a threat only over the immediate target area. Of the 70-strong Berlin force, only 32 aircraft had bombed Berlin. Nine aircraft, three Manchesters, three Wellingtons, two Halifaxes and a Stirling were lost.

Following a raid on Magdeburg, 207 and 97 Squadrons were called on to participate on a raid on Dusseldorf on 16th August. No. 207 sent two aircraft to Dusseldorf and two new crews undertook a shallow penetration raid on Ostend to gain experience. No. 97 Squadron supplied four aircraft: Flying Officer Gardiner and Pilot Officer Keartland were to take-off from Waddington close to 2300 whilst the 97 Squadron force took off between 2247 and 2256.

Dusseldorf / Ostend† – 16th August 1941

Serial	Code	Sqn	Captain
L7423	OF-*	97	F/Sgt D H Rowlands
L7306	OF-*	97	F/L C P D Price
L7383	OF-F	97	F/O H S Blakeman
L7384	OF-*	97	F/L J L Nunn
L7432	EM-Z	207	F/O W G Gardiner
L7311	EM-F	207	P/O H G Keartland
L7380	EM-W	207†	P/O T R Gilderthorp
L7422	EM-V	207†	P/O P C Birch

Nothing seemed to go right in Keartland's aircraft from the very start of the operation. Out on the grass airfield at Waddington it was raining very heavily. The deluge was sufficiently severe that Keartland completely overlooked his usually unvarying custom of 'watering' the tail wheel before boarding. This practical preparation for a long flight had, for many crews, become steeped in tradition and superstition. To miss any part of the routine which had 'protected' them before was regarded as a bad omen.

When engines were started, Keartland found that it was impossible to run them to full power without the aircraft dancing and sliding uncontrollably across the grass. Consequently, L7311 was taxied from the grass dispersal onto the nearby Sleaford main road, holding up the Lincoln-Sleaford bus. Here the brakes were applied and the engines tested to satisfaction. Finally at around 2315 hours they took off through the rain.

Pilot Officers Birch and Gilderthorp took off an hour and a half later at 0140 and 0146 hours respectively. Peter Birch located Ostend docks and dropped two 1,000 lb GPs from 14,000ft, which were estimated to have fallen on a jetty west of the dock. Unfortunately the remaining two 1,000 pounders hung up and despite vigorous manoeuvring it proved impossible to jettison them. Birch returned to Waddington at 0445 hours. Gilderthorp was unable to identify Ostend but eventually found another port to bomb which was subsequently identified as Terneuzen on the River Scheldt. He landed at 0500 hours.

The six Manchesters of the Dusseldorf force were well ahead. In L7311 the concentration level of the crew rose a notch as they crossed the enemy coast inward bound for Dusseldorf. They had dragged L7311 up to 15,000ft but now one of the engines was dropping revolutions. The two pilots, Keartland and Ross, discussed the situation over the intercom. Bill Hart, the rear gunner, recalls that since the performance did not appear to be deteriorating any further and Dusseldorf was a relatively shallow penetration target, Keartland had decided to press on.

Their next objective was to traverse the searchlight belt stretching across eastern Holland without being detected. They appeared to be close to achieving this and had reached a position near to the Dutch/German border, only some 20 minutes flying time from the target, when they were suddenly illuminated 'by the blue searchlight'. All the other searching fingers of light nearby immediately converged on them. With a full bomb load and still carrying the bulk of the fuel load, Keartland was unable to effect any violent evasive action. They were well and truly coned and held by the lights.

In the rear turret, Hart was completely blinded by the glare and could give no warning when, within only a short period after they were located, they were shocked to see and feel cannon and machine gun bullets strike the aircraft. Holes appeared in the perspex turret close to Bill Hart and he was lucky to survive. In the few hectic seconds of the attack he was scarcely aware of what was happening to him. Still the attacker was unseen, but the closing speed of the fighter on the overloaded and underpowered Manchester was such that he overshot the lumbering bomber. In doing so, the fighter

entered the glare of the lights surrounding the Manchester, allowing the snap identification. Hart believed his attacker to be a single engined Messerschmitt Me109. He was a sitting target almost in the rear gunner's sights and Hart immediately pressed the triggers, at the same time operating the turret slewing controls. Nothing happened. The initial attack had severely damaged the aircraft, knocking out all the hydraulic systems and silencing the turret armament, the port engine was set on fire and the flying controls damaged.

Hart lost sight of the fighter as he checked the reason for the turret malfunction, but shortly received a warning on the intercom that the fighter was making another attack on the port quarter. Hart traversed the turret by hand towards the port quarter. As he did so, he fired a short burst. The object was to check whether the first failure to fire was due to a round jamming the guns or alternatively to the hydraulic failure. The short burst was not directed at the fighter and did nothing to deflect it from a second short accurate burst of fire, which this time caused hits in the front fuselage, slightly wounding the second pilot, Sergeant Ross.

Despite his injuries, Ross was the first to regain his faculties, ramming forward the stick and diving the Manchester until it evaded the searchlights. Enquiries have now ascertained that the attacker was the German ace and commander of 1 Stab / NJG1, Hauptmann Werner Streib based at Stade and possibly flying a Messerschmitt Me110. He was to become one of the Luftwaffe's top aces and attain a high wartime rank, surviving the war with a tally of 65 victories in the night skies of Europe. Streib was to claim two Manchesters that night.

Hart was still unaware of the damage up front and now had time to call the pilot on the intercom, still, fortunately, functioning. There was no reply to the first call, the two pilots no doubt having their hands full, and Hart called again. In the front turret, Sergeant Ball had seen little of the attacks and had not been hit. Ross managed to recover from the headlong dive and found they had evaded both the lights and the night fighter. Everything told them that L7311 was doomed. Sergeant Eddie Ball was enveloped in acrid smoke and glycol in the pitch darkness. The port engine was on fire and the flames were spreading. 'Sorry chaps, you will have to bale out', called the second pilot.

Discovering the seriousness of the situation, Hart began to prepare to abandon the aircraft, noticing for the first time as he did so that his left arm and left side of his body seemed numb and useless. His actions thus restricted, he opened the doors in his turret and reached into the fuselage stowage rack for his parachute.

Clipping the 'chute onto his chest harness, he locked on the right clip but was totally

unable to fasten the left. A parachute course had taught him that baling out with one clip fastened should be quite safe, as the rigging lines were linked together guaranteeing a safe and full deployment of the silk. Thus prepared, Hart traversed the turret onto the beam, again one handed.

After what seemed an age, the turret appeared to have traversed far enough for him to fall out of the aircraft. He leant his full weight backwards only to discover, to his dismay, that the doors, so recently opened for him to collect his parachute were now jammed. In desperation he braced his feet in the turret and exerted all the force he could muster on the doors, which burst open allowing him to somersault free.

Hart pulled the ripcord and received a severe jolt as the parachute blossomed above him. For the first time in the hectic encounter with the night fighter, which had probably lasted less than a minute, he had time to collect his thoughts. His left arm still hung down uselessly and he realised that he had indeed been wounded. He could feel blood trickling down his back inside his flying suit. It later transpired he had stopped both a cannon shell splinter and a machine gun bullet, although how these had reached his back when he was sitting facing the gunfire from the fighter is not clear. They may have been ricochets and lost much of their momentum before hitting him.

Meanwhile, Sergeants Curry, Wappet and Ball, the navigator, wireless operator and front gunners respectively, had great difficulty in escaping from the lower hatch in the nose. Ball's parachute had only just deployed when he hit the ground, damaging the base of his spine.

A few fields ahead, the Manchester, still with the bomb load aboard, blew up on impact. L7311, lying shattered at Kruchten, over the German border, must have provided little information for the Germans.

Hart was unable to see the ground, owing to the darkness, and made a heavy landing amongst bushes he could barely discern. Partly paralysed and in great pain, he dragged his parachute over himself and settled down to await daybreak, assess the seriousness of his wounds and get his bearings. Unbeknown to Hart, he had landed at Roermond in eastern Holland.

Within a few minutes of his successful attack on L7311, Streib was manoeuvring to intercept his second Manchester of the night, this time L7384 of 97 Squadron. The crew comprised Flight Lieutenant J L Nunn (captain), Sergeant Ratcliffe (second pilot), Sergeant Wood (observer), Flight Sergeant Ashmore (wireless operator), Sergeant Currie (front gunner), Flight Sergeant Williams (rear gunner) and Sergeant Smith (mid-upper gunner). The night remained hot and sultry even at the take-off time close to midnight. Nunn recalled that even with a load of only six 1,000 lb GPs his take-off from Coningsby was a marginal and unnerving experience.

The aircraft had climbed painfully slowly in the thin air as they headed out over the North Sea at full throttle. As they approached the coast of occupied Europe they were still below 10,000ft and Nunn toyed with the idea of jettisoning one or two of the bombs safe into the sea, so they would be able to climb to a safer height before crossing the searchlight belt. He decided to keep the bombs on board – a decision he would later regret, but one which probably had little effect on the events which followed.

By the time they reached 'The Belt' in eastern Belgium he had still only hauled the Manchester up to 11,000ft. On approaching the searchlights, Nunn began corkscrewing the aircraft. Despite his exertions he was trapped in the beams and illuminated. His efforts to escape the cone became more desperate, but to no avail. Suddenly they were attacked by the prowling Me110 night fighter of Werner Streib, which seriously damaged the Manchester with the first burst of fire. The starboard engine caught fire and the hydraulics were damaged. The undercarriage dropped down, slowing their speed further and making evasion even more difficult.

Nunn feathered the starboard propeller and pressed the fire extinguisher button. Despite the serious damage caused in the first pass the night fighter continued to press home his attack and the next burst of fire caused further destruction including wounding the front gunner, Currie.

It was obvious that the Manchester was doomed. They were descending quickly and there was little time to spare. Nunn ordered the crew to bale out. The second pilot, observer, wireless operator and mid-upper gunner baled out, the rear gunner also jumped, but his body was found later. It is likely his parachute had failed. The remaining four were taken prisoner.

Nunn was in a dilemma, he was alone in the crippled Manchester with his front gunner who was too badly wounded to escape. To bale out meant leaving Currie to certain death. They were within a few thousand feet of the ground and would soon be too low to bale out anyway. The Graviner system appeared to have worked as the fire in the starboard engine died down and appeared to have gone out. At least something in the shattered aircraft worked.

The dying fire helped Nunn to decide to try and save Currie's life by force landing the Manchester. It was a pitch black night with only the stars visible and Nunn could make out no details whatever on the ground. Other than knowing that most of eastern Belgium was fairly flat he would be landing totally blind, with some of the hydraulics shot away and carrying 6,000 lb of bombs plus most of the fuel load. Nunn maintained his resolve.

On the remaining port engine the Manchester sank very quickly so that it was soon too low for Nunn to bale out even if he had changed his mind. His responsibilities to his crew remained uppermost.

As they descended, Nunn pumped furiously on the emergency flap handle but it was not possible to judge whether the flaps had extended at all. In any case the emergency system took a lot of pumping to fully lower the flaps and on his own with the aircraft to control there was insufficient time. Still, the ground beneath was invisible.

At 100ft on the altimeter, still blind to what lay in their path, Nunn throttled back the port engine and pulled back on the stick. The Manchester sank onto the ground in an area of small fields and trees. The dangling undercarriage collapsed and the careering aircraft smashed through several hedges and trees. A large branch smashed the cockpit perspex and then the aircraft ground to a halt. The bomb load, which Nunn had not had the opportunity to jettison, was not fused and remained intact. Nunn was severely shaken around in the impact and deceleration of the landing.

His first thoughts when they finally stopped was of the possibly holed and ruptured fuel tanks and whether the fire in the starboard engine was out or might flare up again. He was shocked and in pain himself, but his immediate thought was for Currie, his front gunner. He struggled forward to the turret and with great difficulty extricated the wounded man. Dragging him up to the cockpit, he hauled the gunner through the broken cockpit canopy. Despite the pitch blackness the aircraft appeared to have survived the ordeal quite well. It was on an even keel, the wings were still in place and it was more or less in one piece. Nunn thinks he lowered Currie the short distance to the ground and followed himself. He laboriously dragged the gunner to a safe distance from the wreck in the expectation that the bomb load would soon detonate, or leaking fuel on the hot engines must soon set the aircraft on fire. They had landed some ten miles west of Maastricht at about 0100 hours on 17th August 1941.

This last effort was all Nunn could achieve and he collapsed beside the wounded gunner. Later, Nunn was to discover that amongst his many injuries were breaks to both his arms. In the circumstances his achievement in extricating Currie showed loyalty and fortitude of the highest order. Currie was much more seriously wounded. Hit in the chest, a bullet had punctured his lung. As a result of their injuries and the exhaustion of escaping from the aircraft they could go no further. They lay there until next morning when they were discovered by Belgian children. Soon the Germans arrived.

They were taken to Maastricht hospital, which was full, so they had to transfer to another hospital nearby. The next day Currie, sadly, died from his wounds. His death cannot detract from the devotion shown by Nunn, risking his own life in the force landing in the attempt to save his disabled gunner.

Flying Officer Gardiner soldiered on to Dusseldorf in L7422, where five 1,000 lb GPs and three small bomb carriers (SBCs) of incendiaries were dropped in the town centre. The searchlight and flak defences were intense but the aircraft escaped damage and returned safely to Waddington at 0350 hours on the 17th. From 97 Squadron, Flight Lieutenant Blakeman's aircraft was repeatedly hit by flak as it traversed the searchlight belt on the outward leg, but all three aircraft bombed the estimated target and returned safely to Coningsby.

During this period in mid-August 1941 cooling the overtaxed Vultures was still a problem and operating oil temperatures were commonly too high for safety. One way of improving the situation was felt to be to enhance the cooling of the oil itself by the lip fitted on the wing upper surface alluded to earlier. This relatively small modification was to have an unforeseen, but dramatic, effect on the aerodynamic efficiency of the aircraft. At this time the aircraft were experiencing severe tail flutter when climbing with a full bomb load. This time it was the whole tailplane and not just the central fin which was affected.

On 25th August 1941 207 Squadron offered seven Manchesters and 97 Squadron two for an operation planned on Mannheim. It was to be a night of high nervous tension and desperate endeavour on behalf of the beleaguered aircrews but, as so often with the Manchester, it was one which produced only the most negligible achievement in military terms. Following briefing, the crews were taken out to their aircraft, the engines and all system checks were carried out preparatory to take-off. At this stage two 207 Squadron Manchesters became unserviceable, one with yet another burst tail wheel tyre, the other with a bad oil leak.

Mannheim – 25th August 1941

Serial	Code	Sqn	Captain
L7308	OF-*	97	F/L C P D Price
L7306	OF-*	97	Sgt T J Mycock
L7300	EM-S	207	F/O W G Gardiner
L7378	EM-A	207	P/O L A Paskell
L7316	EM-U	207	P/O W S Herring
L7317	EM-C	207	F/L W J Lewis
L7432	EM-S	207	P/O P C Birch

The aircraft took off between eight and nine in the evening. The take-offs themselves were unusually protracted, even for the Manchester, and once airborne the most extreme flying difficulties were experienced in several machines. The aircraft seemed more than usually unwilling to climb.

Over the North Sea, after a prolonged struggle, Flying Officer Gardiner was unable to coax L7300 above 8,000ft and persistent severe tail flutter was experienced. He elected to jettison the bombs in the sea and return to base, landing back at 2323 hours. Pilot Officer Len Paskell experienced similar difficulties and dropped his bomb load on Dunkirk docks before returning to base at 0004 hours.

As the remaining crews continued their eastward flight over the continent, the weather deteriorated rapidly. All these aircraft encountered 10/10ths cloud, sleet, rain, icing and electrical storms, making flying conditions extremely uncomfortable. In addition, Pilot Officer Herring in L7316 experienced tail flutter, whilst in L7432 the climbing performance was so marginal and the engines overheating so severely that Pilot Officer Birch had no alternative but to jettison a 1,000 lb bomb to ease the strain.

Flight Lieutenant Lewis was unable to locate Mannheim owing to the extreme weather but dropped four 1,000 lb GPs and 180 x 4 lb incendiaries on an urban area, later tentatively identified as St Goarshausen. At the estimated time of arrival for the target, a break in the cloud below L7432 revealed no sign of it so Birch eventually dumped the load on an unidentified searchlight concentration. Only Herring claimed to have dropped five 1,000 lb and 180 x 4 lb incendiaries on the town centre at Mannheim. Sergeant Tommy Mycock had to abort owing to a hydraulic failure but reported his engines running well.

A close shave for Flying Officer Peter Birch and his crew in Manchester I L7422 'EM-V' of 207 Squadron, following a night fighter attack over the Netherlands en route to Cologne on 31st August 1941. Cockpit perspex was perforated, but damage was mainly concentrated in the rear fuselage and tail. See page 97.
via J M Duncan

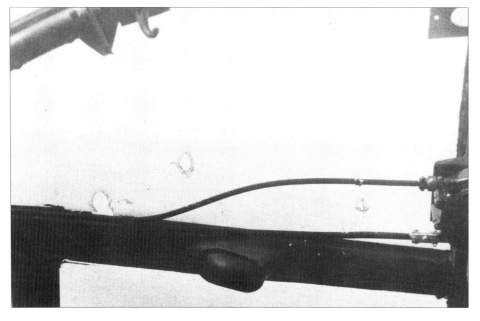

Flight Lieutenant Price was unable to locate the main post office at Mannheim owing to the same cloud cover but estimated his bombs to have fallen in the southern sector of the town. He reported his aircraft behaved perfectly. It remains uncertain whether the 97 Squadron aircraft had the lip fitted to the oil cooling system.

On return, the 207 Squadron crews complained of the truly awful flying performance they had endured with their aircraft. On 27th August Mike Lewis, who had encountered the least problems, was delegated to carry out an altitude test on Herring's aircraft, L7316. There was some suspicion in high places that the crews were exaggerating the poor performance and using it as an excuse not to press home their attacks. Mike Lewis had been Acting Commanding Officer for the week, standing in for Group Captain Boothman who was on leave. Wing Commander K P Lewis became station CO in turn.

Following the fuss which had been raised, the test crew consisted of Group Captain Lewis Roberts, an Avro test pilot, 'Bill' Thorn, Gardiner and Lewis. The aircraft had a full bomb load to simulate the conditions experienced and was found to have a pitiful flying performance. Approaching 14,000ft the aircraft stalled completely with a tremendous flutter in the starboard wing and tailplane.

They concluded the tail buffeting was caused by climbing the aircraft too near the stall and that the best climbing speed was 150mph at 2,850rpm and +6 boost.

A second and separate problem was that the new lips fitted over the oil cooler outlets, whilst improving oil cooling to a limited extent, induced a breakdown in the airflow over the upper wing surface, causing turbulence and a significant loss of lift. The loss of lift was felt to have the greatest effect on those aircraft additionally burdened by a mid-upper turret. Consequently they had

identified another major performance defect which had been created in attempting to solve an earlier problem.

The modifications to the oil cooling system were quickly dispensed with and these extreme climbing and tail flutter problems were overcome.

Later trials with L7320 at the Aeroplane & Armament Experimental Establishment confirmed this diagnosis. Tail flutter could be substantially reduced, it was found by using 10° flap on the climb, but this did little to ease the degradation in take-off performance. The cooling lips were found to be located in the worst possible place and shed 'dirty', turbulent air which impinged directly onto the fin/tailplane junction inducing the vibration. Remedial action had already been taken on the squadrons.

The information came not a moment too soon as 207 Squadron was called upon to operate the very next night, 28th August 1941. The target allocated was the marshalling yards at Duisburg, although the squadron were no more capable of finding such a pinpoint position than they had been in late 1940. On this operation and that dispatched on the following night, the Manchester crews recognised an immediate and noticeable improvement in aerodynamic characteristics and altitude performance.

Although the number of aircraft available for operations remained small, the demands on 207 Squadron continued to be high. For the night of 31st August/1st September 1941 the command asked for four Manchesters to participate. On this occasion the engineering side managed to make six aircraft serviceable. These joined a total of 103 aircraft dispatched to Cologne.

Cologne – 31st August/1st September 1941

Serial	Code	Sqn	Captain
L7419	EM-K	207	P/O A W Hills
L7312	EM-L	207	F/O W G Gardiner
L7373	EM-T	207	P/O W S Herring
L7316	EM-U	207	P/O T R Gilderthorp
L7422	EM-V	207	P/O P C Birch
L7321	EM-D	207	P/O L F Kneil

The aircraft took-off close to 2030 hours and made their separate ways towards Cologne. Soon after entering enemy airspace over Holland L7422 was detected by a Messerschmitt Me110 night fighter. It attacked, seriously damaging the Manchester in the tailplane, blowing great holes in the elevators and making 63 separate holes in the rear turret, knocking out its hydraulic traversing mechanism. The fuselage and cockpit perspex were also holed.

Miraculously, there were no casualties, but as Pilot Officer Birch took evasive action the damage to the elevators resulted in control being lost and the bomber plunged earthward.

Birch eventually righted the aircraft sufficiently for the bomb load to be jettisoned, but control difficulties remained severe. They were near Roermond in Holland. Almost immediately the second pilot, on his first operation and apparently unnerved by his experience, switched on the aircraft's navigation lights, left his seat and baled out of the aircraft via the crew entry door. The lights were soon extinguished and it became clear that as a consequence of the violence of the manoeuvres, assisted perhaps by the return fire of the rear gunner, Sergeant Shadbolt, the night fighter had been shaken off.

Although the aileron and rudder controls remained operative, the airflow was acting alternately on the partly detached upper and lower coverings of the shattered elevators. Still cabled through to the cockpit this was causing the control column to thrash backwards and forwards uncontrollably. The Manchester was climbing and diving in response to the movements of the damaged elevators. Eventually, Peter Birch established that he could reduce and control the switch-backing by means of the tail trimming wheel. Marginally in control, Birch flew L7422 back to Waddington and achieved a safe landing.

Previous histories have reported L7422 as crashing on 1st September 1941, whereas the aircraft survived this encounter, only to be written off in a forced landing on 26th October 1941. L7422 was a triple-finned Manchester I but it is possible that following the severe damage to the tail that it was one of the aircraft modified to Mk.IA configuration by the retrospective fitting of the larger end plate fins.

Meanwhile, L7316 'EM-U', captained by the Australian Pilot Officer T R Gilderthorp, continued struggling for extra height as it ploughed on across Holland. Gilderthorp had been on the high seas en route to England to join the RAF when war was declared. This was the third operation of his first tour. L7316 had reached 7–8,000ft as it entered German airspace when it was suddenly illuminated by searchlights. Immediately they were trapped in a heavy and accurate flak barrage. With the bomb load still on board and before any significant evasive manoeuvres could be undertaken, the Manchester was hit by a burst of flak and immediately caught fire. The shells almost certainly ruptured the wing fuel tanks and shrapnel fragments penetrated the fuselage, one wounding the pilot in the back.

There was obviously no prospect of saving the aircraft, which quickly became a raging inferno. Gilderthorp and the observer, Sergeant Leonard C Parker, baled out from the front hatch before the flames reached them. Wounded and unable to see the ground approaching, Gilderthorp was unprepared for the severity of the impact and suffered further serious injury, including a broken pelvis, in landing. He was rendered unconscious and consequently has no recollection of

The tail of Manchester I L7422 'EM-V' of 207 Squadron, 31st August 1941. Flying Officer Peter Birch made an early return, maintaining marginal control by use of the elevator trim and accomplished a 'wheeler' landing at Waddington. The rear turret was also seriously damaged. Miraculously, nobody in the crew was injured. *via J M Duncan*

where he fell or how he was located and taken to hospital. It was several days before he recovered consciousness and many weeks before he was strong enough to be passed on to the PoW camp. Parker also survived the descent and was captured. L7316, with the remaining members of the crew, fell at Oberkruechen near Cologne, almost certainly before midnight.

The remaining four aircraft all bombed Cologne successfully before returning to Waddington; where Pilot Officer Hills landed back at 0137 hours on 1st September 1941. The heavy cloud cover had again protected Cologne and only a few bombs fell in the city, killing one civilian. The rest of the loads from the 103 aircraft dispatched must have been spread over open country and other built up areas.

That day a conference on crew training on Manchesters was held at the 5 Group Headquarters attended by the commanding officers of 207, 97 and 61 Squadrons, Wing Commanders K Purdon Lewis, D F Balsdon and G E Valentine. It was agreed that 'A' Flight of 207 Squadron would remain operational, whilst 'B' Flight would be withdrawn to concentrate on crew training. The 207 Squadron Operational Record Book (ORB) records that as of this date the squadron had eight Man-

chester captains and ten under training. No. 5 Group had guaranteed that 207 would continue to have priority over other units regarding the supply of new aircraft and crews.

The final and definitive version of the Manchester, the twin finned Mk.IA had started to leave the production lines, being held in readiness at the maintenance units (MUs) for delivery to the squadrons. During August 61 Squadron had only achieved one air-sea rescue sortie and one bombing raid with their aircraft. A large influx of Manchesters was expected now that the engine problems seemed to be overcome and to cater for this 'A' Flight of 97 Squadron was stood down to train crews of 'B' Flight.

On 2nd September 1941 207 Squadron received orders for a raid on a railway station in Berlin. Four aircraft were serviceable and carried out night flying tests, but unfortunately one of these developed engine trouble as it prepared to take-off and had to be withdrawn. The aircraft took off between 2055 and 2126 hours. No.61 Squadron also produced an aircraft, flown by the commanding officer.

Berlin – 2nd/3rd September 1941

Serial	Code	Sqn	Captain
L7388	QR-*	61	W/C G E Valentine
L7373	EM-T	207	P/O W S Herring
L7300	EM-S	207	P/O A W Hills
L7378	EM-A	207	P/O L A Paskell

On the way out across the North Sea, Pilot Officer Hills flew over unbroken cloud at 9,000ft. Pilot Officer Herring reported seeing several groups of German night fighters flying in formation, one group having five and another seven aircraft involved.

All three Manchesters from 207 reached Berlin but failed to locate the railway station owing to haze and cloud. Each of them elected to drop their bombs on the urban area as a secondary target. All found the searchlights and flak defences active and accurate as they ran up to drop their bomb loads.

Herring estimated his 4,000 lb HC and 120 x 4 lb incendiaries fell in the city centre from 17,000ft. Hills experienced an intense flak barrage and dropped his five 1,000 lb GPs on the city centre from 16,000ft. Paskell was able to see his 4,000 lb 'Cookie' burst after it was dropped from 15,500ft but saw no details owing to the haze. His aircraft was peppered by shrapnel from near misses, fortunately without being hit in a vital place.

No. 61 Squadron moved to North Luffenham in July 1941 and the low level of Manchester operations persisted, the squadron continuing to rely on its elderly but reliable Hampdens. The raid on 2nd/3rd September 1941 was Wing Commander Valentine's fifth Manchester operation. In addition to carrying the commanding officer, Group Captain Barrett, the station commander, also went along for the experience. On an earlier operation in the aircraft on 14/15th August 1941 Valentine had bombed Magdeburg from only 1,500ft. He had already declared his intentions of maintaining a low altitude all the way to Berlin before climbing in the target area to identify the aiming point and to reach a safe height above the effects of bomb blast.

A routine radio transmission was received at 2338 hours only half an hour before the briefed time over target. At 0125 European Time the aircraft was engaged by Flakbatterie 1/321 and brought down in the Schönefeld district of Berlin, killing the entire crew, who are all buried in Berlin. Following this loss, orders were issued that station and squadron commanders were not allowed to fly operations without special permission. No. 61 Squadron's Manchester flight was dispersed for a while and several crew members seconded to 207 and 97 Squadrons.

On the return flight from Berlin, Herring saw seven more night fighters patrolling Hamburg but managed to elude them all, whilst Hills received a rousing send off from the flak defences at Bremerhaven. As L7378 was crossing the North Sea a crew member observed a light on the water flashing 'SOS'. They carried out a brief search of the area, but failed to find its source and finally landed back at Cottesmore at 0508 hours due to fuel shortage. The remaining two aircraft had reached Waddington an hour earlier.

As a consequence of the policy change on training between 2nd September and 20th October 207 returned to being the only operational Manchester squadron. Owing to the various postponements and cancellations the next operation, on 7th September 1941, became the second successive return to Berlin. A total of 197 aircraft were sent to the city with a further 51 aircraft diversion to Kiel. Six Manchesters of 207 Squadron stood by for the operation, which was allocated the main telephone exchange in Berlin as its aiming point. As so often was the case, two Manchesters failed to take-off owing to mechanical failure.

Berlin – 7th/8th September 1941

Serial	Code	Sqn	Captain
L7380	EM-W	207	F/L W J Lewis
L7432	EM-Z	207	P/O W S Herring
L7419	EM-Y	207	F/O W G Gardiner
L7378	EM-A	207	P/O L A Paskell

By this time, 'Mike' Lewis had completed his second tour and was scheduled to remain at Waddington to be posted to 44 Squadron as their conversion pilot to the Avro Lancaster. No. 44 were to receive the first prototype, BT308/G, on 16th September 1941. (The '/G' suffix was an indication that the aircraft must be guarded at all times). When the operation was called the squadron commanding officer sought out Lewis and asked him to put in just one more operation. It was a fateful decision. The aircraft Lewis was allocated became unserviceable prior to the night flying test and he had already been obliged to take the reserve. He had carried out a night flying test on L7380 during the afternoon and viewed the aircraft with some trepidation. During the air test he had stopped the engines in turn and discovered that even without a bomb load the aircraft would not maintain height on a single engine. It was, he recalls, 'a clunker amongst clunkers'.

The first three Manchesters took off between 2135 and 2140 hours. Lewis taxied L7380 around to the take-off point, joining a queue of aircraft. Ahead, poised at the Chance Light, was a 44 Squadron Hampden already lined up for take-off, with a second waiting to line up as soon as the first was in the air. They were taking off towards the north east and Lewis watched the Hampden begin to roll on its take-off run. It became airborne, but for some reason the pilot lost control and it piled straight into the ground immediately across the Sleaford road. The bomb load and fuel exploded with a fearful detonation. No radio call of any kind came from the doomed aircraft to hint at its fate. As this aircraft had started its take-off run the second Hampden had lined up on the active runway. The pilot received a 'green' from the control caravan, but sat there apparently frozen in the horror of what had unfolded in front of his eyes.

Lewis, stuck behind, was absolutely champing at the bit. His engines were getting hotter and hotter and take-off could not be delayed. Lewis got on the radio and in no uncertain terms told the Hampden pilot to either take-off or move aside, he simply could not wait. With the urgency conveyed by this call the Hampden pilot finally plucked up the courage and made his own take-off run.

Lewis swung L7380 onto the runway as soon as the Hampden was rolling and commenced his protracted take-off run. It was even more heart stopping than usual for none of them knew whether the whole of the crashed Hampden's bomb load had detonated or not. L7380 rose slowly and reluctantly, with Lewis raising the undercarriage as they passed over the burning wreckage of the Hampden.

Lewis headed for 'The Gate' near Skegness, his usual exit point when crossing the English coast outward bound. He climbed up through a low deck of stratus cloud which was topped at about 3,000ft and levelled out at 8,000ft. Each aircraft proceeded separately along a route chosen by its captain. In order to lessen the risks of traversing the searchlight belt in Holland twice, Lewis elected to take a flight path across the North Sea to hit the German coast just north of the River Elbe, almost due west of Kiel, and from that point he intended to change course towards the south east, heading directly for Berlin. Such a track would have taken L7380 about midway between Kiel and Hamburg and thus for the most part clear of the flak defences of those cities, as well as north of such other major defended city areas as Magdeburg, lying directly west of Berlin. The more northerly route avoided not only the Dutch searchlight belt but also the adjacent flak defences of the Ruhr valley and beyond.

Lewis had decided to complete the crossing of the North Sea maintaining a height of 8,000ft until within striking distance of the north German coast. By this time, he would have burned off almost two hours of fuel, lightening the all up weight of the aircraft to an extent where he was hopeful they could climb to perhaps 14–15,000ft which was the most he could expect from the aircraft without overheating the engines.

Having left the English coast and headed out over the sea the crew settled into a well-established routine. The gunners called in turn asking permission to test their guns. Lewis felt the discernible tremor in the airframe as Warrant Officer Hall traversed the mid-upper turret onto the beam before his short test burst.

With the experience of his two previous tours Lewis had developed his philosophy for operational flying. The aircraft carried a second pilot who, however, did not have a duplicate set of instruments. Thus, Lewis maintained that if he himself became incapacitated the first thing was for the crew to extricate him so the second pilot could take over his position. With this in mind, Lewis had a friend in Lincoln who owned a furniture store, fashion him a comfortable rubber and material covered cushion of the exact proportions to fit into the bucket seat of the aircraft. Instead of the seat pack parachute he wore an observer type of harness and carried a chest pack type parachute in the stowage position behind his seat.

When the aircraft reached cruising altitude Lewis adopted the custom of undoing his seat strap safety harness so he could easily be removed from his seat in the darkness if necessary. At the same time the co-pilot and navigator would swing up the armour plate, giving protection from the rear to the pilot's head and shoulders. On this flight, when Lewis dropped his safety harness, the co-pilot and navigator, for reasons they could not identify in the darkened cockpit, had great difficulty in pushing the armoured plate the last part of the way and eventually had to use considerable force. However, the seat back was finally raised and could be locked in place. The reason for the difficulty was to become apparent a little while later.

The outward flight towards the German coast was uneventful, other than that it suddenly dawned on them that they must have picked up a much stronger tail wind than the 'Met' forecasters had predicted, as they were reaching the enemy coast earlier than expected. Lewis therefore initiated a climb and soon L7380 was slogging up as fast as it could on full climbing power and travelling not much more than 110mph indicated airspeed.

They had reached an altitude of approximately 13,000ft and were still over the sea at a locality a few kilometres west of Tönning in Schleswig Holstein, the time was close to 2200 GMT when 'Dusty' Miller, the rear gunner, suddenly called 'Night fighter astern!' Simultaneously with the call they received a burst of tracer, combined machine gun and cannon fire, which hit the port wing in and around the port engine.

At the low speed Lewis was flying there was no possibility of any evasive action, but an instinctive and fortuitous presence of mind caused him to slam the stick hard forward. The aircraft immediately sank like a stone and the nose dropped. No sooner was this action initiated then a second burst of machine gun and cannon fire soared over them, exactly in the position they had occupied moments earlier.

The fighter had approached from seven o'clock high and in the split second of its approach, 'Dusty' Miller had drawn a bead on the closing night fighter and opened fire. The twin-engined aircraft, provisionally identified as a Junkers Ju 88 or Messerschmitt Me110, was overshooting and as the Manchester disappeared under his nose he broke away above and to port, coming as he did so within the field of fire of the mid-upper gunner, Hall, at a range of only 50-100ft. Miller also fired in the direction of the fighter before it broke away and lost contact completely. There is no positive identification of the night

fighter concerned, nor whether any damage was inflicted by the return fire. With no outward sign that the fire had hit L7380, the pilot may have been unaware that he had caused any damage.

Whilst the gunners kept a sharp lookout lest the fighter should return, Lewis took stock of their situation. Miraculously the aircraft had not caught fire under the hail of tracer bullets. Lewis could vaguely discern the many hits they had taken in the port wing and engine cowling. All engine functions appeared normal but the fuel gauges indicated a serious leak in the port fuel tank. It did not appear that any fire from the fighter had entered the fuselage and there were consequently no injuries.

As a result of the seriousness of the fuel leak, Lewis recognised that it was hopeless going on towards the primary target, Berlin. He accordingly diverted south to Wilhelmshaven, dropped his 4,000lb 'Cookie' and incendiaries on the town and had the navigator work out a course for Waddington. A radio message was transmitted saying they had been attacked by a night fighter and were returning to base. Somehow the position passed with this message became garbled so that the squadron believed the attack to have taken place 50 miles from Berlin, whereas in reality they had barely crossed the coast. L7380 was now heading westwards again over the North Sea at 8,000ft. The fuel had by this time virtually stopped leaking from the wing tank, indicating that the self-sealing mechanism of the tank had eventually worked and staunched the flow.

Suddenly Lewis and Sergeant Powell, the second pilot, noticed that the port engine temperature was rising rapidly. Lewis took a quick look and saw that the whole engine and thin parts of the engine cowling were glowing red hot. By the time he had shut the engine down and feathered the propeller it had become white hot and would probably have seized and caught fire if left a few seconds longer.

After their lucky escapes from the night fighter and from fire when the engine seized, the fight to keep L7380 airborne now began in earnest. A last radio message was received at Waddington, timed 15 minutes later than the first, saying that the port engine was smoking. Lewis set the starboard engine up on maximum power. He was grateful that the port tank had stopped leaking as they would obviously need every pint of fuel they could save if they were going to keep the aircraft airborne and reach the UK flying now into the wind. Relieved of the bombs and part of the fuel load and supported by the denser air at low level, Lewis was determined to make an all out effort. It would be touch and go, as he recalled 'with the starboard engine wide open they were going to chew up an awful lot of gas to reach even East Anglia'.

Lewis immediately turned on the cross-

feed to the port tank and shut off the starboard tank to draw the fuel out of the port wing and cut down the dead weight on the port side. The Manchester had started to lose height at a fairly rapid rate following the engine failure but Lewis had actually encouraged this. Below them was the layer of stratus and they felt like sitting ducks up at 8,000ft on one engine.

Lewis intended to let down slowly until they were immediately above the layer of cloud. Here he reasoned at least they would be safe from attack from below and the gunners could keep a sharp look out in the lighter areas of sky above, if only they could maintain that flying height. They descended to about 5,000ft at which altitude they were within easy reach of the sanctuary of the protective layer of cloud. Unfortunately, despite Lewis' best efforts to trim the aircraft and the use of maximum power on the starboard Vulture, L7380 continued to sink. Slowly they descended into the cloud tops and on down through the cloud layer on instruments until they eventually emerged to see the dark waters of the North Sea beneath. Still the aircraft was showing no sign of maintaining altitude and it began to look certain that within a very short timescale they would have to ditch.

At this point, when they were down to perhaps 1,000ft Lewis decided that, since they would inevitably end up in the water if they maintained their present heading, it would be better to put the aircraft down somewhere on a beach rather than well out to sea where there was the serious risk of losing lives. Thus resigned to not reaching the UK he turned off course to the south until he hit the coast of the Frisian Isles, from which he had been slowly diverging. Having located the coast he again turned westwards keeping the aircraft just offshore. The starboard engine remained at maximum power but still the inexorable loss of height continued.

They were now below 500ft and slowly sank on down towards 300ft. At this height the aircraft began to give the first signs that it might hold altitude and there was suddenly the faintest glimmer of hope that they might remain airborne. The aircraft would fly straight and level for ten seconds or more and then drop a few feet and so on. Unfortunately these downward steps 'on the stairs' continued until Lewis could see by the beach off the port wing tip that they were practically in the water. Lewis deemed that this point, whilst they were flying along an open beach rather than crossing the open stretches of water between the islands, was as good a place as any to set them down.

To carry out the forced landing Lewis needed to be strapped in again and here the problem with the armour plate head protection became apparent, for when Sergeant Powell tried to pass Lewis the safety harness they discovered that the shoulder straps were still over the back of the seat and now jammed by the raised head protection. It was these which had led to the difficulty in raising the plate. To the pilot's dismay the straps were jammed and he was unable to fasten his safety harness. Recognising the problem, Powell and Warrant Officer Macleod, the observer, tried to pull the pins to lower the armoured plate and release the straps, but it was so tightly jammed they were unable to free it. Time was short and a certain amount of confusion arose. Lewis had the co-pilot stand behind his seat and grab him by the shoulders to help reduce the impact. To the rear, 'Dusty' Miller misunderstood their instructions to take up crash landing positions and, thinking they were about to crash, opened the rear side entry door and made to jump out. The mid-upper gunner, Hall, also climbing down from this turret to take up crash position, just had time to grab Miller, pull him back and slam the door.

As Hall settled in position with the aircraft now down to about 25ft, Lewis pulled back the throttle to idle, dumped full flap and carried out a belly landing on the water about 100ft feet out from the water line. There was a terrific shock of the first impact, the deceleration from which was sufficiently small that Powell managed to maintain his hold on Lewis. Immediately there was a second, more severe impact, the aircraft struck the beach below the water, stoving in the bomb aiming perspex dome and bringing them to a shuddering halt. Lewis was catapulted from

the grasp of Powell into the windscreen. A mighty wave of sea water gushed in through the crumpled nose section, rose up beneath the instrument panel and struck Lewis with full force at virtually the same moment that he hit the windscreen. The massive tidal wave no doubt saved Lewis from possible serious injury. He received a severe bang on his head and was rendered semi-conscious, yet still functioning.

To the rear Miller was not yet settled in the crash position and was thrown violently forwards, breaking a small bone in his right hand. At the same time the circular hatch over the former dustbin turret position burst inwards atop a fountain of sea water.

The crew then scrambled to vacate the fuselage in case the aircraft sank. On climbing out of the escape hatches they found to their relief that L7380 had settled down in about six feet of water, facing west south west and lying parallel to the beach. Lewis' next real conscious memory is of coming-to sitting in the escape hatch in the cockpit roof, his feet dangling inside and calling to the crew 'Is everyone out OK?' He was somewhat chastened by the impatience of the response to the query. 'Christ, Skipper, that's the *third* time you've asked us that – *we are all OK!*'

They began to collect themselves and their thoughts. The time was approximately 0100 BST. Looking around there was no indication that their spectacular arrival had attracted any attention. They agreed to take their time and return into the aircraft, finding the interior flooded to knee depth on the flight deck. Having collected the fire axes from their stowage positions they commenced a thorough and systematic destruction of anything and everything which could possibly interest the Germans. They chopped the instrument panel to pieces, the engine instrument panel on the starboard side, the navigation equipment, the radio, the gun sights etc. They pressed the self-

destruct buttons on the confidential items like the bomb sight and identification, friend or foe (IFF) gear but found they had already detonated and then proceeded to demolish these with the axes too. The two wireless operators, Kingston and Hall, between them ate all the night's coded signals they had been issued with at briefing. Although printed on rice paper these were still more than a mouthful!

Having done a thorough job, they decided to make for the shore. Suddenly they heard a hiss and turned to see the dinghy appear from its stowage in the starboard wing root. As it inflated it flopped obstinately upside down into the water by the wing trailing edge. After a struggle this was righted and towed round to the port side. They then walked to the port wingtip and dropped into the sea, which was here only 3-4ft deep. This was of great relief to Lewis, a life-long non-swimmer.

In a group they waded to the shore, pushing the dinghy ahead of them, where a sudden and frightening thought struck Lewis. During 1941, Commando raids by British troops had started in earnest. It came to his mind that surely these exposed beaches on the seaward side of the Frisians must be mined. He held back the crew in shallow water and set off alone up the beach, with a great deal of trepidation, instructing them on leaving that if he made it to dry land they were to follow him in single file stepping in his footsteps. In the event there were no mines and they all made it onto the main part of the island without incident.

There was still no sign of life. They started walking along the beach heading westwards, trying to establish their location and before long found themselves heading back eastwards. This confirmed to them that they were on an island, which was in fact, unknown to them, Ameland. Shortly afterwards they found a large lifeboat at least 25ft long mounted on a cradle consisting of a half-track bogie with wagon wheels at the front, obviously designed for launching by a team of horses. Inspection showed it to be equipped with a mast, engine and fuel. They went through the boat from stem to stern and finding a bottle with a small amount of rum remaining, shared it between them.

They found boards and poles and, working as a team, tried to lever the boat seawards in the hope of sailing it away. They continued to work all night without moving the heavy boat by so much as a fraction. As the dawn rose they saw beyond, at a short distance, a village with a wharf but no sign of other boats they might use. They decided not to involve the local Dutch population for fear of bringing the wrath of the German occupying forces down upon the civilian population. It was a wise decision, for as it turned out there was no way the local people could have helped them to get off the island.

Part of a sequence of photographs showing German servicemen salvaging L7380 'EM-W' which was ditched by Flight Lieutenant Lewis in shallow water on the beach at Ameland on the night of 7/8th September 1941. This event gave the Luftwaffe its first real technical inspection of the Manchester.
via G J Zwanenburg

Above: **With the fins and tailplane and the starboard wingtip and propellers missing, L7380 awaits further demolition. The external completeness contrasted with the devastation wrought by the crew prior to their escape.** *via G J Zwanenburg*

Right: **Block and tackle rigged to lift the starboard Vulture from L7380 on the beach at Ameland.** *No. 207 Squadron archives / R Glynne-Owen*

Below: **Work parties return to the wreck of L7380 and remove the guns. Note how the wavy colour demarcation is oversprayed on a sharp and straight factory finish. In the foreground, the serviceman is using an oxy-acetylene burner.** *via G J Zwanenburg*

At around 0900 hours a German soldier appeared over the dunes. He raised his rifle and shouted to them to raise their arms. Covering them, he called out to others nearby and they were rapidly surrounded and captured.

At more or less the same time that 'Mike' Lewis was setting L7380 down on the beach at Ameland the remainder of the Berlin force reached the target area. Flying Officer 'Junior' Gardiner observed a large fire started by preceding aircraft and dropped his four 1,000lb GP bombs on Aiming Point 'A' from 18,000ft, starting a small fire. Searchlights and flak were as fierce as ever and although Gardiner was not singled out for attack he did see another bomber caught by the lights weaving desperately to escape. At one point this aircraft was seen to fire on a sister aircraft, fortunately with no discernible effect.

As Pilot Officer 'Len' Paskell guided L7378 onto the target at 17,000ft he was in turn trapped and illuminated by the searchlights. More and more lights converged on his aircraft until the crew estimated that 25-30 from all over the city were involved. The heavy flak batteries began to get their range and despite vigorous evasive action the aircraft was hit 15 times, rendering the hydraulics and turrets unserviceable. The crew eventually slipped away into the protective cloak of darkness and returned home, fortunately without being detected by the patrolling night fighters. The results of their efforts could not be observed due to smoke from fires burning near the aiming point.

Flying Officer 'Kipper' Herring and crew had followed a route north east to a point close to Flensburg and then dog-legged across the Baltic to Berlin, entering German airspace between Lubeck and Rostock. En route to the target they observed and successfully evaded patrolling night fighters on five occasions. As they approached the target area they had reached 18,000ft. The defences were thoroughly alerted and intense flak and searchlight activity was evident. As they held a steady course on the bombing run they were trapped in a large searchlight cone and shrapnel from near misses began to pepper the aircraft. Four 1,000lb GPs were released and seen to straddle the target. As the observer closed the bomb doors, and Herring prepared to recommence violent evasive action, the aircraft was suddenly hit by a flak burst. Most seriously hit was the port Vulture, which began to lose coolant rapidly. In quick succession four more flak hits shook the Manchester.

In desperation, Herring put the aircraft into a dive to escape the barrage. As the engine temperature rose he had no alternative but to shut it down and feather the propeller. Unknown to them other damage had occurred, not the least of which was that the bursts had activated the dinghy release. The life raft had inflated and floated down to join the mayhem below. Loss of the port engine meant that the hydraulic supply was also rendered unserviceable, incapacitating all three turrets.

As soon as Herring felt them to be clear of the barrage he pulled out, fortunately they had sustained no further damage. As they levelled out they were relieved to find all the flak bursting several thousand feet higher. In fact they had sustained more than 30 flak hits in the wings and fuselage. The port flank had taken the brunt, with the engine dead and three holes in the wing tank. Fortunately the self-sealing around the tank worked and the fuel loss was contained. Their immediate situation had stabilised but the long term prospect of a single engine return from such a distant target as Berlin was remote. Herring was determined to give it his best shot and a hurried discussion took place. Offered the option of baling out or co-operating in the attempted return, the crew chorused in unison, 'We're staying with you, Skipper.'

As they vacated the target area L7432 began to lose height slowly. Whilst Herring set up the aircraft to fly straight and level and minimise the height loss, the observer, Sergeant Smith, laid out a course in a direct line across the most heavily defended areas of Germany. The wireless operator, Sergeant Riddell, was equally occupied. He transmitted the usual 'Q' code group for duty carried out and that they had encountered heavy defensive action. A coded damage status report followed. He continued listening out for Bomber Command broadcasts of weather conditions during the return flight and began taking bearings to assist the navigation on the homeward leg.

Their predicament, in a Manchester reduced to a single engine and with its defensive armament totally disabled, deep in enemy territory, was precarious in the extreme. Whilst the pilots, observer and wireless operator were fully occupied the two gunners were relieved from their defensive responsibilities. However, L7432 was continuing to lose height and the two were set to work stripping out and jettisoning everything they could get loose from the airframe to decrease their all up weight. This had to be accomplished rapidly but with the minimum of movement within the aircraft so as not to upset the delicate trim. Every foot of altitude was precious and once lost could not be recovered. First Sergeant Everett jettisoned the bombsight, the twin Brownings and all the ammunition from the front turret through the forward escape hatch.

'Tiny' Hallam, the rear gunner, opened the rear hatch and the crew members now formed a human chain passing first the readily dismountable items. The remaining six Brownings from the rear and mid-upper turrets and all their ammunition were dumped. The oxygen bottles, flares etc all went and next the crew set to with fire axes removing parts of the airframe, including even the armoured doors between the cockpit area and the rear fuselage. Despite the critical nature of their situation there was still time for light-hearted banter, Hallam ribbing Smith to the effect that the latter would be missing his date with his girlfriend yet again. This was a crack at Smith having become serious over a local girl to the extent that he moaned loudly every time his scheduled dates were interfered with by unscheduled changes in plan.

Their height was now down to 5,000ft and with the reduction in weight, Herring found L7432 could now maintain this altitude. They were fortunate in evading detection by the defences as they approached the Dutch searchlight belt and Riddell allowed himself to be buoyed up by the prospect that they might at least reach the North Sea with the chance of ditching and being picked up by the air-sea rescue service. Nobody had any idea that the dinghy had been lost. As they crossed the searchlight belt Herring managed to take careful, but spirited, evasive action to avoid detection by the probing beams. The controls started to become sluggish and Herring realised the aircraft was icing up and the aircraft was forced lower still.

Eventually the enemy coast was reached and the long laborious crossing of the North Sea began. The crew could barely believe that the starboard Vulture would continue to keep them aloft for so long, but stagger along they did. L7432 was really a unique Manchester.

After a five hour return flight, in the first light of dawn and on the last dregs of fuel the aircraft reached West Raynham. Having used the emergency system to blow down the undercart 'Kipper' approached the airfield still carrying opposite rudder to counteract the loss of the port engine. He kept the port wing high to minimise the forces on the damaged side of the aircraft and lined up on the grass beside the active runway. Such a cautious approach proved wise when, having touched down on the starboard wheel first, speed was lost before the port wheel was allowed to touch the runway. Unbeknown to the pilot the port tyre was flat, with the result that they swung round sharply to the left, although without further damage to the aircraft. The time was 0600 hours. It was a truly magnificent feat of airmanship and an even more miraculous landing.

When the crew shut down the starboard engine, opened the doors and got out to inspect the aircraft, they found to their amazement that the dinghy, which for some hours they had expected to use, was missing. According to some reports a 1,000lb GP bomb was found to be hung up in the bomb bay, but this has not been confirmed. It was exactly a month since the final spate of engine mods and few could doubt that despite this crews' determination, engine unreliability prior to this time would probably have prevented such prolonged full throttle operation.

L7432 must have looked a wreck, but it was a popular aircraft and following repair returned to the squadron. Herring Christened his mount 'London Pride' and it became much sought after by fellow crews. It was later to experience another engine failure, but once more carry its crew back to a safe landing.

Gardiner and Paskell had returned to Waddington at 0500 and 0520 hours respectively. After the raid, 137 crews reported attacking Berlin in clear weather and many buildings were damaged in the Lichtenberg and Pankow districts to the east and north of the centre; 36 civilians were killed and 212 injured. On the squadron there was dismay at the loss of 'Mike' Lewis and crew but joy and wonder at the near miraculous return of 'Kipper' Herring and his crew.

Within a few days Kipper's crew were invited to the Avro factory at Woodford to be feted by the firm. They had dinner with the Managing Director, Mr Roy Dobson, and Chief Designer, Roy Chadwick, which included, as one was to recall later, the best tomato soup he had ever tasted. Each member was presented with a silver cigarette case to commemorate their achievement. Such was the reputation of the Manchester and the limitations of its military achievements that simply to get one home was an occasion worth celebrating. This fact could not detract in any way from the magnificent feat of airmanship 'Kipper' Herring and his crew achieved.

From early September things had begun, imperceptibly, to improve. The groundings were at an end, serviceability was improving, 61 Squadron had temporarily relinquished its Manchesters, 97 Squadron had reverted to training and 'B' Flight of 207 Squadron was working up to operational status again. On 10th September another development was manifest for the first time. No. 207 Squadron took delivery of its and the RAF's first twin-finned Mk.IA Manchesters, when L7483 and L7484 were received at Waddington. L7483 was the 133rd and not the 21st airframe as all previous histories claim was the first Mk.IA.

With the arrival of these aircraft the Manchester experienced its fourth and final change in colour scheme. The wavy line demarcation between the upper and lower surfaces was replaced by a simpler, straight line. Despite the removal of the central fin, the straight line demarcation continued to sweep up over the fuselage top as if the central fin was still in place.

Two days later, on 12th September 1941, three more Mk.IAs arrived at Waddington, L7485, L7486, L7487. The boys from 'B' Flight of 207 Squadron congregated in front of one of the new Mk.IAs within two or three days and had their photographs taken. The new aircraft were allocated directly to them. The

5 Group commitment to giving the squadron priority regarding the supply of aircraft was being adhered to.

By mid-September 1941 the bulk of the Vulture problems were cured up to a point. Modification No. 44 was being applied to all Vultures in turn by Rolls-Royce and the re-engineered motors finally delivered to Avro for the engineless Manchesters standing idle and forlorn at Cranage, Woodford and Ringway. It seems that the last Avro-built Manchester was completed in late September 1941, whilst Woodford were to complete the last Metrovick aircraft in about November, before switching to Lancasters. At last the equipping of the remainder of 5 Group with Manchesters, albeit now as a stopgap measure, could be considered.

The reduction in rpm from 3,200 to 2,850 reluctantly agreed to by Rolls-Royce, was of great significance in terms of Vulture development and its future potential. It signified the acceptance by the engine designer that it was his star-rod design which was placing an ultimate ceiling on power output in the engine. Opinion within Rolls-Royce was later to be virtually unanimous that it was the star-rod design which killed the Vulture. Only a further major redesign could provide a con-rod configuration capable of absorbing continual increments of power, as opposed to the pegging back represented by reduced con-rod bolt loading.

In late 1941, when the power output from the Merlin was going up in leaps and bounds, the Vulture was operating at the extreme limit it could be stretched to at that stage of its development. By this time only the Manchester was powered by the Vulture and even if the engine had been fully developed and reliable, the Manchester would still have remained underpowered and seriously at risk in the event of one engine failing. As far back as November 1940 it had been recognised that the four Merlin Manchester III, the Lancaster, offered the way forward.

At this stage Rolls-Royce's own assessment of the Vulture was that, to emulate the Merlin and take the first step on the ladder to greater power, the Vulture needed three things: a redesigned con-rod assembly; a two piece cylinder block; a two stage blower.

A Rolls-Royce director and confidant of Lord Hives, Mr R W Harvey-Bailey (Senior), had produced a redesign of the star-rod assembly in the Vulture as a private venture. This reached the model stage and was apparently highly regarded in respect of its innovative design. The redesign envisaged a big-end cap carrying three rods and a union with the fork of the master rod in the same plane as the rod, avoiding the troublesome diagonal junction in the existing star-rod. The low ductility, high brinell con-rod bolts were to be replaced by four long bolts in the steel more commonly used for this purpose by Rolls-Royce metallurgists. These, too, were

oriented in the same plane as the master rod. Power output at altitude was restricted by the two-speed supercharger and the need for a two-speed, two-stage supercharger another essential requirement. Had these three developments come to fruition then possibly the Vulture would have outperformed the Napier Sabre and gone on to a bright future.

In September the brutal truths of the Vulture situation were all too obvious to Rolls-Royce personnel. Eventually Lovell felt sufficiently confident to raise take-off power back up to +9lb/sq in boost and 3,000rpm. This was a mere drop in the ocean,

Roy Chadwick was relentless in pressing Rolls-Royce to increase take-off power still further. Chadwick had enquired whether power could be raised further to 3,200rpm, which would give +11lb/sq in boost. Rolls reflected that this was not covered by type test approval and was already too much for the con-rod assembly.

Chadwick had, moreover, pressed for further increases, mentioning revolutions as high as 3,400rpm. Rolls-Royce commented that at 3,000rpm the Vulture was already using the maximum power obtainable as the engine was full throttle at +9lb/sq in. They pointed out that Boscombe Down had shown that 3,200rpm at +9lb/sq in boost gave no measurable improvement in take-off. The difference between Roy Chadwick's hopes and the reality was stark. In the end wartime expediency killed the Vulture just as that same expediency had thrust it forward into the limelight in 1940, well ahead of its designated time.

Wilfred Stanley 'Kipper' Herring sketched six months after his memorable single engine return from Berlin. By this time he had risen in rank to Squadron Leader. *G R Herring*

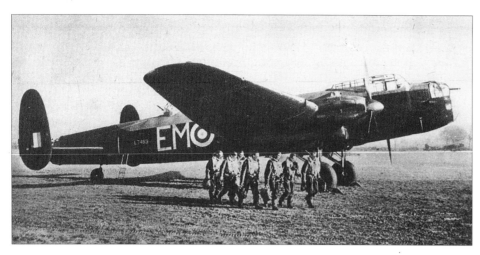

Official photograph of one of 207 Squadron's first Mk.IAs, L7483 'EM-H', at Waddington, circa September/October 1941. Later coded 'EM-O', this aircraft was written off after a forced landing at Martlesham Heath by Squadron Leader K.H.P. Beauchamp. An engine failed outward bound for Dusseldorf on 27/28th December 1941. It was named 'Hobson's Choice' by its crew, a fitting description of their own situation.
Author's collection.

It was about this time that the decision was made to cancel any further development. The Vulture had reached the end and when the decision to abandon the engine went around the Rolls-Royce factory at Derby, the only reaction was a loud and almost universal sigh of relief arising from all sides.

In an unusual interlude on 11th September 207 Squadron entertained a Russian military mission at Waddington. Colonel Fedrovi, a Russian test pilot, and Major Shvetsov, the Air Attaché as interpreter, were given a 45 minute demonstration flight in Manchester L7319 by Flying Officer Geoff Hall, on secondment from 61 Squadron. The evaluation included fighter affiliation with a Boulton Paul Defiant and Colonel Fedrovi had by this time taken the controls. The Russian put the wind up Hall on more than one occasion with unconventional manoeuvres during this close encounter. It steadily became apparent that the visitor was a very competent pilot and Hall had little alternative but to sit back and try to keep calm. After the aircraft disengaged they returned safely to Waddington where the Russians departed following hearty handshakes and lunch in the mess.

The underlying purpose of the visit is uncertain, but it is tempting to suggest that some especially imaginative 'bod' at Air Ministry had devised the ideal solution to the Manchester problem – give them to the Russians! Our Russian Allies accepted everything offered them and palming them off with Manchesters would have been a master stroke. Alas it was not to be!

At this time anyone who was the least bit superstitious would have been excused for believing the Vulture and indeed the Manchester was irretrievably jinxed. As if to strengthen such views an epidemic of propeller feathering mechanism failures now burgeoned in the squadrons. Rolls-Royce compiled a record of these failures with a view to isolating a common cause. The list, dated 17th November 1941, no doubt included failures over much of 1941 as well as those of recent date.

The Rolls-Royce report concluded that the constant speed unit and feathering system had been the cause of the trouble. The airscrew itself appeared satisfactory. A large proportion of the forced landings would not have happened had it not been for a fundamental defect in every Manchester installation, causing the airscrew to lock in fine pitch.

Manchester Propeller Feathering Failures – 17th November 1941

Serial	Operator	Pilot	Date
L7375	**97 Sqn**	**Blakeman**	**28.09.41**

Written off in forced landing near Coningsby. Pressure cut-out switch did not work when feathering, so that airscrew unfeathered again to fine pitch stops, and remained there owing to defect referred to above.

| **L7308** | **97 Sqn** | **Blakeman** | **28.10.41** |

Written off in forced landing near Coningsby. Airscrew feathered itself on take-off, due to defect in constant speed unit. [Aircraft Record Cards indicate this aircraft reincarnated at some stage – Author.]

| **L7520** | **61 Sqn** | **Searby** | **2.11.41** |

Written off in forced landing Roxton, Beds. Port engine cut in flight and airscrew could not be feathered so that aircraft could not maintain height.

| **L7280** | **207 Sqn ?** | **Eustace ?** | **–** |

Landed downwind at Waddington aerodrome. Airscrew feathered itself on take-off due to defect in constant speed unit.

| **L7465** | **97 Sqn** | **–** | **–** |

Vulture No.548. Went to fine pitch stops after unfeathering at Coningsby. Four con-rods broken.

| **R5782** | **207 Sqn** | **–** | **11.11.41** |

Vulture No.166. Went into fine pitch after unfeathering. Engine returned to works after over-revving, no damage done.

| **L7286?** | **207 Sqn** | **Burton-Gyles?** | **4.6.41?** |

Force landed in field near Waddington. Airscrews could not be unfeathered after a silent approach test.

| **L7320** | **A&AEE** | **–** | **–** |

Airscrew feathered itself and then went to the fine pitch stops on take-off. Solenoid switch was stuck. Collided with wireless mast and force landed at Boscombe Down.

| **L7282** | **97 Sqn ?** | **–** | **–** |

Force landed on Waddington aerodrome. Port airscrew would not unfeather after a feathering test.

| **L7292** | **–** | **–** | **27.11.40** |

Force landed on Woodford aerodrome. Airscrew went to fine pitch on take-off due to failure of constant speed unit washer. Con-rod broken.

| **L7322** | **–** | **–** | **–** |

Force landed on Waddington aerodrome. Same as above. Over-revving did not damage engine.

| **L7377** | **207 Sqn** | **Nunn** | **5.41** |

Force landed between the hangars at Scampton. The airscrew feathered itself in flight, and then went to the fine pitch stops due to a short in the electronics.

Miraculously nobody was killed in any of these incidents but they can have done little to bolster confidence in the Vulture or the Manchester. For much of this period 207, 97 and, later in December, 61 Squadrons were engaged on operations and there is no record of any feathering failure in the course of operational flying. In December 1941 Pilot Officer Dave Green was to have a similar failure at low level over the Severn Estuary in L7432. In this case the feathering mechanism remained operational and a safe single engine landing was carried out. Moves towards rectification had obviously been made but quite what and when this was achieved is not established.

With Manchester airframe development finally reaching its ultimate expression and Vulture engine development terminated, in mid-September 1941 the story of the aircraft itself reaches an end. Production had ceased and the Manchester was no more than a stopgap awaiting the Lancaster. Many Manchesters remained engineless and ineffective and it would be the end of the year before enough aircraft were serviceable to begin the task of re-equipping more 5 Group squadrons. No. 207 Squadron remained the only operational unit and it would be early December before 61 Squadron returned to operations, followed in quick succession by 83 and 106 Squadrons.

With many 61 Squadron crews attached to 97 and 207 Squadrons for further training, the remainder of September was principally taken up with testing new aircraft and training new crews. Despite this there were adventures and tragedies aplenty for Manchester crews during the month.

On 13th September Sergeant 'Jammy' Hartley and crew of 97 Squadron had a lucky escape when a main wheel tyre burst on L7306 just before lift off. The undercarriage collapsed and the aircraft spun round and caught fire. L7306 was a write-off. That night

Pilot Officer D E Fox of 97 Squadron ran out of fuel on a cross-country flight in L7383. The aircraft crashed in an attempted forced landing at West Wickhouse, two miles south of the village of North Walsham in Norfolk. One crew member died.

Training of 207 Squadron 'B' Flight crews was progressing over this period and various exercises and night cross-country flights took the aircraft long distances from Waddington. On one such navigation exercise, on 14th September 1941, a 'B' Flight Manchester made a scheduled landing at Millom (or Haverigg) in Cumberland.

It appears that when this Manchester later took off from Millom to continue the exercise a thin paper washer in a hydraulic component in the fuselage failed, causing the fluid under pressure to spurt out in a dense spray. The hydraulic system was of relatively low pressure, in large diameter pipes, involving large volumes of fluid. Such was the suddenness of the rupture and the severity of the leak that the wireless operator incorrectly presumed that the aircraft had hit the sea and was ditching.

Quickly recognising the true source of the fluid, the wireless op – who was nearest to the leak, called the pilot who completed a circuit and landed before all the fluid drained out of the system.

The captain telephoned Waddington informing them of his plight and within a short period another aircraft was made ready, with Eric McCabe and a small team of fitters, who flew up to Millom. When McCabe inspected the unserviceable aircraft the cause of the leak was quickly established, but since all the necessary spare parts were not available, the aircraft and fitters returned to Waddington that night.

Next day, with the necessary spares, Pilot Officer Crump took off in L7318 for Millom. Eric McCabe was due to accompany Crump, but at the last moment a Senior Rolls-Royce representative arrived to discuss engine problems. McCabe handed his flying kit to a Senior NCO who took his place. Later on the 15th September, with the repair completed the two aircraft flew back to Waddington where the repaired Manchester landed safely in the early evening.

An 'op' was planned for 'A' Flight for that night. Six Manchesters were to attack Hamburg, the total force was 169 aircraft. At around 1830 the crews were out on the airfield carrying out their preflight checks. Pilot Officer Paskell and crew were busily 'washing down' the tail wheel of their Manchester when Crump appeared in the circuit in L7318. There would just be time for him to land before the Manchester force took off.

Pilots of 'B' Flight 207 Squadron, Waddington, posed in front of one of their new Manchester Mk.IAs, early September 1941. Left to right: Warrant Officer K A King (unit unknown), Flight Lieutenant Geoffrey Hall (seconded from 61 Squadron), Flying Officer John De Lacey Wooldridge, Pilot Officer Gordon Crump (killed 15th September 1941), Flying Officer David A Green, Pilot Officer John C L Ruck-Keene (killed in action 20th/21st October 1941), Pilot Officer B Derek Bowes-Cavanagh (killed in action 12/13th October 1941) and Pilot Officer George R Bayley (killed in action 8/9th January 1942). *No.207 Squadron archives / R Glynne Owen*

Hamburg – 15th September, 1941

Serial	Code	Sqn	Captain
L7300	EM-S	207	F/O W G Gardiner
L7455	EM-G	207	P/O A W Hills
L7378	EM-A	207	P/O D A Green
L7373	EM-*	207	P/O W S Herring
L7317	EM-C	207	P/O P C Birch
?	EM-*	207	P/O L A Paskell

'Penny' Beauchamp, the 'B' Flight Commander, was on the airfield awaiting the return of his charges. He watched L7318 as it flew past the airfield at about 1,000ft on the downwind leg prior to landing. Suddenly, without any warning or radio call from the aircraft, it put its nose straight down and dived vertically into the ground. There was a large explosion as the aircraft plunged into a field at South Hykeham, five miles west of Waddington. The crash and explosion left a large smoking crater and scattered wreckage far and wide. The aircraft was carrying a total of ten air and groundcrew and there were no survivors.

A member of the groundcrew party sent to the scene soon afterwards, Corporal Terry Flatt, described the horrific sights at the crash site. Near one crumpled section of airframe he came upon the torso of a crew member still strapped in his seat, the head was missing and only the stumps of his four limbs remained. It was a gruesome and tragic loss.

The crash investigation by the Accident Investigation Branch (AIB) proved inconclusive, no defects in the airframe or engines could be found. In the absence of any positive evidence and in view of the timing and position when the crash occurred the AIB inspector hypothesised that, since an extra crew complement was being carried, one or more of them were more than likely travelling in the nose compartment. There was a rule that the aircraft were not to land with any crew members in the nose except on operations. It was suggested that after Crump had lowered the wheels prior to landing he would have called those in the nose to get back into the rear of the aircraft for landing, thus shifting the centre of gravity aft. When the flaps were lowered the centre of gravity would suddenly shift further aft. At such a slow speed lift would disappear, with the result that the nose would drop and the aircraft would crash before control could be recovered. This conjecture was later tested at a safe height in a simulation of the crash. It was found that the aircraft did indeed nose down and lost at least 1,000ft before level flight could be regained.

Despite the shock at witnessing L7318 going straight-in directly in front of their eyes, the 'A' Flight operation had to proceed. Whilst crash crews and ambulances went out to try and find survivors from Crump's aircraft the six Manchesters completed their preflight checks and trundled out for take-off. Pilot

Officer Len Paskell's Manchester, with Sergeant 'Eddy' Edmonds on board, became unserviceable with mechanical trouble before take-off; it is thought the rear tyre burst. Thus only five Manchesters departed in a tight bunch between 1849 and 1852 hours.

Dense cloud was encountered on the outward journey, which became more broken towards the target, allowing details on the ground to be discerned. The aircraft were, at this stage of their operational career, reaching more respectable flying heights, ranging from 13,000 to 17,500ft in the target area. In the target area they encountered ferocious opposition. Searchlights and intense flak interfered with bombing accuracy. The aircraft carried out their attacks between 2133 and 2157 hours.

Flying Officer Gardiner's observer watched his bombs burst in a line across a railway junction within one mile of Aiming Point 'B', whilst Pilot Officer Herring's bombs, which were a mixture of a 'Cookie' and 4lb incendiaries, burst one mile north of the railway junction. The intense opposition resulted in a number of casualties in the attacking force. Gardiner recorded a bomber crashing in flames at 2133 hours. Hills also observed an aircraft in the target area illuminated by searchlights and shot down. Herring saw an aircraft shot down by fighters and another by flak as it was passing over Sylt.

Pilot Officer Dave Green was flying that night with an inexperienced second pilot, Sergeant Thomas. Thomas was to become a capable pilot before being tragically killed with Sergeant Wescombe and crew on 14th January 1942. Sergeant 'Goldie' Goldstraw, the observer in the aircraft, recalls Thomas as a big gangling lad who wore his full Irving jacket and trousers in the cockpit.

On the return flight, when Dave Green judged they were beyond the zone in which German night fighter attacks might be encountered, he suggested that the second pilot should exchange seats with him and obtain some operational experience behind a full set of blind flying instruments. Owing to his size and the cumbersome flying suit, Thomas had some difficulty in making the switch and in doing so unknowingly kicked the flap lever forward, dropping the flaps fully down. At the same time his left elbow inadvertently knocked the autopilot, which was disengaged, to the 'on' position. The autopilot had not been trimmed to fly the aircraft 'hands off' and consequently the aircraft immediately began a vicious climb, which became progressively steeper until, as the speed fell away, the Manchester stalled. Green and Thomas naturally were in a difficult position, not yet strapped in and disconnected from the intercom. As the aircraft reared up both were pushing desperately forward on the control column fighting the autopilot and flaps. Meanwhile the mid-upper gunner was shouting down the inter-

com 'The flaps are down. The flaps are down'. It was pandemonium as the shouted comments were deafening everyone other than the only two who had the means to rectify the situation. The aircraft performed several other manoeuvres it was not designed to do before Dave Green had the chance to slip back into the left hand seat.

In the complete darkness, operating by touch only, Green quickly established which of the many potential combination of variables was not as it should be, pulled up the flaps again and disengaged the autopilot. Slowly they calmed down and breathed again, not for nothing would Dave Green receive an assessment of 'Above Average' as a multi-engine pilot on leaving the squadron. His superb qualities of airmanship had undoubtedly saved the aircraft in circumstances where a less experienced pilot may have been unable to diagnose the combination of changes which was causing the control difficulties.

Pilot Officer Birch had a frustrating experience. Having reached the target area his aircraft, L7317, experienced a bomb release failure. Perhaps whilst stooging around trying to release them his aircraft was coned by searchlights and held. He evaded them by gliding. One 1,000lb bomb was eventually jettisoned in the sea and the remainder brought all the way back. On return he found the hydraulics unserviceable, as did Hills. Both pilots managed to pull off safe landings at Waddington, presumably following the use of the emergency systems to lower the flaps and undercarriage.

They landed back between 0045 and 0130 hours. Hamburg was a heavily defended, hard nut of a target. Throughout his tour, Bill Hills had a premonition he was going to be shot down over Hamburg. He did have some narrow escapes but was ultimately one of those to complete a tour.

On this occasion 207's modest effort was marred only by the persistent malfunctions of the aircraft and all had returned safely. A great deal of damage occurred in Hamburg in this attack. There were 26 fires, seven of them large, 82 civilians were killed and 229 injured. The worst incident occurred in Wielandstrasse where a 'Cookie' fell on a large apartment block which was still occupied, 66 civilians were killed and 171 injured in this single incident.

Later in September there was more excitement at Waddington. The very first Metropolitan Vickers built Manchester delivered to the RAF, R5782, had just been received by the squadron, which by then was also using Bottesford for flying training.

On 27th September 1941 'Penny' Beauchamp was given the job of air testing this completely new aircraft from Bottesford. The test completed, Beauchamp headed R5782 back. They made their circuit prior to landing but on lowering the undercart the port leg

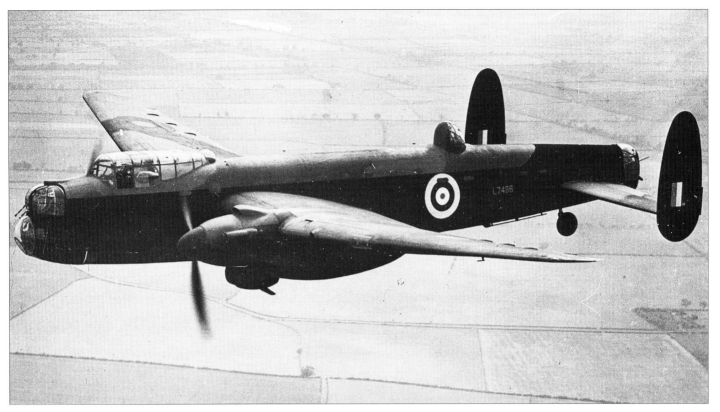

One of 207 Squadron's first Manchester IAs, L7486, caught on a brief air test from Waddington soon after delivery in early September 1941. L7486 was dispatched 19 times as 'EM-P' and 'EM-B'. *J Simpson*

failed to lock down. Overshooting the airfield, Beauchamp decided to divert to Waddington, which had no concrete runways and therefore offered more scope for drifting off-line on landing. On approaching Waddington the undercarriage was lowered again and still the port undercarriage warning light remained a positive red. There appeared to have been a hydraulic failure on one side. Beauchamp had still not run out of options and activated the auxiliary pneumatic system. Still the red light remained illuminated. They toyed with the possibility that the wheel was indeed locked but that there was an electrical fault. Whatever the reason, Beauchamp had to meet the moment of truth.

The aircraft made a careful approach to Waddington, where Beauchamp touched down the starboard wheel first before gently allowing the port wheel to settle onto the grass as the speed died away. The port undercarriage leg slowly collapsed, dropping the wing and spinning the aircraft round with little damage. It was a textbook emergency landing.

Inspections revealed that the hydraulic supply to the undercarriage had failed, but the reason for the non-operation of the pneu-

matic system was more of a surprise. Following propeller icing problems, a de-icing system was developed and installed. This involved a 'slinger ring' installed within the airscrew boss. When activated, de-icing fluid was pumped out through the slinger ring and was spun outward by centrifugal force along the blades. In this instance they discovered that the emergency compressed air actuating mechanism had been inadvertently connected to the slinger ring instead of the undercart, venting the air uselessly through the slinger ring instead of locking the wheels.

Trouble returned to 97 Squadron in a familiar form on 28th September. Flying Officer Blakeman and crew were carrying out propeller feathering exercises in L7375 'OF-B', when a propeller unfeathered itself spontaneously and went to the fine pitch stops and stuck. The engine promptly over-revved itself and the drag on one side caused an immediate forced landing to be made at East Sibsey near Boston, Lincolnshire. The aircraft was a complete write-off and the crew fortunate to survive.

In addition to the Metrovick Manchesters and the new Woodford built Mk.IAs arriving, September was a good month for 207 Squadron in that on the 29th 'B' Flight became operational, doubling at a stroke the number of serviceable aircraft generally available for operations. On 30th September another list of modifications to be incorporated into Manchester and Lancaster aircraft was issued. This time none related to merely keeping the aircraft serviceable and few appear to have been actually installed.

Manchester and Lancaster Modification List – 30th September 1941

1 Parachutist dropping
2 Multi-flare chute
3 Conversion to glider tug
4 Dual control
5 Special armour protection
6 Arrester Gear
7 AD Type H

Of these the most interesting was probably item No.6 and arrested landing trials were later carried out by both aircraft types, as described in a later chapter. During October 61 Squadron began flying from North Luffenham's satellite, Woolfox Lodge. When the squadron returned to operational flying in December it flew all its remaining Manchester operations from this base.

On 4th, 5th and 9th October 1941 the largest force of serviceable Manchesters yet assembled by 207 Squadron were prepared for operations to Emden (twice), Nuremberg and Karlsruhe, each in turn being cancelled for unspecified reasons. On the 10th another operation was set up but due either to weather problems or uncertainties at Group the planned target was changed from Stuttgart to Karlsruhe and later to Essen. Later still an amendment standing down two of the original force of 12 was received. The actual target finally agreed was the Krupps Works. The 207 Squadron Manchester force joined 68 other Bomber Command aircraft in the Essen force and a further 69 aircraft were sent to Cologne

This was apparently the first operation to involve Manchester Mk.IAs. The aircraft took-off between 0026 and 0045 hours carrying either a 4,000 lb 'Cookie' and incendiaries or 1,000 lb GP bombs and incendiaries.

Essen, 207's biggest yet – 10th October 1941

Serial	Code	Sqn	Captain
L7378	EM-A	207	P/O L A Paskell
L7454	EM-M	207	F/O P C Birch
L7483	EM-H	207	S/L K H P Beauchamp
L7485	EM-O	207	F/L W G Gardiner
L7419	EM-Y	207	P/O B D Bowes-Cavanagh
L7317	EM-C	207	P/O L F Kneil
L7309	EM-J	207	F/Sgt G B Dawkins†
L7486	EM-P	207	F/L P C Ward-Hunt
L7484	EM-F	207	F/O J Wooldridge†
L7373	EM-T	207	F/O W S Herring

† First 'op' of second tour.

On the outward flight bad weather was encountered with dense cloud and icing conditions. Pilot Officer Bowes-Cavanagh had crossed the Dutch coast at 12,000ft when flames were seen issuing from the port engine, accompanied by a rise in engine temperature. He located an airfield below and, arming the bombs, dropped his five 1,000 pounders and incendiaries on it. He made an early return, the fire apparently having died down. Later the airfield was estimated to be Haamstede.

As they continued their penetration to the Ruhr, both Pilot Officer Paskell and Flight Sergeant Dawkins had their air speed indicators (ASI) freeze up. With the ground invisible due to cloud and no ASIs it was impossible to plot time and speed for dead reckoning navigation. As a consequence they soon had only the vaguest idea of their location and instead of the Krupp Works reported later that they had bombed the 'Ruhr area'. Dawkins' ASI remained frozen for two hours. On return nobody could be confident they had found the target, although six crews believed they had bombed near Essen. Dense cloud and haze had protected the city as so often in the past.

Perhaps most indicative of all of the severity of the navigation problems and of how far off course a crew could wander inadvertently in a five hour flight at this stage of the war with no adequate navigational aids is the story of Flying Officer Birch's return flight. After blind flying all the operation, Sergeant Stead, the observer, had calculated their estimated time of arrival to descend on approaching the English coast to obtain a pinpoint for the last leg to Waddington. They descended to less than 1,000ft before breaking cloud, only to discover they were still over Holland! Consternation ensued, a check on the fuel situation indicated around 105 gallons still available, which was very marginal to reach base. They continued westwards at the most economical speed and as they pro-

gressed it became likely they would have to ditch. All the necessary preparations were therefore made for a sea landing. To their profound relief Birch had eked out their modest remaining fuel so that they just reached East Anglia, landing on the first approach to Horsham St Faith with the fuel gauges reading zero.

Afterwards the crew were able to tease their observer, christening this operation 'Stead's Folly'. Underneath the frivolity it had been a tense and desperate episode, as well as a stark example of the navigational problems facing Bomber Command at this time. The first aircraft back at Waddington landed at 0537 hours whilst Peter Birch touched down at Horsham at 0721. Dawkins, with ASI problems, got back at 0655, whilst Paskell landed at 0732.

For an operation on 12th October 207 Squadron put up the previously unattainable number of 14 serviceable Manchesters. The target was the synthetic rubber factory at Huls in the Ruhr. Three aircraft were later cancelled by Group. Once more the bomber force was split, Command dispatching 152 aircraft to Nuremberg, 99 to Bremen and 90 to Huls. The eleven aircraft took off between 0130 and 0200 hours.

Huls – 11 up – 12th October 1941

Serial	Code	Sqn	Captain
L7486	EM-P	207	F/L P C Ward-Hunt
L7378	EM-A	207	P/O L A Paskell
L7309	EM-J	207	F/Sgt G B Dawkins
L7454	EM-M	207	F/O P C Birch
L7485	EM-O	207	F/L W G Gardiner
L7487	EM-N	207	S/L K H P Beauchamp
L7322	EM-B	207	P/O G R Bayley
L7422	EM-V	207	Sgt J C Atkinson (1st 'op')
L7373	EM-T	207	F/O W S Herring
L7484	EM-F	207	F/O J Wooldridge
L7312	EM-L	207	P/O B D Bowes-Cavanagh

Pilot Officer Derek Bowes-Cavanagh carried out his pre-flight checks. In his case this included hanging his personal good luck charm – a pair of his girlfriend's French knickers – in the cockpit beside him. As with all such charms and superstitions its function was to ward off evil and keep him safe. So far it had worked it seemed.

Bowes-Cavanagh's observer, Sergeant Jack Cheesman, had laid out a course which picked up a pinpoint on the North Sea coast of Holland close to the Belgian border and thence on across Belgium to the Ruhr. They crossed over the estuary of the Scheldt and were making their way unobtrusively into Belgian airspace. All was calm on board. Quite suddenly and without any forewarning on the intercom, L7312 was riddled from nose to tail by gun fire. Oberfeldwebel Paul Gildner in a Messerschmitt Me110 of II/NJG1 at Leeuwarden had completed a classic night fighter stalk from below and behind in

the dark part of the sky.

Before any assessment of the extent of the damage or casualties could be made, although clearly the aircraft was seriously damaged and on fire, Cheesman was contacted on the intercom by Bowes-Cavanagh and instructed to go forward to the bomb aiming position and jettison the bombs.

Cheesman achieved this within a short time period, which was certainly less than a minute, but by then it had become clear to him that the conditions within the aircraft had deteriorated to such an extent that it was irredeemably doomed. With his parachute already on, Cheesman opened the front escape hatch and baled out. He was the only crew member to survive. The blazing Manchester plummeted down and exploded on the ground beneath. Derek Bowes-Cavanagh's lucky talisman had proved no protection against cannon and machine gun bullets.

In his combat report Gildner claimed the aircraft was a Whitley and gave the time of the attack as 0408 hours. Gildner himself was killed on 24th February 1943 by which time he had 44 victories to this credit. Cheesman himself reached the ground only a short time later near the blazing wreck. He had landed at Eschen in northern Belgium only a few miles from Roosendaal on the Dutch/Belgian border.

Ahead in the glow of the fire from the burning Manchester, Cheesman vaguely discerned moving figures silhouetted in the orange glow. Heading off in the opposite direction to escape the commotion he encountered others heading for the scene. He tried his schoolboy German and then French on them but they did not understand him and he could not follow their responses. Possibly these were Flemish speaking members of the local population. Lost and confused, Cheesman was soon captured and incarcerated for the night somewhere close by.

The next day his German captors returned with him to the crash site, perhaps to confirm that it was indeed the aircraft he had escaped from. It was a distressing and horrifying experience which once witnessed no amount of trying could ever drive out of the mind. In the early morning mist of 13th October 1941 the shattered and burnt bodies and airframe were scattered in confusion, an Alsatian guard dog running around with lively interest. From here Cheesman was escorted, possibly in a motor-cycle combination, to a Luftwaffe night fighter station near Antwerp and later moved by car to Brussels. Thence by train he was sent to Dulag Luft for interrogation.

The rest of the aircraft were due on target at 0315 to 0400 hours, where 10/10ths cloud made target identification problematical. Fires were reported in the target area. The remaining ten aircraft returned safely.

Whilst Jack Cheesman was experiencing his first day in four years of captivity and wondering why he alone had been picked out to survive, back at Waddington plans for another operation on the 13th were proceeding apace. A 60-strong aircraft raid on Dusseldorf was planned, together with a 39 aircraft raid on Cologne. Ten Manchesters were detailed for the operation to Cologne, although one was later cancelled in an amendment order from Group.

Cologne – 13th October 1941

Serial	Code	Sqn	Captain
L7317	EM-C	207	P/O L F Kneil
L7485	EM-O	207	S/L T C Murray
L7484	EM-F	207	F/L W G Gardiner
L7486	EM-P	207	F/O D A Green
L7483	EM-H	207	P/O G R Bayley
L7487	EM-N	207	P/O J C L Ruck-Keene†
L7300	EM-S	207	F/O P C Birch
L7373	EM-T	207	P/O L A Paskell
L7321	EM-D	207	F/O J Unsworth

† First 'op' as captain.

The 13th was a Sunday and Pilot Officer 'Jock' Paskell's crew were already advanced in preparations for the forthcoming operation. Sergeant 'Eddy' Edmonds, his rear gunner, was busy in the hangar when Paskell came in to pass on the good news that Edmonds' posting at the end of his tour had just come through. Edmonds had been with the unit since the time of inception at Boscombe Down. The following Thursday Edmonds was to go to Manby on an Air Gunnery Instructors' Course. Edmonds told Paskell that he was willing to continue flying in the crew until the day of his posting. Paskell there and then determined that he would personally ensure that Edmonds lived to go to Manby and during the day insisted on making out a leave pass that would carry Edmonds from that day until the next Thursday. Paskell felt strongly that Edmonds had done his bit and there was no way he would fly with 207 again.

Neither knew, nor could possibly know, that by this action Paskell had saved Edmonds' life, albeit inadvertently, at the expense of another. Such are the laws of chance in wartime.

Another highly experienced member of Paskell's crew at this time was the observer, Flight Sergeant Ken Houghton, who had already completed one tour with 83 Squadron (Handley Page Hampdens) and won the DFM. He had also had his fair share of narrow scrapes. Whilst returning from operations in a Hampden they overflew Britain in bad weather and were forced to ditch in Cardigan Bay. The pilot, Sergeant Farmer, and wireless operator were drowned but Houghton and the rear gunner managed to stay afloat on the partially inflated dinghy and miraculously survived.

Following the loss of Pilot Officer Bowes-Cavanagh's aircraft the night before, the 13/14th October was to be another tragic night for 207 Squadron. For the second consecutive night, Bomber Command was bound for the Ruhr, the route traversing Belgian airspace. The aircraft took-off between 0125 and 0155 hours and almost immediately the overladen bombers experienced problems, several finding it impossible to reach a sufficient height to make a safe traverse of the North Sea.

Flight Lieutenant Gardiner jettisoned a 1,000 lb bomb safe off Orfordness. Flying Officer Birch similarly released a 1,000 lb bomb 40 miles from the Dutch coast to permit a safe crossing of the enemy coast.

On reaching the anti-aircraft searchlight belt, Pilot Officer Ruck-Keene was coned by the lights near Liege and held. Evasive action was taken and at the same time an enemy fighter, believed to have been a Me109, was caught in the glare of the lights for a few seconds. L7487 slipped the lights and no fighter attack materialised, the fighter pilot possibly having been temporarily blinded.

Rising along with the Me109 was a small group of black painted Me110Cs of I/NJG1 from St Trond in Belgium. The Me110s carried no airborne radar at this stage and were not even connected to the ground radar stations, relying entirely on visual interceptions and co-operation with the searchlights. Oberleutnant Heinrich Griese had taken off in 'G9+KH' at 0343 local time (0243 GMT) with Unteroffizier Scherke as his radio operator and was now patrolling his assigned 'box' in the Himmelbett system over Liege.

Amongst the mixed bomber force strung out across Belgium and the North Sea was Manchester L7321 'EM-D', being flown by Flying Officer Joe Unsworth on the first operation of his second tour. He carried a scratch crew with little experience of flying together, although the wireless operator, Flight Sergeant Moulding, was experienced and also starting his second tour. For this crew the operation had been unusually quiet so far.

Suddenly the searchlights surrounding Liege found their second victim within a few minutes, L7321. This time Griese was nearest the aircraft and closed with his quarry, taking pains to remain in the dark part of the sky and not be blinded by the lights. As he came within range Griese identified the triple tail unit of an RAF Manchester. In the last few seconds he dived to approach from below and then pulled up under the tail of Unsworth's aircraft until he was within 25 metres (30 yards) and certain of a decisive strike. At 0443, Griese entered the searchlight beams fleetingly and opened fire with his fixed nose cannon on a still unsuspecting prey. His first burst struck home with, it seemed to him, devastating effect.

In L7321 Tom Cox, the second wireless op/air gunner, was occupying the front turret

that night and has no recollection of the aircraft being detected by searchlights. The first intimation he had of an attack was when air fired tracer began to fly past his turret on the right hand side. The next few seconds passed in a blur. Unsworth immediately called the rear gunner, Sergeant Dickson, for information on what was happening. Dickson replied that he had been firing at a night fighter for the last ten minutes. If this was the case nobody in the aircraft had been aware of it and Dickson had not informed Unsworth of the developing attack or suggested any evasive action. Perhaps unprepared for this response, Unsworth instructed the experienced Moulding to discover what was happening at the rear of the aircraft.

Within seconds of the attack and before Moulding could take any action the second pilot, Pilot Officer 'Eddie' Carroll, interjected on the intercom to report that clouds of sparks and a few flames were issuing from the starboard Vulture. Unsworth immediately ordered Carroll to press the fire extinguisher button. Carroll carried out the order but coincident with him hitting the button the entire starboard wing burst into flame. Whether the two facts were in any way linked could not be ascertained.

In the Me110 Griese had seen the Manchester catch fire within a few seconds of his attack and it is likely that his shells hit more than just the starboard wing. He has no recollection of any return fire from either of the rear defence positions in the aircraft. Recognising that the Manchester was mortally hit he refrained from mounting a follow-up attack to give the crew a chance to use their parachutes. Griese landed back at St Trond at 0624 hours to learn that the Anti-Aircraft Searchlight Regiment had confirmed his kill.

The intensity and scale of the fire left Unsworth in no doubt that they had only a few seconds before the fuel tanks or bomb load exploded and he immediately ordered the crew to bale out. Receiving the order, Tom Cox climbed out of the front turret, donned his parachute, jettisoned the forward escape hatch and baled out. Carroll was able to follow shortly after Cox. Once his parachute had deployed, Cox was able to watch the blazing Manchester maintain a steady course ahead of him for quite a while before it dived into the ground and exploded on impact at 0444 local time (0344 GMT). The aircraft fell in a small wood at Horion-Hozemont four kilometres (2½ miles) east of Comblain-au-Pont, 17km south of Liège carrying the five remaining airmen to their deaths. Cox found it difficult to understand what had prevented the remaining crew members escaping.

As he approached the ground in the clear, dark, moonless night, Cox realised he was drifting backwards. Shortly afterwards he felt the movement arrested as he, too, fell into a small tree on the edge of a wood.

Looking down he saw he was only about two feet off the ground and so punched his quick release and dropped free to the earth below. He was unable to disentangle the 'chute initially, but as it became a little lighter and he could make out more detail of what was snagging the canopy he made a fresh attempt to release it. As he was doing so he became aware that he was being approached by two young men close to his own age in civilian clothes. They challenged Cox in English and his first contact with the underground group 'Comète' was made. Together they dragged the parachute down and hid it, along with Cox's flying suit. A raincoat to cover his uniform was produced and together they walked to a safe house at Comblain-au-pont.

Pilot Officer Howard Carroll had also been picked up by the underground and joined a small party of escapers, Larry Birk (RAAF), Jack Newton (RAF) and a Belgian, Gerard Waucquez. This band formed the fourth group of airmen guided to Spain by 'Comète'. They were conveyed across occupied Europe by an 18 year old girl, Andrée de Jongh, passing the Pyrenees on 10th December 1941. Carroll eventually reached England, only to be lost flying over Germany later in the war.

Sergeant Tom Cox was passed along the chain of safe houses to Liège, where he was hidden by Monsieur and Madam Debaerts at 82 Rue de Cocq, before moving on to Brussels, Amiens, Paris, Biarritz, San Sebastian, Madrid and Gibraltar. He was joined by Albert Daye (RCAF), Leonard Warburton and John Hutton, forming the fifth group guided by 'Comète' in the capable hands of de Jongh. They reached the Pyrenees on Christmas Day having a party at Anglet near Bayonne before trekking across the mountains. Cox was embarked on a Polish ship, the *Sobieski* and landed back in Britain in March 1942. He remustered as a pilot and saw out the war training glider pilots. The remainder of the crew are now buried at Haverlee War Cemetery near Louvain.

In the target area a ground haze made target identification difficult and the problems were increased by the persistent and accurate searchlight activity. On his bomb run, in L7484, Flight Lieutenant Gardiner was coned by searchlights and hit several times by heavy flak, fortunately without damage to vital parts. Immediately the bomb load was released violent evasive action shook off the flak and the lights, saving them from further damage. Observation of the result of the bombing was impossible.

Flying Officer Dave Green experienced a similar intense and accurate flak barrage on his run up on board L7486. One box barrage of six heavy flak shells burst only 50 yards ahead and directly at their flying height. They were lucky to escape undamaged. Searchlights and flak also troubled Pilot Officer Ruck-Keene and Flying Officer Birch.

Crews at this era of the war had developed and widely held a belief that their identification, friend or foe (IFF) sets could be used to jam the radar guidance system of the master searchlight. There was no logic behind this belief and indeed it was not simply ineffective but later positively dangerous, when German night fighters were able to home directly onto the IFF transmissions. On this night, crews used their IFF sets to try and mislead the radar and not surprisingly reported variable success on return.

Soon after leaving the Ruhr the returning aircrews were once more crossing the airspace of southeast Belgium and facing their next obstacle, the recrossing of the searchlight belt and its flak and fighter defences. In L7373 Pilot Officer 'Jock' Paskell had decided to replace the posted 'Eddy' Edmonds in the rear turret with the second wireless operator/air gunner, Sergeant Arthur Smith, who had more experience operating with the crew. The two new gunners, Sergeants Walter and Compton, occupied the mid-upper and front turrets.

At close to 0410 (0510 local time) whilst flying at a height of 14,000ft in the vicinity of Louvain they were suddenly enmeshed by two large searchlight cones. Paskell began manoeuvring to evade the beams and as he did so Smith in the rear turret observed a Me110 night fighter approaching from the starboard quarter at about five o'clock. Unbeknown to them, this was Gefreiter Bruhnke of III/NJG1 based at Twente in Holland. The Me110 bored in at a fast closing speed and as Smith traversed his turret and called a warning Bruhnke opened fire with his cannon from long range. As Smith opened fire he could already feel the impacts of the shells on the aircraft structure around him, testifying to the accuracy of Bruhnke's initial burst.

Almost immediately the traversing mechanism in the rear turret failed, presumably as a result of a hit in the hydraulic system supplying the power. Smith was still able to fire but could not follow the flight line of the attacking fighter and his return fire was falling short. Paskell continued to take evasive action and the turret guns swung towards the fighter but Smith was unable to draw a bead. As Bruhnke closed in, still firing, Smith heard a call on the intercom 'We're on fire'. Immediately Paskell gave the order 'Bale out!' Clearly this single, sudden attack had been overwhelming and devastating.

Smith disconnected himself from his intercom and oxygen leads and concentrated on his own survival. The rear turret was jammed to starboard such that only the starboard turret door provided access to the fuselage. With a struggle, he squeezed through this narrow space and reached into the parachute stowage rack. Whilst clipping the 'chute on in preparation to moving forward to the lower hatch in the nose, Smith

tried to push open the draught doors behind his turret but found these jammed. Possibly the doors had been distorted by the ferocity of the attack and as Smith was struggling with these his problems multiplied when the entire interior of the aircraft burst into flames.

The added stimulus may have intensified Smith's effort and he was quickly able to burst through the draught doors. He was greeted by a veritable Dante's inferno of fire within the fuselage. All thought of reaching the forward hatch disappeared and as the flames enveloped Smith himself he just had time to register the immobile figure of the mid-upper gunner totally ablaze. Later Smith was to speculate that the gunner may have been hit during the attack as there had been no word on the intercom or return fire from his turret.

Smith could not afford to hesitate. Pulling open the side entry door he dived out, missing the tailplane and then yanking the ripcord. The aircraft flew on for a short while and Smith could see the extent of the flames. Suddenly the blazing wreck nosed forward and plummeted into the ground like a flaming comet, crashing southwest of Lommel and near Louvain.

Unbeknown to Smith, both he and the dying crew were to play vital, if inadvertent, roles in the escape of a second crew member, the observer, Ken Houghton. For 45 years Smith was to believe himself to be the sole survivor and to puzzle why, when the aircraft had flown on straight and level for a spell that no one up front had escaped. In fact they did. When the aircraft was riddled from end to end in the long steady attack the forward area apparently caught fire, rapidly producing choking fumes and dense smoke. Houghton was all but completely overcome by nausea, but with eyes blinded and streaming from the fumes, managed with a superhuman effort to reach the forward hatch and bale out. Apparently his escape was either much earlier or much later than that of Smith.

Whilst flying on previous operations, 'Eddy' Edmonds and Houghton had discussed the procedure they would adopt should they ever need to bale out. Edmonds advised Houghton that in this event he must ensure before leaving the aircraft which side of his parachute the 'D' ring was. Despite the chaos in the aircraft Houghton remembered to check this on his way to the hatch, ascertaining it to be on the right side. On vacating the aircraft it came readily to hand and he made a safe descent.

Within a short interval, the groping searchlights picked up Smith's parachute and held it in their glare as he gently drifted earthwards. Houghton must have been sufficiently separated that he descended undetected. Smith was taking centre stage and holding the Germans' entire attention. Amidst the excitement and enveloped in the covering darkness Houghton reached the ground unnoticed. A German patrol with dogs was waiting for Smith on landing but even without his reception committee it is unlikely that Smith could have escaped. His face was blackened and severely burnt, the skin hanging in strips in places.

Smith was treated with great tenderness and dedication by his captors. He was taken to a first aid post where, at 0800 hours, two German medical attendants and the victorious Bruhnke arrived to care for him and convey him to hospital. The medical orderlies told Smith they had come directly from the wreckage of his aircraft where they had located the remains of the six other crew members. In death the crew had provided a service to their comrade, with Smith in captivity and six aircrew apparently dead there would be no search for Houghton – the Germans believing him already dead. So it was that Smith had covered Houghton's descent and his fellow crew members presented the opportunity for his escape.

The small party caring for Smith set out and took most of the day getting to a hospital in Brussels. Towards the latter part of the day, Smith lost his sight completely, apparently through shock, and had to rely entirely on his captors for guidance. Smith spent two months being treated by a German burns specialist with the rank of General, who proved most kind and attentive. After five days his sight returned and eventually the skill of this doctor saved him from facial disfigurement.

The story of Ken Houghton's subsequent evasion is reconstructed from his conversations with fellow squadron members on return to the UK. Ken was not a man to let slip the opportunity which his fellow crew members had furnished him. Squadron members recall him as having a very slight, almost scrawny build, not at all the physique or temperament of a story book hero, yet there was a true grit about Ken and a deep welling pool of fortitude and stoicism, what was called at the time 'a press-on type'. Having reached the ground uninjured, Houghton hid himself whilst an evasion plan formed itself in his mind. Not being a great linguist he decided to go it alone and avoid both the Germans and the local population. He would hide by day and walk at night using his navigator's skill to reach neutral Switzerland.

During the first day he was able to watch from a safe hiding place whilst the Germans buried the dead members of his crew. How many coffins were buried is not clear. Without assistance Houghton made his way alone across Belgium and France and eventually into Switzerland. Declaring himself to the authorities he was given the option of either internment or of paroling himself. The latter implied him to be free to live and move about within that country but to be bound on his honour not to escape. Adopting the latter

choice, Houghton got a job, according to some sources in a bank and to others with the UK Air Attaché, and progressively assembled enough money to be self-sufficient.

He saved money to pay for the wherewithal for the next leg of his adventure. Amongst other items he paid a handsome bribe to a Swiss doctor to supply him with a 'blood chit' declaring himself to be deaf, dumb and mentally subnormal. Similarly, he obtained forged identity papers and clothes to suit the character. Finally he bought a rail ticket from Switzerland to the Spanish border. Perhaps he considered it incautious to buy a rail ticket all the way to a neutral port or alternatively he could not afford to travel further.

After formally 'unparoling' himself he immediately joined the train, having taught himself to look and act the part he had chosen. Having travelled from Switzerland into France, he changed trains and found himself boarding a train packed with German troops. Thus accompanied and maintaining his theatrical act, he proceeded into Spain and his destination. Houghton had planned to make his way to Lisbon in neutral Portugal and at the start of the next stage he met and teamed up with a Pole who was similarly bound. Together they crossed Spain, again avoiding contact with the local population.

Houghton described this as the worst part of his journey. They had little money, food and water and had to traverse what was virtually a desert. Eventually, at the physical limits of their endurance, they reached the British Embassy in Lisbon. From here he flew back on one of the regular flights across the Bay of Biscay to the UK. Later he was to comment ruefully that his journey to Portugal took six months, whereas his return from Portugal took six hours.

On reaching this country his first move was to seek out his fellow aircrew in 207 Squadron, walking into the mess at Bottesford unannounced, to great rejoicing. A contemporary, 'Scotty' Scott, remembers his arrival well.

Houghton had designs on piloting himself and arranged a transfer to a pilots' training course in Canada. During the course he was to encounter both Jim Duncan and Bob Storey, former 207 Squadron wireless operators, then instructing in Canada. Having qualified as a pilot, Houghton was delegated a Lend-Lease aircraft to fly back to Britain on delivery, only to have it disintegrate around him during a heavy landing in Iceland.

Eventually hitching a ride on another aircraft, he landed up at Prestwick, coming face to face within hours with his ex-fellow crew member 'Eddy' Edmonds. Their greeting was mutual, 'You lucky bugger!' they called to each other delightedly – Edmonds for missing the fateful operation and Houghton for escaping. With great joy they exchanged experiences since their wartime careers had diverged.

Captain L D Gammans MP (suited) visited Coningsby on 21st September 1941, representing the Association of British Malay at the naming of 97 Squadron as the 'Straits Settlements' squadron. Top row, left to right: Flying Officer D S Mims; Flight Lieutenant J Truman; Flight Lieutenant C E Rolfe; Pilot Officer W G Noble; Flying Officer H S Blakeman DFM. Bottom row, left to right: Flight Lieutenant C P D Price DFC; Wing Commander D F Balsdon; Squadron Leader J S Sherwood DFC, Flight Lieutenant L Hinds. *Imperial War Museum CH4055*

Twelve pilots and a 97 Squadron Manchester posed on 21st September 1941 on the occasion of the linking of the unit with the Association of British Malay.
Imperial War Museum CH4056

Houghton was champing at the bit to get back to operations a third time. Regrettably, for that irrepressible man, it was not to be 'third time lucky', for Ken Houghton is believed to have been killed later in the war.

The 'Grim Reaper' had struck at 207 Squadron with a vengeance in the last 24 hours, resulting in three Manchesters being lost to night fighters. 'Jock' Paskell was on the eighth operation of his second tour, whilst Joe Unsworth was on the first operation of his second. In both cases the aircraft had been overwhelmed in a devastating assault, leaving no time to send a radio message to base of their predicament. All the squadron could record was a bald 'Nothing further heard since take-off'.

After the initial months, in which the major threat to the squadrons had been the flak defences in the immediate target area on a particular city, the pendulum had now swung towards the night fighter as the main threat. At a time when the squadrons still had no target finding devices of any kind, the ground and airborne radars now being deployed by the Germans were stripping away the protective cover of darkness to a marked degree. Only the small number of fighters available and early problems with equipment serviceability lessened the impact.

In return for these severe losses the achievements had been minimal. The bombing was scattered at Huls on 12th October 1941 and at Cologne on the 13th only a few bombs landed in the city damaging 17 houses, killing six civilians and injuring five.

The high level of pressure on 207 Squadron continued with operations for four

and ten Manchesters to Cologne and Emden respectively on the 15th and 18th being requested, but later cancelled due to the weather. Finally, on the 20th, the weather improved somewhat and four 207 Manchesters were required for mine-laying operations off Sassnitz in the Baltic. This was a minor diversionary operation in support of main force attacks on four targets. It was decided that the aircraft would take-off from and return to Horsham St Faith to shorten the range. The aircraft departed between 1832 and 1845 hours.

On this night 97 Squadron returned to operations with its training of new crews complete. It continued to operate the Manchester only for another two months but was to have a fateful re-encounter with operational flying. No. 97 Squadron supplied eight Manchesters to attack Bremen. At this time the unit's aircraft had begun to carry individual names under their cockpits on the port side to mark their naming as the 'Straits Settlement' Squadron.

Baltic minelaying and Bremen – 20th October 1941

Serial	Code	Sqn	Captain
L7490	OF-U	97	W/O D H Rowlands
L7463	OF-P	97	F/Sgt R A Fletcher
L7461	OF-R	97	F/Sgt G E A Pendrill
L7453	OF-X	97	S/L J Dugdale
L7489	OF-T	97	W/O T J Mycock
L7464	OF-N	97	Sgt C G Hughes
R5783	OF-V	97	Sgt G H Hartley
L7462	OF-Z	97	P/O W G Noble
L7432	EM-O	207	F/Sgt G B Dawkins
L7422	EM-V	207	F/L W G Gardiner
L7322	EM-Q	207	P/O G R Bayley
L7487	EM-N	207	P/O J C L Ruck-Keene

Two 207 aircraft 'planted' their 'vegetables' in the allocated position, whilst the third failed to locate the pinpoint designated for

laying and jettisoned his load. Manchester Mk.IA, L7487, failed to return. It is presumed that the aircraft laid its mines and was heading for Horsham St Faith on the return leg. It came down in the North Sea approximately 18 miles off the Norfolk coast with the loss of the entire crew. There is no information on the circumstances leading to the ditching of this aircraft. Its reported position presumably results from a radio message or homing obtained by a ground station. It has been suggested that the loss of this aircraft was associated with the continued rash of propeller feathering and engine failures still being experienced on the aircraft at this time, but the aircraft could easily have run out of fuel. The last few hours in the lives of Pilot Officer Ruck-Keene and his crew, the fears, failure and final tragedy, remain known only to God.

The eight Manchesters of 97 Squadron took off in a tight bunch headed for Bremen just before 1830 hours. All appear to have reached the Bremen area where target identification was made difficult by cloud and ground haze. The defences were ferocious, including many searchlight cones involving 19-20 individual lights and intense and accurate flak. Warrant Officer Rowlands' crew also sighted a patrolling Me110 as they ran in to the target, but it apparently failed to see them. Squadron Leader Dugdale's aircraft, L7453, was slightly damaged by flak in the target area. Following bomb release, Flight Sergeant Pendrill put the nose of L7461 down and dived seawards, pulling out at 1,000ft and crossing the coast over a five ship convoy near Cuxhaven. Shortly afterwards they were engaged by an enemy warship.

A message was received at 0030 hours from the crew of Pilot Officer Noble in L7462 on his first operation stating that the wireless telegraphy receiver was unserviceable. The aircraft failed to return and it is presumed to have crashed in the sea due to unknown causes on its return flight. Some days later, the bodies of two crew members were washed up on the East Anglian coast, possibly indicating that L7462 was also close to home when it crashed.

Despite the shallow penetration and fact that the aircraft had only been airborne for six hours, Sergeant Hartley ran out of fuel on return, just managing to reach the Lincolnshire coast before force landing on the salt marshes at Friskney, near Wainfleet. All the crew escaped uninjured. R5783 was recovered by 58 Maintenance Unit but the combination of the damage it had received and the salt water in which it had been partly immersed resulted in it being written off.

The Air Sea Rescue service carried out a sweep with no result. Pressure of further operations prevented 207 Squadron from participating, but on the 22nd and 23rd two and three Manchesters respectively carried out a desperate and fruitless search for a dinghy from Ruck-Keene's aircraft.

This was a period when engine reliability was slightly improved, although the propeller feathering problems remained to be solved. Progress was being made with these and aircraft were to be test flown on 26th October 1941. On the same day a party of ATC cadets paid a visit to Waddington and amongst the days instruction for them was an air experience flight in a Manchester.

The two flight commanders, Squadron Leaders Beauchamp and Murray, divided the group of cadets between them with a view to taking them aloft in the course of the planned air tests for the day. Murray took off on a 55 minute test flight in L7419, with his crew amplified by 11 cadets, a massive complement for a Manchester. Beauchamp got aloft in L7422 'EM-V' with a crew including a new sergeant pilot and a similar number of cadets. L7422 had recently been returned from repair following the serious damage to its tail assembly after the night fighter attack of 31st August 1941.

The object of the test was to obtain sufficient height so that the new second pilot could practice propeller feathering. They soon reached the 1,500ft height deemed necessary to carry out the test. The designated engine was stopped and the propeller feathered. Having accomplished this successfully the restart procedure was initiated.

The rpm and boost increased on the engine and the propeller was unfeathered. However, the engine was giving no thrust and with the propeller now in coarse pitch the drag built up rapidly. A quick check confirmed the rpm and boost readings, suggesting the engine was running, but the 16ft diameter propeller and weight of the engine was actually causing an extremely rapid height loss.

A desperate look around the cockpit failed to provide any information on why the engine was not, in fact, producing any thrust and a forced landing became imminent. The crew and cadets were called to take up crash positions and Beauchamp turned his attention to finding a suitable forced landing field. None appeared large enough, but they had no alternative. Beauchamp turned into wind with the last available height and speed, lowered the flaps but kept the undercarriage up. L7422 bellied into an unobstructed small field, bounced, demolished the boundary hedge, careered on into a second field and ground to a halt. As soon as the aircraft stopped all the hatches were thrown open and crew and ATC cadets scattered in all directions. Figures seemed to appear everywhere, feet running before they hit the ground. Fortunately the wreck did not catch fire. They had come down at Linwood, near Market Rasen in Lincolnshire.

A roll call showed the whole crew were uninjured. A crew member was dispatched to find a telephone and as their jangled nerves recovered and the aircraft steadfastly refused to burn Beauchamp finally felt it to be safe to return. He climbed into the pilot's seat and carefully repeated the restart procedure to try and establish the reason for the engine failure. To his dismay he saw that the fuel taps to the engine they had feathered were still off. He hesitated, if the taps were moved to the 'on' position the accident could be blamed on an aircraft malfunction. In view of the many hours spent recently trying to rectify the persistent propeller feathering failures nobody was likely to doubt him. A moment's reflection was enough to convince him that honesty was the best policy, thereby saving the crash investigators and perhaps Avro and de Havilland many hours work chasing red herrings.

Flying Officer Bob Fletcher at his captain's seat after his Manchester was named *Sri Gajah* (Elephant) in commemoration of the association with the Straits Settlement States of Malaya. All of the aircraft were named after land animals or birds. *Jill* was Fletcher's niece and God-daughter, not a pin-up. L7463 'OF-P' was photographed soon after its fourth operation on 8th November 1941. *R A Fletcher*

Warrant Officer D H Rowlands poses beneath his *Sri Harimau* of 97 (Straits Settlement) Squadron at Coningsby, November 1941. The lion head is overpainted on an eagle with spread wings. *Imperial War Museum CH4150*

Squadron Leader J Dugdale of 97 Squadron, beneath *Sri Matahiri*, Coningsby, November 1941. *Imperial War Museum CH4149*

Cologne – 7th November 1941

Serial	Code	Sqn	Captain
L7453	OF-X	97	S/L J Dugdale
L7489	OF-T	97	F/L E Coton
L7522	OF-V	97	F/Sgt G E A Pendrill
L7463	OF-P	97	F/Sgt L H Adams
L7423	OF-S	97	F/Sgt G H Hartley
R5791	EM-V	207	Sgt J C Atkinson
L7322	EM-Q	207	P/O G R Bayley
L7432	EM-J	207	F/O P C Birch
L7455	EM-G	207	F/O W S Herring DSO, DFM
L7486	EM-B	207	F/L P C Ward-Hunt DFC
L7300	EM-F	207	P/O A W Hills DFM
L7485	EM-D	207	S/L T C Murray DFC
L7484	EM-P	207	F/O J Wooldridge DFM
L7319	EM-X	207	F/Sgt G H Coles

Boulogne – 7th November 1941

Serial	Code	Sqn	Captain
L7491	OF-C	97	F/O J G McKid
L7492	OF-A	97	P/O E E Rodley
L7382	OF-D	97	F/Sgt S E Harrison
?	EM-*	207	?

At the time of the crash L7422 had a new direction finding (DF) device fitted in the cockpit immediately above the fuel taps and partly obscuring them. The presence of this was the most likely reason for both pilots failing to detect that the taps had not been put on again after shutting down. Thus L7422 crashed due to pilot error, as opposed to propeller feathering mechanism malfunction. The aircraft never flew again and was struck off charge and scrapped soon afterwards.

Avro passed a milestone on 31st October 1941 when the first production Lancaster (L7527) made its maiden test flight from Woodford. From then onwards the assembly lines were fully devoted to the new type.

Bomber Command's next major operation on 7th November 1941 proved a watershed in its fortunes for some time to come. Impatient following a prolonged period of bad weather and poor bombing results, the Air Officer Commanding, Sir Richard Pierse, proposed a maximum effort on Berlin. The weather forecast was most unfavourable with thick storm clouds, icing and hail, especially over the North Sea.

Air Vice-Marshal Slessor, the 5 Group commander was vehemently opposed to the attack and finally obtained a partial relief for his crews, being permitted to attack Cologne instead. This proved the salvation of many 5 Group crews. The 392 aircraft dispatched was a record for the Command with 169 allocated

to Berlin, 75 to Cologne and 55 to Mannheim. Smaller groups carried out minor operations to Essen, Ostend, Boulogne and various mining areas.

A total of 17 Manchesters were dispatched from 207 and 97 Squadrons, which were still the only two units operating the type in 5 Group. The raid turned into a disaster, although Slessor's judgement was to safeguard the Manchester force.

Ten 207 Squadron Manchesters with experienced crews were detailed to attack Cologne with the main railway station as the Aiming Point. One Manchester was later cancelled by Group. This Manchester, with an inexperienced crew, was prepared instead for the raid on the docks at Boulogne. The Cologne force departed between 1920 and 1955 hours to make their way individually to the target.

Sergeant Atkinson experienced a burst hydraulic pipe over the North Sea in R5791 which rendered the front and mid-upper turrets unserviceable. The intercom was also unreliable. The aircraft returned early with bomb load intact.

Similarly, Pilot Officer Bayley in L7322 had the rear turret and second pilot's intercom fail some 15 miles north east of Brussels. The captain elected to return and a search for an enemy aerodrome as an alternative target was unsuccessful. L7322 landed at base at 2350 hours.

The force attacked the target under cloud from heights ranging from 12,000-14,000ft generally between 2118 and 2150 hours, although Squadron Leader Murray was an hour later at 2250. Fires were observed burning in the town. All five of the Cologne force from 97 Squadron attacked successfully, although Squadron Leader Dugdale's aircraft was peppered by a flak shell bursting beneath it. The port wing tank was badly holed and lost 200 gallons of fuel before the self-sealing closed across the gash.

Flak gunners near-missed L7319, piloted by Flight Sergeant Coles. A hydraulic line was fractured over the target by a shrapnel fragment. The aircraft experienced a hydraulic failure, the bomb doors fell open, and the rear turret became unserviceable. The intercom also failed at about the same time, whether by coincidence or not is unreported. Coles brought L7319 back to base and effected a safe landing after the compressed air system had been used to lock the undercart in the down position.

Flight Sergeant Pendrill and crew had an eventful night. As the Manchester force headed for Cologne once more, Oberleutnant Heinrich Griese and his fellow NJG2 pilots were rising from St Trond and other airfields to do battle with Bomber Command. For once the boot was on the other foot and the night saw the revenge of the Manchesters.

Pendrill had trained his crew into a well-disciplined and experienced team. Following their take-off at 1852 hours they proceeded to Cologne where they bombed without being able to observe any results due to low cloud. Turning for their return they were soon trapped in the searchlight belt in the vicinity of Liège. Patrolling nearby in 'G9+AH' as usual, Griese and his wireless operator, Scherke, spotted L7522, gave the tally-ho radio signal to the ground and advanced the throttles in their Me110 to maximum. As they approached, Pendrill was vigorously corkscrewing the lightened Manchester and managed to escape the clinging lights. Now the odds were more even with both crews equally free to search in the darkened sky. Unknown to Griese he had already been spotted and reported by Sergeant Jones, the rear gunner in L7522. This time any attack would be less one-sided than when Joe Unsworth had been brought down.

After a few minutes, Griese spotted the Manchester ahead of him, still corkscrewing as it increased its distance from the searchlight belt. Jones kept up a steady commentary and trained his four Brownings on the area of sky the Me110 had to fly through as Griese went into his well-tried attack pattern. Griese entered a steep dive to build up speed and get beneath the weaving bomber. Then, when he judged the instant exactly right, he pulled back hard on the stick to point the nose directly at the Manchester when it passed through his gunsight as he hung on the point of the stall a few metres beneath. Both Griese and Jones judged the interception well, but this time it was the Englishman who was a split second faster, ordering a break from George Pendrill.

As Griese opened fire, the massive black Manchester filling his vision drifted out of the firing line and from a mere 20 metres (22 yards) his tracers flew over the top of the bomber. Jones in turn had been following the track of the fighter for some time and had now depressed his Brownings fully, as the Manchester jinked aside he was presented with the perfect shot looking down onto the top of the attacker suspended, apparently stationary, at the apex of his near-vertical climb. Anticipating the direction of the manoeuvre, Jones opened fire at point blank range and saw tracers entering the crew cockpit and both wing roots. The withering fire killed Scherke outright and badly wounded Griese, the cockpit was devastated and the armoured windshield crazed into opaqueness by direct hits. The port engine burst into flames.

'G9+AH' fell away out of control in its death throes. Griese knew he was weakening fast but managed to haul back the shattered canopy. In his enfeebled state he was unable to jump clear and in clawing his way out found his parachute entangled in the cockpit framing. With his last remaining strength he finally managed to break free and clear the aircraft, pulling the ripcord sharply before fainting from loss of blood.

In L7522 the crew observed a jet of flame shoot up from the ground as 'G9+AH' went in. Griese drifted a short distance from the crash site before hitting the ground unconscious. Unable to control his landing, Griese sustained further injury when the impact broke his left femur. Griese was quickly located and given medical treatment, but it

was 1943 before he was sufficiently recovered to return to flying.

Pendrill and his victorious crew landed back at Coningsby at 0019 hours. Honours that night had been won by the Manchesters, but in the relentless butchery of the bomber war Pendrill and crew had themselves only six weeks to live before they too met 'the Grim Reaper'.

From the Berlin force 21 aircraft failed to return, 12.4% of those dispatched. The bombing was very scattered with only 14 buildings destroyed and eleven civilians killed. The returning crews from the Cologne force reported many fires, but in fact only eight high explosive and 60 incendiaries fell in the town killing five and injuring five more.

The worst results of all related to Mannheim where a specific request to the authorities revealed that no bombs had fallen within the city limits that night. In all 37 aircraft failed to return, more than twice the previous loss rate for night operations. Many casualties were believed to have come down in the North Sea due to fuel exhaustion and icing and a massive air/sea rescue (ASR) was mounted. As a result of this failure, Berlin was not raided in force again until January 1943 and orders were given to conserve aircraft and reduce the scale of the bombing offensive.

These events shaped the immediate operational future of the Manchester squadrons. For 207 the prospect of a move to a new base, and for the Manchesters the temporary winding down in the scale of operations and the bad weather of the winter combined to provide a respite. Before this an ASR, a shallow penetration raid and one final main force attack were to be carried out.

Following the catastrophic losses from the Berlin force on the night of 7/8th November 1941, 97 Squadron was called upon next day to provide two aircraft for ASR operations over the North Sea. L7466 'OF-N' flown by Flight Lieutenant Price and L7488 'OF-F', Flying Officer Blakeman, neither of whom had operated the previous night, took off together close to 1320 in the afternoon. The cloud base was still low with poor visibility and intermittent rain. Both aircraft reached their search areas and began flying overlapping search patterns at only 200ft. Neither aircraft reported any sightings. Blakeman's crew encountered Price's aircraft on six occasions, the last being timed at 1600 hours, shortly before the search was called off. They landed back at Coningsby close to 1800 in the evening. No further sign of Price or his aircraft was ever seen again. Bearing in mind the weather conditions, flying height and falling darkness it is possibly unlikely that L7466 was brought down by the Germans.

Whilst Price and Blakeman were still out searching, three freshmen from 'A' Flight of 97 Squadron and two from 207 Squadron were being prepared for a gentle shallow penetration introductory raid on the docks at Dunkirk, to gain experience. The aircraft departed around 1800 hours.

Flight Sergeant George E A Pendrill in the captain's seat of his Manchester Mk.IA L7522 'OF-V' after it was named *Sri Garuda*. The swastika identifies the victory over Oberleutnant Griese on the night of 7/8th November 1941.
Imperial War Museum CH4157

Oberleutnant Griese's Messerschmitt Me110 'G9+KH' of I/NJG1 at St. Trond, Belgium, in 1941.

Oberleutnant Heinrich Griese photographed whilst serving with I/NJG1 in 1940. Griese's tit-for-tat engagements with Pilot Officer Unsworth's and Flight Sergeant's Pendrill's Manchesters are recounted in the narrative.
Both H Griese

Hamburg / Ostend† – 9th November 1941

Serial	Code	Sqn	Captain
L7309	EM-R	207	S/L K H P Beauchamp DFC
L7322	EM-Q	207	P/O G R Bayley
L7455	EM-G	207	F/O P C Birch
L7485	EM-D	207	P/O A W Hills DFM
R5791	EM-V	207	F/Sgt J C Atkinson
L7319	EM-X	207	F/O J Wooldridge
L7300	EM-F	207	F/Sgt G H Hathersich†

Dunkirk, a freshman's run – 8th November 1941

Serial	Code	Sqn	Captain
L7491	OF-C	97	S/L J S Sherwood
L7476	OF-K	97	P/O E A Deverill
L7475	OF-B	97	P/O E E Rodley
L7300	EM-F	207	F/Sgt G H Hathersich
L7322	EM-Q	207	F/O J H Leland

Squadron Leader Sherwood was unable to attack owing to the glare from the searchlight batteries, whilst Pilot Officer Rodley attacked successfully with ten 500lb bombs.

Pilot Officer Deverill's crew had a harrowing experience. Their aircraft was heavily engaged by flak batteries whilst running up to bomb at 17,000ft. The aircraft was very

severely damaged by a near miss and plunged to 4,000ft with the mortally wounded second pilot, Pilot Officer Hodge, obstructing the controls. Deverill was able to level out and jettison part of the bomb load, the remaining four 500lb bombs were dumped in the North Sea. With the second pilot being cared for on the rest couch, Deverill took stock. All exterior lights were illuminated on the aircraft and could not be extinguished due to a short in the electrical system. The bomb doors were jammed open owing to the failure of the hydraulic system. Deverill was able to return to Coningsby where the emergency system had to be used to lower the undercarriage. Don Hodge, a Rhodesian straight from the Operational Training Unit, was taken to the station sick bay at 2038 hours but died of his wounds at 2300 the same night. So much for shallow penetration operational experience raids!

Finally, the experienced main force crews of 207 were called, early on 9th November 1941, to provide six Manchesters for a raid on the Hamburg shipyards. Finding no respite, Flight Sergeant Hathersich was again called upon to continue his transition to a fully fledged member of the squadron by taking L7300 to Ostend. The whole force took off between 1740 and 1755, Hathersich amongst them.

The usual spate of 'Manchester' problems began to descend upon the unfortunate crews. L7319 was by this time becoming rather long in the tooth for an operational aircraft and Flying Officer Wooldridge, who was taking it on operations for the first time, was appalled by its flying performance. He reported it was extremely slow and would not climb.

Squadron Leader Beauchamp was also having similar difficulties persuading another of the older aircraft, L7309, to climb. Eventually he had no alternative but to jettison one of the four 1,000lb GPs into the North Sea. He eventually coaxed L7309 up to a height of 14,500ft as he approached Hamburg.

Other aircraft were experiencing different problems. In L7322 Pilot Officer Bayley encountered rear turret failure, whilst one of the two Brownings in the dorsal F.N.7A turret went unserviceable. The rear turret in L7455 also packed up and Flying Officer Birch's problems were compounded by hydraulic trouble. Pilot Officer Hills also reported turret failure in L7485.

Beauchamp approached the shipyards close to 2012 hours, impeded by the intense glare of searchlights. Heavy flak was also intense and accurate causing slight damage to L7309. Flight Sergeant Atkinson was similarly impeded by the glare at 13,000ft as he

Manchester IA L7489 'OF-T' *Hoo Flung* of 97 Squadron, Coningsby, with five 'ops' to its credit. Photographed in mid-November 1941, L7489 went on to be 97's joint top scorer with a total of ten 'ops'. It was the usual mount of Flight Lieutenant Elmer Coton. Evidently not all aircraft received Malay names.

Showing the wear and tear of perhaps a long time in a wallet, a print of Flight Lieutenant Elmer Coton at the captain's seat of a 97 Squadron Manchester. *Both R A Fletcher*

threaded his way inland keeping the Elbe in sight 25 miles to one side. He could only report that his 4x1,000lb GPs had fallen somewhere in the built up area of Hamburg. Hills was unable to reach the main target owing to the several cones of searchlights, although L7485 was not held or hit by flak. His 4,000lb 'Cookie' fell in the south east part of the built up area from 16,000ft. Hills must have felt very vulnerable with his turret problems.

These were the only three Manchesters to reach Hamburg. In L7322 Pilot Officer Bayley chose to attack Borkum as a last resort target. His aircraft had only one Browning gun capable of being brought to bear in the event of a rear attack from a night fighter and he would have been justified in aborting the operation. Instead, his bombs were aimed at the seaplane base from a height of 15,000ft.

In the struggling L7319, Flying Officer Wooldridge had eventually reached 12,000ft. His observer mistook Jade Bay for the mouth of the Elbe and Wooldridge elected to attack Wilhelmshaven docks as a last resort target instead of pressing on to the hot bed of flak and fighters over Hamburg. Wooldridge carried out one of the diving glide attacks he favoured. The searchlight and flak defences were intense as he dived from 12,000ft, releasing his bomb load before reaching 10,000ft. The defences were sufficiently ferocious that Wooldridge kept the nose down all the way down to the coast, crossing out at only 1,000ft.

The remaining disabled Manchester, L7455, captained by Flying Officer Birch, with both turret and hydraulic problems might well, with justification, have returned to Waddington. But Birch was determined to leave some mark on the enemy and diverted to Calais, dropping four 1,000lb GPs on the docks from 14,000ft at 2040 hours. Birch's problems were further compounded when the Lorenz homing device failed. Nevertheless, base was reached and a successful landing made in an aircraft in which the port undercarriage leg refused to lock and with no brakes. L7455 had a lot to answer for that night. Of the Hamburg force, only R5791 had not had mechanical or aerodynamic problems of some kind.

Meanwhile, Flight Sergeant Hathersich and his 'freshman' crew reached Ostend docks at 1945 and dropped 12x500lb GPs from 8,000ft. He was undeterred by searchlights and intense light flak but was unable to see the results of his attack.

All in all it had been an extremely unsuccessful operation and a stark indication, if one were needed, that the many problems were far from solved. In military terms such limited results from a relatively major effort was unacceptable. The crews themselves were intensely frustrated. Despite their most determined efforts, the Manchesters were still seeming to prevent them making a significant contribution to the war effort, with the Germans hardly needing to enter the arena.

Bomber Command's successes as a whole were only a little better than the Manchesters'. From the Hamburg operation on 9/10th November 1941, the recorders on the ground established that from the 71 aircraft claiming to attack, three large fires were started, 13 civilians killed and 56 injured.

From this time the level of operational activity declined for a while. No. 207 Squadron stood down on 11th November 1941 to receive 19 Air Ministry Press representatives. The interviews and photographs appeared in the November 1941 edition of *The Aeroplane*. Stories of determined efforts against great odds by the crews, which were true, were interspersed with claims for the complete reliability of the Vulture powerplants, which were not. Despite the heavy censorship, a hint that all was not well was the first admission that in its introduction to operations the Vulture had had its fair share of problems. The crews must have regarded this as the understatement of the century.

Manchester I L7455 'EM-G' of 207 Squadron at Bottesford. Delivered on 10th September 1941, the aircraft was dispatched on 26 sorties by three squadrons. Left to right: Sergeant J Duncan (1st wireless op); Sergeant S Allen (2nd wireless op); Sergeant A Hall (observer), Flying Officer P C Birch (captain); Sergeant N A Lingard (2nd pilot); Sergeant A P Cullerne (mid-upper gunner); Sergeant Boldy (rear gunner). *J M Duncan*

The Manchester airframe and colour scheme shown in their final form on Mk.IA L7515 'EM-S'. The aircraft was delivered to 207 Squadron on 10th October 1941 and photographed during November. It undertook 14 sorties with 207, a further ten with 106 and was not struck off charge until November 1943. *via British Aerospace*

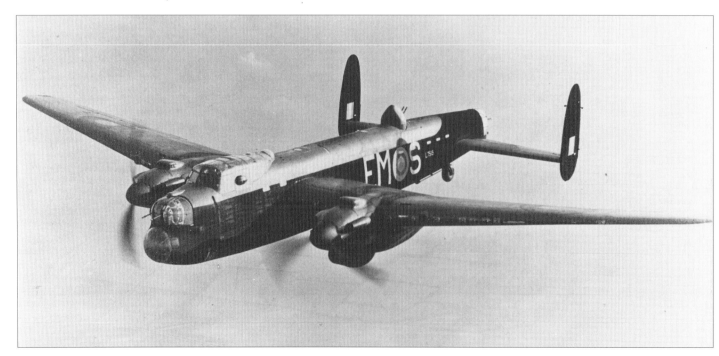

Emden – 15th November 1941

Serial	Code	Sqn	Captain
L7432	EM-J	207	F/Sgt B O Wescombe
L7322	EM-Q	207	F/L W D B Ruth DFC

A 'new crew' operation on 12th November 1941 was also cancelled due to bad weather, but on the 15th two such crews were briefed for an attack on Emden. They took off at 1750-1755 in reasonable weather, which quickly deteriorated when the aircraft encountered an occluded front. There was 10/10ths cloud, total darkness and dense fog with no prospect of locating the target with the equipment then available. To make matters worse, Flight Lieutenant Ruth experienced heavy icing. The autopilot and then the hydraulic system in the aircraft failed. Ruth abandoned the operation and bombed Den Helder with four 1,000 pounders from 8,000ft on the way home.

The observer in L7322, Sergeant Wheatley, was soon unsure of their position and as the ice built up on the airframe the aircraft began to lose height rapidly. Lost over the North Sea and with a sink rate which would take them into the water within a short period, they were clearly in a desperate position. Only a rapid change in their fortunes could prevent a disaster. Sergeant 'Scotty' Scott, the wireless operator, had lost first one and then the second trailing aerial owing to the weight of ice and was consequently unable to get a fix to help the observer in locating their position. In desperation Scott played his final card and deployed his spare aerial. Before he could contact the various stations this too carried away.

The last prospect of contact with the outside world had disappeared. As ice accumulated on the airframe the turrets and cockpit perspex iced over with a white crystalline hoar frost. Not only had they lost their ears, but with the fog and ice their eyes as well. For the moment the engines and ASI were unaffected but the steadily unwinding altimeter indicated the seriousness of their plight.

Whilst Ruth flew the aircraft, the second pilot, Pilot Officer Gerry Ings, slid open the cockpit window and stuck his head out sufficiently to see ahead. A mid-air conference developed and with visions of flying headlong into the ground within a very short timescale, Ruth and others advocated baling out immediately, whereas Scott and the remainder, unaware of what lay below, preferred to hang on until the last minute in the forlorn hope that something would turn up. Soon Ings was sufficiently frozen at his post that it was necessary for him to change places as look out with Scott. The aircraft continued to sink and still they could not be confident whether they had crossed the UK coast. Scott rapidly became chilled to the bone, they were approaching 1,000ft with still no break in the curtain of fog.

Quite suddenly and to his delight Scott saw a hole in the murk with, amazingly, a lighted flarepath at the bottom. Without hesitation, Scott grabbed the second pilot's control column in front of him and shoved it forward, not taking his eyes off the one prospect of salvation for a second. Feeling the stick move in his hand, Ruth shot Scott a startled glance exclaiming 'What the hell are you doing?' 'Scotty' replied with increasing confidence 'There's a flarepath down there!' As the nose dropped Ruth could see it too. 'Good God, so there is!' cried Ruth, galvanised into action. With no more ado, Ruth dropped the flaps and wheels, thankful that at least the emergency systems were working and, lining up on the runway closest to their approach direction, trimmed the aircraft and put the propellers into fine pitch. They would go straight in without the customary circuit. As a result of the steepness of their approach, combined with his restricted vision and the weight of the aircraft, Ruth put L7322 down with a jarring crash, but they were down safely and taxied to the indicated dispersal. As they did so the fog closed in around them again and they were to be marooned for three days.

For Scott, who might, given different circumstances, have been in L7310 with Squadron Leader Kydd on the fateful 21st June night flying test, it was the second escape from the jaws of death. Did he but know it, a further two narrow squeaks would follow in the two years he was with 207. Such flukes of chance could and did separate the survivors from the victims of wartime flying.

On leaving the aircraft and being debriefed they learned first of all that they had landed at Docking in North Norfolk. In conversation with those on the ground they learned that the sound of their engines, as they approached, had alerted the residents who had illuminated the airfield in the hope that the airmen would see them through the murk. Onlookers had seen their Manchester, ghostly white and festooned with ice, appear as though from a solid wall of fog. The touchdown was even more dramatic when, as Ruth dropped the aircraft onto the tarmac, the shock caused the airframe to shed its mantle of ice in a huge shower, which in the glare of the Chance Light produced a dramatic halo effect, momentarily enveloping the entire aircraft. It was a spectacular and unforgettable arrival. For the crew, however, it was sufficient to find their feet once more on solid ground. It must have been an unwelcome introduction to Manchester operations for Flight Lieutenant Ruth.

On 16th November 1941 207 Squadron moved to Bottesford where it continued to operate its mixture of triple-finned Mk.I and twin-finned Mk.IA Manchesters. New Manchesters delivered to the squadron as and when required were Mk.IAs and these invariably had the division between the upper shadow shading and the lower black forming the now standard straight line at the top of the fuselage decking. In all cases the black lower colour continued to sweep up over the rear fuselage in line with the leading edge of the position where the third fin would have been. This should not be taken to imply that the third, central, fin had once been fitted and later removed. These Mk.IAs were built as such in the factory and no-one had apparently thought to alter the colouring instructions. All these aircraft continued to be delivered with a mid-upper F.N.7A turret.

At the same time the squadron continued to soldier on with some of its early Mk.Is. These notably included L7300, L7309, L7317 and L7319. In several cases these Manchesters, despite the authorised change in colour schemes to a straight demarcation, continued to operate with the earlier wavy demarcation unchanged. In the case of L7300, the aircraft continued to operate without the F.N.7A mid-upper turret in the condition it was first delivered back in February. Crews appreciated the lack of fin flutter and the decrease in weight which arose from its absence. There was an additional safety margin which might make the difference between keeping the aircraft aloft in the event of losing an engine. It is known that L7309 did have a mid-upper turret when lost in January 1942 and photographs of L7319 show it to be so fitted.

The first trickle of Metropolitan Vickers built Manchesters was starting to arrive, R5791, R5782 and R5796 being on strength. No evidence as to whether these were delivered as Mk.I or Mk.IAs has come to light, although it is believed all were originally built as Mk.Is.

No. 5 Group had meanwhile become reconciled to soldiering on with its ageing Hampdens and still only 207, 97 and 61 were equipped with Manchesters. No. 44 Squadron at Waddington had been evaluating the prototype Lancaster, BT308/G, since September 1941 and was due to receive the first production aircraft in late December 1941. Next in line was 97 Squadron. In the meantime the Halifax and Stirling squadrons were receiving the bulk of the press, public and, apparently, RAF attention. After all their fervent endeavours with the Manchester, 207 and 97 Squadrons felt themselves to be on the sidelines.

October and November 1941 saw a further resurgence in pressure to develop cannon armed, power operated turrets for the Manchester and Lancaster. A 5 Group minute dated 19th November 1941 identified the increased number of interceptions by German night fighters, the trend for German night fighters to mount cannon armament themselves and the possible use of the bombers for daylight operations as the main justification for renewed pressure to acquire the heavier armaments.

At various meetings the prospect of two 20mm cannon in power operated turrets was re-examined, with an alternative interim solution of two 0.5in Hispano short-barrelled cannon in the semi-manual installation first offered by Rose Brothers in April/May 1941. In respect of the 20mm cannon, the power increase, weight increase and size remained unchanged, whilst structural increases arising from the drag and recoil of the weapons was a major problem. Expulsion of cordite fumes was also a severe constraint. A F.N.4A four gun Browning turret with 2,000 rounds per gun weighed in at 726lbs. In comparison, two 20mm Hispano guns with 200 rounds per gun, belt fed, weighed 400lb on their own, without any turret. Avro had by this time designed a two 20mm belt fed power operated turret with 550 rounds per gun, but it was likely to weigh in at a massive 2,000lb. In the event, for whatever reasons, neither the two 20mm power turret nor the lighter Rose concept attained production status on the Manchester or any other British bomber.

Mid-November spelt the beginning of a miserable period for the personnel of 207 Squadron, co-inciding with its move to a new station. Bottesford was a completely new airfield with concrete runways and rapidly constructed, dispersed facilities. A period of settling in was called for and the squadron stood down from the 18th to the 21st to allow for this. Many squadron personnel never forgot the transition. Bill 'Goldie' Goldstraw, first wireless operator to Flying Officer Dave Green, has indelible memories which probably parallel those of many of his compatriots. He recalls that 'Waddington, being a permanent pre-war station, had all the comforts of a well run establishment, brick built accommodation blocks with central heating, dry and warm, with plenty of washing facilities and hot water, everything to hand. There was relatively limited dispersal of the dwelling and operational facilities, which were separated by made-up roads. On the social side, when stood down from flying, Lincoln was a couple of miles down the road with convenient public transport. On non-operational nights the pubs and cinemas were packed with aircrew from all the airfields around Lincoln. Entertainment of all description and, in short – tastes – was available.'

Bottesford was quite, quite different. For a start virtually the entire site was a sea of mud, still being in the final stages of completion. Wellington boots were the permanent order of the day. The buildings were well dispersed, temporary Nissen huts, often unheated and they leaked. It was cold, damp, muddy and uncomfortable. Goldstraw shared a small room with a rear gunner. The roof leaked, the floor was wet, the bedclothes were wet. They found that the sleeping accommodation was in one area of the airfield, whilst the washing, shaving and feeding facilities were in a communal site with cookhouse, ablutions, messes etc. half a mile distant.

Each morning they had to leave their damp beds, don damp clothes and Wellingtons and walk across the muddy fields to wash, shave and have breakfast. Next they had to walk a mile or so to the operational area where the duty office, briefing rooms and hangars were dispersed.

To add to the extreme domestic inconvenience, aircraft operations posed particular hazards since although the perimeter track, taxiways, dispersals and runways were concrete their recently completed nature meant that they were edged with deep soft mud. Taxying called for extreme caution as immediately a wheel ran off the tarmac it sank axle deep, immobilising the aircraft itself and frequently the remainder of the squadron aircraft snaking and waddling along behind.

The winter of 1941-42 was therefore spent in acute discomfort by the squadron and illness reached epidemic proportions at times. In addition to their immediate domestic and flying problems, Bottesford was a very isolated spot miles from any entertainment. Without public transport and so far from a major centre of population they initially felt trapped and abandoned.

Left to their own devices, they eventually established a system which Bill Goldstraw admits did have its compensations. They organised their entertainment on a squadron basis and since 207 had Bottesford entirely to themselves all the personnel got to know each other far better than at Waddington, where all facilities were shared with another squadron. Moreover, they had another unifying influence – the discomforts and difficulties, which were common to all. After the initial plunge, morale in the unit rose higher than it ever was at Waddington – but this was still some time in the future.

Bottesford had one further drawback in the shape of a portly and odious Station Warrant Officer, who seemed to take a perverse delight in bullying the young and beleaguered junior aircrew at every opportunity. With the pressure of operations lying heavily upon them, this was one unnecessary strain they could well do without. Imagine then their ultimate unbounded joy when said Warrant Officer was accused of illegal homosexual advances by a junior AC2. The Warrant Officer was court martialled and the trial held on the station at Bottesford as soon as legal briefs could be taken. On the day of the court martial a large and expectant crowd had gathered outside the court room to savour every detail of the demise of the unpopular officer. When the doors opened the stampede for places was something to behold.

The prosecution put its case and in the circumstances the evidence direct from the AC2 himself seemed overwhelming. In vain the defence counsel began 'Did you object to W/O 'X' using you in this way?' 'No, Sir'. 'Then what was it that led you to make a complaint?' 'Well, when he wanted me in RAF time I didn't mind, but when he started wanting me on my days off I thought that was a bit much!' The revelations exceeded their wildest expectations and suddenly the public gallery collapsed in a sea of bowed heads, shaking shoulders and barely-contained merriment. The Warrant Officer was found guilty and disappeared immediately from the station. Justice had been done in more ways than one and in the English tradition seen to be done by the grinning horde.

Occasionally, on stand-downs from operations, most of the squadron 'decamped' to Nottingham to drink at 'The Airborne Nag' (Flying Horse) or the 'Trip to Jerusalem'. They reassembled at the 'Palais de Dance' where they sang squadron songs and enjoyed themselves. Eventually they congregated on the milk train next morning back to Bottesford.

Another long serving squadron wireless operator, Sergeant Jim Duncan, has additional memories of Bottesford. The crews were interested to discover large concrete structures to either side of the main runway and repeated at either end. Inspection and further enquiry revealed these to be the anchorage points for an arrested landing system for heavy bombers. Such a system had been designed and tested at the Royal Aircraft Establishment, Farnborough. The system involved taut arrester wires stretched transverse to the runway and a large retractable arrester hook mounted in the bomber. In the event no aircraft were fitted with the system.

By 22nd November 1941 the squadron had organised itself to a sufficient extent that it was once more in a position to mount operations. Next day the two inexperienced crews were required for a shallow penetration raid to Lorient docks in search of U-boats in their lair. Crews carried out night flying tests during the day.

Lorient – 22nd November 1941

Serial	Code	Sqn	Captain
L7432	EM-J	207	F/Sgt B O Wescombe
L7319	EM-X	207	F/L W D B Ruth DFC

During the afternoon Pilot Officer Bill Hills took off from Bottesford to fly to Waddington in one of the longest serving Manchesters, L7300 'EM-F'. Nine persons were on board. These were the regular crew, Bill Hills (captain), Flight Sergeant Plaistowe (second pilot), Sergeants Jackson (observer), Smith (wireless operator), van Puyenbroek (front gunner) and Ward (rear gunner), together with Flying Officer Pattinson who was going off on a course and two air traffic controllers hitching a ride to Waddington. Pattinson's suitcase with personal effects and logbooks was stowed in the bomb bay.

Having raised the undercarriage, Bill Hills then followed a familiar route and adopted a well-established routine. For part of the flight they followed the Lincoln to Boston canal which ran alongside a high embankment carrying the Lincoln to London main railway line. The crews at times got a kick out of flying along the canal at the same height as the bank waving to surprised engine drivers as they overtook them at the same level.

On this occasion they were flying at 500ft along the route when, with a loud rumble and clatter, the port engine suddenly failed. Hills immediately pressed the button to feather the port propeller. The feathering mechanism initially engaged but failed before the blades had fully rotated parallel to the airflow, leaving the propeller windmilling and creating additional drag. Hills raised the wireless operator on the intercom and instructed him to inform the tower at Waddington that they would be 'coming in on one'. He next advanced the throttle of the starboard engine which would enable them to climb to a safer height. Opening the throttle failed to produce any increase in power and instead a severe vibration in the engine and airframe was followed by this engine packing up too.

At low altitude with two dead engines and little excess speed there was minimal time to prepare for and no option regarding the site of, the inevitable forced landing. They simply had to go more or less straight in dead ahead.

By great good fortune there was flat open ground bordering a small tree-lined lake slightly to their left. Hills remembered suddenly that he was not strapped into his seat, but in these few final seconds was unable to take his hands off the controls. A thought flashed into his mind recalling a fellow 49 Squadron Hampden pilot during his first tour who had survived a crash landing in similar circumstances by bracing his feet on the dashboard at the instant of impact.

Accordingly, Hills shouted 'Hold on!' to warn the crew, raised his feet from the rudder bars, bracing them on the instrument panel and yanked hard back on the stick just before the aircraft hit the ground. The nose rose sharply and the tail hit the ground first. The severity of the impact resulted in the rear fuselage and tail unit breaking off immediately forward of the crew entry door. The triple fin tail unit, fortunately unoccupied, tumbled away to come to rest on the edge of the lake.

Twenty tons of uncontrollable, disintegrating, screeching Manchester slithering on its belly was bearing down on the lake at almost 100mph. The scene in the flooded disused quarry now known as Fiskerton Lake could not have provided a more marked contrast – a fishing match was in progress. Competitors were distributed around its margin and one of the organisers was out on the lake in a flat bottomed punt. For this group the afternoon epitomised peace, solitude and an escape from war work.

In an instant the careering Manchester appeared over the bank and pitched forwards into perhaps ten feet of water, throwing up a massive tidal wave as it did so. Fishermen turned and ran as the wave broke upon the bank, whilst the unfortunate occupant of the punt had a grandstand view before the advancing wall of water swept over his craft, rocking it violently and sending cascades of water over its gunwales. Within a few seconds the Manchester had settled and the waves were dissipating, leaving the boatman standing unscathed, soaking wet and transfixed with fear ankle-deep in water, his sandwiches bobbing gently around him.

On impact, Hills must have catapulted over the top of the control column and then down into the nose, as his next recollection is lying in the nose section with water, mud and gravel spurting in on him. They were all shocked and not reacting rationally. Lying beside him was Pattinson, who on feeling the liquid on him shouted 'Look out, petrol!' 'No, it's only water!' replied Hills who, finding he could stand, returned to the cockpit, climbed out of his side window and thence onto the wing.

Moans and groans coming from the rear of the aircraft brought the sudden vivid and irrational thought that he had killed the remainder of his crew. To discover their condition and come to their assistance he then released the aircraft dinghy and was relieved to see it inflate undamaged. Climbing in, he paddled the dinghy round to the gaping hole where the rear fuselage had broken off. As he did so he heard a scream of pain from inside 'Ah! My back, leave me alone!', as one shocked crew member tried to help another.

In his haste and anxiety to help, Hills pulled the dinghy in too firmly against the jagged metal, puncturing it. Despite their injuries the crew came running hell for leather down the fuselage towards him through the water, by now rising inside the rear fuselage. This aircraft was not fitted with a mid-upper turret so that the progress of the crew was unimpeded. As the Manchester settled, the last escaper, van Puyenbroek, found himself completely submerged, but with scrabbling fingers he managed to pull himself clear of the fuselage with the last of his remaining breath.

Although the outer cover punctured and the dinghy partly deflated, the inner skin remained intact and Hills was able to ferry the survivors in groups to the wing of the Manchester, which was still above the water. A head count then established that the entire crew had survived. There were various injuries which were relatively minor in the circumstances; these included van Puyenbroek with a broken arm and skinned fingers and Pattinson with a severely bruised backside. Plaistowe had a cut head and was concussed. They then ferried themselves in stages to the shore. Latterly, the lone sentinel frozen and open mouthed in the punt was galvanised into action and helped them ashore in his swamped vessel.

Bill Hills was left standing on the wing in true captain's style, the last to leave the aircraft, and he found the time to reach inside his soaking clothing and pull out his cigarettes. Finding one still dry he lit it up as he waited his turn to be ferried ashore.

The whole crew was finally assembled on the shore and as they waited for transport to arrive, in their wet clothes began to feel the effects of the extreme November cold. To keep the cold at bay they broached the emergency rations and found seven small bottles of rum. Only Hills and one other crew member liked rum and it certainly did warm them, especially the last bottle.

By this time a private car and ambulance had been rustled up from somewhere and they were ferried to hospital for a check up. The worst injured, including Plaistowe, were stripped of their wet clothes and wrapped in dry blankets.

Hills was by now high on the combined relief from the anxiety of their crash and the effects of the alcohol and insisted in riding up front with the (female) ambulance driver. En route to the hospital the car stopped at a turning and Plaistowe leaped out and raced naked down the street before his compatriots recaptured him. The effects of the concussion were still apparent.

When Hills and the other group arrived in the ambulance at Lincoln hospital those with injuries were taken to the wards, whilst Hills was not only unhurt, but a liability. He was suffering from shock, extreme cold and the alcohol and was immediately bundled into blankets and transferred to the medical wing at Waddington. Here the doctor soaked him in a hot bath and the effects of cold and rum slowly abated. That night he appeared in the mess at Waddington resplendent in a uniform loaned by the squadron doctor.

L7300 was recovered from the lake in early December by 58 Maintenance Unit, assisted by a naval diving team and consigned to the scrap heap. The aircraft still carried its early style wavy demarcation between the black undersides and the disruptive brown and green upper surfaces and never had a mid-upper turret.

An internal Rolls-Royce minute of 26th November 1941 specifies what was possibly the last large scale Vulture problem, although by now it was a problem of more modest proportions. The minute, entitled 'Vulture Progress' remarks on the epidemic of exhaust manifolds failing at 25 OTU Finningley. All the failures occurred at around 60 hours of life. It was suggested that the trouble was accelerated by the large number of take-offs carried out at the OTU. There were also failures at Coningsby and Bottesford.

The troubles stressed the need, the minute went on, for large quantities of 18 SWG manifolds for retrospective fitting. At that time service replacements consisted of reconditioned 20 SWG manifolds returned after 90 hours. In early December 207 Squadron was stood down for several days to permit all the exhaust manifolds to be changed, presumably they were changed sequentially on each unit.

A rider to the minute provides a contemporary check on the status of Vulture deliveries at this date; 37 engines were awaiting Mod 44, the correction of the con-rod assembly. There were 116 more new engines to deliver to complete the contract. The implication that it was considered that Avro were now responsible for any delay in delivery of completed aircraft is found in the claim that Avro still had more engines than they could cope with, and that it had been possible to supply two spare engines to all the stations (a whole two!). This was mute testimony to the perpetual and desperate shortage of all Vulture spares, which reduced squadrons at times to desperate measures.

On checking Vultures returned for inspection after 120 hours, it became apparent that several examples of excessive barrel wear were coming to light, especially of the master-rod cylinder. In an attempt to reduce barrel wear several engines were modified to take nitrided liners which had a greater wear resistance. Vultures Nos. 682, 694, 696 and 698 were fitted to two Metrovick aircraft, R5793 and R5794, and delivered to 25 OTU at Finningley. It appears this modification was not proceeded with.

In respect of the engine problems the pilots were still complaining on return from operations that they had been unable to climb above about 7,000ft. The power available from the twin Vultures was very low but even so they should have been able to reach 15,000ft. Rolls-Royce engineers once again examined the engines and on the 5th December 1941 Flying Officer Dave Green was ordered to undertake a full warload climb in L7486 to simulate the operational problems. Green took off from Bottesford and on this occasion managed to lift the aircraft to about 17,000ft. Before reaching the aircraft's ultimate ceiling, Green made one of his periodic visual checks on the aircraft and noticed that the wire clipped around the engine cowlings to keep them in place was loose and flapping in the slipstream. Assessing the situation, Green checked all the engine control instruments and found them normal. He believed the most likely explana-

tion for this to be that the clasp had become detached or the cable worn through due to the vibration.

Nevertheless, Green decided to make a precautionary landing to establish the true explanation. It was a wise decision. Green throttled back and spiralled down to the airfield beneath. As they descended into the denser, bumpy air closer to the ground his regular checks appeared to indicate that the entire engine was actually loose on its mountings. In the circuit the suspicions were confirmed as the engine was by this time rising and falling to an alarming degree. They were pleased to land and shut down the engines as soon as possible.

Inspection revealed that the aircraft was indeed closer to disaster than the tell-tale clamping wire had initially indicated. The supercharger cooler mounted on the outboard side of the Vulture engine, where it could not be seen by the crew, was mounted too close to the alloy engine bearers. The supercharger commonly overheated and in this case the heat was sufficiently intense that the bearer had begun to melt. Had Green continued for only a short period it is certain that the engine would either have caught fire or the entire engine would have fallen out of the airframe completely, with disastrous consequences. Once more the skill and experience of 207 Squadron's aircrews had saved an aircraft and the crew itself from imminent disaster.

L7300 'EM-F' of 207 Squadron during recovery operations by a naval diving team at Fiskerton Lake, Lincolnshire. The aircraft crashed on 23rd November 1941 when Pilot Officer Hills had a double engine failure. *via N Franklin*

Chapter Six

Against the Battlecruisers

As December 1941 began, Manchester serviceability problems continued to dog the force. Combined with Bomber Command policy to conserve resources following the severe losses of the 7/8th November 1941 raid, this largely neutralised the Manchester units. Notwithstanding these limitations, pressure was beginning to increase from intelligence sources for further and even more vigorous attempts to take out the *Scharnhorst*, *Gneisenau* and *Prinz Eugen*. Reports had revealed that the *Scharnhorst* would soon be seaworthy again following lengthy repairs necessitated by the bomb damage suffered back on the 24th July. Soon this potent force could be rampaging around the Atlantic once more, at a time when Britain's fortunes and resources were at a low ebb throughout the world. The campaign against the German capital ships waged over the next three months was to witness a variety of unusual and desperate measures, a daylight raid on the ships at Brest, numerous night attacks including the use of a novel anti-shipping weapon, widespread mining operations, including an unprecedented daylight attack in Dutch and German coastal shipping lanes when the intended breakout route was appreciated and finally the chaotic daylight bombing attack on the ships *en passage* in the southern North Sea. At the time, it appeared a major defeat for the Royal Navy, Fleet Air Arm and Bomber Command. In fact Bomber Command's efforts had led to three mine explosions and severe damage to the *Scharnhorst* and *Gneisenau* and furthermore it was a Bomber Command aimed 2,000 lb armour piercing (AP) bomb which disabled *Gneisenau* in Kiel by the end of February 1942 and resulted in the final decommissioning of this unlucky vessel.

All this was naturally unknown to the Manchester squadrons as December 1941 began. Amongst a plethora of continuing problems at this time there were a few bright spots. No. 61 Squadron was preparing to return its Manchesters to operations after a three month work up and had finally relinquished its Handley Page Hampdens. As this new phase began a glance at the Manchesters which would participate will set the scene.

Whilst the remainder of the 5 Group squadrons continued to soldier on with their obsolescent Hampdens, now six to nine months overdue for replacement, the Manchester was sidelined with all eyes on the Avro Lancaster. In the meantime, as December began, 83 Squadron at Scampton was delegated to be the fourth unit to receive Manchesters. Conversion began during the month to a unit enviously aware of its more favoured cousins receiving Lancasters at nearby Waddington.

In September and October a rush of the latest factory-fresh Mk.IAs from L7483 onward had reached 207 Squadron at Waddington, with the main batch in October setting up 61 Squadron, still working up at North Luffenham. A few also reached 97 Squadron at Coningsby. Similarly, the first trickle of Metropolitan Vickers built Manchesters reached the three units in October, 61 Squadron again taking the bulk of deliveries. These Metrovick aircraft had been built earlier in the year as Mk.Is but whether they had been retrofitted as Mk.IAs prior to delivery has not been established. No. 61 Squadron found that not all deliveries were fitted with an Elsan, but those that had included a privacy curtain which was rapidly dispensed with as a fire risk.

Alongside these latest aircraft, the earlier Mk.Is, often retaining their wavy camouflage demarcation, continued in service. In 207 Squadron L7309, L7317 and L7319 were still active. Despite the Bomber Command directive in late June to fit or refit the F.N.7A to existing Manchesters a number remained lacking this facility. L7300, just recently written off, had never had the turret and L7309 and L7322 had lacked the turret initially, although L7309 at least had it installed when it was eventually lost in January. Despite the continuing Rolls-Royce Vulture problems and in an attempt to maintain some pressure on the Germans, Bomber Command laid on a main force operation on 7/8th December 1941 to Aachen which was to involve Manchesters from both 207 and 97 Squadrons. Also returning to operating Manchesters after their three month absence was 61 Squadron which was to attack Boulogne docks as a gentle re-introduction to operations but, as with 97 Squadron's return to operations in mid-October, things did not proceed very smoothly. These aircraft joined with 124 other aircraft allocated to the Boulogne. Take-off was unusually late, ranging from 0212 to 0224 hours.

Aachen – 7/8th December 1941

Serial	Code	Sqn	Captain
L7491	OF-C	97	F/L J G Mackid
L7488	OF-F	97	F/O H S Blakeman
L7473	OF-H	97	F/O E A Deverill
L7475	OF-B	97	P/O Keir
L7492	OF-A	97	P/O E E Rodley
L7476	OF-K	97	F/Sgt S E Harrison
L7523	EM-M	207	F/L P C Ward-Hunt
L7432	EM-J	207	F/O P C Birch
L7480	EM-L	207	F/O D A Green
R5796	EM-S	207	S/L K H P Beauchamp
L7468	EM-Z	207	P/O G R Bayley
L7484	EM-P	207	F/Sgt G H Coles

Boulogne – 7/8th December 1941

Serial	Code	Sqn	Captain
L7519	QR-*	61	W/C T C Weir
L7494	QR-*	61	S/L J L Riley
L7496	QR-*	61	F/L P G Sooby
L7472	QR-*	61	F/L R A V Gascoyne-Cecil

Of the six aircraft dispatched by 207 Squadron, three bombed what they believed to be the general target area on the estimated time of arrival (ETA), without any results being observed. A Messerschmitt Me109 passed a mere 50ft beneath L7523 as Flight Lieutenant Ward-Hunt returned.

Squadron Leader Beauchamp was unable to find the primary or any suitable alternative target and brought his bombs back in R5796, releasing only his load of leaflets in the Aachen area. Flight Sergeant Coles similarly failed to locate the primary owing to 10/10th cloud and severe icing in the target area and released his 5 x 1,000 lb bomb load on Dunkirk docks at 0540 hours on the return flight.

In L7432 Flying Officer Peter Birch was encountering almost insuperable serviceability problems, but with irrepressible spirit carried on towards Aachen. First the rear turret went unserviceable, then the intercom to the front turret failed and finally the dorsal turret guns jammed after a test burst of fire. L7432 was defenceless, but incredibly Peter Birch elected to continue.

North of Lille the almost inevitable happened and they were intercepted by a Me109. By skilful use of cloud and evasive tactics, Birch and his crew kept the fighter at bay for a full 30 minutes before it was seen to break off the engagement to attack a nearby Vickers Wellington.

Finally, bowing to the inevitable and with the added complication of engine trouble, Birch diverted to an alternative target. At 0415 the aircraft was down to 3,800ft when it attacked the docks at Calais with five 1,000lb bombs. As a final act of defiance Birch dived to 800ft to permit the front gunner to shoot out searchlights around the town.

From the 97 Squadron force Pilot Officer Deverill returned when both front and rear turrets proved unserviceable when tested over the North Sea. None of the remaining aircraft located Aachen, which was under deep cloud, and most bombed dock areas on the Belgian and French coast as a last resort. No. 61 Squadron had equal difficulty locating Boulogne and Flight Lieutenant Riley, the 'A' Flight commander, failed to return. An attacking aircraft had been seen to explode in mid-air on the run up to the target. Since Riley was the only casualty of the night it must have been his aircraft hit by a flak shell. The aircraft crashed into the sea with no survivors.

Of those dispatched, only 64 aircraft claimed to attack, whereas the Aachen daily report specifies an attack force of 16. Most of the bombs dropped fell in open country to the north of the city and only five high explosive (HE) bombs, two of them duds, and nine incendiaries fell in the city. There were no casualties. A further operation on the 8th was cancelled owing to continued inclement weather and on 10th December the Manchester squadrons were stood down for four days in order to change all manifolds on the Vultures.

The crews returned from a welcome break to find that they were to retrain for daylight formation flying and bombing. At this time, Bomber Command had been plugging away at the *Scharnhorst* and the *Gneisenau* in Brest in the dark for months, with limited effect. Now it seemed from intelligence they may have been on the point of breaking out to ravage the Atlantic convoys, as the *Bismarck* had done in May. Since the first horrific unescorted bombing raids of the war, fighter defences had been provided for shallow penetration raids. Short Stirlings and Handley Page Halifaxes had participated in

Top: **Sergeant Morton (sitting) and Flying Officer Neath in the doorway of Mk.IA L7494 during 61 Squadron's third work up period on the Manchester** *circa* **November 1941. L7494 exploded in mid-air running up to Boulogne on its first operation on 7/8th December 1941. The 'A' Flight commander, Squadron Leader Riley and his crew, were killed.** *L Boot*

Above: **Ken Leyshon on 'ops'! Allegedly one of the few Manchesters on 61 Squadron fitted with an Elsan.** *L Boot*

Below: **Aircrew of 61 Squadron photographed in front of one of their Manchesters,** *circa* **December 1941. The commanding officer, Wing Commander Weir, is flanked by his two flight commanders.** *via H Scott*

Port nacelle and undercarriage dwarfing a 207 Squadron crew at Bottesford, early 1942. The aircraft is possibly L7317 'EM-C'. Left to right: 'Ginger' Hathersich (second pilot); Bob Storey (wireless operator/air gunner); Ken Ferris (air gunner); Frank Belfitt (observer); Jimmy Kneil (captain) and Bob Elliott (air gunner). *K Ferris*

some of the earliest 'Circus' attacks in France and the Low Countries. Manchesters had been spared this ordeal, and were grounded during the summer daylight attacks on La Pallice and St Nazaire.

Now desperation seemed to dictate that the Manchester force could be thrown in with the hope of striking a decisive blow against the capital ships before they lost themselves in the wide expanses of the ocean. The prospect of daylight operations in the Manchester must have filled their hearts with trepidation, but the urgency was such that training began forthwith. In the case of 207, formation flying practice commenced on 14th December. It was obvious there was a lot to learn and great care was needed both on the ground and in the air. Groups of nine aircraft at a time participated. The need for a rapid take-off sequence was paramount, but if a single 207 Squadron aircraft snaking along the narrow perimeter track to the active runway put a wheel off the tarmac it immediately sank up to the axle in Bottesford mud and immobilised those aircraft behind. Such aircraft could only be removed by being towed tail-first back to the hard standings. However rapid the take-off sequence ach-·ieved, the lead aircraft would be 15 miles ahead by the time the last one took off. Such a distance could never be made up by the heavily laden Manchesters. During practice on 14, 15, 16 and 17th December a system was evolved in which the two wingmen of a vic would take-off and join up and then pick up the leader when he took off afterwards.

At the crunch it was 97 Squadron which drew the short straw and was chosen to join the mixed force led by Halifaxes from 76 Squadron, followed by nine Stirlings each from 7 and 15 Squadrons and accompanied by the 97 Squadron force. The operation was planned for 18th December 1941, its urgency heightened by ULTRA intercepts indicating the imminence of the two capital ships breaking out of Brest.

The 97 Squadron force consisted of 11 Manchesters led by the CO, Wing Commander Balsdon, one of which was intended as a spare in case any aircraft should drop out through unserviceability on the flight across England. Wing Commander Balsdon decided to take the crew of Flight Sergeant George Pendrill, still accompanied by Sergeant Les Jones, who had out-fought Heinrich Griese back in early November, as rear gunner. This brought the crew complement to eight. Other crew carried were Sergeant Gibson,

the squadron navigation leader, and Flight Lieutenant Wright the squadron bombing leader. Take-off was close to 0930 hours.

Brest in daylight – 18th December 1941

Serial	Code	Sqn	Captain
L7490	OF-U	97	W/C D F Balsdon
L7453	OF-X	97	W/O D H Rowlands
L7489	OF-K	97	F/Sgt C G Hughes
L7463	OF-P	97†	F/Sgt R A Fletcher
L7492	OF-A	97	S/L J S Sherwood DFC
R5795	OF-W	97	P/O N G Stokes
L7460	OF-J	97	F/O H S Blakeman
L7525	OF-D	97	F/O B R W Hallows
L7491	OF-C	97	F/L J G Mackid
L7425	OF-G	97	F/O E E Rodley
L7488	OF-F	97	F/O E A Deverill

† operational spare

The six Halifaxes from 76 Squadron, led by their new commanding officer (CO), Wing Commander D Young, rendezvoused over Linton-on-Ouse with a further five from 10 Squadron and six from 35 Squadron to make up a 17 aircraft force. The CO of 10 Squadron, Wing Commander Marks, had already aborted with a jammed starboard undercarriage.

In misty weather, course was set for Lundy Island in the Bristol Channel, where the remainder of the bomber force, including aircraft from the Stirling squadrons and the Manchesters, were to join forces. The rendezvous was achieved successfully close to the briefed time of 1120, although a further Halifax aborted and diverted to Boscombe Down with engine trouble. The entire force then headed for the Lizard Peninsula with 18 Stirlings leading the Halifaxes and the 11 Manchesters at the rear.

L7475 'QR-D' of 61 Squadron during daylight formation practice, possibly December 1941. *L Boot*

Over the Lizard the mist cleared and it became sunny with only occasional wisps of cloud. As all the Manchesters remained serviceable, Flight Sergeant Bob Fletcher, the spare, was able to peel away and return to base. Later Flying Officer Deverill had to return owing to a malfunction in the aircraft, reducing the force to nine.

Ahead, a force of Spitfires and Hurricanes had carried out a fighter sweep of the area with a view to bringing up the German day fighters and using up their fuel. As the Manchesters steeled themselves and bunched up even closer for mutual protection approaching the French coast, a jar and roar sent a shock through the tensed up members of Pilot Officer Stokes' crew in R5795 'OF-W', on their first operation. The upper escape hatch had flown off and hit the tail fin. The rushing airstream at 17,000ft brought in the outside air at a temperature of –17°F.

As the first smoke began to drift across Brest Harbour from the smoke pots the intense flak defences opened up in greeting. At around 1230 hours Wing Commander Graham led his 7 and 15 Squadron Stirlings over the target, harried all the way by Me109 fighters, who ignored the dense flak barrage. Next Wing Commander Young led his Halifax force across the French coast in the run up to the target. By the time the Halifax group made their final bomb run, fighter attacks had temporarily abated and they only had the flak to contend with. It appeared that the fighter sweeps had been successful in drawing off much of the Luftwaffe whilst the RAF close escort remained in attendance. Good bombing results seemed to be achieved. Several Halifaxes were damaged by flak and one later ditched in the Channel.

Finally it was the turn of the Manchesters to brave the cauldron of flak over the harbour. As they bored in, maintaining their disciplined three vic formation, the RAF fighter cover finally had to withdraw short of fuel, whilst refuelled and armed Me109s began to reach their height. The Manchesters were on their own.

The flak defences were already having a field day, first a heavy calibre shell burst close to the left side of Flight Sergeant Hughes in L7489, knocking out the port Vulture, which had to be feathered. Hughes was able to maintain his course and, despite dropping back, released his bomb load. Next, only a few seconds prior to bomb release, a savage flak burst on the port side of Stokes' R5795 'OF-W' damaged the port wing and caused the aircraft to yaw to the left, lose speed and fall behind the formation. Sergeant Tom Wade, the observer, released the bombs soon afterwards, but nobody in his crew had the opportunity to observe their fall. Then, a heavy burst exploded beneath L7490 'OF-U', buffeting the aircraft, damaging the rear fuselage and tail and wounding the rear gunner, Sergeant Les Jones. The flak intensity and accuracy was hellish for the clumsy Manchesters committed to their straight and level bombing attack and several other aircraft were damaged.

As they cleared the target, Hughes put L7489 into a dive to put distance between himself and the flak gunners as quickly as possible. Lagging behind the remainder of

Flying Officer Dave Green in the cockpit of his 207 Squadron Manchester *Dopey* at Bottesford, *circa* December 1941. The aircraft is probably L7419 'EM-Y'. *D Green*

the force they were set on by a gaggle of Me109s, which commenced a series of ferocious attacks from astern. Sergeant Gerry McMahon, the rear gunner in L7489, maintained spirited and accurate return fire. Despite being a straggler and being hit repeatedly by the '109s, no vital services were damaged. McMahon claimed hits on four attacking fighters on his return.

Clearing the target, Sergeant Wade closed the bomb doors of R5795 and Stokes put the nose down and turned for home. Ahead the Manchesters streamed out in shallow dives in an attempt to evade the returning Luftwaffe fighters. The straggling Stokes, along with Hughes, last over Brittany and with their escorts already well out in the channel, was one of the first to feel the savage onslaught from the Me109s. Sergeants Fell in the rear turret and Heinish in the mid-upper gave urgent instructions to Stokes to take evasive action as R5795 was rapidly overtaken. Regrettably, at no time after the flak hit did Stokes reply to instructions or take any evasive action. Either Stokes himself was badly wounded or he was fully occupied in flying the damaged Manchester. Sergeant Ike Hewitt was sitting impotent, but prepared, in the front turret as R5795 crossed the coast. At least two Me109s were able to approach from port and starboard quarters and pound the Manchester on its predictable straight and level flight path from long range with their cannon. Fell and Heinish were unable to respond effectively and the first few bursts of cannon fire riddled the rear of the aircraft, incapacitating or killing both gunners. The straggling Manchester was now defenceless to the rear and the Me109s closed in remorselessly, maintaining steady bursts of fire. R5795 was set on fire amidships and the final order was given to bale out. The observer, Sergeant Tom Wade, second pilot Sergeant Thomas and wireless operator, Sergeant Conn got away through the front escape hatch.

Hewitt made a vain attempt to reach the rear gunner in the hope that he was still alive. Fire quickly drove him back and he then became entangled in the front escape hatch as he tried to follow his three crew mates. Finally breaking free, the last to escape, Hewitt pulled the rip-cord to see that his parachute had burnt through in one area. His descent was consequently faster than normal. Stokes had remained at the controls and the Manchester continued to descend on an even keel before plunging into the sea. Hewitt splashed-in shortly afterwards. His watch stopped at 0104 and he found that a heavy sea was running. The crash locality is given as four miles off Brest, whereas when he was picked up just before dark at soon after 5 pm, Hewitt was told he was 20 miles out and lucky to be found. Along with Thomas and Wade he became a prisoner, but Conn was never found.

Cheery groundcrew of 61 Squadron digging out the starboard main wheel of a Manchester which strayed off the peritrack on return from an air test, December 1941. *L Boot*

German fighters also continued to harry L7489, limping along behind on its remaining starboard engine. Eventually the attacks petered out and the '109s withdrew, giving Gerry McMahon in the rear turret more time to take in the happenings around him. As L7489, the last bomber to return from the Brest force, traversed the designated route back, MacMahon was struck by the incongruous thought that if he had been a giant he could have walked back to England using the series of floating ditched bombers they passed over en route as stepping stones. Flight Sergeant Hughes could have elected to land soon after crossing the coast but L7489 was flying well on one and all engine instruments read normal. He decided to press on to Coningsby following the rest.

As they plodded on, slowly falling even further behind, it appears that Wing Commander Balsdon too had radioed ahead his intention to return to Coningsby, despite reporting damage to the rear fuselage, tailplanes and elevators of L7490. Flying Officer Blakeman's aircraft had been hit in the starboard oil tank and as he crossed the Channel his crew monitored the rising engine temperature with growing concern. He wisely decided on a precautionary landing at Colerne in Wiltshire where the engine cut out on the runway.

At Coningsby the returning Manchester force arrived back in the late afternoon with a little evening mist but generally favourable weather. Several Manchesters had already landed when the damaged L7490 made its approach. It is not known whether Flight Sergeant Pendrill or Wing Commander Balsdon was flying. The aircraft made a safe and normal circuit and approach, other than that as it let down it was observed to be slightly above the glide path. When the aircraft was on finals and already over the boundary fence its pilot apparently elected to overshoot, as the engines were heard to open up to full power.

Regrettably and for unknown reasons, instead of increasing speed and climbing away steadily to make another approach, the nose of the aircraft began to rise steadily and uncontrollably. The nose angle steepened and speed dropped off until the aircraft was almost vertical, a few hundred feet above the airfield. It stalled and flicked over until it was pointing nose down, whereupon it crashed in the centre of the field under the horrified gaze of the control tower staff and wives of several crew members.

On impact the fuselage broke in half at the mid-upper turret, the rear half of the fuselage folding forward over the front. The aircraft was consumed in a ball of flame from which there could be no survivors. The wreckage continued to burn for some time. Indeed by the time Flight Sergeant Hughes arrived in the circuit some time later it was quite foggy and the fires in the burning wreckage helped him to judge his single-engined landing alongside.

It was next day before the wreck of L7490 had cooled down sufficiently for the debris to be sorted and removed. Personnel found that the only recognisable debris amongst the ashes were the two wing tips and the propellers. The force of the impact had driven the heavy engines down into the ground and all six blades were bent vertically upwards so that their tips projected from the ground. Bob Fletcher, who was billeted with George Pendrill and Les Jones out at Woodhall Spa, returned next day and walked over to the crash site to pay his last respects to his two friends.

All that remained was a heap of black ash which Fletcher walked through, numbed into incomprehension by the thought that George and Les were part of those very ashes. The raid itself had achieved little and all 5 Group Manchester airfields were closed by fog for the next four days.

Wing Commander Kynoch arrived to take command and 97 Squadron only undertook a few more Manchester operations in early January before they were stood-down to convert to the Lancaster. Formation flying by the three Manchester squadrons continued in expectation of a follow up attack. To their disgust they were even called on to continue their preparations, with a formation flying practice, on Christmas Day.

In the meantime, on 27th December, Group cancelled daylight formation flying and instead specified 207 Squadron to prepare 12 Manchesters for a night operation to Dusseldorf in what was only the third Manchester operation of the month. Later in the day Group cancelled five of the 12. These seven joined a total force of 132 aircraft.

Dusseldorf – 27th December 1941

Serial	Code	Sqn	Captain
L7522	EM-M	207	F/L P C Ward-Hunt
L7455	EM-G	207	F/O P C Birch
L7432	EM-J	207	F/Sgt B O Wescombe
L7484	EM-P	207	F/L W D B Ruth
L7483	EM-O	207	S/L K H P Beauchamp
L7322	EM-Q	207	F/Sgt G B Dawkins
R5791	EM-V	207	F/Sgt J C Atkinson

Take-off on this occasion was well spaced out. Ruth took off at 1701 and Atkinson was last away at 1747. Take-off and climb performance was marginal, as the crews had come to accept with the Manchester. 'Penny' Beauchamp had undertaken a night flying test in the RAF's first Manchester Mk.IA,

No. 97 Squadron aircrew relax in the crew-room at Coningsby. Sergeant Gordon Hartley is slumped in the chair beneath the dartboard with, to his right Sergeant 'Fluffy' Berridge, second pilot to Bob Fletcher. *R A Fletcher*

L7483 and found it to perform adequately.

Close to 1750, whilst outward bound over Orfordness, the aircraft had struggled to a height of 4,000ft when the starboard engine lost power and failed. Beauchamp feathered the starboard propeller, put the nose down to maintain airspeed and continued out to sea. The aircraft was unable to maintain height on one engine with the heavy fuel load, 4,000lb 'Cookie', and two 500lb general purpose (GP) bombs. Reducing their all up weight was an urgent necessity but directly in their path ahead to seaward could be one of our coastal convoys, which had been mentioned at briefing. The thin cased 'Cookies' often detonated on impact even when dropped safe. As a precautionary measure Beauchamp continued east to clear the supposed route of the convoy before the bombs were jettisoned. In the event the 4,000lb bomb did not explode and neither were they troubled by anti-aircraft fire from any convoy which may have been nearby.

L7483 had by this time lost much of what little height had been in hand and was immediately turned inland to return. They continued to lose height even without the bomb load, despite Beauchamp's best efforts. If they were to save the aircraft they would have to find an airfield quickly. Ahead they recognised a single letter flashing PUNDIT beacon showing the coded signal for Martlesham Heath, still at this time a grass airfield. These beacons were mobile and placed at various positions around an airfield. On take-off the crew were given a 'flimsy' showing the chosen codes and the range and bearing of the airfields they marked for that particular night.

Beauchamp called Martlesham on the radio and got a reply from the airman in charge of the flarepath. The airman authorised Beauchamp to land and turned on the flarepath lights. Seeing the position of the air-

field for the first time, Beauchamp shaped to make a circuit at around 1,000ft. On their downwind leg the lights were suddenly extinguished and they lost sight of the airfield completely. It turned out that the airman in charge of the flarepath was 25 miles from his headquarters. He had telephoned his headquarters and informed them he had lit the flarepath for an aircraft, which had fired the colours of the day and identified itself as friendly. Headquarters had insisted the aircraft was a hostile and that the flarepath must be extinguished.

The aircraft was continuing to lose height and there was little time left if they were to get down safely. An irate Beauchamp called the airfield again, by now he was on the base leg of the circuit. The lights came on again. By the lights Beauchamp was able to line up on the runway for finals. Their height was 500ft by then, the undercarriage and flaps were down and they were committed to the landing, with no prospect of a second attempt. Without warning the flarepath lights were extinguished yet again. The airfield disappeared, the whole surrounding countryside was blacked out and in the clear half-moonlight Beauchamp could vaguely and indistinctly see an open space ahead. Judging height and distance in these circumstances was virtually impossible. Beauchamp continued the approach and when finally down to 50ft suddenly saw houses coming up on the far side of the airfield. They were overshooting.

Beauchamp had run out of options. At the last moment the lights came on for a third time but too late to help. He rammed the stick forward, the nose dropped and they dived into the ground with the wheels still down. The aircraft hit and the airframe crunched, groaned and ground itself into the turf. There was no significant shock of the impact or deceleration since the enormous forces were mainly taken up by the crushing of the airframe.

The undercarriage legs were driven up through the wings and the aircraft slithered across the grass on its belly, finally coming to a halt with a wingtip against a pill box and the tail against a dispersed Spitfire on the aerodrome boundary. When the noises of the aircraft tearing itself apart finally stopped the only sound was of gurgling, rushing liquid – petrol! To a man the crew abandoned the wreck as fast as their legs would carry them. The ruptured fuel tanks were emptying their contents and the crew ran through a big pool of petrol almost ankle-deep in places spreading all round the aircraft. Fortunately it did not catch fire. The time was 1807.

The entire crew had escaped uninjured, but L7483 was a sorry sight. Although initially categorised as repairable it never flew again, it was dismantled by 39 Maintenance Unit and passed to 12 School of Technical Training as an instructional airframe.

Unaware of the drama which had befallen Beauchamp and his crew the rest of the pilots nursed their Vulture engines and continued towards Dusseldorf. Soon another Manchester, L7523, flown by Peter Ward-Hunt had to abandon its attempt to reach Dusseldorf when the aircraft experienced first a failure of the electrical supply to the rear turret and later an intercom failure. Ward-Hunt diverted to Ostend, releasing five 1,000 lb bombs from 11,000ft at 1837 hours. Receiving a diversionary signal Ward-Hunt returned to Horsham St Faith.

The remaining five aircraft in the depleted force reached what they took to be the target area, where their effectiveness was further reduced when Ruth had his 4,000 lb bomb hang up and Atkinson was unable to release

Manchester I of 207 Squadron in the snow at Bottesford in the winter of 1941/1942. Former groundcrew will recognise the almost inevitable trestle erected around the starboard Vulture.
No. 207 Squadron archives / R Glynne-Owen

two of his four 1,000 lb bombs. In the target area visibility was good, although one crew had difficulties navigating across the snow covered countryside. Dawkins' aircraft swung at the instant of bomb release with the result that the bombs fell slightly east of the aiming point. Searchlight and flak activity prevented the bomb bursts being observed. Peter Birch in his personalised Manchester, L7455, made a determined attack on the primary at 2010 from 14,000ft releasing five 1,000 lb bombs. The bursts could not be distinguished owing to those from other aircraft bursting at the same time, but were estimated to have fallen in the town centre.

Closing the bomb doors Birch then dived to a roof top height of 150ft to try his hand as a night intruder. As they proceeded westwards the gunners fired on two factories at Bud-erich, a train at Heimoud-Masshese and two small towns. All aircraft landed at Horsham St Faith, the hydraulic system in Wescombe's aircraft failing in the process. Although 96 aircraft claimed to attack the city the records reveal that only 32 HE and three cans of incendiaries fell in the built up area. These caused very slight damage and no casualties.

On 30th December a second daylight attack was mounted on the *Scharnhorst* and

the *Gneisenau* but the three Manchester squadrons were not required. It is clear that Bomber Command still considered the Manchesters fair game for daylight operations as 207 was stood by for a daylight attack on 31st December. On this occasion the weather resulted in both this and night flying training being cancelled.

As 1942 began 207 Squadron was still shouldering the lion's share of Manchester operations. On 2nd/3rd January, 1942 the squadron dispatched ten aircraft to St Nazaire and on 5/6th January ten aircraft returned to Brest, followed by a further raid on Brest on 8/9th January. No. 97 Squadron was able to raise two Manchesters on this date to join the force. All these operations were rendered completely ineffective by exceptionally bad weather, with dense unbroken cloud. This resulted in navigation and target location problems. In the absence of any sight of the ground or any aids to navigation, crews were reduced to pin-pointing the general area of Brest naval base by the flak bursts in the sky. Even searchlights were unable to penetrate the gloom. Many crews jettisoned bomb loads offshore but a few 'area bombed' the flak activity in the vain hope of a hit with their AP and semi-armour piercing (SAP) bombs.

Manchester I L7459 'OF-N' of 97 Squadron following a forced landing when a practice bomb
detonated as Sergeant 'Jammy' Hartley was
taking off from Coningsby on 8th January
1942. Dense smoke blinded and choked the
crew. *R A Fletcher*

In these conditions the weather provided
the best protection for the vessels berthed in
Brest and Bomber Command was impotent
to overcome such conditions. As was soon to
become apparent at the end of January,
when the veil of cloud lifted, Brest naval
base's man-made protection was an equal
match for the weather. Bomber Command's
frustration seemed set to continue. To make
matters worse 207 Squadron lost Pilot Officer
Bayley and his entire crew on the last night.

In continued bad weather 207 Squadron
produced a further two Manchesters and 97
Squadron four on 9/10th January 1942 for a
further desperate assault on Brest. Although
nominally a squadron equipped with Manchesters since early March 1941, by this date
61 Squadron had accomplished a mere 23
sorties in total in the nine month period. This
had been achieved at the expense of three
aircraft lost on operations and a further two
in training! It was hardly an auspicious
record. On this night the squadron was to
contribute a further six Manchesters, although the force was restricted to the docks
at Cherbourg. From this time onwards however, under Wing Commander Weir, the
squadron was to shoulder a major proportion of Manchester operations.

Brest / Cherbourg† – 9/10th January 1942

Serial	Code	Sqn	Captain
L7518	QR-*	61†	S/L A M Paape
L7472	QR-*	61†	P/O G L Tofield
R5789	QR-*	61†	P/O D S Matthews
L7495	QR-*	61†	P/O G W Gilpin
R5787	QR-*	61†	P/O J R Hubbard
R5785	QR-*	61†	Sgt P H G Webster
L7457	OF-Y	97	F/O E A Deverill
L7475	OF-B	97	F/O B R W Hallows
L7455	OF-X	97	W/O D H Rowlands
L7476	OF-K	97	W/O T J Mycock
L7468	EM-Z	207	S/L T C Murray
L7515	EM-S	207	F/O J H Leland

Note: Pilot Officer Gunter undertook a NICKEL *op on
Rennes in R5786, but his sortie is not in any official record.*

The six aircraft of the Brest force departed
soon after midnight, but encountered insuperable difficulties. The ground and sky were
obscured, severely inhibiting prospects for
accurate navigation. Leland jettisoned his
bombs offshore from Brest, whilst Murray jettisoned his load in the target area. His aircraft
became hopelessly lost on the return flight
and he was lucky to reach base. No.97
Squadron crews were similarly impeded. A
compass fault in Deverill's aircraft, sent them
off on a reciprocal course. By the time this
was recognised it was too late to reach Brest.
Neither 'Darky' Hallows, nor Rowlands were
able to locate a worthwhile target and returned with their bombs.

The best effort of the night was made by
Tommy Mycock in L7476. They too had located the general dockyard area from the various calibres of flak shell bursting in the
vicinity. After fruitless circling and searching
at ever dwindling altitude Mycock finally
made a diving bomb run from only 1,500ft.
Breaking out of the cloud at almost mast-
head height, bombs were released when the
target area was in the sight, but no ships
could be discerned. The crew later attributed
this to effective camouflaging of the vessels.
Mycock made his escape at a suicidal 200ft,
hotly pursued by light flak bursts. Possibly the
defenders were concentrating on higher levels, as Mycock was able to escape unscathed.
Tommy was awarded an immediate DFC for
his efforts on return. Despite this desperate
tactic *Scharnhorst* and *Gneisenau* suffered
no damage.

As the Brest force began to withdraw the
feint by 61 Squadron began to come in. Possibly the delayed take-off between 0435 and
0500, was intended to divert the German
defences. For the third consecutive operation (2nd/3rd September, 7/8th December
1941 and 9/10th January 1942) 61 Squadron
were to lose a Manchester. Two of the squadron aircraft carried passengers on this night
and for one it was to be a brief and harrowing
experience. Two Regional Control Officers
(RCOs), Pilot Officer Butler in Tofield's aircraft, L7472, and Pilot Officer Lancaster in

Matthews' aircraft, R5789, were to accompany the raiders. Matthews was setting out on
his first operation in a Manchester. No.61
Squadron's problems began at base. An aircraft had crashed at Woolfox Lodge rendering the airfield unserviceable and the aircraft
had to take-off from North Luffenham
instead.

It was a pitch black night with the same
weather restrictions as the Brest force had
encountered. The underpowered and overloaded 61 Squadron Manchesters laboured
imperceptibly upward. By 0600 Matthews,
with Pilot Officer Wilson as his second pilot
and Lancaster, the RCO, as passenger, had
reached a few thousand feet over the Wilt-
shire/Hampshire border when the starboard
engine lost power and caught fire. The propeller was feathered and the fire extinguished, but their position was immediately
desperate.

With full bomb load and most of the fuel
still remaining, their height loss was rapid
and irreversible. In the pitch darkness Matthews had no idea of their precise position
and bravely elected not to jettison the bomb
load for fear of killing innocent civilians. The
captain first steadied the aircraft whilst six of
the crew baled out. Having safely accomplished this, the two pilots maintained their
discipline and attempted a blind forced landing. Like Derek Pinchbeck and John Nunn
before and Jim Wilkie afterwards, they were
in the hands of fate.

Regrettably on this cruel night fate was
against them and as Matthews flared for
landing the aircraft crashed at a shallow
angle into a belt of trees at Tidworth, near
Wiltshire Cross. Both pilots were killed and
the aircraft burnt and later the bomb load
exploded. To their eternal credit, in forfeiting
their own lives the two pilots saved six more
in the crew and avoided any casualties on
the ground. Crash investigators were later
unable to pin-point the specific cause of the
engine failure and speculated that icing may
have been a contributory cause. Lancaster
and the remainder of the crew escaped with
minor injuries.

Of the remainder of the attack force,
Gilpin, Hubbard and Webster were all unable
to locate Cherbourg and returned with their
bombs. By descending to low level Paape
and Tofield were able to get below the cloud
base and attack. All five returned to base,
landing close to 9 am.

Maritime targets were again the priority on 10/11th January 1942, but for a change Wilhelmshaven was specified to receive the attention of 61, 97 and 207 Squadrons. The aiming point was the main railway station, but with the intention of causing resultant damage in the port area.

Wilhelmshaven – 10/11th January 1942

Serial	Code	Sqn	Captain
L7497	QR-*	61	F/Sgt E W Noble
L7488	OF-F	97	F/O H S Blakeman
L7475	OF-B	97	F/O Keir
L7489	OF-T	97	F/L E Coton
L7522	OF-V	97	F/L D J Penman
L7309	EM-O	207	S/L K H P Beauchamp
R5796	EM-W	207	F/O J Wooldridge
L7515	EM-S	207	F/Sgt G H Coles
L7432	EM-J	207	F/O D A Green
L7378	EM-A	207	F/Sgt B O Wescombe

No. 97 Squadron's aircraft carried one 4,000 lb and four 500 lb GPs whilst three 207 Squadron aircraft carried 4000 lb 'Cookies' and four 500 lb GPs, the remaining two carrying six 1,000 lb GPs. A quarter of the latter are recorded as being fitted with 'Screamers', presumably devices to produce a piercing whistle on the way down. The Germans had taught this lesson well. Take-off was in the late afternoon between 1644 and 1658.

The town of Wilhelmshaven should have been an easy target to locate in good weather, lying as it does on the shores of the Jade Bay. Flying Officer Green experienced severe visibility problems when the windscreen of L7432 iced up for the entire operation at heights above 8,000ft. His debriefing report specifies that the aircraft approached the primary target, the main railway station, by following the railway tracks from the west into the town. His load of six 1,000 lb bombs were believed to have fallen in the target area. Flight Sergeant Wescombe flew down the Jade Bay coastline to release his bombs from 16,000ft at 1930. He pin-pointed the impact position at one mile north east of the railway station and his crew saw the 4,000 lb 'Cookie' explode. Squadron Leader Beauchamp attacked a clearly distinguished target and both Wooldridge and Coles reported that many fires were burning in the target area stoked up by their own bombs. Three 97 Squadron aircraft bombed the primary, whilst the fourth hit Emden. Flight Sergeant Noble had high oil temperature in the port engine and so bombed a seaplane base at Terschelling instead.

Whilst the remainder of the aircraft turned for home, 'Dim' Wooldridge made a slight diversion to the German barrier island of Norderney. Descending to 600ft so the crew could distinguish individual objects on the ground they first dispatched seven bundles of NICKELS. The flak defences of the Frisians were still engaging incoming bombers and

Wooldridge and crew proceeded to disrupt these as much as possible. The Manchester was being used once more by 207 Squadron in the improbable role of low-level night intruder. Wooldridge guided R5796 around various nests of searchlight and flak emplacements, where the gunners took the opportunity to interfere with the defences. The gunners claimed four searchlights doused and one heavy calibre flak gun put out of action on Norderney.

Inevitably, as Wooldridge circled to pick out his targets, the action was not all one sided and a flak burst spattered the aircraft, damaging the hydraulic system. As the precious hydraulic fluid leaked away the bomb doors began to gape and one main wheel leg flopped down, the intercom had also been put out of action. The flak and searchlight suppression was continued for a while but crew co-ordination, speed and manoeuvrability had been impaired. Reluctantly Wooldridge was forced to abandon the interdiction and retrace his route across the North Sea with bomb doors now completely open and the main wheel still down. Fortunately the emergency undercarriage lowering system operated successfully at 2239 hours.

Whatever the limitations of the Manchester there was certainly no lack of determination in many of its crews. The bombing results from Wilhelmshaven, bore little resemblance to the optimistic claims of returning crews. Although a total of 124 aircraft were dispatched the German defenders recognised this as only a light attack with only six civilians injured.

Operations planned for 12th and 13th January were cancelled, but following a light

L7378 'EM-A', the 'King of Manchesters' in the snow at Boscombe Down on 1st February 1942. It completed more operations than any other Manchester; 25 with 207 and a further eight with 106 Squadron. *via N Franklin*

snowfall were on again on the 14th. Since the year end 207 and 97 Squadrons had been called to operate virtually every night and now 61 Squadron had joined in, such were the stakes being played for at Brest and in the war in general. This time eight 207 Squadron Manchesters were to go to the Blohm und Voss shipyards at Hamburg, together with two from 61 Squadron. Following night flying tests the aircraft were bombed up.

Hamburg – 14th January 1942

Serial	Code	Sqn	Captain
R5785	QR-*	61	S/L P G Sooby
L7458	QR-*	61	F/L A M Paape
L7468	EM-Z	207	F/O J Wooldridge
L7515	EM-S	207	F/O J H Leland
L7309	EM-O	207	P/O G B Dawkins
L7319	EM-X	207	F/Sgt G H Coles
L7455	EM-G	207	F/O P C Birch
L7485	EM-D	207	F/O D A Green
L7523	EM-M	207	F/Sgt B O Wescombe
L7486	EM-B	207	F/Sgt G H Hathersich

At briefing the crews were informed of a new tactic to be employed for the first time. Instead of taking off at irregular intervals and making their own way to the target by whatever route captain and navigator favoured, the aircraft were to take off in a close-spaced procession and fly exactly the same route and speed, joining up with other units to form what came to be known as the bomber stream. The object of reversing the previous tactics was to try and concentrate the attack in space and time and so overwhelm the flak and night fighter defences. The new arrangement would be particularly effective against the German night fighter defences in which only one fighter could be controlled in a box 45km wide and 22km deep at any one time. The condensed take-off sequence went smoothly until the last aircraft in line. Wooldridge 1707, Birch 1708, Dawkins 1709, Hathersich 1710, Coles 1711, Leland 1712, Green 1718, Wescombe 1735.

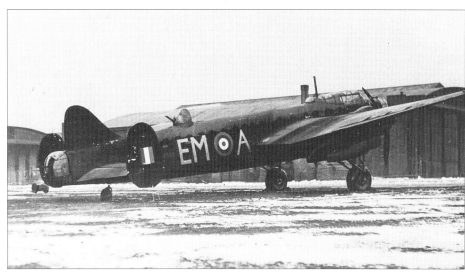

Top: **L7378 'EM-A', carrying its name beneath the cockpit, surrounded by a flock of Westland Lysanders, at Boscombe Down on 1st February 1942.** *via N Franklin*

Above: **S/L Thos Murray accelerating L7378, 'EM-A', for take-off from Boscombe Down on 1st February 1942 en route to Weston-super-Mare for experimental mine trials on behalf of the Torpedo Development Unit.** *via Aerospace Publishing*

The reason for the delayed take-off of Flight Sergeant Basil Wescombe is unknown and indeed nothing further was heard from this aircraft until it mysteriously crashed at 2045 hours in the evening at Cliff House Farm, Holmpton, near Withernsea in Yorkshire, after being airborne for three hours ten minutes, killing the entire crew. After being airborne for such a short period it seems unlikely that enemy action had caused an early return. The elder of three Misses Walker, who with their brother ran Cliff House Farm for more than 50 years, heard a loud popping sound of a throttled back aero engine at low altitude and rushed outside to see L7523 pass low to the south, with flames apparently issuing from the rear. Almost immediately afterwards it hit the ground and exploded. The source of the fire is unknown, but possibly an uncontrollable fire in the port Vulture would have given the same appearance to a ground observer. If attempting to return to Bottesford the aircraft was way off course.

Only a few days earlier on return from an operation to Brest the crew had similarly got off course and blundered into the balloon barrage surrounding Southampton. Only the quick action of the second pilot, Sergeant Thomas, had saved them on that occasion. Sadly on 14th January 1942 they were beyond help. Next morning farm workers found a sorry sight. Soldiers were already guarding the impact point and the tail unit had been thrown over a nearby hedge. Small fragments of airframe were spread over a wide area, the bodies of the crew awaiting collection in a farm building. Apparently the bomb load had already been jettisoned. A freezing rain was falling from a leaden sky and within a short period the farm workers' clothes were frozen stiff. Despite having crashed in Yorkshire, no Aircraft Accident Card summarising results of an investigation has been traced. Flight Lieutenant Paape experienced engine trouble and also had to make an early return, landing back at Woolfox at 1855 hours.

Meanwhile the remaining seven Manchesters held identical courses, a few min-

utes apart, as they traversed the North Sea. The route involved crossing the English coast near Orfordness and flying a 400 mile leg passing between Heligoland and the Frisians to hit the enemy coast in the centre of the mouth of the Elbe estuary. Here they were to turn south east with a view to flying in, parallel to the Elbe, but 20 miles away from the flak defences lining the river. The penalty of being only slightly off track to the south would be to pass directly over the flak defences of Cuxhaven.

It was a bitterly cold night, and with continuous overcast over the North Sea. Unusually for the period, both Flying Officer Leland and Pilot Officer 'Gerry' Dawkins carried only six man crews, lacking a front gunner. Dawkins' regular navigator, Flight Sergeant Nisbet, was sick and Flying Officer P J Edwards was standing in. L7309 toiled slowly upwards on this eastward leg with Dawkins instrument flying in the 'clag'. Shortly after passing between Heligoland and the mainland coast they finally began to clear the top of the cloud layer. Edwards immediately took the opportunity of climbing into the astrodome to try and check the drift so they could adjust their course and ETA to the turning point at the German coast.

Before Edwards had time to take any readings Sergeant Bestel, the Canadian rear gunner, called out a sighting of an aircraft closing from astern. Before he had finished speaking tracer fire started to fly past on the starboard side. The call and tracer fire, coming as it did so quickly after they breasted the cloud layer, galvanised Dawkins into action. Closing the throttle of the port engine he slammed the stick forward and hard left. As he did so the familiar roar and vibration of the four 0.303in Brownings in the rear turret could be heard and felt as Bestel, swinging his turret, loosed off a scaring burst. Dawkins' manoeuvre was not one in the flying regulations, but the pilots had found that it was the only way of jinking a large, slow and overloaded Manchester out of the firing line of a night fighter. The Manchester slewed violently to port, slowed down and dropped like a stone, being swallowed up in the cloud almost immediately. The fighter overshot and as they sank back into the cloud layer Bestel was heard to complain that his return fire had missed the target. Once in the cloud the fighter was unable to relocate them.

The fighter had only been glimpsed for a few seconds and was not identified. It is likely that the night fighter pilot was, in fact, Oberleutnant Rudolf Schoenert of II/NJG2 and that his aircraft had been guided into the bomber stream by ground radar and made a final visual interception. It was Schoenert who, in July 1942, got the blessing of General Kammhuber to test his ideas for fixed obliquely firing armaments in the upper fuselage of a night fighter. Eventually, following his promotion to commanding officer of the

Messerschmitt Me110 equipped II/NJG5, Schoenert had such armament fitted to one of the unit's aircraft and in May 1943 made the Luftwaffe's first kill with what became the widely used 'Schrage Musik' installation. Schoenert went on to make 64 confirmed kills and survived the war.

Gerry Dawkins opened the throttle on the port engine and an immediate check on the cockpit instruments showed all apparently normal. Both engines were running at climbing revs, but it soon became clear that all was far from well with the starboard engine, which was producing no power. The drag from the starboard propeller, still at climbing pitch, was causing the aircraft to slew to the right and the altimeter showed they were sinking instead of maintaining altitude.

Recognising their dilemma, Dawkins ordered the bomb load to be jettisoned and meanwhile reached across to feather the starboard propeller. They felt a reassuring lurch as the bombs fell away, but the propeller steadfastly refused to feather. It became clear that the brief burst of fire from the night fighter had damaged the controls to the starboard engine, which was out of action and with the propeller now windmilling and jammed in fine pitch.

Dawkins turned onto a course of 270° and tried to trim the aircraft to fly home. By experimenting with the engine settings of the port Vulture he found that at maximum power the airspeed hovered close to 165mph, but the aircraft lost height at between 100 and 200 feet per minute. By slowing down to 145mph he found they could maintain height but the starboard wing dropped and they slowly swung to starboard due to the drag of the starboard propeller. It seemed to be a no-win situation. Meanwhile the crew began ditching every heavy item readily detachable from the airframe. In desperation they tried to train the twin Brownings of the mid-upper turret onto the starboard propeller blades and shoot them off. However, the guns could not depress far enough and they were unable to disconnect the externally mounted deflector installed to prevent that very thing happening by accident.

By this time they had descended to 8,000ft and the prospects of getting home on one engine, even if it kept going, with the drag of the starboard propeller disc, were zero. Edwards calculated that they had rather less than one hour of flying time before reaching ground level and Dawkins judged that even if they all survived a ditching they would be unlikely to last more than 20 minutes in an open dinghy in the North Sea. The facts left no room for doubt and having thus exhausted all the options Dawkins reluctantly altered course again, turning due south to hit the nearest point on the German coast. They could but hope that the port Vulture, running at full throttle, would prove equal to the task.

Dawkins then directed the wireless operator, Sergeant Mercer, to break radio silence and relay a message to base informing them of his decision. Mercer tried several times to establish contact but was completely unsuccessful, so they pressed the radio destruct knobs and destroyed the set. Edwards, meanwhile, threw overboard all code books and navigation documents.

They continued south for some 40 minutes and mercifully the remaining motor kept turning. At this point, when they had descended to about 4,000ft and were still enveloped in the blanket of cloud, they were relieved to find themselves on the receiving end of inaccurate light flak. This gave them the satisfaction of knowing they must be traversing the Frisian Islands. As they did so the cloud cover finally started to become more broken and a few minutes later, as they inexorably descended, they reached 3,500ft and came out of cloud just as they crossed the shore of mainland Germany. Dawkins had flown for 45 minutes with the control column held hard over to the left to lift the starboard wing and there was clearly no chance of making a forced landing in these conditions, they could merely fly straight ahead and would be unable to avoid any obstacle on the ground which appeared in their path.

That being so they had prepared to bale out as quickly as possible after crossing the coast. Bestel left his turret and tried to open the rear entry door in anticipation of baling out, but found it to be frozen solid. Sergeant Cadman then moved forward from the mid-upper turret to jettison the forward escape hatch. Clearly they would all have to get out the same way. As he did so for some inexplicable reason his parachute fell through the open hatch and was lost. More precious time was lost in debating how this problem could be overcome and eventually Sergeant Allen, the second pilot, offered to attempt a double descent with Cadman. Sergeant Mercer helped them to get away first with Cadman piggy-backing on Allen. Mercer and Flying Officer Edwards then followed in quick succession. Dawkins still had no hands free and Bestel buckled his parachute on for him before following the crew through the hatch.

Gerry Dawkins was left alone, he only had a single chance to escape because as soon as he released the control column the aircraft would roll onto its back and go out of control. Time was now of the essence. The aircraft was correctly trimmed fore and aft but the stick still had to be held hard left to keep the wings level. Dawkins grabbed the second pilot's stick and held it as he moved first into the right hand seat. Next, having loosed all his intercom leads and straps, he positioned himself to dive through the beckoning hatch. He released the stick and dived straight through, fortunately without getting himself entangled in the process.

As soon as he was clear of the aircraft he pulled the D-ring and breathed a sigh of relief at the jerk of the parachute as it arrested his descent. He was only suspended for a short period but time enough to feel the piercing, numbing cold. The cockpit of the Manchester was very warm and comfortable and he was only wearing his flying jacket and boots on top of normal battle dress in the aircraft. He landed awkwardly, straining himself with the unexpected direction of the deceleration. Close by, the aircraft crashed and exploded.

An unlucky Mk.IA, L7523 'EM-M' of 207 Squadron. Equipment failures occurred on two of the first three 'ops', resulting in early returns. On the fourth, 14th January 1942, it crashed at the clifftop village of Holmpton, Yorkshire, with Flight Sergeant Wescombe in command. *No. 207 Squadron archives / R Glynne-Owen*

Anonymous Manchester of 61 Squadron drawn up on the apron at Woolfox Lodge.
N F Turner

Dawkins found he could stand and his first action was to collect his parachute and walk across to the blazing wreck and throw the mass of silk into the flames. Turning away he began to formulate an evasion plan, but the extreme cold and pain from his fall quickly overtook such issues and with the last of his remaining stamina he approached an isolated farm and gave himself up.

Sergeant Cadman was not so lucky; during the descent he slipped off Allen's back and fell to his death. The remainder of the crew landed safely and having been tracked across the coast by the German radar were soon captured. They had come down at Sandel Moens near Jever, close to Wilhelmshaven in Germany at about 2100 in the evening, the last Manchester to be lost by 207 in the course of air operations. Ironically, but fittingly, it was the result of the loss of an engine and the inability of the remaining Vulture to keep them airborne.

Peter Birch had encountered the same 10/10th cloud with heavy icing conditions over the sea. Having breasted the cloud layer he took to skirting the higher cumulus to cut down ice accretion on the airframe. Darkness and haze led to difficulties in target identification but several crews located and followed the Elbe River. Hamburg was picked out by large searchlight concentrations. 'Dim' Wooldridge reported heavy searchlight concentrations co-operating with night fighters and his rear gunner spotted several, although no attacks materialised. Over the town itself the searchlight and flak batteries were working closely together and the crews received a rousing reception. These prevented Bill Goldstraw, observer to Pilot Officer Dave Green, from observing the fall of bombs.

Wooldridge carried out his customary fast diving attack. Having circled to the east of Hamburg at 12,000ft he dived across the city on a westerly heading planning to release the bomb load at about 8,000ft. Shortly after commencing the bombing run the aircraft was coned and held by searchlights, which

blinded the crew to the extent that the bombs were released prematurely and undershot the designated aiming point. Within a few seconds of bomb release the aircraft was hit by shrapnel from a heavy flak shell bursting nearby, which slightly wounded the front gunner. Soon the speed of the descending aircraft took it clear of the barrage to escape into the enveloping protective darkness and a third loss from the small force was narrowly avoided.

Flight Lieutenant Sooby also found the German flak defences thoroughly roused. He tried approaches from the north, east and south before finally releasing his incendiaries from 13,000ft on an easterly heading and then turning away northwards to escape the clinging searchlights and insistent flak. Good fires were starting from the combined high explosive and incendiary bombs as the aircraft left the target.

As Pilot Officer Green departed from the target area a loud explosion was heard and felt immediately aft of the bulkhead doors, followed by a prolonged hissing. When the startled crew investigated it was found that an oxygen connection had parted due to metal fatigue. The aircraft was undamaged and the only inconvenience arising was that Dave Green had to land at Coningsby without the assistance of brakes. On inspection next morning the bomb doors of Birch's and Green's aircraft were both found to be damaged by flak. The German's own report detailed 12 fires, seven of them large with six civilians killed and 22 injured in Hamburg.

No major raids were planned by Bomber Command during the following week but 97 and 61 Squadrons attacked Hamburg again on 15/16th and then Bremen on 17/18th. The latter date was the last night on which 97 Squadron operated Manchesters. The squadron was already working up on Lancasters and became the first RAF unit to relinquish the aircraft.

Reports of the 25 Operational Training Unit (OTU) Bombing Section fact-finding tour of the Manchester squadrons in late January 1942 provide a fascinating insight into Bomber Command methods. The OTU were trying to ensure that their teaching was as up to date as possible. The disparate findings of the survey were surprising. No uniformity in

bombing tactics was demanded, either by Command or 5 Group. Each squadron formulated its own method, or a variation on methods taught at the OTU. Nos. 97, 83 and 207 Squadrons adopted a jinking level approach with the fixed bomb sight, generally in the height range 12,000 to 18,000ft. Glide bombing, with few exceptions, was not used as the jinking level run up was considered safer and sufficiently accurate. Crews appreciated the need to maintain height in the Manchester, perhaps on account of engine reliability.

In complete contrast, 61 Squadron invariably adopted glide bombing with the tachometric sight, as taught at 25 OTU. For this tactic the glide was commenced at heights between 14,000 and 16,000ft and the bombs released at heights between 7,000 and 9,000ft. After commencing the glide a turn of at least 45° to port was invariably made onto the bomb run. Gliding Manchesters that were picked up by searchlights abandoned the glide, as ground speed increased bombs were released in the target area permitting the attacking aircraft to escape.

Ultra-low level bombing was not liked and seldom done, although reports of very low level attacks were gathered from a number of bomb aimers. When a mixed load of a 4,000lb high capacity (HC) and 250lb GP or SAP bombs were carried the normal practice was to aim the HC and allow the GPs or SAPs to follow 'as they will', of course resulting in an overshoot. Bomber Command tactics still had a great way to go before the rigid control in height, time and approach direction essential when aircraft began attacking as a tightly bunched stream.

January 1942 was to end with a return to Brest and three raids spaced four days apart, largely made possible by an improvement in the weather. On 25/26th 207 Squadron contributed seven and 61 Squadron eight Manchesters to the 61-strong aircraft attack. On this night the squadrons were to find only partial cloud cover and apparently enhanced prospects for successful precision bomb aiming. However, their arrival must have been anticipated well in advance because the Germans had plenty of time to activate the smoke screen. Smoke spread in the wind and blanketed the target at ground level. Flying Officer McNaughton had already returned early in R5785 when the dinghy released itself on take-off and Sergeant Underwood returned soon afterwards with low oil pressure, but the remaining 13 Manchesters were able to attack. All had to aim at the general dock area as an alternative when smoke obscured the ships. Several aircraft were engaged by intense and accurate flak defences, which were especially effective around Brest. Crews believed naval flak gunners had been drafted in from Kiel to bolster the defences. All of the Manchesters involved returned safely.

On 28/29th January 1942, 83 Squadron at Scampton made its operational debut in the Manchester when four crews, including the commanding officer Wing Commander Tudor in Squadron Leader Rainford's aircraft, were briefed for Boulogne. No. 61 Squadron provided four Manchesters, two for Boulogne and the remaining two for Brest. No. 207 Squadron provided a single Manchester to strike Boulogne.

Boulogne, 83 Squadron's Debut, also Brest† – 28th/29th January 1942

Serial	Code	Sqn	Captain
L7521	QR-*	61†	P/O J R Hubbard
L7396	QR-*	61†	F/O I G A McNaughton
L7396	QR-*	61	P/O L Gunter
L7470	QR-*	61	F/Sgt J B Underwood
L7427	OL-*	83	S/L J R Rainford
L7453	OL-*	83	P/O J H Morpett
L7465	OL-*	83	P/O R G W Oakley
L7423	OL-*	83	W/O H H Whitehead
R5791	EM-V	207	W/O C Wathey

Manchester IA L7516 'QR-F' of 61 Squadron at Woolfox Lodge provides a backdrop for its crew. Left to right: Flight Sergeant G E Williams RCAF (captain); second pilot; first wireless operator/air gunner, observer, wireless operator, front gunner, spare gunner, second wireless operator/air gunner. Flight Sergeant Williams was later the sole survivor from a squadron Lancaster. *G E Williams*

All seven Manchesters returned safely having attacked Boulogne, but Warrant Officer Whitehead's introduction was eventful. His autopilot, directional gyro and hydraulics went unserviceable and the undercarriage had to be lowered by the pneumatic emergency system. Both Hubbard and McNaughton made low level diving attacks from 9,000ft and 7,500ft respectively. Warrant Officer Wathey also attacked, he and McNaughton experiencing fierce opposition from flak.

After false starts on the two previous nights, the last day of the month, 31st January/1st February 1942, shaped up to be the biggest Manchester effort since June 1941 and the largest force of Manchesters ever sent out, 19 in all. Spurred on by persistent intelligence warning of the breakout of the battlecruisers from Brest, Bomber Command put together a major operation. After 300 separate RAF raids on the two capital ships in Brest, and with imminent ULTRA warning of their break out from the port, Bomber Command was making a maximum effort and trying every option to cripple the vessels.

No. 61 Squadron contributed nine Manchesters, 83 Squadron six and 207 a total of four. Bomber Command split its effort and its Manchester force between Brest, where 72 aircraft in all were dispatched, and a smaller diversionary raid on St Nazaire. All the 61 Squadron aircraft and two from 207 Squadron were briefed for Brest. The six 83 Squadron aircraft and one from 207 went to St Nazaire, whilst Flying Officer Pattinson of 207 carried out a NICKEL raid on Rennes, acting both as a diversion and training flight.

Manchester Maximum Effort – 31st January / 1st February 1942

Serial	Code	Sqn	Captain
L7396	QR-*	61	F/L H C S Page
L7470	QR-*	61	P/O L Gunter
L7458	QR-*	61	F/O R E Archibald
L7516	QR-*	61	F/Sgt E W Noble
L7492	QR-*	61	P/O A L Searby
R5787	QR-*	61	F/O J R B Parsons
L7521	QR-*	61	F/O I G A McNaughton
L7477	QR-*	61	P/O R E S Smith
L7472	QR-*	61	F/O R D Fraser
R5831	OL-*	83	S/L O Altmann
R5790	OL-*	83	F/L K Cook
R5779	OL-*	83	F/Sgt P A Mackenzie
L7427	OL-*	83	P/O R G W Oakley
L7423	OL-*	83	F/L D A McClure
L7453	OL-*	83	F/O M A Smith
R5796	EM-W	207	P/O M E Doble
R5791	EM-V	207	F/Sgt G H Hathersich
L7491	EM-C	207	W/O C Wathey
L7515	EM-S	207	F/O S E Pattinson

Targets: 83 Squadron and two 207 Squadron to St Nazaire. No. 207 L7515 NICKEL to Rennes. All others to Brest.

At briefing at Woolfox Lodge it was clear that the operation was to be out of the ordinary and that the Royal Navy had 'Got the wind up'. First of all a Naval Sub-Lieutenant was in attendance to give the crews a pep talk. He told them of official concern that the *Scharnhorst*, *Gneisenau* and *Prinz Eugen* were about to break out of Brest, when they might cause untold havoc with the Atlantic convoys.

A 61 Squadron crew pose in front of one of their Manchesters. Left to right: Sergeant Furby (second pilot); Sergeant Boot (wireless operator); Sergeant Smart (observer); Sergeant Tomlinson (second wireless operator/air gunner); Sergeant Crawford (rear gunner); Flying Officer Gunter (captain).

Flight Lieutenant Fraser of 61 Squadron running up L7472 at Woolfox Lodge on 31st January 1942, prior to 'ops' to Brest from which the aircraft failed to return.
Both L Boot

Following the briefing the bomb designer spent some time chatting to Fraser and Hannigan, ironing out last minute details and then accompanied the eight man crew out to their aircraft. Amongst the superstitious crew this intrusion was greeted with the utmost foreboding. Events were to prove their premonitions well founded.

At Scampton and Bottesford the 83 Squadron and 207 Squadron briefings were more routine. The six 83 Squadron and one 207 Squadron Manchesters took off first, starting at 1732 to permit them to travel the extra distance to St Nazaire. This force carried 500 lb or 1,000 lb GP bomb loads.

Right from the start the carefully planned operation began to go awry for Fraser. Whilst the bulk of the force lifted off close to 1800, L7472, despite being on song during its night flying test earlier in the day, developed engine trouble, which delayed the take-off until 1845. They would have to attack without the cover of their colleagues.

On the outward flight R5791 of 207 Squadron was labouring heavily, unable to climb. At 2025, two hours and 20 minutes after take-off, whilst off the French coast near Plouescat, the aircraft had staggered to a mere 8,000ft. Flight Sergeant Hathersich dropped a 2,000 lb AP bomb 'safe' into the sea to permit a climb to a more respectable height. Events proved this to be a wise precaution for as the two squadron Manchesters in the attack force approached Brest they found the town laid out before them like a map, with unlimited visibility. Sergeant Clitheroe in Pilot Officer Doble's aircraft, R5796, released three 2,000 lb AP bombs from 16,500ft but as R5791 started its bomb run, still some thousands of feet below, it was singled out and heavily engaged by the flak defences. A good run up was made and the remaining two 2,000 lb APs released in the target area. Immediately following bomb release the aircraft shuddered from a near miss from a heavy calibre flak shell. The aircraft was extensively damaged taking hits in the centre fin, the bomb doors, throttle box and front turret. None of the crew was injured but the bomb aimer was temporarily blinded by the spray of oil shooting from the hydraulic lines to the turret. As a result the fall of bombs was not observed.

Furthermore the Admiralty did not rule out the possibility that they might be heading for the Mediterranean. Should that happen, he said with emphasis, it might tip the balance and 'we could lose the Mediterranean to the enemy'. The importance of crippling the ships could not be over-emphasised.

In another unusual, but by no means unique departure from normal, an extra crew member, Squadron Leader Burrough from Headquarters 5 Group, was to accompany Flight Lieutenant Page as an observer; for what purpose has not been established because sadly for Burrough and the entire crew it was to be a one way trip. Regrettably, the 61 Squadron Operational Record Book (ORB) records nothing concerning the bomb loads of the aircraft involved. It is likely that most carried three 2,000 lb AP bombs in the hope of hitting the battle cruisers and certainly this was the load carried by the two 207 Squadron Manchesters in the Brest force.

For one 61 Squadron Manchester crew the operation was to prove quite unique, in more ways than one. Pilot Officer Fraser and crew

had been selected to introduce a new anti-shipping weapon to RAF service. Fraser and his crew had a separate briefing after the main event in which the 'boffin' who had designed the new bomb explained its operation and how it should be dropped for maximum effect. The bomb is recalled by the surviving crew as a 4,000 lb armour piercing weapon with a double charge designed to first blast a hole in the armoured deck of a battlecruiser before exploding below. The only weapon which bears any resemblance to this description is the 5,000 lb CS or 'Capital Ship' bomb, of which little seems to be known.

The raid was planned to start at 2000 hours with a large proportion of the force set to cross the target close to 2032, creating a diversion under which Fraser would attack with the special weapon from 2,000ft below the remainder of the attackers. For this special operation Fraser carried, in addition to his normal crew, the squadron bombing leader, Flight Lieutenant Hannigan, whose job it was to aim and release the weapon.

Both Flying Officer McNaughton and Pilot Officer Smith carried out glide bombing attacks on Brest harbour from a low 7,000ft. Both were held for long periods in the intense searchlight concentrations illuminating the clear sky and subjected to heavy and intense ground opposition, fortunately without damage to either aircraft.

Pilot Officer Searby was not so fortunate. He also skirted the French coast and eventually attacked from the south east, gliding down from 12,000ft to 6,000ft before releasing his armour piercing bombs on dry docks Nos. 8 and 9. No results could be observed because in the later stages of its bomb run the aircraft was enmeshed in a blinding searchlight battery and ravaged by the ruthlessly efficient flak defences. Their aircraft experienced several near misses, being holed in mid-fuselage and rear turret. The IFF, hydraulics and pneumatic systems to operate the flaps, undercarriage and brakes were all put out of action.

Also en route to Brest that night from 61 Squadron were Flying Officer Archibald RCAF and his crew, including Sergeant Holmes as his second pilot. Peter Holmes was engaged on his first operation after leaving the crew of the 'A' Flight Commander, Squadron Leader Peter West. For this 'baptism' West had loaned Archibald and Holmes his personal Manchester, L7458 'QR-A', a special aircraft of exceptionally fine flying characteristics. West cherished and guarded the aircraft, to the extent of keeping a careful check of the serial numbers of its two Vulture engines to ensure these were not swopped during maintenance.

Archibald had carried out a long and patient climb en route to the target, eventually reaching 15,000ft, a height with which he felt well satisfied. The only problem experienced on the way out occurred when they inadvertently overflew Guernsey and Jersey and drew some ineffective flak from the alert defences. As they approached the French coast visibility was good. They had been briefed to expect that the *Gneisenau*, sown into the quay wall by camouflage nets, would be difficult to locate, but that the *Scharnhorst* was towed out every night onto a mooring and would be easier to spot.

Archibald was to fly the aircraft during the actual attack and when they reached the target area three circuits of the harbour were made whilst all members searched vainly for the *Scharnhorst*. Fortunately they were not caught by the probing searchlights, although these contributed in no small part to their difficulty in locating their targets. Eventually, they decided to make a bombing run from the west across the length of Brest harbour hoping to spot a target at the last minute. Archibald had become very animated in the last few tense minutes prior to bomb release, even though they had, by chance, still not been illuminated.

On feeling the lift in the aircraft following release of the bombs he ordered bomb doors closed and pulled the nose up sharply and to the left intending a climbing turn onto a nor-north east homeward course. Unfortunately, in his excitement he pulled up too sharply, causing the Manchester to stall and wing over to the left. Soon they were plunging back down in a near vertical dive heading west, with Archibald fighting to regain control and Holmes, his seat folded to permit the observer access to the nose, standing beside him hanging on for grim death as the aircraft went down like a lift. Balloon cables were foremost in their minds as they shot out westwards between the harbour walls at an altitude of a few hundred feet. It had been a nerve chilling 30 seconds, but once clear of the harbour they calmed down and made an uneventful return to Woolfox Lodge.

Sergeant Louis 'Gus' Gunter was captain of L7470 that night. He had managed to drag the aircraft up to 15–16,000ft and headed into the maelstrom over Brest from nor-north east. During the run up to the target they were quickly coned by the searchlights and flak shells began to burst close by. Boxed in by the intense and accurate barrage it seemed that it could only be a matter of seconds before they were hit. In any case the glare of the lights made target location quite impossible. Gunter began throwing L7470 around the sky in an attempt to shake off the lights and guns, but to no avail. In a desperate ploy to evade the remorseless defences Gunter ordered the bombs jettisoned and then dived away, turning to starboard, chancing that they would miss the balloon cables and pulling out at 500ft, by which time the lights were searching for another victim. Once the sheltering cover of darkness was regained they took stock, finding L7470 miraculously unscathed and with all instruments reading normally. Gunter immediately turned for home and began to climb back to regain a safe height for the sea crossing. As they skirted the French coast they suddenly remembered that leaflets remained on board and nipped back over land whilst these were dispatched. They returned safely to Woolfox Lodge.

Flying Officer Parsons and crew in R5787 'QR-M' experienced loss of power in one engine soon after take-off which restricted the height they could attain to only 9,000ft. Parsons nevertheless elected to continue with the dangerous mission. The crew found the night so bright and clear that navigation was simple. Following a southerly course they found the Brest peninsula stark and clear beneath a light dusting of snow. The whole countryside was laid out like a map below. As they lined up for their final approach they were immediately coned by searchlights and heavily engaged by the flak defences. Convinced that they would not survive such murderous flak at such low

level, Parsons turned away westwards and headed out over the Atlantic west of Brest. Here, in consultation with the observer, Sergeant Holmes, they agreed to circle round to the south east of Brest and make a second run in from that direction.

On their second approach from 8,000ft the defences on the south eastern approaches to Brest were just as vigilant and, before the target came into view, they were again coned and engaged by the flak batteries. After a particularly close burst had jarred the aircraft Sergeant Wright looked out from his position in the mid-upper turret and saw that oil was escaping from the starboard engine and streaming back to smother the fin and tailplane. Wright reported this and Parsons feathered the starboard propeller and shut down the engine, meanwhile continuing spirited evasive manoeuvres. Still they were coned and unable to identify any target owing to the glare. Again Parsons turned away from the city to take stock, this time to the west and then north west. By now all hope of attack had evaporated and their main preoccupation was their own survival. Parsons instructed the observer to jettison the bombs to reduce their rapid descent rate. Despite his efforts, Holmes could not achieve this at first, possibly due to flak damage to his bomb aiming panel, but suddenly they felt the bucking of the load dropping away. It was too late to save 'M-Mother'.

Parsons ordered the crew to prepare to bale out because the aircraft was still losing height rapidly on the remaining port engine. The lights finally left them as they headed out north westwards away from the city. By the time the hatches were released and all crew members ready to abandon the aircraft they were down to 600ft and already too low for a safe escape. Parsons altered his orders and instead sent the crew to their crash positions. The Brittany landscape they descended into was one of low relief but with many small fields, surrounded by earth embankments topped by hedgerows. They hit the ground in a series of bone jarring crashes in which the front fuselage of the aircraft concertina-ed and the remainder tore itself apart.

The entire front section of the aircraft was telescoped and on fire, Flying Officer Parsons, Sergeants Holmes, McCaskill and Butterworth already dead. Sergeant Kindred, the second pilot, had been thrown from the wreck with multiple injuries including a badly mangled leg, but was alive. In the rear of the fuselage Wright was badly bruised but still functioning, whilst the rear gunner, Sergeant Griffiths, was lying nearby with a broken leg. After burning his hand badly trying to release the jammed top escape hatch, Wright transferred his attention to the main crew door, which swung inwards easily. A series of loud explosions from the mid-section of the aircraft startled them, but Griffiths recognised them as the oxygen bottles.

Wright was then able to half carry and half drag Griffiths from the blazing wreckage, reaching some 50 yards from the aircraft before both collapsed, exhausted.

They were both aware that the blazing wreck and exploding oxygen bottles and ammunition would soon bring the searching Germans and suddenly the sound of a dog barking nearby was clearly audible. Cutting short the farewells and making Griffiths as comfortable as possible, Wright hurried to the blazing wreck, flinging his 'Mae West', parachute etc. deep into the flames. Then he made off across the fields still unaware of his other crew colleague, Kindred, lying nearby. Wright himself became one of the Manchester evaders, whilst both Kindred and Griffiths were picked up by the Germans and survived the war.

Flight Lieutenant Fraser and crew in L7472 encountered a moonlit sky, with 50% broken cumulus, very suited to locating small targets on the water. Very soon after take-off the troublesome starboard Vulture began overheating and with the prospect of further delay some consideration was given to aborting the operation. Fortified by the exhortations of the naval sub-lieutenant they agreed to proceed and by nursing the starboard engine they steadily hauled the aircraft to 10,000ft at which height it stubbornly refused to climb higher. Traversing the murderous flak defences of Brest in clear weather at less than 10,000ft was a suicidal risk, but one which the crew resolutely accepted.

L7472 made landfall on the Brittany coast at Plouguerneau and headed due south across the narrow peninsula towards Brest. As they steered a steady course onwards, Sergeant Bill Shorrock, the observer in L7472, got the feeling he would be happier if Fraser 'threw her about a bit' and as if to reinforce the feeling a battery of six to eight flak guns out in the countryside loosed off a single salvo in their direction. At his seat directly over the bomb Shorrock flinched as a burst close beneath opened up several small holes in the fuselage to his right. Another shell had burst directly ahead and the smell of cordite filled the cockpit area. There was no indication of any damage to the vital systems of the aircraft.

As Shorrock conned them south towards their target the time came for Flight Lieutenant Hannigan to descend to the bomb aiming position in the nose. All was peaceful in the aircraft for several minutes, until, as the bight of Brest Harbour came into view and Fraser throttled back for the gliding attack, the lights and heavy flak guns began to seek them out. It was a novelty for Shorrock to be a passenger at this vital stage of the operation, but with Hannigan at the bomb sight he took up a standing position behind the pilot to watch the proceedings.

Suddenly the lights flashed across them and locked on. It was bright enough in the cockpit for the crew to have read a newspaper. Next, all hell broke loose as L7472 struck a balloon cable inboard of the starboard engine, which caused a violent yaw to the right. Fraser, briefly unsighted, wrenched the stick over to counteract the yaw, but at the same moment they heard and felt the detonation of the cable cutter and were freed from its drag. Fraser resumed his course, although his visibility outside was restricted by the glare of the searchlights. All the flak guns in Brest Harbour seemed to have concentrated their attention on L7472, but so far there were no more hits. Hannigan called that he could not identify the ships owing to the glare, which was mainly coming from batteries of lights to their right. Over to the left Shorrock could clearly see the inner harbour and the two capital ships. He called 'I see them hard-a-port' and Fraser banked round sharply eastward towards the target. Shortly afterwards Hannigan, having identified the ships, requested slight heading adjustments before calling. 'Bomb away!'.

All the while flak had continued to explode, but now as Fraser pushed both throttles wide open to climb away eastward and began to take evasive action the starboard engine immediately burst into flames and cut out. Fraser was frantically pushing the buttons of the fire extinguisher and propeller feathering mechanism. Neither the extinguishers nor feathering mechanism appeared to be operating and their short and long term situation looked desperate. To add to the problems, another balloon cable caught L7472 in exactly the same position as the first and again slewed the aircraft violently to the right. This time it was more serious because the cable cutters were a one-time device. Their forward motion caused the cable to shear simultaneously at the ground below and the balloon above. The drag of the heavy steel cable compounded that of the windmilling propeller on the dead starboard engine and the aircraft began to shake and vibrate like a cart crossing cobblestones as it steered once more on a southerly heading. By this time they had crossed out over the water of Brest Harbour and were heading for the Plougastel peninsula.

Now the flak finally left them alone, but their situation remained perilous. To counter the drag of the windmilling propeller and cable on the right side, Fraser was flying with full port rudder, his left knee against his chest. The control column was also hard over to keep the starboard wing from dropping. Very little aileron control remained. A ribbon of flame still stretched out past the tail from the starboard engine and they were losing height quickly. Despite the desperate odds there was still plenty of fight left in Fraser, who called for a course for home. Shorrock switched on his intercom and replied, 'Coming up in a minute'.

In their remorseless and rapid descent they had crossed the wide southern expanse of Brest Harbour and reached the low lying Crozon peninsula. As they did so the trailing balloon cable finally shook itself loose and fell away, but did little to ease their descent rate. At the sight of land the second pilot, Sergeant Marshall, decided to take his chance and quickly descended to the nose and baled out by the bottom hatch. By this time they were down to 300ft and to the right the land rose higher than their flying height. They crossed the Crozon peninsula at its narrowest point and at this moment the south shore of the bay at Morgat appeared directly ahead. A row of houses along the sea front barred their way they were so low, but Fraser raised the nose just sufficiently to halt their descent momentarily and they floated over the chimney pots a few feet below. A few seconds later the port engine failed and Fraser carried out an immediate copy book dead stick landing on the water of the bay.

Jettisoning the top hatch, Shorrock observed with relief that the dinghy had already released. He jumped out to attend to it but was called back by Fraser. Sergeant McLean, the new gunner on his first trip, had remained in the nose throughout the entire incident but now, as he struggled to climb up into the cockpit, his parachute harness snagged on some projection, trapping him in the rising water. Fraser and Shorrock heaved with all their strength but could not tear him free. They implored him to go back and release himself but the youngster was too frightened to duck back under the water and disentangle himself. Quickly the water rose up over him and they had to vacate the cockpit and join the remainder of the crew in the dinghy.

Still the fast moving series of events was not over. It was about 2130 hours when they bellied in and a steady 15-20 knot wind was blowing down from the north. Knowing their heading and the general lie of the land they were concerned that if they cut the 50 fathom line tethering them to the aircraft they would be blown out into the Bay of Biscay and rapidly die of exposure. With this in mind, as L7472 sank under them, they paid out the painter until the aircraft settled onto the seabed below and remained moored to it.

They spent a cold night in the dinghy, but at daybreak they discerned that they were more or less landlocked and moreover the wind had steadily backed to the west. They cut the painter and were driven eastward by the wind parallel to the shore. The crew came ashore at a low rocky peninsula about 50ft high and all six survivors were able to climb the cliffs into the hands of the waiting Luftwaffe.

No. 61 Squadron was not finished with its adventures for the night even now. In L7516, Flight Sergeant Eric Noble and co-pilot Sergeant Don Macsporran had circled around the Brest peninsula before attacking the harbour from the south in a glide attack down to 7,000ft. Immediately the course was reversed and the dive continued down to 3,000ft. As the engines were opened up they were suddenly engaged by the ferocious flak defences, but fortunately escaped damage.

As they tracked back over England, they were startled by a loud bang and on checking the instruments found that the pneumatic pressure was zero. A sealing gland had cracked and flown apart on the compressed air bottle and they would now have no brakes for landing. Considering the implications, Noble decided to land at the parent station, North Luffenham, with its longer runway, rather than at Woolfox Lodge. Making a careful approach at the slowest safe airspeed, Noble put L7516 down as near the runway threshold as possible and immediately cut the ignition, leaving the windmilling propellers to create as much air resistance and slow them down as much as possible. Steering was only possible early in the landing run when the airflow over the rudders remained sufficient for them to turn the aircraft. The quietness within the aircraft was a strange sensation with only the rumbling of the undercarriage to be heard. Noble sat poised to whip up the undercarriage and drop L7516 onto its belly if an obstruction appeared ahead. Just as they were rolling to a halt they ran through a Hampden dispersal near the perimeter, the Manchester's port wing passing directly over the parked aircraft. As they finally stopped an 'erk' jumped into the aircraft and told them they had just scared the hell out of him as he had been ·inside the Hampden, trying to start it at the very moment the Manchester loomed silently out of the darkness.

The final sequel occurred next day when Eric Noble was called into the CO's office to explain why he had brought his bombs back. In the excitement the back up jettison action had not been carried out and no-one had noticed that the bombs had hung-up!

Fortunately for Pilot Officer Searby in the damaged L7492, neither of the vulnerable Vulture engines was damaged and they limped slowly back, also electing to land at North Luffenham owing to the absence of flaps and brakes. A fast but safe landing was executed, although on shutting down they found themselves to be at Wittering instead! L7492 had been holed in 58 places.

Most poignant of all was the fate of Flight Lieutenant Page and his crew in L7396. This aircraft had taken off late at 1850, possibly due to a malfunction, but the captain bravely pressed on to the target. By the time he arrived the flak gunners would have few victims to divide their attention and it seems the belated Manchester must have been damaged during its attack. Page pressed on, determined to reach the British coast, but L7396 was failing and losing height all the while. Soon his wireless operator, Sergeant Turner, was sending out SOS messages indicating the imminence of alighting in the sea. Shore stations fixed the last position of the aircraft 50 miles south of Plymouth and two destroyers were detached from a nearby Channel convoy in an attempt to locate the crew. Both vessels searched all night, but abandoned the task the following morning when neither signs of the crew nor wreckage had been seen. The entire crew, including their passenger from 5 Group, were drowned. The final sad chapter came when the body of Flight Lieutenant Page was washed ashore on the Scilly Islands.

From the eleven Manchesters sent to Brest, all had received a savage reception and found the greatest difficulty penetrating the heavily defended port area. Most had hairy experiences and were lucky to escape. Two returned seriously damaged by flak and three failed to return. Several had experienced losses of engine power, making the initial approach to the target hazardous and

all the 61 Squadron aircraft attacked from very low level, mindful of the importance of the attack explained at the briefing. No results were available of the effects of the special weapon, but it seems this night Brest's defences had very much the upper hand.

The St Nazaire Manchester force were completely thwarted by 10/10th cloud, which began at the coastline. Pilot Officer Oakley had experienced a hydraulic failure on the outward trip and was also seriously concerned at the high fuel consumption in L7427. When the port was completely socked-in, at the time over target he wisely jettisoned his bombs and returned. Two aircraft brought their bombs back, whilst two others attacked last resort targets. Flying Officer Smith had only released three bombs but on the return trip his port tank was down to 100 gallons and he jettisoned the remaining five 500 pounders to enable him to reach base. Only Flight Sergeant Mackenzie of 83 and Warrant Officer Wathey of 207 thought they had bombed the primary target.

Wathey attacked St Nazaire successfully in L7491, although cloud cover prevented the bursts being recorded accurately. During the operation the general services generator in the starboard engine failed, whilst potentially terminal for the crew if it had happened earlier, the starboard Vulture cut on landing at Colerne in Wiltshire. Flight Sergeant Hathersich brought the damaged R5791 back safely, diverting to Coningsby.

Manchesters returning from the ill-timed Mannheim raid on 11/12th February 1942 were scattered to the four winds. Flight Sergeant Hathersich brought L7486 'EM-B' down at West Malling, Kent. It is pictured being refuelled prior to return to base.
No. 207 Squadron archives / R Glynne-Owen

Such humour as was to be had in 1941-1942 was often of the black variety. Following the loss of one of 61 Squadron's Manchesters, the 'A' Flight Commander, Squadron Leader Peter West, received a distraught telephone call from a wife whose husband had failed to return from an operation. Before the good lady could be placated she announced her intention of travelling up to Woolfox to obtain such first hand information as was available and hung up. The effect on crew morale of a distressed wife was only too apparent and West immediately dispatched his trusted second pilot, Sergeant Peter Holmes, in an attempt to intercept the wife at one of the train changes en route. Holmes was to try and soothe and offer what little consolation and optimistic prospects could be summoned up in the circumstances. En route, the onerous task ahead weighed heavily on the teenage Holmes who had never been faced with a very probably bereaved wife before. Much practising of appropriate sentiments was rehearsed before he had the good fortune to encounter the upset wife. Taking the lady to one side and sitting her down on a seat on the platform, Holmes chose his most upbeat prospects, emphasising the short period which had elapsed since the loss, the possibilities of baling out, evading and being made a prisoner etc. Only slowly did it dawn on the nervous teenager that the erstwhile partner was actually more concerned with finding evidence for the husband's death, having for some time been involved with someone else! Holmes' entreaties remained equally reassuring: no, no, the chances of survival were remarkably poor. The reassured wife returned hence, as did a bemused Sergeant Holmes!

As February 1942 began and intelligence reports continued to reveal the imminence of the break out of the battle fleet from Brest, Bomber Command applied itself progressively more single-mindedly to thwarting German efforts. Despite increasingly desperate measures the whole of Bomber and Coastal Commands had little to show for a major effort of long duration. The daylight attack of 18th December by the mixed Halifax, Stirling and Manchester formation had achieved nothing. Repeated attacks in January had met with no success and on the infrequent occasions when clear weather permitted a good sight of the target in night attacks, as on 31st January/1st February 1942, the formidable flak and searchlight defences of the naval base proved more than a match. Even the new secret anti-shipping weapon had not got near its target.

During February Bomber Command switched tactics. The Manchesters had not undertaken any GARDENING sorties in January, but in a change heralding the breakout, 68 were to be attempted in February. Less spectacular for the aircrews because they would never hope to see the ships in the cross hairs of a bomb sight and in many respects just as hazardous with the cloud and now the icing of this bitter month, it was none-the-less to prove more effective in the longer run.

In line with the desperate urgency to parry the breakout, Manchesters were kept bombed up during the first days of February, with experienced 61, 83 and 207 Squadron crews standing by in daylight hours. Naturally, this largely neutralised the force for other activities and Bomber Command had to play a guessing game, trying as it must to use its force with maximum efficiency. Various bomb loads came on and off the aircraft and from time to time mines were loaded instead. In a new departure on both the 2nd and 4th of February 207 Squadron attempted their first daylight operations in the Manchester period. On the 2nd three aircraft were prepared in the early afternoon for daylight mining operations, largely thwarted by the weather. One was scrubbed prior to take-off, a second returned immediately and the third was recalled soon afterwards.

Despite its inherent dangers, a further daylight unescorted mining operation was set up for 61, 83 and 207 on the 6th as part of a 46 aircraft force. Fourteen Manchesters were to take-off soon after 1045 in the morning and take advantage of the expected cloud cover to evade searching day fighters. Flying Officer Leland from 207 was scrubbed in L7515 'EM-S' when his port engine became unserviceable prior to take-off, but the remaining crews proceeded. The designated drop zones for the four mines in each aircraft were the shipping lanes of the NECTARINE area along the Dutch barrier island coast. All three squadrons recognised it as a maximum effort with the COs of both 61 and 207 Squadrons participating.

Gardening off Holland – 6th February 1942

Serial	Code	Sqn	Captain
L7433	QR-*	61	W/C T C Weir
L7477	QR-*	61	S/L A M Paape
L7518	QR-*	61	F/O G W Gilpin
L7516	QR-*	61	F/O S J Beard
L7454	QR-*	61	P/O J R Hubbard
R5831	OL-I	83	P/O C R Frost
R5833	OL-N	83	F/L D A McClure
R5779	OL-G	83	F/O N A J Mackie
L7480	EM-L	207	S/L K H P Beauchamp
L7476	EM-K	207	F/O J Wooldridge
R5782	EM-R	207	W/C C Fothergill
L7485	EM-D	207	F/O D A Green
L7468	EM-Z	207	F/O L F Kneil
L7515	EM-S	207	F/O J H Leland

Visibility once airborne was initially bad, with 10/10th cloud at 1,400ft. Squadron Leader Beauchamp returned to base after two hours flying in accordance with orders when he ran into clear skies en route.

The remainder of the force continued in unaccustomed daylight. Flying Officer Wooldridge formated with a Hampden and a Manchester whilst en route to the release area. Wooldridge made landfall at Borkum before turning seaward for a timed run on a compass bearing to the drop site. L7476's load of four mines was released from a height of 500ft.

Wing Commander Fothergill, on his first operation, flew a course to the ETA on the enemy coast. From there he located the west end of Schiermonnikoog, turning seaward for a timed run to the designated area. Fothergill was fired on by a heavy flak barrage on Schiermonnikoog which holed the port wing, necessitating a quick jink into cloud. Later an enemy aircraft was seen and Fothergill again sought the sanctuary of the cloud.

Flying Officer Green pinpointed his landfall site on the south west end of Terschelling and flew a timed course at 600ft to the spot where his four mines were laid. On completion, he formated on two other Manchesters in the area, forming a tight mutual protection group with gunners scanning the skies anxiously for German day fighters.

Flying Officer Kneil also placed his four mines accurately in position. Aerial activity around him was intense and off on the beam two Me109s were seen following a Hampden into cloud. At 1342 L7468 was itself intercepted by a Me110 as Kneil headed homewards. This was shaken off by dodging up into the murk above.

No. 83 Squadron seem to have had less eventful operations. Flying Officer Mackie had the frustrating experience of reaching the drop zone only to have all four 'vegetables' hang up, whilst Pilot Officer Frost's aircraft had a hydraulic failure of some kind. Two of the 61 Squadron contingent had vision problems due to icing. Squadron Leader Paape was engaged by light flak and machine gun fire when he made landfall on the Dutch coast to make his timed run. His gunners silenced two machine guns.

Wing Commander Weir had the most unnerving experience when a burst hydraulic pipe in the port engine put the rear turret out of action. Undeterred, Weir pressed on, only to encounter first flak on two barrier islands and a Dornier Do215 on the return journey. All of these were evaded and all the Manchesters returned safely, most having sown their 'vegetables' in the allotted position. Within a few days perhaps these very 5 Group mines were to play a vital role in marring the escape of the *Scharnhorst* and *Gneisenau* to their German home ports.

Immediately on return the aircraft were refuelled and armed to standby once more for attacks on the *Scharnhorst* and *Gneisenau*, and later stood down. The Manchesters were stood by for operations against the battlecruisers on the 8th and 9th of February which were subsequently cancelled.

In an attempt to maintain pressure on the mainland targets, four 83 Squadron Manchesters were sent in a mixed force to bomb marshalling yards at Bremen on 10th/11th February 1942. Severe icing of seas and rivers made navigation very difficult, whilst visibility and operation of vital systems in the aircraft were impaired. The Manchesters bombed alternative targets in Bremen, Emden and near the mouth of the Weser.

Frustrated by the general lack of activity, Bomber Command laid on a 49 aircraft operation to Mannheim and a second force to Bremen on 11th February, an operation which was to be a tactical mistake. 61 Squadron provided six Manchesters, in addition, 18 Wellingtons raided Brest, five dropped leaflets and one 207 Squadron aircraft was sent on a mining operation. Six 207 Squadron aircraft were delegated for the Mannheim operation, whilst the seventh aircraft, manned by the trainee crew of Flying Officer Pattinson, was briefed to mine an area off the Frisian Islands.

Mannheim / Bremen† – 11/12th February 1942

Serial	Code	Sqn	Captain
L7433	QR-*	61†	F/O R E Archibald
L7474	QR-*	61†	P/O G L Tofield
L7518	QR-*	61†	P/O R E S Smith
R5834	QR-*	61†	F/Sgt J B Underwood
L7473	QR-*	61†	F/O I G A McNaughton
L7521	QR-*	61†	F/Sgt P H G Webster
L7432	EM-J	207‡	F/O S E Pattinson
L7491	EM-O	207	S/L K H P Beauchamp
L7515	EM-S	207	F/O J H Leland
L7484	EM-P	207	F/O J Wooldridge
R5796	EM-W	207	P/O M E Doble
L7391	EM-Y	207	F/Sgt J C Atkinson
L7486	EM-B	207	F/Sgt G H Hathersich

‡ *GARDENING sortie off the Frisian Islands.*

F/O Pattinson took off separately from the rest of the force at 1800 hours and was followed by the main group. Over the English coast, en route to the target Flying Officer Wooldridge lost coolant from the port Vulture in L7484, leading to the engine overheating and spewing long exhaust flames. The maximum height he could reach was only 8,000ft. As a result, he wisely diverted to Dunkirk as a last resort target, dropping six 1,000lb GPs at 1945 from 7,000ft before returning to Manston at 2021. Pilot Officer Doble had to jettison two 1,000lb bombs to cross the enemy coast at a safe height. Flight Sergeant Atkinson was unable to locate Mannheim and bombed a built up area, believed to have been Saarbrücken, as a last resort.

Two aircraft attacked the primary, whilst the remaining two also had to make do with alternative targets. On return all aircraft landed safely, although the weather was so adverse that Beauchamp and Leland diverted to Horsham St Faith, Atkinson found Manston and joined 'Dim' Wooldridge. Doble

landed at Boscombe Down, whilst Hathersich returned to West Malling.

The 61 Squadron force took off much later than the Mannheim raiders, leaving at intervals of a few minutes between 0155 and 0220 hours. The 61 Squadron Manchesters also experienced serviceability problems and as usual it was the Vulture engines which let down Pilot Officer Tofield. Soon after take-off he noted low oil pressure in his starboard Vulture and shortly afterwards a hydraulic pipe burst in the same engine. He landed back at base after only 20 minutes.

On taking off from Woolfox, L7518 steadfastly refused to climb. As they headed eastward Pilot Officer Smith was unable to coax any additional lift for the underpowered and struggling bomber. Nearing the Dutch coast he had found L7518 quite unable to climb above its ceiling of 9,000ft and reluctantly diverted to Terschelling to release his bombs before returning.

Flying Officer Archibald also experienced engine trouble on the outward journey in the heavily loaded aircraft. He pressed on to the target, searching for 35 minutes for the aiming point and being held in searchlight cones for long periods. His aircraft, L7433, was holed by flak in several places but he finally made a gliding attack from 12,000ft down to 7,500ft to release his bombs before returning. Flying Officer McNaughton and Flight Sergeant Webster made similar gliding attacks and turned for home.

On this night Warrant Officer H A Scott was flying his eighth and final Manchester operation and his third in the crew of Flight Sergeant Underwood. Scott had been with 61 Squadron from its very earliest days with a few Manchesters, back in March 1941. He had at first been in the crew of the CO, Wing Commander Valentine, but on 30th July 1941 had been the sole survivor from a 61 Squadron Hampden when Pilot Officer Adshead crashed returning from a raid on Cologne. Scott's injuries kept him in hospital until early September, thus causing him to be unavailable for Valentine's fateful final operation to Berlin on 3rd/4th September 1941. Scott was to have yet another brush with fate on 11/12th February 1942. This night Underwood flew in a Manchester with a very small number of flying hours, R5834, being joined in his crew by Sergeant Usher (second pilot), Warrant Officer Scott (observer), Sergeant Bithell (wireless operator/air gunner), Sergeant Anderson (front gunner), Pilot Officer Bluett (mid-upper gunner) and Sergeant Patey (rear gunner).

As R5834 settled on its outward course across the North Sea, Scott was putting in some practice with a sextant and soon began to suspect that the 'Met' forecast of a wind from a northerly direction was out by 180°. Most aircraft probably drifted off course to the south but Scott was able to correct Underwood's course to such effect that they

became one of the first aircraft in the target area, where they accordingly received more than their fair share of the flak. A gliding attack was made with bombs being released at 9,000ft. At this stage they remained unscathed, turning to a course which would take them back out to sea, passing to one side of Wilhelmshaven. Soon after establishing this return course and whilst in the vicinity of Wilhelmshaven they were coned by searchlights and engaged by a furious flak barrage. They suffered a very near miss from a heavy flak shell just off the starboard wing.

Underwood called the crew on the intercom, informing them of his intention to dive down the searchlight beams in an attempt to escape the flak, but Scott immediately counselled him to keep what height he had and alter course with a view to upsetting the gunners' aim. Underwood swung the nose away from the greatest concentration of lights and they soon escaped into the darkened sky without further near misses, the pilot immediately climbing up to 12,000ft. Close scrutiny soon showed Scott that they had not escaped unscathed.

The starboard engine temperature steadily rose until it passed the danger point. The crew expected it to seize and catch fire at any moment. Accordingly, to preclude this eventuality, Underwood shut it down and feathered the propeller. In this configuration Underwood found he was unable to maintain height and the wisdom of making the extra height after the flak engagement became apparent. By experimentation, Underwood found that he could reduce the rate of height loss to a few feet per minute only at airspeeds of 105mph or less, a whisker above stalling speed. Soon Underwood crossed the German coast between Bremerhaven and Wilhelmshaven.

Despite being determined to try their best to regain the English coast, they were reluctant to strike out due east away from land and turned instead south westwards to fly parallel to the Frisian Islands. They had reached as far as Texel, a few miles to port, when speed momentarily dropped to 100 and R5834 suddenly stalled and fell into a spin. Underwood worked hard, closing the throttle to permit spin recovery before re-opening the port engine as they resumed a generally level flight. Almost immediately they fell into a second spin, made worse on this occasion by the port engine cutting. Closing the throttle with the wheels still retracted caused the undercarriage warning klaxon to sound, increasing their sense of foreboding. Fortunately the engine picked up again. Underwood had to set the aircraft up at a crazy angle with the starboard wing high and a lot of right hand rudder to minimise height loss. The height loss did not seem terminal in the short term and the crew slowly began to recover from the shock of almost spinning straight down into the North Sea.

This page and opposite page: **Repairs in progress on Manchester L7477 'QR-N' of 61 Squadron at Woolfox Lodge, following Squadron Leader Paape's brave attack on the *Scharnhorst* and the *Gneisenau* off the Dutch coast on 12th February 1942. Near misses by several flak shells disabled the hydraulics, putting the turrets and brakes out of action. The trimming gear, starboard fin, tailplane, petrol tank and bomb doors were all holed. Paape and crew were very fortunate to return.** *via Chaz Bowyer*

surface more clearly and were soon gratified to recognise the bow wave of an air sea rescue launch heading directly towards them. It appeared to have been sent out in response to their earlier radio call for, having passed it, Sergeant Patey called to say it had reversed course and was now following them back westwards.

To their intense relief it began to appear that they would reach the English coast, and soon afterwards they crossed the coast south of Yarmouth, still heading steadfastly towards Woolfox Lodge. This happy situation did not continue for long for, en route to Norwich, the port engine spluttered and stopped, apparently short of fuel. With little height in hand there was no prospect of baling out and Underwood rapidly called all crew members to take up their crash positions. The pilot shaped up to force land in a flattish field directly in their path.

Scott had hastened to sit facing rearwards, his back braced against the main spar. He found he had a good view aft as Sergeant Patey had left the rear turret doors wide open. As they bellied in, turf, earth, divots and pieces of aeroplane flew in all directions and they lurched violently to a halt, the aircraft more or less in one piece. Nobody had been seriously hurt, although Underwood had been thrown forward in his straps by the deceleration and was thus unable to avoid being badly bruised across the chest by the thrashing control column.

As all scrambled out to survey the damage and feel solid ground under their feet, Usher had the misfortune to fall through the ice covering a deep dyke which the Manchester was straddling. Despite their ordeal humour had not eluded the crew and Underwood berated him, recalling his two hour struggle to keep Usher's feet dry only for him to fall into the dyke the moment he left the aircraft!

Luckily a farm was nearby and the undersized Ben Usher was soon warmly dressed in decidedly oversized farmer's clothes. Later that day the crew were transported to Horsham St Faith from where they flew back to Woolfox Lodge. The week-old R5834 was a write-off, but at least it had survived long enough to deliver its precious crew back home.

Off on the port beam the wide sandy beaches of Texel were clearly visible in the rising dawn and Underwood offered the crew the choice of an immediate forced landing on the beach or of continuing their attempt to reach the English coast. They unanimously elected to make for home. Efforts were redoubled to trim the aircraft and reduce the rate of height loss. Attempts were made to open the balance cock to transfer fuel from the starboard tank to the port engine. The control was stiff and although it opened eventually Scott was unable to ascertain whether much fuel was transferred.

Sergeant Bithell sent a message to base indicating their predicament and was gratified to receive an acknowledgement. The spin had toppled the gyro in the master unit of the dead reckoning compass, whilst the crabwise, wing high attitude of the aircraft led Scott to be dissatisfied with the headings shown on the P4 compass. Scott asked Bithell to obtain a series of radio fixes as they made their ponderous way westwards.

Despite their best efforts R5834 continued to lose height and it looked progressively more certain that they would have to ditch. The gunners were set to work stripping out and dumping the guns, ammunition, armour plate and any other readily detachable item. Only two guns and a small quantity of ammunition were retained in the rear turret. They reasoned that they might get a few miles closer to the English coast before ditching.

Slowly the aircraft ate up the miles towards the coast, sinking steadily as it did so. With the rising sun they could see the sea

In mid-February Warrant Officer Scott was posted to Manby on a bombing leaders' course and in his absence Flight Sergeant Underwood and crew flew yet another Manchester operation, returning this time with a number of bricks embedded in the leading edge of a wing after colliding with a high chimney stack during a low level escape from the target. Having converted onto Lancasters, Underwood and his crew failed to return from a subsequent operation with the loss of all on board. Warrant Officer Scott was still at Manby. Yet another brave 61 Squadron crew had paid the ultimate sacrifice.

Underwood had bellied in at 0755 hours but two of the 61 Squadron Manchesters were still airborne. Flying Officer Archibald reached Woolfox and landed safely at 0810, whereas Flying Officer McNaughton's crew had left the enemy coast at daybreak but were unable to pinpoint their landfall on the English coast. They flew up and down for two hours until they picked up a course to base, where they landed at 0915 with marginal fuel reserves. Bomber Command's forces were accordingly scattered and exhausted when the Germans finally made their audacious breakout.

The next day witnessed one of the RAF's and the nation's most ignominious encounters. Early on 12th February 1942 the *Scharnhorst* and the *Gneisenau*, together with the cruiser *Prinz Eugen* and with a strong destroyer escort, finally broke out of Brest with the intention of forcing a route through the English Channel, trailing their coats across the very doorstep of the most powerful navy in the world. The Germans had chosen the weather for the sortie with the utmost care. It was atrocious, severe gales, low cloud, poor visibility, snow, sleet and rain all served to shroud the racing ships. Right from the beginning, however, luck was on the German side. Coastal Command had been patrolling the harbour approaches for weeks, day and night, with air-to-surface vessel (ASV) equipped search aircraft to provide forewarning of just such an escape. Irrespective of the weather and unbeknown to the Germans, who had no inkling that our aircraft were so equipped, the patrolling Hudson should have detected the ships in spite of the weather. By a cruel quirk of fate the ASV set in the Lockheed Hudson chose this particular moment to fail and to compound matters the standby aircraft also became unserviceable. The game of hide and seek was on with a vengeance.

Bomber Command were put on a four hour standby to attack the ships during the morning, but serious logistic difficulties manifested themselves. In addition to Coastal Command, the Germans had caught Bomber Command on the hop too. Six of 207 Squadron's aircraft from the previous night's operation were spread the length and breadth of Britain, their crews sleeping in

after getting away from debriefing later than 0100 that morning.

A further difficulty was that the cloud base was so low that there was no prospect of using AP and SAP bombs on the ships. If the aircraft flew at the height sufficient for the bombs to reach the terminal velocity needed to penetrate the deck armour the bomb aimers would have no chance of seeing their target. After months of preparation it looked to be a fudge right from the beginning.

Following frantic telephone calls during the morning the aircraft engaged on the Mannheim raid returned in dribs and drabs to Bottesford. Flying Officer Leland took off from Horsham at 1125 and landed at base at 1210, where groundcrews descended on this and other aircraft to refuel, rearm and load them each in turn with twelve 500lb GP bombs. Such weapons would be almost totally ineffective against the heavily armoured battlecruisers, but there was a faint chance a near miss below the water line might damage the more vulnerable undersides of the vessels. It was a thousand to one chance, but in this weather and with the equipment then at its disposal it was the only option open to Bomber Command.

The aircraft eventually assembled included five Manchesters from both 61 and 83 Squadrons and six from 207. Nos. 61 and 207 provided their COs and both flight commanders. All aircraft carried 12 x 500lb bombs. For Pilot Officer Leland and his crew it was the second of three operations in less than 36 hours.

Channel Breakout, Operation Fuller – 12th February 1942

Serial	Code	Sqn	Captain
L7458	QR-*	61	W/C T C Weir
L7477	QR-N	61	S/L A M Paape
L7475	QR-D	61	S/L P W M West
L7521	QR-*	61	F/O G W Gilpin
L7473	QR-*	61	P/O J R Hubbard
R5831	OL-I	83	P/O C R Frost
L7465	OL-H	83	F/Sgt P A Mackenzie
L7525	OL-O	83	F/O M A Smith
L7427	OL-J	83	F/L D A McClure
L7385	OL-C	83	F/O R W Cooper
L7432	EM-J	207	W/C C Fothergill
L7468	EM-Z	207	F/L P C Ward-Hunt
L7515	EM-S	207	F/O J H Leland
L7485	EM-D	207	S/L T C Murray
L7455	EM-G	207	F/O P C Birch
L7488	EM-Q	207	F/S J C Atkinson

After the heroic attack by Lieutenant Commander Esmonde and the six Swordfish of 815 Squadron, the German ships were once more enveloped in low cloud and squalls. Attempts to shadow the fleet were made difficult by the terrible visibility, the escorting German fighter umbrella and the E-boat and destroyer screen. The obvious intention of the Manchesters was to make a

concerted attack on the ships and so divide the ferocious German flak defences. No. 83 Squadron's Manchesters took off between 1349 and 1502, whilst the 61 and 207 aircraft were due off at 1500 or soon afterwards. The hastily contrived operation began to go seriously wrong from the very first.

Whilst running up for take-off two of the 207 Squadron aircraft from the previous night's raid, L7432, Wing Commander Fothergill and L7515, Flying Officer Leland became unserviceable and were cancelled. There were no reserves for the crews to transfer to. The remaining four Manchesters took off between 1459 and 1525. L7485, which was last away, experienced a hydraulic failure on take-off in the hands of Squadron Leader Thos Murray, who completed a circuit and immediately landed back at Bottesford.

Damaged fin and elevator of an 83 Squadron Manchester (L752?). Two 83 Squadron Manchesters were damaged in the tail area on 12th February 1942 while engaged in Operation FULLER. Flying Officer Smith's rear gunner was injured in L7525 'OL-O'. Flying Officer McFarlane's rear gunner was reported killed, but his operation is not listed in the squadron records. *via Chaz Bowyer*

A force born out of desperation and with little hope of locating their targets, of hitting or of damaging them had thus been reduced by half before the operation started. Despite the most determined efforts by air and ground crew alike the unreliability of the Manchester was their undoing yet again. Small wonder those involved felt frustrated.

Out over the North Sea a motley collection of RAF aircraft searched blindly and in totally unco-ordinated fashion for the fast escaping cruisers. Halifaxes, Stirlings, Wellingtons, Whitleys and Hampdens milled around with the Manchesters on the off-chance of locating the ships upon which they could unload their totally ineffective bombs.

In the air aircraft had to contend with visibility of only 500 to 1,000 yards and a cloud base as low as 500ft. They had to fly and search at low level to maintain any contact with the sea surface. Flight Lieutenant Ward-Hunt searched for three hours, constantly asking his wireless operator, Sergeant Gibson, whether news of any sightings had been broadcast, but to no avail. He returned with bomb load intact. Flying Officer Peter Birch in L7455 had an equally uneventful search before bombing small vessels at The Hook of Holland from 500ft at 1635 as a last resort.

Flight Sergeant Atkinson in L7488 'EM-Q' was one of the few Bomber Command aircraft which did sight the battlecruisers. Having stumbled across the racing fleet, he

noted the position of the capital ships before rising up to 800ft and entering cloud. The visibility was only 700 yards and Atkinson was almost on top of the alerted fleet before his lookouts spotted them. As he circled to a more advantageous position the bomb doors were opened and Sergeant Worthington, the observer, got down into the nose and fused the bombs. As they dived to attack, heavy rain and mist still impeded their bomb run, but they were immediately engaged by the flak defences of escorts and capital ships alike. All 12 x 500 lb GP bombs were dropped from 700ft at 1616 and thought to have straddled a cruiser. As they entered a climbing turn to regain the sanctuary of the cloud the rear gunner, Sergeant Leahy, saw five bomb bursts near the starboard side of the vessel but no sign of a hit or damage. At this very instant the aircraft was hit in the tail by a flak burst. No vital damage was done and Atkinson was able to return safely to Bottesford. He was later awarded the DFC for this attack.

No. 83 Squadron remained in the search area until nightfall. All aircraft carried out square searches but in the low cloud, mist and rain four of the five brought their bombs back. Flying Officer Smith's crew sighted the double column of ships briefly, but as they manoeuvred to attack the poor visibility impeded bomb aiming. As they ran in they were spotted by enemy escort fighters which closed in to attack the rear gunner. Sergeant Duff put up a spirited defence, later claiming two 'Heinkels' shot down. He in turn was wounded. The Form 540 details Pilot Officer McFarlane's rear gunner being killed but there is no record of his operation in the Form 541.

Wing Commander Weir headed off individually at low level for the estimated position of the racing German naval units. Although visibility was poor L7458 was followed twice en route to the target area, first by a Junkers Ju 88 and later a Messerschmitt Me 110. These were evaded by dodging into the plentiful cloud cover. On ETA a square search was carried out without any sighting being made. Eventually one track led them onto the Dutch coast at Zandvoort. Weir flew down the coast to Den Haag (The Hague) before turning west and flying out to sea at low level for 15 miles to commence a second search. Almost immediately the rear gunner, Flying Officer Bluett, spotted the German ships at close range just astern.

Weir advanced the throttles and made a climbing turn up into the enveloping cloud cover. Opening the bomb doors and preparing for the attack, Weir then turned on a reciprocal and headed into a diving attack with all members keeping a sharp look out. On breaking cloud at 400ft the pilot and bomb aimer, Pilot Officer Beach, found themselves running between and in the same direction as the two columns of ships. Beach began directing Weir to a ship in the right hand col-

umn calling 'Right!' then 'Hard right!' as they overtook their target.

At the same time an intense and ferocious barrage of light and medium flak was opened up on them. Weir had banked right and was tightening the turn when a large calibre shell went through the port wing, outboard of the fuel tank, damaging the aileron, which jammed in the up position. Airflow over the port wing then threw L7458 into a steep left hand banked turn, which Weir was fully occupied stopping tightening into a fatal spin.

Pandemonium had broken out with flak bursts all round them, air gunners replying and Beach calling 'Right,' right!' in frustration as Weir, unbeknown to them, strove with might and main just to keep them airborne. A less experienced pilot might have gone straight into the sea there and then, but Weir had an Above Average rating and used all his experience to bring the crippled Manchester under control, still engaged by the German escorts. They had turned sharply left towards the port column of vessels and Weir was still unable to raise the left wing. Quickly closing the throttle of the port engine to half power, he finally managed to get the wings level at about 200ft. Abandoning any prospect of attack, Weir ordered the bombs jettisoned and bomb doors closed, meanwhile descending to sea level for maximum safety. No further flak hits had occurred and as they passed through the left hand column fire became erratic and ineffective. It seemed the poor visibility and risk of hitting their own ships was deterring the enemy gunners. Weir now zig-zagged his way through the convoy, his crew doing all they could to keep the flak gunners heads down as they passed each ship.

Eventually they were clear and Weir was able to climb into the sanctuary of cloud, relaxing slightly after the last hectic few minutes and their close brush with death. In turn he began calling each crew position to check whether anyone had been injured. Last of all was Flying Officer Bluett who replied 'OK sir, that was great, let's go back and do it again!' It raised a wry smile from Weir, who was the only one to appreciate how close they had been to death, and the tension in the aircraft dropped perceptibly. They were able to regain base without further incident.

The 'A' Flight Commander, Squadron Leader Peter West, had set out from Woolfox Lodge in L7475 at about the same time as the remainder of 61 Squadron's Manchesters. Heading out from the English coast, as they climbed out through 2,500ft in bad visibility they met a Ju 88 head-on over Great Yarmouth. Neither crew had any time to respond. They flew on at 3,000ft over a thick and continuous cloud layer. In the howling gale near ground level the air was very turbulent and L7475 was lurching violently. Soon all the gunners were very airsick.

On ETA, West let down to carry out a square search at 500ft just below the cloud base. Shortly afterwards, three Me109s were seen, but they popped up into cloud and evaded them. West reached the Dutch coast, where he obtained a fix on one of the radio transmitters before heading off seawards to resume the search. Suddenly they came across a destroyer screen, which indicated the German capital ships were nearby and West began a search of the neighbourhood. Intense and accurate flak was encountered whenever they ventured out of cloud. However, the larger units could not be located and cloud base was now locally so low that it would be impossible to release bombs without destroying the aircraft.

Thus thwarted, West gave up the struggle and steadily climbed up through the cloud layer with the intention of returning to base. As they breasted the cloud layer they were shocked to immobility to find themselves right alongside a Me110! The German fighter crew were equally taken off guard, staring across with raised eyebrows. Peter West was the first to galvanise himself into action, stuffing the nose back down and calling out irritably to the gunners 'Well, fire at the bastard someone!'

As both aircraft sheared away the fighter passed through the sights of the mid-upper gunner, who was still too startled to respond, but Pilot Officer Kominski loosed off a quick burst from the rear turret from close range. Kominski believed he had disabled the rear gunner in the aircraft. Following this adventure they set course for base, landing with the bomb load intact.

Squadron Leader Paape flew directly to the Dutch coast, locating it at 400ft and obtaining a pin-point. He then returned offshore to make two runs up and down about 10 miles out in the hope of locating the German ships. Having no success, he flew to a distance of 30 miles offshore and recommenced his search, locating the convoy shortly afterwards. His aircraft was immediately engaged by flak and sustained two hits. Climbing through cloud Paape skirted the convoy and made a bombing run on one of the battlecruisers from 450ft. In the excitement his bombs undershot and straddled an escort destroyer.

The anti-aircraft defences may have upset Flight Sergent Halls' aim and as Paape broke for sea level L7477 was hit several more times. The hydraulic lines were severed, brakes and trimming gear shot away, turrets put out of service and starboard fin, tailplane and petrol tank holed. Loss of hydraulic power prevented the bomb doors from being closed. In this precarious condition Paape limped back to base, where a successful 'wheeler' landing was accomplished.

Neither Flying Officer Gilpin nor Pilot Officer Hubbard located the enemy ships and the disconsolate force returned to base with nothing to show for their efforts. It was 61 Squadron's second and last daylight operation in Manchesters.

At the time it seemed that the entire Royal Navy and the RAF had been entirely non-effective in preventing the escape of the capital ships. Indeed it was a frustrating and humiliating day, with none of the aircraft having anything to show for their strenuous efforts. Perhaps the most surprising outcome in the swirling mass of British and German aircraft was that there were no collisions. All of the Manchesters returned.

Whilst this drama was being acted out unseen, all three squadrons were preparing for the final desperate throw of the dice. At Bottesford the groundcrews had worked constantly on L7485 and L7515 to make them serviceable and they were joined by two others for a mining operation to a sea area at the mouth of the Elbe, coded NECTARINE, where the German battlecruisers were believed to be headed. The aircraft each carried four 1,500lb mines.

Gardening – 12/13th February 1942

Serial	Code	Sqn	Captain
L7475	QR-*	61	P/O G L Tofield
L7519	QR-*	61	F/O L Gunter
L7465	OL-H	83	W/O H H Whitehead
R5831	OL-I	83	P/O H G Hazelden
L7427	OL-J	83	P/O J H Morphett
L7391	EM-Y	207	S/L K H P Beauchamp
L7515	EM-S	207	F/O J H Leland
R5796	EM-W	207	P/O M E Doble
L7485	EM-D	207	S/L T C Murray

Despite the participation of the two flight commanders from 207 Squadron, this operation, too, was an unmitigated disaster. The aircraft took off in a group between 2250 and 2258 hours to make their way individually to their designated areas.

Flying Officer Leland returned at 0226 with mines intact after encountering severe icing in nimbus stratus cloud. Squadron Leader Murray in L7485, with hydraulics repaired following his aborted operation in the same aircraft the previous afternoon, located the dropping zone but was unable to release his mines owing to another hydraulic failure, which prevented the bomb doors opening.

Pilot Officer Doble released four mines at the estimated position from 600ft at 0205 only to find that they had inadvertently been dropped 'safe'. Squadron Leader 'Penny' Beauchamp's logbook records him flying the operation in Manchester Mk.IA L7491 to the Frisian Isles, where the bomb doors failed to open. The manual release also failed, necessitating the four mines being returned to base.

In exceptionally bad weather, Pilot Officer Tofield took off and climbed to 8,000ft, where he experienced acute icing conditions. Ice built up on the airscrew blades and was shed in lumps which dented the fuselage and burst through the perspex of the cockpit. The weight caused the aircraft to steadily lose height to a mere 600ft! Next they flew into a severe snow storm and Tofield had no alternative but to abandon the operation.

In contrast, Pilot Officer Gunter elected to fly at 1,500ft but at this height found conditions very bumpy and visibility nil. At 0050 he calculated that he could not reach the drop zone by the stipulated time and turned for home. Only Pilot Officer Hazelden and Pilot Officer Morphett from 83 Squadron laid their 'vegetables' in the designated area.

With few exceptions the crews went to bed exhausted and burning with anguish and frustration. Despite many being continuously awake for more than 36 hours and making a Herculean effort the Manchester had let them down again. From 207 Squadron three out of six became unserviceable on the daylight raid and two out of four on the night mining mission.

The weather had conspired to nullify the efforts of the remainder of the force. They were left feeling that, even if the weather had been better, their chances of dealing the Germans a decisive blow were negligible, whilst the chances of the unescorted Manchesters evading the German fighter screen would have been slight. All in all it was a typical, if somewhat extreme, example of the continuing operational limitations of the Manchester.

As the evening wore on it had become increasingly obvious that the battlecruisers would make good their escape. The only silver lining to the whole endeavour was that, unseen by the attackers, the *Scharnhorst* had hit and exploded mines on two separate occasions and limped into Wilhelmshaven for repair. *Gneisenau* had hit a mine too, but was less seriously damaged, reaching the intended destination, the Elbe, in company with the *Prinz Eugen*. These mines had been laid in the previous few days by the Hampdens and Manchesters of 5 Group, so perhaps 61, 83 and 207 Squadrons did make a significant contribution after all.

Indeed before February was over Bomber Command did draw a line under the activities of one of the German capital ships. *Gneisenau* had limped on to Kiel and a floating dock for repair of the damage caused by the mine explosion.

On 26/27th February 1942 during a 49 aircraft attack on Kiel harbour, in which Manchesters for once did not participate, several bombs fell near the floating dock but one struck *Gneisenau* in the bows, penetrating the armoured deck and severely damaging the vessel and killing 116 of the crew. *Gneisenau*'s all-threatening guns were subsequently removed for use by coastal defence batteries. The hulk laid up at Gdynia, a casualty of persistence.

Chapter Seven

New tactics, New owners

Up to the end of February 1942 the greatest number of Manchesters dispatched on an operation on a single night was 19 and the reader would be excused for drawing the conclusion, based on the groundings and delays of May-August 1941, that the Manchester had already been eclipsed, numerically at least, by the contemporary Handley Page Halifaxes and Short Stirlings. However, daily Bomber Command returns indicate that until late February 1942 the average number of serviceable Manchesters never exceeded 31, whilst of Stirlings and Halifaxes there were never more than 21 and 23 respectively! Throughout much of 1941 and early 1942 the Manchester was thus the major heavy type in service. Cast in the light of these statistics, it is easier to appreciate why Bomber Command strove so determinedly to persist with such an obviously unsuitable aircraft. Stirlings and Halifaxes too had their share of production delays and serviceability problems. A mark of the rapid expansion of heavy bomber units is evident, though greatly exaggerated, by the landmark first 1,000 Bomber raid on Cologne exactly three months later, when 88 Stirlings, 131 Halifaxes, and 73 Lancasters participated in addition to the 45 Manchesters.

The end of February 1942 had marked another sharp change in Bomber Command priorities and is reflected in the deployment of its Manchester forces. Air Chief Marshal Sir Arthur Harris had become Commander in Chief on 22nd February 1942. He held strong views on the employment of bomber aircraft and inherited a force poised on the brink of grasping a range of new techniques. Concentration in space and time, use of incendiaries, application of target finding devices and marking techniques, all were in the offing.

For the Manchester too it was a period of change. Lancaster production was accelerating rapidly and 5 Group squadrons would finally acquire an aircraft capable of making a significant contribution to the war effort. After almost 18 months of service, 12 of them operational, 207 Squadron would rejoice in passing the torch to other units. A short burst of activity in early March was all that remained to it. In turn 106, 50 and 49 Squadrons respectively were to re-equip with Manchesters for only a two month period. By mid-April, 61 and 83 Squadrons passed their Manchesters on to their Conversion Flights and these would only re-appear fleetingly during operations in

the all-risks, maximum effort, 1,000 bomber raids of late May and June.

Despite their rapidly approaching obsolescence, Manchester availability did not tail away. Indeed more aircraft were serviceable in March and April than at any time previously. For a very short time in early April, four squadrons were operational at once.

For the first time units would regularly dispatch strengths of eight, nine and ten Manchesters on a single operation. Previous policy and availability had prevented this. The objective of the new tactics was to greatly enhance the effectiveness and striking power of the bomber force and one corollary of bunching the aircraft into a tightly packed stream was to locally overwhelm defences and reduce losses. Possibly it is surprising then, and a reflection of enhanced German defensive capability, that Manchester losses increased sharply over this period. Roy Chadwick's 1940 prophecy was to be written in blood by the tragic losses in the final three months of operations.

Billancourt – 2nd/3rd March 1942

Serial	Code	Sqn	Captain
L7519	QR-*	61	S/L A M Paape
L7473	QR-*	61	F/L I G A McNaughton
L7518	QR-*	61	F/Sgt J B Underwood
L7480	QR-*	61	P/O R E S Smith
R5832	QR-*	61	F/O L Gunter
L7521	QR-*	61	F/O S J Beard
L7516	QR-*	61	F/L R A V Gascoyne-Cecil
L7497	QR-*	61	F/Sgt E W Noble
L7464	QR-*	61	P/O G L Tofield
R5831	OL-I	83	F/O H G Hazelden
L7427	OL-*	83	P/O R G W Oakley
R5838	OL-*	83	F/O M A Smith
R5775	OL-*	83	F/L K Cook
L7453	OL-*	83	P/O R McFarlane
L7423	OL-*	83	S/L D A McClure
R5837	OL-*	83	P/O J H Morphett
R5780	OL-*	83	P/O P A Mackenzie
L7426	OL-*	83	P/O C R Frost
L7387	OL-*	83	P/O R W Cooper
L7455	EM-G	207	F/O L F Kneil DFM
R5782	EM-R	207	F/L Ward-Hunt
L7319	EM-X	207	F/Sgt G H Coles
L7486	EM-B	207	S/L T C Murray
L7491	EM-O	207	F/L W D B Ruth
L7378	EM-A	207	F/O J H Leland
L7488	EM-Q	207	F/S J C Atkinson

On the night of 2nd/3rd March, Bomber Command planned an experimental maximum effort to take out a precision target. Command required a significant target in good weather and where only modest defences could be expected and chose the Renault factory at Billancourt near Paris. Renault were producing 18,000 lorries a year for the German Army. The briefing called for the attack to be made in three waves, with 235 aircraft to cross the target area in only one hour 50 minutes. The first wave was to be made up of the most experienced crews, who by use of massed flares and incendiaries would light and mark the way for following aircraft. To further ensure concentration on the factory area, aircraft were to go in at very low level. The objective was not only to ensure maximum damage but to avoid hitting French civilians in the adjacent suburbs. The three Manchester squadrons raised a total of 26 aircraft, the largest since the aircraft began operating. No 61 Squadron contributed nine, 83 Squadron ten and 207 Squadron seven.

Soon after take-off, 'Jimmy' Kneil in L7455 of 207 Squadron encountered engine trouble and returned. The remaining 25 pressed home their attacks. Flight Lieutenant Ward-Hunt and Flight Sergeant Coles of 207 Squadron located the target by the bright moonlight and flares and attacked in the first wave around 2030 hours, Coles from a mere 1,600ft. No. 83 Squadron provided seven aircraft for the first wave, all carrying 1,000 lb general purpose (GP) bombs. Pilot Officer Mackenzie went in at 1,000ft to make sure his bombs hit the works, his aircraft being shaken by the blast waves of his own bombs. Pilot Officer Morphett and Squadron Leader McClure came down to 2,000ft to release their bombs. The coloured Target Indicator (TI) bombs used later were not available at this time and these two crews circled after bombing to release the flares intended to mark the target for subsequent waves. Both Pilot Officer Frost and Pilot Officer Cooper claimed to have hit and exploded a gasometer.

The remaining four 207 Squadron Manchesters attacked in the second wave around 2200 hours. By this time the target was ablaze from end to end and readily identifiable. All four Manchesters were carrying a 4,000 lb 'Cookie' plus four 500 lb GP bombs and attacked at heights ranging from

3–5000ft. Squadron Leader Murray reported that his bomb load detonated in the motor vehicle park. On his bomb run a Vickers Wellington following immediately behind and only 100ft above hit the same spot at the same time.

The remaining three Manchesters from 83 Squadron also attacked in the second wave. Crews reported flares visible at the target when they were still crossing The Channel and that the target was already a mass of flames. Their 4,000 lb 'Cookies' demanded a higher safe bombing height but they came in at 5–6,000ft.

The nine 61 Squadron crews joined in the third wave. These aircraft reached the target up to 35 minutes early and had to orbit until their allotted time. Squadron Leader Paape saw his bombs shatter several buildings in the works and red hot metal flew up to 4,000ft. Flight Sergeant Noble reported bricks and rooftops flying up to 1,500ft into the air under the onslaught of their 4,000 lb 'Cookies' and the factory area seemed ablaze from end to end. Whilst the two earlier waves had encountered little opposition, and this from searchlights and the few flak guns, German night fighters began to arrive as this third wave withdrew. Pilot Officer Smith in L7480 was approached by a Junkers Ju 88, which did not attack. Both Paape and Pilot Officer Tofield observed Messerschmitt Me 110s searching the sky, but neither were attacked and Tofield also passed a single engined night fighter head on, but evaded it. Flight Lieutenant Gascoyne-Cecil's aircraft, L7516, was intercepted and attacked near Paris by an unidentified twin engined fighter. The rear gunner, Flight Sergeant Say, replied as the fighter closed in and it turned away at close range and disappeared. There were no casualties amongst the Manchesters and on return all the crews who reached the target were able to give graphic accounts of the point-blank attack on the virtually undefended objective.

The Billancourt factory records confirmed what crews and photo-reconnaissance had suggested, namely that the new tactics were enormously successful. A total of 300 bombs fell on the factory, destroying 40% of the buildings. Of the estimated output, direct destruction or loss of production resulted in a loss of at least 2,300 lorries. Unfortunately the toll of French civilian casualties was grievously high and more than double that occasioned in one night on a German target up till that time – 367 civilians were killed and 341 injured. A major contributory factor to this high casualty figure was that the population had received false air raid alerts on countless previous occasions and had consequently failed to take shelter when a real need arose.

The raid broke many of Bomber Command's records. The 235 strong force was the largest number of aircraft sent to a single target, the concentration of aircraft over the tar-

get, at 121 aircraft/hour, was the highest yet achieved and a record tonnage of bombs was dropped. The raid consequently represented a major milestone for Bomber Command and a marked contrast with its efforts over Kiel only a week earlier, when 68 aircraft were so far wide of the mark that city authorities recorded engine noises only in their diary of events.

The Air Staff had been evaluating techniques for some months and a series of recent directives greeted Harris on his appointment. Notwithstanding Billancourt, Harris was instructed 'the primary object of your operations should now be focused on the morale of the enemy civilian population and in particular of the industrial workers'. To renew this assault the navigation aid GEE was released for use on 14th February. It had a projected lifespan of six months and was to be employed in conjunction with 'concentrated incendiary attacks'. A cardinal principle in the use of GEE was to be 'concentration on one target until its destruction has been achieved'. The initial attack was to be on Essen – 'the supreme target'. Harris did not dissent. During March and April eight large scale raids on Essen were to be dispatched. The results were a great disappointment, the strategic air weapon was not yet fully honed.

The offensive against the Ruhr, with Essen as the focus, began on 8/9th March 1942. To gain the maximum benefit from GEE, Harris had been directed not to take on the enemy and the weather at the same time. For these attacks the SHAKER technique had been developed. For this the bomber force was divided in three groups, first the target illuminators, next the target markers and close-spaced behind, the followers. The Pathfinder force was presaged in this approach, which in all its essential elements mimicked German techniques of 18 months earlier on Coventry and elsewhere.

The 20 GEE-equipped illuminators would arrive in five waves at three minute intervals. Each illuminator would carry 12 bundles of triple flares and was to run along the up-wind side of the target, releasing flares at 10-second intervals. Thus it was intended to sky mark the target for 12 minutes with lanes of flares 6 miles long to assist visual bombing by the target markers. The target markers, also carrying GEE, would release the maximum load of incendiaries to create an unmistakable concentrated area of fire for the high explosive carrying and non-GEE equipped, followers. It required careful timing and discipline from crews in respect of courses, approach direction and belief in their new equipment. Initially this was not to prove evident.

The forthcoming three consecutive nights were to prove an unsatisfactory finale to 207 Squadron's long involvement with the Manchester. Nos. 61 and 83 Squadrons also contributed. On 8/9th March 1942 Bomber Command dispatched 211 aircraft to Essen, 82 of them equipped with GEE. The designated aiming point was the Krupps works. The total Manchester force was 25, of which three were sent mining off Lorient and the remainder joined the followers carrying loads, largely of high explosive. Clearly the Manchesters could not have been GEE equipped.

A fateful photograph of R5779 'OL-G' of 83 Squadron at Scampton on 7th March 1942. The aircraft failed to return from Essen the next night. Left to right: Sergeants Rex, Broad, Dalby, Flying Officer Cooper, Sergeants Cross, Key and Mowatt. *G Rex*

Essen – 8/9th March 1942

Serial	Code	Sqn	Captain
L7518	QR-*	61	S/L A M Paape
L7458	QR-*	61	F/L R A V Gascoyne-Cecil
L7521	QR-*	61	F/O S J Beard
L7471	QR-*	61	F/O L Gunter
L7497	QR-*	61	F/O R E Archibald
L7464	QR-*	61	P/O G L Tofield
L7519	QR-*	61	P/O A L Searby
L7473	QR-*	61	P/O R E S Smith
R5786	QR-*	61†	P/O R E Clarke
L7475	QR-*	61†	Sgt C G Furby
R5831	OL-*	83	S/L D A McClure
R5838	OL-*	83	F/O M A Smith
L7465	OL-*	83	P/O P A Mackenzie
L7387	OL-*	83	F/O H G Hazelden
L7423	OL-*	83	P/O J H Morphett
L7453	OL-*	83	F/L D A J Mackie
L7427	OL-*	83	P/O R G W Oakley
R5830	OL-*	83	W/O H H Whitehead
L7426	OL-*	83	P/O C R Frost
R5779	OL-G	83	F/O R W Cooper
L7378	EM-A	207	S/L T C Murray
L7491	EM-O	207	F/L W D B Ruth
L7455	EM-G	207	F/L P C Birch
L7484	EM-P	207	F/Sgt G H Hathersich
L7391	EM-Y	207†	P/O F A Roper

† These three sent on mining sortie off Lorient.

On this night Flight Lieutenant Peter Birch in L7455 'EM-G' was carrying the redoubtable Group Captain 'Ferdie' Swain OBE AFC, the officer commanding Bottesford, as an eighth crew member. Regrettably it was this crew which had the misfortune to experience troubles with the starboard Vulture, exhaust manifold, autopilot etc. which necessitated an early return from the region of the Dutch coast. The emergency air bottle had also to be used to lower the undercarriage at base.

For two 83 Squadron crews, those of Pilot Officer Chris Frost DFM and Flying Officer Bob Cooper, it was to be their last briefing of the war. They felt the same grim tightening of the stomach when the target for the night, Essen, was announced. Frost was into his second tour and was allocated L7426. Cooper, about to fly his 22nd operation, was allocated in turn R5779 'OL-G'. Bob Cooper was 24 years old, whereas his second pilot, Sergeant Mowat, was still only 18, having lied about his age to join up. Sergeant Cross was the observer, Sergeant George Dalby the wireless operator/air gunner, Sergeant George Rex the second wireless op/air gunner, whose turn it was to fly in the front turret that night, Sergeant Alfred Key was the mid-upper gunner. Sergeant Charles Broad was the rear gunner.

It was about 0115 hours when Cooper finally took off on a bright moonlight night with good visibility. When the German defences were alerted to the forthcoming raid, amongst the night fighters scrambled to meet the threat were Me110s of II/NJG2 at Leeuwarden. Patrolling the coastline searching for incoming bombers was the ace, Oberleutnant Ludwig Becker. He soon latched onto a bomber, identifying it as a Manchester and swiftly brought it to earth in flames. It was Chris Frost in L7426. The blazing wreck plummeted down 2 miles north east of Enkhuizen onto the ice-covered Ijsselmeer, which at the time was 80cm thick. The entire crew were killed outright. The attack has been timed at 0032, but this seems doubtful.

Following behind and some 30 miles to the north east was Bob Cooper in R5779. Some prolonged discussion had arisen between the captain and observer when they were unable to pick up any pin-point on crossing the enemy coast. Eventually they identified a landmark showing them off track to the north. Unbeknown to them the 'Freya' ground radar was already tracking them and Oberfeldwebel Paul Gildner was in the final moments of a classic night fighter stalk in the dark sky beneath their tail. Now Gildner was formating beneath the big black silhouette of the Manchester. Suddenly, when he judged the moment right, Gildner pulled back on the stick, raising the nose and raking the underside of R5779 with his nose guns as the Manchester flew through his sights. The first inkling the seven man crew had was when tracer lanced up through the airframe from stem to stern with a shattering series of explosions. A confusion of voices rang out on the intercom 'We've been hit!', 'We're on fire!', then the strangely detached voice of 18 year old Mowat reporting incredulously that the rear section of the aircraft was on fire.

Cooper was the first to take practical steps to try and save them. He ordered Cross to put the bombs on safe and jettison them. The bomb doors were opened and a few moments later Cross confirmed 'Bombs away safe'. Whilst Cross was busy down in the nose, Cooper did his best to keep R5779 straight and level, and Rex searched vainly for their assailant. In any case, with Cross blocking the nose compartment he wasn't going anywhere. As soon as Cross turned to recover his seat in the cockpit, Rex climbed out of the front turret with a view to helping fight the fire. He was about to climb up into the cockpit when a second attack, more devastating than the first, enveloped the aircraft. Rex could feel hits nearby in the bomb bay.

As Rex continued to climb he found his head suddenly jerked violently to one side and he fell back into the floor of the nose compartment. In his haste he had forgotten to detach his intercom lead. On his knees he raised his head and saw that the space beneath the cockpit floor was a raging inferno, fanned to a blowtorch by jets of air entering through the many shrapnel tears. The floor of the cockpit was already curling like paper. Possibly the hydraulic fluid had sprayed from the piping and caught fire. Suddenly the fire flashed over and enveloped the entire cockpit and nose compartment. Engulfed by fire, Bob Cooper just had time to shout his last order 'Oh hell! Bale out!, bale out!' Rex moved swiftly to obey, yanking out the intercom lead, buckling on his parachute, jettisoning the hatch and diving after it to escape the raging inferno. The transition from noise and fire to cold and silence was such a relief that Rex allowed himself to free fall 2–3,000ft before pulling the rip-cord. Thanks to his leather flying suit and helmet his burns were confined to his eyebrows and hands. He landed at 0220 hours in a clump of young fir trees west of Smilde.

After the second onslaught, Sergeant Alf Key in the rear of the aircraft had decided to leave his turret and try to aid Sergeant Broad, the rear gunner. As he dropped to the floor he found that Gildner's cannon fire had blasted away sections of the flaming lower fuselage, though which Key inadvertently tumbled into the night sky. His rapid departure, coupled with the fact that he was already wearing his parachute, saved him from the conflagration and he was able to pull the rip-cord and descend. They were the only crew members to survive. Witnesses on the ground watched horrified as 'G-George', burning fiercely, came spinning and side-slipping down on them to crash in a field in the small hamlet of Oranji in the district of Smilde. Key injured his foot and was soon captured. Although Rex attempted to escape and had some help from local residents he too was eventually captured.

The rest of the force went on to Essen, but within a few miles of the enemy coast 83 Squadron had already lost twelve men dead that night. Also from 83 Squadron, Pilot Officer Morphett had to release two of his six 1,000 lb bombs into the sea when L7423 steadfastly refused to climb. He pressed on to the target although the aircraft still only reached 9,500ft.

All three of the 207 Squadron Manchesters still airborne ran into heavy and intense flak over the Ruhr and were further inconvenienced by searchlights. Flight Lieutenant Ruth was only able to attack the last resort target. Squadron Leader Murray's aircraft was hit in the tail by flak leaving the target, whilst L7484 piloted by Flight Sergeant Hathersich was seriously damaged by a large calibre flak shell, which fortunately passed through the fuselage without exploding. The shell nevertheless started a fire amongst the ammunition chutes to the mid-upper turret, rounds in which began popping off. With great presence of mind, Sergeant Everett, the wireless operator, beat the fires out with his hands before they got out of control.

The remaining force from 83 Squadron experienced similar savage searchlight and flak defences. R5831 with Squadron Leader McClure was slightly damaged by flak, whilst only Flying Officer Hazelden believed he had hit the Krupps works themselves. The 61 Squadron crews were unable to identify the

Rear of Mk.IA R5830 'OL-L' of 83 Squadron following early return by Squadron Leader McClure on the night of 28/29th March 1942. The aircraft was seriously damaged by a night fighter and equipment had to be jettisoned to remain airborne on the return flight, a frequent Manchester problem.

Aircrew and groundcrew of 83 Squadron at Scampton in front of 'OL-B'.
Both via Chaz Bowyer

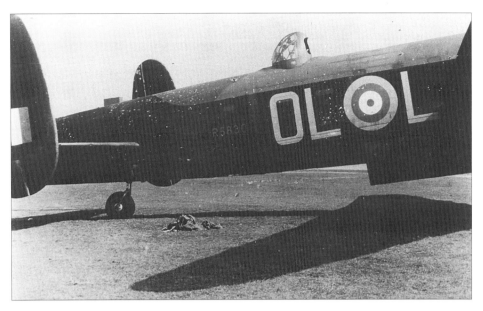

intended concentrated mass of burning incendiaries dropped by the target markers and had great difficulty identifying any target. On the return flight Pilot Officer Smith dived to low level where his gunners could range onto ground targets. They particularly concentrated their attention on searchlights, several of which were extinguished.

The surviving 20 Manchesters from the Essen force returned to base. All had experienced the effects of the ferocious flak barrage, but two had been fatally stalked and brought down by the rapidly expanding German night fighter force. The results of the new technique were a great disappointment, GEE showed itself a navigation aid but not a blind bombing aid. Many crews still had difficulty operating the set and of the 20 illuminators it later transpired that only eleven dropped their flares on the GEE fix.

Out of 43 identifiable photographs, none showed any recognisable feature of the target area. The aiming point, the Krupp factory, was not hit at all and only a few bombs fell on the south part of Essen. Only a few houses were destroyed, ten civilians were killed and 19 missing. The Essen authorities classified it as a light raid. The raid was a great disappointment and a major contrast with Billancourt only a few days earlier. The raids were in many respects a rehearsal for the full blooded Battle of the Ruhr which began almost a year later on 5/6th March 1943. Then, as in March 1942, Bomber Command were to find the Ruhr a very hard nut to crack.

The nights of 9/10th and 10/11th March 1942 were in many respects repetitions of the first assault. Ten and 13 Manchesters respectively were dispatched and there were no casualties. On 9/10th two of 207 Squadron's six Manchesters were scrubbed prior to take-off and a third returned with engine overheating after jettisoning its bombs near the Dutch coast. Two of the remaining three aircraft were damaged by flak. All six Manchesters of 83 Squadron attacked.

Next night 207 Squadron mustered six aircraft. One failed to take-off and three returned early due to engine troubles and inability to climb. One of the two aircraft which did participate was damaged by flak over Essen. All eight 61 Squadron aircraft dis-

patched attacked Essen and, with fire in their bellies, two crews, those of Flying Officer Archibald, L7497, and Pilot Officer Smith, L7518, dived to low level for the return flight and engaged themselves in the increasingly popular searchlight suppression activities. Crews felt safer from both heavy flak and night fighters at ground level and could participate in some offensive activity. On this latter night, cloud cover presented target location difficulties, but still 62 aircraft from the 126 aircraft force claimed to have attacked Essen.

These claims are at marked variance with actual experiences of the residents of Essen. Only two bombs hit industrial targets: the railway lines near the Krupp factory. In the town itself there was minimal damage. One house was destroyed, five civilians killed and 12 injured. Even within this small group not all casualties were a direct consequence of bombing. One of the five killed was a Polish immigrant worker standing outside an air

raid shelter who was hit by a descending unexploded 88mm flak shell! Failures hardly come more total.

With this operation 207 completed its almost 18 months active service with the Manchester and gladly moved on to Lancasters. Right to the bitter end engine problems had dogged the unit and continually conspired, despite everyone's best efforts, to reduce the effective striking power of the unit.

For ten days in March front line Manchester strength fell to two squadrons, but by now a fifth squadron, 106, was working up to operations on Manchesters at Scampton. No. 106 Squadron's involvement with the Manchester was to be deployed mainly over the short six week period between 20th March and 10th May, although it did supply Manchesters for each of the 1,000 bomber raids. During the period, 106 Squadron concentrated to a large extent on mining activities, in which sphere it became expert.

Aircrew of 83 Squadron in front of one of their Manchesters at Scampton.

Manchester I L7465 'OL-H' of 83 Squadron, Scampton. The aircraft was lost with Sergeant Markidcs and his entire crew on a raid to Essen, 25/26th March 1942.
Both via Chaz Bowyer

catching alight and feathered the propeller. They flew in over The Wash and located one of the homing beacons, but were unable to contact base. On one engine, unable to locate a safe landing strip and with control still marginal, Hubbard ordered the crew to bale out at 4,000ft. The pilot himself managed to escape when the aircraft had descended to 2,000ft, the starboard engine catching fire shortly afterwards. The aircraft crashed in flames near Wittering and the crew all descended safely, Sergeant Tom Stanley landing in a tree.

The second Manchester lost that night was L7423 'OL-S' from 83 Squadron, flown by Pilot Officer Bromiley. In a repetition of the recent loss of the two 83 Squadron machines four days earlier, Bromiley was intercepted by a German night fighter whilst en route to the target and shot down at Brockhuizen near Nenlow in Holland. Only two crew members survived, one of whom, Sergeant J Dowd, was to have his story recounted in the famous account *Escape or Die* by Paul Brickhill.

The night of 25/26th March 1942 was an integral part of the most tragic 24 hours in the entire lifespan of the Manchester, with five aircraft written off and many crew members killed. At this time the sixth squadron, No. 50, at Skellingthorpe was taking delivery of Manchesters at the start of its re-equipment programme. Mk.IA L7486 was a newly arrived aircraft recently taken over from 207 Squadron and became the first casualty. In the evening of 25th March Sergeant Atkinson and his crew were engaged in circuits and landings to familiarise themselves with the type. On one of his first approaches at 1915 hours Atkinson held off, ballooned once and stalled the aircraft onto the runway on one wheel from 20ft, collapsing the undercarriage. The aircraft caught fire, but the crew managed to escape with minor injuries. The local fire-fighting facilities were inadequate to prevent the aircraft burning out.

The three operational squadrons, Nos. 61, 83 and 106, were briefed to follow up operations to Essen that night, with an additional Manchester from 106 delegated to 'gardening'. No. 61 produced the major contribution of ten aircraft, 83 produced five, whilst 106 sent four bombers and the 'gardener'. The raid was part of Bomber Command's developing experiments with target location and marking.

Whilst Bomber Command concentrated on the development and refinement of its new techniques, Manchester losses began to increase perceptibly in proportion to the force dispatched. Just how harrowing bomber operations could be for an unlucky crew can be demonstrated from the final three operations of Pilot Officer Hubbard and his crew over just a two week period. How crews could continue to fly and still carry out their orders with such fortitude and bravery almost defies belief.

On 10/11th March Hubbard and his crew in L7473 joined the bomber force attacking Essen. They flew through heavy flak to bomb the target and soon after turning for home sustained a very near miss from a flak burst just below the bomb bay, which jolted the aircraft skywards momentarily and peppered it with splinters. A check of all instruments revealed no sign of damage and they returned safely to England, where an undercarriage check prior to landing produced two reassuring 'greens'. Unbeknown to them the starboard main wheel was punctured. In

the pitched darkness at 0045 this was not apparent to any of the crew until L7473 touched down. Before any speed was lost the aircraft fell onto its starboard undercarriage legs, slewed violently to the right and sheared off the undercart. L7473 was severely damaged but did not catch fire. Hubbard and his crew were shaken and unnerved but suffered only minor physical injury.

On the 13/14th, 61 and 83 Squadrons rostered 16 Manchesters to attack Cologne and Hubbard was down to fly again, this time in L7395. Once again two of the 16 strong force were lost. Outward bound over the North Sea, Hubbard began to experience serious control difficulties and L7395 continually stalled at 150mph as he attempted to climb. In a desperate attempt to save the aircraft and crew, Hubbard jettisoned the bomb load safe 50 miles offshore and turned for home. Control difficulties eased but immediately after establishing the return course a coolant leak developed in the port engine, which overheated and began smoking badly. Hubbard shut down the engine to prevent it

On crossing the enemy coast inbound, the crew of Warrant Officer Whitehead's 83 Squadron Manchester could clearly distinguish sky marking flares over a target ahead, but these had burnt out by the time they arrived. Whitehead followed another aircraft into the target area, which released a load of incendiaries and flares. Whitehead backed up and bombed onto these, but his navigator doubted they had fallen on the primary target. It was a typical Manchester operation in many respects, with Pilot Officer Lumb of 83 Squadron having to release a 1,000 lb bomb over the North Sea to ensure a safe crossing of the enemy coast inbound.

From 106 Squadron the 'gardening' Manchester returned to base when the front and rear turrets both developed hydraulic leaks. The Ruhr was, as usual, hazy, which made target location problematical and most air-

This photograph, together with reports from survivors from Flying Officer Hubbard's aircraft, also lost on the night of 25/26th March 1942, vividly portrays the awesome destructive power of German night fighters. Here, L7497 of 61 Squadron is already disintegrating whilst Oberleutnant Woltersdorf still has his finger on the firing button. Sergeant Furby and his crew fell at Werterbruch, near Bolholt, on the Dutch/German border. Oberleutnant Woltersdorf was in turn killed on 6th June 1942. *Aders / Rapp*

craft chose to bomb on the flares. Anti-aircraft opposition was not heavy on this occasion but Warrant Officer Merralls' 106 Squadron Manchester was damaged by flak. Despite the flak defences being relatively subdued, night fighters were apparently active and engagements were reported by several aircraft.

Sergeant Markides in Manchester L7465 'OL-H' of 83 Squadron was shot down. The aircraft crashed at Lichtaert in Belgium with the loss of the entire crew. It is likely that they were victims of a night fighter. Flight Lieutenant Dunlop-Mackenzie in L7390 of 106 Squadron was intercepted by Oberleutnant Ludwig Becker of 6II/NJG2 at Leeuwarden and crashed on the ice of the Ijsselmeer near Kornwerderzand in Holland. Dunlop-Mackenzie was on his first operation in a Manchester and again there were no survivors in the crew.

Several of 61 Squadron's crews found the flares useful in locating the target and employed their customary gliding or diving attacks. On the return journey Flying Officer Gilpin dived to 4,000ft near the Ijsselmeer to fire at four troublesome searchlights. One light was dowsed and the attack attracted light tracer in reply, which failed to find the swooping Manchester. Squadron Leader McClure of 83 Squadron had already witnessed an aircraft shot down at 52°43'N 04°56'E, from which one parachute was seen to open and then be held in searchlights. Flying Officer Gunter of 61 Squadron observed

an aircraft shot down in flames at the Dutch coast on his return flight. This was possibly Dunlop-Mackenzie or, more likely, his fellow squadron member Pilot Officer Hubbard.

No. 61 Squadron indeed lost two Manchesters. Sergeant Furby in L7497 fell with his entire crew at Werterbruch near Bolholt on the Dutch/German border, following attack by Oberleutnant Woltersdorf, and again were no survivors. Hubbard's aircraft did have two survivors and from them the story of their ruthless and pitiless destruction has been reconstructed. On this night, John Hubbard was allocated Manchester Mk.IA, L7518 'QR-O', and his crew, in addition to himself, were Pilot Officer Buchan RCAF (second pilot, on his first operation), Pilot Officer Heggie (navigator), Flight Sergeant Clelland (wireless operator), Sergeant Baker (front gunner), Sergeant P Jones (mid-upper gunner) and Sergeant T Stanley (rear gunner).

Early on a bright moonlit evening Hubbard took off and headed east for the familiar maelstrom of 'Happy Valley'. Despite their recent close shaves, a grim humour supported the well-drilled crew. The Dutch coast slid beneath them and at 2155 hours they got their first sight of the target, burning, ahead and in the distance. Jones felt the familiar tightening of his stomach as the well practised exchanges between the crew commenced. So far they had traversed the searchlight belt undetected, but as they commenced their bombing run they began to be heavily engaged by flak.

Bob Heggie moved down to the bomb aiming position and after some minutes announced over the intercom that he was 'All set for business'. Hubbard steadied the Manchester as they ran in to the aiming point. Scanning the sky around them Jones took in a Handley Page Hampden to port trapped in a cone of searchlights having the living daylights pasted out of it by the flak gunners. To starboard and below the same thing was happening to a Wellington. In turn, both burst into flames and plunged earthwards. The gunners were knocking three bells out of L7518 too, but Hubbard's approach was unswerving and so far nothing vital had been hit. The release of tension when the bombs dropped free was almost audible. Someone voiced the feelings of all of them, 'Let's get the hell out of here!' and another 'Put the nose down Johnny and let's go home'. The bomb doors closed, Hubbard was only too happy to comply.

Flak continued to pound them, but as they eventually drew clear Hubbard gave a reassuring call to keep up crew morale. 'OK lads, we'll make it'. As they continued to weave and corkscrew back towards the Dutch coast both Jones and Stanley became aware of a new threat. Searchlights were pointing up on either side, forming a lighted avenue down which they were forced to fly. As they moved out of range other lights ahead took over. They took this as a sure signal that night fighter attacks were imminent and immediately redoubled their vigilance. However, there was to be no escape for L7518 that night and their 'charmed life' was approaching a brutal end. Long, tense minutes passed with no sighting of any incoming attack and they had reached as far as the Dutch coastal zone.

They began to hope that attention had passed to other homecoming bombers behind.

Suddenly Jones spotted a twin engined aircraft closing fast and from the lower port quarter. Jones yelled a warning as he traversed his turret and began a disciplined defence, firing off short bursts one after another as the Me110 bored in. Almost at the same instant the fighter opened up, raking them with a devastatingly accurate volley of cannon and machine gun fire. Tracking the Me110 as it rose up over them, Jones was momentarily distracted by a burst of firing from another source. A hasty glance revealed that Tom Stanley, in turn, had opened up on a second stalking Me110, his tracer crossing with that of the additional assailant dead astern. They certainly had their hands full.

The first Me110 broke off above, receiving a parting burst from Jones' twin Brownings, whilst the second dived down beneath, overtaking them. Immediately the guns fell silent Jones was shocked to smell smoke and traversing his turret saw that the front of the aircraft was on fire. Finding the intercom u/s, both gunners vacated their turrets and one elected to go forward for instructions. Pushing open the armoured doors a scene of utter devastation met his eyes. The inside of the fuselage was a shambles, with holes everywhere. To his left the wireless operator, Flight Sergeant Jock Clelland, was crouched unhurt, conscientiously sending out news of their attack to base. Beyond, the observer was slumped over his table apparently lifeless. Stepping forward the gunner discerned the second pilot sprawled dead in the gangway. The pilot was hanging in his straps, head lolling to one side, seriously wounded but doggedly fighting with his remaining con-

sciousness to hold the stick and maintain some control. Flames were leaping up in places and one long glance was enough to convince the gunner that the aircraft and part of the crew were doomed.

He began his retreat aft from the flames and heat, tapping Jock Clelland urgently on the back as he did so. Clelland nodded and rose to follow him, but suddenly turned on his heel and bent to his set to accomplish some final task. As he did so a further fighter attack developed, unannounced and uncontested from dead ahead. As before, the attack had pin-point accuracy and devastating effect. Tracer and exploding cannon shells ripped through the cockpit area again and Clelland folded up onto his set and lay still. The pilot, too, must have been hit again, because the nose went down and the aircraft entered a shallow spiral dive. In a last valiant act the trusty Hubbard summoned his fast draining strength, raised his head and signalled the gunner to bale out.

Flames of renewed intensity flared in the cockpit and there could clearly be little time left. Returning aft the gunner assisted his companion to don his parachute before opening the rear entry door. Sergeant Jones dived out of the gyrating aircraft followed later by Sergeant Stanley. Peter Jones felt a terrific jerk that drove virtually every breath from his body as his 'chute opened, but came round in the cool, sweet, peaceful air in time to see L7518 spiralling down beneath, outlined in fire with both engines still roaring. Tom Stanley was not so fortunate, his jump took him face first into the tailplane as it swung to the right in front of him. The impact broke his nose and almost rendered him unconscious. Racked by pain from his wounds and the injuries received in his collision with the tail, Stanley expended precious seconds before he regained his senses sufficiently to wrench the D-ring of his parachute. There was a merciful explosion of silk above him, but before the 'chute fully deployed and his downward speed was completely arrested, he plunged into the water and mud of what turned out to be a small canal.

Manchester L7518, with its remaining five crew members, had crashed to earth nearby only a few seconds earlier, erupting in a fireball as the flames found the remaining fuel load. Stanley must have taken some time to collect and orientate himself and disentangle

Left to right: Neville Patton (rear gunner); unknown; Peter Kent (second pilot); Ken Leyshon (wireless operator); Eric Noble (captain) in front of Mk.IA L7497 'QR-?' of 61 Squadron at Woolfox Lodge, 1942. L7497 was lost with Sergeant Furby and his crew on the night of 25/26th March 1942. Flight Sergeant Noble and his crew were killed on the night of 6/7th April 1942. *D H MacSporran*

Capturing the essential spirit of the aircraft – L7427 'OL-Q' of 83 Squadron taken from a sister aircraft in March 1942. Released for press publication on 21st April 1942, by which time the aircraft had been lost with its crew on a raid to Hamburg on its 16th 'op' with Pilot Officer Morphett and his crew on 8/9th April. A sortie tally of ten can be discerned just behind the front turret, ahead of the propeller blur. *via Chaz Bowyer*

himself from his 'chute. Painfully he dragged himself up the bank and, seeing figures outlined in the glare from the blazing aircraft, found his emergency whistle and blew it. One figure turned towards him, turning out to be not the expected Sergeant Jones, but the village doctor, Rein Posthuma from the village of Warmenhuizen, a village between Alkmaar and Schagen. Tom Stanley's injuries, in addition to his broken nose and bruised face, included a bullet in the right shoulder, a second in the side and a third in his right thigh, plus numerous shrapnel splinters.

Jones had baled out higher and opened his 'chute earlier, resulting in him reaching ground level last of all. As he drifted lower he distinguished an expanse of water beneath and had no more time than to think 'out of the fire and into the kettle' before plunging into it. Although he had clearly seen the aircraft crash on land, Jones himself was gripped by the fear of the limitless size of the North Sea into which he had the misfortune to descend. He inflated his 'Mae West', unbuckled his parachute harness and struck out for a group of three or four searchlights on the shore some distance away. He took care first to check his watch, being surprised to find it still ticking. Noting the time at 2235,

he took it off his wrist and placed it in the special pocket in his 'Mae West'. The cold was numbing and he rested every 10 minutes or so to regain his strength. He was at the limits of endurance with his own wounds, exhaustion and hypothermia when he reached a muddy shoreline about three hours later.

He lay in a ploughed field sleeping in fits and starts till daybreak when he awoke to find his flying suit frozen solid. Having engaged in vigorous exercise to get the circulation going, he struck off inland, crossing fields and swimming or wading the many canals. Whilst crossing one of these he had no time to hide when a barge rowed by four Dutchmen and with two armed German soldiers appeared. The first soldier raised his machine pistol and with a grin gestured for Jones to put his hands on his head and join them in the barge.

Marched a mile and a half across country to the nearby village, Jones and his guards were met by a car which took them to the nearby airfield. Here he queue-jumped the usual group crowded outside the medical officer's office and could not resist a rueful smile at their shocked response to seeing 'a victim of operational flying' at first hand. He was freezing cold, soaking wet, plastered in mud, his hair matted with dried blood and his body peppered with shrapnel splinters. The station doctor then cleaned him up and dressed his wounds before he was permitted to sleep.

Later he was transported to Amsterdam jail where, after a couple of days, he received a visit from the German night fighter pilot who claimed to have shot them down. German records attribute the victory to the rising fighter ace Hauptmann Helmut Lent of II/NJG2 at Leeuwarden in Holland and the time of the engagement to 0032. The discrep-

ancy in time may be accounted for by the difference in British local time and that in Europe over the war period. The visitor expressed his sympathy to Jones for the loss of five of his crew mates whose bodies had been found in the wreckage. Sergeant Stanley was being held in Amsterdam hospital he was told. Their destruction had been ruthlessly efficient and merciless. No quarter had been asked or given and Jones learned that return fire from the rear or mid-upper turret guns had killed the radio operator/gunner in the night fighter. In their last three operations, 10th March to Essen, 13th March to Cologne and now 25th March to Essen, Pilot Officer Hubbard and his crew had crashed each time. Now they finally had their ultimate disaster.

Four Manchesters had been lost in quick succession on this single night, and from the 28 crew members only two survived. At least three Manchesters were victims of the German night fighters. The Manchester loss rate for the night was four out of 20 or 20%.

Deflected from the Ruhr by its lack of success, Command considered other targets within GEE range. Target location was always easier for coastal sites and if these proved to be only lightly defended they would be all the more appropriate at this stage in the development of area bombing techniques. Eyes fell on Lubeck on the Baltic coast, a medieval town containing a warren of ancient wooden houses. The Bomber Command Operational Research Station appraised it as 'a particularly suitable target for testing the effect of a very heavy attack with incendiary bombs'. Harris' own evaluation was more emotive. It was 'built more like a fire lighter than a human habitation'. Lubeck thus became a target principally on grounds of its operational vulnerability.

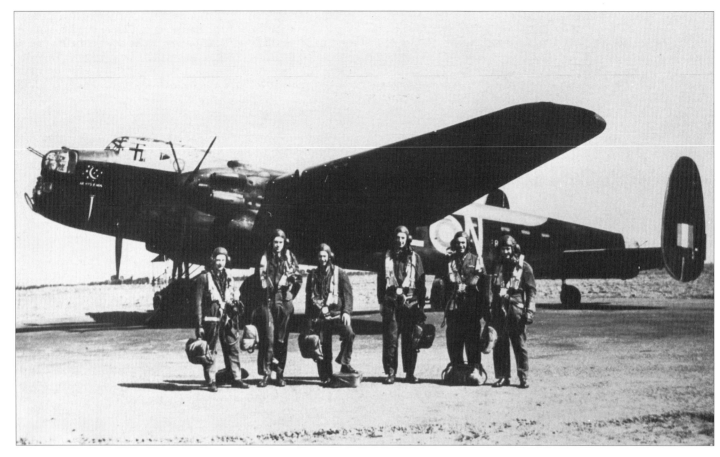

On the night of 28/29th March 234 bombers, guided by GEE for much of the outward leg, attacked Lubeck using the SHAKER technique. Twenty-one Manchesters from 61, 83 and 106 Squadrons were involved. Attacking aircraft released some 300 tons of bombs, almost half of which were incendiaries, in a devastating attack. The old town burned like tinder and the firefighters below were totally overwhelmed. Afterwards some 45–50% of the whole city, 190 acres, were judged destroyed; 1,425 houses were demolished, 1,976 heavily damaged and 8,000 to a lesser extent. More than 300 citizens were killed and 780 injured, making the heaviest death toll inflicted on a German population to date.

Bomber Command had finally shown that it could wreak major devastation from the air and Command itself and Britain in general in these darkest of days, celebrated the achievement with considerable satisfaction. In truth it had required the combined effects of GEE, excellent visibility including a full moon, negligible defences in the target area and an attack from as little as 2,000ft on the wooden fabric, but it had been done. Bomber Command never raided Lubeck again in strength. One Manchester, that of Flying Officer Lumb of 83 Squadron, was lost with the entire crew.

Next night the three serving Manchester squadrons dispatched only eight aircraft between them for mining operations to the NECTARINE area off Terschelling on the Dutch coast. Flight Sergeant Dimond of 106 Squadron and Pilot Officer Churchill of 61 Squadron, both on their first full operation as Manchester captains, failed to return. There were no survivors from either aircraft. This represented 25% of the Manchester force dispatched.

As April 1942 began, for the first and virtually only time, four Manchester squadrons were operational together. No. 50 Squadron at Skellingthorpe had been the sixth squadron to receive Manchesters and had been working up for some time. The overlap only lasted for a few days because 61 and 83 Squadrons were both at an advanced stage in converting to Lancasters. Not surprisingly, squadrons could not get rid of their Manchesters quickly enough.

On the night of 8/9th April 1942, 18 Manchesters were raised for operations from amongst the four squadrons. No. 50 dispatched its first operation, when three aircraft carried out a leaflet raid, being joined by a further two from 83 Squadron. In addition 61, 83 and 106 raised in turn three, five and five bombers to attack Hamburg. Sadly for 83 Squadron they were to lose two more aircraft that night, a total of 11% of the force.

Pilot Officer Hedley Hazelden was one of the seven Manchester pilots briefed for Hamburg. His usual co-pilot, Sergeant Zaleschuk, was replaced by Wing Commander Crighton-Biggie ('CB') who had been posted to command 83 Squadron from a desk job at Air

Manchester IA R5833 'OL-N' of 'B' Flight 83 Squadron at Scampton, 8th April 1942. The crew are, left to right: Sergeant J Bushby; Pilot Officer Billings; Sergeants Dodsworth; Baines; Williams and their captain, Warrant Officer Whitehead. The moon and stars crescent is inscribed in Welsh, *Ar hyd y nos* (All through the night). *via R Low / F Harper, 83 Squadron archives*

Ministry. Crighton-Biggie was one of the giants of Bomber Command, well-known to everyone in 5 Group but who never became a household name like some of his peers. Crighton-Biggie commenced by doing a few trips with second tour captains to gain operational experience. Later he went on to fly operations with every crew in the squadron and was a real tower of strength. His second operational trip was on 8/9th April 1942. Their aircraft that night was L7484, a Mk.IA and the bomb load six 1,000 lb GP.

All went normally on the outward leg, the target was attacked and Hazelden turned L7484 towards home. As they settled down on the homeward leg they soon began experiencing over-heating of the starboard Vulture. By the time they crossed the German coast at 9,000ft, heading out into the Heligoland Bight, they observed wide and rapid radiator temperature fluctuations on the engine. Their initial diagnosis was a faulty gauge, but this theory was hastily abandoned when the engine began throwing trails of sparks from the exhausts, which soon turned to a long tongue of flame.

In the darkened cockpit both 'CB' and Hazelden went for the feathering button, each unaware of the other's action (shades of Bill Hills and Derek Bowes-Cavanagh in 207 Squadron). The feathering buttons were located near the bottom of the instrument panel towards the right hand side. From the pilot's seat, Hazelden leaned across, felt what he thought was the port button and pressed the next on the right, which should have been the starboard. Looking over his right shoulder he watched the propeller wind down and stop. The flames disappeared. As Hazelden tried to retrim the aircraft he was surprised to find little change considering the asymmetry of the thrust.

A casual, if somewhat strained, remark from the wireless operator, Flight Sergeant C J Taylor, on the intercom drew his attention, 'Seems a trifle quiet in here, Skip' and made him glance round at the port engine. That, too, was feathered and stopped! Hazelden's first thought was that somehow both circuits had operated from the single button, but to unfeather the port engine was now urgent and imperative. A torch was produced and used to illuminate the pitch dark cockpit, alerting night fighters by so doing being a lesser risk.

Feathering and unfeathering was achieved by depressing the same button, with separate buttons for each engine. Pressing once and holding-in resulted in feathering. Re-press and hold unfeathered the propeller. On unfeathering, the point at which to release the hold was difficult to judge, to release too soon was meant that the propeller would not have reached the blade angular range for constant speeding, whereas holding too long could easily result in the blade passing straight through the constant speeding range towards full fine pitch, with resultant overspeed. This last eventuality Hazelden was determined to avoid at all costs, with the result that he twice released the button too soon and had to go back to the feathered position and start again. There was much bated breath all round. On the third attempt he was successful and power was restored on the port engine at 4,500ft, exactly half the altitude at which the emergency had occurred.

Using full rated power, Hazelden then set about discovering how to fly the aircraft to maintain height. Strange to say by present standards, they had no information on speeds, heights, weights, power settings etc for single engine flying. Over the next half hour or so they lost a further 500ft and discovered by trial and error that in their condition a speed of 137 knots IAS was best, since at both 140 and 135 knots the rate of descent was greater. Hazelden reckoned this rate of

descent was tolerable as they would reach UK territory before running out of atmosphere. In fact they were able to maintain 4,000ft, probably due to using up fuel, and after running the port Vulture at full throttle for an hour and a half they reached Horsham St Faith and thankfully landed.

The subsequent inquest revealed that in the original emergency 'CB' and Hazelden were both feeling in the dark for the feathering button on the starboard engine. 'CB' found the first button, which was indeed the starboard, and pressed it. Hazelden found what he took to be the port and pressed the next one on the right. This turned out to be the port engine feathering button because what he had found first was the brake pressure gauge.

Pilot Officer Hazelden and crew were consequently more fortunate than two of their fellow crews. Pilot Officer Morphett in L7427 'OL-Q' was one of those who failed to return. His rear gunner was the sole survivor, but unfortunately died whilst a prisoner of war. Manchesters were now highly vulnerable even during the shallowest – penetration introductory Freshman raids, as evident from the loss of the second 83 Squadron aircraft on the night of 8/9th April and a 61 Squadron machine two nights later. Pilot Officer Sproule was on an introductory NICKEL raid on Paris in R5837 prior to commencing his operational career. On 8/9th April he was carrying an eight man crew, with an Intelligence Officer (IO) along to gain operational experience. Unfortunately R5837 was hit by flak near Calais, which stopped one of the engines. Sproule tried to return on the remaining one but was unable to maintain height, eventually alighting on the sea near Margate. An SOS had been sent out but the aircraft settled so swiftly that only Sproule was able to locate the dinghy. The pilot spent 14 hours afloat before being picked up by the Air Sea Rescue Service. A grim sidelight on this tragedy was that when the unfortunate widow of the IO tried to claim a pension on her loss she was told she was not eligible because her man was officially AWOL!

On the night of 10/11th April 1942 the main force operated to Essen. At this time 61 Squadron had about double the number of aircrews as Manchesters. Sergeant Don MacSporran was waiting to fly his first operation as a captain with his own crew. Accordingly he was rostered to take Manchester R5785, 'QR-M', on a 'Nursery' raid to Le Havre.

Wing Commander Weir briefed MacSporran carefully, explaining that R5785 was the squadron's worst Manchester. It was badly in need of a 'ring job' and as a result the engines did not produce as much power as they should, which severely restricted the take-off and altitude performance. Weir made it quite clear that if it became evident that the aircraft was letting them down they were not to hesitate to turn back.

As they droned southwards across England, MacSporran tried to coax the best ceiling he could from the struggling Manchester, but eventually found that 9,000ft was the maximum possible. He had decided to cross the French coast west of Deauville before turning left and carrying out the bombing run on an northerly track, which would carry them out across the Channel and towards home. Having crossed the enemy coast he turned and, heading northwards, entered a gentle dive to let down to 8,000ft at the point of bomb release.

Immediately the bombs fell away the aircraft was enveloped by an intense accurate flak barrage. Shrapnel was slashing through the airframe in many places and the pilot felt a distinctive twitch in the control column as fragments perforated the ailerons.

Converted Mk.IA R5837 'OL-R' allegedly waiting to be bombed up at Scampton on 8th April 1942. That night the aircraft ditched near Margate after aborting a NICKEL raid on Paris with flak damage. The pilot, Pilot Officer Sproule, was the sole survivor. Some sources quote R5837 as 'OL-J'. *via R Low / F Harper, 83 Squadron archives*

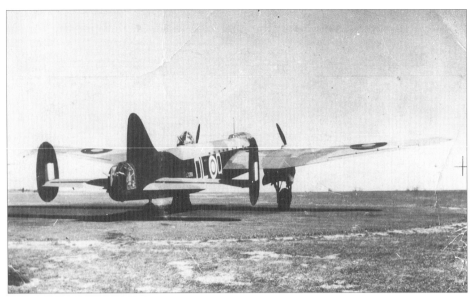

MacSporran had expected to come out of the flak within a short period, but when he looked round for any reason why they were still suffering the unabated fury of the defenders he was shocked to find the aircraft had turned back and was heading inland again. The starboard engine had failed, with the result that the aircraft had yawed to the right and swung back on a southerly heading.

The pilot then feathered the starboard propeller and turned left again towards the good engine and finally made it out to sea. By this time they were down to 4,000ft, their speed had fallen to 120mph and they were descending at 400ft/min. Just before crossing the coast, MacSporran called the crew and gave them all the option of baling out over land, but all decided to stay aboard in the hope of making the English coast.

Regrettably, even with the throttle of the port Vulture fully open, MacSporran could do nothing to prevent them descending into the sea about 20 miles off the French coast. He barely had time to pull back on the stick before they wallowed into the sea at a mere 100mph. The aircraft neither bounced nor skated on the surface, but dug its nose in and stopped abruptly. R5785 sank very quickly under them and they all got soaked escaping from the hatches. As they cast off, the tail swung up, towering over them, and 'M-Mother' plunged vertically to the bottom. All seven crew had reached the dinghy safely.

They remained at sea undetected until the afternoon of 16th April when, in weakened condition, they finally fetched up on rocks on the Cherbourg peninsula only 50 feet off-shore. Four of the crew tried to swim the last few feet but it was at this point that the wireless operator, Sergeant Dave Meikle, finally used up the remainder of his strength, his head dropped forward into the water and he drowned. The dinghy itself finally floated into the shore and the remaining crew were able to disembark to captivity.

A late starter, L7289 from the initial production batch of 20 went initially into store at 37 Maintenance Unit, Burtonwood, being finally reworked at Avro and reaching 83 Squadron on 11th April 1942, where it became 'OL-Q'. It only undertook one sortie before being passed to 50 Squadron, where it failed to return from its first operation with Sergeant Roy.

Mk.I L7385 'OL-C' of 83 Squadron being bombed up with three 2,000lb armour piercers at Scampton, March/April 1942. L7385 met a gruesome fate with 207 'Con' Flight on the evening of 6th August 1942 when Lancaster R5550 taxied head on into it as it flared for landing at Bottesford.
Both via Chaz Bowyer

As Manchester activity diminished from mid-April onwards, with only 50 and 106 Squadrons still active on the aircraft, losses thus remained high. A total of nine Manchesters were lost during April.

Consistent with the continuation and development of its area bombing techniques, Bomber Command had been planning a series of hammer blows on Rostock on the Baltic coast. These fell on four consecutive nights between the 23rd and 26th April. Only six, nine, five and nine Manchesters respectively could be mustered for this assault, the aircraft consequently playing only a minor role. Unlike Lubeck, Rostock contained a number of important industries, shipbuilding, an Arado aircraft factory and the Heinkel works at Marienehe in the suburbs. It, too, was lightly defended and easy to locate. Bomber Command was at this time simultaneously striving to test the twin tactics of a concentrated incendiary area attack combined with a precision high explosive attack. The precision attack was entrusted to the 5 Group squadrons, which had strived to perfect navigational and bombing accuracy.

The first two attacks went in on April 23/24th (161 aircraft) and April 24/25th (125 aircraft) and both were disappointing. Despite clear skies and a bright moon, the Heinkel factory was not hit and most of the bombs fell 2–6 miles wide. No. 106 Squadron lost Pilot Officer Stoffer in the first attack. It is reported that an engine overheated and caught fire. Six of the crew baled out, but the main spar burnt through and the aircraft shed a wing, carrying Stoffer to his death near Tinglev in Denmark.

On the third night of the series of raids on Rostock (25/26th) 128 aircraft were dispatched including 16 from 5 Group. Only 106 Squadron operated Manchesters that night, when Wing Commander Guy Gibson led five. One aircraft made an early return, but the remainder overflew the factory from only 5,000ft. Of 71 night photographs, 30 showed the centre of Rostock, a further 35 were within five miles of the centre and three showed the factory itself. The operation was a triumph. Finally, on the last night (26/27th), 107 aircraft were dispatched, with both 5 and 3 Group going for the Heinkel factory.

P/O Harold Southgate captained one of the four 50 Squadron aircraft briefed for this final raid on Rostock. Only two days previously he had attacked the same target from 7,000ft, rejoicing in the almost total lack of opposition. This night, in L7432, he viewed the 7½–8 hour operation as a 'piece of cake'. The aircraft carried six 1,000 lb GP and Southgate was sufficiently emboldened by his recent experience to elect to attack Rostock from 4,000ft. The outward flight was uneventful and Southgate's observer, Sergeant Shirley, brought them onto Rostock from the agreed approach direction. On the final approach at 4,000ft, with the bomb doors

open, all hell broke loose from the hastily reinforced flak defences below.

Guns of all calibres ranged on the aircraft, shells burst all round and the aircraft jolted steadily as it took a series of hits. In desperation and with little height in hand, Southgate nosed forward to increase their speed in the hope of escaping the defences. Eventually, close to what they believed was the Aiming Point, the observer released the load from an almost fatal 2,000ft. Shortly afterwards the aircraft was punched skyward, as if by enormous fists, as the bombs detonated only a little to the rear. Within a short period numerous other crushing jolts from bombs released by aircraft overhead at a safer height buffeted the aircraft.

Neither the explosions nor the flak had damaged L7432 fatally and Southgate and his second pilot, Flight Sergeant Morgan, working in unison, were able to regain some semblance of control. They had taken several hits. The rudder had clearly been distorted by a near miss, although none of the other vital systems of the aircraft had been damaged. Lateral control forces had become extreme and the two pilots had to use all their combined strength to steady the aircraft. The flak gunners meanwhile appeared to have transferred their attention elsewhere and the two pilots were able to steer a course by bracing one leg locked straight on the rudder bars. In this condition and without any relief from the extreme physical effort they endured the three hour return to Skellingthorpe.

Once in the vicinity of base they radioed ahead for a priority landing, which was safely accomplished after further Herculean effort. Southgate vowed never again to underestimate the Germans' capability to reorganise and redeploy their defences.

On this night, the *pièce de resistance*, 92 aircraft reached the target and of the 52 photographs taken every one showed the target area – 13 showed the factory itself, where most 5 Group aircraft had attacked from 2,000ft. Subsequent reconnaissance showed widespread devastation and a second great victory for Bomber Command so soon after the attack on Lubeck. Furthermore, from the

The distinctive tail unit of a 106 Squadron Manchester, probably L7399 'ZN-X', amongst other wreckage after it crashed at Lilholt near Haderslev, Denmark, with F/Sgt Young, whilst engaged on a 'gardening' operation. Only two crew survived. *Birger Hansen*

four night, 521 sortie attack, only 12 aircraft were lost. Sixty per cent of the built-up area, 130 acres, were destroyed; 204 citizens were killed and 89 injured.

No. 50 Squadron at Skellingthorpe had now been operating Manchesters for three weeks of a desultory eight week period, whilst preparing for conversion to the Lancaster. Despite the rather short period and relatively restricted numbers of aircraft generally dispatched on operations, 50 were to lose 10 Manchesters on operations and another two in training. By this time, too, 49 Squadron at Scampton was working up on Manchesters to become the seventh and final squadron to receive the aircraft with a view to undertaking operational flying. No. 49 operated the aircraft on a small scale basis for less than a month, but were still to lose six Manchesters. Whilst Bomber Command had room to rejoice at the relatively modest casualty list from this period of shallow penetration operations, the Manchester crews were finally reaping the whirlwind for hanging on so long with a vulnerable and obsolescent type.

From late March onwards, 61, 83 and 106 and then 50 and 106 had invested a major effort in mining operations in the North Sea and beyond. No. 106 lost four of the total of its seven operational casualties in mine-laying operations. Frequently, the Manchesters lost during mining operations crashed at sea with no survivors. Just occasionally there were survivors to tell the tale, as was the case on 29/30th April 1942 when 50 Squadron sent five Manchesters to lay their 'vegetables' in the FORGET-ME-NOT, QUINCE, ENDIVE and RADISH marine areas. One aircraft returned early with violent buffeting of the rudders and three others were successful.

The experiences of Flight Sergeant Willett and crew in the fifth aircraft were every bit as harrowing as those of crews lost on attacks on land targets. They were allocated a former 61 Squadron Mk.IA, L7516 'VN-N', to attack Kiel Bay. For wireless operator Hector Macdonald this was to be his seventh Manchester operation in just 12 days. L7516 took off from Skellingthorpe at 2330 hours and all went according to plan until they were over Denmark on the return flight. Willett had just initiated a climb to give them some height in hand and the aircraft had reached 10,000ft, when the observer, Pilot Officer Hannah, reported his suspicion that one of their four mines had hung up. Macdonald took a torch to the observation port at the rear end of the bomb bay and shone it for Hannah, at the forward observation port, to confirm his suspicions. At this moment and without warning they were attacked from behind by a Me110 night fighter.

The Manchester shook under the impact of a number of 20mm shells, following which the fighter broke away. Willett called the rear gunner for a situation report, but, being unable to raise him, sent Macdonald from his intercom position aft of the bomb bay. As Macdonald approached he could see that the turret was fully traversed on the port beam and that Sergeant Williams was slumped over his guns, probably already dead. He was about to operate the 'dead man's handle' to rotate the turret and extricate the inert figure, when a second and devastating attack materialised. Macdonald himself was enveloped in tracer and in Willett's violent evasive manoeuvres was tossed around the rear fuselage.

In this follow up attack the aircraft was fatally damaged. Both engines caught fire, the wing tanks were punctured, the fuselage riddled. A stray round shorted out the lighting circuit turning all the lights, including the

landing lights, on. L7516 was now lit up like a Christmas tree. With the severe bumps and bruises he had sustained, Macdonald did not immediately realise that a shell splinter had severed several fingers on his left hand, which were left hanging by the skin. To add to the cacophony of noise, Sergeant Miners, the mid-upper gunner, loosed off a burst at the fighter as it closed in for the kill. Macdonald, still plugged in to the intercom and still unaware of his wounds, was the first to react when Willett, fighting to control the gyrating bomber, cried out 'Put those bloody lights off!'. Macdonald returned to the fuse box. Speed was the essence, and without taking the time to consult the list of fuse positions, began removing every fuse in turn until he found the one which doused the lights.

During the course of the attacks L7516 had lost much of the height it had gained and was now a fire trap. Macdonald heard Willett give an order to bale out, clearly indicating them to be over land. Moments later Willett called again, cancelling the order and saying they were back over water. An immediate ditching was inevitable. The fighter pilot must have recognised that the aircraft was doomed for no further attacks developed. With the mine still on board and with time for only minimal preparation of the aircraft by Willett, they bellied onto the water between Rantum and Morsum on Sylt. Instead of skating across the compliant surface they found that the aircraft hit a shallow submerged sand bank beneath, which brought them to an abrupt halt. Fortunately Macdonald did not receive any further serious injuries in the ditching. However, the front gunner, Sergeant Scott, and second pilot, Flight Sergeant Packard, were not so fortunate.

It transpired that when the order came to bale out both got down into the nose compartment and jettisoned the lower hatch.

What happened next is unclear, but it appears Scott left the aircraft, without his parachute, at too low a height. After Scott vacated the hatch, Packard, already cut off from the intercom, took his place sitting with his legs dangling in space prior to baling out. He was caught in this posture when L7516 bellied in, being thrown forward and trapped by the legs when the aircraft settled onto the sand beneath.

The captain, navigator, mid-upper gunner and Macdonald himself all scrambled out of the upper hatch. L7516 had settled by now in only two to three feet of water, but notwithstanding this, both engines continued to blaze and the oxygen bottles began to explode sporadically. With the mine still nestling in the wrecked bomb bay, petrol spewing out and 0.303in ammunition nearby, the four survivors hastened to leave the scene. The aircraft dinghy had failed to deploy. At this moment and before they could gather themselves together a splash and gasp from the water revealed the head of Packard bobbing to the surface. They dragged him onto the wing, alive but badly injured in the legs.

The bright moonlight, combined with the fact that a searchlight was trained on them across the water allowed the crew to see the coast. Bearing in mind the risk of explosion they decided to wade to the shore. However, they rapidly discovered that the sand bank was deeply dissected by tidal channels, which were precarious to cross, especially now that they were assisting the wounded Packard. Eventually they agreed to return to the burning wreck of L7516, but not before Hector Macdonald had come across the body of the front gunner floating in a tidal channel, his 'Mae West' inflated. Back at the wreck they perched on the wingtip, keeping as far from the flames as possible.

Soon afterwards an inflatable boat appeared and they were taken prisoner, Macdonald and Packard being conveyed straight to hospital where they had come down, on the island of Sylt. They had ditched at close to 0300 in the morning. Within days they received a stream of visitors, including Oberleutnant Günther Köberich, the pilot of the Me110 based at Westerland, who had shot them down. From him they learned that return fire from their mid-upper gunner had killed the rear gunner in the Messerschmitt.

Rear section of Mk.I L7434 'ZN-J' of 106 Squadron, Coningsby, *circa* May 1942. The aircraft undertook nine operations before being passed to 1656 Conversion Unit. *D Richards / 106 Squadron Association*

When Macdonald and Packard were suffi-ciently recovered from their injuries they were interrogated. It was apparent that the Germans had learned, possibly from mark-ings on their ditched aircraft, that they were assigned to 50 Squadron. Not only did they know the base at Skellingthorpe and the pre-vious history of their aircraft, but questioned them in detail about their CO, Wing Com-mander 'Beetle' Oxley, and his regular pep-talks to the crews in which he urged them to whip up what he called 'Hun-hate'. They had little doubt that Oxley would be high on the Gestapo wanted list.

On 2nd/3rd May 1942, 49 Squadron dis-patched a single preparatory NICKELLING operation as a gentle introduction to Man-chester operations and 50 Squadron a further three. No.106 Squadron dispatched eight Manchesters on a mining operation losing two of the force, or 25%. The Manchesters of Flight Sergeants Hurd and Young came down on land and there were survivors from both crews. Young was on his first operation.

Finally, on 8/9th May 1942, 11 Manchesters from 50 and 106 Squadrons were dispatched on operations. Two 50 Squadron aircraft went GARDENING and the remaining nine bombing at Warnemunde. Of the three air-craft element from 50 Squadron, Sergeant Gruber's aircraft was hit by flak over the tar-get, causing hydraulic failure and the open bomb doors meant severe height loss. They attempted to reach Sweden, but the star-board engine burst into flames over Den-mark. All but Gruber baled out. Sergeant Wilkie's aircraft so badly damaged by flak that it had to be written off on return to base.

From this time onwards Manchester oper-ational activity all but ceased. Lancasters were coming in to replace them and Bomber Command was conserving all aircraft in the

risky attempt to capture the political and military high ground by committing every operational aircraft and all reserves under advanced training to a cataclysmic thousand bomber raid. This would, at a stroke, almost quadruple the bomber force from its current 250–350 maximum. Manchesters still equip-ped 49 and 50 Squadrons as well as the Con-version Flights of many Lancaster squadrons in 5 Group. They had been issued to 44 and 408 (RCAF) Squadron 'Con' (Conversion) Flights and were already working up on 420 (RCAF) Squadron.

Despite mounting losses, Manchesters were still considered fair game for a last ditch and desperate maximum effort.

Mk.I L7425 'EM-C' of 207 Conversion Flight at Bottesford in February 1942. The aircraft retains the older, wavy, demarcation of colours and has the white areas of its national markings darkened. L7425 was first delivered to 97 Squadron on 19th June 1941, passed to 207 Squadron on 21st January 1942 and moved on to 50 Con Flight on 18th March 1942. The six personnel are armourers of 207 Squadron. *No.207 Squadron archives / R Glynne-Owen*

Crew of an unidentified Manchester IA of 106 Squadron prepare for an air test at Coningsby, March/April 1942. *P Cartwight and D Richards / 106 Squadron Association*

Chapter Eight

The 'Thousand' Raids

By early May 1942, the Manchester was slipping unnoticed and unmourned into oblivion. Nos. 61 and 83 Squadrons had both converted to Avro Lancasters, carrying out their final flurry of Manchester operations in early April, save for a brief 83 Squadron effort on 5th May. Manchesters had passed to their Conversion ('Con') Flights. Nos. 97 and 207 were both well established on Lancasters with Manchester 'Con' Flights and 44 Squadron on Lancasters and 408 and 420 on Handley Page Hampdens also had Manchester training flights. No. 49 Squadron had recently been converted to Manchesters with a view to gaining experience in the dual cockpits before they, too, moved on to Lancasters. As a result of the fact that there was initially no intention to carry out operations with the Manchester, 49 received mainly 'the halt' and 'the lame', Manchesters from the initial non-operationally fit batch. Many were still without their mid-upper F.N.7A turret. They were almost without exception the original, triple fin Mk.I variety. This left 50 and 106 Squadrons, of which 106 was at an advanced stage in converting to Lancasters, its Manchesters passing to a recently formed 'Con' Flight, whilst 50 Squadron too had begun the conversion process, although still largely Manchester equipped.

In addition to their obsolescence, Manchesters were now experiencing disproportionate casualties. Whilst crews still tried to get the most out of often very ancient, ill-equipped aircraft, both RAF aircraft performance and the German defences had rapidly outstripped them. To heighten the mismatch further, worn out engines and lack of spares was serving to degrade Manchester performance still further.

It was ironic then that the thousand bomber raids ordered by Harris on 30th/31st May 1942 to Cologne and 1st/2nd June 1942 to Essen were to result in the deployment of the largest Manchester forces ever dispatched. On 25/26th June 1942 the third and last thousand raid of the series, on Bremen, was the final Manchester operation, although by then four squadrons scraped together just 19 aircraft. Ironic too that the Manchester, which had been around during the darkest days for Bomber Command in mid-1941, and itself contributing in no small way to that poor performance, should hang on to see Bomber Command finally demonstrate the enormous striking force of a strategic area offensive.

Following its protracted and inauspicious introduction the Manchester was to make a timely exit, with Bomber Command as a whole on a high note. Yet, for the Manchesters involved and their crews, it was to be very much the recipe as before. In the short period of his tenure as Air Officer Commanding (AOC) Bomber Command, Air Vice-Marshal Harris had grasped the new technology just becoming available and rapidly improved the tactics for area bombing. Now he recognised the need demonstrate the awesome power of the modern bomber. The concept of the mass attack with the 'magic' figure of 1,000 aircraft was born.

In order to strike such a blow, Harris needed to both conserve and assemble his forces. He needed good weather and a full moon period. The last few days in May were earmarked. Accordingly from 9/10th May Manchester operations were heavily curtailed. In anticipation of the operation, work-up and training continued. On the night of 19/20th May a new crew, captained by Flight Sergeant Freeman of 49 Squadron in L7287 'EA-G', were engaged, along with others, in a searchlight co-operation exercise to London. At about 2220 hours they were in collision over Grantham with another unseen Scampton aircraft, the 83 Squadron Lancaster of Squadron Leader Hinton. The underside of the starboard wing of the Manchester lost several square feet of skin, whereas the Lancaster lost its starboard wing tip and the starboard outer engine stopped. Both aircraft returned safely to Scampton after 40 minutes flying, but it had been a lucky escape. L7287 was repaired on site in time to participate in the Cologne raid ten days later.

The planning and build up to the raid needs no repetition here, other than the reminder that as the last few days in May loomed it seemed the weather might thwart the carefully laid plans. Much interchanging of aircraft and crews, accompanied by the drawing together of scratch crews composed partly of instructors and partly of pupils at advanced stages in their operational training, had to occur. Weather forecasts for the night of Wednesday/Thursday 27/28th and Thursday/Friday 28/29th May were unfavourable, as too were those of Friday/Saturday 29th/30th. All crews were confined to base and the appreciation that 'something big' was afoot was unmistakable. The weather was unusually bad for late May with thundery outbreaks and heavy cloud both over the home bases and over the potential German targets, Hamburg and Cologne.

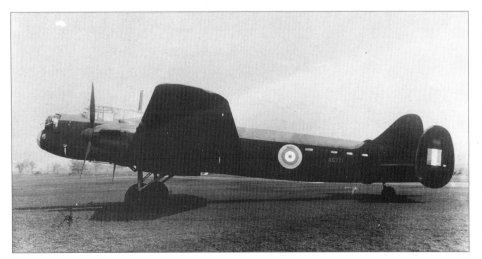

Metropolitan Vickers built Mk.I R5771 assembled 10th June 1941 at Woodford, but stored until late March 1942. After brief periods at 25 Operational Training Unit and 83 Squadron it was passed to 49 Squadron and undertook three sorties. *G A Jenks collection*

Wherever possible, flying training, especially by those crews too inexperienced even to be contemplated as potential participants, continued. On the night of 29/30th May this was to remove two potential Manchester participants from inclusion in the big raid. From 50 'Con' Flight at Skellingthorpe a number of 'Fresher' crews were dispatched on training flights.

Weather conditions were variable with heavy cloud patches, within and below which visibility was poor and rain was very heavy. In Manchester L7492, Sergeant Eyres had been out on a night cross-country, during the course of which a TR9 radio failure occurred. He arrived in the vicinity of the airfield soon after midnight in a heavy rain squall. Air traffic control tried to contact the aircraft to advise the captain to hold off until the rain abated, but were unable to do so. The poor visibility and heavy rain led to the airfield being very difficult to identify. Not having developed the experience and judgement to handle these conditions, Eyres held off too high and stalled on one wheel, causing the undercarriage to collapse and the aircraft to be left blocking the runway. There were no casualties in the crew. Efforts commenced to move the damaged aircraft, but in the meantime other returning crews were diverted to Waddington.

The weather had turned worse than the forecast and was now too difficult for the inexperienced crews. Pilot Officer D W Garland arrived in the circuit at Waddington in R5786 in continuing poor visibility and heavy rain. He touched down well along the grass runway, but the aircraft failed to slow, even when full brake was applied in the later part of the landing run. The aircraft overshot, breaking through the airfield boundary, crossing a road and falling into a field beyond, below the aerodrome level, where the undercarriage collapsed. R5786 was more seriously damaged and two crew members were injured.

At 0920 on the morning of Saturday 30th May, the weather forecast put before AV-M Harris proved decisive. The local thundery showers and convection cloud over the home bases which had undone Sergeant Eyres and Pilot Officer Garland the night before were decreasing. Thundery cloud was likely to be heavy over north west Germany but it would break and decrease south from here and during the night.

Hamburg was out of the question, but Cologne looked possible. Harris gave the orders and Operation MILLENNIUM was underway.

Whilst 97 and 207 Conversion Flights were not to produce any Manchesters and none of the crews of 420 (RCAF) Squadron at Waddington was proficient in their Manchesters, seven other units did cobble together a major force. In all 45 Manchesters were mustered to take part in MILLENNIUM.

Cologne, Operation Millennium – 30th/31st May, 1942

Serial	Code	Sqn	Captain
Balderton – along with 19 Hampdens			
L7401	EQ-Ā	408 CF	S/L L B B Price
Coningsby – along with 11 Lancasters			
L7434	ZN-*	106	P/O J Aytoun
R5796	ZN-*	106	P/O S Cockbain
R5780	ZN-*	106	P/O M Duff
L7391	ZN-*	106	P/O R G Churcher
L7488	ZN-*	106	F/S G Appleyard
Scampton – along with 13 Lancasters			
L7287	EA-G	49	F/L R E R Paramore
L7479	EA-*	49	P/O S T Farrington
L7290	EA-*	49	P/O P W Floyd
L7389	EA-L	49	Sgt H G Burton
L7429	EA-*	49	F/S J P Carter
L7526	EA-V	49	S/L P D S Bennett
R5775	EA-*	49	P/O G S Jeffreys
L7524	EA-*	49	P/O A S Perry
R5794	EA-*	49	P/O W C Shackleton
L7421	EA-*	49	F/S R G Lewis
L7493	EA-F	49 CF	S/L P C Ward Hunt
L7398	EA-*	49 CF	F/S D H Rowlands
L7293†	OL-*	83	F/S J Marchant
L7397	OL-*	83	Sgt R N Williams
L7293†	OL-*	83	P/O J Hodgson
L7308	EA-*	49 CF‡	Sgt T G Irvine
?	EA-*	49 CF‡	P/O A J F Rayment
R5768	EA-*	49 CF‡	P/O J G MacDonald
Skellingthorpe – along with 2 Lancasters			
R5784	VN-*	50	F/S E J Morgan
L7471	VN-*	50	Sgt A Weber
R5769	VN-*	50	P/O H B Martin
L7319	VN-*	50	P/O D A Atkinson
L7468	VN-*	50	P/O J S Bunbury
L7432	VN-*	50	F/O H W Southgate
L7525	VN-*	50	P/O R O Calvert
L7491	VN-*	50	F/L P J Stone
L7476	VN-Z?	50	P/O T Cole
L7460	VN-*	50	Sgt P M Crampton
L7475	VN-*	50	F/O J T Heaton
L7419	VN-*	50	Sgt E Dampier-Crossley
R5833	VN-*	50	Sgt D Gray
L7301	ZN-D	106 CF§	P/O L T Manser
L7456	ZN-*	106 CF§	Sgt J B Wilkie
Syerston – along with 15 Lancasters			
L7425†	QR-*	61	F/S N Turner
L7425†	QR-*	61	Sgt T A Stewart
L7473	QR-*	61	F/O R E Archibald
L7477	QR-*	61	F/O L Gunter
Waddington – along with 10 Lancasters			
L7430	KM-N̄	44 CF	F/O H E Maudslay
L7480	KM-Ā	44 CF	S/L L W S Herring

† Identity as given in the ORB, one or the other in error.
‡ On loan to 83 Squadron. § On loan to 50 Squadron.
Not included are two Manchesters one each from 49 and 61 Squadrons which became unserviceable just before take-off.

Between 2219 and 0030 hours 1,043 crews took off with a view to concentrating the attack in a 90 minute period. The crews of 5 Group were given a 15 minute period, between 75 and 90 minutes after the start of the attack in which to bomb. 'Z' hour was 0055. Most 5 Group Manchesters took off soon after 2300.

The Manchester force soon began to experience problems. As Pilot Officer Perry tried to make height in L7524 the aircraft began to vibrate and lose altitude. He had no alternative but to land at Docking after 45 minutes in the air. Sergeant Weber in L7471 of 50 Squadron had the intercom to the rear turret fail at the Dutch coast and returned early. From 83 Squadron, Flight Sergeant Marchant in L7293 experienced intercom and a rear turret failure and returned to base with his bombs.

Pilot Officer Hodgson lost engine power in his aircraft and had to jettison the bomb load to remain under control. He too returned early. Pilot Officer Rayment in one of the 49 'Con' Flight Manchesters loaned to 83 Squadron also lost power and had to release his bomb load over the North Sea. Squadron Leader Price was delayed taking off in the sole 408 'Con' Flight Manchester, L7401, possibly due to technical problems. It was to no avail because the aircraft experienced a hydraulic failure and had to return with its incendiaries still on board. So six Manchesters dropped out from the initial force of 45 aircraft leaving the remaining 39 to attack Cologne.

On this night, despite their increasing vulnerability, it was believed that the Manchesters could take advantage of the swamping of the anti-aircraft defences around Cologne and not unduly expose their crews to risk. However, the whole operation was a risk, involving as it did so many inexperienced crews.

Many of the Conversion Flight aircraft were old, having in some cases a large number of airframe hours (for a Manchester) whilst a surprising number were from the initial production batch of 20, not considered fit for operations. These had originally been issued to 207 Squadron for crew training and development flying and then handed on successively to 97, 61 and the other units in turn for training purposes. They had flown occasional operations but many had been withdrawn from service and held in store at maintenance units (MUs) for prolonged periods. Amongst this early batch were L7287, L7289, L7290 and L7301.

Arising from their languishing in MUs or being issued to Conversion Flights for second line duties, most remained unmodified to the latest standard. For example, most if not all still retained the triple fins and short span tail of the first 20 Mk.Is whilst most, too, had no mid-upper turret fitted. Indeed in the case of at least one aircraft, L7287, which had been the trials aircraft for the F.N.7A mid-upper turret, by the time of the MILLENNIUM raid the turret had been removed.

Prior to Operation MILLENNIUM there had been little flying at Skellingthorpe. All sorts of rumours had been 'doing the rounds'. No.50 Squadron were in the final days of operating their Manchesters.

A new-looking R5771 in final colour scheme, possibly photographed at Woodford. The F.N.5 front turret is fully slewed to the left. *J Simpson*

Aircrew of 106 Squadron pose in front of one of the unit's Manchesters at Coningsby. *D Richards / 106 Squadron Association*

Few photographs of 50 Squadron's short association with the Manchester have emerged. Mk.I 'VN-Z', possibly L7476, of 50 Squadron at Skellingthorpe, April-June 1942. *No. 50 Squadron archives*

Mk.I R5784 'VN-?' of 50 Squadron is said to be at Hinton-in-the-Hedges, not its home base, Skellingthorpe. *No. 50 Squadron archives via Peter Green*

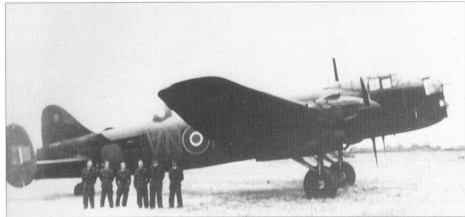

Leslie Baveystock, a second pilot under training, had just commenced a weekend leave and his wife was already on the train from London to Lincoln to join him, when he heard his leave was cancelled and that he was operating that night. He learned he was to fly with Pilot Officer Leslie Manser, with whom he had not previously flown. Manser informed him that they had orders to fly over to Coningsby that afternoon to collect one of the 106 Conversion Flight aircraft, which was used only for circuits and bumps. Baveystock obtained Manser's agreement to at least meet his wife from the railway station and install her in the 'Station Hotel' before returning to base. A scratch crew collected 106 Squadron's aircraft and flew it back to Skellingthorpe, arriving in the late afternoon.

They found they had acquired one of the earliest Manchesters, L7301, now coded 'ZN-D' of 106 Squadron. Despite being received by the RAF on 21st December 1940, L7301 had done very little flying, possibly being one of the initial, non-operationally fit 'pre-production' aircraft. First it had been stored at 27 MU, Shawbury. Later in March 1941 it was sent back to Avro at Ringway ostensibly for an engine change and held there until April 1942, when it was finally reworked to later production standards. Quite which modifications were incorporated is not recorded. It was issued to 106 Squadron Conversion Flight on 28th April 1942. On arrival at Skellingthorpe on the 30th May the ground crews found that the mid-upper turret had still not been fitted and that the lower escape hatch, where the mid-under turret would originally have been fitted, was sealed by a series of permanently mounted metal plates. Consistent with this early batch of aircraft no auto-pilot was fitted.

Time at Skellingthorpe only permitted the barest checking and topping up of oil and coolant levels as the aircraft was hurriedly refuelled and bombed up with 1,260 x 4lb incendiaries in 14 containers. Following briefing and a meal the crew were driven out to the aircraft. Manser had discussed his attack plan with Baveystock and informed him of his intention to bomb from 7,000ft instead of their briefed height of 12,000ft. The prospect of all the light and medium flak at that height, not to mention the falling bombs and incendiaries caused Baveystock an inward shudder.

When they reached the aircraft and got down from their transport Baveystock saw L7301 for the first time, taking in amongst other things that it lacked a mid-upper turret. Why then need they carry Sergeant Stanley King, the second wireless operator/air gunner, who would be a mere passenger with nowhere to sit and nothing to do? At least someone had given some thought to this problem and Baveystock was surprised to see a young Corporal Armourer waiting to greet them. He told Manser and King that he had drawn a pair of Vickers Gas Operated (VGO) machine guns and several pans of 0.303in ammunition from the armoury in lieu of the mid-upper turret and suggested that if they were attacked from the beam Sergeant King might like to 'poke' a hole in the side of the fuselage and fire at the attacker. Of course the entire concept was ludicrous. There was no rack in the aircraft to store the guns or 0.303in pans, no bracket to mount the VGO, no aperture to point the gun through or even windows to sight and aim it. Possibly pre-occupied with more serious and immediate issues, Manser allowed the extra weight of the VGOs, their ammunition and the useless gunner to be loaded in the aircraft.

In addition to expending Sergeant King needlessly in the next few hours even more

was at stake, because L7301 carried not just two but a *third* pilot, that night. Flying Officer Richard Barnes, the observer, was also a pilot.

Over at Scampton both 83 and 49 Squadrons put up Manchesters for the operation. The aircraft were carefully marshalled to permit a streamed take-off. The 12 Manchesters of 49 Squadron were away first between 2250 and 2331 hours, followed by the 83 Squadron Manchesters between 2329 and 2347 and finally the Lancasters of 83 Squadron.

Pilot Officer Roy Calvert was flying L7525 of 50 Squadron and had had an uneventful outward flight, other than the unusual experience of all hands keeping a careful watch for other aircraft in the bomber stream. Both the number of aircraft involved and their proximity in space and time was still a novelty to the crews. They had traversed Cologne on their bomb run at 9,000ft and the bomb aimer had just called 'Bombs away!', when the aircraft was struck by a flak burst in the starboard engine. The similarities with Pilot Officer Manser's experiences later that night, other than the outcome, are astounding. Calvert's starboard engine burst into flame. Calmly, but quickly, Calvert closed the bomb doors, shut off the fuel supply to the starboard Vulture, pressed the extinguisher button and feathered the propeller.

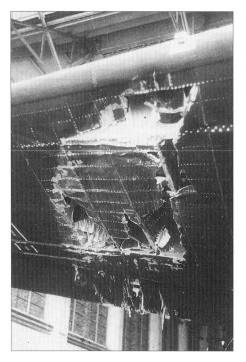

Lucky escape. Damage to the underside of the starboard wing of L7287 'EA-G' of 49 Squadron after Flight Sergeant Freeman and crew were in collision over Grantham with another, unseen, Scampton aircraft on 19/20th May 1942. This was a Lancaster of 83 Squadron flown by Squadron Leader Hinton. The aircraft were involved in a searchlight co-operation exercise to London. The Lancaster lost its starboard wingtip and the starboard outer engine stopped. Both aircraft landed at base after being airborne for about 40 minutes. *via P Gaunt*

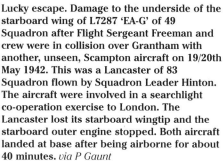

A vic of Manchester Is of 49 Squadron, 'EA-N', 'EA-G' and 'EA-T', airborne from Scampton *circa* **May 1942. 'EA-G', leading, has no mid-upper turret and is probably L7287.** *IWM, FLM2005*

The crew were relieved when the fire diminished and went out and the feathering mechanism worked satisfactorily. Calvert advanced the throttle of the port Vulture and pushed forward the stick, diving to clear the searchlights in the target area as quickly as possible. They cleared the lights at about 7,000ft and levelled out on a westerly heading. As the speed built up in the dive ebbed away, Calvert, having trimmed the aircraft to fly on one, found to his dismay that L7525 was inexorably sinking. It seemed that the inevitable Manchester problem would be their undoing too.

Evaluating their options, Calvert chanced opening the fuel tap on the starboard Vulture and unfeathering the prop to restart the engine hoping for a little help from it. The

engine started, but promptly burst into flames again. Now the situation was potentially terminal because Calvert knew the Graviner bottle would be empty. He refeathered the propeller, turned off the fuel and to his immense relief the fire died down of its own accord. Next he instructed the crew to prepare to abandon the aircraft, but in the meantime to jettison any moveable items on board. The crew turned to with a will and their rate of descent steadily decreased. However, after 45 minutes flying they were approaching the Dutch coast, still without a sign that the aircraft would maintain its altitude.

By now they were down to a critical altitude of 200ft. Soon after crossing the coast they encountered low filmy cloud at sea level and Calvert judged them to be completely safe from attack by night fighters. Thus assured, he ordered the gunners to strip out all guns and ammunition and ditch these through the open hatches. Still they sank inexorably lower, the port throttle was fully advanced and at 100ft Calvert tried another ploy. He closed the radiator flap under the port nacelle, which reduced the drag, increased the speed and lift and permitted a climb to 200ft. Then he quickly reopened the flap to let the engine cool down, gradually losing height to 100ft again. Still they flew on.

This procedure was repeated several times until the crew finally recognised the approaches to the Thames Estuary ahead. By this time, too, more fuel had been burned off and having reached the coast they found there seemed to be fractionally more lift over the land. They were then able to climb to a few hundred feet without overheating. The first airfield they came to was Tempsford, where a precautionary landing was thankfully carried out. Inspection next day revealed a

sliver of shrapnel in the coolant pipe of the starboard engine which had led to the fire.

The story of Pilot Officer Manser's brave and selfless attack on Cologne has been recorded many times. The run across the target was prolonged by Manser's determination to bomb on the edge of a dark patch in the flaming city. In so doing they were trapped in the searchlights and shortly after the incendiaries were released the aircraft was jolted from beneath by a flak hit, which blew off the rear of the bomb doors and damaged the fuselage. Manser immediately thrust the stick forward in an attempt to shake off the lights, but despite their twisting flight path they continued to be held and peppered by a hail of light 20mm flak, until they finally slid out of range of the lights at 700ft. Manser then hauled back on the stick and began climbing to provide the additional height necessary if they needed to bale out. The crew meanwhile assessed the damage around their crew stations.

At 2,000ft there was an explosion and roar from the port engine, which burst into flame. Manser instructed Baveystock to operate the extinguisher and feather the propeller. The extinguisher seemed to have no effect and indeed the fire was trailing aft of the wing and beyond the tail unit. With the threat of the fuel tank exploding or the main spar burning through the crew expected the order to bale out any moment. Manser remained supremely calm and instructed them to wait and see if the fire went out. He obtained a course for Manston in Kent, his determination to reach and bomb the target now replaced by an equal determination to get them home.

Fortunately, at least the feathering mechanism had worked, and in the next few minutes the fierce fire in the nacelle gradually burnt itself out. The short term emergency was replaced by a longer term concern, for they were gradually losing height on the remaining Vulture. As with Pilot Officer Calvert's aircraft in similar straits nearby, the crew set to jettisoning everything removable from the airframe to reduce weight. One of the first items Baveystock ditched were the two useless VGOs and their ammunition from the mid-section.

In the case of L7301, bravery and discipline proved more enduring than the aircraft, for as they crossed into Belgian airspace the starboard engine began to overheat from the strain, speed dropped away further and Manser began to have control difficulties as the port wing kept dropping, causing the aircraft to bank and yaw off course. With the starboard engine temperature rising off the clock and the engine likely to seize and catch fire at any moment, and moreover with their steady descent unabated, Manser made his final and perfectly timed judgement. In doing so he saved six lives and forfeited his own. 'Parachutes on. Prepare to abandon aircraft!' called Manser. Horsley, Naylor and King, the wireless operator and rear and 'mid-upper' gunners stood by the rear entry door, whilst Barnes, the observer and Mills the front gunner jettisoned the lower escape hatch in the nose.

'Bale out! Bale out!' The five crewmen went in quick succession, pulling their ripcords soon after they were free. Baveystock remained behind with the intention of helping Manser into his 'chute. The aircraft was shuddering on the point of the stall and would fall out of control at any moment. Manser thrust Baveystock away. 'For God's sake, get out! We're going down!' Recognising that he could do no more, Baveystock doubled himself up and dropped through the hatch. His tumbling body was arrested partly by his half-open parachute and partly by the 4–5ft of water in the ditch into which he immediately fell.

Ahead, Manser had finally lost control and the Manchester rolled over and plunged into the ground, killing him instantly. They had come down in farmland near Bree in eastern Belgium. Next day the wreck was visited and photographed by a German night fighter pilot, Oberleutnant Baake of II/NJG1, who mistakenly claimed to have shot the aircraft down at 0214 hours European Time.

Baveystock and the remainder of the crew had a remarkable escape and by chance

four of them evaded capture and were eventually able to return to England. On the basis of their report Leslie Manser received a posthumous Victoria Cross. Never was an award more appropriate, but it was also awarded on behalf of the other Manchester crews who had shown equal bravery but whose self-sacrifice had gone unreported.

At least one other 50 Squadron Manchester had an adventurous night over Cologne, from which it too failed to return. Sergeant Jim Wilkie had also flown over to Coningsby to collect another machine from 106 'Con' Flight, L7456. His second pilot was Sergeant Cyril Tobias who had been posted from 455 Squadron, RAAF, with 16 operations to his credit for conversion onto Lancasters as these became available. In the meantime he would do a few Manchester operations. Nineteen year old Wilkie was approaching Cologne at 9,000ft, having tried every ploy to coax the Manchester to a safer height. On the run up searchlights and flak brought down a bomber ahead of them and he swung north to get around this hot spot, only to run into one of his own. The flak defences were fully alerted and the low flying Manchesters were easy meat. His aircraft was coned and heavily engaged by accurate anti-aircraft fire. He threw the overladen aircraft around in a vain attempt to shake off the lights and tried diving. As he did so a flak burst disabled his port engine, which began running rough and spitting fire. Wilkie feathered the engine and operated the fire extinguisher. The deliberate height loss became inadvertent and try as he might Wilkie could not prevent the aircraft from sinking under its heavy load. All hope of reaching the inner city was gone and their entire efforts turned now to survival. The bomb load was jettisoned in the suburbs of Cologne and Wilkie turned away, still enmeshed in the blinding searchlights.

Despite releasing the bombs the aircraft was still unable to maintain height. Wilkie was unsure of his heading and his manoeu-

vres trying to evade the lights cost further precious height, which he could not claw back. Suddenly they passed out of range of the lights, but their height was now critically low and he immediately ordered the crew to bale out. He judged their chances of survival, even at this low level, better than his own in the forthcoming forced landing into the dark unknown ahead.

Jim Wilkie was holding on full left rudder to counteract the asymmetrical thrust of the starboard Vulture and knew that the instant he released it the aircraft would flip over on its back and crash. Like Derek Pinchbeck, John Nunn and other Manchester pilots who had to force land blind in the dark before him, Wilkie had no option but to sit there and accept the inevitable, whatever that turned out to be.

In a desperate attempt to see something in the total darkness ahead, Wilkie, alone now except for second pilot Tobias, flipped on the switch of the landing light. He was shocked to see trees illuminated and flashing by just beneath them. Bowing to the inevitable and hoping for some cushioning by the pine tree tops, Wilkie hauled back on the stick and cut the throttle to belly in into the forest. Instead they felt a jolt and rapid deceleration and dust and grass flew into the cockpit. By pure chance they had carried out a perfect belly landing, but a much greater coincidence was soon to become apparent. Both engines were now burning fiercely and by the glow of the still illuminated landing light, shining across the ground, they made out a fence with houses and gardens beyond. Wilkie and Tobias hurried back down the fuselage, both to escape the flames and check that all crew members had departed. They jumped down and began to flee the blaze, but were almost immediately surrounded by Luftwaffe personnel and captured. Miraculously L7456 had chosen to return to earth in the middle of Dusseldorf airfield!

Manchester Mk.IA L7493 'EA-F' of 49 Squadron taxying at Scampton *circa* **May 1942. Initially delivered to 25 Operational Training Unit, L7493 reached 49 Squadron in May 1942 and undertook two operations.** *IWM, FLM2006*

Top: **A view of the sorry remains of L7301 'ZN-D' which carried Flying Officer Leslie Manser to his death and a posthumous Victoria Cross on the night of 30th/31st May 1942. Photograph attributed to Oberleutnant Baake of II/NJG1, who mistakenly claimed the Manchester destroyed at Kimroy at 0214 hours.** *via P Loncke*

Flying Officer L T Manser, who was awarded the VC posthumously for his sacrifice on 30/31st May 1942 in a 106 Squadron 'Con' flight aircraft allocated to 50 Squadron.
Peter Green collection via A S Thomas

Pilot Officer Atkinson of 50 Squadron had released part of his incendiary load approaching the Dutch coast as his Manchester resolutely refused to climb. Flying Officer Heaton encountered enemy fighters on three occasions but managed to escape detection and attack successfully. All 50 Squadron Manchester crews, other than the early return, found Cologne alight from end to end. The river, cathedral and streets were clearly visible through the dense smoke already beginning to rise. Crews bombed from heights ranging between 5,000 and 10,500ft.

Australian Pilot Officer H M 'Micky' Martin, later to achieve fame in 617 Squadron, participated in the operation with three other Australians, Sergeants Leggo (observer), Foxlee (front gunner) and Simpson (rear gunner), who were to remain in his crew for much of the war. Martin was greatly respected in 5 Group for his piloting skills, but at this time was not known for his respect for discipline or dress. He still proudly wore his dark blue battledress jacket even though it was faded and worn out at the elbows. He attacked Cologne from 7,400ft noting the ineffective flak and stoking up the raging fires.

Amongst the 49 Squadron aircraft heading for Cologne was the elderly L7290, being flown that night by Pilot Officer Phillip Floyd with Sergeant J R M Valentine as observer. L7290 also lacked a mid-upper turret but, as with the similar aircraft sent out by 50 Squadron that night, they still carried a seven man crew. In this case Sergeant Randall flew as a passenger, curtaining himself off in the rest bed reading a novel until the action began to get out of hand. What a ridiculous waste to sacrifice a fully trained airman to the enemy for no possible benefit! Fortunately Randall was to escape with his life.

L7290 was desperately slow, fully loaded

they barely made 150 knots, and Floyd had the familiar fight to gain altitude. Eventually they nursed the aircraft up to 8,000ft, a dangerously low altitude for the well-defended targets of the Ruhr. Urged on by the briefing, Floyd continued across Belgium, seeing Cologne from many miles distant. By the time they arrived, the defenders had recognised the approach direction of the bomber stream and in their run up to the target they were caught in a mammoth cone of searchlights. Floyd began weaving and corkscrewing in an attempt to shake off the lights, always anxious not to lose the precious height they had fought for two hours to gain. Searchlights seemed to extend to the horizon in all directions and the flak gunners appeared to be concentrating on their aircraft, at what was, for them, point blank range. They took a number of hits, one of which shattered the hydraulic lines in several places. Valentine was drenched by the high pressure fluid, the front and rear turrets were put out of commission and the fuselage floor was flooded with the slippery oil.

Floyd recognised the imminence of their destruction if they remained at this height and dived for lower levels to restrict the field of fire of the guns and to throw off the lights. Speed built up and at 3,000ft they left the lighted arena and plunged temporarily into the anonymity of the night. Doggedly, Floyd headed on in towards Cologne and the aiming point, but now a new danger manifest itself for they had come within range of the rapid firing light flak guns. L7290 was raked with tracer.

Monitoring his instruments and still in control of the fast moving train of events, Floyd suddenly noticed that the oil temperature on the starboard engine was rising rapidly. A quick glance from the astrodome revealed that coolant was rippling back across the wing and streaming back in the slipstream. Moments later the engine caught fire. Floyd stopped it and feathered the propeller.

With the bomb load still on board and their descent rate increasing on the remaining engine, Floyd gave the inevitable order to bale out before they descended too low. Whilst Floyd stamped on full right rudder to counteract the pull of the port engine and held the stick hard over to keep up the starboard wing the crew hurried to the exits. Like Calvert, Manser, Wilkie and Carter faced with identical situations that same night in their Manchesters, Floyd knew the odds. As the crew tumbled out Valentine gave Floyd a last few words of encouragement and thanks 'You've done bloody well, Phillip. I'm going out in a second – I hope you'll follow me'. Floyd reached out and shook Valentine's hand and then the latter flung himself down to the forward hatch. He was almost his own undoing when he pulled his D-ring prematurely and his 'chute spilled inside the aircraft.

He bundled it up before it was blown out too far and lunged through the hatch. Sergeant Smith, the front gunner, was still waiting in the nose too afraid to jump, but Valentine could do nothing for him.

The overloaded Manchester was sinking like a stone. Next second the faltering aircraft rolled over onto its back, possibly as Floyd made his own attempt to bale out. It plunged nose down vertically into the ground, its bomb load exploding in the crash. Floyd and Smith were still on board and died instantly. The remaining five in the crew descended safely at Mulheim-Oberhausen and were taken prisoner.

Also engaged on the MILLENNIUM raid was Pilot Officer Carter of 49 Squadron in L7429. Nothing further was heard from this aircraft after take-off, but several bodies from this crew were recovered from the North Sea the next day. Although it remains circumstantial it seems likely that his aircraft also reached Cologne, although at a very vulnerable flying height. It could have suffered similar flak damage to the other four Manchesters whose experiences have been detailed here. Instead of baling out to captivity it seems that Carter, too, had made a 100% effort to save his aircraft and crew.

Of the remaining 49 Squadron aircraft, all made successful attacks. Sergeant Burton turned in an excellent performance, bombing the target despite engine and airframe trouble and an intercom failure. Flight Lieutenant Paramore's aircraft was fired on by an unidentified aircraft but not damaged, whilst Flight Sergeant Rowland's aircraft was approached by a Junkers Ju 88. It closed in twice but broke away on each occasion as soon as evasive action was taken. Most of the night fighters seemed unusually hesitant, although Flight Sergeant Lewis did report an aircraft engaged by a night fighter followed shortly afterwards by an explosion on the ground. All attacked from similar heights to 50 Squadron crews and reported the same extensive area of fires.

No. 83 Squadron had already had three early returns from its force of six and in the target area its problems continued. The crew of R5768, captained by Pilot Officer MacDonald, saw their bombs straddle a factory, but soon afterwards they were engaged by flak which knocked out the hydraulics, shot away the fixed aerial and put the rear turret out of commission. Only Sergeant Williams had an uneventful operation.

Sergeant T G Irvine of 83 Squadron had taken the old 49 Conversion Flight Manchester, L7308. The fact that 49 Conversion Flight may not have had much time for the aircraft may be indicated by the fact that they never tried to operate it. In fact it had been through a major rebuild following a serious accident with 97 Squadron back in September 1941.

Despite its vintage, Irvine managed to bomb the primary target from 12,000ft at a late stage in the raid. His bomb bursts could not be distinguished amongst the many fires. Irvine turned on the return leg and concern soon arose due to excessive fuel consumption. Thirty-two minutes prior to landfall checks revealed 120 gallons remaining in the port tank and only 100 in the starboard. Irvine tried to nurse the aircraft towards Scampton, but on approach his difficulties were accentuated by recognition of a hydraulic failure, which necessitated the undercarriage and flaps being lowered by the emergency system. Soon after this one shot system had been activated their problems escalated sharply, when the starboard engine failed as they turned in on approach to the first available 'drome, which turned out to be Ingham in Lincolnshire. By this time the Manchester was losing height rapidly and the inexperienced captain felt powerless to stretch the glide. In the final moments the port Vulture began to splutter through lack of fuel. L7308 hit the ground ten yards short of the aerodrome boundary, descending like a lift, and the undercarriage collapsed. The aircraft slid through the boundary fence and came to a halt. All the crew escaped without injury.

Meanwhile, in Manchester R5768, Pilot Officer MacDonald also had problems. On return it was found that the undercarriage could not be lowered with the emergency system. MacDonald then carried out a successful belly landing at Scampton, causing only slight damage to the aircraft. No. 83 Squadron had had a rough night, but at least all its Manchesters returned.

No. 61 Squadron had a less eventful night, all four of its Manchesters bombed Cologne. Flying Officer Archibald released his load from only 7,000ft and then dived to ground level for the return. His gunners fired on factories and a gasometer on the return flight. Sergeant Turner climbed to 15,000ft approaching the target and released his bombs in a power dive from 14,000ft.

Likewise, all five of 106 Squadron's aircraft attacked with minimal interference and returned. Squadron Leader Herring reached 17,000ft in his Manchester, bombing the target at 0205 hours. Flying Officer Henry Maudslay was late taking off in the second 44 Conversion Flight aircraft. By the time he arrived the target was well alight and the enemy defences had been overwhelmed. He released his load of incendiaries from 6,800ft at 0213 to add to the conflagration.

In the analysis the raid proved the wisdom of Roy Chadwick's concern for the Manchester. Four of the aircraft whose experiences are related here, and very likely the fifth, had reached the target area and attacked at suicidally low level. Most had proved incapable of climbing above 10,000ft. Amongst the survivors many were less seriously damaged only because their numbers had overwhelmed the defences and prevented them concentrating on individual targets for long.

In every case it was flak not night fighters which had done the damage and in all cases once one engine was put out of action the other had proved inadequate, or in the case of Pilot Officer Calvert, *just* adequate to the task. So Bomber Command's maximum effort coincided with that of the Manchester.

Following their return, the 'Thousand Force' was kept together in the hope that a second, telling, blow could be delivered on Hamburg. Crews were dog-tired and greatly relieved when weather led to the operation being cancelled that night. However, they were on again on 1st/2nd June 1942 and although Hamburg remained cloud covered Harris went for Essen with 956 aircraft. The same seven squadrons were involved, supplying this time 33 Manchesters. However, the raid was to be a total failure with bad weather causing bombs to be scattered far and wide.

Essen, a near Millennium – 1st/2nd June 1942

Serial	Code	Sqn	Captain
Balderton – also 16 Hampdens			
?	EQ-N̄	408	S/L L B B Price
Coningsby – also 9 Lancasters			
L7434	ZN-*	106	P/O J Aytoun
R5796	ZN-*	106	P/O S Cockbain
L7457	ZN-*	106	P/O G Cooke
L7488	ZN-*	106	F/S G Appleyard
L7391	ZN-*	106	P/O R G Churcher
R5780	ZN-*	106	P/O M Duff
Scampton – also ? Lancasters			
L7389	EA-L	49	S/L P M de Mestre
L7493	EA-F	49	Sgt H G Burton
L7398	EA-*	49	P/O A S Perry
L7526	EA-V	49	P/O G S Jeffreys
L7479	EA-*	49	P/O S T Farrington
R5775	EA-*	49	F/L R E R Paramore
L7421	EA-*	49	F/S R G Lewis
R5794	EA-*	49	P/O W C Shackleton
L7397	OL-*	83	P/O J Hodgson
Skellingthorpe			
L7476	VN-*	50	P/O T Cole
L7319	VN-*	50	P/O D A Atkinson
L7432	VN-*	50	F/O H W Southgate
L7471	VN-*	50	Sgt A Weber
L7419	VN-*	50	F/S E J Morgan
R5769	VN-*	50	P/O H B Martin
L7460	VN-*	50	Sgt P M Crampton
L7430	KM-N̄	44 CF†	P/O J S Bunbury
R5833	KM-*	44 CF†	F/S D Gray
?	ZN-G	106 CF†	P/O Q D Beatty
Syerston – also 11 Lancasters			
L7477	QR-*	61	P/O E R Seibold
L7401	QR-*	61	F/S P W Gregory
L7415	QR-*	61	F/S J G Stewart
L7491	QR-*	61	S/L R A V Gascoyne-Cecil
L7458	QR-*	61	F/S N R Meyer
L7425	QR-*	61	S/L A M Paape
Waddington – also 11 Lancasters			
L7480	KM-Ā	44	F/O Maudsley

† on loan to 50 Squadron.

Manchester I L7287 'EA-G' running up at Scampton, probably in May 1942. L7287 was from the pre-production batch and had been used as the F.N.7A trials aircraft. The turret had been removed by the time it was issued to 49 Squadron for operations. It was lost on 6/7th June 1942 with Flight Lieutenant Paramore and crew. *IWM, FLM2004*

Ground crews of 49 Squadron had a battle to get the Manchesters airborne. Seven of the force got away close either side of midnight. Pilot Officer Farrington did not take-off until 0050 hours owing to unspecified problems, whilst Squadron Leader de Mestre was delayed until 0056 with engine trouble. Both returned from the Dutch coast, having insufficient time to reach the target. R5794 with Pilot Officer Shackleton failed to return. An SOS was received at 0219 reporting that the starboard engine had failed but nothing more was heard. There are no further details on the fate of the crew. The remaining crews claimed to attack the primary target.

All 50 Squadron aircraft attacked what they believed to be the primary target and reported very little response from the defences. A flak hit injured Flight Sergeant Stevens, the observer in Pilot Officer Cole's aircraft and a Messerschmitt Me109 followed Sergeant Crampton's aircraft for a while on return, but did not attack.

Three of the 61 Squadron Manchesters returned early. Flight Sergeant Stewart was delayed taking off by intercom failure and returned when it became clear he could not reach the target by the time ordered. Squadron Leader Paape experienced excessive tail shudder, which led him to return early as a precaution. It is not clear why Pilot Officer Seibold returned early. Flying Officer Gregory bombed fires on the ground, having had problems locating the target. Squadron Leader Gascoyne-Cecil claimed a visual on the aiming point and Flight Sergeant Meyer made a good effort. His port rev counter went u/s 150 miles out but be carried on and bombed the target from 10,000ft. On 61's last Manchester operation Pilot Officer Hodgson was unable to locate the primary and believed he hit Oberhausen instead.

All 106 Squadron crews reported attacking the primary, although target identification had been problematical. Flying Officer Maudslay in the 44 Conversion Flight aircraft had to attack an alternate target from 8,000ft when he was unable to locate Essen. Similarly,

Squadron Leader Price in the 408 Conversion Flight aircraft had target identification problems and bombed a built up area he believed to be Essen. In fact the raid was widely dispersed. Some damage was caused to Oberhausen, Mulheim and Duisburg.

Finally, on 25/26th June 1942, during the next full moon period, the force was reassembled once more for another attempt to achieve the results of the Cologne raid a month earlier. This time the target was Bremen and approaching 100 Coastal Command Hudsons joined Bomber Command in raising a force of 1,006 aircraft. It was the last operation of the war flown by Manchesters, but by now only 19 serviceable aircraft could be raised, mostly from 50 Squadron. (See also page 192.) The operation was code-named MILLENNIUM TWO. The aircraft raised were:

Bremen, Millennium Two and Manchester bow out – 25/26th June 1942

Serial	Code	Sqn	Captain
Coningsby – also 17 Lancasters			
R5839	ZN-*	106	Sgt T B Crowfoot
R5780	ZN-*	106	Sgt S E J Jones
Scampton – also one Lancaster			
R5772	EA-*	49	P/O R F Elliott
L7453	EA-T	49	Sgt J W Heard
R5788	EA-*	49	Sgt T V Webster
Skellingthorpe – also two Lancasters			
L7455	VN-*	50	F/S J F Taylor
L7289	VN-*	50	Sgt J C Roy
L7415	VN-*	50	F/S E J Morgan
R5835	VN-*	50	Sgt R C Wiseman
L7496	VN-*	50	P/O T Cole
L7277	VN-*	50	Sgt D Gray
L7521	VN-*	50	F/S A Weber
L7416	VN-*	50	P/O R O Calvert
L7464	VN-*	50	F/L P J Stone
L7401	VN-*	50	P/O J S Bunbury
L7294	VN-*	50	F/O H W Southgate
R5769	VN-*	50	P/O H B Martin
Syerston – also ? Lancasters			
R5835	QR-*	61	F/S F Hobson
L7477	QR-*	61	F/S C P Shriner

The specific 5 Group target in Bremen was the Focke-Wulf factory. However, as at Essen, the large amount of cloud cover prevented a concentrated attack. The three 49 Squadron Manchesters attacked what they believed was the built up area of Bremen instead. From the 50 Squadron force only one aircraft, which came down to 2,500ft, managed to bomb the factory. This was Flying Officer Southgate. Flight Sergeant Taylor had a rear turret failure after being airborne for an hour. He turned north out of the bomber stream, jettisoned his incendiaries and returned to base. Pilot Officer Martin had the intercom to the rear turret fail and bombed Alkmaar airfield as a last resort target before returning. Flight Sergeant Roy and his crew became the last operational Manchester casualty of the war when his aircraft failed to return. It is not known what became of his crew. Both 61 Squadron Manchesters aborted and reports from the two 106 Squadron flight crews are unavailable.

During the last three months the loss rate on Manchesters seemed to be increasing beyond that experienced earlier:

Manchester Losses March-June 1942

Date	Dispatched	FTR	Loss Rate %
8/9th March	25	2	8.0
13/14th March	16	2	12.5
25/26th March	20	4	20.0
28/29th March	21	1	4.8
29/30th March	8	2	5.0
8/9th April	18	2	11.0
10/11th April	16	1	6.3
2nd/3rd May	17	2	11.8
8th/9th May	11	2	18.0
30th/31st May	45	4	8.8
6/7th June	7	3	42.9

Naturally, with such small sample numbers, the variability is high, but clearly the loss rate was sufficiently high to trigger an inquiry within Bomber Command. The report, No. 44 from the Operational Research Section (ORS), apparently assessed various possible reasons for the high losses. It did not have the information available presented in this history and amongst other suggestions a possible problem with the fuel system was considered and dismissed. The only common feature was the low operating height of the Manchester, but Bomber Command

responded by pointing out that there was no technical reason why the Manchester should be operated at a lower average height than other 'heavies', especially the Stirling, which had a more favourable loss rate. The operational ceiling was stated to be almost 3,000ft higher than the Stirling. Any tendency for crews to operate the Manchester at lower heights was considered to be due to a disinclination of crews to overtax their engines. Loss rates were regularly reaching double figures and at times 25% and above. At this rate a Manchester crew would not survive a tour of 30 operations but perhaps four instead.

A look at the fates of operational Manchesters in the appendix possibly gives some clues. Night fighters are prominent and the low flying height possibly made the Manchesters unusually vulnerable to flak. A factor largely absent from the loss statistics of other aircraft is the risk of loss following one of the Vulture engines being put out of service by enemy action, or even at this late stage the direct risk of an unprovoked engine failure. Indeed, minutes circulating in late 1941 and early 1942 had examined the concerns over burning out of exhaust manifolds and of weaknesses in the hydraulic piping in the Vulture engines. This was to worsen as the spares situation deteriorated for aircraft in second line duties.

In the event the ORS report only became available on 10th June 1942, by which time the Manchesters had only one more mission to undertake before being withdrawn. Consequently the matter was not pursued further. The loss statistics served only to reinforce the obvious obsolescence of the Manchester, which could no longer survive in the night skies over occupied Europe.

Triple fin Manchester I L7389 'EA-L' of 49 Squadron aloft from Scampton, circa June 1942. The aircraft served sequentially with 61, 207, 83 (as 'OL-M'?), 49 Squadrons and 106 Squadron 'Con' Flight. A year earlier, on 30th June 1941, as 'QR-J' of 61 Squadron, whilst engaged overnight on intensive engine trials in the hands of Pilot Officer Stevens, the starboard engine failed. In the dark the second pilot inadvertently feathered the port propeller and a dead stick belly landing was accomplished at Fowlmere. *via P Gaunt*

An appropriate photograph upon which to close the operational career of the Avro Manchester. Armourers loading 0.303in ammunition into the rear turret of Mk.IA L7526 'EA-V' of 49 Squadron at Scampton. L7526 was the last Avro-built Manchester and had initially been with 25 Operational Training Unit. *IWM, FLM2003*

Chapter Nine

Second Line Service

As aircraft weights and sizes increased during the 1930s and 1940s, concerns arose from time to time as to whether existing airfields could adequately cope with the increased loads. At this time RAF airfields were grass covered and small in size. Moreover, interest extended to use of launching devices of various kinds to optimise load carrying capability and ease propeller design. As early as 1931, at the RAF Pageant at Hendon, a Royal Aircraft Establishment (RAE) Farnborough-designed accelerated take-off device was demonstrated in public. Trials at Farnborough itself had apparently involved a Vickers Vimy, whereas for the Hendon Pageant a Virginia was used.

The requirement was to accelerate an 18,000 lb weight to a speed of 60mph within 300ft. The solution employed two compressed air engines powering a winch drum. The drum was securely anchored to the ground and the aircraft then located ahead of this, its tail raised into the flying position on a wheeled trolley. A winch wire ran forward from the drum under the trolley and on through the main undercarriage legs to a well anchored frame, which carried a pulley wheel. The wire passed over the pulley and back to the aircraft, where it was hooked beneath the forward fuselage.

By 1936 when the specifications for the 55,000 lb B12/36 and the 45,000 lb P13/36 were drawn up the requirement had escalated to one of accelerating a 60,000lb weight to 110mph for take-off. Both the B12/36 and P13/36 were to be stressed to cope with catapult take-offs. Once more the catapult section at RAE Farnborough was involved. This time they came up with a multi-ram hydropneumatic catapult. In anticipation of the requirement for much larger aircraft, Mr P Salmon of RAE had commenced the design of this system back in 1935. Its design was based on experience in developing catapults for various shipboard applications.

Development of the system continued in parallel with that of the Short Stirling, Handley Page Halifax and Manchester aircraft themselves. However, during this period Air Ministry policy was to change, extension of aerodromes began, together with the policy of installing concrete runways. The need for catapult take-off diminished. Installation of the heavy aircraft catapult was scheduled for a number of bomber airfields and had actually commenced at Harwell during 1938.

Development snags were experienced and this, together with the declining importance arising from the alternative approach to very heavy bomber operations, led to the concept being abandoned in late 1939.

Strategic bomber operations were the mainstay of RAF policy and even with the planned three metalled runways laid out at 120°, it was considered that the heavy bombers might not be able to cope with cross winds. To cater for this eventuality, a new concept for taking off heavy aircraft was considered. This concept was quite unlike and unrelated to the initial requirement in the 1936 specification and this time the Manchester *did* get to use it. A further relevant factor, although no documentation has been tracked down which directly links the two, may have been that not just engine power was considered to be close to limiting performance, but perhaps more so, tyre pressures.

The concept envisaged a so-called 'frictionless take-off' device. It involved a very extended, twin, steel track 4,400ft long and with a gauge of 22ft 9in, equivalent to the main undercarriage track of the Manchester. The track length was more or less equivalent in length to that envisaged for a fully loaded operational Manchester. The principles behind the system involved designing a trolley with few bearing surfaces, such that friction between the track and trolley was minimised, so permitting rapid acceleration. At the same time the trolley was to be capable of cradling the aircraft at an angle to the centre line of the track, such that aircraft could always take off into wind.

As originally conceived, following each launching a tractor would tow the trolley back to the starting point of the accelerator and in this manner, rapid serial launching of aircraft could be facilitated. Moreover, the lowered undercarriage of the aircraft was supported by the trolley such that at maximum all up weight the tyres did not carry any load.

The original drawings at Farnborough, dated 25th November 1938, show the almost one mile of track laid out from Jersey Brow on the airfield in a south westerly direction, into the prevailing wind. A turntable device located at either end of the track could be used to mount the aircraft. In addition to the railway-like rails and turntables the ground installation included the free-running trolley.

The basis of the latter was a massive cylindrical beam or axle between two small multi-wheeled dollies. These were coupled to an upturned V-frame which raised the tail of the Manchester into the flying position.

Close scrutiny of the remaining evidence shows no sign of any attachment point for rams or cables and indeed the very length of the rails suggests that external means of acceleration was never envisaged, although various authors have concluded that such means must have been available. No mountings for winching apparatus are evident on surviving photographs. Similarly, the trolley gives little inkling of how the Manchester could have been mounted so as to be angled-off from the centre-line. Possibly the key to this slewing lies in two horizontally mounted hydraulic pistons which could vary the distance between the trolley and each leg of the V-frame, the length of each V-frame changing accordingly. In June 1940 Avro were requesting funding for a modification to the 'direction controlled trolley'. Based on this information it seems evident that the concept was aimed at taking advantage of angling of the aircraft in some way and meanwhile exploiting the trivial friction in the system using the aircraft's own engines, in the absence of any external boosting.

Mounting the aircraft must have taken some time because the aircraft would first need to have been pulled or taxied onto the turntable and positioned on the trolley. At Farnborough a large hand-operated winch, mounted beside the track, appears to have served this purpose. A pneumatic or hydraulic platform was then raised under the tail wheel to lift the aircraft into flying attitude, subsequent to which the V-strut could be raised and locked in place. The only modification necessary to the aircraft appears to have been a short strut projecting down from the lower fuselage onto which the V-strut was locked.

Following this mounting the platform beneath the tail wheel was retracted and the turntable and aircraft aligned with the accelerator track. In July 1941 demonstration take-offs with a Handley Page Heyford loaded to 12,000lb were carried out at Farnborough. This paved the way for later experiments for which the first prototype Manchester, L7246, was modified to take both accelerator and arrester hook fittings.

Above: Frictionless take-off trials on the accelerator at Farnborough, 5th September 1942. L7246 was aligned perpendicular to the rails and hauled tail first onto the turntable, using the hand winch directly behind it. A ram beneath the tail wheel then raised the aircraft into flying attitude. *Crown Copyright 42278*

Below: The ventral V-strut was fixed to a pylon beneath the fuselage and the tail wheel ram then retracted. Horizontal rams resting on the rails may have slewed the V-frame and permitted the aircraft to be angled off the track centre-line into wind. The 1,470 yards, initially downhill, track, can be seen beneath the belly of the aircraft. *Crown Copyright 42276*

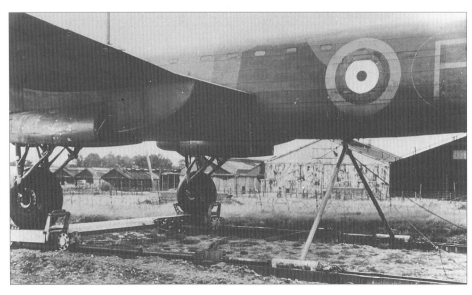

The turntable has been rotated through 90° and L7246 towed onto the track ready to accelerate itself from Jersey Brow, 8th September 1942. *Crown Copyright 42322*

L7246 was painted with white photo-calibration and yellow prototype 'P' markings prior to the frictionless take-off trials at Farnborough, 8th September 1942. The arrester hook has been removed since 5th September, but the fin guards are retained. *Crown Copyright 42321*

Close-up of the V-strut and undercarriage 'bogies'. *via Author*

During trials which extended through late 1941 and until September 1942 L7246 accelerated itself from the rails at Jersey Brow at weights up to at least 38,000 lb, three times that of the Heyford. In later phases attention was given to mounting the Manchester in a cradle with undercarriage already retracted, thus enabling higher all-up weights to be used. As part of the same series, consideration was given to fitting rocket boosters to the trolley to increase the take-off performance still further.

By this time it had become apparent that the launching rate with the system severely restricted its practicality as an operational aid. Moreover, operational experience was revealing that heavily laden aircraft could largely cope with take-off from metalled runways in cross wind conditions and at the tyre pressures necessary. Within a short period, when closely spaced stream take-offs for the bomber force became the norm, the frictionless take-off rails became recognised as anachronistic and a blind alley in development of heavy aircraft. In the event there are no records that either the retracted undercarriage, or the rocket boosting trials were completed.

Records of Manchester trials at Farnborough remain elusive, but it may be that the aircraft participated in a further and unrelated series of experiments in an effort to boost its lamentable take-off performance. Uncorroborated recollections of the RAE test pilot, Group Captain H J Wilson, include fitting two packs of 12 rockets to the underwing centre-section of L7246. These were allegedly wired to fire in sequential pairs to provide a long burn during short take-off trials. The anecdotal evidence specifies a number of successful trials, subsequent to which a group of Air Ministry and Bomber Command dignitaries were assembled at Farnborough to witness a demonstration of the technique. What nobody could discern was that a bracket supporting one of the rocket packs had fatigued. Wilson taxied to the take-off point with the observers in front and to one side, well placed to derive the best appreciation of the spectacular acceleration. The engines were gunned and the rocket firing button depressed. On first firing, one of the paired rockets sheared the fatigued bracket, instantly short-circuiting all cables to the remaining 11 rockets on that side. These fired in one salvo, swinging the Manchester viciously and uncontrollably in an arc towards the assembled group. The unleashed rockets shot forward through the airscrew disc, being chopped into short lengths and spraying amongst the now rapidly retreating figures! There has been no independent route to checking this story and if it did occur, no damage or record of repair of damage to the Manchester reached the aircraft accident cards. Possibly, as usual, the best stories are apocryphal ones?

At the same time as the frictionless take-off experiments were in progress operational experience with night bombers landing on small and poorly lit aerodromes had revealed a significant number of accidents arising from aircraft overshooting runways. As a possible palliative, consideration was given to fitting arrester systems comparable to those in use on carrier-based aircraft. Detailed consideration had been given to the concept extending back to as early as 1938. The initial RAE drawing from 25th November 1938 shows both the accelerator rails and the arrester system installed alongside. In late 1940 and early 1941 development of this system was speeded up. By August 1941 both static tests of the hook system and of the ground based arrester gear were well advanced.

The specification required a 60,000 lb aircraft to be arrested from 70mph with a retardation of 0.5'g'. All four heavy bomber types, Stirling, Halifax, Lancaster and the Manchester were apparently tested in a trials programme, extending until late 1942.

The ground installation consisted of massive reinforced concrete blocks spaced in pairs to either side of a runway to provide anchor points for the wires, as in the shipboard installations. The steel wires had a hydraulic retardation system to decelerate the aircraft at the specified rate. Each cable was stretched across the runway at a height of about 6in supported on a series of upturned V-frames. The wire was located at the apex of the V. An arrester hook was located beneath the rear fuselage of L7246, just ahead of the tail wheel.

RAE evaluated the hooks in a series of static load trials and, after several failures, a hook which maintained its integrity at 60,000 lb and failed at 72,000 lb was eventually developed. Possibly more than one type of aircraft mounting was evaluated because RAE records refer to both arrester hooks and also 'pulley-type' arrester hooks. The trials

programme itself did not progress entirely without incident. Again, according to the unsubstantiated memories of Group Captain Wilson, the earliest tests were conducted prior to metalled runways being installed at Farnborough. The size of the concrete anchor blocks had been carefully calculated to permit them to take the deceleration loads induced. A trials observation group, including those allegedly present during the rocket assisted take-off trials, was assembled to witness the first 'live' arrest. Wilson recalls flaring perfectly to catch a wire, whereupon the weights of the buried foundation blocks proved only a fraction of that necessary and a number of wires and blocks were jerked free, to be catapulted in the vicinity of the rapidly departing observers once more. Again, if any damage to the aircraft ensued, this is not evident in the accident cards.

What *is* documented is that on 1st August 1941 during ground trials at high speed an arrester gear failure resulted in the tail of L7246 rising to a great height, before crashing with great force back onto the runway. The tailplane spar extensions into the fuselage, fuselage bottom skin and fuselage former in this neighbourhood were damaged. Avro working parties attended at Farnborough to effect repairs, which included a new tailplane. The trials programme then continued. Full scale trials progressed satisfactorily, the aircraft flying with the hook retracted against the outer skin of the aircraft and being lowered onto the runway when it was necessary to engage an arrester wire. The fully loaded Manchester was arrested from 72mph in 460 yards during the course of the trials programme.

Early type of heavy bomber arrester hook fitted to Manchester L7246 for trials with the arrested landing system at Farnborough, 6th August 1941. *Crown Copyright 36562*

Amongst those airfields equipped with the mountings for the arrester wires at either end of its main runways was Bottesford in Leicestershire, where 207 Squadron moved in during November 1941. Despite the success of the trials, the installation turned out not to be viewed favourably by Bomber Command, it is suggested because the addition of even the 100 lb tare weight of the installation was considered not to offset the occasional benefit which might materialise from its use. None of the Command's aircraft were equipped with the arrester hook operationally. In the case of Bottesford aerodrome this was just as well because over the first few months aircrews watched the concrete anchors for the arrester wires tilt and subside into the weak soils upon which the airfield was built.

Whereas extensive testing of accelerated take-off and arrested landing systems were undertaken, other projects were stillborn. Amongst the few surviving Avro drawings for the Type 679 is one dated 3rd December 1940 specifying all the plant for tanker and receiver installations for in-flight refuelling. The project, in conjunction with Flight Refuelling Ltd, involved a 1,000 gallon transfer tank in the bomb bay of the tanker aircraft. A large diameter hose drum suspended horizontally from trunnions ahead of the tank projected into the airstream. In this respect the installation presaged the later UPKEEP installation of the bouncing bomb. The hose itself was led from the drum aft to the mid-under position from which it was trailed aft and below to mate with the receiver. Presumably the eventual aim was to install receiver equipment in operational Manchesters.

The intention was for the receiver aircraft to formate beneath the tanker. The reception coupling was to be mounted beneath the rear turret, a windlass on the rear floor was to deploy a hauling conduit with some form of grapnel to snag and recover the trailing hose. Union was to be effected at the coupling beneath the rear turret, from which point twin lines led forward to the two wing tanks. There is no information as to whether this project proceeded any further than the paper stage. Other problems with the Manchester were of a more immediate nature.

In early August 1941, in pursuance of the centre fin vibration problems, which had bedevilled the Manchester since the F.N.7A mid-upper turrets began to be fitted in March, L7320, the trials aircraft arrived at the Aeroplane & Armament Experimental Establishment (A&AEE) Boscombe Down. Presumably arising from wind tunnel tests it had been recognised that the most severe eddies were shed from the turret apex. An inverted 'dishplate' or cap was fitted to the turret top to smooth the airflow and so decrease fin buffeting.

In an unusual test arrangement L7320 was not only fitted with the enlarged Lancaster-type twin fins and rudders but also the Mk.I Manchester central fin. Flight tests were carried out at 185, 225, 250 and finally at 310mph with various turret angles. Only at the highest air speed did centre fin vibration become severe. It was concluded that the 'dishplate' would provide a major benefit, but by this time a decision had been made to adopt the twin fin arrangement thereby eliminating the centre fin vibration problems. An unexpected secondary benefit was that the dishplate also reduced vibration in the F.N.7A, making it a more stable gun platform even at speeds up to 310mph. On these grounds A&AEE recommended that despite elimination of the centre fin, incorporation of the 'dishplate' was recommended for all aircraft fitted with the F.N.7A. This recommendation was not acted upon.

At the end of the trial L7320 was dived to 320mph and the turret slewed to the port beam. Vibration in the centre fin increased and the pilot could feel this in the rudder pedals despite the centre fin not being connected to the controls. This was due to the 'panting' of the fabric cover to the fin. As speed increased the fabric cover ballooned on either side of the fin. Suddenly the fabric on the port side split vertically and tore away, followed rapidly by the ribs and fabric breaking away and detaching. As L7320 was eased out of the dive only the leading edge, spar and their adjacent fabric remained in place. With this front section only remaining, L7320 returned to Boscombe Down having tested the modification to destruction.

L7246 with yellow under surfaces and the final arrester hook lowered during the trials programme at Farnborough, 8th November 1941. Note what appear to be cable deflectors under both fins. Two Hurricanes and a Spitfire are in the background.
Crown Copyright 37963

Still from a trials film dated 14th February 1942, showing the Manchester prototype L7246 engaged in arrested landing trials. The aircraft is taxying at high speed with the hook lowered. The first wire is mounted on a low V-frame (extreme left). *IWM, FLM2143*

A few seconds later, the hook has engaged the first wire. Short white sections of the wire were a visibility aid to the pilot. *IWM, FLM2148*

Novel and fascinating as these various special trials may be, the main non-operational uses of the Manchester were more mundane and involved crew training during 1942 and 1943. Initially training was carried out on the squadrons. It was closely interwoven with early trials and has been discussed earlier. As 1941 drew on and the delays and engine problems increased it became apparent that operational squadrons had more than enough to contend with without the additional burden of crew training.

In a minute from Headquarters Bomber Command, High Wycombe, dated 9th May 1941 concerning modification to early Manchesters, a policy decision to establish 25 Operational Training Unit (OTU) for crew training was stipulated. As such aircraft would not be used for operational flying, only four major modifications had to be incorporated: modified engines, 33ft tailplane, Avro-fixed olive couplings in the hydraulic system and, if possible, de-icing equipment. Balloon barrage cutters and auto-pilots were not required. The minute specified that 12 Manchesters were to be allotted, but later lists an Initial Establishment of six with three in reserve. It was recommended that a total of 14 aircraft should be modified to this status with those unallocated being held in reserve to replace any wastage. L7280, L7283, L7286, L7276, L7279, L7284, L7291, L7292, L7294, L7282, L7288, L7290, L7298 and L7299 were earmarked. The aircraft listed above were disposed at the time at Waddington (three), Hemswell (six), and Coningsby (five). This would leave two aircraft from this initial batch, L7281 and L7295, to be modified at some later date.

No 25 OTU began to receive these Manchesters as early as June 1941 at Finningley. It is suggested aircraft may have been coded 'PP- ', but no proof of this is available. In addition to flying from Finningley, night circuits and landing practice was carried out from the nearby grass satellite, Bircotes. No. 25 OTU had the same problems with their Manchesters as the operational squadrons, although they at least were not over the North Sea or enemy-held territory.

In November 1941 the unit lost its first Manchester when the port engine of L7428 caught fire in flight. Flight Sergeant Adams was possibly in the company of several other pilots taking turns taking off and landing, and delayed feathering the propeller, with the

result that the aircraft lost height rapidly and struck the ground through a hedge, killing three and injuring the remaining two on board. The crash occurred at Scaftworth near Bawtry. It is not known when 25 OTU finally gave up its Manchesters, but if the aircraft accident cards are any indicator this could have been soon after March 1942.

In November and December 1941 Manchesters finally began to receive their modified engines and in rapid succession 83, 106, 50 and 49 Squadrons re-equipped. Insufficient aircraft were available for both the squadrons and the OTU. With the increase of Manchester squadrons it was decided in late 1941 that a number of formal Conversion ('Con') Flights would be attached, replacing the earlier and rather haphazard conversion training on the squadrons. In each case the initial complement would be four Manchesters, often from the earlier pre-production batches. On 6th January 1942 formal authority was given for such establishments manned by tour-expired aircrews from the squadrons themselves. By the end of the month 44, 97 and 207 Squadrons all had Manchester Conversion Flights.

Manchesters were semi-ideal Lancaster conversion aircraft, having identical instrumentation and layouts and comparable flying characteristics. When lightly loaded the Manchesters flew well and, unlike the Lancasters, were equipped with a second seat and extensions for all flying controls. Aircraft instruments were not, however, duplicated.

Nos. 61 and 83 Squadrons may have had Manchester Conversion Flights soon after, but certainly on 27th March 1942, when 61 Squadron at Woolfox Lodge was ordered to re-equip immediately with Lancasters, a Conversion Flight establishment of two Manchesters and two Lancasters was specified. Soon afterwards both Squadron and Conversion Flight moved to Syerston. Two weeks later a Conversion Flight was attached to 83 Squadron at Scampton, similarly equipped with two Manchesters and two Lancasters. Plans to re-equip 83 Squadron were also in hand. Nos. 97 and 207 Squadrons had already re-equipped, their Manchester complements being retained in their Conversion flights or transferred to other squadrons and Conversion Flights. No. 106, 50 and 49 were in the process of re-equipment.

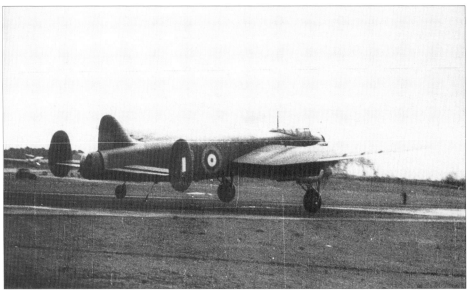

Early 1942 was truly a period of rapid interchanges of Handley Page Hampden, Manchester and Lancaster aircraft. By early May, Manchesters had already been superseded by Lancasters in 106 Squadron and a number of Lancasters also reached its Conversion Flight. In many cases Conversion Flights continued to train from the operational parent base, causing unnecessary congestion and loss of sleep to the operational crews. All this suggested the need for a further re-organisation, facilitated by the rapid introduction of the Lancaster, which in turn released more Manchesters for training. The operational life of the Manchester was rapidly drawing to a close, albeit after a period of almost 18 months – a long time period for an under developed and unsuccessful aircraft.

On 19th May 1942, 1654 Conversion Unit (CU) came into existence at Swinderby to standardise and provide badly needed conversion facilities for 5 Group. The new CU received eight Manchesters and eight Lancasters. In the same month both 49 and 50 Conversion Flights began to receive Lancasters to commence their respective conversions to this type. In turn 408 and 420 Squadron Conversion Flights formed with Manchesters. These two flights were both subject, five weeks later, to cancellation due to a decision to retain Hampdens on the parent squadrons for the time being.

On 18th May 1942, Squadron Leader Dave Penman found himself posted to Waddington as the sole instructor to convert 420 (RCAF) Squadron to Manchesters. L7386, L7400, L7402, L7416 and R5771 were allocated. Over the next few weeks squadron crews continued to fly Hampden operations, with the result that conversion was a protracted business. The first five pilots commenced dual instruction on 23rd May, but with other squadrons receiving Lancasters directly 420 were somewhat reluctant to embrace the Manchesters.

Matters came to a head on the night of 11th June 1942 when Penman was giving dual to Flight Sergeant Hiley, with three other crew members, in L7402. It was a clear dark night with no wind and the aircraft was taking-off and landing towards the east across the grass, slightly downhill, towards the Lincoln road. The flare path was a mere four or five goose-neck flares. Sitting in the right hand seat of the Manchester, the goose-necks disappeared on the final approach as the tail came down for each landing. A number of successful landings were accomplished until, with the goose-necks out of view on one more circuit, Penman had the feeling, as Hiley cut the throttles, that L7402 was a little high.

Over-riding Hiley's action, Penman opened both throttles just as the Manchester began to sink. Such action would have saved a Lancaster, but the two Vultures were simply not responsive enough and L7402 dropped so hard onto the grass that both undercarriage legs collapsed, the aircraft skidding to a halt in a cloud of dust. The retaining leg of the second pilot's canvas, fold-up chair jumped out of its seating with the impact, projecting Penman and the seat forwards and down into the bomb aiming position. Fortunately the aircraft did not catch fire and all five crew members scrambled out safely. The accident seemed to settle matters as far as the Canadians were concerned and they retained their Hampdens until August, when they transferred to 4 Group and converted to Vickers Wellingtons instead.

On 20th May 1942, Sergeant A J McHardy and crew of 106 Conversion Flight were nearing the end of their training and undertook a long cross country flight from Coningsby. The five man crew made a routine radio transmission as they crossed the Pembrokeshire coast en route for a turning point at the Scilly Isles and were never heard of again.

Above left: **Belly shot looking aft, showing the hook just engaging the wire – tail wheel behind. Note the spoon shape of the hook with what may be a locking bar ahead to retain the wire.**
IWM, FLM 2146

Above right: **L7246 flares for landing with the arrester hook lowered, 4th April 1942. First wire may be adjacent to the blurred figure ahead, beside the runway.**
IWM, FLM 2145

In late May 1942, it became clear something unprecedented was in the offing, with no operations, all leave cancelled and a maximum effort in prospect. Not only operational but training unit aircraft were required. Indeed it was aircraft availability as opposed to aircrews which presented the major problem. All Conversion Flights provided their aircraft, often with scratch crews, combinations of experienced captains with other crew members at an advanced stage in their training. Much interchanging of aircraft took place to optimise aircrew and aircraft availability. The participation of Conversion Flight Manchesters in the 'thousand' bomber raids on Cologne and Essen has been outlined in the previous chapter.

Following these two nights, Conversion Flight Manchesters never operated again, but reverted to their true role of training. This included all aspects of operational flying. Circuits and landings to train the pilots were followed by air-to-air firing for the gunners, bombing for the pilots and navigators at various nearby ranges and later extended navigation training on a variety routes around the United Kingdom coast. Finally crews carried out a simulated raid on a blacked out British City, later called a BULLSEYE, as a final dress rehearsal for operations.

One day a Westland Lysander target tug approached Waddington and landed hesitantly. After a short run, it stopped in the centre of the airfield, its engine running, impeding any further aircraft movements. Attempts to contact the pilot by radio failed, and a vehicle was sent out. Its driver found the Lysander pilot dead from bullet wounds incurred from wayward fire from a Manchester mid-upper gunner under training.

By the end of June 1942 the Manchesters were withdrawn from first line service and made generally available to the many Conversion Flights and to 1654 CU at Swinderby. Manchesters also went to 9 and 57 Squadron Conversion Flights.

On 5th June 1654 CU moved to Wigsley, 'Wicked' Wigsley, the most desolate and depressing station in 5 Group and the only station without a pub in striking distance. There were, however, moments of excitement. At about 1800 hours on 3rd July, two Junkers Ju 88 intruders appeared unannounced at low level over the airfield and fired on one of the Manchesters at its dispersal point. No one was hurt and only slight damage was done to the aircraft.

On 6th August 1942 a tragic accident occurred at the 207 Squadron airfield at Bottesford, when Manchester L7385 collided on the runway with Lancaster R5550 causing four fatalities. Only ten days later Flight Sergeant Dickenson in a 50 Squadron Conversion Flight aircraft, L7475, encountered what was to become a frequent Manchester accident, one which mirrored the squadron losses with relentless precision. Following a landing at Talbenny near Cardigan, Dickenson took off again at 1530 hours to continue his exercise. At 150ft, at a critical stage after take-off, the starboard engine caught fire. It was shut down and the propeller feathered, but Dickenson was unable to maintain height on the port engine alone. The captain was fortunate in carrying out a belly landing in a field at nearby Narloes. The aircraft was totally burnt out but only one crew member was injured. Following questioning the crew and inspecting the wreckage, accident investigators concluded a fuel line had cracked and the high octane had ignited.

On 21st August 50 and 83 Conversion Flights were both posted from their parent units and sent to Wigsley and on 22nd August 61 Conversion Flight moved into Swinderby, being joined next day by 207 Conversion Flight from Bottesford. The way was open to merging the various Conversion Flights into more effective training echelons. On 24th August 1942 authority was given in principle for a build up of all Conversion Flights to an establishment of eight aircraft, four Manchesters and four Lancasters. This was not an adequate solution to training problems.

By October 1942, it was recognised that the policy of having most of the heavy bomber training undertaken by small sub-units attached to each squadron was becoming increasingly impractical. It was decided that the future policy would be for the conversion of aircrew to heavy bombers to take place entirely on dedicated Conversion Units, to be known as Heavy Conversion Units. Normal establishment would be 32 aircraft in four Flights, 16 Manchesters and 16 Lancasters.

Two cycling teenagers, later RAF aircrew, photographed a large, and no doubt highly secret, aircraft out in the meadows bordering Farnborough in the winter of 1941-42. Close inspection reveals it to be Manchester L7246, complete with lowered arrester hook. *No. 207 Squadron archives / R Glynne-Owen*

Avro drawings of the Type 679, tanker (upper) and receiver (lower) Manchesters. Drawing A.1611 prepared by Flight Refuelling Ltd at Malvern, dated 3rd December 1940. *via Chaz Bowyer*

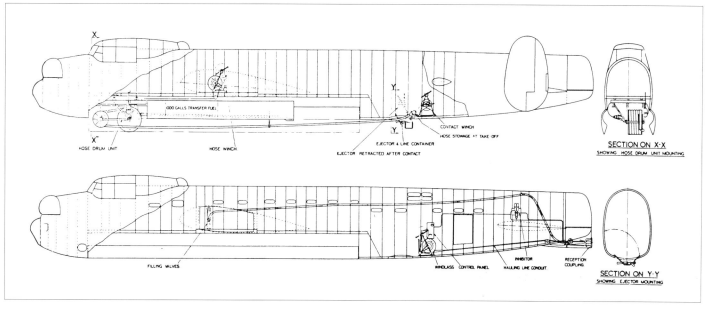

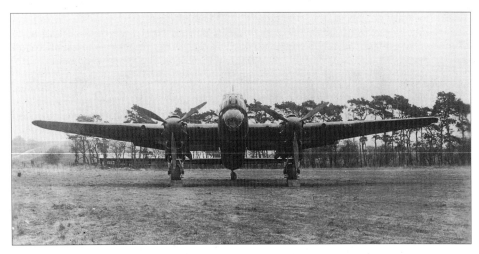

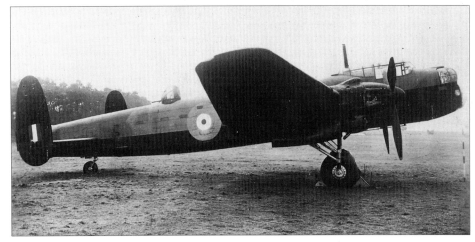

No. 1654 (H)CU was already in being, but shortly 1656 HCU was established with three Flights at Breighton, soon moving to Lindholme. No. 1660 HCU was established at Swinderby and 1661 HCU at Skellingthorpe with four and three Flights respectively.

At the CFs and HCUs some of 5 Group's most senior and experienced tour expired pilots were responsible for crew training. These were the fortunate few to have already survived two tours of operations with 5 Group, men like 'Kipper' Herring, Peter Ward-Hunt, Micky Martin. Some, like Wing Commander 'Junior' Gardiner and Charles Stenner were regulars, having joined the RAF at Halton as Aero Engine/Motor Transport Apprentices in the early 1930s. Stenner had completed 68 operations by this time and had learnt from his earliest training to nurse his engines. To him the two big Vultures were like sewing machines and although he had to take off at maximum power he always climbed and ran the engines at less than the stipulated maximum settings. Few can have flown more Manchesters than Gardiner. He flew 62 of the 202 aircraft built, starting with L7300 on 15th February 1941 and finishing with L7307 on 12th September 1943, a total of 337 hours operationally and in training.

Together, all these experienced pilots attempted to instil discipline and confidence

The trials aircraft, L7320, dispersed at Boscombe Down. *A&AEE HA447-3*

into their fledgling crews on the CFs and HCUs. The reputation for engine fires and alleged inability to fly on one engine were well known and the Manchester still retained its fearsome reputation. To try to counteract this Stenner would frequently shut down one engine with trainees on board and circle the airfield demonstrating the single engine performance. Gardiner, similarly, appreciated the giant bomber's flying characteristics, likening it to a big Avro Anson with no vices and very responsive in the roll.

Despite their best efforts the Manchesters continued to live up to their reputation, even when flown lightly loaded at the training units. Again it was almost invariably engine failures, often leading to fires in the air, which led to crashes. By now though component shortages, fatigue failures and burn outs of components long overdue for replacement were a contributory factor. Acute spares shortages were to finally lead to the aircraft being declared obsolete. The aircraft crash cards and resulting inquiry summaries of findings itemise large numbers of such failures, whilst the appendix lists numbers of

Manchesters from 1654, 1660, 1661 HCU, 57 CF and 1485 Bombing & Gunnery Flights written off in crashes following engine failures or fires.

In mid-December, changes occurred to the equipment of the four HCUs, 1654, 1656, 1660 and 1661, all hitherto operating 16 Lancasters and 16 Manchesters. The Lancaster complement was reduced to 12 and the Manchester increased to 20. As 1942 drew to a close and 1943 began the spares situation, especially for the Rolls-Royce Vulture engines, became steadily more acute. Even in 1941 certain components were in such critical short supply that squadron groundcrews were want to cannibalise usable engine components from crashed aircraft before the accident investigators arrived on the scene. By the time the aircraft reached the CUs components were having their lives extended well beyond normal just to keep aircraft flying. Arising from this, small components began to burn out, often leading to major engine fires and accidents.

On 10th September 1942 Squadron Leader Long was conducting flying training in R5784 of 57 Conversion Flight at Scampton when the starboard engine caught fire in the circuit. The aircraft made a normal landing and the station fire service extinguished the blaze. Investigation revealed the fire to have been caused by the 'D' block engine exhaust pipe burning out. The loss of L7386 of 57 CF on 5th October 1942 was later found to have its primary cause in the cracking of a light alloy hydraulic pipe which then sprayed inflammable fluid onto the red hot exhaust manifold.

When 1654 CU lost R5772 on 26th January 1943 the investigators found that the primary cause of the engine fire was the failure of No. 3 exhaust valve on the port engine due to burning through of the valve head. This in turn led to the flame traps burning through and igniting the engine itself. On 14th February 1943 L7286 of 1660 CU belly landed at Waddington after the starboard Vulture caught fire at 1,000ft. The flame traps in 'A' and 'B' blocks were burnt through. A similar incident at Swinderby on 24th March 1943 led to L7453 making a belly landing. In this case the fire started from the burning through of the exhaust manifold of 'A' block on the port engine.

Only three weeks later a fire in the vicinity of 'B' block on the starboard Vulture of R5841 of 1660 CU at Swinderby led to a serious crash, with three killed and three injured in the crew. Further incidents involved L7468 of 1660 CU at Swinderby on 1st May 1943 and L7297 of 1661 CU at Winthorpe on 19th May 1943. In both cases fires in the flame traps were the primary case. Despite all that the experienced flying instructors tried in order to instil confidence in their fledgling crews, the Vultures continued to warrant their evil reputation.

On 1st January 1943 No.1661 HCU had moved from Skellingthorpe to Winthorpe. The aircraft complements were further adjusted on 16th March 1943. Later still, further movement and expansion ensued and in September 1943 the move to 'Group Stations' was formalised and each Group allotted either two or three numbered bases, each consisting initially of either three or four stations. Swinderby housed 51 Base in 5 Group and had 1660 HCU in occupation, this base also controlling 1654 HCU at Wigsley and 1661 HCU at Winthorpe. No.1656 HCU was transferred to 11 Base in 1 Group.

By this time, however, the Manchesters had virtually disappeared from RAF second line service. Declared obsolete at the end of June 1943 due to severe spares shortages, a few soldiered on into the early autumn. Rows of Manchesters at each unit stood forlornly as spares aircraft, steadily being cannibalised. The Manchester era had ended but the child it spawned was on the way to be-

coming a war-winner. An anachronism before it even entered service, the Manchester nevertheless had served the RAF during three years of war from autumn 1940 to autumn 1943. By the time it went out of service it was unnoticed, by-passed by the great advances in bomber design it had in part contributed to. Its demise was, nonetheless, a marked contrast to the expectations attendant on its specification, design and early development.

Manchesters also served with the Torpedo Development Unit (TDU) at Gosport, although the name itself was something of a misnomer because the unit was responsible for developing and testing almost all the air dropped weapons used by Coastal Command. The TDU comprised a Headquarters Section, the Torpedo Development Flight and a Torpedo, Mine and Bomb Section, all controlled by the Ministry of Aircraft Production. The unit regularly sent detachments for trials at Pembrey and Weston-super-Mare. Each of these three aerodromes were adjacent to a particular trials area.

In the case of Weston-super-Mare the attraction was the high tidal range of the Severn Estuary. At high water on spring tides coastal sites at Sand Bay and nearby Pawlett Hams would be covered by 40ft of water which drained completely at the next low tide only six hours later. This allowed the performance of various weapons to be tested in

relatively deep waters, as well as readily retrieved from the seabed for examination. In October 1941 the unit had a range of aircraft allocated for trials purposes including Bristol Beauforts, Blackburn Bothas, Westland Lysanders, Fairey Albacores and Swordfishes, Handley Page Herefords and Hampdens.

At various times requirements developed for other trials aircraft and Manchesters were detached on an 'as available' basis for specific trials from the operational squadrons. The TDU Operational Record Book (ORB) and Appendices specify Manchester aircraft as being involved from as early as November 1941 and continuing until July 1943, by which time an Albacore and Manchester were at last supplemented by a Lancaster. From late 1941 through to April 1942 TDU relied entirely on Manchesters seconded from the operational squadrons. In that month the unit received two aircraft of its own from the previously unconverted Metropolitan Vickers batch, R5773 and R5774 being allocated.

Manchesters seem to have been used almost exclusively from Weston-super-Mare and occasionally from nearby Lulsgate Bottom, both a short distance from the Sand Bay and Pawlett Hams ranges. In the main, serial numbers of aircraft used at TDU are not recorded in its ORB, whereas for such second line duties little or nothing is recorded in squadron ORBs.

The twin fin (Avro Mod No. 390) trials aircraft, L7320, airborne from Boscombe Down. This view emphasises the bulk of the Rolls-Royce Vulture engine. *via Chaz Bowyer*

The entries in the TDU ORB are a laconic recitation of the various trials, in the main conducted at fortnightly intervals coincident with spring tides. Were it not for aircrew flying logbooks and personal recollections of aircrew concerned, little would remain discoverable on this aspect of Manchester service.

As a general rule it appears squadron air and groundcrew were detached with all necessary tools and spares, whilst TDU detached a working party of six men to provide weapon loading and dropping facilities to Weston. The range of weapons tested during the period November 1941 to July 1943 included depth charges of many marks, a wide range of mines with various fuses and the parachutes used to deploy them, as well as a variety of anti-submarine bombs, ranging from 600 to 30 lb. Tests varied from air photography of ballistics to ricocheting behaviour off water and the seabed. More uncommon devices included anti-surface vessel buoys, JW Bombs, flame floats, Schermully 'water snowflakes' and the mysterious and enigmatic 'Special Stores'.

The only hint of events untoward is the record for 28th August 1942 revealing that the TDU Manchester flown to Weston by Sergeant Thornton on 24th had become unserviceable and he returned by train to collect the reserve Manchester aircraft. This presumably relates to R5773 and R5774. However, like everything concerning the Manchester, all was by no means as routine as the records imply.

On 31st January 1942, Squadron Leader Thos Murray's 207 Squadron crew were detached to Weston for a week's mining trials with the unit. Murray and crew, plus 12 groundcrew members and all their equipment and personal kit took off from Bottesford in L7378 and flew to Boscombe Down to prepare for the trials. Next day they flew from Boscombe to Weston to be briefed and for L7378 to be got ready for the trials programme. Finally all was ready and on 3rd February 1942 L7378 took off from Weston loaded with the experimental mines. After 1hr 40 min flying the aircraft had to make an emergency landing at Chipping Warden, fortunately without injury to the crew or damage to the aircraft. The groundcrew at Weston were alerted and four fitters travelled to Chipping Warden, where repairs were effected. It was not until 5th February 1942 that L7378, complete with air and groundcrew, could return to Weston. The mining trials were resumed with flights on 5th and 7th February before the aircraft, crew and 12 groundcrew returned to Bottesford on 8th February.

'Dishplate' fitted to the apex of the F.N.7A 'Botha' turret for trials in L7320, aimed at reducing turret/centre fin interactions. Unusually, L7320 had the enlarged twin 'Lancaster' fins and also the standard centre fin for this trial. The 'dishplate' reduced both turret and centre fin vibration, but the switch to twin fin configuration led to the abandonment of the 'dishplate'. *A&AEE HA447-1*

At various times L7320 evaluated tail vibration induced by the rotation of the F.N.7A turret, the twin fin installation and the erosion of climbing performance caused by the oil cooler lips installed on the upper wing surface outboard of the engines. Close inspection shows the F.N.7A is fitted with the 'dishplate' but the aircraft is not equipped with the centre fin. L7320 finally met the same fate as many other Manchesters, forced landing and being written off after engine failure. *via Chaz Bowyer*

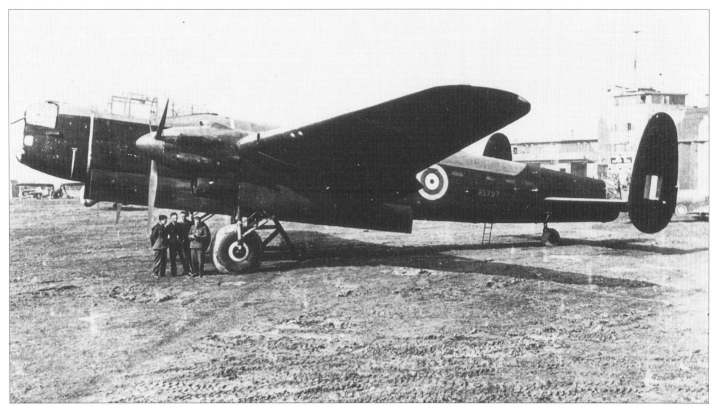

R5797 at Tollerton early in 1942, with members of a wireless fitting party from West Drayton who had uprated the wireless by installing a new Marconi T1154/R1155. Used only as a trials installation aircraft, including work on the Mk.XIV bomb sight, R5797 has nevertheless been modified to Mk.IA status and is fully armed. *S Hall*

Following the slight hiccup during this trials programme, Flying Officer Dave Green was the pilot on a second detachment to Weston on 8th March 1942. This time the aircraft participating was L7432 'EM-J', still reverently referred to on 207 Squadron as 'Kipper's Aircraft', it being the Manchester Herring had successfully brought back from Berlin on one engine on 7/8th September 1941. Aircraft, aircrew and the necessary supporting groundcrew were detached for a week to be at the disposal of the naval commander for the purpose of undertaking a series of trials with small, 30lb anti-submarine bombs. The objective was to release the weapons at various low levels, below 1,000ft, and speeds, to study their ballistics, trajectory and how they survived impact with the water. The drops would be made at high water at Sand Bay and the fragments collected for examination at low water.

At Bottesford, L7432 was loaded with

everything necessary for detached duty for a week. In addition to personal gear, this included trestles, tool boxes, bomb loading winches, armaments and the ten engine and airframe fitters who would accompany the seven aircrew. The aircraft was consequently very heavily loaded on take-off from Bottesford and, moreover, the overload weight could not be jettisoned in an emergency.

They flew down to Weston in daylight with clear instructions of how to signal the airfield defences to lower the defensive balloon barrage around the airfield to permit them to effect a safe landing. The Manchester was to announce its presence to the naval unit by diving over the observation post on the end of Weston Pier at 500ft. The duty officer would then telephone the airfield and instruct them to lower the balloons. They accordingly made a pass over the pier, which produced no response. A second pass was made with the same result. On the third overpass from the land, running along the length of the pier, they dived to 200ft and finally received a flashing light response as they headed out across the Severn Estuary towards Cardiff.

At this precise moment the constant speed unit of the starboard propeller disintegrated with a loud bang, followed by a louder howl as the propeller ran away out of control. By chance, Green had sitting with him in the cockpit, right by the engine controls, one of the best engine fitters on the squadron. Taking instant action without having to be instructed, the fitter immediately pressed the feathering button and also turned off the fuel

supply. Miraculously the feathering mechanism worked and the windmilling blades began to turn to present their edges to the airflow, slowing down as they did so. To be able to feather the propeller on the dead engine was a significant element in their favour, but the immediate situation was extremely grim. They were at 200ft over the turbulent, unforgiving waters of the Severn in an overloaded Manchester on one engine with a 17 man crew.

Many Manchesters would not even maintain height on one engine whilst lightly loaded. At 200ft they had neither the time nor the capability to lighten the load they were carrying. Dave Green acted immediately, advancing the port throttle and working quickly and efficiently to set the aircraft up to fly on one engine. As a precaution against the inevitable, Green ordered the entire crew to ditching stations. As they held their breath L7432 responded wonderfully once more to the challenge, not only were they not losing height but they were almost imperceptibly climbing.

For a Manchester to maintain height on one engine was unusual, to be able to climb was exceptional, but to be able to climb in such an overloaded condition must have been virtually unique. Suddenly the situation did not seem quite so grave and Dave Green was even able to think in terms of attempting a return to Weston-super-Mare. By this time they were some 7–8 miles north of the airfield. If only they could reach 1,000ft and if only the port Vulture would keep turning they might make it.

Air and groundcrew pose in front of the fifth
production aircraft, L7280 'OL-X' of 83 'Con'
Flight at Scampton. Built with an F.N.21A mid-
under and 28ft span tail, the aircraft was
reworked but still did not operate after being
allocated to 83 Squadron on 2nd April 1942.
Note the C1 type roundels. *via R Low /
F Harper, 83 Squadron archives*

No. 4 Manchester air gunners' course.
via Author

L7484, L7473 and R5791 were amongst air-craft used.

It has been suggested that Manchesters were allocated to Lancaster Finishing Schools and Air Gunnery Schools. Study of Aircraft Movement Cards confirms that the final allocation of a number of Manchesters was one of a range of Air Observer Schools, Air Gunnery Schools and Schools of Technical Training. When aircraft flew with a unit for any significant period minor and major accidents would lead to them quickly appearing in Aircraft Accident Cards and no accidents are recorded for any of these latter units. It would appear they were allocated as ground instruction airframes.

In early June 1943 one of the last and, as it turned out, stillborn twists in the Manchester saga is an Air Ministry directive dated 9th June 1943 specifying that Manchester aircraft had been earmarked for transfer to the Americans and they were not to be broken up when the type was declared obsolete at the end of the month.

It turns out a small number of expendable aircraft had been requested for 1478 Flight as flying wireless telegraphy stations. The aircraft were required for a special United States operation with the Tactical Air Force in North Africa. Aircraft were to be ferried to North Africa, where the nature of the operation required a good duration but a flying life of only 80 hours per airframe.

Initially two specially equipped Manchesters were considered, but their rapidly approaching obsolescence and critical shortage of all spares demanded a substantial number of airframes to be allocated for possible cannibalisation. Furthermore, concern was focus-ed on the lack of provision for tropicalisation of the Vulture engines. The Air Ministry minute affirms that it was lack of spares which had forced the RAF to declare the aircraft obsolete. After a few days of deliberation it was suggested to the Americans that they were more likely to obtain the results they needed in North Africa by providing two of their own Douglas Dakotas. The final record is a telegram confirming that 'The Americans do not, repeat not, want Manchesters'. Possibly someone had tipped them the wink on what they might be letting themselves in for?

Dave Green began a gentle turn back towards the airfield and eventually levelled off at 1,200ft. This gave him enough of a safety margin of height to ease back a little on the port throttle and nurse the engine home. When they got within sight of the aerodrome again they were relieved to see that the signal had got through and the balloons had been lowered. The approach had to be right, they would have only one chance. Green did a normal circuit, lined up onto the active runway and made a successful landing without damaging the aircraft. Switching off they all tumbled out, breathing immense sighs of relief. Dave Green's superb airmanship had got them down safely once more and the reputation of 'Kipper's Aircraft' increased.

There was, of course, no prospect of carrying out the proposed trials programme. The naval unit must have wondered at the bravery of young men who daily flew around in aircraft which, at so little provocation and at such frequency, fell out of the sky. On 9th March 1942 Flight Lieutenant Huntley-Wood flew down to Weston in L7515 then returned to Bottesford with the two aircrews and part of the groundcrew, leaving the engine fitters to replace the engine on L7432. Dave Green and crew eventually returned to Weston in R5835 on 14th March and undertook the anti-submarine bombing trials during 12 flights lasting until the 23rd. A small boat was moored close to the target buoy filming the drops – Sergeant 'Goldie' Goldstraw marvelled at the film crew's confidence in his bomb aiming.

The only other unit to make significant use of the Manchester was 1485 Bombing & Gunnery Flight (B&GF) at Dunholme Lodge, which mainly used the aircraft for air gunnery, fighter affiliation and bombing training in the period August 1942 to February 1943.

Chapter Ten

Reckoning

History has tended, not unnaturally, to judge the Manchester harshly. Official histories dismiss the aircraft, and with it the crews and their endeavours over 18 months, in a few words – as a failure and a disappointment. To many of the crews who flew the aircraft and lived with the constant and high risk of failure of the Rolls-Royce Vultures the aircraft too is best forgotten. Its achievements were indeed eclipsed by the Handley Page Halifax and the Short Stirling and ultimately by its offspring, the Avro Lancaster.

Performance in war, tends like all human activity, to be judged on attainment with little recognition for those who, despite giving all, have little tangible to show for their skill, fortitude and dedication. As a result, the efforts of the Manchester crews have been neglected and they have been assigned to the role of peripheral bystanders in the mainstream of war, which passed them by and consigned their efforts to obscurity, along with their aircraft.

A judgement on the aircraft itself depends upon perspectives. Those regular and auxiliary aircrews flying at the time of the Munich Crisis in 1938, who faced the prospect of war with a well-armed Germany in single-engined Hawker Hart and Hind biplanes and gained their operational experience in Handley Page Hampdens saw some salvation in the Manchester, with all its foibles. Technology had made giant strides for them in two short years.

In contrast, for the aircrews who initially served in Manchesters and later progressed to the Lancaster, their trepidation over the Vulture provided a marked contrast to the confidence they had in their four Merlins. The same airframe was transformed from rating only a few lines in the official history, to the machine which fulfilled the military strategists' dream.

Despite the years of frustration and failure, the Manchester did at least ease the transition to operational status of the Lancaster. The Manchester, and in turn its aircrew, were simply a victim of circumstances. By all reasonable standards an aircraft as advanced and untried as this should never have been expected to fly operationally before all its development problems had been overcome. But the Manchester was introduced at the blackest time of the war for the Allies. Britain and its far-flung Empire stood alone, its army

virtually disarmed at Dunkirk and its navy heavily committed in all the oceans of the world. Notwithstanding the severe limitations of the Vulture engines, production and operational flying continued. What the RAF needed was aircraft, *any* and *every* aircraft, as soon as it could get its hands on them. Thus, despite being reduced to the role of a stop-gap type until the more capable Lancaster became available, the aircrews had no alternative but to get what they could from the Manchester.

Almost all the problems with the Manchester can be laid at the feet of the Rolls-Royce Vulture. Yet it was that same wartime expediency that forced the Manchester to centre stage before it was halfway ready, which in turn, killed off the Vulture before its capabilities could be proved and extended.

Only enough effort was available in Rolls-Royce to cater for the Merlin and to prepare for its offspring, the Griffon. By brilliant design, power output from the Merlin was increasing monthly, whilst the Vulture was ultimately pegged back by the Achilles' heel of its star-rod design.

Had Rolls-Royce had equivalent skill and manpower to lavish on the Vulture, for which a superior con-rod design and split crankcase was already at an advanced stage, then it too could well have followed the pathway of steadily increasing power output, keyed to the reliability which attended its stablemates. Viewed with hindsight, it must be clear that far too much was being expected of Rolls-Royce and of an engine at the start of its development life.

When Vulture problems became critical, Avros turned initially to the Napier Sabre and Bristol Centaurus of equivalent power. A pair of Centaurus engines were reportedly installed in an airframe but never test flown. Viewed in the perspective of these two engines it is hardly surprising that the Vulture proved unequal to the task in 1940. The Sabre was not available in the Hawker Typhoon until 1942 and then gave untold trouble during the first year, whilst the Bristol Centaurus did not appear in the Hawker Tempest until after the end of the war in 1945.

Nor can Vulture output be considered wasteful. In addition to the Hawker Tornado, Vickers Warwick, Blackburn B20 and Hawker Henley test installations, a bare minimum of 404 Vultures were required to equip the

202 Manchesters produced. In this context it is remarkable that Vulture production terminated at 538 units. With such a small engine change capacity it was small wonder that Vulture spares were perpetually so critically limited.

In many respects the evil reputation the Vulture earned for unreliability and catching fire was richly deserved and in the circumstances it is perhaps not surprising, compounded as it was by the secrecy of the Air Ministry, that this reputation should at times get out of hand. In September 1941, when 61 Squadron temporarily relinquished its troubled Manchesters, the crews were convinced amongst themselves that the official reason was that Manchesters spontaneously caught fire over the target area.

At the development stage at which it was abandoned the Vulture was still to all intents and purposes an experimental engine, even though it was to remain operational in the Manchester for a total of 18 months. At this distance in time the faults and mistakes with the Vulture seem obvious and its premature service use can only be understood and appreciated from the standpoint of the extreme and desperate situation in which Britain found itself in the early war.

One elementary mistake in the Vulture, not readily explained, was the omission of the balance pipe between the two coolant pumps and the prolonged delay before this was appreciated and rectified. More fundamental and equally difficult to explain was the designer's choice of the low ductility, high Brinell steel for the con-rod bolts. Many engineers in Rolls-Royce were to reflect that this was the real killer, which finally doomed the engine. The choice of this material was dictated by the unusual star-rod design and the forces on the con-rod bolts arising from the four pistons. Fifty years ago the metallurgical properties of this material were poorly understood.

To this major step in the dark in materials and their properties must be added the fact that for many months Manchesters flew on operations with uneven and arbitrary tensions on the con-rod bolts. Only when multiple failures and write-offs occurred were con-rod bolt loads recalculated and the need for even and lower bolt tensions to withstand the extensions of normal use brought forcibly home.

Avro workers cluster around an early Manchester in the final assembly shop at Woodford in 1940. Note the profusion of wooden access ladders, benches and boxes, all built to order by the extensive woodwork shop at Woodford. Sandbagging against the assembly shop wall can be seen to the left.
G A Jenks collection

Finally, it was this recognition of excessive bolt loads and how close they perpetually came to failure that led Lovesey to take the wholly exceptional step of ordering that bolt loadings must be substantially reduced by decreasing maximum rpm from the initial 3,200 to a safer 2,850. For an engine designer this was an admission of defeat. In truth the bolt head loads had simply been wrongly calculated. With bolt loads at the very limit of safety, even at 2,850rpm, it is easy to see why the engine was not capable of achieving enhanced output without the major redesign of the con-rod finally recognised as essential.

The use of the two long and two very short con-rod bolts was the inevitable consequence of the unusual design adopted for the star-rod assembly in the engine. The odd combination of a master and one subsidiary rod on one side and a cap with the remaining two rods had dictated the diagonal split line and in turn the untried combination of short and long bolts in a strong material of dubious ductility. All these were the undoing of the Vulture and insurmountable obstacles to further development without the sweeping redesign outlined earlier.

Although serious problems had been experienced with the bearings these had been overcome by the development and adoption of A4 silver materials by the time the engine was abandoned. It was not considered that the four con-rods on a single bearing resulted in an excessive or unreasonable load. Indeed radial engines employed single bearings with large numbers of con-rods to a single bearing. The prolonged problems with bearing materials in the Vulture had other origins. So the Vulture passed into history with none of its systems being perpetuated through into other engines. It was a dead end.

It is an oft repeated 'fact' that more Manchesters were lost on operations due to engine failures than to enemy action. Modern analysis of losses can at least lay this ghost. Although in the period up to August 1941, 207 and 97 Squadrons did lose a number of Manchesters due to engine failure, from this time onwards such operational losses became remarkably few, as is apparent from the appendix of individual aircraft histories. The efforts of Rolls-Royce to improve the reliability of the Vulture, especially in the critical May-August 1941 period are well reflected in the loss statistics.

Although far fewer Manchesters were lost due to engine failures than wartime rumour suggested, it is equally apparent that many Manchesters continued to be lost following often quite superficial damage to just one engine. This exposes to scrutiny yet another of the popular myths of the aircraft, which has continued to be debated with some vehemence by those directly involved, as to whether the Manchester could maintain height on one engine. Again the answer seems clear. Some aircraft could and others decidedly could not, whereas some highly skilled and experienced pilots could and others, less proficient, could not. With the possible permutations of aircraft and pilots this breaks down to a ratio of one in four chances of remaining airborne. This, naturally, is an indication of the odds, not of the statistical chances, because aircraft and aircrew performance cannot be retrospectively established.

A feature of this history which perhaps stands out above others is the many examples of the most determined and desperate attempts at bringing home Manchesters on a single engine. In this respect, amongst others, we find examples of the increased stress factors which Manchester aircrews faced. In addition to the numerous examples presented in the narrative where crews baled out of, crash-landed or ditched their failing Manchesters, it is not surprising too that numerous other examples of successful single engine returns have come to light.

Clearly, 'Kipper' Herring and his crew on 7th September 1941 were by no means alone in their experiences. Examples of Manchesters returning successfully from well out in the North Sea, from the German coast, from Brest and the Ruhr are on record. What still endures is that Herring did complete the longest single engine return. His gallantry award was richly deserved, but the experiences of his peers in equivalent circumstances lead one to wonder if, as was suggested, anyone who flew Manchesters on operations against such odds was equally eligible.

Possibly a further manifestation of the success of Rolls-Royce efforts to improve engine reliability, albeit within the narrow limits of the serious under-powering, was that almost all of the successful single engine returns took place after the May-August 1941 spate of engine modifications. As with 'Kipper' Herring's achievements, those of Leslie Manser have several parallels. Many equally courageous and selfless endeavours and sacrifices in Manchesters went unrecognised and unrewarded and are recorded in this account for the first time. In this, however, the Manchester was no different from other wartime aircraft.

Avro themselves had started with problems equally as serious as Rolls-Royce with their 'side of the deal'. The initial flying surfaces had all been ridiculously undersized and all had been extended. The original predictions of speed for the Manchester, at 341mph maximum, had been way above what was realistic and the weight had risen alarmingly.

The airframe weight, fixed military load and crew complement had all spiralled upwards. Even the weight of a pair of Vulture engines was more than one ton greater than that initially forecast by Rolls-Royce. Small wonder then that Chadwick was worried and had so soon turned to the four Merlin alternative concept. Despite these weight increases, power output from the Vulture remained much as originally envisaged. By sheer hard work, Avro had overcome their problems and indeed, in the main, had done so much earlier than Rolls-Royce had come to grips with theirs. Chadwick was later to recognise and accept that his initial forecast of 12 months between the start of the design and the first flight was over-optimistic.

However, during this phase he had many,

often stillborn, changes foisted on him by the Air Ministry. In turn the unrealistic ancillary roles of dive bombing, torpedo bombing and troop carrying were abandoned, but not before months of precious time and effort had been squandered on them. Not just basic problems, but also ancillary problems like the hydraulic system were solved. All this was undertaken at the same time as major constructional innovations were being proven.

These problems had largely been ironed out in the Manchester, which nevertheless was perpetually handicapped by its catastrophic under-powering. Yet, behind this failure, something quite outstanding was waiting to emerge. Thankfully that occasional combination of far sightedness and good fortune came together.

The Manchester was basically an aircraft with outstanding stability and flying characteristics, which reached their peak in the perfectly proportioned Mk.IA. It was easy to fly and possessed of light, well harmonised controls, and gave unequalled manoeuvrability for such a heavy aircraft.

On the production line the Manchester had evolved rapidly. Only nine, ten or eleven airframes had the unsatisfactory F.N.21A mid-under turret and these were removed before operations began. Only the first 20 had the short span 28ft tail. This was replaced by the 33ft tail from the 21st aircraft onwards. The twin fin 'Lancaster' tail replaced the triple fin on the 133rd aircraft. By this time, other than in respect of its shorter span and greater leading and trailing edge taper of its mainplanes, the aircraft was to all intents and purposes a Lancaster in appearance. However, much additional restressing and beef-

ing up of the structure internally was necessary to create the Lancaster.

Total production came to 202 Manchesters – two prototypes, followed by 157 production aircraft by Avro and 43 by Metropolitan Vickers – before output transferred to the Lancaster. Its operational roles were confined to bombing, mining and leaflet dropping, in which capacity a little over 1,260 sorties were dispatched. Seven operational squadrons and two conversion flights undertook operations. No. 207 Squadron contributed the lion's share of Manchester operations, followed by 61.

In spite of early engine failures in service the loss statistics show a pronounced trend in which the earliest squadrons have the best and the later squadrons a sequentially worse loss record. The vulnerability of the Manchester, largely due to the inadequate power and unreliability of its Vulture engines, was soon appreciated. This did not prevent a number of audacious and desperate daylight bombing and mining operations, the latter at low level, being attempted. By the same token, throughout 1941 and early 1942, as the role of the strategic bomber was just emerging and before the regimented flying heights, times and courses were specified, the more determined crews did not think it out of the ordinary to descend to ground level and become night intruders on homeward operational flights.

The clear, clean lines of the Manchester, Mk.I L7284 'EM-D' of 207 Squadron.
No. 207 Squadron archives / R Glynne-Owen

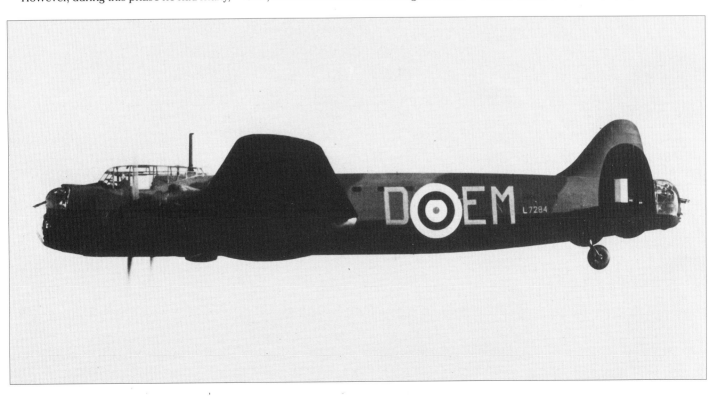

Above and below : **Following its withdrawal from active service, L7420 was used by both the RAF and USAAF for dinghy and ditching training. On 13th June 1956 it was salvaged from a flooded gravel pit of the Lincolnshire Sand & Gravel Co on the Burton Estate by aircrews from USAF Sturgate. The longest surviving Manchester, it is assumed to have been scrapped following recovery. L7420 was struck off charge on 19th November 1943, and never undertook 'ops'.** *Lincolnshire Echo via Peter Green.*

Shipping convoys, trains, airfields and anti-aircraft installations were all considered fair game in this informal aggressiveness. Latterly, low level searchlight suppression operations were officially sanctioned for the returning bombers. Determined, yes, but foolhardy, never, these often experienced second tour crews had a clear perception of how dire their plight would be if return fire caused a Vulture failure at such low altitude.

With 202 Manchesters contributing just over 1,260 sorties the average attempted lies close to six per aircraft. However 15 Manchesters were dispatched on 20 or more occasions, of which L7378 is the clear leader, having attempted 33 operations. At least 40 Manchester pilots undertook ten or more operations as aircraft captains. No captain completed a 30 operation tour exclusively on Manchesters, but Pilot Officer Gardiner holds the record for setting out on 27 occasions.

Set beside the context of the small number of Manchesters built, and its acknowledged limited military achievements, it should be pointed out that the aircraft was in squadron service for 20 months, operational for 17 of these and throughout 1941 and the first part of 1942 remained, on average, the most numerous heavy bomber available for operations in Bomber Command. Engine serviceability notwithstanding, of the total Manchesters built, total airframe hours for slightly less than 30% have survived. If this group is considered to be representative of the whole then 66% of aircraft completed more than 100 hours flying, 9% (five aircraft) more than 400 hours and R5835 achieved the ·highest airframe total, 471¼ hours. Judged on these grounds, Bomber Command derived commendably efficient service from the Manchester.

Of the 200 production Manchesters built, 77 were lost on operations and 20 more in accidents by the operational squadrons prior to withdrawal from first line service at the end of June 1942. A further 24 were lost in non-operational flying accidents by second line units, making 121 in all. The operational squadrons lost 12 of their aircraft as a direct consequence of engine failure, the non operational units lost a further 21. The circumstances of a further 28 losses on operations could not be established. In addition, there were an unknown number of engine failures following which aircraft landed on one engine or were damaged to various degrees but not destroyed.

Manchesters for the most part were well served by their aircrews, amongst whom were highly experienced regulars, second tour crewmen and a significant number of the small percentage of pilots with 'Above Average' ratings. Peter Burton-Gyles, Charles Kydd, 'Kipper' Herring and Guy Gibson were amongst the Manchester 'giants' who served with exceptional distinction and failed to survive the war.

Another pilot, who also went on to become a leading night intruder on de Havilland Mosquitoes, was John De Lacy Wooldridge. Not only was he an exceptionally audacious pilot but also an author, composer and musician! He wrote *Low Attack* describing his Mosquito experiences, as well as the script for *Appointment in London* made into a play and film. His music was performed by the New York Philharmonic conducted by Leonard Bernstein.

Above all 'Dim' Wooldridge was a great character. Visiting a hotel on a rare spell of leave, he registered and was approached by the hall porter who asked if there was luggage to be carried to his room. 'Yes,' replied 'Dim', rifling through his pockets until he came across his toothbrush, which he presented to the startled porter before following him up the staircase!

Exceptional qualities were to be found not only amongst the pilots but also other trades. A number of the air gunners and gunnery leaders were of the highest quality and several had multiple claims for German fighters to their credit. From the ranks of 'hostilities only' aircrews were more outstanding individuals, none can represent the calibre of these better than wireless operator/air gunner Sergeant Maxwell Riddell. Known universally in 207 Squadron as 'Mad Max', he not only stood foursquare and flew his Manchester operations with distinction but was perpetually to be found hanging about the crew room door when 'ops' were pending, hoping to scrounge spare trips over and above his commitment.

Flying bomber operations was perpetually stressful, frightening and occasionally harrowing for the crews involved. For the Manchester crews it was arguably worst of all. They were flying operations in a general wartime climate of successive military reverses. Germany and Japan were becoming stronger daily it seemed. In their immediate sphere, experienced crews detected a perceptible stiffening of German defences. Whatever the target, they were forced to steel themselves for a double crossing of the searchlight belt in Holland, which was often more dangerous than the bombing run itself. Flak defences, especially the highly mobile light guns, were increasing rapidly in numbers and efficiency. The night fighters too were beginning to get going and presented an ever more serious threat. Targets, too, were becoming better defended and radar prediction of guns and searchlights further increased the risk. On top of this very frequently was the inclement weather of Northern Europe.

Whereas the earlier Hampden crews with their reliable Bristol Pegasus engines, had flown with relative impunity across blacked out Germany night after night, generally able to keep below cloud to ease navigational difficulties and have the satisfaction of seeing

and hitting their targets, by the time of the Manchesters it was quite different. Manchesters had to fly higher and take to the clouds for their own self protection. Now the frustration increased. They could rarely find their targets, had no navigational aids and spent long, dangerous periods quartering the sky looking for gaps in the cloud to pin-point their position. Only very rarely did they have the satisfaction of seeing their bombs explode on the designated aiming point. In all these respects the Manchester crews were in no worse a position than other RAF bomber crews.

However, the stresses imposed upon the aircrews by operating the Manchester were enormous. At a time when a tour on Hampdens would be completed in as little as four months, some 207 Squadron aircrews joined the unit in November 1940 and did not complete their tours until March or April 1942 after the Manchesters were replaced by the Lancaster. The many engine failures during the work up period made it a dangerous time for the crews and they had been operational for over a year.

There was also the major additional stress factor resulting from the extremely unreliable nature of the Vulture engines. Even when not directly threatened by the enemy in the air the many possible sources of engine failure were a cause of profound worry. Unlike other aircraft, which could take a lot of punishment, crews knew that just one flak or fighter hit, or even a spontaneous leak in any of the cooling or lubricating lines to one engine meant the almost inevitable loss of the aircraft. Manchesters carried abundant threats from within!

All Bomber Command aircrews went through the same emotional steeling process in the lead up to an operation and this took its toll irrespective of whether the operation was carried out or cancelled at some time before take-off.

Weather and other operational reasons led to cancellations. For example, 207 Squadron embarked upon 94 separate operations during its Manchester era, whilst at least a further 59 were briefed but cancelled prior to the squadron becoming airborne. Frequently military or weather problems would lead to crews being at readiness for five or six consecutive days.

Even when operations were mounted a crew often went through the entire physical and mental preparation only for their aircraft to become unserviceable in the hours prior to take-off or soon after becoming airborne. This induced an extreme frustration and anger in the crews, who naturally felt their aircraft was letting them down, whilst they had precious little to show in military terms in return for their efforts. Commonly such failures resulted in a sufficiently serious hazard to the aircraft that they were as dangerous as any enemy action.

The prototype Avro 683 Lancaster, BT308/G.
First flown at Woodford 9th January 1941.
Peter Green collection

The second prototype Lancaster, DG595. It
carried the definitive oval shaped tailplanes,
dispensing with the middle fin. The tailplane
was of 33ft span. *Peter Green collection*

A further factor which preyed on the minds of aircrew through much of 1941, although this was common throughout Bomber Command, was that the concept of a tour of a predetermined number of operations had yet to be introduced. The crews went on flying until they were lost on operations or their squadron or station commanders decided they had earned, or more likely needed, a rest. Not surprisingly the crews felt they were on a treadmill with only one possible escape.

Bob Fletcher, a 97 Squadron Manchester pilot, was caught up in this 'never ending treadmill feeling' along with the rest. He managed to get in eleven Manchester operations in nearly 12 months of a seemingly nightmarish prolonged torture. Fletcher likened the experience to walking in a dark tunnel with no light at the end and could never envisage himself completing one tour, let alone his eventual two. His happiest recollection was of seeing the last of them and moving onto the Lancaster.

As the war progressed Chadwick's visionary design achieved its full potential. Not only was the Lancaster superior in performance to the Halifax and Stirling but just as importantly it was a production triumph for Avros. Construction as major sub-assemblies not only eased transport but also repair. The Air Ministry was so impressed by the superiority of the type that the Ministry of Supply

decided to evaluate Avro's production techniques with a view to making them standards throughout the aircraft industry. On 6th January 1944, Mr R Lubbock and Professor Postan visited Chadwick at the Chadderton works for an extensive interview. In respect of the design, Chadwick emphasised the early importance he had attributed to the bomb compartment and bomb gear, followed closely in his judgement by the undercarriage. By concentrating all fuel in the wings and bombs in the fuselage this was certainly one major area in which his design surpassed the Halifax and Stirling. Furthermore, his undercarriage was lighter than that in the Halifax and far superior to the terrible contraption used in the Stirling.

His long, slim, low set Merlin installations contrasted with the short and high-set engine mountings in the Halifax. As a consequence the propellers in the latter were located in the up-current of air rising over the wing leading edge. Each blade rotation took it alternately through the upstream airflow on one arc and the downstream airflow on the other. Engine and airframe vibration resulted. Although Chadwick may not have itemised it to Lubbock and Postan, Alec Harvey-Bailey Jnr of Rolls-Royce recalls that in one three month period he had 95 reduction gear failures from Merlin Halifaxes through his hands, 75 of which were from the port outer engine. To counteract this, Merlin Halifaxes were seen

with four-bladed propellers, often fitted to the port outer only from this time.

By now the cautious comments of Type 679 and Lancaster supporters in November 1940, that there seemed no reason to suppose that the 'Manchester III' should not at least match the Halifax in performance were in the past. In respect of production Professor Postan mentioned that Sir Frederick Handley Page had also tried to cater for the split assembly methods, perfected by Chadwick, but had clearly been less successful. Unusually for him, Chadwick's response included the gentle jibe that Sir Frederick's principal contribution to the war effort had been to try to convince Lord Beaverbrook that there should be only one heavy bomber, the Halifax, and that the Lancaster was no good.

So, from the modest and humble beginnings of 'Hettie' Hyde and a few others in the pre-production Manchesters, a mighty strike force of Lancasters was created. Avros had given birth to a line of bomber aircraft which developed sequentially into the Lancaster, the York, the Lincoln, and the Shackleton. It was a distinguished family line which served the RAF for 50 years. Clearly, once released from the burden of its under-developed and unreliable engines, the airframe justified all the aspirations of its makers, the aircrew and the RAF. Even 50 years later the Shackleton had bomb bay components constructed from Type 679 drawings.

Historians have evaluated the extent to which unreasonable restrictions and reparations imposed on Germany after the First World War, Hitler and his henchmen, the Peace League, public opinion in Britain and the politicians in general contributed to the outbreak of the Second World War. Wherever responsibility lies, it was the staffs of Avro and Rolls-Royce who paid the price in exhaustion arising from seven day a week, 18 hour days in bringing the premature Manchester and its Vultures into service. Uniquely though, the 5 Group aircrews operating their engine test-beds into the very heart of enemy airspace on more than 1,200 occasions, paid their price in blood.

The least we can offer is to remember them.

Above: The Manchester airframe went much further than the Lancaster. The design can be traced through three other Avro products. The prototype Type 685 York transport (LV626) first flew on 5th July 1942. C.1 TS792, illustrated, was built in 1945 and went on to serve with BOAC as G-AGNO.

Right: The Type 694 Lincoln was designed in advance of Specification B14/43 calling for a developed Lancaster, with thoughts of the war against Japan. The prototype (illustrated) PW925, made its first flight on the 9th June 1944.

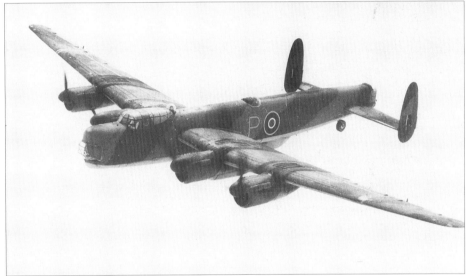

Below: The final development of the line was the maritime development of the Lincoln, and initially referred to as the Lincoln III. The Type 696 Shackleton prototype VW126 first took to the air on 9th March 1949. No.220 Squadron MR.1A WB831 is illustrated.
All Peter Green collection

Appendix A

General Arrangement Drawings

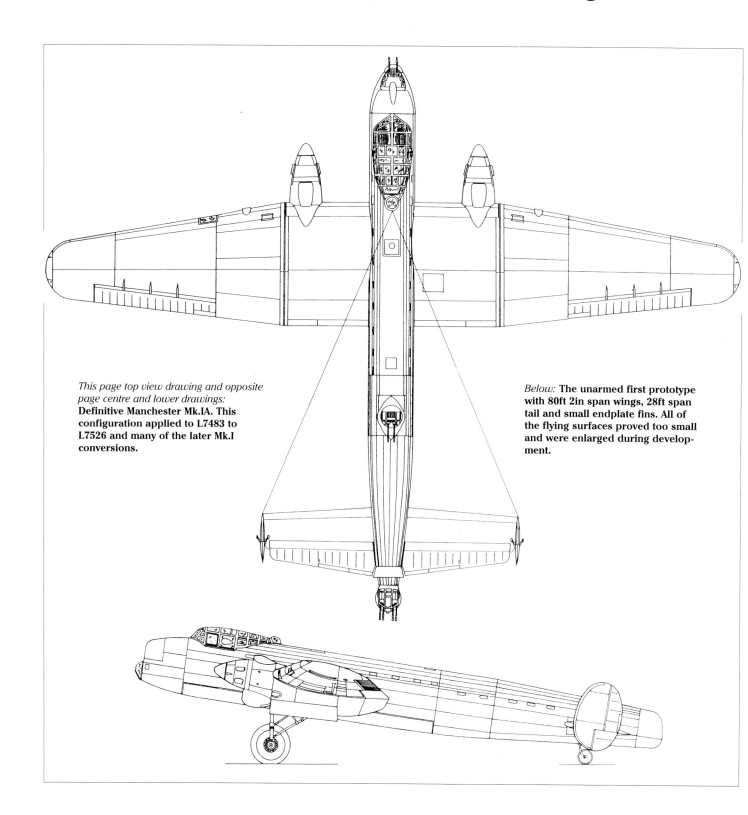

This page top view drawing and opposite page centre and lower drawings: **Definitive Manchester Mk.IA. This configuration applied to L7483 to L7526 and many of the later Mk.I conversions.**

Below: **The unarmed first prototype with 80ft 2in span wings, 28ft span tail and small endplate fins. All of the flying surfaces proved too small and were enlarged during development.**

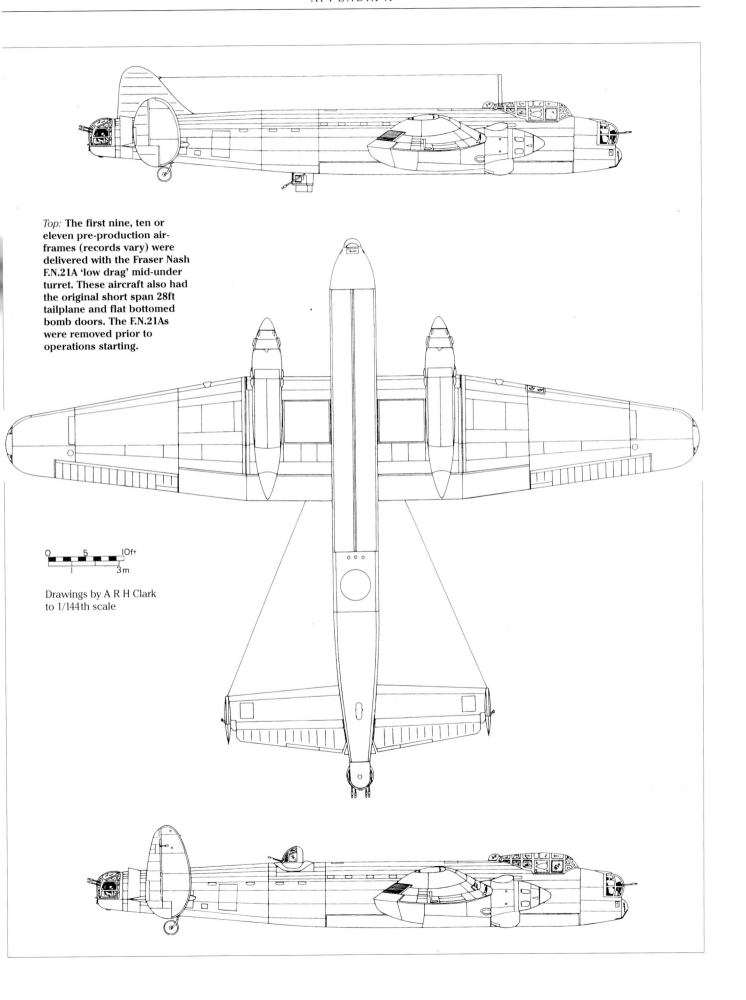

Top: **The first nine, ten or eleven pre-production airframes (records vary) were delivered with the Fraser Nash F.N.21A 'low drag' mid-under turret. These aircraft also had the original short span 28ft tailplane and flat bottomed bomb doors. The F.N.21As were removed prior to operations starting.**

0   5   10ft
1   3m

Drawings by A R H Clark
to 1/144th scale

Appendix B

Manchester Units

OPERATIONAL SQUADRONS
in order of equipment

207 Squadron (code EM-)

First Manchester toc	6th Nov 40 (L7279)
First Manchester Op	24/25th Feb 41
Final Manchester Op	10/11th Mar 41

Commanding Officers:

W/C N C Hyde	1st Nov 40 to 8th Apr 41
S/L C J F Kydd (as	8th Apr 41 to 30th Apr 41
Acting CO)	6th May 41 to 21st May 41
W/C J N D Anderson	30th Apr 41 to 6th May 41
W/C K P Lewis	21st May 41 to ?? 41
W/C C Fothergil	?? 41 to 10th Mar 42

Bases

Waddington, Lincs	1st Nov 40 to 17th Nov 41
Bottesford, Leics	17th Nov 41 to 11th Mar 42.

97 Squadron (code OF-)

First Manchester toc	25th Feb 41 (various, 8 del'd; L7282 recorded as on charge the following day)
First Manchester Op	8/9th Apr 41
Final Manchester Op	17/18th Jan 42

Commanding Officers

W/C D F Balsdon	25th Feb 41 to 18th Dec 41
W/C J H Kynoch	18th Dec 41 to 17/18th Jan 42

Bases

Waddington, Lincs	25th Feb 41 to 11th Mar 41
Coningsby, Lincs	11th Mar 41 to 17/18th Jan 42.

61 Squadron (code QR-)

First Manchester toc	8th Mar 41 (L7307)
First Manchester Op	21st/22nd Jun 41
Final Manchester Op	25/26th Jun 42 (Conv Flt – CF)

Commanding Officers

W/C G E Valentine	1st Mar 41 to 2nd/3rd Sep 41
W/C T C Weir	2/3rd Sep 41 to 25/26th Jun 42

Bases

Hemswell, Lincs	1st Mar 41 to 17th Jul 41
North Luffenham, Rutland	17th Jul 41 to ? Oct 41
Woolfox Lodge, Rutland	? Oct 41 to 5th May 42
Syerston, Notts	5th May 42 to 25/26th Jun 42.

An unidentified Mk.IA of 61 Squadron at Woolfox Lodge, 1942. Note the pale patch ahead of the tailplane, co-incident with the First Aid Kit.
G E Williams

83 Squadron (code OL-)

First Manchester toc	10th Oct 41 (L7382)
First Manchester Op	28/29th Jan 42
Final Manchester Op	1st/2nd Jun 42 (CF)

Commanding Officers

W/C S O Tudor	Dec 41 ?

Base

Scampton, Lincs	? Dec 41 to 1st/2nd Jun 42.

106 Squadron (code ZN-)

First Manchester toc	20th Jan 42 (L7390)
First Manchester Op	20th/21st Mar 42
Final Manchester Op	25/26th Jun 42 (CF)

Commanding Officers

W/C R S Allen	Feb 42 ?
W/C G P Gibson	

Base

Coningsby, Lincs	? Feb 42 to 25/26th Jun 42.

50 Squadron (code VN-)

First Manchester toc	25th Jan 42 (R5778)
First Manchester Op	8/9th Apr 42.
Final Manchester Op	25/26th Jun 42 (CF)

Commanding Officers

W/C J M Southwell	30th Mar 42 to ?
W/C Oxley	

Bases

Skellingthorpe, Lincs	30th Mar 42 to 20th Jun 42
Swinderby, Lincs	20th Jun 42 to 17th Oct 42.

49 Squadron (code EA-)

First Manchester toc	18th Apr 42 (L7287)
First Manchester Op	2nd/3rd May 42
Final Manchester Op	25/26th Jun 42 (CF)

Commanding Officers

W/C L C Slee	17th Apr 42 to ?
Second CO not identified	

Bases

Scampton, Lincs	17th Apr 42 to ? .

44 Squadron Conversion Flight (code KM-)

First Manchester toc	26th Feb 42 (L7382)
First Manchester Op	30th/31st May 42
Final Manchester Op	1st/2nd Jun 42

Commanding Officer W/C Smales

Base Waddington, Lincs.

(44 *Squadron*'s first Manchester, L7382, was taken on charge 27th Dec 41. They undertook no operational flying as an all-Manchester unit, however, L7430 'KM-N', captained by P/O S T Farrington on loan from 49 Squadron, undertook the MILLENIUM TWO raid to Bremen on 25/26th June 42, together with eleven of 44 Squadron's Lancasters. See page 168.)

408 Squadron RCAF Conversion Flight (code EQ-)

First Manchester toc	17th May 42 (L7425)
First Manchester Op	30th/31st May 42
Final Manchester Op	1st/2nd Jun 42

Commanding Officer W/C J D Twigg

Base Balderton, Notts.

CONVERSION FLIGHTS & UNITS

9 Conversion Flight

First Manchester toc	13th Sep 42 (L7425)
	(9 Squadron's first Manchester, R5838, on charge 8th Aug 42 – no operational flying)
Representative acft	L7464 'D'
Formed	8th Aug 42 at Waddington
Disbanded	7th Oct 42 by merging into 1661 Heavy Conversion Unit.

44 Conversion Flight

First Manchester toc	26 Feb 42 (L7382)
Formed	Jan ? 42 at Waddington
Disbanded	7th Oct 42, by merging into 1661 Heavy Conversion Unit.

49 Conversion Flight

First Manchester toc	18th May 42 (L7429)
Representative acft	L7296 'Y'
Formed	16th May 42 at Scampton
Disbanded	7th Oct 42 by merging into 1661 Heavy Conversion Unit.

50 Conversion Flight

First Manchester toc	18th May 42 (L7521)
Formed	16th May 42 at Skellingthorpe
Moved	17th Jun 42 to Swinderby
	21st Aug 42 to Wigsley
Disbanded	7th Oct 42 by merging into 1654 Heavy Conversion Unit.

57 Conversion Flight

First Manchester toc   No allocation has been traced to 57 'Con' Flight, however, R5771 and L7386 were issued to 57 *Squadron* on 6th and 8th Sep 42 respectively – no operational flying.
Formation and disbandment dates unknown.

61 Conversion Flight

First Manchester toc	19th Apr 42 (L7286)
Formed	27th Mar 42 at Nth Luffenham
Moved	5th May 42 to Syerston
	22nd Aug 42 to Swinderby
Disbanded	7th Oct 1942 by merging into 1660 Heavy Conversion Unit.

83 Conversion Flight

First Manchester toc	17th Apr 42 (L7280)
Formed	11th Apr 42 at Scampton
Moved	21st Aug 42 to Wigsley
Disbanded	7th Oct 42 by merging into 1654 Heavy Conversion Unit.

97 Conversion Flight

First Manchester toc	16th Feb 42 (L7457)
Formed	? Jan 42 at Coningsby
Moved	? Aug 42 to Woodhall Spa
	? Sep 42 to Skellingthorpe
Disbanded	7th Oct 42 by merging into 1660 Heavy Conversion Unit.

106 Conversion Flight

First Manchester toc	15th Apr 42 (L7457)
Formed	5th May 42 at Coningsby
Moved	1st Oct 42 to Skellingthorpe
Disbanded	7th Oct 42 by merging into 1660 Heavy Conversion Unit.

207 Conversion Flight

First Manchester toc	4th May 42 (L7385)
Formed	? Jan 42 at Bottesford
Moved	23rd Aug 42 to Swinderby
Disbanded	7th Oct 42 by merging into 1660 Heavy Conversion Unit.

408 Conversion Flight

First Manchester toc	18th May 42 (L7400)
Formed	16th May 42 at Syerston
Disbanded	19th Jun 42.

Unknown crew pose in front of R5790 of 83 Squadron. The area around the codes shows clearly that it has been overpainted, the aircraft was previously with 207 Squadron as 'EM-N'. Squadron Leader McClure had been badly wounded by a flak burst while captaining this aircraft on 6/7th April 1942, during operations against Essen. *via Roy Bonser*

420 Conversion Flight

First Manchester toc	16th May 42 (L7400)
Formed	16th May 42 at Waddington
Disbanded	19th Jun 42.

460 Conversion Flight

First Manchester toc	1st Oct 42 (L7464)
Formed 22nd May 42	Holme-on-Spalding Moor
Moved	26th Sep 42 to Breighton
Disbanded	7th Oct 1942 by merging into 1656 Heavy Conversion Unit.

1654 HCU

First Manchester toc	22nd May 42 (L7281)
Representative acft	L7288 'UG-J', L7419 'UG-B'
Formed as 1654 CU	16th May 42 at Swinderby
Moved	? Jun 42 to Wigsley
Became 1654 HCU	7th Oct 42 on absorbing 50 and 83 CFs
Disbanded	1st Sep 45, at Woolfox Lodge.

1656 HCU

First Manchester toc	1st Oct 42 (L7325)
Representative acft	L7434 'BL-Y'
Formed as 1656 HCU	7th Oct 42 from 103 and 460 CFs at Breighton
Moved	26th Oct 42 to Lindholme
Disbanded	10th Nov 45.

1660 HCU

First Manchester toc	20th Oct 42 (L7283)
Representative acft	R5768 'TV-A'
Formed as 1660HCU	7th Oct 42 from 61, 97, 106 and 207 CFs at Swinderby
Disbanded	? Sep 46, into 1653 HCU.

1661 HCU

First Manchester toc	8th Nov 42 (L7425)
Representative acft	R5839 'GP-G'
Formed as 1661 HCU	7th Oct 42 from 9, 44 and 49 CFs at Skellingthorpe
Moved	1st Jan 43 to Winthorpe
Satellite at Scampton	9th Nov 42 to 1st Jan 43
Disbanded	24th Aug 45.

OTHER MANCHESTER UNITS

1485 Bombing & Gunnery Flight

First Manchester toc	13th Aug 42 (L7391)
Formed	Skellingthorpe, date unknown
Disbandment date unknown.	

25 Operational Training Unit, 'D' Flight

First Manchester toc	7th Jun 41 (L7420)
Formed	1st Mar 41 at Finningley
Disbanded	1st Feb 43.

Torpedo Development Unit

First Manchester toc	27th Apr 42 (R5774)
Formation and disbandment dates unknown.	

Notes

For uniformity, in the tables within the Appendix and within the main narrative, the following abbreviations have been used to denote rank :

F/L – Flight Lieutenant; F/O – Flying Officer; F/Sgt – Flight Sergeant; P/O – Pilot Officer; Sgt – Sergeant; S/L – Squadron Leader; W/C – Wing Commander; W/O – Warrant Officer.

Appendix C

Sortie and Dispatch Statistics

Manchester Sorties Dispatched by Pilots as Aircraft Captain (Ten or more operations)
Tours of operations on Manchester squadrons often took up to 15 months to complete. Arising partly from groundings of the Manchester in mid-1941, no pilot is known to have completed a tour of exclusively Manchester operations, most being mixed in various proportions with Handley Page Hampden sorties or completed after conversion to Avro Lancasters. Dispatched is defined as having taken off from base. Rank is given at the time of service on Manchester.
(See Appendix B for rank abbreviations.)

Name and Rank	Unit	Notes	Total
P/O W G Gardiner	207		27
P/O P C Birch	207		25
P/O W S Herring	207 (20)	KIA	21
	44 (1)		
S/L T C Murray	207		20
S/L K H P Beauchamp	207		17
W/O W L Young	106	FTR 2/3.5.42	17
F/O W J Lewis	207	FTR 7/8.9.41	16
F/Sgt G H Coles	207		16
F/O H S Blakeman	97		16
F/O D A Green	207		15
P/O A W Hills	207		15
F/L A M Paape	207 (8)	KIA	15
	61 (7)		
F/O J H Leland	207		14
F/O J de L Wooldridge	207		13
F/L W D B Ruth	207		13
F/O C A J Smith	83		13
P/O L F Kneil	207		12
P/O H W Southgate	50		12
F/O I G A McNaughton	61	KIA	12
F/Sgt G Appleyard	106		12
F/Sgt G H Hazelden	83		12
F/Sgt J C Atkinson	207		11
F/Sgt G H Hathersich	207		11
F/O P R Burton-Gyles	207	KIA	11
F/L P C Ward-Hunt	207 (10)		11
	49 (1)		
F/L D J French	207 (6)		11
	97 (5)		
Sgt L R Crampton	50		11
F/L D A J McClure	83		11
F/O P G W. Oakley	83		11
W/O D H Rowlands	97		11
P/O G L Tofield	61	KIA	11
P/O R E S Smith	61		11
P/O J Gunter	61		11
P/O A L Searby	61	KIA	11
P/O G R Bayley	207	FTR 8/9.1.42	10
P/O W N Whammond	106		10
F/O S J Beard	61		10
F/O R E Archibald	61	KIA	10
F/Sgt E W Noble	61	FTR 6/7.4.42	10
W/O H H Whitehead	83		10

Notes: FTR – failed to return, date missing from a Manchester operation. KIA – known to have been killed in action during Second World War. Sgt Jim M Duncan, W/Op, A/G, who served with 207 Squadron 22nd Dec 1940 to 15th Jul 1942 undertook 36 Manchester and one Hampden sorties.

Manchester Sorties Dispatched

Unit	Bombing Sorties	Mining Sorties	Other Sorties	Unit Total
44 Con Flt	4	0	0	4
49 Sqdn	28	6	14	48
50 Sqdn	70	34	22	126
61 Sqdn	163	40	6	209
83 Sqdn	103	30	12	145
97 Sqdn	141	8	2	151
106 qdn	81	63	5	149
207 Sqdn	370	48	12	430
408 Con Flt	2	0	0	2

'Other' sorties refer to NICKELS, ASR etc.

Grand Total Manchester 'Ops'				1,264

Sortie Records

Record	Unit	Sorties
Most Operations	207 Squadron	430
Most Bombing 'ops'	207 Squadron	370
Most Mining 'ops'	106 Squadron	63
Most 'ops' in one month (Apr 1942)	106 Squadron	74

Most sorties in one operation

Unit	Total	Date
50 Squadron	15	30/31.5.42
49 Squadron	12	30/31.5.42
50 Squadron	12	25/26.6.42
97 Squadron	11	18.12.41
207 Squadron	11	12/13.12.41

Manchester Losses by Unit

Unit	Operational Losses	Per cent Losses	Per cent loss Less 'other'
44 Con Flt	0	–	–
49 Sqdn	6	12.5	14.7
50 Sqdn	10	7.9	9.6
61 Sqdn	16	7.7	7.8
83 Sqdn	9	6.2	6.0
97 Sqdn	10	6.6	6.0
106 qdn	7	4.7	4.9
207 Sqdn	19	4.4	4.5
408 Con Flt	0	–	–

Loss statistics are affected by the fact that 49, 83 and 97 Squadrons each lost one aircraft during 'other' ops.

Statistics show a general trend in which loss rate increases in relation to the timing of equipment and inversely with the total number of operations dispatched. The major departure is provided by 106, which flew a larger proportion of mining operations.

Manchesters dispatched on 20 or more sorties

Serial	Del'd	Squadrons Allocated and Total Sorties Dispatched	
L7378	13. 4.41	207 (25), 106 (8)	33
L7319	6. 3.41	207 (22), 106 (4), 50 (5)	31
L7432	4. 7.41	207 (18), 50 (8) FTR 3/4.6.42	26
L7455	10. 9.41	207 (15), 97 (1), 50 (10)	26
R5796	18.11.41	207 (14), 106 (12)	26
L7317	25. 2.41	207 (17), 106 (7) FTR 14/15.4.42	24
L7515	10.10.41	207 (14), 106 (10)	24
L7475	28.10.41	97 (5), 61 (9), 50 (9)	23
L7485	12. 9.41	207 (15), 106 (7), FTR 16/17.4.42	22
L7488	15.10.41	207 (4), 97 (6), 106 (12)	22
L7322	17. 3.41	207 (20) FTR 8/9.1.42	20
L7468	9.11.41	207 (15), 50 (5)	20
L7480	9.11.41	207 (5), 61 (8), 50 (5), 44 (2)	20
L7484	10. 9.41	207 (15), 83 (2), 49 (3)	20
L7486	12. 9.41	207 (19), 61 (1)	20

Anonymous Mk.IA 'ZN-D' of 106 Squadron at Coningsby, early 1942. *D Richards / 106 Squadron Association*

Appendix D

Aircraft Losses by Unit

Entries give date, aircraft serial number and the
surname of the captain. Refer to Appendix E for
greater detail.

49 Squadron
30/31.5.42	L7290	Floyd
30/31.5.42	L7429	Carter
1/2.6.42	R5794	Shackleton
6/7.6.42	L7287	Paramore
6/7.6.42	L7469	De Mestre
20/21.6.42	L7387	O'Brien

50 Squadron
25.3.42	L7486	Atkinson
17/18.4.42	R5782	Baker
29/30.4.42	L7516	Willett
8/9.5.42	L7489	Gruber
8/9.5.42	R5778	Wilkie
13.5.42	L7519	Blake
30/31.5.42	L7456	Wilkie
30/31.5.42	L7301	Manser
3/4.6.42	L7432	Heaton
5/6.6.42	R5833	Garland
6/7.6.42	L7471	Beatty
25/26.6.42	L7289	Roy
16.8.42	L7475	Dickensen
5.9.42	L7521	Carter

61 Squadron
26/27.6.41	L7304	Webb
29.6.41	L7315	Colborne
2/3.9.41	L7388	Valentine
2.11.41	L7520	Searby
7/8.12.41	L7494	Riley
9/10.1.42	R5789	Matthews
15/16.1.42	L7495	Beard
31.1/1.2.42	R5787	Parsons
31.1/1.2.42	L7396	Page
31.1/1.2.42	L7472	Fraser
10.2.42	R5834	Underwood
16/17.2.42	L7433	Webster
13/14.3.42	L7395	Hubbard
25/26.42	L7518	Hubbard
25/26.3.42	L7497	Furby
29/30.3.42	L7454	Churchill
6/7.4.42	L7470	Noble
10/11.4.42	R5785	MacSporran

83 Squadron
21/22.2.42	L7522	Rainford
8/9.3.42	L7426	Frost
8/9.3.42	R5779	Cooper
13/14.3.42	L7423	Bromiley
24/25.3.42	R5831	Price
25/26.3.42	L7465	Markides
28/29.3.42	R5781	Lumb
8/9.4.42	L7427	Morphett
8/9.4.42	R5837	Sproule

97 Squadron
10/11.5.41	L7323	Ayton
15/16.5.41	L7324	Bird
26/27.6.41	L7374	Eustace
12/13.8.41	L7424	Little
16/17.8.41	L7384	Nunn
13.9.41	L7306	Hartley
13/14.9.41	L7383	Fox
28.9.41	L7375	Blakeman
20/21.10.41	R5783	Hartley
20/21.10.41	L7462	Noble

8.11.41	L7466	Price
24.11.41	R5792	Hill
18.12.41	R5795	Stokes
18.12.41	L7490	Balsdon
8.1.42	L7459	Hartley

106 Squadron
12.3.42	L7474	Carter
25/26.3.42	L7390	Dunlop-Mackenzie
29/30.3.42	L7394	Dimond
14/15.4.42	L7317	Worswick
16/17.4.42	L7485	Scatchard
23.24.4.42	L7463	Stoffer
2/3.5.42	R5840	Hurd
2/3.5.42	L7399	Young
20.5.42	L7418	McHardy

207 Squadron
13/14.3.41	L7313	Matthews
20/21.3.41	L7278	Harwood
27/28.3.41	L7303	Siebert
8/9.4.41	L7302	Hyde
2/3.5.41	L7379	Pinchbeck
18.5.41	L7393	Mackintosh
21.6.41	L7310	Kydd
21/22.6.41	L7314	Withers
12/13.8.41	L7381	Smith
12/13.8.41	L7377	Taylor
16/17.8.41	L7311	Keartland
31.8/1.9.41	L7316	Gilderthorp
7/8.9.41	L7380	Lewis
15.9.41	L7318	Crump
12/13.10.41	L7312	Bowes-Cavanagh
13/14.10.41	L7373	Paskell
13/14.10.41	L7321	Unsworth
20/21.10.41	L7487	Ruck-Keene
26.10.41	L7422	Beauchamp
23.11.41	L7300	Hills
27/28.12.41	L7483	Beauchamp
8/9.1.42	L7322	Bayley
14/15.1.42	L7523	Wescombe
14/15.1.42	L7309	Dawkins
6.8.42	L7385	Pearson

25 Operational Training Unit
18.11.41	L7428	Adams
10.2.42	L7478	Siebold

1654 Heavy Conversion Unit
5.7.42	L7496	Lancey
30.8.42	L7416	Picken
1.9.42	L7298	Knight

24.1.43	L7457	Taylor
26.1.43	R5772	Schnier
25.2.43	L7400	Hendry
2.3.43	L7277	Stone
4.4.43	L7291	See Appendix E.
15.4.43	L7294	Eager
17.5.43	L7491	Walters

1656 Heavy Conversion Unit
19.10.42	R5780	Horner

1660 Heavy Conversion Unit
2.1.43	L7482	Goodyear
14.2.43	L7286	Keeffe
11.4.43	R5841	Whitwell
30.5.43	L7389	See Appendix E.
4.7.43	R5770	Cooper
16.11.43	L7421	See Appendix E.

1661 Heavy Conversion Unit
1/2.12.42	R5836	Desmond
12.3.43	R5838	Knight
24.3.43	L7453	Oakley
19.5.43	L7297	Clifford

Miscellaneous Units

Rolls-Royce
26.5.41	L7295	Kirlew

Aeroplane & Armament Experimental Establishment
12.12.41	L7320	Robinson

Royal Aircraft Establishment
16.4.42	L7285	See Appendix E.

57 Conversion Flight
5.10.42	L7386	Walsh

1485 Bombing & Gunnery Flight
6.10.42	L7473	Taylor
11.2.43	L7391	Eyres

Torpedo Development Unit
31.10.43	L7276	See Appendix E.

Australian P/O N G Stokes looking down apprehensively from *Sri Ribut* of 97 Squadron. Stokes and crew failed to return 18th December 1941 in R5795.
Imperial War Museum / CH4151

Appendix E

Individual Aircraft Histories

Information culled from Aircraft Movement Cards and Aircraft Accident Cards, cross referenced to Squadron Operational Record Books, Raid Summary Books, Personal Experience Report Files, Flying Logbooks and contacts with former air and ground crew. Particular care has been taken to show the entries on the Aircraft Movement Cards in the order they are given. Where date structures are clearly, or quite possibly, wrong this has been denoted by (ce) noting corrupt entry.

Allocation and delivery dates often differ but, for brevity, are not differentiated. Where both are known only the former are listed. They usually differ by a few days.

No attempt is made to append records of internal system failures in aircraft on operational or non-operational flying except where these led in turn to major ensuing damage.

Aircraft Accident Cards are only available up to 26th July 1943. A number of known accidents are not in Aircraft Movement Cards. A number of apparent repairs in Aircraft Movement Cards do not have an equivalent Aircraft Accident Card.

Only 28% of aircraft have total airframe hours preserved of which R5835 has the maximum, 471 hours 15 minutes (given as 471.15 in the tables). Where known, flying hour totals are given at the end of each entry. Also given at the end of each entry is the total number of operational sorties known to have been undertaken by that aircraft. Where no figure is given, the aircraft in question is not known to have undertaken any 'ops'.

For accidents a standard approach has been made to note crew circumstances. Beyond details of the loss (often prefixed with MFO – missing following ops) will appear a linked listing of data. For example:
'QR-O', P/O J R Hubbard–7–2–Essen.
This shows aircraft code (where known), captain, number in crew, number of survivors, sortie. In many cases the sortie will be the name of a town or city, eg Dortmund, in which case that was the duty target for the particular op. Other examples of sortie may include details of a GARDENING op, or a training duty etc.

ABBREVIATIONS

In order that the individual histories do not take up an inordinate amount of space, it has been necessary to use an extensive amount of abbreviations. These should present few problems to readers, especially following reference to this section prior to referring to the histories themselves.

Units/Departments

A&AEE	Aircraft & Armament Experimental Establishment
AAS	Air Armament School
AFEE	Airborne Forces Experimental Establishment
AFU	Advanced Flying Unit (possibly corrupt attribution?)
AFW	? possibly corrupt
AGS	Air Gunnery School
AMDP	Air Member for Development & Production
AOS	Air Observers School
B&GF	Bombing & Gunnery Flight
CF	(Squadron) Conversion Flight.
CU	Conversion Unit
DGRD	Director General of Research & Development
DTD	Director of Technical Development
LFS	Lancaster Finishing School
1 MPRU	Metal Produce & Recovery Unit, Cowley

MU	Maintenance Unit. The following are referred to : 6 Brize Norton; 27 Shawbury; 37 Burtonwood; 38 Llandow; 39 Colerne; 46 Lossiemouth
RAE	Royal Aircraft Establishment
Sqn	Squadron
SoTT	School of Technical Training. The following are referred to : 1 Halton; 3 Stanley Park, Blackpool, but a large number of airframes kept at Squire's Gate (Blackpool Airport); 12 Melksham
TDU	Torpedo Development Unit

Accident Damage Categories & Equivalents

Pre-1941		1941-42
Cat.U	Undamaged	
Cat.M(u)	Capable of being repaired on site by operating unit.	Cat A
Cat.M(c)	Repair beyond unit capacity.	Cat Ac
Cat.R(b)	Repair on site not possible. Beyond repair on site. Aircraft must be dismantled and sent to a repair facility.	Cat B
–	Allocated to instructional airframe duties.	Cat C
Cat.W	Aircraft a write-off	Cat E
–	Write-off but considered suitable for component recovery.	Cat E1
–	Write-off, suitable only for scrap	Cat E2
–	Aircraft is burnt out.	Cat E3
–	Aircraft missing from an operational sortie.	Cat Em

also postscripts, eg:

Cat E(FA)	Write-off as a result of flying accident.
Cat E(FB)	Write-off as a result of flying battle damage.
Cat /OR	Category varies. Operational reasons.
Cat /MI	Category varies. Major Inspection required.
Cat /MR	Category normally E. Major repair required.

Loss Abbreviations
Country in which aircraft crashed or force landed:
B – Belgium; D – Denmark, F – France; G – Germany; N – Norway; NL– Netherlands.

Operational Abbreviations
In addition to standard RAF examples:
(D)- daylight raid. NF – night fighter.

RAF Semi-official

A/c	Aircraft
AC2	Aircraftsman Class 2
AP	Aiming point
ASR	Air sea rescue
ATC	Air traffic control
Aw/cn	Awaiting collection
C & L	Circuits & landings
Dd	Delivered (if Avro, to Flight Shed)
Ff	First flight
F/G	Front gunner
FTR	Failed to return
43 GDA	Group Deposit Account. Used to dispose of lost or damaged aircraft from units to salvage and repair organisations. Often pre-43, denoting 43 Group, Andover.
GI airfr	Ground instruction airframe
IAS	Indicated air speed
IFF	Identification friend or foe
MFO	Missing from operations, used to denote despatched on an 'op' and lost either en route, over or returning from the target.

MUG	Mid-upper gunner
NFD	No further details
NFT	Night flying test
ORB	Operations record book (made up of Forms 540 & 541)
Ops	Operations
R/G	Rear gunner
RIW	Repaired in works
ROS	Repaired on site
RPM	Revolutions per minute
SAS	Service & Supply (back up organisation)
SOC/ PSOC	Struck off charge/ Presumed struck off charge
TA	Target area
TI	Trial installation
TO	Take (took) off
TOC/toc	take(n) on charge
U/c, u/c	Undercarriage
u/s	Unserviceable
W/Op	Wireless operator

General

BA blister	Bomb Aimer's (perspex) blister
br	bracket
circs	circumstances
cl	closed
corr	corrosion
cr	crashed
ct	caught
dam	damaged
eng	engine
exs	exercises
fd	found
fr	front
fter	fighter
gd	ground
ht	height
jett	jettisoned
lg, ldg	land, landing
mntn	maintenance
nr	near
pt	port
rec	recovery
rep'd	reported
stbd	starboard
twd	towards
vibr	vibration
wt	weight

L7246 approaches the wire at Farnborough with the arrester hook lowered, 4th April 1942. Note the vertical light coloured stripe ahead of the cockpit. *Imperial War Museum FLM 2147*

The second production Manchester, L7277, with FN.21A turret fitted, at Boscombe Down during the frantic and superficial trials programme of late 1940. *RAF Museum*

NOTES ON PRODUCTION BATCHES

L7246 first prototype, initially unarmed.

L7247 second prototype. Full turret armament including F.N.21A mid-under.

L7276 to L7302 – 27 aircraft. All Mk.Is. First nine, ten or 11 aircraft (including L7247 – records vary), delivered with F.N.21A mid-under turret. Some reached 207 Squadron but all removed prior to first 'op'. First 20 aircraft delivered with early 28ft span tail and triple fins. Twenty-first and subsequent aircraft fitted with 33ft span tail and triple fins. First 20 not retrofitted with 33ft tail until late 1942. Up to L7302 (?) all delivered lacking mid-upper turrets. Last aircraft delivered without mid-positioned turrets unknown. L7309, outside this range, known not to be fitted with F.N.7A mid-upper initially. Some airframes, (ie L7303?), may have had F.N.7A retrofitted. Early aircraft from this production batch not fully operationally fit and rapidly withdrawn for conversion training and development. All service aircraft had F.N.7A removed during June/July 1941.

L7303 to L7482 (?) – 103 aircraft (?). All Mk.Is. Early airframes delivered lacking F.N.7A mid-upper turret which in some (? all) cases was retrofitted. Remainder carried standard three turret armament from factory. All delivered with 33ft span, triple fin tail. L7313 had first F.N.7A.

R5768 to R5841 – 43 aircraft. All delivered to Avro Woodford for assembly as triple fin Mk.Is. Retained at factory and at dispersed sites until September 1941 from which time issued as required fitted with improved Vulture engines. All carried standard three turret armament.

L7483 to L7526 – 27 aircraft. All Mk.IAs. Only aircraft delivered direct with twin fin, 33 ft span tailplane. All aircraft carried standard three turret armament.

From the Avro (L-serials) and Metropolitan Vickers (R-serials) production runs a number of airframes were retrofitted with twin fins on their existing 33 ft span tails becoming Mk.IA. No reliable record of those so fitted has come to light. All previous lists have concluded that no more than 20 Mk.Is were built, the remainder being Mk.IAs. In fact, only 27 Mk.IAs were delivered direct from the factory. Known Mk IA conversions are noted in italics in the individual histories.

PROTOTYPE & PRODUCTION CONTRACTS

L7246 to L7247 – prototypes to Contract No 624973/37 dated 30th April 1937.

L7276 to L72584 – 200 aircraft. Contract No 648770/37 dated 1st July 1937. Batches as follows: L7276-L7325, L7373-L7402, L7415-L7434, L7453-L7497, L7515-L7526 all completed as Manchester Is. L7527 onwards completed as Lancaster Is.

R2671 – Contract No 7625/39 dated 25th July 1939 for cannon turret trials aircraft.

R4525 to R4744 – 150 aircraft. Contract number not recorded, date not traced, but likely early September 1939. Ordered from Fairey but cancelled. Batches as follows: R4525-R4554, R4572-R4611, R4630-R4649, R4670-R4694, R4710-R4744.

R5273 to R5477 – 150 aircraft. Contract No 982865/39, undated. Ordered from Armstrong Whitworth, but cancelled. Batches as follows: R5273-R5320, R5339-R5380, R5397-R5426, R5448-R5477.

R5482 to R5763 – 200 aircraft. Contract number and date not recorded. Batch ordered as Manchesters, built as Lancasters.

R5768 to R5917 – 100 aircraft. Contract No 982866/39. By Metropolitan-Vickers. Batches as follows: R5768-R5797, R5829-R5841.

W1280 to W1498 – 150 aircraft. Contract No B.982865.39 shown as placed with the Armstrong Whitworth Group and dated 12th January 1940 and valued at £4.5 million. All cancelled. Batches as follows: W1280-W1299, W1319-W1350, W1374-W1410, W1426-W1475, W1488-W1498.

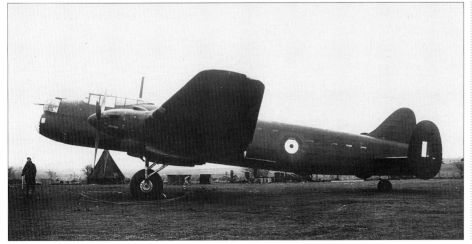

Avro 679 Manchester Prototypes ordered to Contract No 624973.37 of 30th April 1937.

L7246 First flown 24.7.39. Force landed 29.11.39 Charnos Hall, Staffs on delivery to A&AEE when port eng stopped after inadvertent running on reserve. Force landed 12.12.39 after engine failure outside Boscombe Down. Force landed 23.12.39 after eng failure outside Boscombe Down. RIW by Avro 12.4.40. A&AEE/AMDP 9.7.40. Avro/AMDP 24.8.40. A&AEE 14.10.40.43 GDA undated. RAE Farnborough/DGRD 18.12.40 frictionless take-off and arrested landing trials. Damaged in trials 1.8.41 ROS. To 3422M at 1 SoTT 20.11.42.

L7247 First flown 26.5.40. A&AEE/AMDP 9.7.40 and recorded again 13.9.40. Avro/AMDP 8.10.40. A&AEE/AMDP 25.11.40. Avro 21.2.41. To 2738M at 1 SoTT (allocated 8.10.41) ?.5.42.

Avro 679 Manchester Is built by Avro at Woodford to Contract No 648770/37 of 1st July 1937. 157 aircraft, delivered between August 1940 and November 1941. L7483 to L7526 (27 aircraft) completed and test flown as Mk.IAs. Others converted to Mk.IA.

L7276 A&AEE 5.8.40. 61 Sqn undated. 25 OTU undated. Avro 31.8.41. 39 MU 9.7.42. TDU 12.43; Cat.E 31.10.43. No accident card. A/c movement card cites this as date scrapped. Other sources say it crashed at TDU Gosport.

L7277 A&AEE 25.10.40. Avro/SAS 28.2.41. 1654 CU 1.6.42. 408 Sqn 8.6.42. 1654 CU 16.6.42. 1467 Flt 24.8.42 (ce). 130 Flt 23.9.41 (ce). 1654 CU 10.10.42. Cat. E 1500 hrs 2.3.43. Feathering demo to trainee pilot. Port prop would not unfeather. Undershot aerodrome on force landing attempt due to premature lowering of u/c. Attempted belly landing, struck tree, at North Searle*, Notts. A/c caught fire. F/L P J Stone–6–6–trng. Feathering practice discontinued following this incident. SOC 16.3.43. Ops 1. (*As on history card, perhaps Scarle?)

L7278 27 MU 31.7.40. Avro/AMDP 7.10.40. 207 Sqn 10.11.40. Cat.E 20/21.3.41 as MFO. 'EM-A', Sgt F B Harwood–6–2–Lorient. 0.5% silver bearing failure 15 min after take-off. Cr at Wymondham, Leics. Ops 3. 80 hrs.

L7279 6 MU 22.10.40. 207 Sqn 6.11.40. 61 Sqn 15.4.41. Avro/SAS 14.7.41. 39 MU 10.8.42. RAE 11.6.43. 39 MU 21.8.43. Cat.E2 11.10.43. No accident card. SOC 11.10.43. Ops 1.

L7280 Avro/AMDP 4.8.40. 27 MU 11.11.40. 207 Sqn 2.12.40. Avro/SAS 13.6.41. 44 CF 6.3.42. 83 Sqn 2.4.42. 83 CF 17.4.42. 1654 CU 10.10.42. Cat.Ac 1100 hrs 19.10.42. Heavy landing at Wigsley. 1654 CU 7.11.42. Cat.A 1030 hrs 2.1.43. R5796 struck by L7280 whilst both taxiing. 1660 CU 11.7.43. Unknown allocation 22.9.43. Cat.E2 15.10.43. No accident card. SOC 18.10.43.

L7281 Avro/AMDP 4.9.40. Avro/DGRD 19.10.40. A&AEE/DGRD 2.11.40. 6 MU undated. Avro 12.1.42 for engine change & conv to *Mk.IA*. 1654 CU 22.5.42. 49 Sqn 26.5.42. 49 CF 29.5.42. 49 Sqn undated. Cat.B AE(?) 13.7.42. No accident card. ROS 20.7.42. 49 CF 1.8.42. 1661 CU 9.11.42. Cat.E2 undated. No accident card. SOC 14.9.43. 327.25 hrs.

L7282 6 MU 29.10.40. 207 Sqn 21.12.40. 97 Sqn 20.2.41. Avro/SAS 17.8.41 engine change & *Mk.IA*. 39 MU 10.8.42. 12 SoTT 4.6.43. SOC undated.

L7283 6 MU 29.10.40. 207 Sqn 28.11.40. Avro SAS 13.6.41. 25 OTU 27.3.42. 97 CF 15.4.42. 1660 CU 20.10.42. 10 AGS 23.6.43 as inst airframe 3743M. SOC undated.

L7284 27 MU 29.10.40. 207 Sqn 29.11.40. U/c failure 24.2.41, force ldg ex ops at Waddington. 43 GDA 25.2.41. 207 Sqn 6.4.41. 61 Sqn 15.4.41. Avro SAS 14.7.41. 39 MU 12.9.42. SOC undated. 1 op.

L7285 Unknown allocation 29.10.40. 27 MU 1.11.40. 37 MU 7.7.41. Avro 29.3.42 for mods. 83 Sqn 11.4.42. RAE undated. Cat.Ac 16.4.42. U/c coll on a/c parked at Farnborough. Avro 16.4.42. RAE 24.4.42. 39 MU 13.10.42. SOC 15.6.43.

L7286   6 MU 29.10.40. 207 Sqn 7.12.40. Avro/SAS
        13.6.41. 61 CF 19.4.42. 83 Sqn? 20.4.42? Cat.Ac
        16.5.42 at 61 CF Syerston. Hydraulics, then
        emergency system failed. Stbd wheel only
        lowered for landing. ROS undated. 83 Sqn
        25.7.42.1660 CU 20.10.42. Cat.Ac 1100 hrs
        14.2.43. Stbd eng caught fire at 1,000 ft. A/c belly
        landed Waddington. Flame traps to A & B
        blocks burnt through. Sgt N C Keffee–?–all–trng.
        SOC 7.3.43. 2 ops. 218.05 hrs.

L7287   Avro/DGRD 16.8.40. DGRD 11.12.40. Avro/SAS
        undated. 83 Sqn 16.4.42. 49 Sqn 18.4.42. Mid-air
        collision with 83 Sqn Lancaster 19.5.42. Not in
        accident cards. Cat.E MFO 7.6.42. 'EA-G'. F/L R E
        R Paramore–7–0–Emden. NFD. 5 ops. 88.10 hrs.

L7288   6 MU 17.11.40. 207 Sqn 7.12.40. 97 Sqn 26.2.41.
        61 Sqn 22.4.41. Avro/SAS 24.7.41. 1654 CU
        29.6.42. Avro (Waddington) 12.5.43. PSOC.
        2 ops.

L7289   37 MU 5.7.41. Avro 27.3.42. 83 Sqn 11.4.42. Heavy
        landing. Pilot held off too late, a/c bounced and
        wing touched ground 0250 hrs 25.4.42. ROS
        27.4.42. 83 Sqn undated. 50 Sqn 5.6.42. MFO
        25/26.6.42. Sgt R G Roy–7–0–Bremen. Shot
        down by flak. Cr Gramble, Germany. 2 (?) ops.
        110.15 hrs.

L7290   27 MU 17.11.40. 207 Sqn 31.12.40. 97 Sqn 26.2.41.
        Avro/SAS 11.6.41. 1654 CU 24.5.42. 49 Sqn
        25.5.42. Cat.E MFO 30/31.5.42. P/O P W
        Floyd–7–5–Cologne. Hit by flak, stbd eng failed.
        5 baled out. A/c rolled onto back and crashed
        at Mulheim-Oberhausen, Germany. 2 ops.

L7291   46 MU 17.11.40. 207 Sqn 3.1.41. 97 Sqn 26.2.41.
        Avro/SAS 11.6.41. 106 Sqn 13.5.42. 50 Sqn
        14.5.42. 420 CF 17.5.42. 1654 CU ?.7.42. Cat.Ac
        1100 hrs 19.10.42. Heavy landing at Wigsley.
        ROS 29.10.42. 1654 CU 7.11.42. Cat.E (Burnt)
        4.4.43. No accident card. SOC 15.4.43? At
        Wigsley, but no confirmation in accident
        records. 1 op.

L7292   46 MU 17.11.40. 207 Sqn 3.1.41. 97 Sqn 30.3.41.
        61 Sqn 22.4.41. 43 GDA undated. Avro/SAS
        28.7.41. 39 MU 25.7.42. TDU 1.12.42. Avro/MR
        RIW 7.1.43. AW/CN 6.3.43. 39 MU 15.3.43. Cat.E2
        6.11.43. No acc card. SOC 10.11.43. 2 ops.

L7293   37 MU 15.7.41. Rolls-Royce (Derby) 10.3.42.
        Avro/mods 2.4.42. 83 Sqn 18.4.42. 49 Sqn
        11.6.42. 61 CF 2.8.42. 207 CF 22.9.42. 1660 CU
        20.10.42. GI afrm 3773M. SOC 15.10.43. 2 ops.

L7294   27 MU 24.11.40. 207 Sqn 29.12.40. 97 Sqn 26.2.41.
        61 Sqn 27.4.41. Avro/SAS 24.7.41 engine change
        and Mk. IA. 1654 CU 11.6.42. Cat.E 1850 hrs
        15.4.43. Eng misfired & caught fire. A/c stalled
        on app, cr & burnt out. Sgt W H Eager–7–7–trng.
        SOC 26.4.43. 5 ops.

L7295   Allocated to ukn unit 24.11.40. Rolls-Royce/
        DGRD 4.12.40. Avro/DGRD 21.2.41. Rolls-Royce/
        DGRD 9.3.41. Uncontrollable eng fire due to
        uneven coolant distrib. Undershot & crashed
        Ternhill 26.5.41. Mr R Kirlew–4–3–test. SOC
        undated.

L7296   6 MU 24.11.40. Avro/SAS 28.2.41. Eng change &
        Mk IA. 49 Sqn 25.6.42. 49 CF 22.7.42. 1661 CU
        9.11.42. Avro/ROS 30.4.43. No accident card.
        1661 CU 8.5.43. RAF Benson 5.10.43. Cat.E2
        15.10.43. No acc card. SOC 18.10.43. 404.10 hrs.

L7297   37 MU 15.7.41. Rolls-Royce (Derby) 10.3.42.
        Avro 17.4.42. 83 Sqn 28.4.42. 207 CF 7.6.42. 1661
        CU 30.10.42. Cat.A 1.4.43 R5769 blown back in
        gale, damaged L7297 parked at Winthorpe. Cat.
        E 1215 hrs 19.5.43. Engine fire in flight. Emerg
        landing Winthorpe, u/c retracted to stop on over
        -shoot. Flametraps in A & D blocks had burnt
        out. Sgt J Clifford–?–all–trng. SOC 26.5.43. 1 op.

L7298   6 MU 24.11.40. 207 Sqn 24.12.40. 97 Sqn 26.2.41.
        Avro/SAS 24.7.41. 1654 CU 29.6.42. Cat.E 2315
        hrs 1.9.42. Eng fail on ldng. Belly landed outside
        aerodrome. Partial closure of fuel master cock
        caused fuel starvation. Sgt L G Knight–?–all
        –trng. SOC 9.9.42. 1 op. 157.50 hrs.

L7299   46 MU 24.11.40. 207 Sqn 3.1.41. 97 Sqn 26.2.41.
        Avro/SAS 9.7.41. 39 MU 11.7.42. Cat.E2
        31.10.43. No accident card. SOC 4.11.43.

L7300   6 MU 21.12.40. 207 Sqn 3.2.41. Avro 10.10.41.
        207 Sqn undated. Cat.E 23.11.41. Double engine
        failure. Cr Fiskerton Lake. SOC ?.12.41. 'EM-F',
        P/O A W Hill–9–9–trng. 17 ops.

L7301   27 MU 21.12.40. Avro/SAS 18.3.41. 106 Sqn
        28.4.42. Cat.E 30/31.5.42 MFO. 'ZN-D', F/O
        Manser–7–6–Cologne. Port engine fire after flak
        dam. Crashed nr Bree, Belgium. 106 CF a/c
        on loan 50 Sqn. 2 ops.

L7302   46 MU 21.12.40. 207 Sqn 16.2.41. MFO 8/9.4.41.
        'EM-R' W/C N C Hyde–6–6–Kiel. Sqn CO.
        Damaged by flak, eng caught fire. Crew baled
        out. Cr Hostrup, Germany. 8 ops. 59 hrs.

L7303   6 MU 22.12.40. 207 Sqn 11.2.41. MFO 27/28.3.41.
        'EM-P', F/L J A Siebert–6–5–Dusseldorf.
        Encountered flak, eng failure and night fighter
        piloted by Oblt Herzog 3/NJG1 Eindhoven.
        Cr Bakel, NL. 2 ops. 27 hrs.

L7304   6 MU 22.12.40. 207 Sqn 11.2.41. 61 Sqn 15.4.41.
        MFO 26/27.6.41. F/O K G Webb–6–0–Kiel.
        Cr near Brunsbuttel, Germany. 4 ops.

L7305   27 MU 22.12.40. Avro/DGRD 6.1.41. 25 OTU
        22.1.42. 106 Sqn 18.4.42. 106 CF 19.5.42. Cat.A
        9.6.42. Collided with trestles when turning at
        downwind end of flarepath on C&L. 1660 CU
        20.10.42. To GI 4279M 22.9.43, 3 SoTT. SOC
        undated. 1 op.

L7306   27 MU 22.12.40. 97 Sqn 15.4.41. Three bombs fell
        thro' bomb doors before reaching enemy coast.
        This & other unserviceabilities caused early
        return 26/27.8.41. Cat.E 13.9.41 tyre burst on
        take-off at Coningsby. U/c collapsed & a/c
        swung to right. Eng ct fire, Graviner button
        pressed but a/c burnt out.Sgt G H Hartley–7–
        7–non-op. SOC undated. 6 ops.

L7307   46 MU 22.12.40. 97 Sqn 18.3.41. 61 Sqn 18.3.41.
        207 Sqn 10.9.41. 97 Sqn 15.9.41. 25 OTU
        21.10.41. 1654 CU 10.7.42. 1660 CU 11.7.43
        (probably incorrectly sequenced entry).
        3 SoTT 22.9.43. 1668 CU 12.10.43 (ce?). 5 LFS
        undated (ce?) 4118M. SOC 12.9.45. 1 op.

L7308   46 MU 22.12.40 97 Sqn 1.3.41. Cat.B 28.10.41.
        Pt airscrew feathered itself on take-off from
        Woodhall Spa. Unable to maintn height. Force
        landing in field. Tail torn off, u/c & props dam.
        SOC 13.11.41. Avro/RIW 22.11.41. Aw/cn
        12.5.42. 49 Sqn 25.5.42. Cat.B 30/31.5.42. Loaned
        to 83 Sqn. Stbd eng failed due to fuel shortage
        on retn from ops. Force ldg at Ingham. ROS
        4.6.42. 49 CF 2.8.42. Cat.Ac 20.10.42 damage
        found on inspection at Wigsley. (?) ROS
        24.10.42. 49 CF 31.10.42. 1656 CU 1.12.42. 39 MU
        14.12.42. ?.5.43 force ldg in field adjacent to
        Woodhall Spa due to both props feathering. No
        accident card. SOC 26.5.43? 5 ops.

L7309   6 MU 21.1.41. 97 Sqn 1.3.41. 207 Sqn 6.3.41.
        Cat.Ac (FB) 8.4.41. Flak shell passed thro'
        mainplane on ops. ROS. Hit maintenance tres-
        tles at Waddington 29.4.41. 43 GDA undated.
        Cat.Ac(FB) 10/11.5.41. A/c attacked by 2 Me
        110s and damaged in fins, elevators, tailplane,
        pt & stbd wing tanks, mainplanes & u/c doors.
        Heavy ldg at base. 97 Sqn 22.8.41? Hit trestles
        taxying to dispersal with 207 Sqn 19.10.41. Slight
        flak dam on ops 9.11.41. Ca OAC [sic] 14.11.41.
        RAAA 29.12.41. 207 Sqn 31.12.41. MFO
        14/15.1.42. 'EM-O', P/O G Dawkins–6–5–Ham-
        burg. Shot down by Oblt Schoenert II/NJG2.
        Crashed at Sandel/Moens, nr Jever, Germany.
        13 ops.

L7300 following its dramatic 'dunking' in Fiskerton
Lake 23rd November 1941 after double engine failure. The triple fin tail rear fuselage remained
onshore and the aircraft had never been fitted with
an FN.7A mid-upper. via Neville Franklin

The burnt and mangled remains of F/O Manser's
L7301 'ZN-D' near Bree in Belgium on 31st May
1942. The 106 Squadron Conversion Flight aircraft
had been loaned to 50 Squadron for the MILLENIUM
raid on Cologne. via P Loncke

L7310 27 MU 21.1.41. 207 Sqn 11.2.41. Taxying on muddy ground Waddington, tail swung into fence 26.2.41. 21.6.41, force landed & hit embankment. 'EM-H', S/L C J F Kydd–3–1–tng. Loose tappet nut led to valve blockage and eng failure on take-off. Cr at Dunstan Pillar, Lincs. 43 GDA undated. Avro/SAS 7.8.41. SOC undated. 5 ops.

L7311 46 MU 21.1.41. 207 Sqn 11.2.41. MFO 16/17.8.41. 'EM-F', P/O Keartland–6–6–Dusseldorf. Shot down by Me 110 (?) of I/NJG1 Venlo, pilot Hpt W Streib. Cr at Kruchten, Germany. 10 ops. 119 hrs.

L7312 6 MU 21.1.41. 207 Sqn 11.2.41. U/c collapsed in 'normal' landing Waddington 28.2.41. 43 GDA undated. 207 Sqn 13.6.41. Flak dam on ops 29.9.41. MFO 12/13.10.41. 'EM-L', P/O D B Bowes-Cavanagh–7–1–Huls. Shot down at 0408 by Me 110 of II/NJG1 Leeuwarden, pilot Ofw P Gildner. Cr Eschen, Belgium. 9 ops.

L7313 6 MU 24.1.41. 207 Sqn 11.2.41. MFO 13/14.3.41. 'EM-C', F/O H V Matthews–6–1–Hamburg. Shot down by Ju 88 intruder, pilot Oblt H Hahn I/NJG2 Gilze-Rijen. Cr at Whisby, nr Lincoln. 3 ops.

L7314 27 MU 24.1.41. 97 Sqn 1.3.41. 207 Sqn 17.3.41. MFO 21/22.6.41. 'EM-Y', F/O J G D Withers–7–0–Boulogne. Attacked in error by 25 Sqn Beaufighter. Crashed at Wollaston, Northants. 4 ops.

L7315 46 MU 24.1.41. 97 Sqn 18.3.41. 61 Sqn 18.3.41. Held off too late on local night landings, u/c collapsed, 10.4.41. 43 GDA undated. 61 Sqn undated. 29.6.41. Eng failed during circuits 29.6.41. A/c abandoned on catching fire. P/O C G Colborne–2–1–non-op. Con-rod bolt failure led to fire. W/Op baled out. Pilot killed nr Grantham. SOC undated. 3 ops. 85.55 hrs.

L7316 27 MU 24.1.41. 207 Sqn 13.4.41. Form 540 gives L7317 hit by flak on ops 2/3.5.41. Form 541 identifies a/c as L7316. Intercepted by Me 110 & dam by flak on ops 9/10.5.41. MFO 31.8/1.9.41. 'EM-U' P/O Gilderthorp–6–2–Cologne. Hit by flak on app to target. Caught fire. Crashed at Oberkruechen, Germany. 15 ops. 136 hrs.

L7317 6 MU 23.2.41. 207 Sqn 13.4.41. See L7316 above. Refers to a/c of F/O Romans. Cat.Ac (FA) 22.1.42 Main wheel ran off peri-track taxying. Forced back on by burst of eng power. U/c collapsed, at Bottesford. 207 Sqn 21.2.42. 106 Sqn 12.3.42. MFO 14.4.42. P/O J A Worswick–7–7?–Dortmund. Lost, ran out of fuel & force landed in sea 1 ml NW of Lee-on-Solent. 24 ops.

L7318 6 MU 23.2.41. 97 Sqn 1.3.41. 207 Sqn 6.3.41. Cat.E 15.9.41 1810. 'EM-K', P/O E D G Crump–10–0 –trng. Nosed down in circuit nr Waddington. Crashed at South Hykeham. SOC undated. 1 op.

L7319 27 MU 23.2.41. 97 Sqn 1.3.41. 207 Sqn 6.3.41. Cat.Ac (FB) 7.11.41. Shrapnel severed hydraulic pipe on ops causing total hyd failure. Cat.Ac (FB) 2/3.1.42. A/c dam by flak on ops; 106 Sqn 12.3.42. 50 Sqn 16.5.42. 50 CF 17.7.42. 1654 CU 10.10.42. Cat.Ac 1500 hrs 6.11.42. Damaged oleo taxying over small trench. ROS undated. 1654 CU 12.12.42. Cat.B 25.2.43. No accident card. SOC 1.4.43. 31 ops.

L7320 Avro/DGRD 28.2.41. A&AEE/DGRD 23.3.41. Cat.E (FA) 12.12.41. Lost power on stbd eng with full bomb load. Lost height. Force landing in field. Sgt F J Robinson–2–all–test. Came down at Potts Hill, Elstead. Avro (Bracebridge Heath) 20.12.41. SOC 1.1.42. 117.3 hrs.

L7321 97 Sqn 1.3.41. 207 Sqn 17.3.41. MFO 13/14.10.41. 'EM-D', P/O Unsworth–7–2–Cologne. Shot down by Me 110 'G9 + KH', Oblt Griese, I/NJG1 St Trond. Cr at Hozemont, B. 8 ops. 146 hrs.

L7322 207 Sqn 15.3.41. Cat.Mu 11.6.41. Struck trestle & small pile of logs. Cat.Ac (FB) 11/12.10.41 single flak hit on ops. 207 Sqn undated. MFO 8.1.42. 'EM-Q', P/O Bayley–7–0–Brest.Cr in sea nr Ile Longue, France, at 0600. NFD.

L7323 97 Sqn 15.3.41. MFO 12.5.41. 'OF-A', P/O R S Ayton–6–6–Berlin. Ditched in North Sea after eng failure. Crew PoWs. 4 ops. 32.2 hrs.

L7324 97 Sqn 15.3.41. MFO 16.5.41. F/L G O L Bird–6–0 –Berlin. Ditched nr Borkum in N Sea after failure of both enginess in turn. 4 ops. 30.4 hrs.

Mk.IA L7320 of the Aeroplane & Armament Experimental Establishment on 29th September 1941 during the FN.7A 'dishplate' trials. The censor has erased the serial number. *via J Simpson*

L7325 97 Sq 22.3.41. Attacked by Defiant NF returning from ops 22.6.41. 43 GDA undated. 97 Sq 26.8.41. Cat.R 11.10.41. Eng ct fire landing at Coningsby. 25 OTU 21.10.41. Avro/RIW 11.11.41. No accident card. RAF Finningley 15.12.41. Avro 1.2.42. 25 OTU undated. Cat.Mc 29.1.42. Heavy ldg, bounced, landed on 1 wheel, u/c collapsed, Bircotes. 25 OTU 7.3.42. 49 Sqn 20.4.42. 9 CF 12.8.42. 57 CF 11.9.42. 1656 CU 1.10.42. 39 MU 31.12.42. To 12 SoTT 4.6.43 as 3751M. SOC 10.?.45. 2 ops.

L7373 97 Sqn 22.3.41. A&AEE/DGRD 13.4.41. 207 Sqn 16.5.41. Many flak hits on ops, none serious, with 97 Squadron (poss mistaken identity?) 26/27.6.41. Sgt Hall fell on floor in heavy landing ex-ops with 207 Sqn 13.8.41. MFO 13/14.10.41. 'EM-T', P/O L Paskell–7–2–Cologne. Shot down by Gefr Bruhnke of III/NJG1 Twente. Cr SW of Lommel. 13 ops. 163 hrs.

L7374 97 Sqn 22.3.41. MFO 27.6.41. F/O F Eustace–7–0–Kiel. A/c reported R/Gnr killed by enemy fire from NF. Later cr in N Sea at Sud-erkoog, G. 1 body washed up at Westerhever, Frisian Is. 4 ops. 81.5 hrs.

L7375 97 Sqn 21.3.41. 43 GDA undated. 97 Sqn undated. Many flak hits on ops, none serious, 26/27.6.41. 97 Sqn 9.9.41. Cat.R(B) 28.9.41. Props failed to unfeather during exercise. Height could not be maintained. Belly landed E Sibsey. Feathering exs prohibited below 3,000 ft and must be gliding dist from aerodrome. 'OF-B', F/O H S Blakemore–2–2–non-op. Avro/ SAS 3.10.41. NFD. PSOC. 2 ops.

L7376 97 Sq 21.3.41. 3 AGS undated and probably incor sequenced. 25 OTU 24.12.41. 106 Sqn 14.4.42. 1654 CU undated. Collided with gunpit whilst taxying at Swinderby, u/c damaged 18.10.42. ROS undated. 1654 CU 24.10.42. To 3747M. SOC 11.5.43. 5 ops.

L7377 97 Sqn 21.3.41. 207 Sqn 13.4.41. MFO 12/13.8.41. 'EM-G', S/L G R Taylor–6–1–Berlin. Shot down by flak. Cr at 0200 nr Gross-Beeren/Teltow, nr Berlin, G. 4 ops.

L7378 97 Sqn 21.3.41. 207 Sqn 13.4.41. Cat. Ac (FB) 2/3.9.41. Hit by flak on ops. Cat.Ac (FB) 7/8.9.41. A/c hit 15 times by flak on ops. A/c hit by flak on ops 21/22.10.41. Cat. Ac 28.10.41 NFD. No accident card. 207 Sqn 11.12.41. Cat. Ac (FB) 8.3.42. A/c hit in tail unit by flak. 106 Sq 12.3.42. 50 CF 6.7.42.1654 CU 10.10.42. Avro 19.10.42. 39 MU 8.12.42. To 12 SoTT 17.6.43 as 3752M. PSOC. 33 ops.

L7379 97 Sqn 9.4.41. MFO 2/3.5.41. 'EM-T', F/O D Pinchbeck–6–6–Hamburg. Damaged by flak. Crew baled out. Pilot force landed nr Hamburg, Germany. 1 op. 10 hrs.

L7380 207 Sqn 13.4.41. MFO 7/8.9.41. 'EM-W', F/L W J Lewis–6–6–Berlin. Dam by unk night fghtr near Kiel at 0100. Force landed on beach at Ameland Is, Frisians, Netherlands. 5 ops.

L7381 207 Sqn 13.4.41. MFO 12/13.8.41. 'EM-R', F/O M Smith–6–0–Berlin. Shot down by Do 215, pilot Oblt L Becker IV/NJG1 Leeuwarden. Cr 0050 Lange Dijk, Groningen, Netherlands. 9 ops.

L7382 97 Sqn 23.4.41. Attacked by Me 110 over N Sea 26/27.6.41. A/c took several hits. MUG slightly wounded in head. 83 Sqn 10.10.41 (10.12.41 more likely). 44 Sqn 25.12.41. 44 CF 26.2.42. 83 Sqn 2.4.42. 83 CF 17.4.42. Cat.Ac 1705 hrs 10.8.42. A/c thrown into air on touch down & tail bounced twice. Due to rough surface of aerodrome. ROS undated. 83 CF 22.8.42. Avro 23.9.42. No acc card. RIW. AW/CN 10.10.42. 39 MU 16.10.42. To 3753M. 6 AOS? (ce?). Reduced to spares 13.3.45. 5 ops.

L7383 61 Sqn 16.4.41. 97 Sqn undated. Repeated flak hits on ops 14/15.8.41. Cat. W force landed out of fuel on cross country 14.9.41. Both engines cut. 'OF-F', P/O D E Fox–6–5–no-op. Cr at West Wickhouse, Norfolk. Pilot did not do ops. SOC 26.9.41. 10 ops.

L7384 97 Sqn 23.4.41. Cat.Mc 6.5.41. Glide approach slightly slow. Landed too high & tail down. 43 GDA undated. Avro (Flight Trials) 25.5.41. 97 Sqn 1.6.41. MFO 14/15.8.41. F/L J Nunn–7–5–Dusseldorf. Attacked by Hpt W Streib I/NJG1 Venlo in Me 110. 5 baled out. Force ldg at Kimroy. 2 ops.

L7385 61 Sqn 16.4.41. Avro (Mods) 12.10.41. 83 Sqn 9.1.42. Cat.M(u) 12.2.42. Attempted to land on side of runway at Scampton to avoid crashed a/c but weight of a/c with 6, 000 lb bombs and slippery surface made response sluggish & a/c collided with wreck. 83 Sqn undated. Cat. Ac 2040 hrs 24.3.42. Touched down in front of metalled road crossing 'drome. A/c bounced & tail wheel landed heavily. Roadway being removed. ROS 29.3.42. 83 Sqn 7.4.42. Dam by flak on op 8/9.4.42. 44 CF 30.4.42. 207 CF 4.5.42. Cat.Ac 1515 hrs 21.5.42. Swung off runway on landing during circuits & evidently damaged tail wheel which collapsed after further swing. ROS 27.5.42. 207 CF 13.6.42. Cat.E 0050 6.8.42. Lan-casterR5550 'EM-B', taxied onto flarepath & was hit by L7385 landing.'EM-U', Sgt Pearson–5–3–trng at Bottesford. SOC 13.8.42. 4 ops. 112.4 hrs.

L7386 RAF Cranage 6.5.41 for eng change. Avro (Woodford) 5.12.41. 25 OTU 24.12.41. Cat.A 24.3.42. Overshot thro' hedge into field adjoining Bircotes. 49 Sqn 20.4.42. 420 Sqn 23.5.42. 1654 CU 12.7.42. 9 CF 9.8.42. 57 CF 8.9.42. Cat.E 5.10.42. Stbd eng caught fire in air. Attempted to stretch approach to Scampton but a/c touched outside boundary & bounced onto aerodrome. U/c collapsed. Fire due to cracked hyd. pipe. P/O M E Walsh–?–all–test. SOC 16.10.42. 2 ops. 151.5 hrs.

L7387   61 Sqn 24.4.41. 207 Sqn 10.9.41. 97 Sqn 15.9.41.
Cat.Ac wheel bounced in heavy ldng, opened
throttle too quick & choked engines. U/c leg
collapsed 10.10.41. 97 Sqn 9.11.41. 83 Sqn
4.12.42. Cat.Ac 1615 hrs 4.4.42 landed diagonally
in front of road crossing 'drome which caused
a/c to become airborne again, . Stbd rudder
struck ground. ROS 8.4.42. 83 Sqn 9.5.42. 49 Sqn
7.6.42. Cat.E MFO 21.6.42. Sgt J H O'Brien–7–0–
search sortie. Cr at sea. 1 of crew buried in
Sweden, another at Schiermonnikoog, NL.
5 not recovered. SOC 26.6.42. 10 ops. 220.30 hrs.

L7388   61 Sqn 24.4.41. MFO 2/3.9.41. W/C G E
Valentine–7–0–Berlin. Sqn CO. Attempted
morale-boosting low level raid by senior crew.
Shot down by flak and cr near Berlin, G. 6 ops.

L7389   61 Sqn 24.4.41. Cat.R (B) 30.6.41. Stbd eng failed
in flight. 2nd pilot feathered pt prop in error.
Belly landed Fowlmere. Recommend luminous
paint on buttons. Avro/SAS 8.7.41. RAE?
24.10.41. 207 Sqn 25.11.41. 83 Sqn 9.12.41.
Cat.Ac (FB) 12.2.42. Presumed a/c of P/O
McFarlane. Attack by day fighter. R/G killed. Not
in unit ORB. ROS 17.2.42. 83 Sqn 10.4.42.
49 Sqn 23.5.42. 106 CF 19.7.42. 1660 CU 20.10.42.
1 SoTT 30.5.43 as 3763M. PSOC. 6 ops.

L7390   Avro/SAS 24.4.41 eng change etc. Avro
(Woodford) 21.12.41. 97 Sqn 9.1.42. 106 Sqn
20.1.42. MFO 25/26.3.42. F/L R J
Dunlop-Mackenzie–7–0–Essen. Shot down by
Oblt L Becker 6 II/NJG2 Leeuwarden. Cr in
Ijsselmeer nr Kornwerderzand, NL. 2 ops.

L7391   Avro/SAS 24.4.41 eng change. Rolls 1.12.41. No
accident card. Avro (mods) 1.1.42. 207 Sqn
17.1.42. Parked a/c struck by lorry 21.1.42.
Avro/ROS 24.1.42. 207 Sqn 31.1.42. Escape hatch
blown off & hole made in bomb bay doors by flak
9.3.42. Pt windscreen blown in & many holes in
bomb doors by flak 10.3.42. 106 Sqn 12.3.42.
Flak dam on ops 26/27.3.42. Rear turret dam by
flak 2/3.5.42. 106 CF undated. Cat.Ac 1500 hrs
11.6.42. Eng failed in flight, NFD. 1485 B&GF
undated. Air-air firing ex stbd eng failed at
1,200 ft 1540 hrs 11.2.43. Ht could not be maintd.
Belly landed nr Boston. F/S R Eyres–?–all–trng.
SOC 27.3.43. 13 ops. 160 hrs.

L7392   Avro/SAS 24.4.41 eng change. AFEE (Ringway)
9.2.42. 39 MU 3.9.42. Cat.E2 24.10.43. No
accident card. SOC 26.10.43.

L7393   207 Sqn 27.4.41. Cat.E2 18.5.41. Stbd eng failed
in flight. Force ldg Perranporth, retracted u/c to
stop. 'EM-V', S/L J C Mackintosh–5–5–trng. Avro/
SAS 1.6.41. To 2660M GI airframe with 25 OTU
7.9.41. SOC undated. 6 ops.

L7394   RAF Cranage 2.5.41 eng change. Avro (Mods)
7.2.42. 83 Sqn 27.2.42. 106 Sqn 27.2.42. Slight flak
dam on ops 25/26.3.42. MFO 29/30.3.42. F/S E R
Dimond–7–0–NECTARINE. Presumed lost at sea on
their first op. 4 ops.

L7395   RAF Cranage 2.5.41, eng change. Avro (Mods)
28.1.42. 61 Sqn 13.2.42. Lost on Ops 13/14.3.42.
P/O J R Hubbard–7–7–Cologne. Engine failed
over Wash on return. Abandoned. A/c cr 1.5 mls
south of Wittering. 1 MPRU Cowley 20.3.42.
1 (?) op.

L7396   RAF Cranage 6.5.41. Engine change 23.12.41.
Avro (Mods) 3.1.42. 61 Sqn 22.1.42. MFO
31.1/1.2.42. F/L Page–8–0–Brest. Cr in Eng
Channel, possibly on return. Body of pilot only
recovered. NFD. SOC 2.2.42.3 ops.

L7397   Avro/DGRD 24.2.41. 2 AGS (Probably
incorrectly seq'd & corrupt). Avro 15.4.41.
83 Sqn 29.4.42. 49 Sqn 3.6.42. 207 CF 2.8.42.
1660 CU 20.10.42. To 3762M. PSOC. 3 ops.

L7398   RAF Cranage 13.5.41. Eng change 14.12.41. Avro
(Mods) 13.10.41. 97 Sqn 9.1.42. 106 Sqn 20.1.42.
49 Sqn 2.5.42. Cat.Ac 20.6.42. Structural defect
on Frame 35. ROS undated. 49 Sqn 4.7.42.
97 CF 3.7.42 (note chronological error). Cat.Ac
1400 hrs 23.8.42. Overshot, ran over 2 ditches in
field. Stbd oleo leg coll following air firing ex.
97 Sqn 31.10.42. 1661 CU 20.1.43. 1660 CU
28.1.43. SOC 30.4.43. 8 ops. 286.05 hrs.

L7399   Rolleston Av/SAS 14.5.41. Still stored Rolleston
31.12.41 awaiting mods. 106 Sqn 26.4.42. MFO
3/4.5.42. 'ZN-X', F/S W L Young–7–2–GARDENING.

Cr Lilholt,14 km W of Haderslev, D. NFD. 1 op.

L7400   Rolleston Av/SAS 15.5.41. Still stored awaiting
mods 31.12.41. RAE (Farnborough) 7.5.42. ? CF
18.5.42. 49 Sq? 19.5.42. 1654 CU 25.6.42. Cat.A
25.2.43. Practice bomb exploded in bomb bay
prior to take-off, Wigsley. Sgt Hendry. Accident
not in a/c movement card records. SOC 11.9.43.

L7401   Rolleston Av/SAS 17.5.41. Still stored awaiting
mods 31.12.41. 408 Sqn 20.5.42. 1654 CU 10.6.42.
1485 B&GF 11.9.42. 1654 CU 25.4.43. 1661 CU
6.5.42. RAF Kidlington (?) 6.10.43. Cat.E2
15.10.43 crashed. No accident card. ORBs also
give ops for this aircraft with 50& 61 Sqdns
making up total of three if correctly attributed.
SOC 16.10.43. 3 ops. 366.45 hrs.

L7402   Rolleston Av/SAS 18.5.41. Still stored awaiting
mods 31.12.41. 49 CF 19.5.42. 420 CF undated.
Cat.Ac12.6.42. Pilots could not see flarepath.
Too high, landed heavily, u/c coll. ROS
15.6.42. 420 CF 5.9.42. 1661 CU 7.1.43. Cat.E1.
No accident card. SOC 31.3.43.

L7415   Rolleston Av/SAS 20.5.41. Still stored awaiting
mods 31.12.41. 408 Sqn 27.5?.42. 1654 CU
16.6.42. Uknown allocation 26.8.42. 1660 CU
6.11.42. 1661 CU 25.2.43. RAF ? 20.9.43. (If
correctly attributed, ORBs give the 3 ops with
50, 61 & 106 Sqns.) SOC 1.10.43. 3 ops. 207.
30 hrs.

L7416   Rolleston Avtn/SAS 24.5.41. Still stored awaiting
mods 31.12.41. 1654 CU 4.6.42. 420 Sqn 6.6.42.
1654 CU 16.6.42. Cat.E 1630 hrs 30.8.42. Landing
cross wind with no brakes, swung & cr into
trees, Wigsley. Air pressure line blown. P/O W J
Picken–?–all–trng. ORB gives the op to 50 Sqn.
SOC 5.9.42. 1 op. 82.25 hrs.

L7417   RAF Cranage 20.5.41. Eng change 28.12.41. Avro
(Mods) 25.2.42. 61 Sqn? undated. 106 Sqn
19.3.42. 106 CF 19.5.42. 1660 CU 20.10.42. Cat.B
29.10.42. Accident card gives 'Cause unknown'.
SOC 9.11.42. 5 ops.

L7418   RAF Cranage 20.5.41 eng change. Avro (Mods)
13.2.42. 83 Sqn 26.2.42. 106 Sqn 27.3.42. Cat.E
19.5.42 lost in Celtic Sea on cross country. Sgt A J
McHardy–5–0–non-op. Last heard crossing
Pembroke coast,on nav ex prior to going
operational. SOC 20.5.42. 4 ops.

L7419   Avro/SAS 22.5.41. 207 Sqn 2.7.41. Cat.B 2.11.41.
Failed to level out soon enough on app. Flew
into ground & bounced. ROS 10.11.41. 207 Sqn
20.11.41. Cat.R 27.1.42. Heavy landing on night
flying trng. Iced up windscreen & falling snow
made it impossible to see even thro' open clear
viz panel. U/c collapsed. ROS 29.1.42. 207 Sqn
10.3.42. 50 Sqn 26.3.42. Cat.Ac 13.4.42. Pt eng ct
fire when taxiing due to failure of hyd pipe to
hot air control. Fire temp controlled by a/c
extinguisher & finally by stn fire tender. ROS
22.4.42. 50 Sqn 25.4.42. Slight dam to bomb door
by flak 30/31.5.42. 408 Sqn 5.6.42.1654 CU
10.6.42. Cat.Ac 21.9.42. Damage found on
inspection. ROS 22.9.42. 1654 CU 3.10.42.
4 AGS undated. 3748M GI airframe. SOC 10.8.44.
14 ops.

L7420   25 OTU 7.6.41. 44 CF 3.5.42. 207 CF 4.5.42. 1660
CU 20.10.42. 1661 CU 25.2.43. 1660 CU 13.4.43.
Cat.E2 16.11.43. No accident card. SOC 19.11.43.

L7421   25 OTU 11.6.41. Cat.Mc 2.1.42. Tailwheel
collapsed on landing due to rough surface at
Bircotes. A lighter type of a/c to op from this
newly laid grass aerodrome in future.
Manchesters to Finningley. ROS 11.1.42. 25 OTU
14.2.42. Cat.Ac 29.3.42. Tailwheel found
dam on inspection. Attrib to fair wear & tear &
repeated C&Ls. ROS 2.4.42. 25 OTU 25.4.42.
49 Sqn 2.5.42. CAT.Ac 9.6.42. Frame 35 failure
found on insp, ROS undated. 49 Sqn 27.6.42.
Cat.Ac 0005 hrs 7.7.42. Heavy ldg. Pilot flew into
ground, bounced & corrected with throttle. Tail
damaged. ROS undated. 49 CF 8.7.42. 106 CF
5.8.42. 97 CF 28.8.42. 1660 CU 20.10.42. Cat.A
17.5.43 stabilising fin torn away in flt during
bombing practice. Attachment corroded.
Whole structure weakened by vibr & corr.

Cat.E2 16.11.43. No accident card. Poss date
scrapped? SOC 19.11.43. 4 ops.

L7422   Avro/SAS 20.3.41. 207 Sqn 26.6.41.Cat. Ac (FB)
31.8/1.9.41. Attacked by NF causing loss of
control. Bombs jettisoned. Made early return.
Severe tail dam. Conv to Mk.IA
during repairs. 43 GDA 1.9.41. 207 Sq undated.
Cat.E2 26.10.41. After unfeathering stbd prop
pilot failed to switch on ign. Lost height & belly
landed. 'EM-V', S/L K H PBeauchamp–13?–
13?–trng. Cr Hardings Farm, Linwood, Lincs.
ORBs show ops with 61 & 97 Sqns as well as 207
in this 11. SOC ?.9.43. 11 ops. 70 hrs.

L7423   97 Sqn 12.6.41. Landed Martlesham Heath
29/30.10.41 with slight damage after aborted op.
Holed by flak on ops 7/8.11.41. 83 Sqn 22.1.42.
MFO 13.3.42. 'OL-S', P/O J Bromiley–7–2–
Cologne. Shot down by NF and crashed near
Broekhuizen, NL. 12 ops. 23.17 hrs.

L7424   97 Sqn 1.6.41. MFO 12/13.8.41. F/O J A
Little–7–Berlin. Cr nr Munster. Crew poss baled
out over Holland on rtn. Signal received 0228 hr.
NFD. 2 (?) ops.

L7425   Avro/SAS 10.6.41. 97 Sqn 26.6.41. 207 Sqn
21.1.42. 50 Sqn 18.3.42. 408 Sqn 16.5.42. 408 CF
17.5.42. Cat.Ac 9.6.42 defect discovered on
inspection. ROS 15.6.42. 408 CF 4.7.42. 1654 CU
12.7.42. 9 CF 9.8.42. 1661 CU 8.11.42. 8 AGS
undated, 3741M as GI airframe. SOC 13.2.47.
3 ops.

L7426   61 Sqn 26.6.41. Cat.Mc 4.7.41. Eng failed in flt
during intensive flight trial. Overshot thro'
hedge at Rearsby. U/c collapsed in ditch. 43
GDA 4.7.41. 83 Sqn 10.12.41. Flying accident, but
no accident card, ROS approx 17.1.42. 83 Sqn
14.2.42. MFO 8/9.3.42. P/O Frost–7–0–Essen.
Shot down at 0032 by Oblt Becker II/NJG2.
Ditched off Enkhuizen, NL. SOC 10.3.42. 2ops.

L7427   Avro/SAS 14.6.41. 97 Sqn 26.6.41. Cat. R(B)
3.7.41. Stbd eng failed in flt during intensive eng
trial. Yawed, unable to maintain height. Force
lnd in field 2 ml E Spalding. 43 GDA 3.7.41.
83 Sqn 9.1.42. Avro/ROS 10.2.42, no accident
card. 83 Sqn 14.2.42. MFO 8/9.4.42. 'OL-Q',
P/O Morphett–7–1–Hamburg. Cr Ermke, G, at
0010. R/Gnr died while PoW. NFD. 16 ops.

L7428   25 OTU 11.6.41. Cat.W 18.11.41. Pt eng failed in
flt. Prop not feathered. Ht lost rapidly. Belly
landed thro' hedge at Scaftworth nr Bawtry. F/S
L H Adams–5–2–night trng. Avro (Bracebridge
Heath) 4.12.41. SOC 2.1?.42. 56.35 hrs.

L7429   25 OTU 12.6.41. 97 Sqn 21.10.41. 25 OTU
31.12.41. 49 Sqn 28.4.42. 49 CF 18.5.42. MFO
30/31.5.42. P/O J P Carter–7–0–Cologne.
Cr in North Sea, poss on retn,bodies recovered.
NFD. SOC. 1 op.

L7430   25 OTU 11.6.41. 44 CF 30.4.42. Cat.? 26.9.42.
Collided with parked Tiger Moth on landing at
Kingstown, Cumb. Error of Judgement. 1661 CU
8.11.42. 27.3.43 Cat.Ac. Frame 46 found
damaged at Winthorpe. ROS 31.3.43. 1661 CU
7.4.43. 1654 CU 12.6.43. 1661 CU 16.7.43. RAF ?
22.9.43. SOC 30.9.43. 1 op. 449.15 hrs.

L7431   25 OTU 11.6.41. Cat.Ac 8.11.41. No accident
card. 25 OTU 24.11.41. Cat.B. 2.1.42. Sodium
flarepath ldgs. Pt eng emitted loud bangs &
panel behind air intake blew off. Unable to
maintn ht, belly landed Cotterill Woods Farm,
Woodsetts. 25 OTU 8.1.42. 1654 CU 6.7.42.
Cat.Ac 2130 hrs 10.8.42. Heavy ldg with drift at
Coningsby. Stbd u/c coll. ROS 15.8.42. 1654 CU
3.10.42. To 3772M GI Airframe. SOC undated.

L7432   207 Sqn 13.6.41. 43 GDA undated. 207 Sqn
undated. Flak hit stopped pt eng over Berlin
7/8.9.41. Crew jettisoned loose gear to keep ht.
Single eng retn to West Raynham. 207 Sqn
16.10.41. 50 Sqn 25.3.42. Bird strike thro' BA
blister on ops 8/9.4.42. Severe flak hits in target
area 26/27.4.42. Most serious, distorted fins.
Landed safely after difficult return. MFO 4.6.42.
P/O J F Heaton–7–2–Bremen. Shot down by Maj
Radusch IV/NJG1. Crashed at Zwiggelte, NL.
26 ops. 245.35 hrs.

L7433 97 Sqn 13.6.41. 6 MU 6.7.41. 61 Sqn 13.12.41.
Cat.Ac (FB) 10/11.2.42. Holed by flak in several
places. MFO 16.2.42. F/S P H G
Webster–7–0–GARDENING. Hit by flak and cr in
North Sea nr Terschelling, NL. NFD. 5 ops.

L7434 97 Sqn 13.6.41. 6 MU 6.7.41. 25 OTU 13.12.41.
106 CF 15.11.42. 1656 CU 25.11.42. 39 MU
31.12.42. To 4221M GI airframe. Cat.E2 13.10.43.
No acc card, poss date scrapped? SOC 16.10.43.
(Ops with 106 Sqn.) 10 ops.

L7453 Avro/SAS eng change 5.7.41. 207 Sqn 29.8.41.
97 Sqn 26.9.41. A/c dam by flak on ops
20/21.10.42. Pt wing & fuel tank holed by flak
7/8.11.41. Presumed ROS 11.11.41. 97 Sqn
26.11.41. 83 Sqn 22.1.42. Cat.Ac (FB) 20.3.42.
A/c damaged by Me 110 NF. ROS 29.3.42. 83 Sqn
16.5.42. 49 Sqn 23.5.42. 44 CF 2.8.42. 1661 CU
8.11.42. Cat.B 1525 hrs 14.3.43. Pt eng caught fire
shortly after take-off Swinderby. Feathered prop
& belly landed. Fire due to burning of exhaust
manifold of 'A' block pt eng. S/L Oakley–?–all-
trng.RIW 5.4.43. ORBs show ops with 49, 106 &
83 Sqns. Recat E1 1.5.43. SOC 1.5.43. Alternative
fate has mid-air collision with Halifax at
Winthorpe 1.5.43 and SOC. 16 ops.

L7454 Avro/SAS eng change 5.7.41. 207 Sqn 10.9.41.
Cat M(c) 31.10.41. Unable to see ground due to
rain & mist at Waddington, heavy ldg with drift.
U/c coll. ROS 8.11.41. 207 Sqn 3.1.42. 61 Sqn
24.2.42. MFO 29.3.42. P/O C S Churchill–7–0–
GARDENING. Pres lost at sea. 7 ops.

L7455 Avro/SAS eng change 12.7.41. 207 Sqn 10.9.41.
50 Sqn 17.3.42. 9 CF 4.8.42. 1661 CU 8.11.42.
8 AGS 21.5.43. To 3742M as GI airframe. SOC
23.5.44? 26 ops.

L7456 Avro/SAS eng change 12.7.41. 6 MU 26.11.41.
25 OTU 16.12.41. 106 Sqn 7.5.42. MFO 30/31.5.42
whilst on loan to 50 Sqn from 106 CF. Sgt Wilkie–
7–4–Cologne. Hit by flak, pt eng caught fire.
Force landed on airfield at Dusseldorf. 1 op.

L7457 Avro/SAS eng change 12.7.41. 207 Sqn 13.9.41.
97 Sqn 13.9.41. Dam by flak on ops 4/5.11.41.
97 CF 16.2.42. 106 Sqn 15.4.42. Cat.Ac 21.5.42.
Tailwheel found damaged due to previous
heavy landing. ROS 25.5.42. 106 Sqn 15.6.42.
83 CF 11.6.42. Cat.Ac 14.9.42. Collision with
air raid shelter taxying at Wigsley. ROS 15.9.42.
83 CF 26.9.42. 1654 CU 10.10.42. Cat.E 1510 hrs
24.1.43. Pt eng caught fire in flight. Crew slow to
feather prop. Unable to maint ht. Force landing
Highfield Farm, Saxilby. F/S Taylor–?–all–trng.
SOC 24.1.43. 13 ops.

L7458 Avro/SAS eng change etc 23.7.41. 83 Sqn
10.12.41. 61 Sqn 11.12.41. 12.2.42. Daylight op.
Serious dam to port wing by ships flak caused
near loss of control & bombs to be jett. Cat.Ac
23.3.42. Tailwheel shimmy on ldg caused tail to
rise & tail wheel unit then fell out. Attributed to
previous heavy ldg. ROS 26.3.42. 61 Sqn 9.5.42.
61 CF 17.5.42. 1660 CU 20.10.42. Cat.Ac 10.11.42.
Tailwheel collapsed during landing run at
Swinderby. ROS 10.11.42. 1660 CU 5.12.42.
3 SoTT 22.9.43 as 4280M GI airframe. PSOC. 9 ops.

L7459 Avro/SAS eng change 19.7.41. 97 Sqn 27.9.41.
Cat.E 8.1.42. Practice bomb exploded on
take-off blinding & choking pilot. Throttled back
& stalled onto ground at Coningsby. 'OF-N', Sgt
G H Hartley–7–7–non-op. SOC 16.1.42. 1 op.
78.45 hrs.

L7460 Avro/SAS engine change etc 23.7.41. 83 Sqn
10.12.41. 97 Sqn 11.12.41. Cat.Ac (FB) 18.12.41.
Hit by flak on daylight op. Stbd oil tanks holed.
Eng cut on landing Colerne. 97 Sqn 8.1.42. 97 CF
16.2.42. 83 Sqn 2.4.42. 50 Sqn 16.4.42. 57 CF
8.9.42. 1656 CU 1.10.42. SOC 26.7.43. 8 ops.

L7461 Avro/SAS 19.7.41. 97 Sqn 19.9.41. 29/30.10.41
Form 540 gives 'Shot up by enemy fighter and
jettisoned bomb load'. Form 541 gives 'A/c
damaged by flak and returned with bombs
Cat.Ac'? ROS 1.11.41. 97 Sqn 22.11.41. Cat.B
10.12.41 Hyd & emerg system failure led to
inability to lower flaps or u/c when ldg at
Coningsby. ROS 14.12.41. 97 Sqn 19.12.42. 106
Sqn 2.3.42. Cat.B (FB) 10/11.4.42. A/c severely
dam by flak. Crew ordered to bale out. Control
regained. Force ldg at Martlesham Heath. ROS
14.4.42. 106 Sqn undated. 1661 CU 8.12.42. 1654
CU 12.6.43. 1660 CU 22.7.43. To 3 SoTT 23.9.43
as 4278M. SOC undated. 6 ops.

L7462 Avro/SAS 26.7.41. 97 Sqn 26.9.41. MFO
20/21.10.41. 'OF-Z', P/O Noble–7–0–Bremen.
Crashed in sea. NFD. (Intense & accurate flak
rep over target.) 1 op.

L7463 Avro/SAS 26.7.41. 97 Sqn 26.9.41. 106 Sqn 20.1.42.
MFO 23/24.4.42. 'ZN-L', P/O H M Stoffer–7–6–
Rostock. Eng overheated & caught fire. 6 baled
out. Mainplane broke off. Crashed at Visgard,
3km E of Tinglev. 1st op for crew. 11 ops.

L7464 Avro/SAS mods & eng change 26.7.41. 97 Sqn
9.1.42. 61 Sqn 23.1.42. 50 Sqn 13.4.42. Cat.Ac
13.4.42 on delivery North Luffenham to
Skellingthorpe. Misjudged ht, pt wing dropped
& struck gnd. Pilot opened throttles to make
further circuit but pt eng failed, a/cswung to pt &
u/c coll. Error of judgement. ROS. 50 Sqn
18.6.42. 57 CF 12.9.42. 460 CF 1.10.42. 1656 CU
2.10.42. To 1 AAS as 3624M GI airframe 26.3.43.
PSOC. 12 ops.

L7465 Avro/SAS Mods & eng change 26.7.41. AW/CN
22.12.41. 83 Sq 24.12.41. MFO 25/26.3.42. 'OL-H',
Sgt P Markides–7–0–Essen. Crashed Lichtaert.
NFD. 8 ops. 47.20 hrs.

L7466 Avro/SAS mods & engine change 26.7.41.
AW/CN 22.12.41. 97 Sqn. 26.9.41. Damaged
by Me 109 night fighter on ops 23/24.10.41. ROS
30.10.41. 97 Sqn. 3?.11.41. MFO 8.11.41. 'OF-N',
F/L C P D Price–7–0–ASR (D). Search for poss
survivors from previous night's Berlin op.
Reported 6 times by sister a/c. Last time at 1600.
NFD. 3 ops.

L7467 Avro/SAS 30.7.41. 25 OTU 10.10.41. Cat.Ac
30.10.41. No accident card. 25 OTU 31.10.41.
97 CF 7.5.42. An AC2 walked into prop when
going to assistance of gnd crew member
attempting to remove wheel chock 1.6.42.
1660 CU 20.10.42. 1661 CU 25.2.43. 1660 CU
12.6.43. ?50 MU 21.9.43. Cat. E2 25.9.43. No
accident card. Reported crashed. SOC 25.9.43.

L7468 Avro/SAS 2.8.41. 207 Sqn 9.11.41. Cat. Ac (FB)
14/15.1.42. F/G slightly wounded by flak burst on
ops. 50 Sqn 28.3.42. Cat.Ac (FB) 30/31.5.42. Hit
twice by flak. Bomb release inoperable. ROS. 50
Sqn 20.6.42. 9 CF 9.8.42. 50 CF undated. 1660 CU
10.11.42. Cat.Ac 1.5.43. Eng faltered in circuit &
failed compl as turned into wind. Eng ct fire on
ldg. Flame trap on 'A' block had failed. To 12
SoTT June 1943 as 3732M GI airframe. SOC
12.1.4?. 16 ops.

L7469 Avro/SAS 2.8.41. 25 OTU 10.10.41. 49 Sqn
21.4.42. MFO 6/7.6.42. Act S/L P M De Mestre–7–
0–Emden. 'A' Flt CO and crew, cr at sea. 1 body
recovered. NFD. SOC 13.6.42. 3 ops. 192.40 hrs.

L7470 Avro/SAS 2.8.41. 61 Sqn 11.10.41. MFO 7/8.4.42.
F/S E W Noble–7–0–Essen. Shot down by Oblt
von Bonin in Me 110 of II/NJG1 St Trond and
cr near St Trond, Belgium. 8 ops.

L7471 Avro/SAS 9.8.41. 61 Sqn 9.11.41. 50 Sqn 19.4.42.
MFO 6/7.6.42. F/O A D Beatty—7–6–Emden. SOS
fix MBQ 4801 0140 hrs. 3rd class, Heston. NFD.
16 ops. 159.40 hrs.

L7472 Avro/SAS 9.8.41. 61 Sqn 11.10.41. MFO 31.1/
1.2.42. F/L Fraser–8–6–Brest. Set on fire by
flak over Brest and snagged balloon cable.
1 baled out too low. Ditched 1/4 mile off shore.
6 escaped, 1 drowned. 4 ops.

L7473 Avro/SAS 9.8.41. 97 Sqn 28.10.41. 61 Sqn 28.1.42.
Cat.Ac (FB) 10.2.42. Ops to Bremen. NFD in
ORB. ROS? Cat.Ac 0045 hrs 11.3.42. Returning
from ops a/c made heavy lding with glim lamps
to stbd, bounced, slewed, tyre burst, u/c
collapsed. ROS 15.3.42. 61 CF 9.9.42. 50 CF
3.10.42. 1485 B&GF undated. Cat.E 1400 hrs
6.10.42. Eng failed at 50 ft. Made short circuit &
crash landing at Dunholme Lodge. SOC F/S H H
Taylor–?–all–trng. SOC 17.10.42. 12 ops. 213 hrs.

L7474 Avro/SAS 9.8.41. 97 Sqn 28.10.41. 106 Sqn
26.1.42. Cat.E 12.3.42 Iced up on cross country
training. U/c damaged in attempted landing at
Coningsby. Crew ordered to point a/c toward N
Sea & abandoned. Cr Winceby. Sgt G K Carter–
7–7–non-op. SOC 18.3.42. 2 ops.

L7475 Avro 16.8.41. 97 Sqn 28.10.41. 61 Sqn 23.1.42. 50
Sqn 8.4.42. 50 CF 17.7.42. Cat.E 1530 hr, 16.8.42.
Stbd eng ct fire at 150 ft after take-off. Ht could
not be mntnd, belly landed in field & burnt out at
Talbenny. F/S Dickensen–?–all–non-op. SOC
21.8.42. 23 ops.

L7476 Avro 16.8.41. 97 Sqn 27.9.41. Hit by flak 8.11.41.
Bombs jett on run up to aiming point. 2-nd pilot
died of wounds on retn. 207 Sqn 29.1.42. 50 Sqn
23.4.42. Cat.B 13.7.42. Fire on ground during
refuelling at Swinderby. Cause obscure. Hit by
flak in target area 1/2.6.42. Nav wounded. 50 CF
17.8.42. 1654 CU 10.10.42. SOC 26.4.43. 14 ops.

L7477 Avro 16.8.41. 61 Sqn 12.10.41. Several flak hits on
ops 25/26.1.42. Cat.Ac (FB) 12.2.42 Opn FULLER,
in daylight. Hit by flak. Bomb doors, brakes,
flaps, trim gear, turrets all u/s. Stbd fin, tailplane
& fuel tanks hit. ROS 17.2.42. 61 Sqn 25.4.42. 61
CF 29.4.42. No acc card but ROS 30.10.42. 1661
CU 7.11.42. 1485 B&GF 4.3.43. 1654 CU 22.4.43.
Avro (Waddington) 12.5.43. SOC 6.6.44. 8 ops.

L7478 38 MU 16.11.41. 25 OTU 23.12.41. Cat. W 1430
hrs 10.2.42. Eng failed in flight, A/c yawed &
undershot aerodrome. Pilot had failed to
diagnose fault as RPM & boost indic remained
normal & erroneously approached at 120 IAS
with u/c and flaps down. 2nd pilot
inadvertently cut off fuel to stbd eng instead of
closing radiator shutters. Cr N of Bawtry. P/O E R
Siebold–7–6–trng. SOC 16.2.42.

**Mk.IA L7485 'EM-D' of 207 Squadron photographed
from a sister aircraft during formation flying practice on December 16th 1941, flown by F/L Peter
Ward-Hunt. Note the darkened white area of the
fuselage roundel. This was in anticipation of a daylight 'op' to Brest.** *D Green*

L7479 Avro 23.8.41. 25 OTU 26.11.41. 49 Sqn 13.5.42. Cat.Ac 19.6.42. Structural defect in Frame 35. ROS 21.6.42. 49 CF 4.7.42. 1656 CU 20.10.42. SOC 15.7.4?. 3 ops.

L7480 Avro 23.8.41. 207 Sqn 9.11.41. 61 Sqn 16.2.42. 50 Sqn 11.4.42. 44 CF 2.5.42. 1661 CU 8.11.42. No accident card but ROS 2.2.43. SOC 30.4.43. 20 ops. 260.50 hrs.

L7481 Avro 23.8.41. 6 MU 2.11.41. 46 MU 14.11.41. 25 OTU 24.11.41. Tyre burst on runway 15.3.42. A/c swung, u/c collapsed. ROS 19.3.42. 25 OTU 16.5.42. 39 Sqn 27.6.42. 44 CF 16.7.42. 1661 CU 3.11.42. Cat.E2 – no accident card. SOC 14.9.43. 323.25 hrs.

L7482 Avro 23.8.41. 25 OTU 26.11.41. 97 CF 7.6.42. 1660 CU 20.10.42. Cat.E 2.1.43. Inadvertant landing at Coleby. Erroneously tried to fly on to intended destination at Waddington. A/c abandoned by crew due to severe icing whilst attempting to climb thro' snowstorm. F/O H C Goodyear–?–all–trng. Snow cover caused error. Cr nr Metheringham, Lincs. SOC 21.1.43. 244.2 hrs.

L7483 *Mk.IA* 207 Sqn 29.8.41. Cat.B 27.12.41. Stbd boost & revs dropped & lost ht outwd leg on ops. Bombs jett offshore. U/c coll in emergency ldg Martlesham Heath. 'EM-O', S/L K H P Beauchamp–7–7–Dusseldorf. Avro 15.1.42 for repair but recat.E. AW/CN 14.11.42. 39 MU 8.12.42 (dismantled). To 12 SoTT 17.6.43 as 3749M GI airframe. PSOC. 4 ops.

L7484 *Mk.IA* 207 Sqn 29.8.41. Cat.Ac (FB) 13/14.10.41 several flak hits on ops. Cat.Ac (FB) 8/9.3.42. Dud flak shell passed through fuselage. Ammu nition exploded & fire started which W/Op beat out with hands. RIW 17.3.42. AW/CN 28.3.42. 207 CF 3.4.42. 83 Sqn undated. Eng failed due to flak dam on ops 6/7.4.42. Single eng retn to Hor- sham St Faith. 83 Sqn 18.4.42. 49 Sqn 22.4.42. 408 Sqn 27.5.42. 1654 CU 20.7.42. 9 CF 2.8.42. Cat. Ac 1600 hrs 9.8.42. Eng failed & stbd mainplane dam by oil tank bursting. Investigation showed wooden blanking plug not removed from tank vent on installation. ROS 11.8.42. 9 CF 15.8.42. 1485 B&GF 23.9.42. Cat.Ac 26.9.42. During fighter affil ex, severe vibration exp in a/c after evasive action. Landed Dunholme Lodge where rivets on tail fr & rear spars found to be loose. ROS 3.10.42. 1485 B&GF 3.10.42. 1654 CU 22.4.43. 1 AGS 17.6.43 as 3776M GI airfr. SOC 19.10.4?. 20 ops.

L7485 *Mk.IA* 207 Sqn 12.9.41. Cat.Mu 1745hr 6.1.42, 1745 hr. Struck bomb trolley on edge of runway at Bottesford taxying in bad viz. 106 Sqn 12.3.42. Several flak hits on ops, 10/11.4.42. MFO 16/17.4.42. P/O Scatchard–7–0–GARDENING Deodars. Presumed lost in Eng Chan. Crew's 1st op. 22 ops.

L7486 *Mk.IA* 207 Sqn 12.9.41. 50 Sqn 17.3.42. Cat.E 1915 hrs 25.3.42. Held off, ballooned &stalled a/c onto runway on one wheel from 20 ft. A/c burnt out but deemed that it could have been saved with more adequate fire fighting facilities at Skellingthorpe. Sgt D Atkinson–?–All–Non op. SOC 2.4. 42. 20 ops.

L7487 *Mk.IA* 207 Sqn 12.9.41. MFO 20/21.10.41. 'EM-N', P/O J C L Ruck-Keene–7–0–GARDENING Sassnitz. Ditched off Yarmouth ret from op. NFD. 4 (?) ops. 26 hrs.

L7488 *Mk.IA* 97 Sqn 14.9.41. 207 Sqn 21.1.42. Cat. Ac (FB) 12.2.42 Opn FULLER in daylight. Hit in tail by ship's flak. 106 Sqn 12.3.42. 50 CF 7.6.42. 1654 CU 10.10.42. Avro. No accident card but RIW 19.11.42. Aw/cn 12.12.42. 39 MU 22.12.42. To 12 SoTT 23.6.43 as 3750M. GI a/fr. PSOC. Ops 22.

L7489 *Mk.IA* 97 Sqn 14.9.41. 50 Sqn 12.2.42. MFO 8/.9.4.42. Sgt M Gruber–7–6–Warnemunde. Abandoned & cr at Marienborg, D. 14 ops.

L7490 *Mk.IA* 97 Sqn 24.9.41. Night of 29/30.10.41 – confusion in records. Form 540 says a/c dam by flak & retn with bombs. Form 541 says a/c attacked by enemy fighter & jettisoned bomb load. MFO 18.12.41. 'OF-U', W/C D F Balsdon–8–0–Brest (D). Stalled on o'shoot & cr at Coningsby. Thought due to flak dam. 7 ops. 89.45 hrs.

L7491 *Mk.IA* 25 OTU 27.9.41. 97 Sqn 21.10.41. 207 Sqn 21.1.42. Cat.Ac (FB) 9.3.42 BA blister blown in & 10 flak hits in fuselage on ops. ROS 12.3.42. 207 CF 3.4.42. 50 Sqn 16.4.42. 1654 CU 25.10.42. Cat.E 1155 hrs 17.5.43. A/c swung on take-off at Wigsley. Attempted to correct but stbd u/c coll. Susp stbd brake seized. P/O A Walters–?–all trng. SOC 26.5.43. 19 ops.

L7492 *Mk.IA* 25 OTU 1.10.41. 97 Sqn 21.10.41. 61 Sqn 22.1.42. Cat.Ac (FB) 31.1/1.2.42. Holed in 58 places by flak esp mid-fus & rear turret. IFF, hyds & brakes all u/s. ROS 15.2.42. 61 Sqn. 4.4.42. 50 Sqn 18.4.42. Cat.Ac 0015 hrs 30.5.42. Ct in heavy rain attempting to land at Skellingthorpe on return from night cross country. Stalled on one wheel & u/c collapsed. TR9 radio failure in a/c prevented ATC advising a hold. ROS 2.6.42. 50 CF 22.8.42. 1485 B&GF 7.10.42. 1654 CU 22.4.43. To 4 AOS 20.7.43 as 3985M GI airframe. SOC 22.6.4?. 6 ops.

L7493 *Mk.IA* 25 OTU 1.10.41. No accident card. ROS 19.3.42. 25 OTU 28.3.42. Avro/MR 20.4.42. No acc card. AW/CN 9.5.42. 49 Sqn 12.6.42. 49 CF 1?.5.42. 1660 CU 9.11.42. RAF B???? 7.10.43. Cat.E2 15.10.43. No acc card. Poss date scrapped. SOC 18.10.43. 2 ops. 397.05 hours.

L7494 *Mk.IA* 61 Sqn 4.10.41. MFO 7/8.12.41. S/L J L Riley–7–0–Boulogne. 'A' Flt Cdr. An a/c exploded in mid-air and cr in sea in target area. Night's only casualty. NFD. 3 ops.

L7495 *Mk.IA* 61 Sqn 20.10.41. Cat.Ac 14.11.41 Sqn non-operational, no acc card. 61 Sqn 21.11.41. Cat.E 16.1.42 MFO. Made landfall at mouth of Humber lost & short of fuel on return ex ops in bad weather. A/c abandoned. F/O Beard–7–7– Hamburg. A/c cr at Grimoldby, Lincs. 3 ops.

L7496 *Mk.IA* 61 Sqn 4.10.41. Cat.R(B) 8.1.42. Undershot & hit step where existing & runway extention meet. U/c coll. ROS 11.1.42. 61 Sqn 28.3.42. 50 Sqn 13.4.42. 420 Sqn 22.5.42. 1654 CU 17.6.42. Cat.E 1635 hrs 5.7.42. Stbd eng failed when throttles opened to carry out overshoot at Wigsley. Landed str ahead. Cr & ct fire. F/S Lancey–?–all–trng. SOC 16.7.42. 3 ops.

L7497 *Mk.IA* 61 Sqn 10.10.41. Rear turret dam & R/G slightly wounded by flak on ops 25/26.1.42. MFO, 26/27.3.42. Sgt C G Furby–7–0–Essen. Shot down at 2209 by Oblt Woltersdorf of NJGI and cr at Werterbruch on NL/G border. 4 ops.

L7515 *Mk.IA* 207 Sq 10.10.41. Cat M(c) 22.11.41. Taxied off runway and became bogged at Bottesford. Dam on recovery. ROS 26.11.41?. 207 Sqn 11.12.41. 106 Sqn 11.3.42. 49 CF 2.8.42. 1656 CU 21.11.42. Avro RIW 30.1.43. No accident card. AW/CN 6.3.43. 39 MU15.3.43. Cat.E2 14.11.43. No acc card. Poss date scrapped. SOC 16.11.43?. 24 ops.

L7516 *Mk.IA* 61 Sqn 10.10.41. 50 Sqn 13.4.42. Bomb doors damaged by light flak on ops 24/25.4.42. MFO 30.4.42. 'VN-N', F/S T Willett–7–5–FORGET-ME-NOTS. Shot down by Me 110 of II/NJG3 Westerland, pilot Oblt G Koberich. Force landed on tidal flats at Sylt, Germany. 18 ops.

L7517 *Mk.IA* Burnt out in works. Not delivered. Contract reduced by one.

L7518 *Mk.IA* 61 Sqn 15.10.41. MFO 25.3.42. 'QR-O', P/O J R Hubbard–7–2–Essen. Shot down at 0032 by Hpt Lent II/NJG2 Leeuwarden & crashed near Warmenhuizen, Netherlands. 10 ops.

L7519 *Mk.IA* 61 Sqn 20.10.41. 50 Sqn 13.4.42. Cat.E 1645 hr 13.5.42. Dived into grnd from 800 ft and ct fire on impact at Thurlby, Lincs. A/c had been flown by others that day with no problems. Suggested autopilot was engaged before pilot was strapped in. F/S P J W Blake–5–0–Non op. SOC 18.5.42. 9 ops.

L7520 *Mk.IA* 61 Sq 21.10.41. Cat.E Pt eng cut 2.11.41. Used incorrect method to feather prop. Unable to maintain ht. Force landed in field, Ekinsfield, Colden, Beds. P/O A L Searby–?–all–non–op. SOC9.11.41. 1 op.

L7521 *Mk.IA* 61 Sqn 25.10.41. Cat.Ac (FB) 27.3.42. No ops this day & no acc card. RIW 9.4.42. Aw/cn 9.4.42. 61 Sqn 8.4.42. 50 Sqn 11.4.42. 50 CF 18.5.42. 1654 CU undated. Cat.E 1215 hrs 5.9.42. Stbd prop failed to unfeather following exercise.

Emergency approach to Waddington but baulked by an incoming Oxford. A/c turned sharply whilst semi-stalled. Cr short & burnt out. S/L Carter–?–all–non-op. SOC 17.9.42. 19 ops. 346.40 hrs.

L7522 *Mk.IA* 61 Sqn 25.10.41. 97 Sqn 27.10.41. ROS 2.12.41, no acc card. Unkn allotment 21.12.41. 97 Sqn 31.12.41. 83 Sqn 31.1.42. MFO 22.2.42. 'OL-N', S/L J R Rainford–7–0–Stavanger (D). Shot down by Me 109 during 5 a/c attack on Stavanger airfield, Norway. 8 ops.

L7523 *Mk.IA* 207 Sqn 31.10.41. MFO 14/15.1.42. 'EM-M', F/S Wescombe–7–0–Hamburg. Cr at Cliff House Farm, Holmpton, nr Withernsea, Yorks, at 2045. Airborne 3.10 hr. 4 ops.

L7524 *Mk.IA* 6 MU 2.11.41. 46 MU 14.11.41. 25 OTU 11.12.41. Cat M(c) 11.12.41. Undershot practising flapless landings. Dropped heavily on uneven ground at edge of peritrack at Bircotes. U/c coll. ROS 14.12.41. 25 OTU 17.1.42. 49 Sqn 15.4.42. 1485 B&GF 1.10.42. 1661 CU 25.4.43. RAF Kidlington 7.10.43. Cat.E2 15.10.43. No accident card. Poss date scrapped. SOC 16.10.43. 2 ops. 275.35 hrs.

L7525 *Mk.IA* 38 MU 15.4.41. 97 Sqn 10.12.41. 106 Sqn 25.1.42. 83 Sqn undated. 12.2.42 Op FULLER. A/c damaged& R/G wounded by day fighter. ROS 17.2.42. 83 Sqn 11.?.42. 50 Sqn 13.5.42. Stbd eng hit by flak in target area & caught fire, jettisoned all moveable gear to reach Tempsford 30/31.5.42. 1485 B&GF 18.8.42. 1661 CU 25.4.43. SOC 24.8.43. 3 ops. 423 hrs.

L7526 *Mk.IA* 25 OTU 26.11.41. Cat M(c) 1.1.42. Tailwheel fork failed & tyre burst ldg on rough ground at Bircotes. ROS 5.1.42. 25 OTU 30.1.42. 49 Sqn 15.6.42. 207 CF 5.8.42. Cat Ac 1515 hrs 2.9.42. Tailwheel collapsed toward end of landing run at Woodhall Spa. 207 Sqn 12.9.42. 1656 CU 22.10.42. SOC 15.7.43. 3 ops.

Avro Manchesters built by Metrovick Trafford Park for erection at Woodford. Contract No 982866.39. 43 aircraft, delivered from March 1941 to March 1942. (First 13 destroyed by enemy action at the works on 23rd December 1940. Serials re-allocated.)

R5768 Avro 10.3.41. Retained & conv *Mk.IA*. 83 Sqn 18.4.42. Cat.B (FB)30/31.5.42. Badly dam by flak. Force landing at base on return. ROS 4.6.42. 83 CF 26.9.42. 1656 CU 23.4.43. Cat.E2 16.11.43. No accident card. Poss date scrapped. SOC 19.3.43. 2 ops.

R5769 Avro Cranage 20.3.41. Stored, mods & eng change. 25 OTU 27.3.42. 106 Sqn 15.4.42. 50 Sqn 16.5.42. 9 CF 12.8.42. 1661 CU 8.11.42. Cat.Ac 1.4.43. Blown into L7297 in gale at Winthorpe. ROS 12.4.43. 1661 CU 1.5.43. SOC 2.9.43. 4 ops. 284.45 hrs.

R5770 Avro for mods etc 9.4.41. 25 OTU 8.3.42. 106 Sqn 15.11.42. 1660 CU 3.1.43. Cat.E 4.7.43. Eng failed on take-off. A/c swung, u/c raised to stop. Foreign matter found in carb. P/O J L Cooper–?– all–trng. SOC 13.7.43. 5 ops. 213.5 hrs.

R5771 Avro/SAS 10.6.41 for mods etc. 25 OTU 27.3.42. 83 Sqn 3.4.42. 49 Sqn 15.4.42. 420 Sqn 23.5.42. 57 CF 6.9.42. 50 CF 23.9.42. 1654 CU 10.10.42. To 2 AGS 27.5.43 as 3746M GI Airframe. SOC 6.12.4?. 3 ops.

R5772 Avro for mods etc 27.4.41. 25 OTU 2.4.42. 49 Sqn 16.4.42. 83 CF 26.7.42. 1661 CU 10.10.42. Cat.E 26.1.43. 1st solo on type. Pt eng cut circling aerodrome. On attempted restart it caught fire. Force ldg in field. Burnt out. Primary cause failure No 3 exhaust valve. F/S Schnier–1–1– trng. SOC 8.2.43. 1 op.

R5773 Avro/SAS 23.7.41. RAE (Farnborough) 24.4.42. TDU 2.5.42. Cat.B. No accident card. Avro MR RIW 25.11.42. TDU 24.12.42. NFD on service. To 3892M GI airframe ?.3.43. SOC 1.11.4?

R5774 Avro/SAS 26.7.41. TDU 27.4.42. Running up stbd eng at Weston-super-Mare 1440 hrs, 12.9.42. Stbd wheel chock slipped whilst eng at 1,500rpm. A/c lurched forward & pushed over platform on which Cpl Smith was working. ROS 5.10.42. TDU 10.10.42. Cat.B. Avro RIW 25.11.42. No accident card. Aw/cn 31.12.42. TDU 2.1.43.

To 11 SoTT as 3890M GI airfr 30.6.43. Reduced to spares 21.2.4?

R5775 Avro 18.6.41. 408 CF 27.5.42. 49 Sqn 28.5.42. 83 CF 26.7.42. 1654 CU 10.10.42. 1660 CU 19.4.43. 3 SoTT as 4281M GI airframe 22.9.43. SOC 12.10.44. 3 ops.

R5776 Avro 18.6.41. 1 AGS – probably incorrectly seq'd. Avro 5.8.41. 1654 CU 1.6.42. 408 CF 7.6.42. 1654 CU 16.6.42. Cat.A 10.8.42. Collided with armourer's lorry; To ? as 3745M GI airframe ?.3.43. SOC 14.5.43.

R5777 Avro 18.6.41. 1654 CU 29.6.42. Cat.B 0040 hrs 16.7.42. Bounced & yawed in heavy ldg. Stbd u/c leg collapsed at Wigsley. RIW. AW/CN 8.5.43. 39 MU 22.5.43. 1654 CU.? Cat.E2 31.10.43. No accident card. SOC 4.11.43.

R5778 Avro 18.7.41. 207 Sqn 17.1.42. 50 Sqn 25.1.42. Cat.Mc 9.2.42. Struck concealed gun pit whilst making way for departing a/c and u/c coll. Gun pit hidden by nets & snow. ROS 13.2.42. 50 Sqn 14.3.42. Cat.E 9.5.42. Aborted bombing mission after being hit by flak, knocking out pt engine. Resulting dam led to a/c being SOC on return. Sgt Wilkie–7–7–Warnemunde. SOC 15.5.43. 7 ops.

R5779 Avro for storage, mods & eng change 1.8.41. 83 Sqn 24.12.41. MFO 8/9.3.42. 'OL-G', F/O R W Cooper–7–2–Essen. Shot down at 0329 by Obfw Gildner of II/NJG2. Cr nr Smilde, NL. 4 ops.

R5780 Avro for storage, mods & eng change 1.8.41. 83 Sqn 27.12.41. Oil cooler burst on ops 29.3.42. Dam by flak on ops 23/24.4.42. 106 Sqn 13.11.41 (ce). 49 CF 29.6.42. Cat.Ac 15.7.42. Undershot Scampton, hit mound, bounced, landed heavily tail down. Tailwheel unit collapsed. ROS 16.7.42. 49 CF 8.8.42. 57 CF 7.9.42. 1656 CU 1.10.42. Cat.E 19.10.42. Unauthorised low flight by Australian crew. Hit tree beating up local pub and nose dived into ground, bursting into flames. 2 ml ENE of Lichfield. P/O R D Horner–6–0–trng.SOC 9.11.42. 14 ops.

R5781 Avro 1.8.41. 83 Sqn 9.1.42. MFO 28/29.3.42. 'OL-I' (?), F/O T A Lumb–7–0–Lubeck. Cr Gemeinde, Ploen, Germany. NFD. 2 ops. 23.45 hrs.

R5782 Avro 3.9.41. 207 Sqn 19.9.41. Cat.B 27.9.41. Both hydr & emerg pneu system failed after air test. Pt u/c locked on landing & stbd semi-retracted. ROS 6.10.41. 207 Sqn 24.10.41. Cat.Mc 23.12.41. Dam in error during formation flying practise by Spitfire. ROS 29.12.41. 207 Sqn 15.1.42. Cat.Ac (FB) 3.3.42. Bomb doors slightly dam by flak while GARDENING in daylight 6.2.42. Top of port wing dam by flak. 50 Sqn 18.4.42. MFO 17/18.4.42. P/O G Baker–7–5–Hamburg. Cr 10 km N of Hamburg, G at 0355 hrs. NFD. 12 ops. 118.25 hrs.

R5783 Avro 3.9.41. 97 Sqn 23.9.41. MFO 21.10.41. 'OF-V', F/O G H Hartley–7–7–Bremen. Ran out of fuel on return & force landed at Friskney, Lincs. 2 ops.

R5784 61 Sqn 4.10.41. Cat.Ac31.1.42. Failure of Former 35 disc on inspection, app due to unrep'd heavy ldg. ROS 17.2.42. 61 Sqn 4.3.42. Avro Cat.B 5.5.42. No accident card. RIW. AW/CN 6.5.42. 50 Sqn 12.5.42. 9 CF 9.8.42. 57 CF 8.9.42. Stbd eng ct fire in circuit 1635 hrs 10.9.42. A/c made normal ldg. 'D' block exhaust had burnt through. 1485 B&GF 28.11.42. 1660 CU 9.1.43. Avro 21.1.43. No accident card. ROS? 1660 CU 30.1.43. 9? AFU 20.7.43 (prob incorrect attribution). 26.7.43 Cat.Ac. Pilot of No 3 Ferry Pool experienced alarming tail flutter in flight. Precautionary landing at Hawarden. Blamed on faulty construction; Became 3984M GI airframe ?.7.43. SOC 22.6.4?. 4 ops.

R5785 Avro 3.9.41. 61 Sqn 12.10.41. MFO 11.4.42. 'QR-M', Sgt D H MacSporran–7–6–Le Havre. Stbd eng failed after flak hit over target. Ditched in English Channel 20 mls off S coast. Crew made PoWs. 1 drowned. 8 ops.

R5786 Avro 2.9.41. 61 Sqn 10.10.41. Cat Ac (FB) 14.1.42. Failed to hold off. Flew into gnd, bounced, swung. Tyre burst, u/c coll returning from ops. Dk night, no floodlts. ROS 18.2.42. 61 Sqn 14.3.42. Mainplane holed by 20mm flak shell 1.4.42. A/c persistently stalled on next op & early retn was nec. 50 Sqn 11.4.42. 50 CF 18.5.42. Cat.B 0250 hrs 30.5.42. Overshot in poor viz & heavy rain. Full brake failed to check. Ran across road & fell into field below 'drome level at Waddington. U/c coll. Had diverted from Skellingthorpe due to cr. a/c (L7492). ROS 2.6.42, 1654 CU 18.7.42. Unknown allocation 21.12.42. Cat.B MR 25.1.43. Avro. No accident card. SOC 28.1.43. 9 ops.

R5787 Avro 22.9.41. 61 Sqn 20.10.41. MFO 31/1.2.42. 'QR-M' F/O J R B Pasons–7–3–Brest. Hit by flak over Brest. Force landed at St Renan, F. 2 ops.

R5788 Avro for Storage, mods & eng change 3.10.41. 207 Sqn 10.10.41. Cat.Mc 17.11.41. Held off too high. Heavy ldg. Tailwheel dam. RIW 24.11.41. 83 Sqn 13.12.41. 49 Sqn 8.6.42. Cat.Ac 1100 hrs 6.7.42. A/c landed, ran 200 yd, u/c lock warning horn sounded & u/c coll. On approach horn silent. ROS. 49 CF 31.10.42. 1660 CU 9.1.43. 1 AFU 20.7.43 as 3983M GI airframe. SOC 1.11.44. 2 ops.

R5789 Avro 3.10.41. 61 Sqn 20.10.41. MFO 9.1.42. P/O D S Matthews–8–6–Brest. Engine ct fire over England. 6 baled out. 2 Pilots killed in force ldg at Wiltshire Cross, Wilts. Captain on 1st op. 1 op.

R5790 Avro 7.10.41. 207 Sqn 22.10.41. Cat.Ac 11.11.41. No accident card. 207 Sqn 10.12.41. 83 Sqn 11.12.41. Dam by flak on ops 6/7.4.42. Pilot wounded. Control lost. 2 baled out. 2nd pilot recovered a/c & returned to Coltishall. 49 Sqn 8.6.42. 44 CF 20.6.42. 1661 CU 8.11.42. Cat.Ac 5.12.42. Tail oleo failed at Waddington. ROS 11.12.42. 1661 CU 19.12.42. Became 3774M GI airframe. SOC 26.9.45. 16 ops.

R5791 Avro 8.10.41. 207 Sqn 29.10.41; 31. Cat. Ac (FB) 31.1/1.2.42. A/c took flak hit imm after bomb release. BA temp blinded by hyd fluid from front turret. Centre fin, bomb doors & throttle box also hit. ROS 3.2.42. 207 Sqn 6.3.42. Cat.Ac 1346 hrs, 21.4.42. V heavy ldg Bottesford. Pilot failed to keep a/c straight. Pt wheel ran into ditch at edge of runway. U/c collapsed. ROS 24.4.42. 207 CF 14.7.42. 1485 B&GF 25.8.42. No accident card but ROS 3.10.42. 1485 B&GF 17.10.42. Cat.B 7.11.42. Tailwheel collapsed taxying at Fulbeck. ROS 13.11.42. 1485 B&GF 12.12.42. 1654 CU 22.4.43. Became 4001M at 3 SoTT 26.7.43. To Henlow 27.5.44. To spares 6.2.45. 10 ops.

R5792 Avro 10.10.41. 97 Sqn 29.10.41. Mid-air collision with Hurricane, 24.11.41, no accident card. Cr Walpole St Andrew. F/O H T Hill–7–0–non-op. Hurricane from 57 OTU, unauthorised mock

attack.SOC 5.12.41. 1 MPRU Cowley 5.12.41. 1 op.

R5793 Avro 30.10.41. 25 OTU 16.11.41. 49 Sqn 27.4.42. 16.6.42 Cat.A 16.6.42. Eng sluggish. Tail swung & hit lorry. 83 CF 5.8.42. 1656 CU 17.11.42. 39 MU 24.12.42. SOC 26.5.43.

R5794 Avro 4.11.41. 25 OTU 16.11.41. 49 Sqn 13.5.42. MFO 1/2.6.42. P/O Shackleton–7–2–Essen. SOS received at 0129 stating stbd eng failure. Fix given THPJ 3207. Dead buried Holland. NFD. 2ops. 136.45 hrs.

R5795 Avro 4.11.41. 97 Sqn 22.11.41. MFO 'OF-Z' P/O N G Stokes–7–3–Brest (D). Shot down by Me 109s & cr in sea 4 mls offshore,Brest. 2 ops. 27.55 hrs.

R5796 Avro 8.11.41. 61 Sqn 18.11.41. 207 Sqn 21.11.41. Cat.Ac (FB) 10.1.42. Embarked on low level interdiction after bombing. Flak dam hydraulics & bomb doors & 1 wheel lowered. Diverted to Coningsby on retn. ROS 2150 hrs 24.2.42. GARDENING. ORB says hit at 500 ft on stbd side by fire from flak ships. Dam rear fus. wing & elevators. Raid Summary Book says attacked by Me 109 at 2225 hrs. 106 Sqn 13.3.42. Dam by flak on ops 30/31.5.42. 57 CF 8.9.42. 50 CF 23.9.42. 1654 CU undated. Cat.Ac 11.10.42. Damage discovered on daily insp, Wigsley. ROS 19.10.42. 50 CF 31.10.42. 1654 CU undated. A/c struck by L7280 whilst taxying 1030hrs 2.1.43. 1654 CU 16.1.43; 1660 CU 11.7.43. Cat.E2 16.11.43 MR. No accident card. SOC 19.11.43. 26 ops.

R5797 Avro 11.11.41. To Flight Shed 19.11.41. AW/CN 23.11.41. DTD 24.12.41. Avro Ringway 22.2.42. TI work incl Mk XIV bombsight at Finningley. Avro Ringway. Became 3778M 2.7.42. Prop tests GI airframe ?.6.43. SOC undated.

R5829 Avro 29.11.41. 25 OTU 17.12.41. Cat.Ac 12.3.42. Swung off runway on take-off & hit Chance light. ROS 17.3.42. 25 OTU 16.5.42. 1654 CU 4.8.42. 3 AGS 18.6.43. SOC 15.7.43.

R5830 Avro 7.11.41. A&EE 11.1.42. 83 Sqn 13.2.42. Cat.Ac (FB) 29.3.42. Early return, dam by fighter. Gear jett to mntn ht. ROS 2.4.42. 83 Sqn 25.7.42. 1656 CU 16.11.42. 39 MU 5.2.43. Cat.E2. 14.11.43. No acc card. SOC 16.11.43. 5 ops.

R5831 Avro 7.11.41. 83 Sqn 9.1.42. Slight dam by flak on ops 8/9.3.42. MFO 25/26.3.42. 'OL-I', Sgt E M Price–7–0–GARDENING Gironde. Cr Warden Point, Kent. NFD. 1 op. 82 hrs.

R5832 Avro 2.12.41. 61 Sqn 28.1.42. Cat.B (FB) 11.2.42. A/c did not operate that night. No accident card. NFD. 61 Sqn undated. Cat.Ac 0145 hrs 30.3.42. Uncertain of position on return from ops. Attempted landing small aerodrome at Westwood, Peterboro. Poor viz. Overshot. ROS 4.4.42. 61 Sqn 13.6.42. 61 CF 16.6.42. 1660 CU 20.10.42. 1661 CU 25.2.43. To 3744M GI airframe, ?.4.43. SOC 30.4.43. 7 ops. 410 hrs.

Mk.IA L7493 'EA-F' of 49 Squadron.
Imperial War Museum FLM 1007

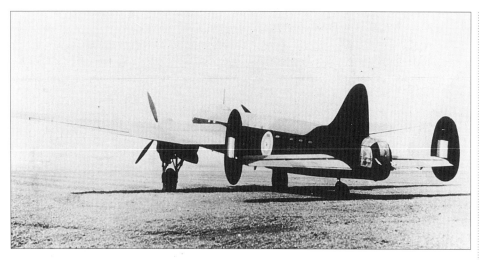

Mk.I R5771. Following its brief operational career, it passed in turn to 420 Squadron, 57 Squadron Con Flight, 50 Con Flight, and 1654 CU before becoming an instructional airframe, 3746M.
G A Jenks collection

R5833   Avro 2.12.41. 207 Sqn 6.2.42. 83 Sqn 1.4.42. 50 Sqn 15.4.42. MFO 6.6.42. P/O D W Garland–7–1–GORSE. Cr near Ile de Quiberone. NFD. 11 ops. 142 hrs.

R5834   Avro 2.12.41. 61 Sqn 28.1.42. 11.2.42 Cat.R(B) force landing at Horsham St Faith after ops. Stbd engine knocked out in target area. Fuel transfer problems. Port eng cut for lack of fuel on finals. Belly landed and struck ditch. F/S J B Underwood–7–7–GARDENING. RIW 9.3.42. SOC 15.4.42. 1 op.

R5835   Avro 2.12.41. 207 Sqn 6.2.42. 83 Sqn 1.4.42. 49 Sqn 24.4.42. 408 Sqn 23.5.42. 1654 CU 22.6.42. Cat Ac 4.7.42. Damaged in raid by enemy intruders. 1654 CU undated. Cat. Ac 26.2.43. Tailwheel oleo failed whilst on tow. ROS 3.3.43. 1654 CU 13.3.43. 1661 CU 11.7.43. RAF Benson 29.9.43. SOC 6.10.43. 2 ops. 471.15 hrs.

R5836   Avro 2.12.41. 83 Sqn 13.2.42. Cat.B (FB) 19.3.42. Last op, 13/14.3.42, was uneventful. Poss flying accident. No accident card. ReCat Ac ROS 19.3.42. 83 Sqn 13.6.42. 49 Sqn 25.6.42. 49 CF 22.7.42. 1661 CU 9.11.42. Cat.B 1.12.42 Came in too high. Failed to take overshoot action promptly. Stalled from 15 ft u/c coll. ReCat.E 2.12.42. P/O J M Desmond–?–all-trng at Scampton. SOC 3.12.42. 2 ops.

R5837   Avro 1.1.42; 83 Sqn 13.2.42. Slightly dam by flak on ops 5/6.4.42. MFO 8/9.4.42. 'OL-J', P/O M A Sproule–8–1–NICKELS Paris. Ditched in English Channel nr Margate, flak dam. 11 ops.

R5838   Avro 5.2.42. 83 Sqn 13.2.42. Poss dam on mining op 20/21.3.42. No accident card. ROS 24.3.42. 83 Sqn 1.4.42. Cat.Ac(FB) 12/13.4.42. Badly dam by NF. R/G killed. One eng failed at Dutch coast. Ret to Coltishall on one. ROS 15.4.42. 83 CF

25.7.42. 9 CF 8.8.42. 1661 CU 8.11.42. Cat.B 12.3.43. Demo prop feathering at 5,000 ft. Port prop failed to unfeather. Attempted ldg at Wickenby. Overshot into ditch. Stbd u/c coll. W/O E Knight–?–all. ReCat.E. SOC 24.3.43. 11 ops.

R5839   Avro 7.2.42. 61 Sqn 28.2.42. 106 Sqn 28.2.42. Cat Ac 20.3.42. Early retn from ops. Hyd failed after take-off. A/c carrying 6,000lb of mines. Permission given to land Coningsby. U/c coll after ballooning due to rough surface of 'drome. ROS 1.4.42. 106 Sqn 18.5.42. 49 Sqn 29.6.42. 1485 B&GF 29.8.42. 1661 CU 25.4.43. RAF Kidlington 6.10.43. Cat.E2 15.10.43. SOC 18.10.43.2 ops. 298.30 hrs.

R5840   Avro 7.2.42. 61 Sqn 28.2.42. 106 Sqn 28.2.42. Dam by flak on ops 6/7.4.42. MFO 2/3.5.42. F/S Hurd–7–7–GARDENING. Shot down & cr Pellworm Is, Germany. 14 ops.

R5841   Avro 9.2.42. 61 Sqn 10.3.42. 106 Sqn 10.3.42. Cat.B 26.3.42. Overshot Exeter returning from mining op. ROS 12.4.42. 106 Sqn 4.7.42. Cat.Ac 26.7.42. No accident card. 106 CF 24.8.42. 1660 CU 30.10.42. Cat.E 1850 hrs 11.4.43. Stbd eng failed & ct fire during circuits. Cr Swinderby. Expect fire reached cockpit before ldg. Seat of fire est as 'B' block in stbd eng poss due to hydraulic pipe failure. F/L J M Whitwell–6–3–trng. SOC 21.4.43. 2 ops. 189.35 hrs.

Select Bibliography

Aircraft of the Royal Air Force since 1918: Owen Thetford, 8th edition; Putnam, 1988

The Airfields of Lincolnshire since 1912: Ron Blake, Mike Hodgson, Bill Taylor; Midland Counties Publications, 1984

Architect of Wings – A Biography of Roy Chadwick, Designer of the Lancaster Bomber: Harald Penrose; Airlife, 1985.

Avro Aircraft since 1908: A J Jackson; Putnam, 1990.

The Avro Lancaster: Francis K Mason; Aston Publications, 1989.

Avro Manchester – Profile No.260: Chaz Bowyer; Profile Publications Ltd, 1974.

The Bomber Command War Diaries, An Operational Reference Book 1939-1945: Martin Middlebrook & C Everitt; Viking, 1985.

Bomber Group at War: Chaz Bowyer; Ian Allan, 1981.

Bomber Squadrons of the RAF and Their Aircraft: Philip J R Moyes; MacDonald & Co, 1964.

Bombing Colours, Part 25 – The Avro Manchester: Michael J F Bowyer; Airfix Magazine, 1971.

British Military Aircraft Serials 1878-1987: Bruce Robertson; Midland Counties Publications, 1987

Cologne – The First 1,000 Bomber Raid; C Messenger; Ian Allan, 1982.

The Design & Development of the Lancaster: D C Wood; Royal Aeronautical Society, Manchester Branch, 1991.

Escape or Die: Paul Brickhill; Evans Bros Ltd, 1952.

Flying the Manchester: W J (Mike) Lewis; CAHS – Journal of the Canadian Aviation Historical Society, Vol 32 No 2, Summer 1994

For The Duration – Extracts from the diary and letters of F/Sgt W G Hawes: D Rope; Mackenzie Publications (Australia), 1984.

Gunner's Moon – A Memoir of the RAF Night Assault on Germany: J Bushby; Ian Allan, 1972.

The Hardest Victory, RAF Bomber Command in the Second World War: Denis Richards; John Curtis & Hodder & Stoughton, 1994

An Ill Fated Bird: 21st Profile, Vol 1 No 6

Lancaster at War, Volume 3: Michael Garbett & Brian Goulding; Ian Allan, 1984.

Lancaster – The Story of a Famous Bomber: Bruce Robertson; Harleyford Publications Ltd, 1964.

Lincolnshire Air War 1939-1945: Sid Finn; Aero Litho Co (Lincoln) Ltd, 1973.

The Manchester Aeroplane, Two Vulture Engines: Air Ministry, Air Publication (AP) 1660A, 1941.

Manchesters: Aeromilitaria; Cliff Minney, Air-Britain, Vol 2, 1990.

Operation Millennium, Bomber Harris's Raid on Cologne, May 1942: E Taylor; Robert Hale, 1987.

The Right of the Line, The Royal Air Force in the European War 1939-1945: John Terraine; Hodder & Stoughton, 1985

Rolls-Royce Aero Engines: Bill Gunston; Patrick Stephens Ltd, 1989.

Rolls-Royce – Hives, The Quiet Tiger. Historical Series No.7: A Harvey-Bailey; Sir Henry Royce Memorial Foundation, 1985.

Royal Air Force Bomber Command Losses of the Second World, 1941: W R Chorley; Midland Counties Publications, 1993.

Royal Air Force Bomber Command Losses of the Second World, 1942: W R Chorley; Midland Counties Publications, 1994.

Squadron Codes 1937-56: M J F Bowyer & J D R Rawlings; Patrick Stephens, 1979

The Squadrons of the Royal Air Force & Commonwealth 1918-1988: J J Halley; Air Britain, 1988

The Strategic Air Offensive Against Germany, vols I-IV: Sir Charles Webster & Noble Frankland; HMSO, 1961

The Thousand Plan – The Story of the First 1,000 Bomber Raid on Cologne: Ralph Barker; Chatto & Windus, 1964.

Wartime RAF Aircrew Training in the UK: R Sturtivant; Aviation News, Vol 11 No 12, 5-18 November 1982.

World War II Aircraft Fact Files, RAF Bombers, Part 1: William Green & Gordon Swanborough; Macdonald & Janes, 1979.

No.83 Squadron 1917-1969: F E Harper & R G Low, privately published by R G Low, 1992.

207 Squadron 1942-1943: Barry Goodwin & Raymond Glynne-Owen; Quacks Books, 1994.

Index

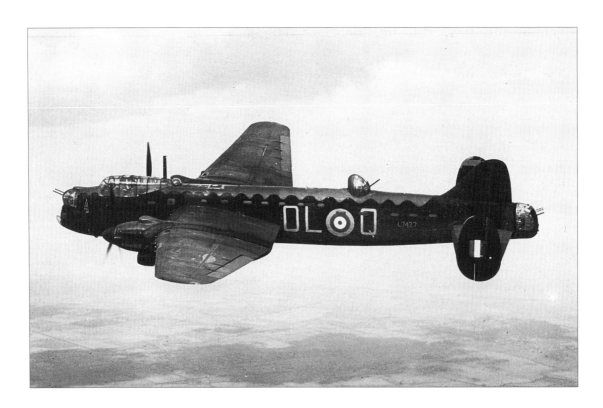

**A fine portrait of Bomber Command's twin-engined
'Heavy', taken during the well-publicised air-to-air
photo session of March 1942.
The Avro Manchester filled a gap in the
RAF's strategic offensive portfolio at a crucial time.
Proudly displaying a sortie 'tally board' of ten on
the nose, L7427 of 83 Squadron went the way of
many Manchesters on the night of 8/9th April 1942
– it failed to return from 'ops'.**
via Phil Jarrett

We hope that you have enjoyed this book . . .

Midland Publishing Limited titles are carefully edited and designed by an experienced and enthusiastic team of specialists. A catalogue detailing our aviation publishing programme is available on request from the address on page four.

In addition, our associate company, Midland Counties Publications, offers an exceptionally large range of railway, aviation, spaceflight, naval, military, astronomy and transport books, and videos, for sale by mail-order around the world.

To order further copies of this book, or to request a copy of the appropriate mail-order catalogue, write, telephone or fax to:
  Midland Counties Publications
  Unit 3 Maizefield, Hinckley, Leics, LE10 1YF
  Tel: 01455 233 747   Fax: 01455 233 737